THE QUEEN'S SCOTLAND

THE NORTH-EAST

THE SHIRES OF
BANFF, MORAY, NAIRN,
WITH EASTER INVERNESS AND
EASTER ROSS

By
NIGEL TRANTER

HODDER AND STOUGHTON
LONDON SYDNEY AUCKLAND TORONTO

BaD
643569

TOWNS AND VILLAGES, ETC.

A key to the towns, villages and natural features of Banff, Moray, Nairn, Easter Inverness-shire and Easter Ross shown on the map and mentioned in the text.

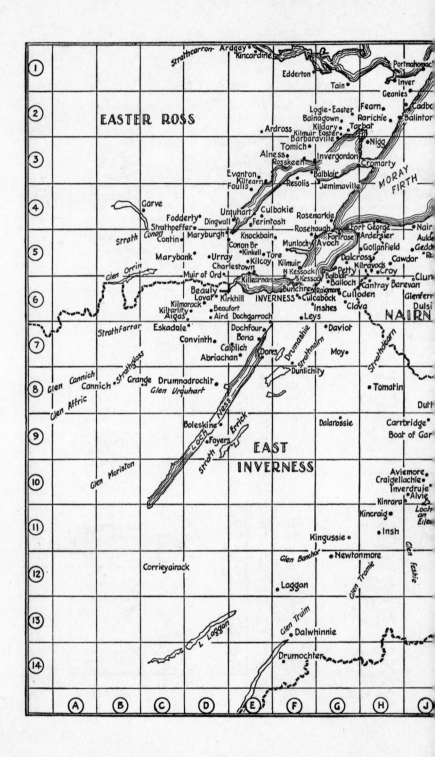

SCOTLAND
THE NORTH-EAST
IN 5-MILE SQUARES

LIST OF ILLUSTRATIONS

All photographs by Brian Long

BANFFSHIRE

This county is possibly one of the least-known and understood in Scotland—save in one respect. It is safe to say that only a very small proportion of the Scots population has ever been there, knows much about it, or realises its size, potentialities and characteristics. There are good reasons for this. It occupies a position remote from large centres of population; it is not really on the road to anywhere else—although the Aberdeen–Inverness highway, A.96, does pass through the county; it contains no large town of its own, Buckie, with 7600 people being much the largest of its burghs; and most of its area is in fact empty mountains and heather moors—yet so far, not adequately "discovered" by tourism. Which is strange, for there is a greal deal here to fascinate and entice the visitor and holiday-maker. Probably, most people, if asked, would say that Banffshire was indeed one of the small counties of Scotland; whereas it ranks fourteenth in acreage, with nineteen smaller, at 440,000 acres or 630 square miles; and eighteenth in population, with fourteen smaller, at 46,000 people. It is, in fact, larger than neighbouring Moray, in extent, and almost as populous. Because Banff town itself is on the coast, and most of the population live on the coastal plain, possibly few realise that Banff-shire extends 60 miles inland, deep into the Cairngorm Mountains indeed, where the well-known summits of Ben MacDhui and Cairn Gorm itself actually mark the boundary-line. The shape of the county is somewhat awkward and irregular, a very elongated triangle, and narrow, based on a 30-mile coastline but essentially following the valleys of Deveron, Spey Avon, Livet and Fiddich.

Yet despite misconceptions, ignorances and so on, Banffshire is renowned the world over, in one respect at least; it is the acknow-ledged "capital" and centre of the distilling industry, the home *par excellence* of Scotch whisky, the site of more famous distilleries than any other county—although neighbouring Moray does run it fairly close. The very names of Glenlivet, Glenfiddich, Glenfarclas, Mortlach, Dufftown, Balvenie, Strathisla, Macduff, Ben Rinnes and the rest, sing their own songs for the knowledgeable. There are literally scores of famous distilleries clustering in these upland valleys, and their distinctive blue-white plumes of smoke-cum-steam, rising above deep glens and pine forests, are a notable feature of the county. From Tomintoul to Ballindalloch, from Craigellachie to Keith, the distilleries proliferate. Some are highly attractive, some rather ugly; some very old, part of the landscape, some highly modern with a severely clinical aspect. And they all tend to have their associated housing, for most of them are far from towns or villages, and they form their own communities, prosperous-looking and self-contained communities, whitewashed, trim, compact, usually in highly scenic surroundings. The water, the peat and the cunning of ages, have

brought them here. Banffshire contributes revenue out of all proportion to its size, for the national exchequer. The Chancellor, especially,
has reason to bless this fairly remote county of North-East Scotland.

But Banffshire is famous for more than its whisky. Its fishing
industry is one of the most important in Britain, as distinct from
the deep-sea trawlers of Aberdeen and Peterhead. Drifters, seine-
netters and light-trawl boats by the hundred, which work from
or are manned from, Buckie, Macduff, Findochty, Cullen, Portknockie, Portsoy, Portgordon, Sandend, Gardenstown and many
another tight little village of this Moray Firth coast. This preoccupation with fishing and the sea has had a pronounced effect on the
coastal population, who are of a markedly different sort and character
from the inland and more Highland folk. Thus there is a very distinct division in the county, not only geographically but in the
people. There is a stern, tough, no-nonsense, yet very religious strain
very evident along Banffshire's 30 miles of coastline, reaching its
extremes in the Close Brethren, a very exclusive sect; but there is
great kindness here too, and the sort of enduring strength engend-
ered in communities at constant grips with the sea. It is a great pity
that, today, the fishing grounds have largely shifted to the West
Highland seaboard, so that the crews of hundreds of these vessels
have to leave their boats at west-coast ports like Kinlochbervie and
Mallaig, and travel home in cars and vans right across Scotland
each week-end, on entirely inadequate and ill-aligned roads, only
to return again early on Monday mornings—an unnatural and inconvenient, as well as expensive proceeding for the entire community.
So that there is a notable lack of menfolk about these fishing villages
and towns throughout many weeks of the year.

As well as distilling and fishing—with its processing, boat-building
and ancillary industries—Banffshire's agriculture is highly important, for the coastal plain is fertile, as are the lower valley-floors, and
the hillfoot areas support great numbers of cattle. Indeed cattle-
rearing here has been raised to something of a fine art, to rival
Aberdeenshire, and there are numerous very famous herds. It is
significant that the great English firm of Sainsbury has its beef-pro-
ducing farms in the Spey valley at Kinermony, near Aberlour.
Forestry is a growing industry, although not on the same scale as in
Moray to the west, one of the most heavily wooded areas of Britain.
So the county is fairly prosperous, in the main—although with its
own problems, like every other rural region today lacking a large
urban centre of its own.

Tourism is now being actively encouraged, and the North-East
of Scotland Tourist Association, with the local constituent bodies
and the town councils of the burghs, are doing a good job to publicise
the very great attractions of the entire area—as well they might.
For this is one of those fortunate regions where there is a marked
variety of natural beauty, allied to topographical and historical
interest and sporting facilities, all comparatively unspoiled. Because
of the extraordinary range of scenery, from the highest mountain

range in Britain to some of the most dramatic rocky coastline, from the great forests and splendid fishing rivers to renowned golf-courses, yachting havens and picturesque ancient burghs, there is something for almost every taste here, with the added bonus of being uncrowded. One especial feature of Banffshire which must strike the visitor is its dramatic geology. For the naked frame of the land makes itself very evident here, in spectacular fashion. This is best seen along the coast, naturally, where a long succession of precipices, deep coves, strange rock-formations and stacks, caves, skerries and thrusting headlands, provide endless and fascinating exploration. The Findochty and Portsoy regions are particularly rich thus. But geology is also responsible for the striking ravines, gorges and waterfalls of many of the river and burn valleys. Another aspect of the subject is the interesting varieties of marbles, serpentine, rock-crystals, soapstone and semi-precious stones to be found here, and which have long supported small industries, Portsoy marbles being especially famous.

This, then, is a very distinctive land, the iron-bound coast with its innumerable havens and fishing communities, full of character, giving place to the gently rising coastal plain, cut through by the waters of Deveron, Boyndie, Durn, Deskford, Buckie and Tynet, and interrupted by a scattering of prominent, isolated hills, sometimes crowned by Pictish forts, such as Durn Hill, the Bin Hill of Cullen, Knock Hill, Hill of Maud and so on. Then the quite wide central vale of Strathisla, parallel with the coast but a dozen miles inland, joining Deveron, wherein lies Keith, the second largest burgh with 4100 of population, and ancient Aberchirder of the Thanes. Thereafter the green foothills begin to rise, cattle-clothed, to be succeeded by the endless heather ranges, scored by the deep valleys of Fiddich, Livet, Avon and their feeders, the whisky country, hundreds of square miles of it. Whereafter the true mountains take over, the land of the stag and the eagle, climbers' country too, from Tomintoul onwards, empty wilderness reaching up to 4000 feet, womb of waters where are born the great rivers of Don and Deveron.

For the antiquarians, and those interested in history, even in a small way, the county is a rich quarry also. For here was where Highlands and Lowlands joined, the edge of the unruly House of Gordon's territories, with others almost equally unruly in possession —Inneses, Ogilvies, Grants. Here were the raiding grounds of the Highland caterans from the mountains—including that royal cateran, the Wolf of Badenoch. It behoved lords and lairds of the lower lands and straths to defend their lands and households, and the castles arose, large and small—Auchindoun, Ballindalloch, Balvenie, Blairfindy, Boyne, Crombie, Cullen, Findlater, Gauldwell, Inchdrewer, Kinnairdy and the like, right down the alphabet, some now long ruinous, some still occupied. And long before these, the Stone and Bronze Age people, and their successors the Picts, left their monuments of stone-circles and standing-stones, symbol-stones, forts and burial-cairns; and the Celtic saints such as Brandan, Colman,

3

Fumac, Marnan and so on, left their cells, holy wells and ecclesiastical communities, from which stemmed the medieval church. Banffshire had no abbeys, like the richer Laigh of Moray, though there was a priory on the Deveron just south of Banff itself, allegedly founded by Robert the Bruce; but there were many fine and interesting churches, some of which remain, intact or otherwise, especially notable being those of Cullen, Deskford, Mortlach, Fordyce and Inveravon.

Banffshire is particularly rich in burghal architecture of the 17th and 18th centuries, and after the inevitable period of neglect, much of this is now being restored and refurbished, in heartening fashion. Banff town itself has led the way in this excellent work, with the Banff Preservation Society, formed in 1965, showing what can be done. Portsoy, also, is to be congratulated on its splendid facelift which has transformed the characterful old harbour area.

Of prominent historical events of a national scope the county has none of first rank importance, its position precluding such. The Battle of the Bauds took place near Findochty against an invading Danish army around 961. Queen Elizabeth de Burgh, the Bruce's wife, died at Cullen in 1327, two years before her husband. Mary Queen of Scots stayed at Boharm, or Bucharin, now called Gauldwell Castle, in 1562, when she came north to put down the power of the Gordons; and one of her Maries, Mary Beaton, married Ogilvie of Deskford, and came to live hereabouts. Thirty-two years later was fought the Battle of Glenlivet, when the Catholic Gordons under Huntly defeated a Protestant army under Argyll, allegedly with the loss of only 14 "Catholic gentlemen" for 700 of the opposition. In 1645 the great Marquis of Montrose held a council-of-war in Balvenie Castle. A small defeat of government forces by Jacobites took place at the Auld Brig o' Keith in 1746. And so on. None earth-shattering events, save for those taking part, but at a comfortable distance in time imposing a pleasant and picturesque patina to the scene.

Banffshire, then, must be *terra nova* for many—which, in a way, is their good fortune, since there is so much of interest, variety, beauty and satisfaction awaiting them in this fine county by the Moray Firth.

Aberchirder. This like its county, must surely be one of the least known and visited small municipalities in mainland Scotland, set in the centre of Marnoch parish deep in central Banffshire, and not on the road to anywhere particular—although the A.97 Turriff to Banff road does pass by. It is a small neatly planned place of only 700 inhabitants, situated on a slight ridge above a shallow vale, but has been a police burgh since 1765, with its own provost and town council—and heir to a very ancient tradition. Not that it is ancient in itself, having been built here only in 1746 by the Gordon laird of Auchintoul. But the name is very old, and formerly applied to the whole parish of Marnoch —and indeed was old long before civil parishes were invented, for it was a well-known and important thanedom of the polity which succeeded the Celtic mormaorships. These thanes ranked below the

old earls but above other landowners, and were a hereditary appoint-
ment with special duties. Aberchirder means the confluence of the
dark brown waters, and refers to the junction of the major Burn of
Auchintoul and the Deveron, near Bridge of Marnoch. The original
community was sited near there, and Kinnairdy was its fortalice; but
the Gordon laird in 1746 objected to it being in sight from his windows at Auchintoul, and had it moved up here, out of view, as was
the way of 18th century landowners. The last Thane of Aberchirder,
Sir David of that Ilk, left only an heiress, Janet, who at the end of
the 14th century married the 9th Laird of Innes, in Moray. So the
Inneses came to Banffshire, and remained at Aberchirder for long,
seated at Kinnairdy Castle. But in the troubled 17th century they
lost the lands. Sir Thomas Innes of Learney, the late Lord Lyon
King of Arms, fairly recently recovered Kinnairdy and Crombie
Castles, also Edingight in the adjoining Grange parish.

The little town is regularly built, in granite, in long parallel
straight streets, climbing a gentle hill to the south-west, a trim place
but without especial character, and with considerable modern
housing developments to the lower north-east end. Here is the *quad
sacra* established church of 1840, built in Greek Revival style, large
and bright, opposite a play and recreation park. Not far away is the
large and handsome modern school which, owing to recent changes
in education policies, has been demoted from secondary—for which
it was built—to primary only, for which it seems altogether too
grand. The fire-station adjoins somehow unlikely in these surroundings. There is a small central square, with a Victoria Jubilee fountain, and the modernised Fife Arms Hotel of 1790. And in North
Street is the Marnoch Memorial Hall, also fairly modern. St.
Marnan's episcopal church of 1824 stands at the top end of the
town, overlooking all. The name of Marnan or Marnoch is inter-
changeable. St. Marnoch was a Celtic missionary from Ireland who
died here about A.D. 650 and was much venerated. And not only in
this area, for Kilmarnock and other places are called after him.
Indication of this veneration is provided by the one-time custom of
taking the saint's head out from its keeping place at Marnoch Kirk
one Sunday of every year, and washing it amidst a blaze of candles
and the prayers of the clergy, the water thereafter being drunk as a
curative for sundry ailments. The skull was carried in processions all
over the province of Moray. Marnoch was called St. Ermin in
Ireland, and was the patron of the Innes family.

The country around Aberchirder is described under Marnoch
parish.

Aberlour, Craigellachie and Edinvillie. Charlestown of
Aberlour, to give its full name, is a small burgh of less than a
thousand population, on the Spey, at the south-west of Banffshire,
little more than a village but with a large parish of nearly 15,000
acres, once known as Kirkdrostan, which includes the lofty and
famous mountain of Ben Rinnes (2755 feet). Craigellachie is a

well-known angling and distilling village 2 miles to the north-east, at a renowned crossing of Spey; and Milltown of Edinvillie is another village, set fairly remotely up on the northern slopes of Rinnes. This is part of the great Banffshire/Moray distilling area, and there are distilleries at all three of these communities, as well as elsewhere in the parish.

Charlestown of Aberlour is perhaps best-known for the large Episcopalean Orphanage founded here in 1875, which has done so much for underprivileged children and achieved nation-wide significance. Fairly recently the character of this institution has been drastically altered to suit modern sentiments, the children dispersed over a wide area in small establishments and houses, and the extensive buildings here either demolished or given over to other uses, such as housing a fire-station and a scrap-yard. The fine Episcopal church of St. Margaret is still there, however, to the east of the site, an ambitious structure of 1875 also, with chancel, clerestory, marble pillars somewhat over-decorative, and much stained-glass, standing in grounds amongst trees, with a few graves. There is also a significant war memorial monument to former pupils of the Orphanage.

The burgh consists mainly of a single long street, with shops, hotels, offices and a masonic hall, lining the A.95 Keith–Grantown road on the south side of Spey, though there is some wider development at the west end, climbing the higher ground. It was founded in 1812 by Charles Grant of Wester Elchies, who managed to have it erected into a burgh, although with only 250 inhabitants—North-East lairds seem to have made a hobby of founding burghs around that period. It is not a particularly distinguished place architecturally or scenically, but is quite pleasant, with its grey granite houses and wooded surroundings, the hills in the background. There is a square towards the west end, with a garden rather than a green, in which is the burgh war-memorial in the style of a mercat-cross; also a Victoria Jubilee fountain and a commemorative tablet to Laird Grant's foundation. The present parish church stands at the north or river side, a large building of 1861, Romanesque in style, with a battlemented clock-tower. It replaces one of 1812, which was burned down; and this in turn replaced the early St. Drostan's kirk in the old graveyard, still in use at the very west end of the burgh. Here is the south gable-end and a fragment of walling of the pre-Reformation kirk. Its very massive old stone font is mounted oddly on a pedestal near by. There are some very old gravestones propped up around the walling, and many old tombs, including a heraldic monument dated 1664 to Innes of Kinermony and his Barclay wife. There is a handsome Grant mausoleum of no great age. All is in good order. The parish hall adjoins; and across the road, where the Aberlour Burn comes down to Spey, is the large Aberlour–Glenlivet Distillery. A suspension footbridge crosses the river here. In the grounds of the distillery is St. Drostan's Well.

On the higher ground above the distillery are a number of features,

The Bridge of Alvah. Beauty spot

Balvenie Castle, Dufftown. Early Stewart and Innes stronghold

Cullen Church:
the Ogilvie Memorial

Deskford:
the sacrament-house within the
ruined old parish church

including the Fleming Cottage Hospital and modern Health Centre, the Fleming Hall of 1896, bowling-green, tennis-court and curling-pond. And a little higher, amongst terraced modern housing, the small Catholic church of the Sacred Heart. In the open foothills above the town is a broom-clad, large burial-cairn beside the road, known as the Fairy Knowe. This may be the cairn-plus-stone-circle alleged to be on Hatton Farm—which is near by, higher; if so, the standing-stones have gone, and no others to be seen.

At the north-eastern end of Charlestown commence the wooded grounds of Aberlour House, an impressive mansion in the Grecian style, now preparatory school for Gordonstoun. On its lawn soars a lofty Doric column of Aberdeen granite 84 feet high, commemorating the Grants—and added to at the top by the Findlays, of the *Scotsman* newspaper, who bought the estate. The old House of Aberlour, a Gordon place, was just to the east of the present mansion, but has wholly gone. Behind are the Blue Hill quarries.

A mile along A.95 north-eastwards is Craigellachie, a busy distilling village, road and hotel centre. There is another Craigellachie at Aviemore in Inverness-shire some 40 miles south-west, and these two, with their rocky bluffs, were supposed to represent of old the east and west limits of the Clan Grant's Strathspey domain—though their lands soon spread far beyond. "Stand Fast, Craigellachie!" is the Grant slogan. The old bridge across Spey here, recently superseded by a modern one less of a hazard to traffic, was built by Telford in 1815. It was a fine achievement, and of enormous advantage to the whole area; but it did have a most difficult northern approach at right angles, cut out of solid rock. As well as the distillery here, there is a large and renowned hotel, other accommodation for visitors and Spey anglers, and a small and fairly modern Established church with a clock over the porch, all in the picturesque scenery of the wooded river-valley.

Most of the North-East used to be divided up into davochs, or daughs, a convenient arable land measure; and Aberlour parish is still rich in these. There are Daughs of Aberlour itself, Edinvillie, Ruthrie, Kinermony, Allachie, Carron and Drumfurrich, etcetera, usually valley-bottoms. The Dauch of Kinermony stretches to the west of Charlestown, and here is an attractive small mansion, not ancient but on the site of a Knights Templar establishment, with lovely views down the Spey valley. Here also the large farmery of Sainsbury's Aberdeen-Angus herd. A side-road striking southwards leads to the foothills of Ben Rinnes, and soon to the Daugh of Ruthrie, wherein is the very modern distillery of Glenallachie, with an ornamental pond and associated housing; a fine scenic setting. On the Burn of Aberlour near by is the Linn of Ruthrie waterfall.

In the same general foothills area, a mile to the south, is the Daugh of Edinvillie and the village of Milltown thereof, pleasantly sited, the old milling hamlet down in the winding valley, the large Ben Rinnes Distillery, housing and school on the higher ground of the hillskirts. Three great clusters of ancient burial-cairns dot the heather slopes just above. The prospects are wide and entrancing. Still higher, 2 miles behind Edinvillie, a spectacular pass called the Glack Harnes separates Rinnes from Meikle Conval Hill in Mortlach parish, a deep defile over a mile long, with a track leading through to the B.9009 Glen Rinnes road. A small part of Aberlour parish is inconveniently situated over here in Glen Rinnes, on the south side of the Ben, 400 feet higher than the rest, and this pass and track used to be the access. From the top of conical Rinnes, the highest summit for a large area, can be seen an enormous vista, from the Grampians to Caithness and Sutherland.

The Daugh of Carron lies near the parish's western boundary along Spey, in pretty, wooded country. Daluaine Distillery lies deep, hidden in this vicinity beside a tree-lined gorge, with the mansion of Carron at the river-side. There was once a pre-Reformation chapel here, with a Chapel Well. The village of Carron itself, however, lies across the Spey, in Moray.

Alvah. This is a quite large and wholly rural parish of 11,500 acres, on both sides of the Deveron immediately south of Banff, a picturesque and pleasant tract of country with no actual village but many features of interest. It includes the well-known beauty spot of Bridge of Alvah, beloved of artists and photographers, a lofty and fine single-arch of 1772, 55 feet high, spanning the Deveron's pronounced vale where it narrows into a dramatic rock-ribbed defile 3 miles upstream from Banff Bay. It was erected by the 2nd Earl of Fife, builder of Duff House, and lies within that great estate, so carrying no public road. It may be seen, however, from the Kirktown's road to the south, at Mill of Alvah—and may be crossed on foot by all, but not driven over. There is no other bridge across Deveron south of Smeaton's Banff Bridge until Turriff is reached, a rather extraordinary—and inconvenient—gap of about 14 miles. The Craigs of Alvah, where the bridge is situated, form a highly impressive gorge, narrowing the river to only 27 feet and causing it to deepen to nearly 60 feet, also to cause flooding higher on occasion.

Half a mile south of the bridge, the Kirktown of Alvah stands high amongst green braes, a pleasing place with attractive views of the great valley. Here is the parish church, of 1792, very plain with a belfry, its bell dated 1645. It is not used now for weekly worship, the Trinity-Alvah church at Whitehills, 5 miles away, being linked. An ancient heraldic panel, with lion rampant, dated 1589, is built into the outer vestry wall, presumably coming from the earlier St. Colm's chapel, for Alvah was only established as a civil parish in the 17th century, being formerly part of Forglen. The hillside graveyard has many old tablestones, and is still in use. On the ridge behind the Kirktown's scattered houses can be seen the Stirling Cairn, an eliptical prehistoric burial-mound 8 feet high.

The former pre-Reformation chapel of St. Colm stood amongst whin-covered braes half-a-mile to the north-west, at the junction of the Kirktown side-road and A.97, on the farm of Tipperty. There are grassy traces of foundations only; but higher a little, 200 yards southwards, amongst old apple trees, is St. Colm's Well, now piped into a cattle-trough, still producing fine clear water—allegedly 27 gallons a minute which used to supply Banff with water. Presumably the Banff folk were neither great washers nor drinkers, not of water anyway. This St. Colm was probably St. Colman rather than St. Columba. In the early 14th century the then Countess of Atholl, daughter of the Earl of Mar, gave Alveth Kirk to the Abbey of Coupar in memory of her husband, a friend of Bruce, who was captured with Nigel Bruce and the Queen at Kildrummy and executed in London.

Across the river near here is Montcoffer, a wooded estate, the old, but not ancient, mansion of which stands deserted on a south-facing attractive terrace. Montcoffer also belonged to the Earls of Fife, and the Bridge of Alvah led across to it from the Duff House policies. There is a cylindrical doocot standing near by, to the east.

Two miles southwards, along the Kirktown side-road is Auchenbadie, with a pleasant old farmhouse of probably the early 18th century, with circular stair-tower. To the south-east is a steep broom-clad knowe above the green valley of the Brydock Burn, called the Ha' Hill, partly artificial, on which presumably once stood a hall-house type mansion. With the sparkling stream and a mill at the foot, it makes a pretty picture.

Soon after this side-road joins B.9121 over a mile southwards, is the oddly named Pole of Itlaw, where there is a post-office and which, with the nearby Bridgend of Montblairy with former school, makes up a roadside hamlet. Montblairy itself is a former large estate and barony, lying to the south on the Deveronside, the mansion, of 1791, now demolished. There was the motte of an ancient castle of the Comyns here, and also a chapel, both gone. Not far to the west, on B.9121 again, is the farm of Burreldales, on higher ground where, amongst trees in a field, is a stone-circle of four monoliths.

Just across the Deveron's deep—and uncrossable—valley from Montblairy is the attractively sited and mellow Georgian mansion of Dunlugas, dating from 1793, but replacing an ancient castle. It is now the seat of Sir Robert Abercrombie of Birkenbog, whose predecessor, the first baronet (1636) was known as "a main Covenanter" and opponent of King Charles. But then Charles was notable for his strange and not very effective policy of trying to buy over his opponents with titles. A large number of Britain's proud titled families owe their rank to their enmity to the King who granted it. Dunlugas in those days, however, was the castle of a powerful branch of the Ogilvie family, from whom stemmed the Lords Banff and others. Less than a mile to the south-east of the mansion on the farm of Boghead, the Carlinkist Cairn and a standing-stone are situated on the valley-side. This eastern area of Alvah has to be reached from the Macduff-Turriff A.947 road.

The southern and western portions of the parish consist of higher and mossy farmlands, practically devoid of woodlands, or indeed of outstanding features. The Burn of Brydock rises here and flows into Deveron at Auchenbadie aforementioned. Mill of Brydock stands where A.97 crosses this burn 2 miles south-west of St. Colm's Well, an old meal-mill, still working but converted into a thriving mill for cattle-feed.

Ballindalloch, Inveravon and Glenlivet. These are well-known names. Inveravon is a huge parish of 50,000 acres, more than half as large again as Clackmannanshire, comprising the lower valley of the Avon and all that of the Livet; and Ballindalloch is a great and ancient estate and district, where the Avon joins the Spey, at the northern edge of the parish, with the parish church near by.

This whitewashed church, isolated on a wooded shelf high above Spey, although highly inconveniently sited for most of the parish, is a delightful place in its old graveyard amongst trees, with its fine manse beside it. A side-road from A.95, with a small school at the junction, leads down to it a mile north of Dalnashaugh Inn. The building of 1806 is successor to one dedicated to St. Peter, and long the seat of the Chancellor of the Diocese of Moray. The church is attractive inside and out, bright, with a small gallery. Against the outside south wall are three Pictish stones and a fragment. The largest, known as the Peter Stone, displays a fine eagle and two mirror symbols. Another has the Celtic beast, or elephant, with cresent and V-rod. And the third, as well as crescent and V-rod has a triple disc and cross-bar, with mirror. The fragment has part of an uncertain symbol. They make a precious group. There is an imposing mausoleum for the Macpherson-Grants of Ballindalloch, and many old gravestones.

Down at the level haughlands of Spey to the south of the church, a mile, stands the imposing and interesting Ballindalloch Castle, in large wooded policies with many notable and ancient trees, home of a famed Aberdeen-Angus herd as well as of a great family. The castle has developed from a 16th century fortalice on the Z-plan with towers projecting diagonally at opposite ends of the main block. Then in 1602 a handsome circular stair-tower was erected midway, rising a storey higher and finishing in a corbelled-out watch-chamber, with a fine oriel window, very unusual, and a small stair-turret to give access, this latter having a machicolated projection for dropping missiles on intruders. There were further extensions in the 18th and 19th centuries. Internally there has been much alteration inevitably, but the basement is vaulted and there is much of interest. One fire-place is dated 1546. Originally there was a Ballindalloch of that Ilk family; but the Grants were not to be contained in upper Strath-spey, and in the early 18th century the Laird of Grant was in the position to give Ballindalloch to Colonel William Grant, second son of Rothiemurchas; and his daughter and heiress married George Macpherson of Invereshie, in Badenoch. This family produced a long line of renowned soldiers, and were given a baronetcy in 1838. The present baronet still lives at Ballindalloch. Many stories are told of these Grants. One must suffice. A culprit named Rob earned the wrath of the laird—who of course had the power of pit and gallows. He was being duly led to execution when he decided to make a break for it, and looked like getting away. His wife, however, watching near by, called out: "Och, Rob—be quiet and dinna anger the Laird!" The appeal brought Rob to his sense of duty and he died like a lamb. There is a doocot of 1697, a mausoleum to General Grant, hero of St. Lucia in 1779, and St. Peter's Well, in the policies.

The main A.95 Strathspey highway has to make a major re-entrant hereabouts to cross Avon incoming to Spey, and at the head of this hairpin bend is Dalnashaugh Inn, a hotel perched on the hillside. Across the Avon by the picturesque 18th century single-arch bridge is the farm of Lagmore, on the south, with, in the field by the roadside, a stone-circle with three uprights and two fallen. The Cragganmore Distillery lies down a side-road near by, at the former Ballindalloch Station, with an isolated but still-used auction-mart, opensided and circular, with cattle-pens. The western boundary of the parish is soon thereafter.

On the eastern side of Ballindalloch and the church, a mile, lies the roadside hamlet of Marypark, with post-office. Here the B.9138 turns off, down to the iron bridge at Blacksboat, formerly a ferry across Spey. Once there was a railway-station here also. There is a small community on either side of the river. Up on the main road is the Ballindalloch Animal Feed Plant, at the head of the Daugh of Carron near the eastern parish boundary. South of this, on the skirts of the Ben Rinnes foothills, is the well-known Glenfarclas Distillery.

Although Inveravon parish is not very wide near its mouth here, a mere 5 miles, it probes very deep into the mountains to the south, about 17 miles to the Braes of Glenlivet. From Dalnashaugh Inn the B.9008 strikes due southwards up the lovely deep and narrow glen of the Avon, on its east side, with another, lesser and dead-end road serving the west side, referred to hereafter. Immediately we are into a Highland atmosphere, with birch and pine forest flanking the road above the rushing river and the heather slopes of the Rinnes outliers, Knocknashaig (1900 feet) and Cairnacay (1605 feet) rising on the left. High on the side of the former, 2 miles east of Dalnashaugh, is a cluster of burial-cairns beside a waterfall of the Burn of Lyneriach. The forested road continues in fine scenery nearly 4 miles to the junction of Livet with Avon at the Downan–Drumin area, where B.9136 branches off to the right to follow Avon up 8 miles to Bridge of Avon just south of Tomintoul; and B.9008 continues up Livet eventually to cross the watershed—after sending off a side-road to Braes of Glenlivet—also to reach Tomintoul by a longer route.

Where B.9136 strikes off and crosses a bridge in the hollow, crowning the wooded hill beyond, in the steading of a large farm, is the ancient castle of Drumin, in a strong site at the junction of the rivers. Here are the shattered remains of a massive square keep of the 14th century, formerly the main seat of the important barony of Inveravon and a stronghold of the Wolf of Badenoch, Alexander Stewart, Earl of Buchan, son of Robert the Second. He gave these lands to his bastard son Sir Andrew Stewart, whose heir Sir William sold them to the Gordons. Not far north of this, on the green tongue of high moraine between the rivers, is a stone-circle of three uprights and two fallen, beside a conical knoll which might be a cairn. Directly west of Drumin half a mile, but on the other side of Avon and so only reachable by the aforementioned *west* side-road, is the ruined chapel and abandoned graveyard of Kilmaichlie, with its holy well, and a burial-cairn near by, at the farm of Chapeltown. And a mile back north, on a wooded shelf high above the river, and visible from the other, or main, road, is yellow-washed Kilmaichlie House, now a farm. This is an interesting laird's house of the early 17th century, on the T-plan, with a square stair-tower and crowstep-gabled watch-chamber. There has been an angle-turret at one corner, but only the base corbel, in the shape of a mask, remains. The barony of Kilmaichlie was part of the great Inveravon domain of the Stewarts, and when Drumin and the rest was sold to the Gordons, they retained this property. It was purchased from them however in the 18th century by the Laird of Grant, and has remained part of Ballindalloch estate. Here the Dowager Lady Grant lived late that century, and was visited by her godson Henry Mackenzie, friend of Scott and author of *The Man of Feeling*, who wrote of the old lady and life at Kilmaichlie in words described as "the tenderest portrait before Sir Walter". It is certainly a lovely place.

After Drumin the B.9136, heading south, passes out of the parish into that of Kirkmichael in under 2 miles, with a large group of burial-cairns on the hillside to the left just before the boundary. But almost directly after the castle, a side-road strikes off south-east-wards, and this leads, by a small roadside school, to the large farm and former Gordon lairdship of Minmore, a pleasant oldish house with fine prospects. In a field by the roadside here is a single stand-ing-stone of quartzite. Near by is the famous Glenlivet Distillery of 1884, less pleasing to look at than most, despite its renown and splendid setting. Its predecessor stood on higher ground to the south, behind Blairfindy Lodge. This was all but the birthplace of malt whisky as we know it, and at the close of the 18th century there were said to be over 200 illicit stills busy hereabouts—which the Distillery Act of 1824 brought to book, so that only five authorised distilleries succeeded them—officially.

South-east of the distillery, prominent on a hillock, stands Blair-findy Castle, a ruinous Gordon fortalice of the late 16th century, still entire to the wall-head however and capable of being saved. It is a tall L-planned building with angle-turrets, a slender stair-turret, machicolated projection, shot-holes and a heraldic panel above the arched doorway with the Gordon arms and date 1586. The basement is vaulted, and there is a great arched kitchen fireplace with oven and stone drain. This stronghold, after Drumin was abandoned, commanded the important pass of Livet from Aberdeenshire and Strathbogie into Banffshire and the North, and also served as a hunting-seat for the Earls of Huntly. The Battle of Glenlivet was fought in 1594, just 4 miles to the east, when Blairfindy's owner, Huntly, defeated the Protestant forces under Argyll, with the slaughter of 700 for the loss allegedly of only 14 Catholic gentlemen. The site of the battle is fairly high on Carn a Bhodaich (2149 feet) above the great planted forest.

Back from this Drumin area to the B.9008 again at Downan, the road follows up the Livet. This famous river, rising in the Blackwater Forest very close to both the Fiddich and the Deveron, part of the Ladder Hills, is only 9 miles long but has made sufficient name for itself, one way or another. Where the Blairfindy side-road sends down a spur to join it, by a picturesque 18th century bridge, is the old graveyard of Downan, in a pretty position, with some old stones. This is almost at the post-office of Glenlivet near where the Deskie Burn comes in from the east, and here is the Glenlivet Caravan Club's site. The Deskie area is another old lairdship, formerly also with a chapel, in a fertile side-valley, up which, on the left, is another large cluster of cairns. A mile on, where B.9009 strikes off eastwards from the B.9008, for Dufftown 11 miles, is Glenlivet and Craggan *quod sacra* parish church, at the hamlet of Achbreck. This former Royal Bounty mission church, rebuilt in 1825, is now a very handsome place of worship internally, owing to the prosperous distilling interests here, well-furnished, with good woodwork, carpeting and much stained-glass. One of the windows is unusual in commemorating a baptism, rather than a death. The renovation of the church was carried out by Margaret Smith Grant, of the distilling family, in memory of her father Robert Anderson, in 1956. An unlikely feature to see near by, in such purely rural surroundings, is a seemingly thriving branch of the Clydesdale Bank. A little further on, a single standing-stone rises on the bank above the road, at Aucharachan farm.

Another mile up Livet, with the glen shallowing and forestry planting in evidence, is the Tomnavoulin–Tombae area, a busy community to find thus far up a mountain glen. It is distilling again, of course. Here, over the single-arch Bridge of Livet, of 1829, is a village with post-office, school, hall and considerable housing, with the Tamnavulin–Glenlivet Distillery, at a widening of the valley where the Crombie Water comes in. It would be interesting to know why many distilleries spell their names differently from the accepted local usage? Something to do with southern customers, perhaps. Across the main river, reached by a side-road forking off before the bridge, is Tombae, where there is a large Catholic church of 1829, with its own burial-ground. Such places are always the sign of a large R.C. population, and this has always been so in Glenlivet and the Braes thereof, ever since the great Catholic house of Gordon held sway here. The church interior is colourful in pinks and blues, with a groined ceiling. In the graveyard is the burial-place of the Gordons of Minmore; also their successors the Gordon-Smiths and Smith-Grants of the distilling family. Tomnavoulin is remembered as the seat of a laird who, with his son, was savagely murdered by James am Tuim Grant, the freebooter from Carron, merely for once having declared that the countryside was better lacking his presence. The Tombae side-road peters out presently into a track—but a long one. For this used to be a drove road which went right up upper Glenlivet and over the watershed at 1279 feet, in Glen Suie, and so down Glen Fiddich to the Dufftown area, and thence south.

After Tomnavoulin the B.9009 leaves the Livet and climbs gradually up towards a watershed, through much new planting, reaching 1235 feet at the parish boundary, 6 miles to Tomintoul. Half-way to the boundary is the Pole Inn, with the cottages of the scattered hamlet of Achnaharrow, an isolated community under the great lumpish hill of The Bochel which rather dominates this area. The North of Scotland College of Agriculture has an establishment here. Opposite the Pole Inn a side-road strikes off due eastwards, a road well worth following, for it leads into something of a world of its own. Once past The Bochel, as guardian, the uplands open out into a vast amphitheatre of the hills, some 4 miles in diameter, dotted with small farms and crofts, and entirely ringed-in by mountains. These are the Ladder Hills, a little-known range, along the summit-ridge of which, at an average of 2500 feet, runs the Aberdeenshire border. The name is probably derived from *leitir*, meaning a regular or lengthy slope. This great basin, with its quite large population, is known as the Braes of Glenlivet, a place of far-flung vistas and great skies, cut off from all else save by this little side-road. In the centre is Chapeltown, with its post-office, school and hamlet. And of course the quite large Catholic chapel of St. Mary, of 1829 which gives it its name, a fairly ambitious edifice to find in such a spot, with a painted Madonna in a niche above the door, and a square tower. There is a memorial inside to the founder of this mission, Abbé Paul Macpherson, who died in 1846. There is a high painted wood ceiling, and seats for a large congregation. It had a Catholic school attached, now closed, dated 1860, with accommodation for 196 pupils, significant indication of the former population of this little world-unto-itself. The metalled road stops at Chapeltown, but a dirt-road goes on a mile to Scalan, where once there was actually a Roman Catholic college and presbytery of which the famous Blairs College, near Aberdeen, is the successor. Tracks cross the hills beyond, by the Clash of Scalan pass, to the Lecht and Strathdon.

Banff. The royal and ancient burgh of Banff is one of those pleasing, dignified and characterful little towns in which Scotland is so happily rich, attractively situated on its wide bay at the mouth of the Deveron, flanked by sands and links and with the hills not far behind. It is also a civil parish of 6,700 acres containing much that is interesting and scenic. Just across the Deveron estuary, to the east, lies Macduff, a separate and rival burgh—although sharing sundry municipal services—a very different town of almost the same size, providing an effective foil.

Banff has a population of only 3723; but it has style, the patina of age, and an almost aristocratic atmosphere largely contributed to by the great number of excellent 17th and 18th century houses still in use—probably a greater proportion of the whole than any other town in Scotland. Happily, nowadays at least, Banff recognises the worth and advantages of these, and has, through the admirable Banff Preservation Society, embarked on an ambitious programme of conservation and restoration—by no means too soon, for not a few fine buildings have gone. It is the county town—although not the largest burgh, which position goes to Buckie, the fishing town 20 miles to the west—and here a large number of the local lairds had their town-houses in the past. This is a feature of old Scotland which we are perhaps apt to forget. The landed gentry tended to desert their castles and country seats during the long, cold winters, and to congregate in the companionable environs of a suitable centre, often only 3 or 4 miles from their homes but so much more convenient and comfortable. And rewarding for the social and cultural life of the said towns. Frequently these town-houses were fine architectural specimens, adorned with heraldry, carved-work, panelling and the like. Banff was particularly rich in this respect. It is interesting to note that the lairds wintering here were not confined to Banffshire, some of the Gordon, Forbes, Ogilvie and Baird gentry coming from well over the Aberdeenshire border. Banff was sufficiently isolated to attract from a wide area.

Despite this emphasis on the ancient and the aristocratic, the royal burgh is nevertheless no sleepy hollow. It may not bustle quite so vigorously as does Macduff—whose splendid harbour gives it the edge for things maritime—but it is quietly go-ahead in its own way, with no lack of interest and development in the present and the future. It has a small industrial estate to the west, at Tannery Road, amongst the modern housing—and though the tannery has gone, Mac Fisheries have here a thriving factory. The foundry down near the harbour is also a casualty, like the former ropeworks and brewery; but these are replaced by engineering works, an aerated-water factory, a large laundry and a distillery a mile to the west, at Inverboyndie. There are flour-mills, agricultural suppliers, builders and other services, besides excellent shops, banks and offices. There are many hotels, including the handsome Fife Arms, built in classical style by the 4th Earl of Fife in 1843, on the site of the ancient Black Bull inn in Low Street. This Black Bull was a famous place—although the ever-critical Dr. Johnson described it as indifferent, and was the scene of the murder, in 1771, of a local gentleman by a military officer over one of the hostelry's maids, for which the officer was never brought to trial. There are caravan-sites to the east and west of the town. The *Banffshire Journal* flourishes—typically, in an 18th century building of some character which once was the grammar school.

Banff claims that its first charter as a royal burgh was granted by Malcolm the 4th in 1163, and that this was confirmed by Robert the Bruce in 1324. The earliest extant charter is dated 1372, by Bruce's grandson, Robert the Second. Little remains to be seen in the town from so early a period, save for the site of the ancient castle. This lies above the shore to the west, in Castle Street, an extension of High Street, and though the present building on the site is called The Castle, it is in fact a typical 18th century mansion with hipped roof. However, at its back, part of the original castle's curtain-walling survives, with its arched postern gateway. This is claimed to be of the 11th century, but is undoubtedly later. The early moat and flanking green banks do date almost certainly from that period, when the castle was the seat of a thanedom which passed to the Comyn Earls of Buchan by marriage. In due course it came, by similar means, to the Ogilvies of Deskford, who became Earls of Findlater; and the present house was built by James, 6th Earl, in 1750, to William Adam's designs, as a jointure or dower house. It is now a Community Centre, its 7 acres of ground a recreation park. In its predecessor was born in 1613 the ill-fated Archbishop Sharp, murdered at Magus Muir in 1679. His father was Sheriff-Clerk of Banffshire.

The original parish church was the pre-Reformation chapel dedicated to the Virgin Mary which stood down near the harbour, and is now represented only by the 16th century burial-aisle of the Ogilvies of Dunlugas, later Lords Banff, vaulted, with a rather fine stone-tracery window with rectangular astragals and a double-moulded arched doorway. Near by is the recumbent effigy of a knight in armour, with helmet on tasselled cushion and lion at feet, dated 1636—George Baird of Auchmeddan. The graveyard is notably crowded with many fine examples of sepulchral monument —but unfortunately sadly neglected for a town so appreciative of things ancient. At its gateway is inserted a heraldic panel, dated 1658, referring to Alexander Douglas, Provost and Sheriff murdered in Low Street.

The present parish church is also called St. Mary's, situated at the east end of High Street, a large building of 1790, based on the design of St. Andrew's Church, Dundee, with a rather good steeple in the Georgian classic style added in 1849. It is bright and very fine within, with a splendid marble-floored apse and chancel, unusual in a Presbyterian parish church. There is a back gallery, and amongst other features, a silver plaque commemorating the Norwegian Brigade, which had its headquarters in Banff in the winter of 1941/2. Crown Prince Olav addressed the Brigade in this church.

There is another handsome established church not far away, in Castle Street, formerly the Free church, of 1844, in the Grecian style, with pillared portico and cupola and an unusual beamed roof within. It is now called the Trinity-Alvah Church, the neighbouring parish of Alvah having become linked with this town congregation. The episcopal church of St. Andrew dates from 1833, Gothic in style, built by Archibald Simpson, with good stained-glass and old pewter communion vessels. There is also a Catholic church dedicated to Our Lady of Mount Carmel—maintaining the link with the former Carmelite Priory of Banff, the site of which is partly occupied by Carmelite House, in Low Street, a good former town-house built by Admiral William Gordon in 1753, standing back from the street. There was a bede-house, or almshouse, here also. Likewise the Knights Templar had an establishment at Banff, a reminder of which is the Spittal Mire not far away. While on the subject of religious establishments, there is the so-called Elf Kirk down on the west shore beyond Scotstoun, but this is merely a rock-feature.

Banff Academy, founded 1786, used to occupy a very dignified classical edifice of about 1835, on a prominent terraced site at the east end of the town, designed by William Robertson, reminiscent of the Royal High School of Edinburgh on a smaller scale. It has recently been superseded by the usual large modern glass-and-concrete complex, in Bellevue Road, but will probably continue in educational use. It is the successor of the grammar school of 1544.

The main town centre is called the Plainstones—not exactly a square but a widening street-junction at the west end of Low Street, allegedly the place where James Macpherson, of *Macpherson's Rant* fame, was executed in 1700 (although another account puts the spot on top of Gallows Hill). He was a noted Highland freebooter, allegedly an illegitimate son of Cluny Macpherson himself, by a tinker woman, declared as "holdin, known and reput an Egyptian" and a renowned piper and fiddler also. He was a composer too, and his spirited and splendid *Rant* he actually played as he marched to his execution, offered his fiddle at the gallows-foot to anyone who would take it, and when none reacted, snapped it across his knee— the fiddle-neck thereafter becoming an heirloom in the chiefly Cluny Macpherson family. Burns who visited Banff in 1780, wrote:

> *Sae rantingly, sae wantonly, sae dauntingly gaed he;*
> *He played a spring and danced it round below the gallows tree.*

At the Plainstones, in front of the Town House, rises the Mercat Cross, a highly unusual tall and fluted column with a 16th century crucifix finial, with which is represented also the Virgin and Child, Banff's emblem. The Cross has been moved around various sites but stands very near its original position. Close by is an old cannon dated 1855, captured at Sebastopol. The Town House here is a plainly massive building of 1796, designed by James Reid—who however did not obtain his hotly disputed 20-guinea fee until two years thereafter. The fluted, tapering clock-steeple with its odd oval apertures was built earlier, 1764, probably by James Adam. There are some interesting portraits and relics in the handsome council-chamber. On the adjoining premises are built-in some heraldic and other panels, including the Royal Arms of 1634 and the Virgin and

Child dated 1628. Banff is full of built-in panels from demolished buildings. A particularly handsome one, with the Gordon arms impaling Scott, and dated 1675, enhances a gateway across the road from the old kirkyard.

At the eastern end of Low Street, near the Fife Arms, is the Sheriff Court building on the site of the town-house of Lord Byron's grandmother, Lady Gight. The County Hall is here also. And round the corner, in an open site beside the car-park is the Collie Lodge, a distinguished though small Ionic edifice, now used as the Information Centre, and formerly a lodge-house of the great Duff House estate, dating from 1836, a building, like the Academy, worthy of any metropolis.

Low Street oddly enough outranks the High Street as the principal thoroughfare of Banff; but there is much of interest in the latter also, set higher on the hillside and linked to Low Street by steep, climbing lanes such as Strait Path. Nos. 1 to 5 High Street make a typical 18th century group, the last, fourstoreyed and substantial, being the former town-house of the Lords Banff. Other groups in this street include a 17th century range with attractive semi-dormer windows in the steeply sloping roof, with a close-mouth pend; and the Shoemaker Incorporation block of 1787—for Banff had its guild-brethren like greater places—with good arched doorway under the gablet.

It would be quite impossible here to give any list of even the major fine buildings and former town-houses with which this little burgh abounds—but mention must be made to a few representative and outstanding groups, some saved by the efforts of the Preservation Society. Particularly fine is that at High Shore (not to be confused with High Street, indeed lower than Low Street). No. 1 is a gem, almost a little castle, with prominent angle-turret, crowstepped gables and good moulded windows. A corbel projecting beneath the turret is dated 1675, but the house appears to be somewhat older than this. It is in process of being restored, and will make a notable residence for some fortunate citizen. Next to it is a somewhat later house, still dignified, and beyond that the old Market Inn, still a hostelry, which claims to be the oldest occupied house in Banff, a pleasing, whitewashed building with a pend through to an inner courtyard. Here is a remarkable mask-stone, dated 1585, showing a rather sinister man's face with handlebar moustaches. The present building is hardly so old as this, but probably incorporates earlier work.

Further along the same High Shore is the very interesting group, partly 17th century, at the corner of Water Path, again with crow-stepped gabling and a pend through to a courtyard, known as Ingle-neuk. And up the Water Path, flanked by the former's lofty garden-wall, is the fine gable-end of Path House, fronting the steep street, with other good buildings behind. Fernlea in this area is also worth a mention. The harbour is in this vicinity, quite famous once, before the Deveron changed course somewhat and caused it to silt up. It was improved by both John Smeaton and Thomas Telford; and many of its old warehouses are still in use, although the fishing fleet has moved to Macduff. And boat-building still continues. The fine Robertson's Granaries complex is typical and authentically Old Banff. Beyond lies the former fishing hamlet of Scotstoun, straggling along the shore of Boyndie Bay westwards, a long row of cottages, with Banff's Seatown, rather similar, on a higher level of the bank. There is a sandy beach here, although most of the seaboard is rocky, and a good coastal walk offers fine views on a clear day.

Up on the higher level, near the quite attractive Railway Inn, is the joint laundry and aerated-water works complex. This is a very characterful and lengthy building, erected as a brewery in 1704, where Butcher Cumberland housed some of his troops after Culloden. Battery Green has also military echoes, for here was sited a battery of cannon to repel possible French invasion during the Napoleonic Wars—but which never found a target. Near by is Chalmers Hospital, and in the adjoining St. Catherine's Street is the house of the same name, built in granite around 1830 in classical style, and now housing the Hospital's Board.

Mention should be made of Banff's museum, in the High Street, once reputed to have a very fine collection. Unfortunately this establishment seems to have sunk in status and is seldom open— although a curious painted notice says that it is open Today and Tomorrow. None of the three days that the author called, unfortunately happened to be either today or tomorrow. The library, housed in the same building, has evening opening however. The noted Pictish bronze swine's head from this museum is now in the Museum of Antiquities, Edinburgh.

At the other, eastern, side of Banff, rather further out, are two notable features—Smeaton's fine 7-arched bridge over the Deveron, built in 1779 and widened in 1881, carrying the main A.98 highway; and the great Duff House estate. The former is called Banff Bridge. There was a ford here anciently, then a ferry-boat. The first bridge was swept away by flood in 1768.

Duff House is a major architectural landmark, by any standard. Enormous, yet attractive in its impressive magnificence, it was built to William Adam's designs in 1725–40 as a more baroque version of his Hopetoun Palace, for the ambitious and vigorous William Duff, then 1st Lord Braco and later 1st Earl of Fife and Viscount Macduff. The Duffs, risen dramatically from comparatively lowly origins, partly on the shrewd purchase of Jacobite forfeited estates, were dead-set to become a power in the land—and achieved their end, the 6th Earl eventually marrying Edward the Seventh's daughter, the Princess Royal, and being created Duke of Fife, in 1889—from bonnet-lairds to dukes in 150 years. Duff House is their monument. Although it is no longer the Duke of Fife's seat, donated to the two burghs in 1906, and standing empty, it is maintained as an ancient monument by the Ministry of Works and its spacious grounds are used to provide Banff's Royal Duff House Golf Club with a course, also a football-pitch, while its far-flung Deveronside policies offer delightful walks for the citizens.

A good mile up-river, in these extensive wooded grounds, is the once-impressive mausoleum of the Duff family, now badly neglected and vandalised, a large Gothic temple with ornate memorials, on the site of an ancient chapel and priory founded before 1324 allegedly by Robert the Bruce. Against the southern outside wall of this is a good recumbent effigy of a knight in armour, within an arched alcove, with decorative panels. This monument has an interesting and revealing story. Local tradition has connected it with the Bruce himself—which is ridiculous. It is probably the effigy of the aforementioned Provost and Sheriff of Banff, Dr. Alexander Douglas, a notable man, murdered in 1658; and was formerly placed over his tomb in Banff old kirkyard. It was removed from there by the second Earl of Fife, and brought to this private mausoleum, presumably to give the impression that it referred to one of the Earl's own ancestors. If this raises eyebrows, let it be remembered that he did exactly the same thing with another effigy, so anxious was he to give the newly ennobled Duffs a suitably ancient and chivalrous background. In 1792 he extracted the effigy of a Duff of Muldavit from Cullen old kirk, and brought it to this same mausoleum, where he recut the lettering and date to suit his ancestral ambitions, changing the mid-16th century to 1404. Not content with this, he altered another knightly incised slab at Cullen, belonging to a member of the Innes family, with the same 1404 date and change of name—which slab is now back on the outer wall of Cullen's church. The effigy itself was removed from the Duff House mausoleum in 1965 and taken back to Cullen, where it belonged. It all makes rather a pathetic tale, especially when we consider how powerful and influential the Duffs did indeed become, all over the North-East, in their own right. Today many of Scotland's proudest families are glad to incorporate the Duff name.

If, in all the foregoing, over-much emphasis has been placed on Banff's past glories and attractions, architectural in particular, perhaps this was inevitable. But the town is noted as a holiday resort, attracting many who have no interest in the past; and it exploits its many potentialities in that direction. It has good sands, fine rock scenery, excellent sporting facilities—and the splendid Tarlair swimming-pool at nearby Macduff—plus the sunny climate of the Moray Firth area. The caravan-sites are well appointed, there are facilities for sea-fishing and water-skiing, and the Banff and Macduff Angling Association, which controls nearly a mile of fishing on both banks of the Deveron, allows visitors to partake. There is even Kart Racing at Boyndie near by. Banff, with its many hotels and guesthouses, makes an ideal centre to explore an unusual and attractive countryside.

Banff parish stretches inland in a long, narrow ellipse for almost 7 miles, to south-west, averaging one and a half miles in width and including much high ground of green hills and moorland, Ord and

Culbirnie Hills, 573 and 518 feet, at the extreme south-west, the loftiest points. At Ord is a former chapel-of-ease of 1836, constituted a *quod sacra* parish in 1869, and still in occasional use, the plain church with belfry and weather-vane standing remotely in open ground amongst wind-blown trees 6 miles from Banff parish kirk.

Inchdrewer Castle, a prominent landmark, stands on a bare lofty ridge 3 miles south-west of Banff, and has only recently been restored from complete ruin by an enthusiast from London, with Ogilvie ancestry. It represents a most admirable effort by all concerned for, a few years ago, most would have considered the remains quite incapable of restoration. But the work has been done lovingly, carefully and authentically, using the old fallen masonry, the result a notable credit to the vision of owner, architect and builder; and shows the way for others, as to what *can* be done in bringing back into enviable use and habitation these fine fortified mansions of our exciting past—even one so far gone as this. Inchdrewer was originally a property of the Barclays of Towie, but passed to the Earl of Crawford in 1414. It was in other hands however when Sir Walter Ogilvie of Deskford, or his son Sir George, purchased it at the end of the 16th century, and it is from this period that the present castle dates. Their greater castle of Boyne is only 5 miles to the north-west, so this was probably intended as seat for the son. It was an L-shaped tower-house with a slender stair-turret in the re-entrant, over a squinch. Then a later wing was added to the south, plus a round tower with open platform roof. A courtyard with circular flanking-towers extended to the west, and this also it is the proprietor's intention to restore. The Hall on first floor has been given larger modern windows, the only external non-authentic feature—but surely permissible for a house which is lived in.

Part of Inverboyndie hamlet is actually in Banff parish, where the Burn of Boyndie reaches the sea near Swordanes Hotel. But since the major part is in the parish of Boyndie itself, it is more suitable to describe it thereunder.

Boharm, Mulben and Maggieknockater. This large west Banffshire parish of Boharm, 16,750 acres, has undergone considerable confusion of nomenclature in its history, and still does to some extent—for one of its two hamlets, formerly known as Blackhillock, is now called Mulben, although it is in fact the Kirkton of Boharm; the other being the renowned Maggieknockater. Boharm itself used to be called Bucharin, and comprised parts of the former parishes of Arndilly and Dundurcas—the latter over Spey, in Moray. And the former Castellum de Bucharin is now known as Gauldwell Castle. All very confusing—as Mary Queen of Scots' French-educated secretary, Ogilvie of Cardell, found it when writing up her northern itinerary, with resultant mistakes which have been perpetuated ever since.

Boharm lies immediately west of Keith 3 miles, and comprises a hilly, wooded and very picturesque area between there and the

Spey, including the fairly dominant hill of Ben Aigen (1544 feet), Knockan (1219), much of the great Rosarie Forest, and part of the vast Wood of Ordiquish, itself now a section of Speymouth Forest. It is threaded by two main roads, the A.95 Keith–Grantown, reaching Spey at Craigellachie, and the B.9103 Keith–Elgin, crossing Spey at Boat o'Brig.

The parish centre—though in fact not very central—is now at Mulben, 5 miles west of Keith, with Messrs Buchanan's Glentouchers Distillery at the roadside near the parish boundary. The former Free church here, at Mulben, is now the parish kirk of Boharm, grey-harled with a small belfry—although its immediate predecessor, less conveniently situated at Balnabreich a mile to the south-west, is still in good order and used in summer time. The small village of Mulben clusters round the cross-roads of the A.95 and B.9103, with post-office, school and village-hall—and, as has been said, was formerly called Blackhillock. The barony of Mulben, from which it takes its present name, lies down a side-road to the north, where the handsome House of Mulben stands beside its farm-steading on the bank of a burn. It is a pleasing and fairly large building, mainly of the late 17th century, with later extensions; but the eastern portion almost certainly incorporates older work, possibly a late 16th or early 17th century tower-house. It is typically tall, harled, steep-roofed and crowstep-gabled. In the east gable are inserted two former dormer pediments, one with Grant heraldry, dated 1696, the other with the monogram of Ludovick Grant and his wife. The Grants of Freuchie, later of Grant, got Mulben through marriage with a daughter of the great Cumming or Comyn family in 1506, and the property remained linked with the chiefly family. The 6th laird, Sir John, was knighted for fighting against the rebel Catholic Gordons under Huntly, at Glenlivet, in 1596. He eventually succeeded as Grant of Grant. He got the Mulben lands erected into a barony in 1616. The Ludovick mentioned was his grandson, who built the older part of the present house. He may have been forced to this when their former seat, the castle of Balnabreich, was destroyed by Claverhouse's troops prior to Killiecrankie in 1689, he having taken Dutch William's side. The Grants, now Earls of Seafield, still own much territory hereabouts, but Mulben has been in the good hands of the well-known Macpherson family, the Aberdeen-Angus breeders since 1888.

The castle of Balnabreich is now wholly gone, but the parish church of 1793 still stands high on the hillside there above A.95, in trees, an isolated position by present-day standards. It is a small-ish, plain, harled building with belfry, a typical 'preaching-kirk' with varnished woodwork. The house close by was not its manse but a former parish school of 1807, now converted. The manse itself is down below the main road, dating from 1811, an excellent Regency house of four storeys, with forestair, which has recently been delightfully restored as a private residence. It has a most attractive site, and is now known as the House of Boharm.

Inchdrewer Castle, Banff, recently restored from complete ruin

Findlater Castle, Sandend

Crovie village, Banffshire coast

High Shore, Banff. No. 1, the turreted house on the left, being restored

Across the valley not far away, on a fine terraced site, rises the large mansion of Auchlunkart, dating substantially from the early 18th century, though with wings and a pillared portico of 1800. It is a most pleasant house in a lovely woodland setting, looking down the valley eastwards, with the heather of Knockan and Ben Aigen behind. It was long a Steuart house. The first of them, Andrew Steuart of Tannochy, was "out" in Mar's Rising of 1715. They retained the estate until 1947.

Three miles on along the A.95 is the ruined still earlier parish church—though still not the earliest—on a steep bank above road and burn. Here is the parish kirkyard, with the west gable remaining of the church of 1618, still retaining its belfry and bell—cast in Elgin—with the burial-vault of the Grants of Arndilly and the Steuarts of Auchlunkart. There is an unusual round stone here carved with a crown and motto, and dated 1618, allegedly commemorating the building of the church at the private expense of James the Sixth—why is not explained—when its predecessor at Gauldwell Castle became inadequate. There is also a Grant of Mulben burial-place, and, in a separate enclosure just outside the graveyard proper is buried William Steuart-Menzies, chief of Menzies, who died in 1961. There are many old gravestones in this picturesque spot.

The hamlet of Maggieknockater lies athwart the main road half a mile on, a small place of a few houses, a former school and a well-known apiary, on the edge of the den of the Altdernie Burn, with farmlands rising in swelling folds on either side. The name is renowned for its oddity, but almost certainly is no more than a corruption of *magh* meaning a plain or field, and *fucadair*, a fuller, the field for waulking of cloth. Maggieknockater—the accent on the *knock*—used to be larger than it is today.

Massive fangs and fragments of masonry and tumbled foundations, in a strong position above the steep ravine where the Altdernie joins the wider vale of Glen Fiddich, a mile on from Maggieknockater, is all that is left of the once great and important Castle of Gauldwell, with its pre-Reformation chapel, which was the parish church until 1618, close by. The castle was built about 1200 by the famous Freskins of Moravia, from Duffus, Moray, ancestors of all the Murrays. Here Mary Queen of Scots stayed on her expedition of 1562 to put down the Gordon power. It seems to have been a large keep within a towered curtain-walled enclosure, and it is reckoned to have been one of the earliest stone castles in the North-East. When and why the name was changed from Bucharin or Boharm to Gauldwell is not clear. Nothing now remains of church or graveyard.

The A.95 passes out of the parish down a wooded winding brae to the Spey a mile on, at Craigellachie. But just before this, a side-road strikes off northwards, through old Scots pine woodland, high above the east bank of Spey, to Arndilly. This used to be a separate small parish, called Ardentol, but is now only a large wooded estate.

The road is highly scenic, flanked by the Wood of Arndilly on the west side of Ben Aigen. There was a parish church set on a shelf above the river nearly 2 miles along, but this has wholly gone, its site being covered by extensions to the mansion of that name. This is a very handsome and unusual house, dating from 1750 to 1850, with later work, in a delightful setting, with curvilinear gabling and ogee-roofed semi-turrets, stringcourses and quoined angles. Also unusual is the fine Pictish symbol-stone inset in the walling to the west of the front doorway, almost square, displaying double-discs and tuning-fork and Z-rod symbols. The views are superb. The side-road is a dead-end, terminating 3 miles on beyond Aikenway, in the Dundurcas area, where are the embankments of a former defensive structure, on a spur at a tight bend of the river.

Back at Mulben the B.9103 proceeds due westwards, in consistently fine country, for nearly 3 miles to the Spey and the county boundary at Boat o' Brig. This is, of course, an odd name, since boat means ferry and one hardly looks for a ferry where there is a bridge. The reason is that anciently there was a wooden bridge here, where the Burn of Mulben enters Spey by a deep gorge. It must have been a large structure, and was important enough to have a Hospice of St. Nicholas established to look after bridge and travellers. It is claimed that it was built by the Romans, though this is as may be. At any rate, Alexander the Second, in 1232, granted provisions for a chaplain here. The bridge was however washed away, and not rebuilt until 1820, when the present suspension-bridge was erected, with a typical toll-house of the period at the eastern, Boharm, end. Just when the wooden bridge was swept away is not known, but it was after the Reformation; presumably in the putting down of the "Popish" establishments, St. Nicholas Hospice also went, and there was nobody to keep up the bridge—which must have been an enormous loss to the whole North, for there was no other bridge over Spey for great distances. So for about 250 years there was only a ferry—hence the name. The hospice is wholly gone, but locals say that snow never lies on its site, near the bridge-end. The area, with its steep wooded banks and the great river, is very fine scenically. A railway-bridge now crosses Spey alongside. Delfur Lodge is pleasingly placed just to the north. Skene makes the Pictish town of Tuessis, of the Vacomagi, hereabouts, mentioned by Ptolemy in the 2nd century.

Before reaching Boat o' Brig from Mulben, a side-road leads away northwards, highly picturesque, with sharp bends and gradients, by deep wooded ravines and through ancient and planted forests, leading 6 miles to Fochabers in Moray, a most delightful run with breathtaking vistas every so often, by the estate of Cairntry, the Crags of Cuildell and the great Wood or Ordiquish. There are many woodland walks.

Botriphnie and Drummuir. This rather oddly named smallish parish of Banffshire lies amongst green hills in Strathisla, along the

Aberdeenshire border south-west of Keith, extending to 9500 acres. It has a little village of the same name, but the great estate and district of Drummuir tend to dominate. There is also a hamlet of Auchindachy on the Keith boundary to the north, where the Water of Davidston joins the Isla.

The parish church lies actually just within the policies of Drummuir Castle, fairly central in the parish, above the river. It is a pleasant sylvan site, in its old graveyard, the present building dating from 1820, a fairly typical preaching kirk with central pulpit and semi-circular gallery, all in good order. Preserved inside is an interesting early Celtic incised wheel-cross on a grey-stone slab, somewhat broken at top. Also a very shallow stone basin, presumably a stoup from the earlier church. There is a collection of good pewter jugs, of 1831, and some cups of 1843, these from the former Free church. In the graveyard are the scanty remains of the earlier kirk, dedicated to St. Fumac, now a burial-enclosure for the Duffs of Drummuir. There are some very old gravestones around the outside of this, and a dormer pediment, built in within, dated 1617, and other 17th century memorials. St. Fumac, one of the Celtic missionaries, had a wooden image which used to be washed yearly on 3rd May, in pre-Reformation times, when there was a Fumac's Fair, the water being considered of healing quality. The saint's well still flows strongly just outside the kirkyard to the east, indeed starts off a small burn.

Drummuir Castle is a huge and impressive Gothic castellated mansion of 1850, built and still owned by the Duff family, standing deep in a large wooded estate, but easily seen from the A.920 Dufftown road. In the policies is the narrow Park Loch, over a mile long but only 100 yards wide, flanked by woodland. The castle's predecessor stands over 2 miles away, on the side-road B.9115, almost on the Aberdeenshire border, and is now a farm called Mains of Drummuir, a very modest establishment compared with the huge modern mansion. But it is interesting, nevertheless, an L-shaped house of the early 17th century, on a steeply sloping site so that it has three storeys at the front and only two at the back. It is severely plain, with crowstepped gables, very small windows, and a number of shot-holes. A built-in dormer pediment has the weather-worn monogram A.A.D. The outside forestair is modern. In the 16th century, Drummuir was a Leslie of Kininvie property, and the famous Covenanting general, Alexander Leslie, first Earl of Leven, came of this family. William Duff, merchant in Inverness, son of Duff of Clunybeg, was the ancestor of the Duffs here, dying in 1715. The same year Alexander Duff of Drummuir, Provost of Inverness, seized that town in the Jacobite interest, unusually rash behaviour on the part of the Duffs, always so cannily sure to be on the winning side.

The small village of Botriphnie lies along the A.920, a short distance east of the church, and has a school, post-office, smiddy, disused mill and some modern council housing. Further along this road towards Keith is the Towiemore Distillery and also a lime-works. And 2 miles further still is Auchindachy, which also has a mill, a farm, an old toll-house and a former railway-station, all under a hillside of picturesque scattered Scots pines.

There are some quite lofty hills in this wholly rural parish, on both sides of the central Isla Valley, Carran Hill to the south reaching 1367 feet, and Knockan to the north 1219 feet.

Boyndie and Whitehills. Boyndie is a parish of 7000 acres, lying immediately to the west of the town and parish of Banff, once called Inverboyndie—and still there is a hamlet of that name. Whitehills is a large and growing fishing-village on the peninsula of Knock Head, 2 miles west of Banff, and the only major community. The parish is very long and narrow, extending inland for about 8 miles to the high mosses of the Ord district, but for most of that distance measuring little more than a mile in width. It widens towards the coast however, and has 4 miles of seaboard, with the Bays of Boyndie and Boyne—a little confusing, this similarity of names—and the headlands of Knock, Whyntie and Stake Ness, on a rock-bound shore.

The Kirkton of Boyndie is only a hamlet, at a junction of side-roads 2 miles south of Whitehills—but having near by to the east the large Banffshire Mental Hospital of Ladysbridge, dating from 1865, with extensive associated housing, almost a village in itself, with much modern building. The parish church, still using the old designation of St. Brandan's, is a plain substantial building of 1773, with belfry but without kirkyard, and a rather fine old manse near by in trees. There was alleged to have been a stone-circle near the church once, but this is not now known—although there is a recumbent flattish monolith lying on supports in the manse garden, which may have come therefrom. There are cottages, some new housing and a school here at Boyndie.

The original church of St. Brandan's was 2 miles to the west, at Inverboyndie, where still is the graveyard. This is a more interesting site, where the Burn of Boyndie winds its way through green undulations to the Bay with a narrow 18th century double-arched bridge crossing. The remains of the old church stand high, and consist only of the west gable and a detached vaulted aisle with wide arched doorway, now used only for storage. The gable, apparently of the 17th century, has an unusual and interesting corbelled projection at either side of its summit to support the belfry. Otherwise there are no special features remaining. The kirkyard is crowded with ancient and modern monuments. Just to the west stands the former manse, which has been a good 17th century building but has been completely gutted for use as a farm-store. This church was abandoned in 1773. Brandan was a Benedictine monk and friend of Malcolm the Second, said to have died about A.D. 1000. To the north-east is the large Banff Distillery.

Whitehills, almost a small town, is a typical North-East fishing village, close-knit, clean, with crowded gable-end cottages in the old part, with narrow lanes and considerable modern housing also. There is a good harbour, busy when the fishing-boats come in, with warehouses, fish-curing yards, old greens for drying nets, and a Lifeboat Station recently disused. The church stands on the higher ground to the south, not old, with a tall, thin clock-steeple, and is called Boyndie-Trinity, a linked charge. At the east end of the village, really at the other side of Knock Head's narrow peninsula, is the detached old haven of Blackpots, where there is an ancient tile-works, still functioning during the summer months, with pictur-esque and lengthy pantiled storehouses and kilns. The tiny harbour cut in the rocks has a rather Hebridean atmosphere and, now disused, is to be converted into a swimming-pool for the children's playground which shares the peninsula with the tilery. All very pleasing. Whether this atmosphere would have survived the erection of a great new nuclear power-station planned for Whitehills, to cost £100 million, is another story; but this may never eventuate. Knock Head here is interesting as allegedly the place where grey rats first came to Scotland, swimming ashore from a wreck on the reef.

Between Whitehills and Ladysbridge is a cross-roads of B.9121 and B.9139, and in this vicinity are a number of features. Quite close to the north-east of the cross-roads is an ancient circular well, with stone-lined shaft, still holding water, and the remains of a small building. There are other similar wells not far away, including one famed as a mineral spring, the Red Well, with a domed roof, presumably all connected with St. Brandan. There are also encamp-ment sites, supposedly Roman but more likely Pictish, amongst whins north and south of the B.9139. The site of the ancient Ogilvie mansion of Buchragie is also near by, but nothing remains.

Two miles to the south-west, beyond Boyndie Kirkton, lies the large farm of Rettie, or Reattie, which was once important enough to be the seat of the Masters of Banff. There is quite a large Rettie area, and on the Moor of Rettie was placed a war-time airfield, now disused save for farming purposes and as site of a Kart-Racing track. This area is also called Whyntie. There are large quarries working the hillsides to the west, just back from Boyne Bay, in a quite attractive position for such.

The Boyne Burn, in its deep wooded den marks the western bound-ary of the parish—as the Boyndie Burn does the eastern—and in the ravine, less than a mile back from the Bay and not far from the quarries, the large and spectacular ruins of Boyne Castle rise amongst the trees, in a strong site at a bend in the den. This has, in fact, been one of the finest castles in the land, and it is shameful that its hopeless ruin should have been hastened on by the tearing out of every item of dressed stonework from windows and doorways, philistinism all too common in the immediate past. It is a large quadrangular pile around a central courtyard, with circular towers at all angles, and a twin-drum-towered gateway formerly reached across a wide moated area where the site is not protected by steep slopes. The castle appears to have been built all at one time, and although it is of the style of early great baronial strongholds of the 13th and 14th centuries, it probably dates only from the end of the 16th century, when Sir George Ogilvie of Dunlugas bought the estate, in 1575, from another branch of the Ogilvies. There was a more ancient building for the old barony nearer the sea; and it is significant that the doocot is on the *wrong* side of the deep ravine, and of a rather unusual crowstepped gabled design, indicating perhaps that the original castle was on that side. The present extensive but shattered remains reveal a most ambitious structure, with six circular towers, much corbelling, many stringcourses, shot-holes and gun-ports. There have been vaulted buildings on three sides of the courtyard. Despite its ravaged state, it makes a highly romantic sight. The Ogilvies were all-powerful in this area from an early period, an offshoot of the Angus stem, their branches having many ramifications and reaching the peerage as Lords Deskford and Banff and Earls of Findlater. Much of the land is still owned by the Ogilvie–Grant Earls of Seafield. The Boyne line it was that became the Lords Banff.

The B.9139 road sends off a steep branch to Portsoy near the castle, and this crosses the river by an old single-arch narrow bridge in the wooded den. Here are the ruins of Scotsmill of Boyne, of 1626, very picturesque; also of a former lime-kiln. About half a mile upstream, on a side-road, is the ruined L-planned Lintmill, also of the 17th century, with a pan-tiled roof and the remains of a walled-garden, now all much neglected.

Deep inland the parish has less of interest to offer. Three miles south of Boyne is the farm of Raggal, formerly a bonnet-lairdship. Here was born in 1674 the celebrated Thomas Ruddiman, author, scholar, Latinist, Keeper of the Advocates' Library; also Mrs. Elizabeth Buchan, founder of the Buchanite sect. The neighbouring farm southwards is Baldavie, where the late 17th century whitewashed farmhouse, with its coped chimneys and crowstepped gables, recalls the Duff pretensions to ancient lineage mentioned under Banff—Duff of Muldavit and Baldavie being the line to which the new Fife earls made claim to belong. It had been an Ogilvie property.

A mile west of this, on the higher ground, almost moorland, stand the St. Brandan's Stones, on the small farm of Lodgehills Croft, behind a wood. This is a stone-circle, one of the few that have survived in this area, consisting of two large and clumsy uprights and some five fallen stones, one with cupmarks. Presumably Brandan had a cell linked with this place of ancient worship.

Buckie and Portgordon. The thriving burgh of Buckie stretches for 3 miles along the Moray Firth seaboard, the largest town in Banffshire. But even so it is not so very huge, with a population of no more than 7688; for it does not reach far inland, lining the coast at sea-level and along the bank above, to no great depth. It includes the former fishing communities of Buckpool, Seatown of Buckie, Gordonsburgh, Ianstown and Portessie. Portgordon, a mile west of Buckpool and near the Moray border, is now more or less a suburb also, though retaining some individuality.

Although the main shopping street, East and West Church Street linked by Cluny Square, lies along the higher level, the true nerve-centre of Buckie is down at the harbour, *raison d'être* for its existence, for this is one of the most active and go-ahead fishing-ports in Scotland, with a huge herring and white-fish seine-net and light-trawl fleet working from it, many boats and crews from the surrounding little burghs and villages all along the coast using it also. The port has all the facilities and ancillary trades available. Cluny Harbour is large, with four basins and an outer haven, and can accommodate up to 400 fishing vessels. £300,000 was spent on improving it in 1932, and other refinements have followed. There are the extensive fish-market sheds, ice-works, merchants' offices, curing establishments, engineering shops, ship-chandlers, sail-makers and boat-building yards, all a stirring scene of industry, especially when the fleet comes in. There is a Coastguard Rescue Station at Buckpool. Not all the industry is connected with fishing, however; there is the large Buckie Works of Messrs. Thorn, making electric bulbs and equipment, with a factory covering 40,000 square feet and employing 350 people. It won the Queen's Award to Industry in 1968, for export achievements. There is also the Inchgower Distillery a mile inland.

All this has grown up comparatively recently. In 1793 Buckie had only 14 boats and a population of 700, with merely a boat strand and no harbour. The first harbour, of timber piers, was built at the Hythie (another name for small haven) in 1843, but was swept away by storm. Then another harbour was built at Buckpool in 1855, by Gordon of Letterfourie and the Board of Fisheries. This proved inadequate, and in 1872 Gordon of Cluny started the great new refuge for shipping, on this sometimes exceedingly dangerous coast, at a cost of £60,000. Since then Buckie has gone from strength to strength, the Town Council now owning the harbour works. The tall tower of the Moray Ice Company's establishment is prominent, in notable contrast to the vaulted old ice-house along the shore at Portgordon, though both for the storage of fish.

As to more ancient history Buckie has not much to show. It has been a Gordon place since 1358, and the Gordons of Buckie came into prominence, first when one of them was the only important casualty in a clan-battle with the Forbeses in 1572; and again in the famous affair of the slaying of the Bonnie Earl of Moray at Donibristle in 1592, when Gordon of Buckie it was who struck the first blow at the unfortunate Moray and then urged his chief, Huntly, to finish off the job. For actual historical incidents on the site, only the Battle of the Bauds near by, A.D. 961, in Rathven and Cullen parishes, calls for mention. Large quantities of human bones were dug up some years ago near Cluny harbour, and it is thought that many of the invading Danes were slain as they sought to re-embark.

Buckie became a burgh in 1888, with its own Provost, magistrates and Town Council. The Town House is in Cluny Place, near the Square, and was formerly the Masonic Institute of 1887. Strangely, there is another municipal building called the Town House East, in East Church Street, where are offices. At Cluny Square are the *County* offices, for some of Banffshire's administration is based here. In the centre of the Square is the impressive war-memorial, the bronze group designed by Birnie Rhind, considered to be one of the finest in Northern Scotland. The large Fishermen's Hall, seating 1000, is down on the lower level at Pringle Street, near the former Seatown. The shopping facilities are good.

Buckie was made a *quod sacra* parish, within Rathven civil parish, in 1876, formerly having been only a chapel-of-ease. This church is situated in Easter Buckie, dating from 1835, and now called the North Church. Its crown-tower is a prominent landmark. It was rebuilt in 1880. There is a South Church in the High Street, and an All Saints Episcopal church, formerly a Methodist building of 1875. But the most imposing ecclesiastical edifice is undoubtedly the large, twin-spired St. Peter's Catholic church at the west end of the town, on an island site and very impressive, dating from 1857. This has long been an area with strong Roman Catholic links, and this great church is an indication thereof. Other denominations, including the Exclusive Brethren, are also well represented. A bridge over the Buckie Burn near St. Peter's celebrates Queen Victoria's Jubilee.

There is a large secondary High School, with modern extensions, and also primary and infant schools, to the south-west of the town. Not far away is the Seafield Hospital, including a maternity wing. In this area is a great deal of municipal housing, not all of it distinguished by any means. Indeed, apart from the churches, especially St. Peter's, Buckie is scarcely notable architecturally or from a civic-planning point of view. But there are many parks, open spaces and recreational facilities, including the Linzee-Gordon public park, the Merson park, Queen Street park, and the Victoria park, with bowling-greens, putting-greens, tennis-courts, football and cricket pitches and games areas. There are two 18-hole golf courses, the municipal one to the east, at Strathlene, and a private one at Buckpool to the west, both open to visitors. There is also a large open-air swimming-pool at Strathlene, and bathing facilities are available along the coastline at various points. Boats and fishing are also catered for, with sea-angling a specialty; so the visitor need not be inactive. The Buckie Thistle Football Club flourishes.

The smaller fishing-villages which have been swallowed up by Buckie have some identity still. Buckpool on the west has its harbour and harbour-head area, with somewhat dull housing. The Seatown of Nether Buckie has its rows of fishermen's houses and the seaward area known as the Yardies, no doubt formerly net-drying open ground, now largely built up. Along the coast are former sheltered strands and bays called Little Hythe, the Nook, Whale's Wig, Peter

Hythe and Slough Hythe. The last three are east of the harbour of Gordonstown, which runs into Portessie. This last remains rather more of a distinct entity than the others, and was incorporated in the burgh only in 1904, a quieter place with brightly painted cottages, some gable-end to the street in traditional fashion, and its own school and Methodist church. The Muckle Sands stretch towards Strathlene. The Ianstown area lies on the higher level here, where the Rathven Burn comes down to the sea.

Eastwards of this lies the large caravan-park and camping-site, and the Strathlene golf course, the former mansion now a hotel.

Portgordon, at the other side of Buckie, is still a separate village, founded in 1797 by the 4th Duke of Gordon—the Gordons seem to have vied with each other in establishing fishing communities hereabouts. It stands where the A.990 approaches the coast from the A.98, near the Moray boundary, with its own harbour, which once supported no fewer than 100 boats, and used to import coals and salt and export grain and salt-fish. It has a church, now linked with Enzie, and a former toll-house of 1820. The afore-mentioned ice-house stands to the east, between road and shore, its vault now grass-grown.

Cabrach. This is one of those names about which people tend to be confused—and understandably. It is a huge, mountainous parish of 34,000 acres, but its centre is only a tiny hamlet of the same name—which used to be in Aberdeenshire but is now in Banffshire. The greater portion of the parish is also in Banffshire, and so I deal with it thereunder; but some is still in Aberdeenshire—all very confusing. The total population for an area of 10 miles by 8 is only about 500, so something of the nature of the terrain may be gauged. It is the headwaters-basin of the Deveron, and all is dominated by the tor-tipped Buck of the Cabrach (2368 feet), although there are many other lofty summits and ridges around the 2000 feet contour, and little of the parish lies below 1000 feet. There is a great stretch of planted woodland in the eastern section, an outlier of the vast Aberdeenshire Clashindarroch Forest. The parish is dissected by the A.941, well-known in weather-reports as the Rhynie-Dufftown road, so often one of the first to be closed by snow. The only other area of population to the Kirktown, hardly to be described as a hamlet, is in the Inverharroch, Bridgend, Milltown, Lesmurdie and Corinacy district to the north-west. The scenery is consistently fine.

Approaching Cabrach from the A.97 at Rhynie, the very attractive road climbs through rising farmlands, past the early Gordon lands of Scurdargue and Lesmoir and the former little parish of Essie (all described under Aberdeenshire) with fine backward views towards the Don valley and Correen Hills. Then for 2 miles the A.941 runs through the planted forest, which suddenly stops at the county boundary, at a col 1370 feet high, and a mighty prospect of heather mountain lands opens dramatically in a vast amphitheatre. It is all heather and bracken thereafter. Two miles further is the

Kirktown, the Cabrach shooting-lodge standing out whitewashed in a small group of trees—for this is a large deer-forest.

The Kirktown is a scattered community with its modest harled grey kirk of 1786 standing isolated beside a deep den, and its large and substantial manse across the dip. It has a belfry, windows on only the south side, and a graveyard with a few old stones. Not far away is the post-office of Upper Cabrach, the former school and a few cottages, in an area of small farms, all dwarfed by the surrounding hills. Peat-stacks are evident.

Westwards, under 2 miles, one of these small croft-like farms is called Aldivalloch, celebrated for the spirited song, *Roy's Wife of Aldivalloch*. Here is a cluster of 18th century croft-houses, some now in picturesque decay. Dead Wife's Hillock (1781 feet) rises behind.

Two miles north-east where the Aldivalloch side-road rejoins A.941 and the Allt Deveron enters a little pass called the Bank of Corinacy, is a pedimented roadside well, with inscription to the effect that it was erected out of the surplus funds of a bazaar held to pay for the six bridges built on the road between Dufftown and Cabrach—evidently a highly successful event. No doubt the well was already an old one. Near by is the remote hostelry, the Grouse Inn; and further on, the hump-backed late 18th century bridge over the Blackwater, a large tributary which turns the Allt Deveron into a sizeable river. Blackwater shooting-lodge stands in highly remote isolation 4 miles up this stream.

Bridgend, at the road-junction a mile on, has the Lower Cabrach post-office and a tiny branch of the county library in a shed. A little way east, along the side-road here, is the former United Presbyterian church of 1873, still in occasional use and linked with Mortlach, plain and rather bare within, above the road. Inverharroch, the large farm and former mill near by, once had its own castle, now gone, no doubt Gordon. Lesmurdie, now also a farm and once a well-known Gordon lairdship, is a mile further on, above the steep bank of the Deveron, and below this bank, in a most inaccessible position, is the site of a chapel and little graveyard of the Leslies—who presumably succeeded the Gordons in the property. These Gordons were evidently cadets of Lesmoir—at a price. We read in the Privy Council Records of 1600 that James Gordon of Lesmurdie entered a bond of £2000 that Alexander Gordon of Lesmoir would not harm James Gordon of Knockespock; and again in 1604 he subscribed another £1000 that the same Alexander would do no harm to three Gordons of Scurdargue. And so on. There is a cairn-circle on the hillside above.

The Catholic Gordon clan assembled here, under their chief Huntly, before the Battle of Glenlivet in 1594, when they defeated the Protestant force of 10,000 under Argyll. The battle was fought about 10 miles to the west, beyond Blackwater Forest.

Malcolm Canmore is said to have had a hunting-seat in the Cabrach, at what is called the King's Haugh, at Spenwell.

32

Cullen. The royal burgh of Cullen occupies a terrace site above the shore of Cullen Bay 14 miles west of Banff, where the Cullen Burn reaches the sea—indeed, it used to be called Invercullen. It is most famous for the splendid Cullen House, seat of the Earls of Seafield, a notable treasure-house; also for its fine pre-Reformation church of St. Mary's, still parish kirk—for Cullen is also a small civil parish of less than a thousand acres.

The royal burgh, although it dates its burghal privileges from William the Lion at the beginning of the 13th century, and has its own Provost and Town Council, is not very large, with a population of only some 1300. Nor is the present town itself of any antiquity, for Old Cullen, its site still so called, was close to Cullen House, within what are now extensive policies; but, being too close to the laird's windows for his taste, was moved to its present position half a mile away in 1822, and most of the old houses demolished. The burgh now has a wide and climbing main street, inevitably called Seafield Street, not especially attractive, with a central square, also on the slope. Here stands the Mercat Cross, on an elaborate crown-type base, with octagonal shaft and an animal holding a shield for finial, also the representation of the Virgin and Child, the town's emblem. The cross is said originally to have come from the Castle-hill, just west of the burgh, where on a green eminence are the remains of a vitrified fort and allegedly the foundations of a medieval castle. Robert the Bruce's queen, Elizabeth de Burgh, died at Cullen in 1327, two years before her husband, and it may be that this hill-top site was the scene of her death.

There are no particularly notable buildings in this New Town. The Seafield Church, of 1839, in the main street, is used nowadays for evening services, the old parish church being half a mile off. The Seafield Arms Hotel dates from 1822, at the corner of the square, but is thoroughly modernised. There is a large modern primary school at the top of the town, and the usual shops, banks and offices.

The former railway line, elevated on lofty viaducts, rather dominates the lower end of Cullen, and here the main A.98 highway curves down to the shore-level, past a wood-carver's workshop and show-room, to reach the western end of the one-time fishing community of Seatown, of typical North-East coastal cottages, many gable-end on to the street. Here is the harbour, built in 1817 by the Earl of Seafield and enlarged 1834, not now so important as once, when it used to sustain a large fishing-fleet and import coal and salt and export fish, grain and timber. There were once rope, sail and boat-building works here, a woollen mill and a brewery. Now the town is geared rather to the holiday-makers for whom there are many attractions. Just west of Seatown is the Seafield estate caravan-park, tucked into the wooded ravine of the Cullen Burn. And just beyond is the fine, long sandy beach, out on the links of which rise the three extraordinary rock formations known as the Three Kings, traditionally said to commemorate a semi-legendary battle with the invading Danes. The fine 18-hole golf course extends westwards, with a

33

putting-green. And still further west, half-way to Portknockie and the Scar Nose headland, is the well-known Cullen Bay Hotel, standing isolated on a bank, on the site of the former laird's house of Farskane.

To the east of Seatown there is considerable modern development, with villas, guest-houses and the like extending into municipal housing. Here, on the clifftop, is the burgh caravan-park, camping-site and playing-fields, with fine views over the rock-bound coast and cliff-walks leading to Logie Head at the other end of Cullen Bay, and Findlater Castle beyond—see Fordyce. Cullen has tennis-courts, bowling-greens, bathing and other facilities for the visitor.

Cullen House and the old parish church stand close together within the Seafield estate, the former open to the public in summer, three days a week, the latter always open. The house, whose interest and treasures can only be hinted at here, deserves a volume to itself. Originally a small monastic establishment connected with the collegiate church, it was after the Reformation built up, on this strong site above the ravine, into a typical L-planned tower-house in 1600. Sir Walter Ogilvie of Deskford and Findlater decided to leave the dramatic but inconvenient Findlater Castle on its cliff and come here. "Upon ye xx day of Mche 1600 yeares the Laird's hous in Culane was begun and the grund cassin." The fortalice has been hugely extended since then, notably in the 18th century, by Robert Adam, and in 1861 by David Bryce, to become the impressive castel-lated pile of today—but still on the L-plan. The original fortalice may still be distinguished however at the angle of the L, especially from the inner or west side, where the handsome ornamental door-way occupies the usual place in the re-entrant, surmounted by her-aldry, and above is an unusual gable flanked by two corbelled angle-turrets. The richness of the decorative stonework is notable. Intern-ally the house is quite magnificent, and particularly famed for its restored tempera-painted ceilings, especially in the King Charles Salon, others of decorative plaster, its carved doors, fireplaces and the interesting staircase with the pulpit-like summit. The furnishings, tapestries and paintings are quite splendid, the latter of great import-ance, including portraits by Kneller, Dahl, Raeburn, Allan Ramsay and many others. The armoury of 17th century guns and pistols is almost unique in Scotland. The Ogilvies are still at Cullen. The 4th Earl of Findlater became Chancellor and was created first Earl of Seafield in 1701—he who remarked that the Treaty of Union was "the end o' ane auld sang"—and when the 7th Earl died in 1811, his Seafield earldom could pass on to his far-out heir, Sir Lewis Grant of Grant descending from a daughter of the 5th Earl, who took the name of Ogilvie-Grant and became 5th Earl of Seafield, Viscount Reidhaven, and Lord Ogilvie of Deskford and Cullen—though the Findlater earldom became extinct.

The ancient St. Mary's church stands very close—indeed it is said to be linked by an underground passage—and is a highly interesting cruciform building of 1543, incorporating an earlier rectangular church, enriched by Robert the Bruce in memory of his wife. He did not *found* it, as is often alleged, for there was a church here in 1236. The tradition is that Elizabeth de Burgh's "interiores" were buried here when her body was carried south to be buried in Dunfermline Abbey, where her husband presently joined her. If so, there is nothing to mark the spot. At any rate, Robert left an endowment for the perpetual saying of masses for the soul of his beloved Queen at Cullen St. Mary's. In 1543 the church was made collegiate, with a provost, six prebendaries and two singing boys, when also the chancel was lengthened and the transepts added. This is the fine building which is still the parish kirk, one of the most interesting in the land. There are some good heraldic panels on the external walls.

Almost a superfluity of items of interest fill the fairly modest interior. There is a pre-Reformation sacrament-house in the chancel, with carvings of angels and a gospel inscription above, less handsome than that at Deskford old church, and no doubt presented by the same donor, Alexander Ogilvie of Deskford, who was one of the endowers of the collegiate foundation. He and his wife, Elizabeth Gordon, are buried here, and the very imposing recumbent effigy and memorial, highly decorative, is almost too grand for its surroundings. He died in 1554. Near by is a notable example of laird's-loft, or private gallery, in timber, dated 1602, with much heraldry and a short stairway up to it. Across from this is another elaborate memorial, in marble this time, to the Chancellor, 4th Earl of Findlater and 1st of Seafield, one of the architects of the Union of Parliaments, for better or worse—and he lived to try to undo the said Union. This great plaque at least is splendidly done. Behind the pulpit to the left, is a modern mosaic, gifted in 1960 and rather fine. In the St. Anne's Aisle is a memorial to another of the collegiate-endowers, the pious Elena Hay, mother of John Duff of Muldavit, a small lairdship which used to lie just across the Cullen Burn. Here are links with the strange genealogical confidence-trick perpetrated at Duff House mausoleum, Banff, in which the 2nd Earl of Fife removed a recumbent effigy from here, and altered the inscribed dates to make it seem as though this was a much earlier ancestor of his own. The effigy has now been brought back and is in its proper place. Above the alcove is inscribed, in very odd spelling which may be interpreted thus: "John Hay, Lord of the Forest of Boyne, Enzie and Tullibody, grandfather to Elena Hay, who built this aisle, gifted a chaplainry here to sing, personally of his lands of Ordinhuf." Outside the church is a sandstone grave-slab upended, with a very fine incised rendering of a knight in armour, now seeming to relate to the aforementioned Duff of Muldavit but probably referring to one Alexander Innes, the date again very obviously recut to read 1404 instead of about 150 years later. Yet the maligned John Duff himself was innocent of all deception, and appears to have gifted one of the windows of St. Anne's Aisle.

It is surprising that the old church is in so excellent a state today, considering that, on the way to Culloden, the Duke of Cumberland

35

stayed at Cullen House for several days, and stabled his horses in this church. Montrose's forces also plundered Cullen, but they may not have harmed the kirk. In the crowded kirkyard are many old and interesting memorials, especially table-stones. But, oddly enough, out here it all looks rather neglected.

In the Seafield estate not far away is a fine single-arch bridge by Robert Adam, dating from 1741, across the ravine of the Cullen Burn. And a triumphal arch by James Adam graces the main driveway entrance. To the south is the small Crannoch Loch, its islet apparently an artificial crannog.

A mile to the south of Cullen is the hamlet of Lintmill, in a pleasant site at the waterside of the Burn of Deskford—which about here changes its name to Cullen Burn. There is some modern housing development and a post-office. A little to the east of this is the former distillery of Tochieneal, of 1824, now an agricultural store. The Bin Hill of Cullen (1053 feet) rises prominently to the south-west, with great woodlands wherein are cairns and the site of a Pictish fort.

Deskford. Deskford is one of those places which are scarcely well-known or important of themselves, but of which the name is celebrated. This is because of the prominent part played in the country's story by the Ogilvie lairds thereof, who became Lords Deskford and finally Earls of Findlater and Seafield. It is a medium-sized civil parish of 8000 acres, more regular in outline than most in Banffshire, 5 miles long by 3 wide, forming a rectangle south-west of Cullen, flanking the quite pronounced vale of the Burn of Deskford, and threaded centrally by the B.9018 Cullen-Keith road. There is only one village, the Kirktown, with its nearby burnside hamlet of Berryhillock, of late 18th century cottages; but there are many farms, and considerable afforestation, three areas in particular having large woodlands, partly Forestry Commission. In the Greenhill area to the south-east, as well as plantations there are some old Scots pines growing out of heather. The parish boundary lies along the summit of Lurg Hill (1028 feet), to the south.

Deskford's interest centres mainly round the churches, ancient and modern, at the Kirktown, crowning a high bank above the wooded valley, a pleasant place now becoming rehabilitated after lapsing into some sort of decay. Here was also Deskford Tower, once the seat of the Ogilvies who gained the lands by a marriage with the Sinclair heiress in 1437. The modern parish church dates from 1872, and is in the usual Gothic tradition of that period, in trees, with the war-memorial, and the school opposite. Its predecessor stands in a sloping graveyard not far to the east, a roofless ruin but with some notable features. Its sacrament-house is a particularly fine example, now kept under protective glass by the Department of Environment, and is dated 1551. It is a highly decorated aumbry for the reservation of the holy elements, with angels, vine-scrolling and heraldry, plus the inscription: THIS PNT LOVEABLE VARK OF SACRAMET HOUS

MAID TO YE HONOR & LOVIG OF GOD BE AN NOBLE MAN ALEXANDER
OGILVY OF YAT ILK & ELIZABET GORDON HIS SPOUSE THE ZEIR OF GOD
1551. This pair are buried in the parish church of Cullen, where
there is another sacrament-house of their providing. Here at Deskford are also two holy-water stoups in the south wall and two pointed
aumbries is the east gable. There is a built-in dormer pediment
dated 1669 with the initials W.O. and M.S.; and another oddly
shaped heraldic memorial, like a pear, to Master Walter Ogilvie.
The pre-Reformation church was dedicated to St. John, and lower
down the hillside is the site of the former St. John's Well. Against
the north outer wall of the church, but actually in the garden of the
adjoining Muckle Hoose, are the scanty remains of Deskford Tower,
the early fortalice. When, well over a century ago, the abandoned
castle fell into a bad state it was pulled down to prevent any damage
to the church. Only some creeper-clad parts of a basement vault
remain. Clearly, however, the building now called the Muckle
Hoose is built on and may partly incorporate some of the castle.
Sir Walter Ogilvie, descended from the Angus Ogilvys of Lintra-
then, who married Mary Beaton, one of the Queen's Maries, was
created Lord Ogilvie of Deskford in 1616.

The wooded valley of the Deskford Burn is very picturesque here;
indeed the entire little strath is attractive. There are a number of
waterfalls, not large, and one called the Linn, south-east of the
Kirktown, is rather fine. Beyond Berryhillock hamlet, south of this
area, is Mains of Skeith, where once was a Castle of Skeith, now
gone.

Another castle stood at Inaltrie, a farm lying on a side-road over a
mile north-east of the Kirktown. Here a massive length of walling
still stands, 40 feet long by 10 feet high, probably part of the curtain-
wall. There was an artificial mound in the immediate vicinity, now
removed, known as the Law Hillock, no doubt the seat of baronial
jurisdiction. This is still in the vale of the Deskford Burn.

Before leaving Deskford mention must be made of the unique
Pictish relic found here on the farm of Leitchestown, a mile north-
east of Inaltrie. This is a remarkable boar-headed trumpet-bell in
sheet bronze, with open jaws—in which once was a wooden tongue
or clapper—part of a Celtic war-trumpet. This fine piece of the
warrior art of our Pictish ancestors, is on view at the Museum of
Antiquities, Edinburgh, on loan from the Banffshire Education
Authority.

Dufftown. The small burgh of Dufftown, nestling under Ben
Rinnes and the Conval Hills, may have a population of only 1500
but it is much more important than its size suggests, owing to the
concentration here of famous and prosperous distilleries, of which
there are at least eight in the immediate vicinity. It stands at the
junction of the Dullan Burn with the River Fiddich, in the large
parish of Mortlach, 10 miles south-west of Keith, and is hidden in
hills until the visitor is almost upon it. The aspect from the higher,

southern approach on B.9009, from Tomintoul, is very fine, this end of the little town being attractive, with trees left amongst the modern housing, and the small Episcopal church of St. Michael's, of 1880, overlooking all.

Dufftown consists basically of two long streets, crossing each other, with lesser avenues and lanes off, and in the centre a square in which rises the tall and massive Town House tower. This battlemented building of pink granite is unusual in more ways than one. It looks rather like an old tolbooth, but dates only from 1836—although built partly as a jail, in the old tradition. Also, it is all tower, with no main block, the town-council chamber being included, despite the modest dimensions. It has a clock, to mark Queen Victoria's Jubilee—she visited Dufftown in 1867—and is surmounted by a strange ogee-roofed metal belfry, as it were on stilts. A plaque commemorates the 1st Duke of Fife (and 6th Earl) munificent benefactor of the burgh, who died 1912.

Dufftown, as its name implies, was founded in 1817 by James Duff, 4th Earl of Fife, a general in the Spanish army during the Peninsula War, and a Lord of the Bedchamber. The burgeoning and ambitious Duffs liked doing this sort of thing, and no doubt this one wished to be upsides with his uncle, the 2nd Earl, who had founded Macduff 30 miles away.

Being a considerable distance from any other town, it is quite a shopping centre with banks, insurance offices and a famous Customs and Excise establishment—where once the two novelists Neil Gunn and Maurice Walsh served together as officers. There are two hospitals, the County being now geriatric and the smaller, the Stephen, founded by Lord Mount Stephen in 1889, for maternity cases. The parish church is that of Mortlach, a notable and highly interesting place with many features—the Kirktown of Mortlach lies immediately to the south, on the lower ground, now a sort of suburb of Dufftown, and described separately as a parish. St. Mary of the Assumption Catholic church, of 1825, is small, on the hill at the east end of the town. There is a fire-station and auction-marts in Hill Street, and a small park, with war memorial, playing-field and bowling-green. Limestone is prevalent, and there are quarries to the north and east, with old limekilns still standing near by. And Balvenie Castle, a magnificent ruin of the 13th, 15th and late 16th centuries, lies less than a mile to the north.

The malt distilleries, however, are the most pronounced and significant features of Dufftown, and employers of labour. Glenfiddich in especial, near Balvenie Castle, being a great attraction as having a whisky museum and reception-centre for visitors. It was founded in 1886 by the famous Major William Grant of Glenfiddich and his seven sons, who more or less erected the original building with their own hands. But everywhere you turn in these deep winding valleys you find these busy establishments, which make Dufftown, for its size, probably the largest earner of foreign currency in the British Isles.

Craigmin bridge in the Letterfourie Estate

Duff House, Banff

Macduff: boatyard

Findochty. The little burgh of Findochty—pronounced locally Finichty—is one of those strung-out fishing communities which line the Banffshire coast of the Moray Firth, from Port Gordon to Cullen, lying midway between these two, 2 miles west of Portknockie and an equal distance east of Buckie and Portessie. It is almost the same size as neighbouring Portknockie, with 1300 population, but is rather different in character, the coastline here being less dramatic and the harbour larger. It was founded as a haven and village in 1716 by a colony of Fraserburgh fishermen, and in 1885 had no fewer than 140 boats working from it. The harbour was much improved in 1882 by the Fishery Commissioners; but the proximity of Buckie, with all its port facilities, draws the trade away.

The town climbs a lofty bank rather than a cliff, and has the usual stone cottages, brightly painted, the older ones gable-end to the street. The main street flanks the harbour, down at that level. At the west end of this is a very fine piece of modern sculpture, of an old fisherman, seated and gazing out to sea, inscribed: "These see the works of the Lord and the wonders of the deep." It was sculpted by an art student at Aberdeen, and erected by an appreciative art master who was formerly a member of Findochty Town Council—a very worthwhile feature.

The Hythe Church stands on a lofty eminence above the town, and acts as a landmark—although it is the usual plain and rather dull building of the 19th century, with small pointed belfry. This presumably was an innovation, for until 1887 the congregation was summoned to worship, perhaps appropriately, by foghorn. There is a Methodist church to the west on lower ground. At the east end of the harbour is quite a large bakery factory, serving the area.

Further east, after a sandy beach, the rock scenery becomes increasingly interesting, and a cliff-path leads past the stack of the Priest's Craig, with its well, to the lofty Three-Mouthed Cave and Canty's Cave (where a Jacobite fugitive lurked after Culloden) and on to the Needle's Eye natural arch and Tronach Head. A path leads along the shore westwards of Findochty also, by further caves to the lesser Craig Head. Flanking this is the Strathlene golf course (Buckie) with other recreational facilities, open to visitors.

Inland a short distance, and west of the town, on Mains farm, are the ruins of Findochty Castle, a very small fortalice crowning a rocky mound. Quite a lot of it survives, an L-shaped tower-house on a miniature scale, with a square tower to the north and the western gable still standing, the rest fragmentary. It dates from the late 16th century, is well supplied with shot-holes, and the window-embrasures have red-stone surrounds. Two vaulted basement chambers remain, one in the foot of the tower quite tiny. The property belonged to the Gordons but passed to the Ogilvies. The Law Hillock, rising in the golf course seaward, was the seat of baronial jurisdiction.

Inland stretches the Moor of Findochty, merging into the Bauds of Cullen a rather bleak and featureless area, wherein are many

39

cairns thought to represent the burial-places of the slain at the Battle of the Bauds, with invading Danes, around A.D. 961.

Fordyce and Sandend. Fordyce is a small, old-world village 4 miles south-east of Cullen, and a large civil parish of 17,400 acres; and Sandend is a thriving and quite picturesque fishing-village 2 miles to the north. The burgh of Portsoy is also in this parish, but is treated separately. The parish, like so many in coastal Banffshire, is elongated, running inland for 8 or 9 miles, and terminates on the lofty pointed summit of Knock Hill (1412 feet).

Fordyce village is tucked away pleasingly on its own burn at the foot of an extension of the Hill of Durn (653 feet)—which is crowned by the remains of a Pictish fort, and has a large quarry on its north-east face. It is a tight-packed little place of narrow winding lanes, romantic of aspect and with the very unusual feature of a castellated laird's house of the late 16th century plumb in the centre of the main street. Fordyce Castle is a highly attractive fortalice, small, traditional, L-planned, with crowstepped gables, conical angle-turrets at two corners and a stair-turret in the re-entrant. It is well-provided with shot-holes, and the stair-turret corbelling is remarkable in that all eleven courses are of different design. The basement is vaulted, and although the house has been much altered internally over the years, there is hope that it is now to be properly restored. It dates from 1592. There is a 17th century block added to the east, also picturesque. The castle was built by Thomas Menzies, an Aberdeen burgess whose family supplied many provosts to that city. Fordyce village was made a burgh of barony in 1499 at the behest of the famous Bishop Elphinstone of Aberdeen, Lord Chancellor.

The ancient and ruined church of Fordyce, dedicated to St. Tarquin, or Talcritan—there was a Tarkin's Well here—stands in its crowded graveyard just to the north, also pleasing. The ivy-clad remains consist of a vaulted square tower with belfry, and pended porch beneath, with an outside stair leading up to a priest's room on the first floor, with aumbry and fireplace. Near by is the vaulted burial-aisle of the Abercrombys of Glassaugh, with its own little belfry, also a good heraldic panel on the north gable. Here commemorated is General James Abercromby "a strict but genteel economist". There is likewise an Ogilvie tomb of the 16th century, with fine pointed recess but now no recumbent effigy. Here are the remains of an old massive stone font. The kirkyard is notably full of old tumbled gravestones, and a rather attractive former manse stands to the east. The present parish church, dating from 1804, is typically large and plain, and now in use only once or twice a month. It stands at the other, west, end of the village. Fordyce, although at a cross-roads, is not on any main highway, and tends to be passed by; which is a pity, for it is a most interesting place with an air of settled peace. There is a school, successor of Fordyce Academy founded in 1790 by a Bombay nabob for the education and board of nine boys of his own name of Smith. Old cottages are being renovated, and there is some modern housing. All Hallows Fair used to be held here. The countryside round about is pleasant, undulating, with more woodland than in many parts of Banff.

The Glassaugh estate lies about a mile to the north, but the massive and rather plain mansion, much enlarged in the early 19th century, is now a hay-store. Glenglassaugh Distillery, however, is still going strong, although some Ordnance maps proclaim it disused, on the seaward side of the A.98. It has the usual hamlet of associated housing. Near by is the massive base of a circular windmill, a very unusual relic for these parts.

The Sandend road-end is not far westwards, and the village lines the west side of Sandend Bay on the way to Garron Point. Modern housing at this end does not improve the prospect, but most of the place has the cheerful and pleasing atmosphere of a traditional fishing-village, with gable-end cottages, a small harbour and quite a number of smoke-houses for curing smokies and kippers, also some small fish-merchants' establishments. Many boats still serve Sandend, and are crewed from here, but work out from Buckie. The sandy beach is an attraction for holiday-makers, and there is a caravan-park. There are caves along the rocky shore east of Sandend Bay, and at Redhythe Point, half-way to Portsoy, former lime-kilns.

A mile north-west of Sandend, beyond Crathie Point but reached by a side-road striking inland by the farm of Barnyards of Findlater, is the dramatic site of Findlater Castle, a former stronghold of the Ogilvies, clinging precariously to a stack of the cliffs above the seething tides. Part of the castle is indeed excavated from the rocks themselves. It has obviously been a very grim, strong place. The site was fortified, with the Crown's consent, in 1445, by Sir Walter Ogilvie of Auchleven; but there may have been an earlier fortalice. Little remains now—but sufficient to demonstrate the sort of romantic, wild hold it was. Findlater was involved in the affairs of Mary Queen of Scots. Ogilvie of Cardell, her Secretary when in France, was true heir of Findlater, but was disinherited by his father in favour of the Earl of Huntly's second son, Sir John Gordon, a murky business. Sir John, a swashbuckling character with a reputation as a lady-killer, had the temerity to desire the hand of the young Queen, and when his cavalier advances were rejected, refused the Queen's requests to deliver up Findlater. Out of this developed the Battle of Corrichie, with the Gordon power having to be put down, where Huntly was defeated and Sir John executed at Aberdeen, still railing at the Queen. The Ogilvies got Findlater back, and in 1638 were elevated to be Earls thereof. The 7th Earl, who was also 4th Earl of Seafield, died in 1811, and only the Seafield title went on, to his Grant cousin. There is a good circular doocot of probably the 16th century inland a little way, near the Barnyards farm.

A mile south of Barnyards, not far from the A.98, is the ancient property of Birkenbog, in a meadowy vale below the afforested Cotton Hill. This has been a delightful place, but it is now a rather dejected farm and steading, though nothing quite obliterates its picturesque character. The long, low hallhouse behind its forecourt, has a good moulded doorway with a heraldic panel above displaying the arms of Abercromby quartered with Gordon and dated 1693. The fine walled-garden and sundry subsidiary buildings have gone to seed. Yet this sad establishment gives title to the Abercromby baronets of Birkenbog, since 1636, who have the fine mansions and estates of Forglen and Dunlugas not far away. A standing-stone is situated on the remote high ground of Ley farm about a mile due south.

The further inland parts of the parish, like so much of Banffshire, are high and moorish, with small farms and few features of interest. The impressive and lofty Knock Hill dominates all this area, but most of it is in Grange parish. There are large forestry plantations at Roughilly Wood and Moss of Reid.

Forglen. This is an attractive, rural Deveron parish of 6250 acres, of farms and estates and woodland, situated just west of the Aberdeenshire border near Turriff, about 9 miles south of Banff. Although only disjoined from Alvah and set up as a civil parish in 1642, it has an ancient identity, William the Lion granting "Forglint" to the Abbey of Arbroath in 1204. Long before that, however, it was known as Tennan, a corruption of St. Eunan, which was a modified form of Adamnan. That stalwart saint and scholar, friend of Columba, founded here his principal chapel and mission amongst the Northern Picts in the 7th century. Here was long preserved the famous Brecbennach of St. Columba, carried at Bannockburn, which came to be known as the Monymusk Reliquary.

The ancient ecclesiastical site is on a shelf above the Deveron not much more than a mile west of Turriff, although on the other side of the river, a picturesque and sequestered spot with the ruined church and still-used graveyard, and large former manse near by. Only a fragment of St. Eunan's chapel remains, with however, a small piscina still in the north wall, and to the west an inscription declaring that this church was re-edified by George Ogilvie, Master of Banff, in 1692. In the kirkyard are many 18th century table-stones. The parish church was removed to a higher site in 1806, above the B.9025 road less than half a mile to the north, but this is now closed down and the congregation conjoined with one in Turriff.

The nearest thing Forglen has to a village is at Bogton, a hamlet on a side-road less than 2 miles north-west of the old church, in pleasant undulating country. Here is the post-office and shop, and a row of 18th century cottages and school, nicely modernised, with a hall on the main road and the Mill of Ribrae in the hollow. This side-road leads on south-westwards to Carnousie, a large and wooded Deveronside estate which has seen better days. Old Carnousie House was replaced by a more modern mansion half a mile away, and became Mains of Carnousie, then was abandoned and allowed to decay. When first the present author visited it, the house was actually being used as a piggery. Happily it is now being restored. For it is a fine

L-planned fortalice of the late 16th century, with an 18th century wing added. It is typically tall and steep-roofed, with a square crowstepped-gabled tower at one end and a circular, conical-roofed one at the other. There are stair-turrets in the main and southern re-entrants. The basement is vaulted and the Hall on first floor has a handsome carved-stone overmantel with lions and unicorns. There is considerable good pine-panelling throughout. Carnousie was early a property of the great Dunbar family, passing to the Ogilvies in 1530—they were seated at nearby Dunlugas. In 1622 Sir George Ogilvie complained to the Privy Council that Robert Innes of that Ilk and sundry others "hound and chaise the cattle off the commonty of Carnousie, threaten their herds, cast faill, dovett and uther fewall on the lands, and commit uther acts of evill nycht-bourheade". The Gordons got Carnousie in the mid-17th century. It is good to see this fine building being saved.

There is much woodland on this estate, and between the old and later mansions, on the slight ridge of Whitehill, is Cairn Ennit, a large cairn-circle with stone outliers, fairly readily discovered. But another stone-circle marked hereabouts on the Ordnance map is less easily found amongst the many piles of large stones, bracken and tree-stumps. At the other side of Carnousie, a mile to the north, on a side-road, is the small, remotely set Free church, still functioning—a reversal of the usual situation, with the parish church closed down.

Forglen estate is large, and the principal seat of the baronet family of Abercromby of Birkenbog—although the present Sir George lives at Dunlugas. The large mansion, in castellated style, was built only in 1842, incorporating an ancient fortalice of the mid-15th century and later. Inset here is a heraldic stone dated 1577, and the cynical motto HOIP OF REVAIRD CAVSES GVID SERVICE, with below a lengthy oddly spelled inscription. The Abercrombys obtained Forglen by marriage with the Ogilvies of Dunlugas, who became Lords Banff. Dunlugas House itself is pleasantly set on the east bank of Deveron, 2 miles to the north. The present medium-sized mansion dates from 1793, but the estate is very ancient, having been the main seat of the Ogilvies, who became so important in Banffshire. The Carlinkist Cairn burial-mound stands on higher ground a mile to the south-east.

Gamrie and Gardenstown. Gamrie is the extreme north-easterly parish of Banffshire, and far from typical. Although extending for some 10 miles along the coast, it reaches inland for an average of only 3 miles, comprising 17,300 acres. The seaboard is spectacular, especially towards the east, with great cliffs, headlands, bays, caves and skerries, culminating in Troup Head right on the Aberdeenshire border, a mighty promontory rising almost sheerly to 365 feet. Gardenstown is a picturesquely sited and quite large fishing-village on Gamrie Bay. The burgh of Macduff is situated in this civil parish, but is dealt with separately.

Gardenstown village has an extraordinary position, climbing what

43

is almost a cliff-face in a succession of narrow terraces linked by steep winding braes. It was founded in 1720 by Alexander Garden of Troup as a fishing community, and its good harbour is still in use for that purpose where many another is not. There are many warehouses, offices, a coastguard rescue-station and other facilities. It is almost a little town, with bank, shops, school and much modern housing, both council and private. There is a plain gaunt church, of 1875, without churchyard, half-way up the steep slope, built as a chapel-of-ease of Gamrie parish church, Gardenstown being made a *quod sacra* parish in 1885. There is a small sandy beach at the west end of the village.

Gamrie Church itself stands remotely, over a mile inland, a rather bleak landmark within its kirkyard, commanding wide prospects, a large, harled preaching kirk of 1830, with valuable communion-plate dating from 1620. There is a large manse near by. But this church is itself only the successor of the original pre-Reformation chapel of St. John, situated in a now rather inaccessible position below Gamrie More Head on the west side of the bay. It is a simple, roofless rectangle dating from 1513, though on a site sanctified since 1004, when reputedly, in battle with invading Danes, the Mormaor of Buchan vowed he would erect a church to St. John if given the victory. A less dramatic version is that he merely rebuilt a chapel demolished by the Danes. At any rate, three skulls of Danish chiefs long decorated this building, in grisly evidence of the victory. In its graveyard are the burial-places of the Gardens (some say originally Gordons) of Troup, and of Patrick Barclay of Towie-Barclay in Aberdeenshire, the latter having a tablet dated 1547.

Troup House estate lies at the easternmost end of the parish, backing on Troup Head, a large and distinctly grim-looking mansion of 1770 now superseded by a more modern house, its policies pleasingly wooded in a somewhat treeless countryside. The eastern side of Troup Head is particularly exciting scenically, with towering cliffs riven and slashed. Here are the well-known Lion's Head, Hell's Lum and Needle's Eye features, to be viewed only from cliff-walks. Here also, almost in Aberdeenshire, is Cullykhan, flanking Pennan Bay, where a dirt-road leads down from B.9031 to a noted cliff-top archaeological site where excavation is currently taking place into a Bronze Age settlement. A unique crucible, 2500 years old, was found here recently, a sort of ladle for bronze-making. There has been later Pictish and Roman occupation—indeed a medieval strong-point was also sited here.

A notable feature of this district is the deep and lengthy den or ravine known as the Tore of Troup, cutting inland for 3 miles towards the Hill of Troup (661 feet). It contains, about half-way along, on the Aberdeenshire side, a holy well and site of another pre-Reformation chapel. This valley marks the county boundary. There are other somewhat similar steep dens scoring the parish, their burns frequently producing waterfalls.

Between Troup Head and Gardenstown is the extraordinary little coastal village of Crovie, beloved of artists and photographers, some forty cottages clinging like limpets to the shoreline at the cliff-foot, with insufficient space even for a linking street or back-gardens. There is a small pier, a brief shingle beach at low tide, and the road down has a gradient of 1 in 5—so that, wisely, certain of the cottagers garage their cars high above at the cliff-top. Crovie is no longer a fishing-village, most of the houses now being holiday-homes.

Inland, near the southern edge of the parish, is the Minnonie area, somewhat bleak and Buchan-like country, with a rather remarkable winding rush-floored watershed valley known as Bog of Minnonie. Near by is the fragmentary ruin of Pitgair Castle perched on the Ha' Hill of Pitgair farm above the ravine, a very early stronghold allegedly linked with the name of William Wallace. Other features of this large parish include the fossil-rich deposits of Findon just south of Gardenstown—where also was once a stronghold marked by its Castle Hill; the Law of Melrose, a pointed cliff-top hillock, rising to 403 feet, midway between Gardenstown and Macduff, another former defensive site; the Longman Cairn, a whin-grown chambered-cairn beside a deserted farmhouse 3 miles south-east of Macduff, 200 feet long by 11 feet high, joined by a neck to a lesser mound; and the Law of Balgreen, over 2 miles further south, one more ancient baronial site now only a green wooded hummock.

Grange, Knock and Edingight. Grange, more properly Grange of Strathisla, is an inland parish extending to some 6400 acres just east and north of Keith, based on the valley of the Banffshire Isla. It has no real village or sizeable community. Knock is the pronounced conical hill at its eastern extremity, reaching 1412 feet, with an area to the south of the same name, including Knock Distillery. And Edingight is an ancient lairdship of the Innes family, in the centre of the parish.

The parish church is inconveniently sited at the extreme south, above the Isla's meadows. The present building dates only from 1795 and was built more or less in the site of a former fortified strength, or castle, the Gallows Hill for which is near by. Remains of the moat may still be traced. The graveyard is across the side-road, on a sloping site, and here is the burial-enclosure of the Innes family of Balveny and Edingight. The church itself is plain, with lateral windows on the south side only, and end gallery, and all rather dull. At the other side of the Gallowhill Wood, to the north, is the site of a group of prehistoric burial-cairns; and a mile to the east, Roman camp site—although why so close to another (less than 2 miles) is not explained. Midway between cairns and camp, at a side-road junction, is the former Free church and manse, the church no longer in use. Just below it at the roadside is a well, which may be the Well of the Cross, known to have existed in the parish not so very far from Our Lady's Well, which is to be found at the side of the Strathisla road, A.95, a little east of the parish church, still functioning and now used as a war-memorial, an unusual development. It takes its name from the pre-Reformation chapel here, dedicated to the Virgin Mary, now gone. Grange, as its name implies, was a farming estate belonging to the Abbey of Kinloss, the house of the sub-prior being the aforementioned castle. Secularised at the Reformation, the property was broken up into a large number of small farms and bonnet-lairdships. Braco, now a large farm a mile to the east, was one of these—and thereby hangs a story. The feuar thereof, about a century later, one Alexander Duff, was an acquisitive man. He was standing on the hillside above Braco one day, with an acquaint-ance, and remarked on the many smokes rising from all the small laird's houses to Strathisla, saying that one day he would make all the smoke go up one vent. And he did, by buying them all up, by one means or another, the Jacobite troubles helping a shrewd man on the make. His son was William, first Lord Braco and later Vis-count Macduff and first Earl of Fife; and in 1885 the 6th Earl married the Princess Royal and was made Duke of Fife.

To the west of Our Lady's Well, in the haugh of the Isla, are two sites, once allegedly a Roman and one a Pictish camp. Little is now to be discerned of either. There is a rather good old single-arch bridge over the Isla, to Cantly, opposite the Well, and this was erected by Alexander Christie, tenant in Cantly, in 1699, to enable the good folk to attend church. It was widened in 1783.

To the east of the church area in fertile Strathisla is the former Grange railway-station, now Garrowood Hotel, with post-office, just across the river and under the huge planted forest of Bin Hill, through which runs the Aberdeenshire border. A little further to the east is Nethermills, a one-time milling hamlet, now a scatter of rather decayed-looking buildings, the mill now a grain-drying establishment. Up on the main road above is the large King Memor-ial Hall, built by a prosperous former native, and rather pretentious-seeming for a rural area.

The parish boundary follows the Shiel Burn which joins Isla near here from the north-east. Three miles up, under Knock Hill, is Knockdhu Distillery and its associated cottages, post-office and large farm, the largest community of the parish. On Knock Hill's south-western flanks, amongst the heather, are a great cluster of ancient burial-cairns, declared to cover the slain at one of those traditional battles between Scots and invading Danes. Near by, at Whitehill, is another disused Free church, of 1771–1897, in a notably isolated position, now used only as a straw-store. Glen Barry, a defile through which runs the main A.95 highway, lies over a mile to the east, and here, at the parish boundary, stands an inn, at a road-junction. Inserted in the gable is a good heraldic panel inscribed: "The arms of William Duff of Braco, afterwards first Lord Fife, for 200 years on the house of Balveny, removed here 1932." William Duff was not created Earl of Fife until 1759, and Balveny House not built until about 1765, so the inscription exaggerates a little. Why it was inserted here is not clear.

The views open out from here, southwards, towards the high hills.

Edingight lies 2 miles to the west, in undulating country but still under the dominance of Knock Hill. The old house of Edingight, a long, low hallhouse of probably late 17th century date but with older nucleus, stands some way to the north of the later mansion in its wooded policies, and is marked on the map as Mains of Edingight. It has fairly recently been restored and occupied by Malcolm Innes of Edingight, Lyon Clerk and a noted herald, son of the late Lord Lyon, Sir Thomas. As is to be expected, there is some excellent modern heraldic carving here. A skew-putt is decorated with an old stone mask. The Innes family derive from one Berowald, who in 1160 was granted the barony of Innes, in Moray, by Malcolm the Fourth. Sir Alexander, of that Ilk, the 9th, married the heiress of the Thane of Aberchirder, in this area, and the Inneses of Balveny and Edingight descend from a son of the 11th chief. They were granted a baronetcy in 1628. The family took a full share in the stirring activities of the North-East.

The north-western section of the parish is an elevated moorland tract known as Aultmore, with small farms amongst the mosses but few features of interest, traversed by the B.9018 Keith–Cullen road. The names, Foggy Moss, Bogs of Paithnick, Greenbog, Windyhills and Myres speak for themselves. Much limestone is available in this parish, and there are many old kilns.

Inverkeithny and Conveth. This is a fairly small, remote and scarcely important farming parish of 7700 acres, of a peculiar S-shape flanking the south side of the Deveron at the Aberdeenshire border, between Turriff and Huntly, and seeming to belong more to that county than to Banffshire. It was, in fact, disjoined from Strathbogie only in 1701. The parish church and small village is at Inverkeithny, at the narrow western loop of the S, but the Conveth area, once a pre-Reformation parish of its own, to the east, is larger, although lacking even a hamlet.

Inverkeithny, picturesquely situated deep in the Deveron's wooded valley, narrowed here, has a slightly decayed air, with an empty school and abandoned cottages. The church and graveyard are still in use, however, and stand at the east end, on a slight bank above the river, with trees around. The building dates only from 1881, in the Gothic style, but is on the site of an earlier church, and the kirkyard is crowded, especially with a great many 18th century tablestones, which gives the impression that the parish was formerly more populous than today. The old bell is in the modern belfry, and there is communion plate of 1633, gifted by the first Viscount Frendraught, the famous Crichton. There used to be a ferry-boat across the Deveron here, but the bridge is across the Burn of Forgue (not the Keithny, as one might expect from the name). The Deveron itself is not crossed till 2 miles further west, at Bridge of Marnoch.

Steep hills lead down into Inverkeithny from both sides, and the general level of the undulating parish is much higher than the 200 feet of the valley-floor here, especially to the east, where the hills of

Tollo and Carlincraig reach 738 and 629 feet, with the site of hut-circles on the latter. To the west there is little of interest to note, although at Mains of Auchingoul at the parish boundary near Bridge of Marnoch is the site of a small Roman post which guarded the ford here, covering 4 acres and marked as Earthwork on the maps. The farmhouse of Auchingoul used to have a fine chimney-piece, probably once a dormer pediment, displaying a viscount's coronet and the Crichton crest, now destroyed. There is a hamlet of Auchingoul flanking the A.97 which here, at the borders of Marnoch parish and Aberdeenshire, makes a brief excursion into this parish. The hamlet is mainly noticeable for its large and unsightly scrap-iron dump. There is a Skene-Murray Mission Hall, up a lane, with a few cottages and a larger house.

The road eastwards from Inverkeithny climbs high on a terraced hillside with splendid prospects over a pleasant land of narrow glens, green hillsides and scattered trees. It leads to the Conveth area, which name has all but disappeared save for a small school in the Fortrie–Tollo area. At Mains of Tollo, in the stackyard, is the site of the pre-Reformation chapel and graveyard, although nothing now remains. Robert the Second in 1380 granted a charter of Conveth to his notorious son, Alexander, Earl of Buchan, Wolf of Badenoch. St. Kryle seems to have been the patron saint, for there is a St. Kryle's, or Creel's Well near the school.

A mile to the north rises the low green hill of Drach Law (483 feet) and on its south flank is the farm of Backhill of Drachlaw where there is a stone-circle in a field, visible from the B.9024 road, of 6 remaining stones. At Cairnrieve, on slightly higher ground a little further north, is a very large monolith, somewhat shattered. Presumably this is the Carlin Stone marked on the map—although there is another single standing-stone only about 400 yards away on the other side of the road. At Feith-hill farm, 2 miles to the south, are two more standing-stones, known as the Hairstanes, on a ridge. And still further south-west, on the county boundary near the remote mossland farm of Reid's Well, is another quite small boulder at the roadside, called the Wolf's Stone locally, said to mark the Buchan boundary. Whether the name refers to the aforementioned Wolf of Badenoch or to some more humble predator, is not now known. Conveth, therefore, if lacking in more recent notable features, is well supplied with stones of the past.

Keith and Newmill. Keith, the second largest town in Banffshire, in its own large parish of 18,250 acres, lies in Strathisla, in the centre of the county, and acts as link between the very distinct Upper and Lower districts. It has a population of 4200 and a burgh charter going back to Charles the Second. Keith is much older than that, however. Working back, the barony thereof is referred to in 1539; and in 1195 a charter of the lands—not the burgh—of Keith, or Geth (from *Gaoith* the Gaelic for wind) in Strathisla, was granted by William the Lion to the Abbey of Kinloss. If that is not antiquity enough, Keith Cairds will tell you that the famous St. Maolrubha, Abbot of Applecross, a follower of Columba (after whom Loch Maree is called) established a cell here, amongst the Picts, in A.D. 700. The name became corrupted as time went on, first to Keith-Malruf, then to St. Rufus and so to Summerius; and the great fair held here annually eventually got named Summereve's Fair—however ridiculous, since it was always held in September. This affair, lasting a week, was one of the most famous occasions in the North, with thousands flocking to it and turning the entire countryside into a dormitory. Keith's parish used to be known as the Kingdom of Keith, and was supported by thirteen lairdships, largely in Gordon hands but two in Ogilvie. Most of these properties still survive as farms.

The municipality has three constituent parts, Old, New and Fife Keith, though the two former are now hard to distinguish apart, the latter, distinct on the west side of the Isla, being founded by the Earl of Fife in 1817. The oldest part of the main town is that on the lower eastern slopes of the river-bank, where the old kirk, graveyard and bridge remain, with climbing terraces of cottages behind. New Keith stretches in fairly regular rectangular fashion on the higher ground, laid out in 1750 by the Ogilvie Earl of Findlater. For a place that has long been important, Keith has a surprisingly small and modest castle as representing the seat of its former power, the little ruined tower of Milton-Keith, down at the wooded riverside, north of the town. But undoubtedly this is only a fragment.

All the most ancient features are near the river. The former church of St. Maolrubha is represented now only by scanty pieces of masonry supporting memorials, on a mound in the old but still-used grave-yard, attractively sited on different levels, at a bend in the Isla. It was abandoned in 1819, when the new church was built some way to the south-east. The major fragment enshrines a good 17th century heraldic memorial known as the Thornton Tomb, with the initials S.I.S. for Sir James Strachan of Thornton, Baronet, and D.M.R. for his wife, a Rose. He was actually Episcopal minister of Keith until deprived of his living for non-conformity in 1690. There are many old gravestones. An old drawing shows the former church as lengthy, with three outside forestairs and a central tower, with steeple, which contained the town jail, with stocks. It was rebuilt in 1569, and used to be the actual seat of the Court of Regality under the Abbots of Kinloss, which tried even the pleas of the Crown, barring only treason. Handy near by in the river was the Gaun's Pot, for drowning women; and there was also a gallow's hill for the men not far away. We are regaled by the story that, so interested was one male malefactor in a witch's punishment going on contemporaneously, that, although his ear was nailed to the gallow's tree he wrenched his head free the better to watch the drowning.

Close by is the picturesque narrow hump-backed Auld Brig of Keith, with its steps up to the crown, a single-arch graceful structure built in 1609 by a husband and wife, Thomas Murray, in Auchorties and Janet Lindsay, tradition varying as to the reason, either that they could not sleep soundly for the cries of unfortunate travellers crossing the ford, or that their own son was drowned here. It is now used only for foot-passengers, the busy A.95 traffic using a bridge with the inscription G. 111 R. R. S. 1770. At the north of the old bridge-end is a huge boulder partly covering a deep cavity. This is known as the Campbells' Hole, referring to sundry Hanoverian Campbell soldiers alleged to have hidden therein after a small defeat of the government forces by Jacobites in 1746. They must have been small Campbells.

In this vicinity of the riverside are the auction-marts, and a cooperage making barrels for the local distilleries. The river offers free trout-fishing; and there is a pleasant grassy walk along the bank, with seats.

Beside the main road, on its climb up to the town proper, rises on a terrace the fine modern parish church of St. Rufus, a large and impressive structure of 1816–19, with a clock-tower 120 feet high and seating for over 1500. It is considered to be one of the finest examples of Perpendicular Gothic in Northern Scotland. Internally it is fairly plain, but handsome and well-lit, with galleries on all sides save the east where there is a high pulpit and organ. Dry rot in the roof necessitated recent repairs, costing the congregation £7000—all raised in one year. In the vestibule are preserved a Deid Bell, traditional wooden collection-ladles, a huge old key from the former church, a pewter baptismal bowl and two very large and handsome pewter communion flagons and platters replaced by solid silver in the late 18th century. Also a large collection of communion-tokens. There is a double carved-wood war-memorial doorway. No graveyard surrounds this later church, but there is the pleasant little Matthew Stewart Memorial Garden on the slope adjoining, commemorating that well-known minister here who became Moderator of the General Assembly. Just opposite is the small St. Rufus Park, with a bandstand gifted by Colonel Kynoch in 1947—rather a strange amenity to see in Keith. There are a number of other parks, including the larger Fife Park and cricket pitch. The former Keith Grammar School derived from one that was old in 1647, stands near by, rather sternly institutional in aspect; but its modern successor is on higher ground off the Banff road to the north-east, spacious in glass-and-concrete on an open site and with a fine new indoor swimming-pool being built alongside. Close at hand are two other modern schools, Senior and Junior Primaries, with, just opposite, a rather good modern housing enclave called Green Court. The Longmore Hall of 1872, presented by a local distiller, is in this north-east vicinity, now developing as a centre for music, dancing and drama.

The main shopping centre, Mid Street, strikes off the A.95 highway to the south, a long and fairly narrow thoroughfare lined with shops and offices, climbing to Reidhaven Square. The Seafield Arms Hotel here dates from 1762. This is New Keith, a symmetry of parallel streets joined by lanes. At the extreme south end is the

Seafield Park, where is held the renowned annual Keith Show, one of the big agricultural events of the North-East, successor of the aforementioned Summereve's Fair, and which attracts attendances of over 30,000, its championships for livestock prized far and wide, with show-jumping, racing and other sports an added attraction.

To the west of Reidhaven Square, on the Cuthill higher ground, is the R.C. church of St. Thomas, whose unusual copper dome makes a striking landmark. It is an ambitious and interesting building altogether, of 1831, modelled on that of St. Maria-de-Angelis at Rome, with an impressive frontage displaying a Latin text from 1st Timothy. It has a striking baroque interior, notable for the fine painted altar-piece of the Incredulity of St. Thomas, presented in 1828 by no less than the Emperor Charles the Tenth of France. In the vestibule is a memorial to the Blessed John Ogilvie, one of Keith's greatest sons, tortured and then martyred in Glasgow in 1615 for his faith, and born in Milton Castle here in 1580. There is a modern St. Thomas's Primary School beside the church.

Amongst other religious establishments is the quite large Holy Trinity Episcopal church of 1882, in the so-called Geometric Gothic style, situated down amongst the large villas of Seafield Avenue to the north. In its chancel is the Seabury Chair, the throne from which Bishop Kilgour consecrated Samuel Seabury the first bishop of the American Episcopal Church in 1784, at Aberdeen. Across the road is a recreation park, with putting- and bowling-greens, tennis-courts and a paddling-pool.

In this lower-lying area near the river are the distilleries, not too evident amongst old trees. In Seafield Avenue itself is the Strathisla–Glenlivet establishment of 1786, on the site of an old mill, still with its wheel. Built into the gable of an entrance-lodge are two stones, one heraldic dated 1695 and the other with a coronet initialled L.M.O., for one of the Lords Oliphant, and coming from the castle of Milton-Keith. The ruined remains of this stand above the river just behind the distillery, near an old bridge, with the rapids of the Linn close by. Only a small rectangular gabled shell subsists, scanty of feature, but there must have been a much larger fortalice once. It was built about 1480 by George Ogilvie who had gained the former Gordon lands of Drumnakeith by marriage with a daughter of the Earl of Huntly. It was repaired by Margaret Ogilvie in 1601, but passed again by marriage in 1707 to the 7th Lord Oliphant, before being finally abandoned in 1829 and being used as a quarry. On the other side of this is another large distillery, the Glenkeith–Glenlivet, the riverside here being extremely attractive and but little spoiled by this industry. Not far away to the north-east are the large Isla Bank Mills of Messrs Kynoch, founded in 1805 and manufacturing the tweed suitings, scarves and ties with the well-known black Scots Terrier trade-mark, 90 per cent of which products go for export. They employ over 300 people. There is another woollen firm in Keith, the Seafield Mills of Messrs. Laidlaw, who make clan tartans as well as knitwear and tweeds. Other industrial undertakings include the large Shellstar Fertiliser Depot, limeworks and the smaller factories of a little industrial estate at Waterton Road. But dominating the prospect from the north are the series of great new bonded warehouses of Messrs. Chivas, where famous blends of whisky mature.

The Turner Memorial Hospital of 1880 is situated on the high ground of the Cuthill; and there is an 18-hole new golf course to the west. Notable also are the woodland walks at Cottage Wood and Den Wood, the latter leading to the picturesque Falls of Tarnash, a mile to the south of the town, not large but enclosed in jaws of rock. There is much planted forestry to this eastern side of Keith.

Newmill, although near to Keith, is an entirely distinct community, lying across the Isla a mile to the north, on the south-facing slope of the Aultmore plateau. It is a planned village, a *quod sacra* parish of its own since 1877, within Keith civil parish, founded likewise in mid-18th century but never growing as New Keith did. It consists of three long, parallel streets, fairly wide, linked geometrically by lanes, on an open terraced site, with a square towards the east end, all lying west of an attractive wooded den. In the centre of the square is a tall clock-tower war-memorial erected in 1923, impressive for a comparatively small place. All is very neat. The church, built as a chapel-of-ease in 1870, is a plain, smallish, harled edifice standing isolated in trees well to the east. Newmill may not rival Keith, but it is at least the "capital" of its own quite large kingdom, that of the Aultmore. This is a strange, detached and interesting area, a quite lofty undulating plateau of as much as 20 square miles, rising towards the north to heather and mosses around the 1000-foot contour, but its southern half averaging perhaps 650 feet above sea-level and dotted with innumerable crofts and small farms, quite a world unto itself. Peat-stacks stand outside the houses still—indeed this was always a renowned area for fuel-gathering, for anciently it was covered by Scots-pine forest and the buried roots of these trees were long much sought-after by Keith folk. Wide views and great skies prevail up here, a vast terrain criss-crossed by little roads and tracks, but no-through-roads—though it is flanked, east and west, by the lower-lying B.9018 and B.9016, 4 to 5 miles apart. The names indicate the type of land—Broadrashes, Herrick's Moss, Greenbog, just Bog itself, Todholes, and both a Foggy and a Foggie Moss. Aultmore stretches well over into Rathven and Deskford parishes to north and east, where the plateau is highest and least populated. At the extreme west of the area is the distilling village nowadays using the name of Aultmore, on B.9016 about 3 miles from Keith, where there is a very modern large distillery and associated housing, a village-hall and a former school. The Aultmore has other ex-schools, Banff county obviously having been ruthless about closing down such small rural places, unfortunately.

At the very bottom south-west corner of this area, just above the valley-floor, is the large farm of Haughs, once one of the thirteen lairdships of the Kingdom. On the farmhouse west gable is built-in a heraldic panel, weatherworn but displaying the buckles of Leslie. Below is the great range of bonded warehouses of Messrs. Chivas, looking like aerodrome hangars. Two more of the lairdships lie immediately to the west, Allanbuie and Muldearie, both now merely farms, with no special features remaining. Hill of Muldearie, rising behind the latter to 1019 feet, is forested almost to its conical summit, on the border of Boharm parish. Just north of Allanbuie is the rather attractive old oatmeal mill of Crooks, beside a single-arch 18th century bridge, off the A.96. In a similar situation at the other, east side of the Aultmore, is the large farm of Glengerrack, once an important Gordon lairdship, referred to hereafter.

All this is north of Keith. To the south rises Caird's Hill (968 feet) from which the Keith folk get their popular name, cairds being tinkers or gipsies. There was formerly a stone-circle crowning this hill, now gone. The hamlet of Auchindachy, with a 3-arched 18th century bridge, lies at the western foot of the hill, but this is just over in Botriphnie parish. On the south flank is the ruined castle of Pitlurg, just on the Aberdeenshire border. This was quite a prominent Gordon stronghold, a 16th century courtyard-type castle built on a rock, of which only a circular tower 30 feet high remains, with a basement vault and squared gunloops, the upper part fitted as a doocot.

To the south-east of this large Keith parish rises another of its enclosing hills, Meikle Balloch (1200 feet) heavily forested, with a long ridge along which runs the Aberdeenshire border. Two more of the thirteen lairdships share its northern flank, Birkenburn and Auchaynanie, now both large farms, though the latter retained a turreted ruined fortalice until comparatively recently. Both were Gordon places.

Apart from the tuilzie with the Campbells and Jacobites in 1746, Keith was the scene of two other military confrontations, one national, one local. Here, in 1645, the great Montrose and Covenanting General Baillie came face-to-face, and on this occasion the master-strategist chose not to risk an encounter, with the other in greater force and a very strong position. Five years later Montrose, betrayed and captured after Carbisdale, and led bound to his execution at Edinburgh, passed an uncomfortable night at Keith, to be railed at publicly the next day, Sunday, in a lengthy sermon by the parish minister, Kininmonth. The local affray was in 1667 when the noted freebooter, Patrick Roy MacGregor, and his supporters, were soundly worsted by the townsfolk under the young Gordon of Glengerrack, and Patrick Roy duly sent to Edinburgh to be hanged. Another freebooter—for the Highland line is near here—Macpherson of *The Rant* fame, was captured at Keith in 1700—but sent this time to Banff for his famous execution, when no one would accept his dying gift of his renowned fiddle.

Macduff. The thriving and busy burgh of Macduff is inevitably linked with the neighbouring royal burgh of Banff only a mile across the Deveron estuary and Banff Bay, yet maintains a very distinct individuality. Indeed a sort of love–hate relationship prevails here, sharing certain services and features as they do. Macduff is the brash, go-ahead, modern and industrially aligned town, whereas Banff is the ancient, dignified county-centre—something like Glasgow and Edinburgh in miniature, only so much closer together. Macduff indeed was only founded as a burgh of barony in 1783, by George the Third, in favour of the up-and-coming Duff 2nd Earl of Fife, prior to which it had been only a tiny hamlet called Doune—the Hill of Doune, crowned by its classical Temple of Venus, memorial to a former Countess of Fife, dominating to the south-west.

Macduff is a well-planned place on a steeply sloping site above an excellent and extensive harbour, improved in 1966, busy home of a large fishing-fleet, and with a fine new fish-market which cost over £160,000 and other attendant facilities including a boat-building yard, fish-salesmen's establishments and a Customs and Excise building. There is a large distillery called the Glendeveron, but this is at Gelly Mill under Doune Hill to the south-west, facing across the river.

The church rather dominates the town, sited on a spur of Doune Hill, a commodious and handsome building of 1805, built as a chapel-of-ease for the new burgh by the 3rd Earl of Fife, unusual in allegedly Italianate style, with a tall clock-tower with domed roof. Internally it is bright, with a three-sided gallery, and prominent pulpit flanked by stained-glass. Sharing the mound with the church is the likewise highly unusual Mercat Cross, on a plinth, with a heavy and blunt cruciform finial, its grassy site making a fine viewpoint for the town, harbour—which has stolen the Banff fishing traffic—and the fine sandy beach to the west, between it and the neighbouring royal burgh. A lofty tower-like war-memorial crowns another green spur near by.

There is a senior secondary school here, as at Banff, on the high ground towards the south, successor of the Institution founded by one, Murray, a London canvas-manufacturer, in 1849. Like Banff too, Macduff has a large Fife Arms Hotel—as well as others, of course—with an entirely modern frontage to contrast with the Banff one's dignified classicism. These two hotels, indeed, might sum up the difference between the burghs. Each town has likewise its major golf course, both "royal". The Royal Tarlair lies east of Macduff along the cliff-top heights, with splendid rock scenery available for the less dedicated. There are also bowling and tennis clubs, and an angling association. And Macduff is deservedly proud of its fine open-air swimming-pool at Tarlair, in a corner of the cliffs amongst some fantastic rock scenery, claimed as unrivalled in the North of Scotland. Here is a restaurant, and entertainment facilities, with a pipe-band to play on summer Sunday afternoons. Tarlair was famous before its pool and golf course however; for here, in 1770, was discovered the renowed Well of Tarlair, a mineral-spring, for which Lord Fife built a well-house and to which visitors flocked

Portknockie: Bow Fiddle Rock

Portsoy, where many excellent restorations are proceeding

Tarlair Swimming-pool, Macduff

Towiemore Distillery, Banffshire

from far and near to take the waters—and which was partly responsible for the rise of Macduff. Unfortunately a war-time mine, washed in on the tide, destroyed all.

Macduff has a population of 3708 against Banff's 3723. It can lay claim to half of Banff's famous 7-arched bridge across the Deveron, built by Smeaton in 1779. The town lies in Gamrie civil parish, so that its country environs are described thereunder.

Marnoch. Marnoch is a large civil parish of central Banffshire, of 15,000 acres, based on the Deveron, with the burgh of Aberchirder at its centre (treated separately) but no real village otherwise. There is much of interest, however, and the scenery generally attractive, in farming country.

The Kirkton of Marnoch is not even a hamlet, and stands at the southern limit of the parish, on the river-bank, in picturesque wooded surroundings. The old church was right at the riverside, where still is the graveyard, with the former manse adjoining; but the present kirk is on an eminence a little to the north, actually built within a former stone-circle, of which two uprights remain, one massive and tall within the church-garden, the other, smaller, in the adjoining farm steading—an interesting example of the continuing tradition of worship. The church is plain and quite large, built in 1792. Some slight traces of the old kirk, dedicated to St. Marnoch, remain down in the graveyard amongst the crowded tombstones. Somewhere here Marnoch himself was buried, about A.D. 650. Interesting is the two-storeyed mort-house of 1832, with a vaulted basement for the keeping secure of corpses for two months until they were sufficiently decomposed to be of no value to the anatomical body-snatchers. The upper floor was the parish school. What the scholars thought of these premises is not recorded. There are some good heraldic monuments in the kirkyard, one to the Inneses of Muiryfold and another, to the Gordons of Avochie, dated 1692, with the unusual upright effigy of a very arrogant-looking man wearing a ruff. Also a fine memorial to the Reverend George Meldrum, Laird of Crombie and Episcopal minister of Glass, of the same period. There are two former holy wells near by, St. Marnoch's and Our Lady's; and there was a St. Marnoch's Ford just below the church. The manse is now a private house, where the proprietors run the Innes Weavers, a handloom craft.

Ardmeallie House stands high in its wooded estate half a mile to the north-west, a pleasing 18th century mansion on a terrace site, looking down the vale.

Striking due north from the Kirkton a side-road runs up the shallower vale of the Crombie Burn. Over a mile up, on the left, is Crombie Castle—pronounced Cromie—a plain and massive fortalice of the mid-16th century, with a farmhouse now attached, the castle itself no longer occupied. It is L-shaped, of three storeys and a garret, rising from a basement plinth to crowstepped gables, the rather unsightly open rounds crowning the wing gables being

55

modern. The doorway is guarded by a gunloop and with a machicolated projection above for the casting down of missiles. The basement is vaulted, and the kitchen has a large arched fireplace, two
mural ovens and a water-stoup. The Hall on the first floor has two
rather evident spy-holes for the laird to observe what went on, from
a tiny chamber above reached via a trap-door—a very furtive provision. In 1453 Sir Walter Innes, 12th of that Ilk, had a charter of
the barony of Crombie, obtained no doubt through the marriage of
the 9th laird with the heiress of the last Thane of Aberchirder near
by. The castle was probably built by James Innes, who fell at the
Battle of Pinkie in 1547. John Innes of that Ilk, successor of Alexander of Crombie who murdered a kinsman in brutal circumstances
in 1580, was himself put to the horn in 1624 for "striking and dinging
the kirk officer of Aberchirder". A sign that lairds were not what
they had been. The lands passed to Urquharts, Meldrums and
Duffs, until fairly recently recovered by the late Sir Thomas Innes
of Learney, Lord Lyon.

A mile north of Crombie, off the same road, is the old hallhouse of
Culvie, a rather fine example of its type, long and low with coped
chimneys, of the late 17th century, and now a farmhouse. It was an
Ogilvie property.

To the east of the Kirkton less than a mile, is Bridge of Marnoch,
which carries the A.97 across Deveron, a double-arched structure of
1806. Half a mile to the east again, reached by a winding side-road,
is Kinnairdy Castle, a most interesting tall tower-house in a romantic
position above a small ravine crossed by another old bridge, once
the fortalice of the ancient thanage and barony of Aberchirder.
The original castle has been an oblong keep of the mid-15th century,
with parapet and wall-walk; but an early alteration re-roofed the
upper storeys and added crowstepped gables and a lower wing to the
east. The crowsteps were formed out of the original parapet corbels.
The stairway, in the south-east angle, is surmounted by a small
gabled watch-chamber. The basement has a notably high vaulted
ceiling; and the Hall above is graced by the celebrated oak-panelled
aumbry, with carving reputed to be the finest in Scotland, dated 1493
and displaying the heads of Sir Alexander Innes, 13th, and his wife
Dame Christian Dunbar. This Sir Alexander was extravagant—as
witness his carvings imported at great expense from Flanders—and
he was shut up by his relatives in Girnigoe Castle, Caithness, as "ane
misguided man and prodigious, and has wastit and destroyit his
lands and guids without ony reasonable occasion". It is perhaps
significant that the Dunbars were a Caithness family. Kinnairdy
was sold to Crichton of Frendraught, involved in the celebrated
tragedy, and in 1647 to the Reverend John Gregory. He was succeeded by his brother, the famous David Gregory, medico and inventor, who produced the first barometer here. He had twenty-nine
children and died aged 95, in 1720, Kinnairdy was also bought back
for the Innes family by Sir Thomas, the late Lord Lyon.

On the other side of the A.97 a mile to the north-west, on the farm of Sheep Park, are the remains of a stone-circle, the stones now prostrate in an arable field. A mile further north on the same road is Auchintoul estate, a former large Gordon property, the mansion now standing empty and used as a straw-store. It has grown from a late 17th century nucleus, round three sides of a courtyard, tall, with a wide semi-circular stair-tower, and has been a handsome house once. It was the seat of a famous General, Alexander Gordon, who learned his soldiering under Tsar Peter the Great, took a prominent part in the Jacobite campaign of 1715, commanded the Highland brigade at Sheriffmuir and was attainted for treason but escaped execution and forfeiture by a flaw in the indictment. Not far away, on the other side of the A.97, is the attractive whitewashed 18th century bonnet-laird's house of Janefield, in a pleasant setting. At the extreme north-west corner of the parish, on the high ground of Wether Hill (890 feet) are a cluster of ancient burial-cairns. There is much high mossy ground, with small farms, over all this northern section.

Mortlach, Glen Fiddich and Glen Rinnes. Mortlach is a large hill parish of upper Banffshire, of 34,000 acres, 11 miles long, comprising most of the glens of Fiddich and Rinnes. The burgh of Dufftown is the main centre of population, but this is dealt with separately. It is in the heart of the distillery country, indeed might well claim to *be* the very heart itself, with many distilleries in the parish, at least eight clustered round Dufftown. All these are hidden away in the deep, steep valleys, and so not evident except for their smoke.

Mortlach is also famous for its church. This is on the outskirts of Dufftown, to the south, and serves that burgh; but there is a distinct and much more ancient Kirktown of Mortlach. The church claims to be one of the oldest in the land, and worship has been continuous here since St. Moluag founded his cell in A.D. 566. Mortlach was one of his three main foundations, the others being Lismore and Rose-markie. At first sight the building does not appear so very old, it having been reconstructed in 1876 and again in 1931; but much old work survives, more evident internally than outside. The oldest remaining portion is probably that section of the north wall around the postern door, once the only door, with its lepers' squint, and may date from the 12th century. There is considerable altercation as to dates, the old claim that Malcolm the Second added to the Columban Church's cell after a victorious battle with the Danes in 1010 being denied by others who say it was Malcolm the Third's work. Mortlach is sometimes also claimed to be Scotland's second see, with St. Bean its first bishop, before the see was removed to Aberdeen; but there seems to be no evidence that it was ever a bishopric. However, be all that as it may, the three lancet windows of the chancel date from the 13th century, although the glass, representing Faith, Hope and Charity, is modern. There is much good stained-glass here, some by the famous Cottier, of Paris, some

57

by Scotland's own Strachan. One window commemorates the Lord Mount Stephen, a local man who rose to prominence as a builder of the Canadian Pacific Railway, and gave liberally to his native parish. Near by is the fine war-memorial enclave, with more stained-glass and flags. The entire church interior is pleasing, with white walls and much excellent woodwork, including the ceiling.

There are many treasures here. In the vestibule is a notable Pictish Class 1 symbol-stone, displaying the Celtic beast, or elephant, and another strange symbol, broken in five pieces but admirably bound together. Also four good heraldic grave-slabs, one, the Lochtervandich Stone of 1417, and another dated 1533 showing a floriate cross and two-handed sword, for Gordon of Brodland. In the chancel is a fine recumbent effigy of a knight in armour, one of the Leslies of Kininvie, dated 1549, with other Leslie memorials near by. Opposite is a mural memorial to the Duffs of Keithmore, of 1694. There is a low-set rectangular aumbry here. In the vestry are preserved many items, much excellent communion silver and pewter, with no fewer than eleven chalices, mainly of the 18th century. There is a Deid Bell, for funerals, a pair of jougs, a sermon hour-glass, a large collection of communion-tokens and a meat-fork used at Culloden. Built into the walling are four small stones, one with Leslie initials dated 1607.

In the graveyard, which occupies a pleasant sloping position above the Dullan Burn, stands the Battle Stone, another Pictish monolith, tall and narrow, on one side a cross below two fish-tailed creatures, and on the other a serpent, bull's-head, and a horseback rider with hound, all rather weather-worn. St. Moloch's Fair used to be held round this stone—although not on this site. It is named presumably after the 1010 battle with the Danes, but is of much older date. There is a Priest's Well near by. A small, low, six-sided watch-house, precaution against grave-robbers, is now used as a heating-chamber for the church. There are many old gravestones, from the early 17th century onwards.

The Dufftown–Glenlivet Distillery adjoins to the south, on the Dullan. And directly above is the former bonnet-laird's house of Pittyvaich, now a dairy-farm, a quite attractive crowstep-gabled house of 1750 with coped chimneystacks.

This is really the mouth of Glen Rinnes, near its junction with Fiddich, the Dullan being its stream. About a mile further up the wooded glen, on a narrow side-road, is the picturesque den in which are the features known as the Giant's Chair and Cave and the Linen Apron Waterfall, down from the road in the ravine. Neither cave nor waterfall are large, and no giant would get into the former. This is a very lovely country of gentle green hills, woodland and broom-covered braes, backed by the tall heather masses of Meikle and Little Conval and Ben Rinnes itself (1867, 1810 and 2755 feet respectively). On the summit of Little Conval, in this parish, is a Pictish fort, 680 by 400 feet, with a large cluster of burial-cairns on the far, west, side. Further up Glen Rinnes, now threaded by the

B.9009 road, a side-road strikes off again to the south flank; and here at the junction is a well to commemorate the coronation of Edward the Seventh and Queen Alexandra—something seldom seen in Scotland. Near by is the former small lairdship of Recletich, now only a farm but with its 17th century lean-to doocot still surviving in battered form. There is alleged to be a feature, of three large stones known as the King's Grave, either here or on the adjoining farm of Milltown of Laggan, but this is not now known. Another mile along the same side-road, under Ben Rinnes, is the church of the *quod sacra* parish of Glenrinnes formerly the Auchnastank chapel-of-ease, of 1883. It stands in an isolated but very peaceful position in a small and not ancient graveyard, and is still in occasional use.

Glen Fiddich is the major valley, and much more populous, Dufftown standing just where the Dullen meets the Fiddich, amongst all the distilleries. Almost a mile north of the burgh, on the west side of Fiddich, stands the splendid ruin of Balvenie Castle, on an elevation in the valley and readily seen from the main A.941 road. Now happily in the care of the Department of the Environment after long neglect, it is especially interesting as demonstrating the development of castle-building over a long period, with 13th, 15th and late 16th century work. From outside the courtyard the impression is of great age and strength, the curtain-walling reaching over 25 feet in height and enclosing a large quadrangle. This is entered by an arched pend, over which are the Royal Arms and those of Stewart of Atholl, with the practical motto FYRTH FORTVIN AND FIL THI FATRIS, meaning Forth Fortune and File thy Fetters. Within the enclosure is the 15th century addition, but this is overshadowed by the late 16th century house, taller and more elaborate, with two stair-towers. There is a circular well in the courtyard. Balvenie anciently belonged to the great De Moravia family, passing to the Douglases and then the Stewarts—who retained it until the 17th century, so most of the work here is theirs. In 1614 it was sold to Robert Innes, 5th of Innermarkie, created a baronet in 1631. Here the great Montrose held a council in 1645, Innes being a staunch loyalist. He suffered much in the Civil War period, and in 1687 Balvenie had to be sold to the up-and-coming Duffs.

Two distilleries flank the castle, and one, Grant's Glenfiddich, has a reception centre and whisky museum. Near by is the alleged site of a lost Pictish stone called the Aqua Vitae Stone, said to bear oghams and symbols. Ploughmen are said to have scraped their shares over it, so it ought not to be too difficult to unearth. There is a later 18th century Balvenie House over a mile down the valley.

On the other side of Fiddich 3 miles north of Dufftown, is the interesting property and fortalice of Kininvie, high above the river. Here is a tall old tower-house, apparently of the late 16th century—although there is an older nucleus—whitewashed and pleasing, attached to a large modern mansion, the former seat of an important branch of the Leslies. It is L-planned, of five storeys, with a higher circular stair-tower corbelled out to the square at top to form a typical watch-chamber, known as the Charter Room. The walls are rounded at the angles, with small windows, a diamond-shaped shot-hole guarding the door. The basement is vaulted. There is a circular doocot near by. A charter of 1521, by the 3rd Stewart Earl of Atholl, grants Kininvie to Alexander Leslie, a son of Leslie of Balquhain in Aberdeenshire—whose effigy has been mentioned in Mortlach Church. James the Fifth is said to have hidden in the kitchen here, during one of his escapades as Gudeman of Ballengeich. A daughter of the 5th Leslie of Kininvie was mother of the ill-fated Archbishop Sharp. Another Leslie house, Buchromb, stood not far away across the river, replaced by a modern baronial structure in 1873, and this itself is now only a shell.

On the south side of Dufftown, the Fiddich fairly quickly takes a great bend eastwards, with the B.9014 branching off the A.941 to follow it. Along here, just over a mile, but not readily seen from the road, is another magnificent ruined castle, Auchindoun, a former Gordon stronghold. It tops an isolated green hill 200 feet high, in most impressive fashion; but though the ruins still make a fine and fair picture, the central keep is so shattered as to retain little of its original appearance. The so obviously strong site was formerly occupied by a Pictish fort, the banks of which may still be discerned. The present castle appears to date from the 15th century, and was built by James the Third's unpopular favourite, the architect Cochrane, though there had been a castle here since the 11th century. It consists of a high curtain-walled courtyard, still tolerably entire, with a massive L-planned keep within, vaulted on two floors, the upper Hall ceiling being finely groined vaulting, the walls up to 10 feet thick. It came to the Gordons in 1535. Sir Adam Gordon of Auchindoun, 6th son of the rebellious 4th Earl of Huntly, defeated the Forbeses at the Craibstone in 1571; and his brother, Sir Patrick, was one of the signatories of the notorious Spanish Blanks, and was slain at the Battle of Glenlivet in 1594. Mary Queen of Scots deliberately passed by in 1564; but Queen Victoria came here for a picnic.

Not far from Auchindoun, within the same great bend of the river, is the large farm of Keithmore, its 18th century house with coped chimneystacks and central courtyard now only a farm-store, the lands Crown property. The Duffs were lairds here, and their monument, of 1694, is mentioned in connection with Mortlach Church. One of Keithmore's sons became Duff of Braco, and ancestor of the Earls and Dukes of Fife. The Milltown of Auchindoun is an attractive spot.

Two miles due south of this, where the A.941 threads a little pass on its way to Rhynie, at 1197 feet, called the Glacks of Balloch (both of which words in Gaelic mean a defile) is the scene of the action of the song "Roy's Wife of Aldivalloch". Aldivalloch itself, in Cabrach parish, is about 3 miles further on.

Mortlach is a highly interesting parish, as will be apparent.

Ordiquhill and Cornhill. The rather strangely named Ordiquhill, meaning allegedly the hollow beside the height, is a small
Banffshire inland parish of 5000 acres, lying some 6 miles due south
of Portsoy; and Cornhill is its village and only real community,
situated near the northern limits of the very irregularly shaped
parish.

Cornhill used to be called Corncairn, and is a pleasant, medium-
sized place, regularly planned, on a gently sloping hillside site, the
land rising gradually from the Burn of Boyne to the Corn Hill itself
(710 feet), behind the large estate of Park. The village gives no
appearance of antiquity but is in fact old and used to be a burgh of
barony with six annual markets. It must have been laid out largely
since 1839, when there was a population of only 60. The main street
is wide, and really only a part of the A.95 highway, the village
clustering round the crossroads with the B.9023, with the whitewashed Gordon Arms Hotel, dating from about 1800, at the corner.
There is a former United Free church, with tower, of 1844, rebuilt
1904, at the east end; and a distinctly ambitious-looking Hay
Memorial Hall on the other side of the road. Also some rather good
modern housing. The general impression is open, pleasing and trim.

The church at Cornhill is not the true parish church. That stands
in an isolated situation on higher ground, 2 miles to the south-west,
not far from the road-junction hamlet of Gordonstown, with its
school. This church is unusual in having a hipped roof, yet with a
belfry on a gablet, a somewhat difficult composition. It is square,
with a rather squat appearance, and dates from 1805, standing in its
kirkyard on a mound in open country. Here is the Gordons' of Park
burial-enclosure, representing an earlier church, with heraldic
panels, one dated 1665. Presumably the original pre-Reformation
church was dedicated to St. Colman, one of the many hereabouts,
for there is a St. Colm's Well sited in a field to the south of the side-
road half a mile to the east, in the Culvie area, still retaining its
circular stone shaft and surround. Culvie Wood, to the south-west
on a low ridge, is old extensive woodland. There is an attractive,
tall, whitewashed farmhouse called Overtown, standing behind the
church, overlooking the vale. This is all at the southern edge of the
parish. A mile to the west rises the prominent conical Knock Hill
(1412 feet) which dominates all this area, Ordiquhill sharing its
summit with the parishes of Fordyce and Grange. At its eastern base
is the shallow defile of Glen Barry, down which the parish boundary
runs, with an inn in the centre.

There is only the one large estate here, the ancient property of
Park, situated a mile south of Cornhill. The mansion is rambling
and extensive, greatly enlarged in 1829; but the nucleus is a mid-
16th century Z-planned fortalice, not very readily perceived
externally but evident on closer inspection. The main block lies
north and south, with wings projecting at the north-east and south-
west; and it is the latter re-entrant, with its slender stair-tower,
corbelling and moulded arched doorway, now reduced to the status

of window, which reveals the original work—though the gable itself is of the 18th century. A good heraldic panel, weatherworn but apparently displaying the Gordon arms, is skied at second floor level here. The walling being harled, it is difficult to trace the limits of the earlier work. A range of vaulted cellars occupies the basement. Alexander the Second granted a charter for Park in 1242. The Gordons of Park took an active part in the affairs of the North-East, and in 1745 Sir William Gordon was engaged on the Jacobite side, and escaping to France, was forfeited. However, he had just previously taken the precaution of marrying Jean Duff, the daughter of the up-and-coming first Earl of Fife—who of course was always on the right side in politics—and the Duffs thereafter saved the estate and moved in. They are still at Park, bracketing the name of Gordon.

Portknockie. This is a small Banffshire fishing burgh of 1250 population, sited on the thrusting promontory of Scar Nose at the west end of Cullen Bay, 2 miles west of Cullen and an equal distance east of Findochty. It is now a *quod sacra* parish of its own, within the old civil parish of Rathven. The seaboard here is highly dramatic, even though the flanking area, known as Bauds of Cullen and Moor of Findochty, is bare and treeless and lacking in interest.

Portknockie was founded as a fishing haven in 1677, and inevitably its harbour, below the cliffs, was its centre. Today, with the centralising of the fishing-fleets at Buckie near by and Macduff, it no longer is used as a port, though many vessels are still owned here and worked from Buckie, and many crews live at Portknockie. In 1885 it had 99 large fishing-boats and 42 smaller ones. The harbour now shelters only sundry small craft, and lobster and pleasure boats. But it remains picturesque. The holiday-maker is now catered for here, and there is much to attract, with magnificent rock-scenery, caves, paddling-pool and the sands of Cullen Bay with its 18-hole golf course just to the east.

The little town is itself in places quite picturesque, with its neat clifftop cottages all brightly painted, many of them gable-end to the narrow streets. There is modern housing and development on the higher ground inland. The *quod sacra* parish church is now in the centre of the town, a plain, low building with belfry, replacing the earlier Seafield chapel-of-ease of 1840, set on the southern extremity and now disused. It was not beautiful either.

It is the sea-cliff area which draws the visitor. Here are many spectacular features. The lofty projecting spur named Green Castle is central, a grass-topped promontory formerly bearing ruined defensive masonry of an early fortification, just east of the harbour. East of this again is the yawning cavern of the Whale's Mou'. And still further, an extraordinary isolated tall sea-rock with a large natural arch known as the Bow Fiddle. Beyond all is Scar Nose Point itself, the most northerly projecting headland of the entire Banffshire coast. To the west of the harbour area are the Linn Links, flanking a series of small, pretty bays, dotted with skerries, to Tronach Head with its caves. There was a Tronach Castle once, of which little or nothing remains.

A name that has practically disappeared from the map here is Farskane, where the Cullen Bay Hotel now stands, less than a mile to the south-east of Portknockie. This was quite an important laird-ship once, with a pre-Reformation chapel, a laird's house of 1677, and a lengthy cave on the nearby shore, where the Gordon laird and two other local gentlemen lived for five or six weeks, in apparent comfort, to avoid trouble during Mar's Rising of 1715.

Portsoy. Portsoy is a typical Banff former fishing-burgh and port, 6 miles west of Banff town, now geared to other activities, an old-world place in its original parts, with steep streets leading down to the harbour, and many fine buildings. From the present main Sea-field Street this is hardly apparent, the undoubted character and atmosphere of old Portsoy being scarcely evident there. It is prob-ably best known today for its Portsoy marble, a handsome green or pink serpentine, long appreciated for its beauty—indeed which pro-vided two chimney-pieces for Louis 14th's Palace of Versailles. Portsoy is not large, with a population of only 1700, but it is quite a go-ahead place, now the centre of a farming area and a holiday resort. In Fordyce civil parish, it was created a burgh of barony in 1550, for Sir William Ogilvie of Boyne, and its charter ratified in 1581. There was a castle here, just where is not now known, al-though the hill named Castle Brae should help to locate its site. The burgh is still governed by its Provost and Town Council of nine members, and this has provided over 200 council houses. There is a Portsoy Town Improvement Association with a wide remit, even to the extent of sponsoring open-air theatre.

The old heart of Portsoy, as might be expected, is around the harbour area. The first harbour was built by Sir Patrick Ogilvie of Boyne in the 16th century, and was considered to be the safest in North-East Scotland. A lively trade with the Continent and England grew up, and indications of this are seen in the excellent vernacular buildings and warehouses clustered around, some of which have been delightfully restored of recent years, or are in process of being so. The Ogilvie–Grant Earl of Seafield in 1825–8 built a new harbour, but a storm swept this away in 1839. It was reconstructed in 1884. But by that time the day of small trading ports was ending, and Portsoy is too near the large modern harbours of Buckie and Macduff to retain its former fishing-fleet. Today only a lobster-boat or two, and a salmon-coble, ply from here. But there is a yacht club and pleasure-boating.

Some of the 17th and 18th century buildings flanking the harbour call for special mention. The finest probably is No. 10 Shorehead, a tall and commodious merchant's house of three storeys and a garret, crowstepped-gabled and L-planned, with three doorways all pro-vided with drawbars and slots. The date 1726 is on a skew, but the building is older than this. It is in process of restoration. Near by is

63

the Corfe's Warehouse building, a lofty plain structure now restored to house the Portsoy Marble Workshop and also the Pottery. Many delightful and useful articles are made here, and sent all over the world, with craftsmen working with local materials. Other houses round about have been saved, and, harled and whitewashed, make an attractive picture especially from the harbour. The Old Star Inn, of 1727, on the waterfront, is one of these. And Soy House, another 17th century town-house up the climbing Church Street, is a fine example of what can be done with the authentic material of these characterful old buildings. Rows of 19th century fishermen's houses have also been modernised and given a face-lift, to add to the picturesque scene.

The coast itself is spectacular here, with fantastic rock formations, headlands, caves and inlets. To the east of the harbour is the old fishertown of Seatown, overlooking Links Bay. Down in the grassy amphitheatre below is a sandy beach, the large caravan-park and camping-site and the playing-field area. Here too, where the Burn of Durn reaches the sea, is the old burial-ground and site of the pre-Reformation chapel dedicated to St. Colm, a busy missionary hereabouts. St. Colm's Well is situated in a semi-subterranean vaulted chamber in the grassy knoll in this graveyard, restored in 1883. There are no remaining tombstones earlier than mid-18th century. It is a pleasant place. At the other, western, side of the harbour, set snugly amongst the rocks, is the Sandypots swimming-pool, a delightful spot on a summer's day.

The main Seafield Street, and thereabouts on the higher ground, later development, is not so picturesque, but there are features of interest here too, as well as the necessary shops and offices. There has been a switching round of church buildings. Portsoy was made a *quod sacra* parish within Fordyce in 1871, and the chapel-of-ease which became its parish church, on the north side of Seafield Street, is now a community centre, while the former Free church of 1843, rebuilt 1869, Gothic with a slender spire, is now the parish church and stands to the west, on the Cullen road. Between the two is the Episcopal church of St. John the Baptist, 1840, replacing a timber building burned by Cumberland's troops on the way to Culloden. The communion-cup was rescued from the flames and hidden in a ditch, and is now used in the present church. There is also a Catholic church of The Assumption at the east end of the town, built 1829. A large modern secondary school stands near by.

In the centre of the town, beside a little sunken green, on the burn that drained the Loch of Soy, is Ewing's oatmeal mill, still functioning in heartening fashion. There is quite a large development of modern housing to the west of the burgh, and here is the small Campbell Hospital, on the verge of open country. Portsoy has many sporting and recreational facilities, including bowling, tennis, putting and sea-angling, as well as the yachting and bathing. There are a number of hotels. The area is geologically rich and interesting, in more than the serpentine deposits; lime-stone is quarried and soapstone used to be worked here also. The Loch of Soy used to be quite large, but has been drained away.

The country environs are dealt with under Fordyce parish, as is the village of Sandend 2 miles away.

Rathven, Letterfourie and Enzie. Rathven is a very large civil parish of 23,500 acres lying in the north-west of Banffshire, and including within its bounds the burghs of Buckie, Findochty and Portknockie, with their adjacent fishing-villages, all dealt with separately. These other articles cover the entire parish coastline of nearly 10 miles, so here it is necessary only to deal with the inland area, which includes the districts of Letterfourie and Enzie. The parish is roughly rectangular, wider at the west end than the east, and lies approximately parallel with the coast to an average of 5 miles deep. Apart from the string of fishing burghs there are no sizeable communities, Rathven kirkton itself being only a very small village; and the hamlets of Arradoul, Drybridge, Cowfurach and Clochan being modest indeed. But the area is fertile, with many old estates and farms, and heavily forested in the eastern section, on the slopes of Bin of Cullen, Little Bin and Hill of Maud (1053, 802 and 900 feet respectively). At the extreme south is a lofty area of moss and moorland, reaching 987 feet at Millstone Hill. There are two large burial-cairns on heights in this vicinity, Tor Sliasg and Peterkin Hillock a mile apart. Near by is the oddly named boggy stretch called Broken Moan—but the moan is only a corruption of *moine*, Gaelic for moss or morass, and broken is doubtless *breacadh*, meaning speckled.

Rathven's kirkton lies just over a mile south-east of Buckie, inland from the coastal suburb of Ianstown, at a junction of side-roads, a rather lost-looking place, with burgeoning Buckie drawing away its importance and individuality, despite some undistinguished modern housing. The parish church is here, dating from 1794, large, plain and harled, with tall windows to the south and a small belfry with ball-finial. Near by, across the road, is the old graveyard and the site of the original church, now represented only by a vault of 1612 used as the burial-place of the Hays of Rannas and Lenplum, from 1421 to 1789, ancestors of the Marquis of Tweedsdale's branch of the family. Above the marble memorial hangs a painted wooden hatchment with the Hay arms. In the crowded kirkyard are also the tombs of the Gordons of Farskane and Findochty, and also of Cairnfield. There are many early stones here, and a modern extension of the cemetery across the road. A bede-house used to stand near the old church, founded in 1226 for 7 bedesmen or pensioners, originally to be lepers. It was still there in 1840, likewise some of the bedesmen, though no longer lepers, each having half an acre of croft-land and certain other privileges from the estate of Rannas. The pre-Reformation Vicarage of Rathven sank as the collegiate church of Cullen rose. Rathven also used to be a barony, so there would be a castle somewhere near.

The Moor of Findochty and Bauds of Cullen area lies immediately to the east, rather bare and windswept. Here was fought, in approximately 961 the Battle of the Bauds, allegedly between Indulphus, 77th King of Scots, and the Danes, at which the invaders were soundly beaten but King Indulphus died. This is all semi-legendary; but there are cairns in this area said to be the burial mounds of the slain, and a farm at the Rathven end is called Moor of Scotstown, so presumably the Scots attacked from the west. In the woodlands now growing on the flanks of Bin Hill, immediately to the south, are other cairns, in one of which Indulphus himself is said to be buried. In the 19th century an Earl of Seafield built a circular road to the top of Bin Hill.

The estate of Rannas lies at the foot of Bin Hill. The former Hay mansion is now a farmhouse, reduced to two oblong and disjoined blocks, that to the north being probably of the late 17th century, on the edge of quite a steep ravine. It has been badly altered however, its roof lowered and hipped. It has a semi-octagonal stair-tower and massive old chimney-stack, with corbels to support the ceiling of the ground-floor kitchen with its old stone ovens. The portion of the house opposite is a more recent replica. The old walled garden with its high coped walling and arched entrance adjoins, with fruit trees, but much neglected. The Hays of Rannas were a military family, who eventually became allied with the Leiths of Leith-hall in Aberdeenshire and were called Leith-Hay. General Alexander Hay or Rannas distinguished himself in the Napoleonic wars and founded the Royal Aberdeenshire Regiment. The last of the direct line was killed in the late war, aged 21.

Two miles to the west, along the A.98 and a mile inland from Buckie, is Bell's Inchgower Distillery, at the roadside, with its own associated housing, almost part of the Arradoul community—which is scattered and hardly a hamlet, centred round a large farm and former bonnet-lairdship. There was a small Episcopal church established here in 1788. Inland, just over a mile southwards is the hamlet of Drybridge on the Burn of Buckie, and near by lies the old estate of Letterfourie, still in the hands of the original family of Gordons. The present large Georgian mansion dates only from 1776 but has an ancient nucleus, also ornamental gardens and pond. And in the wooded grounds is the remarkable Craigmin bridge, a unique composition, consisting of a single arch over a deep ravine supporting a 3-arch superstructure with scalloped parapet, highly picturesque and probably of the late 18th century. The Gordons of Letterfourie descend from the 2nd Earl of Huntly, and in 1625 obtained a baronetcy of Nova Scotia. An earlier Sir James commanded James the Fifth's first Scots fleet.

There is an interesting group of small lairds' houses, now all farms, in the Letterfourie estate vicinity. Walkerdales is a fine old L-planned and crowstep-gabled whitewashed house of 1677, with the Gordon arms over the door. Birkenbush adjoins on a ridge to the north-west, a tall early 18th century building with a curvilinear gablet and coped chimneys, and the tradition that Robert Burns visited here and left his signature on a window-shutter since destroyed. And Thornybank to the north is a traditional white-washed house in trees, dated 1759 on the gable. It is unusual to find three such houses so close together. The smaller estate of Cairnfield, also a Gordon property with a mansion of 1802 lies in woodland to the west. And an equal distance to the south-east is Greenbank House, of the late 18th century, with a doocot with a weathercock.

Further inland, to the north-west of this area, is the remarkable feature of a great, isolated, Roman Catholic church, at Preshome, miles from anywhere on a side-road in foothills country. It is almost large enough to be a small cathedral, dating from 1788, with an old orchard in front and a presbytery-house at the side. It is massive, harled, with an Italianate ornamental gable, and internally extraordinarily fine, if somewhat over-decorated for a country church. Here resided the Bishops of Germanicia. Bishop John Kyle built the presbytery, and is buried here. This part of Banffshire is a traditionally strong Catholic area, and 2 miles to the south-west, at the farm of Chapelford, in the Enzie district, site of an earlier chapel, is a large R.C. burial-ground, St. Ninians, in the open fields. Here are two buildings, both modern, a small private family chapel and also a good burial-vault for clergy, all in good order. Some of the gravestones go back as far as the 17th century. It is known locally as the Banffshire Bethlehem.

This Enzie area is one which has declined, so that today the Ordnance map shows only Braes of Enzie farm. But it was once an important barony, and the title of Earl of Enzie was created by James the Sixth for the 6th Earl of Huntly, when he was promoted Marquis. There are two hamlets in the district—Clochan, small with school and post-office, at a cross-roads; and Cowfurach, where is the small *quod sacra* established church of Enzie, of 1785, rather attractive, with an apse. Cowfurach is remotely situated out in the fields, and has an 18th century group of cottages.

Rothiemay. The River Deveron makes a large S-bend 6 miles north of Huntly and here, on the north side, is the very rural parish of Rothiemay, with the river forming the county boundary with Aberdeenshire. It covers just under 10,000 acres, with only the village of Milltown of Rothiemay, at the riverside, and not even another hamlet. It was quite a famous name in Scottish history however, because of the activities of the Gordon lairds of Rothiemay Castle.

The village is a pleasant sequestered place, in the green valley, compact and not large. The parish church, replacing the earlier St. Drostan's chapel in the castle grounds, stands at the north end in its graveyard, with a burn running by, small, granite-built with a belfry, erected in 1807, but with an arched doorway under an angel's head and wings built into the north wall. This came from the original St. Drostans, demolished in 1752, then incorporated in the

67

castle buildings, and finally brought here in 1959 when the castle itself was demolished. There is also a massive old stone font from the same source. Near by, in the hilly playing-field park, is a modern granite monolith to the memory of James Ferguson, F.R.S., 1710–76, a one-time herd-boy and self-taught astronomer who became very famous. A nice touch, amongst the signs of the zodiac around the plinth, are also the names of his friends and patrons. There is a working smiddy across the road, and further down, by the riverside, is a former corn-mill, functioning until recently and now converted into a very attractive house. Opposite this, beside the old bridge over the Deveron, is the old-fashioned but very pleasant fishing-hotel, the Forbes Arms, in whose bedrooms the river's murmur is always present. Not far from this, tucked in behind cottages, is the unexpected feature of a thriving caravan agency supplying trailers over a wide area of Scotland, built up by a local man. Near the B.9117, half a mile north-east of the village, is a stone-circle in the field, with four uprights remaining and a huge recumbent 15 feet long, with cupmarks. Further north-west, on the B.9118, in an isolated site, is the built-up stone arch which was the doorway of the Free church of 1843, dismantled 1958; also its bell, dated 1857 with quotation from a psalm—an unusual memorial and much better than the usual abandoning of a kirk to decay or become a cart-shed.

East of the village street is the impressive heraldically decorated gateway to Rothiemay estate, which still functions as such although the castle is gone. An attractive small modern house rises on the site, incorporating the old doorway and an iron grille in one of the windows. The position is a fine one, on a terrace overlooking the valley, with delightful views. Just below, in the haugh, is Queen Mary's Bridge over a burn. Here also was the site of the afore-mentioned St. Drostan's chapel. The castle was a large composite edifice incorporating a fortalice in which Mary Queen of Scots stayed in 1562, when she made her progress into the North to bring down the power of Gordon. The property, like so many others, passed to the Duffs, Earls of Fife. Gordon of Rothiemay featured in the famous Frendraught tragedy of 1630, his son also being burned to death in the subsequent feud.

There is not much of interest on the higher ground of the parish, though it is pleasant country, with a large planted forest at Tarry-blake Wood to the north-west. But 2 miles eastwards, along the Deveron valley, is the estate of Mayen. There is a large mansion of 1788 hidden in its wooded policies, but near the B.9117 roadside is the highly attractive predecessor, now called Mains of Mayen, an L-planned house of the early 17th century with circular stair-tower, crow-stepped gables and dormer windows, recently well restored. A pleasingly coloured heraldic panel with the Abernethy arms impaling Halkett, dated 1680, is over the moulded doorway, but there is obviously much older work here, the very thick western wall containing a mural garderobe with its own tiny window. David the Second bestowed Mayen on William de Abercromby in the 14th century, and in 1445 the Abercromby laird became the first Lord Saltoun. The Gordons got the property in 1612. But it was bought by William Halkett, Sheriff-Clerk of Banff in 1649, and his heiress daughter, marrying an Abernethy, carried it back to that family. An extraordinary case developed in 1683-91, too complicated to go into here, involving hidden papers torn from court proceedings and hidden in the walling here, stealthy search while the family were asleep, and finally the reversal of court proceedings, all very romantic. The Abernethys stayed on, however, until one had the misfortune to shoot dead Leith of Leith-hall at an election-meeting in mid-18th century. Happily he had married one of the rising, rich and powerful Duffs, who came to the rescue—and in due course inherited the estate. One of *them* it was who built the more modern mansion of 1788.

Tomintoul, Kirkmichael and Glenavon. Everyone knows the name Tomintoul (the last syllable pronounced towel, by the way) one of the highest villages in Scotland and, remotely set as it is, one of the first to feature in the B.B.C. weather reports as being cut off by snow and wild weather, all its access roads being exposed, more especially that from the south, the famous Cock Bridge–Tomintoul by the Lecht. It lies towards the north end of one of the largest parishes in North-East Scotland, Kirkmichael, of 76,000 acres, basically the basin of the Upper Avon—just as its neighbouring parish to the north-east, Inveravon, not quite so vast, comprises the basin of the Livet and lower Avon. Glenavon is the huge south-westerly section of the parish which flanks the stripling river and probes for about 16 miles above Tomintoul deep into the lofty heart of the greatest mountain-range in Scotland, now known as the Cairngorms but properly the Monadh Ruadh, the Red Mountains, where the Avon has its source in Loch A'an at 2250 feet, under mighty Ben MacDhui, the second highest summit in these islands. The parish of Kirkmichael, then, reaches right up to these summits; indeed its boundary, which is on one side also the county boundary with Inverness, and on the other with Aberdeenshire, runs along the ridge of Cairngorm—Cairn Lochan—Ben MacDhui—Ben a Bhuird—Ben Avon, so touching all the main Cairngorm giants save Braeriach and Cairn Toul. It is therefore, by any standards, an extraordinary parish.

Tomintoul is one of those geometrically planned villages of the North-East, often, as here, set in bare and seemingly inhospitable surroundings, the foundations of "improving" lairds of the late 18th and early 19th centuries, concerned with resettlement of dispossessed crofters in the aftermath and clearances following on the Jacobite troubles, the bringing of their great barren peatlands into cultivation during the blockade of the Napoleonic wars, and enhancing the value of their estates—and at the same time adding to their own prestige. In this case it was the 4th Duke of Gordon who did the founding, first in 1750, but not until 1780 was there any considerable settlement, on his lands of Campdalemore, along the line of the new military road of General Wade. It may have been a bit of a disappointment to the Duke, at first—for when Queen Victoria visited here in 1860, she described it as: ". . . the most tumble-down, poor-looking place I ever saw—a long street with three inns, miserable, dirty-looking houses and people, and a sad look of wretchedness about it. Grant told me that it was the dirtiest, poorest village in the whole of the Highlands." It may have been one of the Queen's "off" days—and it probably was raining. At any rate, Tomintoul is not like that today—even though it is not really beautiful, nor distinguished architecturally; but when the sun shines, it can look quite pleasing, and certainly has an aspect of air and space. It is still basically one very long main street, with a central square, and parallel flanking streets with lanes linking. It is situated at 1160 feet, and has a population of just under 500. Today it is, strangely enough, something of a tourist-trap, with every other shop selling souvenirs and otherwise catering for the visitors, hotels and guesthouses prominent—for Tomintoul is now on the map for the bus-tour and the motorist, after long, rather notorious, isolation; which is of course, an excellent development. Many people like to say that they have stayed in the highest village in Scotland, or indeed the British Isles; but in fact Wanlockhead in upland Dumfriesshire has this distinction, being at 1350 feet, no less.

The hotels are grouped round the grass-planted square, where is a fountain presented by Dr. Robert Grant. Tomintoul is not the site of the parish church, which lies down Avon about 4 miles to the north; but it was made a *quod sacra* parish in 1833, and its church, built in 1826 was renovated in 1877. It is not very large, and has its own graveyard. The Catholic church of St. Michael, of 1837, not on the main street, is a handsome building, and also has a graveyard, sign of a large Catholic population, probably more than a third of the total; this no doubt an echo of the old Gordon Catholic influence. There is also a convent and school. The hotels offer facilities for angling, and winter sports are becoming important. There is a small youth hostel; also a fire-station.

The mile-long village flanks the A.939 along a recognisable ridge —the name should be *Tom an t-Sabhail*, the knoll or ridge of the barn —here joined by the B.9008, from Glenlivet and Ballindalloch. It makes a good centre for exploring a highly interesting and comparatively little-known countryside of great extent.

Half a mile to the west, on lower ground, is the farm of St. Bridget, where Gordon of Glenbucket, one of Prince Charlie's best officers, lived for a while after the Forty-five. It has an 18th century farm-house, and had long been a residence of these Gordons, hereditary principal bailies for Huntly and the Gordon chiefs. There was a pre-Reformation chapel here dedicated to St. Bridget or Bride; but the lands themselves used to be called Camdelbeg, or Campdalebeg. This was the important place of the area, before the erection of the village.

A little further west the land descends to the River Avon, a most notable water with its linns and cataracts and dramatic ravines, the Spey's largest tributary. The public road, however, goes only a couple of miles south of Tomintoul, whereafter it becomes private, sending one branch far up the Avon itself, and another up the quite major valley of the Water of Ailnack—this also being a quite spectacular stream, with a fine gorge quite near its confluence with Avon. Near the joining of the waters is the ancient estate of Delnabo, the mansion set deep in the valley, and now all fairly modern. It was a Grant lairdship from 1638, before which it was part of the surrounding Gordon lands. Oddly enough, one George Smith, of Minmore, Glenlivet, established a Cairngorm Distillery here, as adjunct to his Glenlivet one, between 1850–8; but it was not continued thereafter.

A vast portion of Kirkmichael parish, as far as acreage goes, lies south of this, comprising the valleys and watersheds of the two rivers. But with no public road, and little population, they must remain little known, save for the energetic walker. The Ailnack valley is practically uninhabited, with a splendid ravine some 6 miles up. But the Avon is wider, more wooded, and contains a number of hill-farms and estate houses, as well as the large shooting-lodge of the Glenavon estate at Inchrory, 10 miles up. The Forest of Glenavon, with its river, goes another 14 miles beyond that, before Loch A'an is reached, so something of the size of this little private kingdom may be realised. Inchrory, handsomely set amongst trees at the junction of Glen Builg with Glen Avon, under the rocky crags of Ruigh Speanan, this also a former junction of drove-roads, is a large white-washed lodge and associated buildings. Queen Victoria rode here from Tomintoul in 1860, and described it in her Journal, noting two eagles she saw alighting on the crags above. The present house dates only from 1847, built by the then Duke of Richmond and Gordon. There were Grants here in 1546, but the Gordons obtained it in the 17th century. Because of its strategic importance on the drove-roads, General Wade stationed patrols here during the "pacification" of the Highlands after the Jacobite risings. These glens used to be quite heavily populated, and there are numerous ruined croft-houses and farmsteads. Summer sheilings for the cattle grazing were also much in evidence in these uplands. Down in the Delavorar area, only 3 miles south of Tomintoul, are two large groups of burial cairns, one on either side of the river, a mile apart. Delavorar was a tacksman's house, held by a branch of the MacGregors, under the Gordons, far from their own lands—a family which produced many notable men, one of whom, Sir William, was Governor of Newfoundland. Another became Chief Justice of Jamaica. Montrose in his campaigning, is supposed to have encamped here.

Around Inchrory the hills average about 2300 feet in height, rising steadily westwards through some of the wildest and most remote country in these islands until the 4000-foot contour is reached, around the crescent of mighty summits which cradle Loch

A'an; that lonely and dramatic water, with its famous Shelter Stone.

North-west of Tomintoul, the A.939 drops down towards Bridge of Avon, passing quarries and lime-works, still in use. The bridge itself, a fine double-arched military structure, with a slight hump, stands gracefully amongst picturesque woodland and was partly rebuilt in 1831. An inn used to stand near the farm of Camdelmore, here. The last tenant thereof went off to the Napoleonic Wars, taking his wife with him, as sutlers or suppliers of liquor to the troops—and did so well that they never required to return to their little Highland inn.

Just before the bridge, the road forks, a branch, B.9136 continuing northwards down the Avon valley, on the east side of the river, to Drumin, where it joins the Glenlivet B.9008. A lesser road, across the bridge, likewise goes down the west side of the Avon, referred to hereafter. The parish church of Kirkmichael stands in its old graveyard at the roadside nearly 3 miles down B.9136, in a lovely setting. The small yellow-washed kirk dates only from 1808, and was partly destroyed by fire in 1950. Restored, it is pleasingly simple and bright within. There had been previous churches on the site from the 13th century. Kirkmichael was threatened with fire on an earlier occasion when, at the end of the 15th century, the Gordons allowed most of their Stewart of Strathavon neighbours and rivals to take their seats one Sunday, then locked them in and piled brushwood against doors and windows, announcing that they would set all alight unless certain gainful concessions were made by their fellow-worshippers. The Stewarts wisely agreed. It is also recorded that these Stewarts used to be great salmon-spearers, and had a habit of bringing their spears to church with them, leaning them against the walling, for sport on the way home. The kirkyard is interesting in that it contains the very ancient St. Michael's Cross, of stone, about 5 feet high—not a cross-slab—uninscribed but with small hollows in the centre of each side. Like some others, this cross is said to have been removed from its site several times, but always found its way back to Kirkmichael. There are many very thin gravestones. Many tell tales of Strathavon men who have made their mark on unnumbered foreign fields.

Not far below the church is the Tomintoul–Glenlivet Distillery, at road and river side, near the attractive 18th century farmhouse of Ballantruan. Fuaran na Cloiche, the Well of the Stone, close by, is used to supply the distillery. At the other side of the church, half a mile to the south-east, a side-road strikes off back in the Tomintoul direction; and along this a short distance stood the former parish school of Kirkmichael, at Tommachlaggan. This tiny institution was productive of great educational results, one former pupil listing no fewer than 66 university graduates existing therefrom, in his own day. One parish schoolmaster went on from here to become Professor of Greek at Aberdeen.

The same side-road leads up the valley of the Conglass Water, which passes half a mile to the east of Tomintoul. Two miles along is the ancient former Gordon lairdship of Croughly, with its 18th century house. This family of Gordons achieved as spectacular a record as the nearby school, although in the military sphere—for James Gordon of Croughly (1726–1812) had no fewer than 6 sons, 14 grandsons and 8 great-grandsons commissioned as officers, all of the name of Gordon. Of these one was a lieutenant-general, two were major-generals and one a surgeon-general, two of them knighted.

South of Croughly, another 2 miles up the Conglass and near Tomintoul itself, is Auchriachan and the Milton thereof. The family of Farquharsons holding this bonnet-lairdship had their own prominence. One son went to Paris to attend the Scots College there, but instead of becoming a priest became Captain of the King of France's bodyguard. His son was created a nobleman, and took the title of Baron d'Auchriachan. What the French made of this title is not recorded. The Conglass continues southwards for a further few miles, followed by the well-known Lecht Road, A.939 to Cockbridge and Donside. Up here, near the county boundary with Aberdeenshire, is the Well of the Lecht, where there is a tablet, dated 1754, declaring that five companies of the 33rd Regiment, Lord Charles Hay Colonel, made this road from here to the Spey. Ironstone used to be mined hereabouts.

Back at Bridge of Avon, north of Tomintoul, where the road divides, the "back road" down the west side of Avon branches off a mile along the Grantown road, and goes for five picturesque miles down, to rejoin the B.9136 at a bridge at Inverourie. Past the three former Gordon farms of Fodderletter, under the steep wooded hill of Knock Fergan, is the little former Free church of 1844, now converted into a dwellinghouse, at Dalvrecht. High on the hillside above is Fergan's Well, where, oddly enough, a fair used to be held (also sometimes called the Market of Creudenwell). A stranger site for a fair would be hard to imagine; but before the present afforestation it might have been very different, however steep a position. Anyway, the fair was finally transferred to Tomintoul, not allegedly on account of convenience but because of a notorious brawl over a cheese, of all things, which became known as the Battle of the Kebbuck. There was a Knockfergan slate-quarry up here, too, run by the Gordons of Croughly. Who Fergan was is not clear—presumably a Celtic missionary.

Back on the main A.939 to Grantown, 2 miles on from Bridge of Avon is the still more renowned Bridge of Brown, or more properly Bruan, in its dramatic, deep and steep-sided valley of Glen Bruan, in the old days a distinct traffic hazard. This is still on the former military road. There is a fine linn just a stone's throw from the bridge, and the entire situation very scenic. Here is the Banffshire boundary. The road rises steadily and impressively thereafter over the open braesides of the southern end of the Hills of Cromdale, reaching 1424 feet in 3 miles. The views westwards from this point, over Speyside and the Cairngorms are superb.

INVERNESS-SHIRE, EASTER

The vast county of Inverness, by far the largest in Scotland—or England, either—covers 2,695,094 acres, or over 4250 square miles, far too large an area to be considered or described conveniently as a piece. Moreover, it stretches not only right across Scotland from the North Sea to the Atlantic, but out to the far Outer Hebrides also, so that Vallay in North Uist, for instance, is 150 miles away from its county town of Inverness. For the purposes of this series of volumes, it is convenient to treat the North-Western Highlands and Islands as an entity in themselves, and West Inverness-shire represents a large part of that colourful area. In this book, therefore, the author has arbitrarily drawn a line down the map, from the Ross border near Garve to the Perthshire border near Rannoch Station, passing the head of Loch Ness east of Fort Augustus—and described all to the east of it as Inverness-shire Easter. This line is approximately the watershed and spine of Highland Scotland anyway.

Even so, we are left with a huge area of possibly a million acres, containing a score of civil parishes, some of them the largest in the land, and including a vast variety of scene, territory and conditions, almost impossible to consider as any sort of entity. Contemplation of it all makes one perceive something of the problems and difficulties which face its county council and administrators.

Why should Inverness-shire be all one county, anyway, one might well ask? Historically it was all once part of the important Province of Moray, so much vaster than the present county of that name. Not that the Earls of Moray, or presumably their predecessors, the Celtic mormaors thereof, ever had any real control over much of the wild and mountainous clan lands to the west. It may be that Crown and parliament recognised that it was impossible ever to form a county, or any acceptable administrative unit, of the far-flung territories of the warring clans, and so decided that they must be put under the at least nominal authority of powerful low-country and "civilised" lords to the east, who could be encouraged to make occasional punitive and flag-flying expeditions into the interior in the name of government. And in later times, something of the same attitude has prevailed, aided by the population imbalance, for there is no town in the county west of Inverness save Fort William, with its population of only 3000, and nothing but sheer land and scenery of which to make another county. The total population of the entire county is only 83,000, of which Inverness burgh accounts for 30,000, and its immediate lowland surroundings probably another 10,000. Which does not leave a great deal for the rest.

Even the area under consideration here is one for superlatives. Here is the highest range of mountains in Britain, the Monadh Ruadh or Cairngorms. Here is perhaps the emptiest large area in these islands, that covered by the Monadh Liath or Grey Mountains to the west, some 800 square miles without a single village. Here rise some of the most famous rivers, for salmon and scenery, in the country—the Spey, the Findhorn, the Beauly and the Nairn. Here are the greatest pine-forests in the United Kingdom—Rothie-murchus, Abernethy, Strathspey, Glenurquhart and the rest. Here is some of the most glorious scenery in these islands. And so on.

All these make up tremendous assets nationally and for the visitor; but until comparatively recently represented little but huge problems for the local folk, save for a handful of landowners. Even today, the enormous potentialities of the area, for the tourist trade and as a recreation-ground for the rest of the country, are little developed. The mid-Strathspey district, from Newtonmore to Grantown, admittedly has been exploited on a major scale, almost over-exploited some would say, with intense development centred on Aviemore, Glenmore and the Cairngorm ski slopes. But this is in fact a very small proportion of the whole. For instance, half a mile *west* of Aviemore itself the wilderness begins, and the vast Monadh Liath stretch across most of the rest of Scotland, empty, trackless, unknown, an area much larger than the Cairngorms, extraordinary to exist in these allegedly overcrowded islands. The mountains do not rise so high, of course—but reach almost to the height of Snowdon, nevertheless, and average about 2600 feet. It is surprising how few people, even mountaineers and hill-walkers, ever venture into this lonely upland. Other areas are almost equally neglected. The great mountain tract immediately south of the Cairngorms, where the Rivers Feshie, Eidart, Geldie, Tarff and Tilt rise, is another *terra incognita*, vast, spectacular, seldom feeling the tread of man. On a different scale and level, the delightful, sequestered stretch of country south-east and parallel to the Great Glen and immediately north of the Monadh Liaths, Upper Strathnairn and Stratherrick, 25 miles long by 4 or 5 miles wide, though served by good roads is by-passed by the vast majority of even knowledgeable and country-conscious travellers, yet is full of interest, variety and history. The splendid attractions of the great forest of the ancient Caledonian pines are becoming better known, thanks to the Cairngorm National Forest Park, the Outdoor Education centres, pony-trekking establishments and other influences—and, oddly enough, the return of the ospreys to nest in the Loch Garten area, much aiding in bringing the delights of the mighty Abernethy Forest to the attention of many. Not, of course, that any saturation of these quiet and lovely places by hordes of visitors is something to be desired; and many of us, undoubtedly, would selfishly prefer to keep them, unknown, empty, inviolate—save for ourselves! But the larger, longer-term, kindlier view is surely the right one, as the age of leisure allegedly advances upon us. The vast majority will never seek out this wonderland anyway. Those who do should be guided to learn what a heritage and opportunity is there for their delectation, to take some of the pressure off Strathspey and to bring life, money, employment to a land which needs it all.

Apart from the tourist industry, there is only forestry an an important employer of labour in all this territory today—with, of course, sheep-farming plus the game-keeping and stalking on the deer-forests and grouse-moors. This is, in a way, tragic. For, once, these far-flung uplands supported many people, the entire clan system—and supported them on cattle. The hillsides and glens produced cattle by the hundred-thousand. This was the basis of the clan economy, not sheep. It was stamped out, of course, deliberately, after the Jacobite risings, as government policy, and the people, also by the hundred-thousand, evicted in the infamous Clearances, mainly overseas to Canada and elsewhere, with sheep and deer substituted for the cattle-herds. No longer were the vast droves assembled each autumn, in the Great Glen, Strathspey and Glen More, to be driven over the Corrieyairack, Drumochter and Cairngorm passes to the Lowland trysts, thousands upon thousands of beasts at a time, from these now empty lands—whose drove-roads may still be traced on ground and map. They could do again, and should, were governments in far-away London concerned, interested —and let no one shake heads over the alleged non-availability of winter feed to tide the breeding-stock over the long hard winters. The Canadian Government feed millions of caribou, in the barren-lands, from the air, by dropping baled hay, for no commercial but only conservation purposes—while our authorities sigh over the inhospitable Highlands, and import frozen beef from the Argentine.

Forestry today is in good heart in this, some of the best tree-growing land in Europe. But again, not as it used to be. The timber trade of Rothiemurchus, Abernethy, Glenmore, Kinveachy and so on, in the days of two centuries ago and more, was on a scale which we can barely conceive. Many hundreds of men were regularly employed in felling, trimming, dragging and floating the logs; also in wood-milling and pipe-making and charcoal-burning. The rivers were harnessed, with log-floating dams and sluices, to carry the timber down to the Spey, where vast rafts were assembled to float in convoys down to the sea—the working of these a highly spectacular and dangerous profession. Ship-building yards at Garmouth and Kingston there turned the great Caledonian pine logs—some 20 feet in girth and regularly producing planks 6 feet wide—into ocean-going ships, over 300 of which were built here, many world-famous clippers. Some idea of the scope of this great industry may be realised when it is quoted that, from the Duke of Gordon's estate of Glenmore alone, apart from the main bulk of the timber which went for ship-building, £40,000 worth of wood was disposed of annually otherwise—and money was then worth twenty times what it is today.

For a country of allegedly hard-headed, practical folk, Scotland has squandered its resources direly.

As might be expected, antiquities are not very thick on the ground in the mountainous parts—although even here there are interesting items to be located. But in the straths and low-lying belts there is much of interest. Of things prehistoric there are some especially good features. The famous Boar Stone at Knocknagael, just south of Inverness itself is a fine example of a rough Pictish monolith incised with a spirited carving of a wild boar, as well as the double-disc symbol. This Bona parish hillfoots area is also rich in chambered-cairns and stone-circles. The renowned Clava Stones, to the east, are in a class by themselves, a group of large and well-preserved chambered-cairns within stone-circles and linked by causeways, near the site of the Battle of Culloden. The plain and foothills west of Inverness and south of the Beauly Firth are also well-endowed with cairns, cup-marked stones and the hill-crown vitrified fort of Craig Phadraig. A still more spectacular fort is that of Dun Dearduill, at Inverfarigaig, 8 miles south-west of Dores on the south side of Loch Ness, crowning the summit of a great fang of rocky hill, a dramatic place. The entire district between the Great Glen and the Monadh Liath is dotted with outstanding Pictish forts and duns and ring-cairns. There are many more forts in the Strathspey area, parti-cularly around Boat of Garten, indicating how important this territory was to our early ancestors. Not far away, at Lynchat near Kingussie, is a large and notably well preserved souterrain or Pictish earth-house.

There are no abbeys in the area, but Beauly Priory, a Vallis-caulium establishment, one of only three in Scotland—the others being at Pluscarden and Ardchattan—has a ruined Early Second Pointed church surviving, of probably the 14th century. There are a few good ancient parish churches, notably those of Insh, Alvie and Kincardine. The fine 17th century Lovat Mausoleum in Kirkhill churchyard, with its belfry and "pepper-pots", is worth noting.

Of medieval castles and fortified strengths there is no lack, from the very simple 13th century Castle Roy, near Nethy Bridge, a former Comyn stronghold of most elementary character, to the fine late 16th and early 17th century fortalices of Castle Stuart, Dalcross and Erchless Castles, the last two of the Mackintosh and Chisholm chiefs, all still occupied and in good order. Loch an Eilean Castle, on its island, is a renowned beauty spot, linked allegedly with the Wolf of Badenoch—another Comyn stronghold, as was the motte-hill castle of Ruthven, near Kingussie, now known as Ruthven Barracks, from the 18th century fort superimposed thereon by government to counter Jacobite activities. A little-known but picturesque and interesting small castle is that of Muckerach, near Dulnain Bridge, a 16th century fortalice of the Grants, ruinous but fairly complete to the wallhead. Greatly more ruinous castles are sited at Urquhart, Daviot, Moy and Inverlaidnan. Of a later period, but an interesting feature of the area, especially of Strathspey, is the large number of very attractive and authentic 18th century tacks-men's houses, small mansions, now usually farmhouses—tacksmen being, of course, principal tenants of clan chiefs, often kinsmen, under whom the clan lands were parcelled out in later times. In speaking of fortified strengths, mention might be made of the very impressive citadel of Fort George, built in 1748 on a thrusting penin-sula of the Moray Firth, a vast and complicated fortress, set up to dominate the East Highlands and to ensure that there were no further Jacobite adventures. It still supports a military presence.

The echo of Jacobite campaigns still rings fairly loudly in these parts, inevitably, especially with Culloden battlefield-site a place of pilgrimage for scores of thousands each year. But East Inverness-shire was the scene of battles and stirring events innumerable long before that grim period of the 18th century; for here all roads lead, confined between the vast re-entrant of the Moray Firth and the 23-mile barrier of Loch Ness in the Great Glen, here Highlands and Lowlands meet, here the clans' lands marched with the Laigh, here was the key to the far North and the North-West. So hereabouts, next to the vital Tweed crossings and that strategic hub of Scotland, Stirling, was the most disputed area in all the land. And from Pictish times, when Inverness was the capital of King Brude, whom Columba came to convert, right down Scotland's vehement story, this district proved a testing-ground, a bone of contention, or a cherished prize. Here Macbeth lorded it as not only Thane of Cawdor but Mormaor of both Ross and Moray; here Bruce campaigned, as did his descendants Kings James the First, Third and Fourth; here Mary Queen of Scots hanged a rebellious governor during her only progress into the North; here successive Lords of the Isles raided and sacked and pillaged; here Montrose fought, and, a few years later, Oliver Cromwell clamped his iron fist. And so on. It is a vast territory, now as then, but scarcely a square mile of it has not been fought over—for the clan wars and feuds took over whenever the national campaigns left off, with the Mackintoshes and Macphersons, the Grants and Frasers, the Chisholms and Munroes and Rosses all jockeying for position, land and advantage.

Something of all this may be discerned and demonstrated, as it were on the ground, instead of merely read in books. For, as well as in its castles and sites, this area is particularly rich in rather special museums, for want of a better description. Landmark, at Carrbridge, is a most notable and valuable Visitor Centre, where the past, from the Ice Age right down to modern times, is brought graphically and vividly to life against the background of its ecology, wild-life, geology and topographical development, in dramatic sequence. And at Am Fasgadh, further south at Kingussie, is another splendid if very different Highland Folk Museum, displaying the social and domestic life of the area down the ages. While still further south, at Newtonmore, is the Clan Macpherson Museum, a more conventional but very telling establishment, which recounts still another side of the long story. And the military museum at Fort George should not be forgotten, adding still another dimension.

A modern aspect of the area which must not be overlooked is the development of hydro-electric power, which made such strides hereabouts in the middle years of this century. There is still debate as to whether or no this was a truly beneficial development—for the local people, that is. It brought the advantages of electricity to the Highlands and Islands, so that remote crofts and lonely shepherds' houses were linked up to the grid before many more central and populous places were. The building of these vast undertakings employed large numbers of engineers, contractors and navvies, but few of these were local folk; and the finished installations themselves require little in the way of labour. And, of course, by the very nature of the schemes, huge stretches of the so-valuable valley-floors were inevitably flooded, destroying the winter-feed-growing capacity of the glens, on which stock-rearing in the mountain lands depends; for though the hillsides provide pasture during the months from May to October, stock must be kept alive on hay and oats and turnips during the long winter, and a hill-farm which cannot grow these on its low ground is out-of-business. This has been the fate of many a glen and farms innumerable, in the provision of the electric power which is then exported to other areas, mainly in the populous parts—a balance-sheet insufficiently scrutinised when the demand for hydro-electric development was so strong. This development is not yet finished, despite the advance in oil-fired and nuclear generating, for a great new scheme is at present under way at Foyers, on the south shore of Loch Ness, where Scotland's third pump-storage project is using the dramatic drop of some 600 feet, between the Stratherrick shelf and Ness, to drive the turbines at Ness level, and then in off-peak hours to pump the water back up again to Loch Mhor, for re-use thereafter.

Before leaving this necessarily very brief survey of Inverness-shire in general and Loch Ness-side in particular, a word should be said on the entity which makes the area familiar in name, at least, to untold millions the world over—the Loch Ness Monster. This phenomenon remains a strange and unending source of interest, speculation, hilarity and derision, something upon which no one is expert—and therefore on which we are one and all entitled to hold forth, according to taste and temperament. On the Monster, no one seems to be neutral, however uninformed or far away. One either believes that there is something there, or one believes that the whole thing is either a will-o'-the-wisp, a folly, or a clever hoax. The fact that many scientists have spent much time and money in the search to prove it, cuts no ice with other scientific folk who dismiss it all as nonsense, a perennial boost for the tourist-trade. But local folk do not so dismiss it—not out of excessive credulity nor yet economic gain. For, of course, *this* monster is but the tip of the iceberg, the one which gets talked about, because the busy A.82 highway runs down the lochshore for 23 miles, and everybody can watch. The fact is that the tradition of monsters in Highland lochs is age-old. Even the early Celtic missionaries wrote of them—and who knows, some of the strange monstrous creatures in the typical Pictish symbol-stones may represent the same. Many other lochs than Ness allegedly have their strange denizens, and a round dozen and more are actually called Loch na Beiste, or similar names. Not a few of these lochs, like Ness, are of enormous depths, and strange creatures from time to time have appeared therefrom. The Kelpie, the water-horse, the *uilebheist*, the monster, are part of the Highland story—and undoubtedly will continue to be so, whether or no searchers produce satisfying proofs, of one or more, from Loch Ness, for the world's sceptics.

Abriachan and Caiplich. Abriachan is a surprising place, in more ways than one. To be within a dozen miles of Inverness, it is remarkably remote, in fact as in atmosphere; and to be only a mile and a half from the busy Great Glen highway of A.82, down Loch Ness-side, even more so. But it lies 750 feet higher than that highway, and its steeply twisting access road, with a very awkward turn-in from the A.82, is perhaps not such as to entice the uninformed traveller. Which is a pity, for Abriachan is a place to be visited. Caiplich is an extensive former crofting area, occupying a wide upland valley some way further on.

Abriachan also is a crofting and farming community and district, rather than any village or hamlet. It is rather extraordinary to find so many crofts and houses scattered about these very high braes and lofty slantwise shelves amongst the heather hills—obviously this was an area which was never cleared in the notorious Highland Clearances. Although there is now no church hereabouts, there was a school until recently—of which more hereafter. Yet Abriachan had its religious significance also, once, for down at the lochside is the little abandoned graveyard of Killianan, where formerly was the cell or church of St. Fianan or Finnan, quite a famous shrine— indeed, it is thought to have been here that the parish of Bona had its original church. No trace of a building remains. The graveyard is readily found, just above the highway near the steep Abriachan road-end, because of the tall cypress trees which still distinguish the site. There is a little pier below, but this is not easily seen from the road.

The graveyard was long neglected, but has recently been somewhat tidied up and cared for by the pupils of Inverness High School, as part of an excellent countryside project. Brambles and bracken still cover much of the surface, but certain tombstones are now clear. There is one fine early slab of red sandstone, alleged by some to have been brought from Iona—but this seems ridiculous, for it is typical, and why carry a heavy grave-slab all that way? Several other inscribed stones are said to have been thrown into Loch Ness at the Reformation period. Above the graveyard, on the wooded hillside about 100 yards behind the cottage here, is the stone which made the shrine famous, now called the Holed, or Font Stone. It is a flattish boulder, somewhat heart-shaped, with a deep socket-hole in the centre, 6 inches across, filled with water. The tradition is that this is always filled, whatever the weather—and it was certainly a dry spell when the present writer saw it. Allegedly it was, in fact, the font stone from which Columba baptised the Pictish King Brude, and so brought Christianity to the North-East. Like other stones or wells linked with Columba's name, the water from this was supposed to be good for child-bearing women. The hole may in fact have been the socket for St. Fianan's cell's roof-post. There is claimed to be another interesting boulder, called the Handfasting Stone, still further up the hill, with a cavity capable of accommodating the hand in three different positions—used no doubt for hand-fast marriage ceremonies, before they were blessed by the Church. The present writer did not find this.

Near by, the Abriachan or Killianan Burn descends the very steep hillside in a wooded ravine and a series of cascades and waterfalls, some of them quite picturesque. The little side-road zigzags its way up dramatically, with ever finer views out over the Great Glen. At about the 650-foot contour the land begins to open out again, and the crofts and farms to appear. Near the road here is the small disused mill of Balbeg. The scene becomes very attractive, with Scots pines growing out of the heather, and wide vistas. A little way up is the former school, now a private house, and close by the small community-hall. This was being used, at time of writing, to house a small museum of items collected and maintained by the Inverness High School pupils, who were in process of restoring the croft-house of Druim, further up, to house it all. It is a most admirable project, and congratulations are due to all concerned. The exhibits include a great variety of objects relative to the crofting life, costume, furnishings, implements, nature-study and so on. The young people have also excavated and restored the croft's well.

Abriachan and Caiplich were long a possession of Holy Church, part of the Bishop of Moray's barony of Kinmylies (see Inverness). After the Reformation they passed to the Frasers who sold them to the Grants. Because of its remote situation, Abriachan was a sort of sanctuary for hunted men and the landless, in the clan feuding days. It was also a great place for independent distillers, and excise-men used to roost in the school for weeks at a time, trying to catch out the offenders. Sometimes the school had as many as 100 pupils. It was closed in 1958.

Half a mile beyond the school and hall is Loch Laide, itself half a mile wide, amongst the heather braes. There are stories of water-kelpies here, and older folk did not like to pass that way at night—which was probably convenient enough for the whisky-distillers active around it. There is forestry planting up here now.

The narrow road continues over the hills to Glen Convinth, and the Kiltarlity–Glen Urquhart road, A.833, about 6 miles further, reaching the 1000-foot contour in the process. On the right, stretching far north-eastwards, is the wide and shallow upland vale of Caiplich, still with its scattering of crofts and small sheep-farms, down which runs the Allt Mor finally to join Ness at Dochgarroch quite near Inverness. The Caiplich vale and moss is almost 10 miles long, and is dotted with burial-cairns. The Battan planted forest occupies much of the area now, on both sides. The name means the place of horses, and it was a noted summer sheiling. Most of all this area is in Bona parish, but part of Caiplich is in Kiltarlity.

Alvie and Kinrara. Alvie is one of those vast Central Inverness-shire civil parishes, covering no less than 135 square miles, or 86,000 acres, larger than Kinross, West Lothian or Clackmannan shires, comprising parts of both the Monadh Liath (Grey Mountains) and Monadh Ruadh (Red Mountains—usually called The Cairngorms) systems. Yet Alvie itself is scarcely even a hamlet, on the shores of Loch Alvie 3 miles south of Aviemore. Kincraig village is in this parish, but is dealt with separately. Kinrara is an old and very attractive estate between A.9 and the Spey, with an interesting background. The population, even in 1880, was only 700; today it will be considerably less.

The Spey valley at Alvie is very pleasant, with the birch-wooded slopes of the Monadh Liath rising to the west and the tree-clad hogs-back of Kinrara in the centre, while the high Cairngorms loom to the east. Embosomed in this, Loch Alvie is gentle, sylvan, nothing wild about it but picturesque, irregularly shaped, a mile long and half that in width. On a peninsula to the south stands the parish church on a knoll, in its old graveyard, a delightful spot. It has been the site of worship for untold centuries and the kirk has been restored several times, notably in 1798, 1833, 1880 and recently in 1952 when Sir Basil Spence was the architect. It has a typical whitewashed exterior, save for the belfry gable, and in the kirkyard are many old stones. Interred here are the ashes of Lord Bilsland of Kinrara, who did so much to found the Scottish Council (Development and Industry); also Sir George Henschel, the musician. The interior is bright, with plain-glass windows (always an asset when the views are so fine) and light-coloured woodwork. Features are the ship's-bell from H.M.S. *Loch Alvie* presented 1944, wooden collection-ladles, and a list of parish-ministers since 1567, including the Reverend William Gordon who was summoned before the Duke of Cumberland in 1746 for giving shelter to refugees from Culloden—but survived the interview. Near by, across the loch, is the quite large Lynwilg Hotel, pleasingly situated, on the A.9 but standing isolated amongst the birchwoods.

Kinrara estate lies just opposite, across the main road, embracing a lofty wooded ridge between road and river, one of its two summits reaching 1775 feet, and both being crowned by tall monuments, one to the famous and sprightly Duchess of Gordon and the other to her son the 5th Duke. This Duchess—who was so renowned in her raising of the Gordon Highlanders, allowing each recruit a kiss on the lips—lies buried at a spot she chose in the policies below. Also crowning a tor in the estate is the Waterloo Cairn, erected in memory of the officers and men she raised, who fell in the Napoleonic Wars—two sides of a coin, this. Kinrara was long a seat of the Gordons, and indeed still gives the Gordon–Lennox family the subsidiary title of Earl of Kinrara, in the dukedom of Richmond and Gordon. The mansion is a large and attractive whitewashed pile in a lovely woodland setting, easily seen from across the Spey, basically a Regency house of 1820 with additions. It was visited by Leopold of the Belgians the year after it was built. Kinrara became the Highland home of Steven Bilsland aforementioned. In the policies also is the site of St. Lata's pre-Reformation chapel and well.

In the opposite direction from the parish church, south-west past the roadside Dalraddy Caravan-park, is another sporting estate, Alvie Lodge, with its extensive woodlands, deer-forest and large mansion. To the north of the Lodge nearly a mile is Delfour, Easter and Wester, estate farms where is also a tree-nursery, the view from here across the strath to the Cairngorm flanks being superb. At Delfour is a splendid cairn-circle, with a double ring of large stones, the inner ones slightly smaller, and with a single tall monolith standing guard outside 20 feet to the west.

These features of Alvie parish lie approximately along the main A.9 highway and the valley-floor. But the vast stretches of empty mountains stretch away north-west and south-east for 22 miles, so that it includes the headwaters of the Dulnain to the north, and those of the Feshie and the Geldie south on the borders of Aberdeenshire and Perthshire, a quite enormous area. Footpaths and stalkers' tracks offer walkers tramps through the Monadh Liath from Balavil, Kincraig, Alvie Lodge and Lynwilg, some of these of great length. The eastern side is dealt with under Kincraig and Glenfeshie.

Ardersier and Fort George. Ardersier is a small coastal parish of only 3800 acres, 10 miles east of Inverness, containing the village of the same name, or Campbelltown, and the famous and very impressive military establishment of Fort George, jutting on a low peninsula into the Moray Firth. It is rather a strange and atypical area to find so near both Inverness and Nairn, with its population concentrated only along a mile or so of coast and otherwise almost deserted and fairly level carseland. About a quarter of the parish area is taken up by the extensive Carse Wood, and the Carse of Ardersier itself is largely given over to a military firing-range. It seems always to have been an unproductive area, for in 1792 the total rental of the parish was only £365.

Little is nowadays eloquent of antiquity, although the hill-fort known as Cromal's, or Cromwell's Mount, its old name Tom Mhoit, rises above the north end of the village, with traces of ramparts. Nevertheless, there was a barony of Ardersier in 1574, held by the Campbells of Cawdor—hence the name of the village. This was created a burgh of barony in 1623 for John Dhu Campbell of Cawdor, with a mercat cross, town house, bailies and a fair held each 15th July—though this was changed to a Lammas Market held on 12th August. It became a small port also, but with no harbour, only a long timber jetty, which still survives in a decayed state. There was a population of 1000 in 1840; and though this declined, what with military developments and the place being within commuting distance of Inverness, modern housing has again built up the population. It is hardly a lovely village, although the setting is pleasing enough, straggling along the shore for almost a mile, with some old fishermen's cottages to the south, one or two still thatched with marram-grass, and with cruik construction; and some houses gable-end to the street further north. There is a school, war-memorial-hall, shops and a Free church of 1886. The former West church in the village, an undistinguished Gothic edifice of 1880, is now the parish church, supplanting one, inconveniently placed and isolated, half a mile to the east. The village street widens at the north end, with a few trees and a drinking-well, rather more attractive. Here is the Gun Lodge Hotel.

The former parish church stands inland, on higher ground in bare open country, at a road-junction, surrounded by its graveyard. The building is small and plain, with a belfry, with windows only to the south, dated 1802. There are no very old stones in this kirkyard. The older burial-ground and the site of the still earlier church lies, still more remotely, about a mile to the north-west, on a narrow side-road, amongst the whin-grown carseland which is now the firing-range. The church has wholly gone, and the abandoned farm-steading of Kirkton adjoins. The graveyard is crowded with old to very old stones, all overgrown and neglected, many of them relating to military men and their families from Fort George. There is a former watch-house. It is all rather desolate and depressing.

Fort George, however, is far from that, a most impressive and interesting establishment which lies over a mile due westwards, occupying the tip of a pointed peninsula which projects westwards towards Chanonry Point on the Black Isle shore of Easter Ross, so that between them they narrow the Moray Firth here to barely a mile, creating distinct inner and outer portions thereof. The site of the fort is very strong, and is heavily defended by deep ditches and moats; and its effectiveness against any sea-borne invasion is obvious. Less obvious is its use to overawe the Highland population, for it seems oddly out on a limb here. Yet it was built in 1748 for that very purpose, after the Forty-five Rising, to replace Cromwell's fort at Inverness. It cost the then enormous sum of £160,000, much more than planned for—and this is understandable when its ramifications are considered. It must be one of the latest purely military forts built in these islands; and before the days of modern artillery or aerial bombing would be well-nigh impregnable. It covers 16 acres, and, in the former military parlance, is defended on the landward side by a ditch (enormous), a covert way, a glacis, two lunettes and a ravelin. Seaward, it is polygon-shaped, with six great bastions, its hundreds of yards of parapets gapped by many cannon-ports. A wall-walk, pleasant on a good day, with magnificent views all round but especially to the Ross coast and the far Highland hills, runs round the perimeter. There is much typically military building within, including barrack blocks for over 2000 men, a hospital, storehouses and ammunition bunkers. Also a highly attractive chapel, of 1767, strangely peaceful inside, amongst all the warlike exterior, with old battle flags and many memorials. William Adam, who was Master Mason of the Ordnance, with John Adam, helped to create it all. Long the depot of the Seaforth and the Cameron Highlanders, despite all the reorganisations of units and regiments today, Fort George remains the centre of military activity in the North of Scotland. There is a regimental museum on the premises. The public are admitted to both fort and museum.

There is considerable modern housing east of the fort, married quarters and so on. And further east still a tall castellated tower rises, a prominent landmark in the flat carseland. Actually it is only an elevated water-tank building for supplying the fort, but with houses in the flats below.

Two roads run laterally through the small parish, the B.9092 to Nairn and a side-road from the Fort area passing the aforementioned Kirkton. Most of the eastern part of the area is covered by the Carse Wood. The two roads join at the Nairnshire boundary, and near here is Balnagowan, Muir, Milton and Mains. In the woodland near the side-road is an ancient earth-work, with two parallel lines of tumuli. At Baddock, a mile westwards on the same road, the unfortunate old woman who was alleged to have bewitched the 17th century Campbell of Cawdor so that he fell off his horse at Drumdivan, was burned. Much of the land of this parish once belonged to the Knights Templar. Out in the Moray Firth, the last mile of the extraordinary and lengthy sandy spit, known as Whiteness Head, is in Ardersier, while its base is in Nairn parish. North Sea Oil supporting developments are going on here.

Aviemore. This is, of course, the mountain holiday resort boom-town, the winter-sports mecca of Scotland, which has in the last few years blossomed out into one of those go-go areas which the age of leisure and young people's affluence has produced, really the only one in Highland Scotland. Mind you, although the £3 million Aviemore Centre is new, as are the large modern hotels, motels, High Range Chalets and so on, Aviemore has been a popular holiday-place for a long time. But, before this burst of development, it was the proximity of the great Rothiemurchus pine-forests, the Spey fishing, and the mountaineering challenge of the Cairngorms, which brought devotees and their families back and back to this village, where Badenoch merges with Strathspey; now it is largely the snow-slopes of the north-facing corries which, providing long-lasting ski-runs, which have brought the enthusiasts—and those who like to be doing the fashionable thing—plus of course the entrepreneurs, from all over Britain, and indeed abroad, skiing being one of those sports which are very much with-it today. Which, of course, is splendid. Commercial interests were quick to see the possibilities, and money and ideas have poured into Aviemore, and continue to do so. If some of the older generation of holiday-makers shake their heads and say that the place is spoiled—well, that is the price which falls to be paid for development. It certainly is *not* the place it used to be. But it is a heartening, lively and exciting place today, for all that, with

85

people there, and all the year round, earning their livings in this one-time remote area, employing and catering for more. Bustle and crowds are not what we are apt to associate with the Highlands—and it would be unthinkable if this sort of thing was to spread over any large part of them. But that is improbable, to say the least of it, and the Highlands can absorb Aviemore. So long as the wonderful Forest of Rothiemurchus is not spoiled, Scotland should almost certainly be grateful for the developers here—or most of them. There *are* some features which seem rather evidently out of place.

Aviemore was only a railway-station hamlet in 1880, with a post-office. Even today, despite all the spectacular multi-storey hotels, theatre, cinema, swimming-pool, skating-rink, chalets etcetera, it is still quite a small place in fact. The last census I have noted shows a population of only 650—although it may now be nearer a thousand. New housing is spreading to the north, and the bounds of it keep stretching; but even so it is only a village, no larger than Newton-more, for instance, and smaller than Kingussie. Developing as it has done, it never had the atmosphere of a true village however, with no recognisable centre—as distinct from the striking modern complex called the Aviemore Centre today—and is really only a collection of facilities, shops dotted down, the railway-station, hotels, two churches and patches of housing spread along the A.9 highway for about a mile. If that does not sound wildly attractive—well, the fact is that Aviemore as a place is *not* wildly attractive. Interesting, vigorous, effective, stimulating, yes—and of course its setting superb, with the most wonderful prospects of the mountains and forest-clad foothills; but as a village it cannot be compared in aspect or picturesqueness with any of the other Speyside resorts. That has to be said. On the other hand, it has much that the others have not.

It is unnecessary here to go into details over the well-publicised attractions and facilities which the highly organised forces of development have to offer, in accommodation, catering, entertainment and so on, over and above the sporting activities of skiing, canoeing, sailing, pony-trekking, climbing, skating, golf, even gliding and kart-racing. Most things are catered for, from conferences to trampolining, dancing to hairdressing and Interflora. Extraordinary really, that a range of lofty north-facing hill-slopes should have produced all this.

One or two features of the village call for mention. Its position under the crags of Craigellachie, for one. Speyside is notable in having two Craigellachies, outstanding rocky bluffs, the other 47 miles to the north-east, near Rothes; and these represented of old the main bounds of Clan Grant territory—the clan's motto, of course, is "Stand Fast, Craigellachie!". The Grants still own much of the countryside hereabouts, although there have been inroads, the Ogilvie-Grants of Seafield, Grants of Rothiemurchus and Macpherson-Grants of Ballindalloch, remaining very much powers in the land, even if no longer exercising their almost regal sway. The birch woods which flank this western Craigellachie are a great

Castle Urquhart, Loch Ness

Aviemore

Clava. One of the fine group of chambered cairns, burial-mounds within stone-circles, dating from 1800–1500 BC

asset to Aviemore, and the modern features rising amongst them are
thereby made a deal more acceptable. At the south end of the
village, dotted amongst these glades, are the chalets, the Youth
Hostel and a Catholic church being rebuilt in modern style to match
all else. A large caravan-park is here, too, in the woods, with
another down on the Spey levels. This end, where the Rothiemurchus and Cairngorm road strikes off eastwards over a new bridge
—and an extraordinarily wide speedway it is to find in such surroundings, emphasising still further the constrictions and inadequa-
cies of the main A.9 highway—is the most pleasing part of Aviemore.
The central section is useful but uninspiring, and the northern
end fairly humdrum—except for the views—with council housing,
the granite St. Andrew's church, and the Nature Conservancy local
headquarters. One intriguing feature here is the presence, behind
the very modern fire-station, of an ancient cairn-circle, its five
standing-stones guarding an inner burial-place. There is another
stone-circle over a mile northwards at Loch nan Carraigean, the
Loch of the Standing Stones, on this same eastern side of the A.9, not
readily seen, the railway intervening. And just a little further is the
small, shallow loch of Avielochan, on an otherwise rather un-
interesting stretch of the road. Beyond, where the A.95 strikes off
eastwards for Grantown and Moray, is the Kinveachy area of Boat
of Garten, described separately. Also treated separately are the
highly attractive districts of Rothiemurchus and Glenmore, east of
Aviemore.

Beauly. The name of Beauly is probably better known than that of
most little towns of only 1400 inhabitants—which is not even a
burgh, strangely enough—partly because of the Beauly Firth, the
Beauly River and the fame of Beauly Priory; and also because the
main highway to the North of Scotland, the A.9, runs through it—
to its no great advantage, today. It stands 13 miles west of Inverness,
just where the River Beauly begins to widen towards the estuary and
Firth, but where it still may be bridged—at the Lovat Bridge of 1811
—and only a mile from the Ross boundary. The name, so remarkably "un-Highland", is believed to be a corruption of the French
beau lieu, meaning a beautiful spot, given to it by the Burgundian
monks introduced here in 1230; although some would have it a
corruption of Bealaidh Achaidh, a broom-field. Another Gaelic
name was *A 'Mhanachain*, the Priory; but even in the very early days
Beauly seems to have preferred exotic names, for it was called
Prioratus de Bello Loco in 1300. Beaufort Castle, Lord Lovat's seat
near by, has the same French basis, also of early origin.
The town, or very large village by Highland standards, is a
pleasant open place, laid out as a planned township in 1840, more
attractive perhaps than most Highland towns—which are by no
means always the most scenic additions to a glorious countryside. It
has two rather distinct sections; the main shopping area to the north,
and a residential area to the south, separated by a burn and bridge.

Both reach down to the estuary at the east. The famous Priory ruins lie at the extreme north.

The town centre surrounds a wide and open square, which is a great boon traffic-wise, as well as for amenity. Here are most of the shops and offices—for Beauly is quite an important shopping centre. In the square stands a tall monument, erected in 1905, to commemorate the raising of the Lovat Scouts Regiment by the 16th Lord Lovat, for service in the Boer War. North of this is the entrance to the Priory grounds, still used as a churchyard, and with some rather unusual modern and quite massive hog-backed tombstones. The old Mercat Cross of Beauly stands at the gateway, a slender shaft 6 feet high, on a two-stepped plinth. For this was the burgh of barony and market town of the Lords Lovat; and fairs used to be held here in a big way, no fewer than seven a year, indeed.

The Priory has long been in ruins, and nothing now remains of the conventual buildings, only the mainly roofless shell of the Early Second Pointed church, with some foundations to the south. This was one of only three Valliscaulium foundations in Scotland, all in the Highlands—indeed the only three outside of France, the others being at Pluscarden in Moray and Ardchattan in Argyll, all founded in 1230. This Order had its origins in the Val des Choux, in France. The founder of Beauly Priory was Sir John Bisset of The Aird and Lovat, whose castle of Lovat lay just across the river haughs a mile to the east, on what is now Wester Lovat farm—described under Kirkhill. Much of the church dates from the 13th century, but the nave was largely rebuilt by Prior Robert Reid (1530–58)—who also managed to hold down the offices of Bishop of Orkeny and Abbot of Kinloss! He bequeathed 8000 merks in 1558, to found Edinburgh University. His nephew Walter adopted the Reforming faith, and managed to remain Commendator and lay Prior, which helped to prolong the Priory's existence to the end of that troubled century—whereafter Cromwell, in his insatiable search for easy building materials for his great citadel at Inverness, pulled down the conventual buildings here, as he did with so much else. On the north side of the nave are the remains of a chapel of the Holy Cross, built by Hugh Fraser of Lovat in the early 15th century, the Frasers having succeeded the Bissets, by marriage with the heiress. The north transept was restored in 1901, as the burial place of the Mackenzies of Kintail, chiefs of the name.

This north transept is very fine, the ceiling originally having been groined vaulting in two bays. Here is an excellent recumbent effigy to Sir Kenneth Mackenzie of Kintail, ancestor of the Earls of Seaforth, in full armour, dated 1491, with Latin inscription. The transept is kept locked, as the Mackenzie vault, with a number of graves. Here is also preserved a Pictish symbol-stone, brought from Wester Balblair near Kilmorack—Beauly is in Kilmorack parish—displaying the crescent and V-rod symbols and three small fishes. In the choir, to the east, is a double piscina. Also another arched tomb for the Prior Mackenzie of the 16th century. There is a monument to The Chisholm, and his wife, who died in 1793, and on the floor a large inscribed slab depicting another knight in armour, also with Latin inscription, referring to the Fraser chief slain at the Battle of the Shirts, 1544. The choir or chancel is heavily buttressed; and its large traceried window is of the 16th century. The south transept led to the conventual buildings and was called the St. Katherine Aisle, with lancet windows of the 13th century. The nave, to the west, has another aumbry and piscina, also a holy water-stoup, and fine windows. There are three medieval cross-slabs here, one at least commemorating one of the Fraser lords.

There is a tradition that Mary Queen of Scots stayed at the Prior's house—but it is highly doubtful if she ever moved north of Inverness, in 1562. The Priory is now in the care of the Department of the Environment.

Beauly was a port at one time, before the silting up of the estuary —and even had a harbour-master until 1916. No trace of jetties or harbour-works now remain at the riverside. There was a ferry here, before the bridge. It was also a small Spa.

The present Established church, in Croyard Road to the west, is now really the Kilmorack parish church also. Not far away is the Free church; and a third church building has been converted into a gymnasium. There is also a masonic hall in this street. At the extreme north end of the town, beyond the Priory, is the Catholic church of St. Mary.

There are no particular features in the easter section beyond the bridge, this being mainly devoted to modern housing. But there is a large timber-yard at the railway-station, and other minor industry.

Boat of Garten and Kincardine. This area of Strathspey belongs very much to the Abernethy–Grantown part of Speyside, although Boat of Garten itself is only some 5 miles north-east of Aviemore, and the present Cairngorm winter-sports development inevitably spreads its influence hereabouts. But Boat of Garten was a popular holiday-place long before the skiers found it. Although the lower green hills of Pityoulish and the Glenmore range may seem to isolate this area from the Cairngorm giants, they are in fact quite close, as the crow flies. Kincardine, one of the many places of that name in Scotland, is the ancient parish, long merged with Abernethy but still having its old parish church.

The village of Boat of Garten, with a population of about 500— much increased by holiday-makers in the season, needless to say—is quite large, in a pleasant position at the western edge of the great Abernethy Forest, on the west bank of Spey. There was a ferry here, of course, as the name implies, before the long, wooden and narrow bridge was built in 1898. It is a wide-scattered place on a slight rise amongst open woodlands, L-shaped, with the oldest part, naturally, near the river at the east end, and the main development spreading westwards, at right angles, along the road to the A.9 at Kinveachy. There are good shops, a modern granite church of St. Columba, of about 1900, with one of the slated belfries which are something of a feature of this area. Also a public hall of 1896 (clearly when development first came to Boat of Garten) with billiard-room and sports-centre, and the White Mountain and Mogul Ski Schools establishments. Hotels and guest-houses, needless to say, are the main feature of the place, with the old Boat and later Craigard Hotels prominent. Facilities are available here for a wide variety of holiday pursuits—fishing, riding and pony-trekking, tennis, curling, skiing and of course golf. For Boat of Garten has long been a favoured golfing centre, with a fine 18-hole course across the Spey to the east, tuition facilities and competitions held throughout the summer. There is a caravan-park. And the Osprey Sanctuary at Loch Garten is not far away.

The school for Boat of Garten is placed more than a mile off, at the Chapelton–Glebe of Deishar area to the west, where the village road joins the A.95 from Grantown on the way to the A.9, rather remote a situation but pleasant. No doubt this district was more highly populated originally, with presumably a pre-Reformation chapel and glebe. There is a little Loch Ban in the open moorland behind the school, the northernmost of a string of such between here and Aviemore.

Loch Garten is a larger and famous stretch of water, wholly embosomed in the Abernethy pine-forest 2 miles east of the village. It is a very lovely place, with the wooded walks around it quite enticing, a great venue for picnickers and swimming parties. Here the ospreys have returned to Speyside after being driven away from their ancient haunts on Loch an Eilean 10 miles to the south, and their nesting-site in an old pine is now guarded by bird-protection enthusiasts, from the unscrupulous egg-collectors who have already raided it. There is an observation-post and hide, exceedingly popular, for watching these fine fish-hawks through powerful binoculars. Not far to the south-west is the smaller and less-known Loch Mallachie, with two islets. One wonders whether this little loch was named after the colourful Celtic saint Mallachy-O'Moore? The Abernethy Forest itself is better described under Nethybridge and Abernethy; but mention should here be made of the very interesting Tulloch area of the Glenmore foothills immediately to the south of Loch Garten, a fascinating district of green hillocks and birch-clad braes, dotted with a great many old crofts and small farms, all linked by a network of little roads and tracks, covering a large acreage. I have seldom found an area more apt for getting delightfully lost in, even in a car. On this east side of Boat of Garten the B.970 Grantown to Newtonmore road passes the road-end to the bridge and village. Southwards down this road a mile is the oddly named Street of Kincardine, no doubt once a village but now no more than two or three houses and a former mill, still with its waterwheel. Almost 2 more miles on along the east bank of Spey, a little way off the road, is Kincardine Church, standing isolated above the valley of the Milton Burn flowing down from the Slugan pass. It is a pleasant sequestered spot, the whitewashed little church seeming to speak quietly of peace. Yet it was the scene of horror in the 16th century when the Grants burned it, with its heather-thatch roof, to exterminate the Cummings, or Comyns, who had taken refuge therein after murdering the Grant chief. Whether repaired thereafter or not is unclear, but it had long been roofless when, in 1897, it was restored. Much of the woodwork is modern, but there are two old box-pews; also stained-glass windows to members of the Dunbar family. The building is said to date originally from the 12th century, and the lepers' squint is still there—to enable sufferers from that dread disease to observe Mass from outside, without risk to the congregation. There are a great many old flat stones in the graveyard, grass- and moss-grown. An interesting feature is the presence of dwarf-elder here. The story is that these lands were held by descendants of the notorious Stewart Wolf of Badenoch until 1683. The 5th Baron of Kincardine married a daughter of Cameron of Locheil, and this lady expressed the wish to be buried in her native soil of Lochaber. Rather meanly, perhaps, the soil was brought from the West, rather than the lady taken there, and she was interred amongst it. Some left over was thrown down a bank—and this contained the seeds of the dwarf-elder, not known locally. It was known as the Lady's Flower thereafter.

An old two-arched bridge carries the road over the Milton Burn near by. And across the Spey is the whitewashed Georgian tacksman's house of Kinchurdy, with its lochans behind. The road runs on southwards, and 2 miles further is the attractive area of Pityoulish, under the hill of that name, with its delightful birch-bowered loch and laird's-house. There is the site of a Pictish fort near the track up to the aforementioned Slugan pass to the east, with a burial-cairn on the other side.

Back at Boat of Garten, the road out to the north passes a huge timber-yard and sawmill on the bank of Spey, reminder of the old log-floating days when an enormous trade in this Abernethy, Rothiemurchus and Glenmore timber was floated down to Garmouth. Soon after this, the short side-road joins the A.95 main Strathspey highway, and here is the little roadside community of Drumuillie. Not far off is the farm of Lynchurn, from which a Pictish symbol-stone was removed to an unnamed museum; however, there is still a cup-and-ring-marked stone at the burnside above the farm. On the other, south, side of the road are two early features, the fort of Tom Pitlac, of the 10th century; and further east a much earlier chambered burial-cairn, near the farm of Tullochgorum, of famous name. This is a circle of comparatively small stones, with four remaining uprights, easily seen from the road. Tullochgorum itself was long the seat of the Clan Phadrick Grants. The famous reel-tune, composed by William Marshall, presumably had some reference. The farmhouse is now unremarkable—though once it boasted a brownie in the guise of a small boy. Beyond this we come into the Dulnain Bridge area.

West of Boat of Garten, where the A.95 joins the A.9 at a well-known junction, is Kinveachy. There is a roadside hamlet, amongst woodlands which contain the unseen Loch Vaa, east of the road, with the modern burial-ground of Laggantygown (no church) to the south of it, pleasing amongst trees but beside a bad bend caused by a railway-bridge. Kinveachy is mainly interesting for its mansion, and great timbered estate which clothed the Monadh Liath slopes here, much of it ruthlessly cut down during the last war. Kinveachy has long been a hunting and shooting lodge of the chiefly Grant family, and still is used personally by the Earl of Seafield. The Lodge is finely set on a high terrace, with the most splendid views over the wooded strath to the Cairngorm Mountains. The house is fairly modern Scottish Baronial, though said to have an early nucleus.

An interesting development in the Boat of Garten area is the taking over by steam-train enthusiasts here of the 5-mile stretch of disused track to Aviemore. The Strathspey Railway Company plan to run steam locomotives on this line, for their own satisfaction and as a tourist attraction. They also hope to build a railway museum.

It is very noticeable how Boat of Garten has today almost wholly superseded Kincardine—for which the Boat used only to be an access-ferry. Yet Kincardine was not only a parish but a powerful barony, once. The Gaelic poet John Roy Stuart or Stewart, was born at Knock of Kincardine in 1700.

Bona, Dochfour and Dochgarroch. This area flanks the River Ness and the Caledonian Canal to the south-west of Inverness, below the wooded range of the lowish Dunain and Dochfour Hills, at the foot of Loch Ness. It is all part of the great civil parish of Inverness and Bona, which covers also the Ness plain and hillfoots lands on the other, eastern, side of the river, separately described under Raigmore, Culcabock etc.

Bona is still the parish "centre", however inconveniently placed for the largest part of the area—for there is no bridge across the Ness save that at Inverness town. It makes one wonder what sort of long-ago bureaucrats decided to unite ancient Bona parish with that across the river—even though there used to be a ferry across Loch Dochfour at Bona. Bona church itself has rather an odd history, for the small building, a little beyond Lochend on the west side of the A.82 highway down the Great Glen, is fairly modern, and the attached residence no longer the manse; yet the church standing in the old parish burial-ground at the Kirkton, almost a mile to the north-east, on the other side of the road, is actually the Free church, although built on the site of the original parish church—a situation I have not met with before. Neither building is of especial interest; but there are one or two features in the kirkyard of the latter—and the former's position is a splendid one. An inscription on the gate-posts of the kirkyard records how one Ewan Cameron, 1865, collector of the Revenue at far-away Liverpool, bequeathed a sum of money for the repair of the little church and the enclosure of the burial-ground—surely an unusual activity for a tax-gatherer; and an old stone in the kirkyard wall commemorates a youthful colonel, aged 25, James Baillie Younger of Dochfour, who died in 1796 on his way to the West Indies, with a complacent-looking effigy with folded arms and sword-belt. There is a watch-house to guard against body-snatchers, and a number of old tablestones. A group of council houses is near by, at Lochend, beside a curious detached lagoon of Loch Dochfour, called Abbar Water. The ferry aforementioned used to ply across the loch's link with the great Loch Ness here, with Bona Lighthouse to mark the entry and exit.

Dochfour itself is a large wooded estate on the slopes of the quite steep Dochfour Hill, above the road and loch the mansion, on a pleasant terrace site, easily seen from the A.82. It is a large, yellow-washed, somewhat rambling building in the Venetian style, cluster-ing around a late 18th century core, which Prince Albert, when he visited here in 1847 described as "new and very elegant". The Baillie family have been long settled here, and the present 3rd Lord Burton is the 15th Baillie of Dochfour. The first of the line, Alex-ander Baillie, Constable of Inverness Castle, was a cousin of the then Earl of Huntly, who granted him these Gordon lands as a reward for services rendered in Huntly's defeat of the Earl of Crawford at Brechin in 1452. Below the policies, the main road crosses the loch in rather unusual fashion, not by a bridge but on a sort of causeway.

The similarly sited, and named, Dochgarroch House lies nearly 2 miles nearer Inverness on another wooded terrace, a smaller edition of Dochfour. It has a hamlet prettily placed below the road, at the canal-side, where is the Dochfour estate-office, and nearby Dochfour caravan-park. There is a confusion of names here, for though all part of the extensive Dochfour district, Dochgarroch is an entity of its own. The Dochgarroch Lock of the Caledonian Canal is a regulating device for preventing winter floods on Loch Ness from affecting the canal navigation. There is a yacht anchorage, a village hall and a scattering of houses, all rather attractive.

The site of a Roman station near Bona Ferry, oblong with rounded corners and ditches, has been suggested as the Banatia Urbs of Ptolemy. Here too was a later medieval strength known as Castle Spiritual, its remains swept away when the canal was built. Clearly this crossing-place has always been strategically important.

Carrbridge and Duthil. Where the main A.9 highway crosses the Dulnain River 7 miles above its junction with Spey, is the well-known holiday-resort of Carrbridge, lying in the old civil parish of Duthil, 7 miles north of Aviemore. Duthil parish has long been united with that of Rothiemurchus, and together they comprise an enormous tract of land reaching deep into both the Cairngorm and Monadh Liath Mountains, over 200 square miles. Most of this area is dealt with in various other articles, and we are here concerned only with the territory approximately within 4 or 5 miles radius of Carrbridge. The Kirkton of Duthil itself is a tiny place. The word is derived from *Tuathil*, meaning the northern section, as distinct from *Deishal*, the southern, which name is still perpetuated by Glebe of Deishar, near Boat of Garten. In those days the entire parish was called Glencarnie, Glencherny or *Glen a cheathernich*, the Heroes' Glen. We read of Sir Gilbert Comyn of Glencherny in 1280. The Comyn lords' ancient seat was at Drumuillie, near Boat of Garten.

Carrbridge has long been a favourite village for holiday-makers, not large but well equipped with facilities to attract and cater for visitors; and the recent winter-sports boom has, naturally, much widened its scope. It takes its name from the picturesque 18th century high and narrow single-arch bridge over the rocky Dulnain, just at the west side of the present main-road bridge. Like so many another Speyside resort, Carrbridge would be a much more pleasant place if it could be by-passed by the heavy traffic of the busy A.9. Fortunately there is much of the village well back from the road, on either side. Today the prime attraction is undoubtedly the large, imaginative and exciting Landmark, Europe's first Visitor Centre and Environmental Exhibition, winner of the British Tourist Authority's main award for outstanding development, 1970. This most admirable and comprehensive establishment was set up by Mr. David Hayes, in the pine-woods to the left of the road, and includes a notable exhibition-cum-museum; an ambitious, circular multiscreen auditorium and cinema, with continuous performance, on the history and development of Scotland over 3000 years; a bookshop; craftshop; restaurant; woodland garden, and even nature-trail amongst the pines. The buildings are attractive, in timber and glass, there is a large car-park, and everything is done with taste and a sure hand. This is one of the most exhilarating ventures to be seen in Scotland, and is deservedly popular, fulfilling a real educational need as well as providing excellent entertainment. It cost £165,000 to start with, and is continually being improved. In spite of a recent serious fire, the Centre is still functioning.

Carrbridge has, of course, many hotels, guest-houses and bed-and-breakfast places. Also ski-schools—for this was a pioneer in the winter-sports development. There is a large, modern craft-and-woollens shop, with its own car-park. The established church stands above the road on a grassy eminence, an unusual building, of low line, fairly modern, with hall adjoining. This is really the parish church now, for that at Duthil has recently been closed. There is also a Free church. A 9-hole golf course lies to the north, where the A.938 strikes off eastwards for Grantown. The main development of the village stretches along a side-road, also eastwards, on the south side of Dulnain, rather pleasant. At the other, west side, a less obvious road follows the riverside through woodland, with scattered houses, to the still-used railway-station, half-a-mile, where there is a huge timber-yard and sawmill—for this district is very much in the heavily wooded Strathspey country, with Scots pine prevalent. Hidden in the pines near by is a pleasingly placed modern cemetery and the village war-memorial, with woodland walks around. This

Ellan area has a footbridge across the Dulnain to Dalrachney on the north side.

The side-road does not stop at the station, but proceeds up the south side of Dulnain for some miles into the Monadh Liaths, a little-known but delightful route through open woodlands of natural forest and green foothills. At Sluggan, about 2 miles up—and not very readily found amongst the trees—is a very handsome and lofty packhorse bridge over Dulnain, now disused, larger than that at Carrbridge, indeed 75 feet high, single-arch without parapets, replacing the Wade bridge built a few years before and carried away in a flood. A mile further up, a modern bridge leads over to Inverlaidnan. This is an interesting place, a whitewashed tacksman's house, still occupied, with in the haugh below the substantial ruins of a large defensive house of 1736, although probably with earlier nucleus, provided with a shot-hole and traces of surrounding courtyard-walling, its unusually wide gable crowstepped. It was the Baron Bailie's house of the western portions of the great Grant estates. Prince Charles Edward called here in February 1746, and got a cold reception, the laird absenting himself and his wife refusing food and drink. Instead, word was sent to the Earl of Loudoun, government commander, that if he hurried he might capture the Prince. The small Jacobite victory of the Rout of Moy, some miles to the north, was the result. Still further, over a mile, at Dalnahatnich, the road now peters out. A branch used to cross the river and proceed northwards, across the low hills, to the Slochd area on the A.9, now impassable for vehicles. There is a monument across the river to a famous piper, one Ian Beg MacAndrew, hero of a famous clan-fight.

Directly north of Carrbridge, a short side-road leads along the north bank of Dulnain, serving the Dalrachney area, but only for a mile before becoming private. Above it the main A.9 continues northwards through fine forest country with magnificent backward views of the Cairngorm range, and then across wide moorland. After 4 miles, it reaches the quite dramatic pass of The Slochd, or throat, through which both road and railway must climb. This is one of the places where it is claimed the last wolf was killed; and certainly this area used to be infested with the animals, and as late as the 1842 Statistical Account there is reference to the number of wolf-traps still to be seen, with stories of ravages. The Slochd is also renowned for the wild-goats sometimes seen here—although more are to be observed up Strathdearn to the north. Just before the start of the pass, a side-road leads westwards along the flank of quite a deep valley of the Allt an Aonaich burn, beginning beside a former little school. It goes pleasantly, to end at a gate, where there is a small early single-arch bridge over the burn—for here is the line of the old military road, which took a different route to the Slochd Pass from the present highway, from the Kinveachy area well south of Carrbridge. The bridge in fact dates from 1729, and has no parapet. A network of tracks fan out into the hills from here, and the continuation of the military road follows the northern flank of this valley back to the Slochd. The pass itself is bare and narrow, with steep sides, the road rising to 1332 feet, and the railway 17 feet less. Thereafter the A.9 passes into Moy and Dalarossie parish.

East of Carrbridge the A.938, flanking Dulnain to the north, reaches Duthil after 2 miles, passing the isolated but still functioning school on the way. Just beyond this is another hump-backed bridge of 1800, over the Duthil Burn. A little further, the B.9007 strikes off directly northwards on its lonely way to Forres, 23 miles. This is rather an extraordinary road by any standards, climbing through and over the hills, well-surfaced and with good gradients, but rising from 866 to 1229 feet in a few miles, and seeming endlessly to bestride the heather moors, with never a house to be seen for most of the way. It crosses the county boundary into Moray in 4 miles, and in another 4 enters Nairnshire, coming eventually down out of the emptiness to settled lands again at Glenferness, 13 miles. In winter it must frequently be closed by snow.

Duthil itself is half a mile east of this road-end, and something of an anticlimax as the name-provider for a huge parish. There is only the newly closed parish church, the large former manse, and two or three cottages. The church itself, high, harled, plain, with a small belfry, dates only from 1826, its interior remodelled in 1938. The most interesting features are the twin mausoleums of the Grant of Seafield family, built by Playfair in 1837, almost identical but one within the kirkyard wall and one without, in odd fashion—the former inscribed, the other not. Is there a story here? The chiefly Grants were buried in this parish from 1585 onwards. The last of the Comyn, or Cumming, lords of Glencherny, Gilbert or Gibbon, had only an heiress daughter Maud, who married Sir John Grant in 1364, since when the Grants have reigned. The kirkyard is somewhat neglected, with many old table-stones. Fairs, strangely enough, used to be held in this graveyard.

Beyond Duthil the A.938 runs into the Tullochgribbon area, passing the reedy Loch Mor amongst heather moors with much forestry plantation, and a large commercial sand-pit near by. Dulnain Bridge, described separately, is then reached.

South of Carrbridge, the A.9 runs through mainly woodland country to Kinveachy in the Boat of Garten district, dealt with thereunder, where the other main Strathspey road, A.95, heads off for Grantown, 10 miles.

Culloden, Balloch and Clava. Culloden has for long been a famous and ominous name in Scotland, and far beyond it, synonym for a lost cause and for shameful succeeding barbarity, where the monarchial hopes of the House of Stewart received their death-blow in 1746. While this fame, surely, will never fade, it may be that Culloden will before long come to take on a totally new significance as well. For hereabouts, and to be called by that name, is planned to be erected a complete new town of 20,000 inhabitants, with all accompanying facilities and industries—even the provision of the long-desired Highland University of Inverness is envisaged for here. And although all this is as yet at the drawing-board stage largely, nevertheless beginnings have already been made to implement the plan on the ground. Culloden, topographically, is today a large and recognisable area, commencing some 3 miles east of Inverness, including part of the pleasant lower Strathnairn, partly in Nairnshire, and including portions of the parishes of Croy and Dalcross, Petty, Daviot and Inverness itself, which it is convenient to treat here as a distinctive district. Strangely it has never been a parish on its own, although always very much an entity. There is no village of the name, but a well-known and ancient estate of Culloden, a moor, a modern planted forest, a former railway-station, and of course the battlefield area with its buildings and memorials. Included in the district are the large village of Balloch, today growing fast into the kernel of the new town, and already a commuters' suburb for Inverness; and the modern saw-milling hamlet of Smithtown. Clava is the extraordinary Nairnside district, just south of the battlefield, where are some of the finest prehistoric remains in the land.

To deal with the renowned battlefield area first, this is no place to enter into any description of that grim and highly significant engagement. But it is perhaps worth considering an aspect of it all which is seldom mentioned or even fully understood at the present time. Today, all Scotland, Scots everywhere, tend to look on Culloden as a national disaster; the sympathies of almost all Scots, and a great many others, are wholly with, and aligned to, Prince Charles Edward's Jacobite army there. Indeed many, even writers on the subject, talk about the Scottish and English armies at Culloden. It would be a brave Scot, of any persuasion, who publicly raised three cheers for the *victory* of Culloden. Yet that is exactly what the majority of Scots said and did after the battle of 1746. And, of course there were as many Scots fighting in Cumberland's army as in the Prince's; more, probably. Why this change in outlook and historical perspective has come about is difficult to perceive— although probably it is largely on account of the barbarities perpetrated by the victorious Duke of Cumberland and his troops thereafter, which gradually have percolated through to the Scots population, and from which all wish to be disassociated. That, and the decay of religious dogmatism. The fact remains that most Scots at the time hailed Cumberland as their saviour, and hastened to do him honour. The towns and cities competed with each other to offer him their freedoms, silver caskets, loyal addresses of thanks and so on. Banquets and bonfires celebrated his success; odes, poems and songs were composed in his honour. It must not be forgotten that it was largely a matter of religion. From James the Seventh and Second's time, save for Queen Anne, the Stewarts had remained staunchly Catholic; and this was what prevented Scotland from rising in favour of their ancient royal house against the unpopular but Protestant Germanic newcomers. Presbyterian Scotland saw

Culloden as the removal of the dreaded threat of the reimposition of Catholicism—and rejoiced. It was the largely Catholic Highland clans which supported the Prince—although there were many Protestant loyalists too, of course. But the romantic nostalgia was to come later—with a conscience for the savageries of Butcher Cumberland, which was far from evident at the time. Culloden is a place of almost universal pilgrimage today, and rightly so, but it should make the Scots very thoughtful indeed.

The battlefield lies on that long and broad ridge, of Drummossie Muir as it then was called, which swells between the valley of Strathnairn and the coastal plain, near the 500-foot contour, now largely planted forest, but in 1746 a bleak waste of heather and bog. Most battlefields are somewhat hard to trace satisfactorily today; not so Culloden. It has not been built up, or greatly altered, save for the trees which do change the aspect somewhat. It was in 1881 that the then proprietor and others really began to cherish the site; and the National Trust for Scotland is to be congratulated in having taken over from them so excellently. Their large modern Information Centre and Museum, the preservation of the Leanach Cottage and other significant features, is praiseworthy. This is at a hub of side-roads, where the B.851 and B.9006 meet and are crossed by a lesser road. Here is the Cumberland Stone, a huge boulder-outcrop from which the Duke is supposed to have superintended the battle. Near the Information Centre is the preserved and restored Leanach Cottage, a typical low-browed little heather-thatched farmhouse of the period. In its adjoining barn, now only foundations, took place that disgraceful incident, typical of so much else of the terrible aftermath. Two days after the battle, Cumberland sent out parties of his troops from Inverness to scour the neighbourhood and round up any possible wounded survivors. Thirty Highland officers and men, who in the interim had dragged themselves to the shelter of this barn, were discovered, locked in and the heather-thatch set alight over them. All burned to death. Even this was perhaps less unmerciful than some of the Butcher's reprisals, especially on women and children, much of which he personally ordered and superintended. And yet he was declared to be a personable young man, favoured son of the King, only 25 years old—a year older than his cousin Charles—and himself courageous.

The government army advanced from the east, in no certain mood, recollecting the defeats of Falkirk and Prestonpans; and the Prince's reduced force lay to the west, where is the woodland today. Tired after an abortive night sally to attack Nairn, the Jacobites should undoubtedly have retired across the Nairn on their right and there awaited the arrival of the substantial reinforcements shortly expected—for a large proportion of their army had retired north by the inland route and were still in Badenoch. There was however much bickering and disagreement amongst the Prince's officers, and the fatal decision was made to attack, even though the enemy was known to have double their former numbers of 5000. The result is too well known to recount here. The graves of the clansmen, dotted on either side of the B.9006 road, and marked by stones with the clan names, or by cairns, make an affecting sight in that now peaceful woodland. Here is the Well of the Dead, where the heroic Mac-Gillivray of Dunmaglass, chief of his branch of Clan Chattan and colonel of that regiment, fell with his lieutenant-colonel and major. He is buried in Petty kirkyard, along with others who died that day. Some 1200 men are thought to have fallen in the actual battle, on the Prince's side, apart from the great numbers slain afterwards. A great cairn, 20 feet high, has been erected to commemorate the generality of casualties not covered by the clan stones.

The Information Centre here was opened in 1970. Over 100,000 people visit this place each year.

A great many visitors to Culloden take the opportunity also to inspect the famous Stones of Clava while they are in the vicinity. These extraordinary relics, of the dead of a vastly earlier period, lie only a mile to the south-east, but on the other side of the River Nairn, reached by the road which strikes southwards at the Cumberland Stone and crosses the river at Clava Lodge—a former Forbes mansion now a hotel, near the spectacular Nairn railway viaduct. What are called the Clava Stones are a series of late Stone Age and early Bronze Age chambered cairns or ring cairns, each surrounded by tall standing-stones. These are all close together in open woodland just to the north of the road—save for one or two of the standing-stones on the south—and consist of inner circles of close-set smaller uprights packed in with great heaps of small stones to form mounds with hollow domed central chambers reached by narrow passages. These are all in a much more complete state than usual, and are linked by cobblestone causeways. They date from 1800 to 1500 B.C., and are burial cairns with some special religious significance, a highly interesting feature, now in the care of the Department of the Environment. This Nairn valley area is rich in prehistoric remains, with further ring-cairns at Balnuaran and Culdoich not far to the south-west, and at Cantraybruich, Cantraydoune and Dalgrambich, in Croy and Dalcross parish to the north-east. But the Clava group is outstanding.

A mile east of the Cumberland Stone crossroads, on the B.9006, is the community of Culloden Moor Station, the railway-station itself out-of-use but some small industry established there. Some crofts and also modern housing, with a Caravan Club park, are near by.

To the north of the battlefield area, a mile through woodland, on the north-facing slope above the coastal plain, with magnificent views, is the rapidly developing village of Balloch—pronounced with the accent on the loch. It is rather absurd to call it a village now, for it has sprouted rows and rows of modern housing, in the Cullernie area, almost all private development, just 4 miles from the centre of Inverness. If the houses themselves are not always a delight, the prospects certainly are, especially northwards and westwards to Ross and the Highland mountains. The old part of the village, with one or two shops and the usual facilities—but no church as yet—lies on the lower ground. Here may be inspected a board with the planned Culloden new town development—and very ambitious it is. Industrial zoning, new trunk roads, shopping centre, a new secondary school, as well as a conservation and recreation area, are marked out, plus the site for the hoped-for university in the Culloden estate policies. The township will spread over the low ground eastwards and northwards, towards the Airport and Dalcross Industrial Estate; and its projected 20,000 people may not be an over-estimate, with North Sea Oil development coming into the picture. Inverness itself has just under 30,000 population, so this development will require a careful control if the essential balance and character of the area is not seriously to be altered. But it is an exciting proposition.

The Culloden House estate, so important to the project, lies to the west, the mansion itself a mile south-west of Balloch. It is a splendid house of the Georgian period, very large, with a massive central block flanked by pavilions, standing in timbered parkland. It is in the main of date 1772–83, but is built on the vaulted foundations of an earlier castellated mansion, destroyed by fire. It was the seat of a long succession of Forbes lairds, from Duncan Forbes, M.P. and Provost of Inverness, who bought the property from the Mackintoshes in 1626. His great-grandson was the famous Lord President Forbes (1685–1747) inevitably greatly involved in the Jacobite upsets, but a man respected by all. The Forbeses retained Culloden until 1897. The house was, fairly recently, used as the headquarters of the Highland Development Board. It is at present planned to be a luxury hotel. Near by, to the south-west, is an unusual chapel, of 1799, looking more like a barn save for its pointed windows, but still in use. An 18th century doocot stands close at hand, with conical slated roof and dormer entrances for the birds, now somewhat dilapidated. In the driveway in front of the mansion, stands a simple monolith, not ancient, but marking the site of the former baronial hanging-tree.

A mile further south-west, still in the estate, is the saw-milling community of Smithtown of Culloden, now quite large, with considerable modern housing, amongst woodland. And south of this another mile, in the Culloden Forest area, is the pre-Reformation St. Mary's Well.

To the north of the Culloden area, between the ridge and the sea, is the Allanfearn district, another place which gained prominence by means of a now abandoned railway-station, just east of the Petty parish boundary. At the side of the A.96, opposite Lower Cullernie farm, is another ring-cairn, now only fragmentary. The site of the former Tobar na Clerich, or Minister's Well, on Lower Cullernie, is still visible. This used to be a more important place, seat of Mackintosh of Kyllachy, who in the 16th century slew the Baron of Brackley. To the other, western side of Allanfearn is Stonifield House, a small Georgian mansion of 1820, with a pilastered doorway. And down near the shore is the old Seafield toll-house of 1845, squat, with an Italianate tower. We are here on the edge of Inverness itself.

Dalcross and Cantray. Dalcross is part of the conjoint parish of Croy and Dalcross, united in the 15th century; and partly in Nairnshire, under which the Croy section is described. The Dalcross part is more conveniently dealt with under Inverness-shire, excluding the important Culloden area which deserves an article to itself. This item therefore deals with that part of the conjoint and very irregularly shaped parish west of the Nairn county boundary and north of Culloden and Clava.

Dalcross itself is a district, nowadays, which has rather spread its name around untidily, so that Inverness Airport is called Dalcross, although it is not in the parish but in Petty to the north—presumably because of the former Dalcross railway-station on the Inverness–Aberdeen line, which is itself outwith the parish. As also is the Dalcross Industrial Estate, on the north-western edge of the airfield, again in Petty, two miles from Dalcross proper. All a little confusing.

There is no village or even hamlet of Dalcross, and the site of its original parish church is lost. But there is still the fine Castle of Dalcross. This handsome 17th century fortalice, although formerly ruinous, is now fully restored and occupied. It stands in a commanding situation with splendid views, on the long Dalcross–Feabuie–Culloden ridge which rises between Strathnairn and the coastal plain of the Moray Firth, about 7 miles east of Inverness and 8 miles west of Nairn. It was built in 1620 by the 8th Lord Lovat, but passed to the chief of Mackintosh about the end of that century, with whose descendants it remains. It is a tall and commodious house of five storeys, on a variation of the L-plan, whereby the two wings join each other so as to give two re-entrant angles. A square stair-tower rises in the eastern re-entrant, finishing in a gabled watch-chamber with a circular angle-turret. Three others of the crow-stepped gables are crowned by angle-turrets. Many of the windows still retain their iron grilles or yetts; and the warm red sandstone walling is pierced by numerous gunloops and shot-holes. Heraldic panels over the door and near by display the arms of Mackintosh, dated 1720, and those of Fraser dated 1620. The door is provided with a draw-bar and slot. The basement is vaulted, and unusual is the vaulted passage running round the base of the turnpike stairway. A lower 18th century wing extends to the north, and there is a courtyard with a draw-well. At Dalcross the government troops marshalled prior to the Battle of Culloden. And here the dead 19th chief of Mackintosh lay in state from 9th December 1703 to 18th January 1704, whereafter no fewer than 2000 of his clansmen escorted the body to burial in Petty kirkyard.

On the adjoining farm of Dalcross Mains, crowning an eminence in a field to the north-east, is a cairn-circle, with a complete inner circle of close-set uprights. Almost a mile to the east, at a crossroads, is the small Free church of 1852, in an isolated position.

To the south of Dalcross, on the south-facing braes of Strathnairn, is the Cantray district. This covers quite a wide area of the strath, from Easter Brae of Cantray, a mile west of Croy village, to Cantray-bruich farm, over 2 miles to the south-west, near Culloden Station, with the Cantraydoune and Galcantray farms on the far, north-facing side of the strath, in Nairnshire. Cantray House is a pleasant whitewashed modern mansion, successor of two which were both burned down. It was an early Chisholm property, passing by marriage to the Roses of nearby Kilravock, and thence to the Dallas family. Later it was held by the Davidsons. There is a small hamlet near by amongst fields of raspberry-canes, in pleasing country with wide vistas. A number of crofts still scatter the Wester Brae of Cantray area; and a single standing-stone rises in a field below Dalgrambich farm, near the river-bank, of conglomerate, 6 feet high but oddly dog-legged in shape, probably all that remains of a stone-circle. Across the river at Cantraydoune is a prominent green mound, obviously artificial and presumably the site of a former fortified strength. A burial-cairn at Cantraybruich is now so neglected as to be little more than a site. The rather remarkable Nairn railway-viaduct is very evident hereabouts, the largest such in Scotland, and partly curved, a notable engineering feat of 28 arches of 50-foot span and one of 100 feet, built in 1898.

Cantray Mill lies at the other end of the area, 2 miles to the north-east, at the Nairn-side. The 18th century mill is now abandoned, although the buildings remain. It is interesting in having had two mill-wheels side by side, only one of which survives. There was a grain-drying kiln to the south. Crossing a quiet stretch of the river here is Cantray Bridge, of 1764, replacing one of 1641, a panel from which is built into the present structure, hard to distinguish below the west parapet. The bridge has two arches, cut-waters and is harled.

The famous Clava stone-circles are in this parish; but being so close to Culloden, and usually visited along with the battlefield area, are better described thereunder.

Dalwhinnie and Drumochter. Dalwhinnie is the first community the traveller from the south reaches after the long ascent from Atholl and the bleak constrictions of the Pass of Drumochter, mile upon mile of bare and empty heather and rock, with at last the lower and lovelier lands of Badenoch and Strathspey beginning to beckon ahead. Something of the barren grimness still persists at Dalwhinnie admittedly, on the 1000-foot contour, at the head of lengthy Loch Ericht; but there is an opening of prospects, a tree or two, and promise ahead. It is a scattered, strung-out place, with little of the atmosphere of a village, from the large Loch Ericht Hotel, renowned for fishing, and once a government inn, at the south end, to the equally large and well-known Buchanan's distillery at the north, a mile apart. In between these there is the station—Dalwhinnie grew up as a railway-station community—a school, a

Falls of Divach, Drumnadrochit

Culloden House

Inverness: Huntly Street

small modern church, another hotel and some catering establishments, and housing dotted here and there. Dalwhinnie is in a corner of the vast civil parish of Kingussie and Insh; but much of its surroundings are in Laggan parish. Any attempt to differentiate would be pointless. The unfortunate General Cope encamped his force here for one night in 1745. And Queen Victoria and her husband stayed *incognito* at the hotel in 1861 "supping off two miserable starveling Highland chickens, with only tea and without any potatoes, and in the morning receiving a visit from Cluny Macpherson".

Southwards, beyond the Loch Ericht Hotel, there are glimpses of the loch. Loch Ericht is one of those huge but lonely and inaccessible sheets of water—although its name means the Loch of Meetings—with only a private road running half-way down one side and nothing else, but 20 miles long in a steep-sided and not particularly attractive valley. The loch however provides free fishing for the large Ferox trout, with boats for hire. The great Ben Alder (3757 feet) rises on the west, its remoteness making it a secure haven in 1746 for Cluny Macpherson, whose "Cage" up on its slope was famous—a hidden shelter made out of entwined branches, amongst scrub woodland, not a cave as is often stated—where Prince Charles Edward joined him for six days of hiding after Culloden. All these empty mountains now form Benalder deer-forest with its Lodge at the end of the private road. Beyond is only trackless heather, bog and hillside for 25 miles. The planted Loch Ericht Forest now clothes the lower slopes for some 5 miles on the west side. Traditionally there is said to be a flooded village below the waters of the loch.

South of the hotel, on the A.9, stands the Dalwhinnie war-memorial cairn, in an isolated position. And a mile further is a graceful but abandoned double-arch Wade bridge, near the modern roadside. It is so marked on the Ordnance map, but of course the General himself did not design all these military road-bridges, many engineer officers contributing over quite a long period.

It is 5 miles on, southwards, to the famous Pass of Drumochter, the highest point reached by the railroad in Britain (1484 feet). Wade built the original road through the pass—the earlier drove-roads had found their way through the hills considerably more to the east, by Loch an-t-Seilich—but Telford redesigned and re-routed it somewhat in 1829; traces of Wade's road may still be seen here and there. The Perthshire boundary crosses the summit—the pass is some 3 miles long—with the great lumpish hills of the Boar of Badenoch and the Sow of Atholl frowning over all from the west. There are a few houses at Dalnaspidal Station, slightly to the south, for railway personnel—for maintaining the line here is a major preoccupation in winter. The A.9 itself has been greatly improved here in recent years, and now provides no hazard for motorists, as once it did, save in blizzard conditions. The burns rising near by form the River Truim, and approximately where they unite is the shooting-lodge of

Drumochter, east of the road, its clump of trees a welcome break in
the heathery monotony. On the other side of the valley, the summit
of a lofty ridge is crowned by a group of standing-stones.

Just north of Dalwhinnie the A.9 sends off a fork north-westwards
to Laggan and the A.86 cross-Scotland road (the A.889) 7 miles to
Laggan Bridge, rising to 1241 feet on the way, very much a moorland road almost devoid of features but with fine views. On the
north side it descends through more interesting country scenically to
Catt Lodge and the upper Spey valley. The lonely Loch Caoldair
lies under the crags of a great corrie a mile to the west, midway.

East of Dalwhinnie for endless miles are only the vast empty tracts
of Gaick deer-forest, reached from Glen Tromie; and then the
equally large Glen Feshie Forest reaching to the Aberdeenshire
border some twenty more wild and roadless miles away. It is in
places like Dalwhinnie that talk of this overcrowded island tend to
ring hollow.

Daviot. The parishes of Daviot and Dunlichity were united in
1618; but this by no means makes them into a recognisable entity,
and an oddly shaped and proportioned parish they make, 22 miles
long but in some places as little as half a mile wide, flanking the
River Nairn from 7 miles south of Inverness, south-westwards into
the Monadh Liath Mountains. It is convenient therefore to deal
with them separately, especially as each retains its parish church, 6
miles apart, and has totally different features and character, one
almost Lowland, the other wholly Highland.

Daviot is much the better-known, and much the smaller component, lying athwart the main A.9 highway at a great hairpin bend
and a long brae thereon, its prominent little church a noted landmark. Once the Daviot district is passed, the hills are left behind,
and there is only a 6-mile-long slant down northwards to Inverness
and the coastal plain. There is the kirkton hamlet at the roadside;
and for our purposes it will be best to describe here that area and the
parish north and east of the main road, leaving all south and west to
Dunlichity and Strathnairn.

The eye-catching kirk on the green hillside makes the obvious
starting-point, small but dominant, whitewashed, with a high square
bell-tower with weather-vane, dating from 1826. There is a fragment of the original church, with inset stones, in the graveyard
amongst many old tombs. Here is the burial-place of the old chiefly
Mackintosh family, this area being long dominated by that clan.
Very unusual is the presence of a cup-marked stone at the side-door
of the kirk. There is an early 19th century watch-house. The old
manse near by has a gablet, and dates from 1763. There are some
ten houses and a little school in the kirkton area; but other houses
are scattered over the wide valley sides. At the foot of the hill, near
where the road bridges the Nairn at the apex of the hairpin bend,
the war-memorial cairn stands at the start of the section of the B.851
which runs up Strathnairn to Dunlichity.

Just west of Daviot Kirkton rises the small hill of Dun Daviot (947 feet) crowned by traces of a fort and signal-station, 120 by 90 feet, one of a chain guarding the low lands from Cawdor to Loch Ness. Unfortunately a large quarry is engaged in eating out the side of the hill. An extensive section of the Culloden Forest of planted conifers lies to the north and west, the northern portion called Daviot Wood, the A.9 piercing this.

Two side-roads strike off north-eastwards from the main road hereabouts, the eastern section of the B.851 on the north side of the Nairn; and a lesser but longer road on the south side leading eventually to Cawdor, 11 miles away. The latter, starting at Craggie a mile south of the kirkton, after crossing the sylvan den of the Craggie Burn, runs through pleasant but more or less featureless country and out of the parish in just over a mile. The former Daviot station, on the main railway-line, was in this Craggie area, now gone. There is more of interest on the northern B.851 road. Half a mile along this, pleasingly situated in a wooded estate, on a terrace above the steep descent to the river, is Daviot House, a large Georgian mansion, built in 1821 by Alexander 24th chief of Mackintosh. And just north of the mansion, on the lip of the bank, are the now scanty remains of Daviot Castle, some grass-grown mounds with the more substantial ruins of a circular flanking-tower, still retaining its garderobe and chute, the last of four such surrounding a powerful courtyard castle in a strong position. It was allegedly built by David, 3rd Earl of Crawford, in the early 15th century. He was father of the notorious Tiger Earl, Beardie, and was slain while trying to prevent the Battle of Arbroath. The remains of the flanking-tower, however, look at least a century later than that. No doubt the mansion is largely built from its stones.

Half a mile further east, in a field south of the road, is a large ring-cairn, consisting of an inner ring 45 feet across, of smallish stones with one large, and only two stones left upright of the outer circle, one 9 feet high. There are numerous other stone-circles in the Dunlichity section of the parish. The wooded estate of the modern Nairnside House lies beyond.

The hillier portion of Daviot lies to the south, but there are few items of interest here. Just before the parish boundary with Moy is reached, the former shooting-lodge of Meallmore, at the A.9 roadside, is now converted into a large hotel. Meall Mor hill itself near by reaches only 1611 feet.

Dores and Drumashie. The village, parish and district of Dores lies at the foot of Loch Ness, on the south side, immediately beyond Inverness parish, its northern boundary only 4 miles from Inverness centre. Strath Dores, as it is called, is hardly a true strath, flanking the south side of the River Ness, Loch Dochfour and the larger loch for about 4 miles; and at the south end of this is Dores village. The parish is irregularly shaped, very long and narrow, and the southern end of it is more conveniently described under Stratherrick, Foyers and Boleskine. The top section, where it widens considerably, is dealt with here, an area of some 5 miles by $3\frac{1}{2}$, the higher eastern portion around Loch Ashie being known as the Moor of Drumashie, a fairly featureless expanse—not to be confused with the larger Drummossie Moor to the east, famed as the site of the Battle of Culloden.

Dores village is pleasingly set at Loch Ness-side, just where it suddenly widens by almost a mile, at Tor Point, 2 miles from its foot, to form a considerable bay. On the A.862 this is the first glimpse of the loch. At Dores that road turns away southwards to climb over Drumashie Moor to Errogie, while the B.852 continues on for many miles along Ness-side. The fair-sized village, by Highland standards, has some old cottages and a venerable-looking lochside inn; also considerable modern housing. The parish church stands a little way north of the rest, at a mill, and is not particularly beautiful, dating from 1828, with high, narrow, pointed windows and a small belfry with pinnacle. There is a low-set watch-house with eaves-course, having two small chambers with fireplaces. The kirkyard is entered by a rather ambitious memorial arch commemorating the First World War dead, recast and not entirely successful. There are many old tombstones, mostly undecipherable. Close by, to the north, is the former mill, its buildings ruinous but interesting, including a kiln for drying the grain. The grind-stones are still in position; and the mill cottage occupied and picturesque. On the high ground just behind is Old Clune House, a rather attractive tacksman's house of the Fraser-Tytler family, grown from a small nucleus.

A mile north-eastwards along the A.862 is Dores school, far from the village. Half a mile further, a small side-road strikes off eastwards past another tacksman's house, Darris, now a farm. The little road forks beyond this, and the right-hand branch climbs through birch woodland, past the site of the former Free church—now demolished and its manse a private house—to an interesting feature, the MacBain Memorial Park. This is simply a little walled enclosure of the birch-and-heather hillside, planted with shrubs, and having a good wrought-iron gateway, paths and some seats. It has a disarming notice: "No burial ground, no bodies around, just fond recollections and ancestor connections." It was established in 1961 by Hughston MacBain of MacBain, 21st chief of this branch of the Clan Chattan federation, who lives in America, in memory of his ancestors who held Kinchyle near by from before 1568, as a plaque at the crown of the knoll states. Actually the MacBains lost the lands through an action for debt while Donald MacBain was away fighting the French in Canada in 1760. There are two lifelike bronze wild-cats guarding the plaque, indicative of the prevailing cat symbol of all the Clan Chattan tribes. And the bronze coat-of-arms shows a demi-cat holding a targe or shield, with the motto "Touch not the Cat bot a Targe"—an interesting variation on the usual ". . . bot a Glove". This is a pleasant place. The property of Kinchyle itself lies over a mile northwards, on the other branch of the aforementioned fork, past Antfield. It is a picturesque and secluded whitewashed tacksman's house with good 18th century features, underground cellars and former walled garden, now a farmhouse. On this Kinchyle property half a mile north-west, where the side-road joins the A.862, is a chambered cairn and stone-circle, a little difficult to distinguish amongst all the whin-bushes but close to both roads, consisting of 6 megaliths still upright, ringing a tight inner circle of stones.

At the other side of the A.862—which here follows the line of Wade's military road—is the large estate of Aldourie, formerly another Fraser-Tytler property. Aldourie Castle though now Victorian Scots Baronial, incorporates 18th century work with a possibly earlier core. It was the birthplace of Sir James Mackintosh of Kyllachy (1765-1832), the eminent author, historian and statesman, who wrote vindicating the French Revolution. In one month, May 1820 he introduced six bills in the House of Commons. Further north, between main road and River Ness, is the historic property of Borlum, now a large farm, once the lairdship of the famous Brigadier Mackintosh, Jacobite leader. It is a pleasing tall and whitewashed tacksman's house, the older 18th century part to the rear. There is a suggestion that an older castle stood on an unidentified site near by. Beyond Borlum is the property of Scaniport, where is now a caravan-park, and the Speyroc Scaniport Works. Here is the northern edge of the parish.

Eastwards from Dores village the parish swells notably on to the 600-foot higher ground of Drumashie Moor, very different land from the wooded Ness-side, bare and open. Here are many lochs, three large—Loch Ashie itself, Loch Duntelchaig and Loch Ruthven, the last two half in Dunlichity parish. These are now part of Inverness's water supply. Ashie is fairly bare and featureless, 2 miles long by half a mile wide, surrounded by levelish moorland, with some new forestry planting at its south end. Near by, but very hard to find in long-cut-down woodland is a cluster of three ancient burial-cairns, one said to have been surrounded by concentric circles of 80 feet diameter with cupmarked stones. Half a mile south-east of this is the site of Dun Richnan, the Castle of the King of the Ocean allegedly, where the semi-legendary Fingal is said to have won a great victory over Ashi, son of a Norse king. Much more evident is another dun 2 miles to the south-west, near the junction of A.862 and the Ashie side-road, crowning a finely projecting isolated eminence above Loch Duntelchaig. This looks to be a far finer and stronger position than the alleged site aforementioned for a major stronghold. Perhaps there has been a mistake.

Loch Duntelchaig itself is a very much more attractive water than Ashie, twice as long and a mile wide; much deeper also, reaching 200 feet, described also under Daviot and Dunlichity. Only half a mile separates its southern end from Loch Ruthven, a long, narrow crescent, 2 miles by a quarter-mile, impressively set under the crags of Craig Ruthven and Stac Gorm on its south shore, with woodland on the north. At its north-west end is the property of Dalcrombie, where is the site of an old castle of the Frasers.

Dulnain Bridge and Skye of Curr. Strathspey is rich in attractive holiday villages, amongst pine-woodland and beside fine rivers, and Dulnain Bridge is probably the smallest of these, but by no means the least picturesque, set a mile north-west of where the Dulnain joins Spey, 3 miles north of Nethy Bridge, 3 miles west of Grantown and 6 miles east of Carrbridge. The situation is pleasant, by the rushing river and the dark pine trees, under the long heather hills which cradle Lochindorb, looking southwards to the mighty Cairngorms. The older crofting community of Skye of Curr is now almost a "suburb". The county boundary of Inverness-shire and Moray actually runs through Dulnain Bridge, so that it could be described under either county, but since most of the features here mentioned are in Inverness-shire I shall place it thereunder.

The village has no true main street or centre, and clusters round the modern bridge, replacing one of 1791. It is also a rather complex road-junction, the A.938 from Carrbridge here joining the A.95, and the Skye of Curr and Finlarigg side-roads striking off south-west and north-west. There is a small granite church, rather pleasant, with miniature steeple and belfry, and a hall adjoining; while across the road, the war-memorial, in the form of a high Celtic cross, is set in a little garden. Hotel accommodation here is fairly limited, but there are private houses which take guests.

Skye of Curr lies on its side-road bending away to the west, fairly distinct, and pleasing in a different way, lining the road for well over a mile along a slight ridge, with detached small croft-type houses each in its own patch of land, many now holiday homes.

The other side-road climbs northwards to Finlarigg, passing on the way a lime-kiln, with a house built almost on top of it. There are a number of kilns in this area. Finlarigg House is a good 18th century tacksman's house, tall and dignified, in a commanding position looking southwards to the mountains, half a mile up this dead-end road. Laggan Hill rises to the north-east, and up on its ridge is a cup-marked standing-stone. There is the site of a former chapel and burial-ground, called Finlaggan, beyond a green rise to the north-west.

West of the village, along A.938 less than a mile, is Muckrach Lodge, now a hotel. Before reaching this, opposite a roadside cottage, in the middle of the Dulnain which here runs parallel to the road, is a very large boulder, traditionally called The Fish Stone, which until recently had a wrought-iron fish on top, of which only the base remains. Whether there was some earlier significance to account for the name, perhaps a sculptured representation of a fish, does not appear to be known now locally. Beside it, on the bank, are the remains of a small water-mill, with lade and wheel.

Beyond Muckrach Lodge, amongst green braes back from the road on the north, is the interesting ruin of Muckerach Castle, once also called Over Finlarigg, a former important Grant stronghold. It is a fairly typical late 16th century tower-house on the L-plan, four storeys high with vaulted basement, having a circular wing corbelled out to the square to form a watch-chamber, and a slender stair-turret supported on a squinch-arch in the re-entrant angle. The west gable is badly riven, and although the building is fairly complete to the wallhead, it is in a bad state of repair, and greatly deserving of saving. Traces of courtyard curtain-walls and a flanking-tower remain. In 1583 John Grant of Freuchie, 14th Laird, gave these lands to his second son Patrick, who built the castle. He was knighted by James the Sixth and died 1626, the progenitor of the Grants of Rothiemurchus. A lintel-stone from here, dated 1598, with his arms and motto, is built into the walling at the Doune, Rothiemurchus.

At the other, western, side of Dulnain Bridge there are two or three features. The farm of Ballintomb, below the road, was an important entity in the old clan days, and here was the laird's gallows. A burial-cairn is sited in woodland a mile from the village, on the north side of the road. On this side is very notable rock formation, great slabs of outcrop, smoothed by glaciation. Opposite, below the road some distance and near the river, on the farm of Gaich, is a single standing-stone on a green mound. The Grantown area lies just ahead.

The A.95 crosses the bridge at Dulnain and strikes southwards to round the large and thrusting Curr Wood hill, which contains another burial-cairn. Nearly 2 miles on, at the bend of this hill, a side-road leads northwards to Nethy Bridge, at Broomhill Station, on the former Aviemore–Grantown line, to cross Spey by a long trestle-bridge of 16 spans, built in 1894. Beyond Broomhill, on the A.95, are the lands of Tullochgorum, now a farm, a name famed as the seat of the Clan Phadrick Grants, a wild lot. These Grants were alleged to have a familiar spirit, or brownie, called Mag Molach, in the shape of a small hairy boy, who used to conduct the laird home of a dark night, with a special candle—very useful.

Glen Affric. This is renowned as one of the loveliest glens in all the Highlands, and deservedly. It opens, in rich woodlands, about two and a half miles south-west of Cannich village in Strathglass, where the Affric River comes down in a series of cascades to join the Amhuinn Deabhas, to form the Glass, with the Fasnakyle power-station near by. After this road sends a fork southwards to Tomich and Guisachan, it begins to climb, quickly but steadily, narrow and winding but mainly of good surface, with ever widening vistas. In 2 miles it has risen from 240 feet to 600, passing the large white house of Fasnakyle, a shooting-lodge with its own group of half-a-dozen houses, far below. The river comes down this major descent in rapids and waterfalls through rock gorges, the Badger and Dog Falls being notable—though not readily seen from the road above, because of the steepness of the slope and the thickness of the trees. This entire area is heavily wooded, of natural and very beautiful forest, birches and Scots pines. Three miles up a large hydro-electric dam closes the foot of Loch Beneveian, a long and very lovely sheet of water, dotted with wooded islets and headlands, with the high mountains impressive ahead. The road follows the north shore of this loch for 6 miles, with attractive woodlands most of the way, the enclosing mountains becoming ever more imposing. Near the head, Glen Fiadh comes in on the north, with its sizeable and rushing river providing a quite large waterfall about half a mile up. The glen probes narrowly up into the lofty corries between Sgurr na Lapaich (3401 feet) and Tom a Choinich (3646 feet). The road becomes private here, but continues for another 2 miles up the main valley to Affric Lodge, which lies at the foot of another loch, Affric itself.

Loch Affric is over 3 miles long; and beyond it the glen continues for another 4 miles or so, in very wild country now, roadless, but carrying the well-known walkers' track which eventually climbs over the watershed, by Alltbeith and Camban, to the Croe and Kintail. For much of this way it is really West Highland territory, and beyond the scope of this volume. The Affric's headwaters rise on the massive flanks of Ben Attow and the Five Sisters of Kintail, amongst a magnificent welter of peaks, such as the shapely conical Sgurr nah Ceathreamhnan (3771 feet), so utterly remote-seeming from Kintail, and the mighty Mam Soul (3862) and Carn Eige (3877), the highest summit, north of the Great Glen, very much climbers' country.

No metalled side-roads strike off the Glen Affric road, only tracks; and there are no houses on the south side of the river or lochs—and precious few on the north. It is, in fact, a very lovely wilderness, and in most countries undoubtedly would be something in the nature of a national park. The valley divides up naturally into three sections —the upper area, from Ben Attow to the head of Loch Affric, marshy and fairly bare amongst great heather mountains; then the central area containing the two connected lochs, Beneveian the more beautiful, with the pine and birch remnants of the ancient Caledonian Forest; lastly the lower portion, down to Fasnakyle and Strathglass, where the river tumbles in a series of rapids and falls through the wooded gorges of the Chisholm's Pass. It is worth realising that the main valley is very much a hanging one, in that it lies mainly about the 700–800-foot contours, a good 500 feet above neighbouring Strathglass. The Amhuinn Deabhas, the other tributary which, with Affric, makes the River Glass, runs parallel only about 2 miles to the south, yet is only about the 350-foot contour for much of its length. The value of Glen Affric and its head of waters, to the hydro-electric engineers, therefore needs no stressing.

Glen Cannich. Compared with its neighbour Glen Affric, Glen Cannich is less famous and somewhat shorter. But it is in fact almost as beautiful, and its public road almost as long. It lies immediately north of Affric about 4 miles distant, and like Affric is a hanging valley, some 450 feet higher than the Strathglass valley which it joins. After 10 miles its road reaches the foot of long Loch Mullardoch, with its great dam, and the valley is thereafter roadless—though once it had a road, now flooded. Glen Cannich itself, however, continues for a further 10 miles or so, though all its floor is under water.

The glen road strikes off the A.831, from Beauly to Drumnadrochit, at Cannich village, and at once commences to climb quite steeply, past the little Established church, rising 400 feet in less than a mile, with the River Cannich itself far below on the right. Partway up this hill, at the roadside, is a monument erected in 1968 by the Clan Chisholm Society "within former Clan Chisholm territory", with splendid views over Strathglass.

The woodlands commence.

Over a saddle, the road dips fairly deeply again, to rejoin the river, but soon both start to rise once more, with waterfalls on the latter. The glen becomes steep and winding, and presently the Cannich widens to Loch Craskie, which is really only a broadening of the river. A mile or so on, the road crosses to the north side by a bridge, and the glen begins to open out. Another widening of the stream is Loch Carrie. Now the woodlands of birch and old scattered Caledonian pines die out, and in 2 miles more is another widening, larger this time, Loch Sealbhanach. On the north shore of this is the large whitewashed Cozae Lodge, with Glencannich Forest spreading far and wide to the north, and Fasnakyle Forest to the south, treeless deer-forests. There is still another of these little lochs, called a' Bhand, below the tall and massive dam. This great engineering construction of 1952 has raised the level of Loch Mullardoch by no less than 113 feet. A tunnel carries some of the water southwards to Loch Beneveian in Glen Affric, this dam being the principal one in a great hydro-electric system.

Only a very rough walkers' track now continues westwards. A little way along this is a modern cairn and tablet, erected where traditionally The Chisholm held his councils with his leading clansmen. The cairn has inset stones from Australia and Canada, brought by clansmen, the Australian fragment coming from the spot where the first Chisholm emigrant settled in 1793.

Ahead lie the huge trackless mountains and the Ross boundary. To the north rises another Sgurr na Lapaich (3773 feet) not to be confused with the similarly named mountain, only 6 miles away as the crow flies, north of Loch Affric. And further west is the enormous, bulky ridge of An Riabhachan, with its three main summits of 3696, 3559 and 3503 feet, and its great rock precipices and corries.

The far end of Loch Mullardoch now includes Loch Lungard, so that the entire sheet of water is about 9 miles long. At the remote head of Lungard, tributary glens come in out of a wild jumble of mountains, through which a walkers' track winds and climbs its way over a pass to Glen Elchaig, north of Kintail, and salt water. Beinn

Fhionnlaich (3294 feet) rises in a fine peak just south of Loch Lungard, with Carn Eige (3877 feet) and Mam Soul (3862 feet) near by. The country flanking the deep and narrow Glen a' Chailich, which strikes due southwards from Lungard, must be amongst the most wild, inaccessible and dramatic in Scotland.

For less ambitious climbers, the good peak of Sgurr na Diollaid (2676 feet) may be reached much more readily from the bridge across the Cannich between little Lochs Craskie and Carrie aforementioned.

Glen Cannich is highly attractive, and some even prefer its scenery to that of Affric.

Glenmore and Loch Morlich. Although of recent years this area of the Cairngorms' northern slopes has become Scotland's winter-sports and mountain playground, Glenmore had long had its own renown, its great woodlands, the eastern part of the Rothiemurchus Forest, having played their part in Central Highland history, as a source of wealth in timber, a place of refuge for fugitives and marauders and a Highland base for the great Clan Gordon. Long after Huntly and his clan had lost Ruthven Castle and other Badenoch possessions, they retained Glenmore, which was something of a strategic asset, the dead-end strath of the Luineag River, embosomed in high mountains and easily closed and held; yet commanding two convenient passes to the north and east, the Slugan and the Ryvoan.

The strath called Glenmore should probably include all the vale of the Luineag, which flows out of Loch Morlich, to its confluence with the Druie (coming from the gut of the Lairig Ghru) down at Coylum Bridge. But that part is dealt with under Rothiemurchus, and for our purposes it is convenient to consider Glenmore as the area lying east of the western end of Morlich—where indeed is the Rothiemurchus estate boundary. In the other direction Glenmore estate, now publically owned and comprising the Forestry Commission lands, Glenmore Forest Park and the Cairngorms Nature Reserve, stretches eastwards for 4 miles to Ryvoan, and of course high into the mountains southwards, where is the ski-development, and northwards to the Slugan pass between Pityoulish Hill and the end of the Glenmore range, this section being known as The Queen's Forest. Although most of the woodland area is now modern planted forest, representatives of the ancient Caledonian pines still persist, although not in the numbers they do on Rothiemurchus.

Loch Morlich is a fine stretch of water, very different from neighbouring Loch an Eilean in that, although surrounded by pine-forest and backed by mountains, it all gives the impression of openness, of space and distance. It is a mile long and three-quarters of that in width, so that it is less than twice the size of the other; but because the mountains lie much further back and the flanking slopes are much less steep and high, it seems larger and more spacious. The background of the high Cairngorms seen across the water can be breathtaking, and is of course highly photogenic. Few lochs are so beloved of photographers. And Morlich has the added advantage of having at its eastern end a large and wide sandy beach, much appreciated by picnickers, bathers, canoeists and others.

At the western end, close to the road, the Luineag River issues, and here is the site of one of the former weirs and sluices for the log-floating activities of the 18th and early 19th century, when vast quantities of the Caledonian pines were felled and sent in surges down to Spey, there to be floated in great rafts to the sea at Garmouth, the shipbuilding-yards at Kingston converting them into some of the finest sailing-ships and clippers which the world has known. The timbers of many a famous vessel started floating here. The Duke of Gordon, we read, sold in 1784 all the trees round Loch Morlich to Messrs. Dodsworth & Osborne, Kingston, for £10,000, some of these ancient giants being 18–20 feet in girth, and yielding planks 6 feet in width. Thereafter the area was exploited to produce a trade of up to £40,000 a year, an enormous sum for those days, multipliable by at least twenty times to reach today's prices. Replanting went on, of course; but the real giants would take half a millennium to replace. The log-floating gangs were a notable factor on the human scene in Badenoch and Strathspey, and were inevitably a mighty tough lot. The name of Collie, still prominent locally, is a corruption of *coille*, meaning wood, and derives from these vigorous woodsmen, mainly Grants probably. The ancient Caledonian pine, of course, is a very special tree, bushy-shaped, mighty-trunked, slow-maturing and one of the most splendid things that grows.

A footbridge crosses the Luineag as it emerges from the loch, and may be used for a delightful walk round Morlich, and for sundry routes into the mountains or back to the crossroads' path-junction in Rothiemurchus.

The road goes on for some 4 miles, to end at the car-park (600 cars) in Coire Cas, at 2000 feet, the highest tarmac road in Scotland. After passing the sands at the head of Morlich, where the sails of canoes are apt to be seen flapping as learners struggle with the Cairngorm down-draughts, and family parties disport themselves when the sun shines, development begins to make its presence known. There is a store, post-office and restaurant, an Information Centre, the boathouse for canoeing activities, a large camp-site and caravan-park and Glenmore Lodge itself, once the hunting-seat of the Dukes of Gordon, now the headquarters of a mountaineering training and outdoor activities centre, established here long before the skiers came. The large whitewashed house on the terrace site has now sprouted many outbuildings, chalets and the like; also near by are the houses of the forestry workers, all sharing a quite magnificent prospect. From Glenmore Lodge parties of young people head into the mountains all the year round, practising climbing, hill-craft, orienteering, camping techniques and so on, under experienced and qualified leaders, a most admirable development, supported by education authorities all over the country.

The road runs on below the Lodge, across the levels at the head of the loch, and then begins to climb through the pine-forest in highly picturesque fashion. There was a deal of trouble finding a proper line for this pioneering effort, for winter spates and storms washed away some of the earlier attempts. It zig-zags up the mountainside of Cairn Gorm itself, gaining height rapidly but with no really difficult bends or gradients, running out of the tree-level at 1500 feet. Soon after this a side-road branches off to the east for the Coire na Ciste ski-runs. By the time that the main car-park is reached, the immediate surroundings have inevitably become rather bleak, bare heather, peat and rock; but the superb distant vistas draw the eye. A little higher is a snack-bar restaurant, and thereafter the bottom terminal of the chairlift, which rises most of the way to the top of Cairn Gorm, with an adjacent smaller car-park. The chairlift rises in two sections to 3600 feet, with the White Lady Sheiling, refreshment and toilet facilities midway, and the Ptarmigan Observation Restaurant at the summit, an extraordinary place. As well as the chairlift there are six T-bar ski-tows, one at Coire na Ciste, serving the various ski-runs, altogether giving a lifting capacity of 5200 people per hour, something scarcely credible for what was a few years ago merely empty mountainside. All this has been achieved largely by Cairngorm Sports Development Ltd., and the Cairngorm Winter Sports Development Board, a private concern, though with financial aid from the Highlands and Islands Development Board, and aid by Army sappers in the engineering.

Cairn Gorm itself (4084 feet) is not the highest of the mighty Monadh Ruadh range, Ben Macdhui (4300 feet), Braeriach (4248 feet) and Cairn Toul (4241 feet) all outdoing it. But it has given its name to the whole range, popularly, largely because of the activities of the Aberdeen Cairngorm Mountaineering Club, which had its base here. Together they form the loftiest and most dramatic land-mass in Britain (only Ben Nevis, an isolated peak 75 miles to the south-west, being higher) even though the summits are really only comparatively slight eminences rising out of a tremendous alpine plateau around the 3800-feet level, a place of extraordinary character and contrasts—and considerable dangers for the unwary, or unsuitably clad and equipped. Queen Victoria climbed Ben Macdhui on a pony, in 1859—long before there were today's aids. The county boundary between Inverness-shire and Aberdeenshire runs along the summit-ridge here, above the mighty cliffs and corries of Cairn Lochan.

If, at Glenmore Lodge, a left fork is taken instead of following the ski-road, it is possible to drive for another mile or so eastwards. This leads through the forest to a gate at the mouth of a deep gut between the south end of the Glenmore range and the first outliers of the Cairngorms proper—the Ryvoan pass, a major defile through which runs a private road which eventually reaches Forest Lodge in Abernethy. The defile's flanks are steep and rocky, but wooded in the lower levels. Half-way along is the interesting feature of Lochan

Uaine, the Green Lochan, directly under the stony screes of Creag nan Gall (2040 feet). This small loch, hidden behind a roadside bank, has an air of lonely stillness, and its waters are notably green indeed—caused, it is said, by mica from the surrounding stone. Almost a mile on, at the eastern mouth of the pass, is the isolated bothy of Ryvoan. Just before this, the road sends off a track southwards into the Cairngorm wilderness, by way of another and somewhat larger loch amongst the peat-hags and heather, Loch a' Gharbh Choire. This was a well-known old drove-road to Deeside, by the Lairig an Laiogh, the Pass of the Calves. It crosses the infant Nethy over a mile up, and thereafter climbs over the high open heather slopes for long miles, to pass the tor-crowned summit of Bynack More (3574 feet) and on to the deep valley of the Avon, issuing from Loch A'an behind Cairn Gorm itself. Beyond that it climbs high again, by continuous passes, skirting north of the Ben Macdhui group, to Glen Derry and so to the Dee. It was a renowned route for more than cattle-droves, and must have been of great advantage to the Gordons.

The other pass out of Glenmore is very different. A forestry-road strokes off northwards near the head of Loch Morlich and runs pleasantly through the trees for 2 miles, past the lonely farmstead of Badaguish at the foot of the Glenmore range, and on beyond, where a dog's-leg bend brings it to join another of these private roads coming from near the *foot* of the loch. Level for another mile, the road then starts climbing, and lifts up over the slopes of The Queen's Forest, as it is called, to the narrow *bealach* or pass of The Slugan, over into the Boat of Garten area of Strathspey. The views backwards to the Cairngorms are magnificent. Much of this area was badly devastated by the aforementioned great fire, and though replanting has proceeded the scars are very evident. Before the summit is reached a red granite monument at the roadside commemorates the Silver Jubilee of King George the Fifth, 1935. The forestry-road is here high above the steep, narrow floor of the pass, a quite dramatic place.

There are, of course, innumerable forest-walks to be taken, explored and "permutated" all over the Glenmore area, with the aid of an inch-to-the-mile Ordnance map for preference. It is surprising, considering the huge numbers of cars that drive up the main access-road here, how very seldom one ever comes across a walker in all this widespread loveliness. How much is missed by the car-bound, the unenterprising and the merely lazy!

The famous reindeer-herd of Mikel Utsi, the only such in Britain, falls to be mentioned here. Established in 1952 in the Moormore area north of the access-road, it has now been moved to higher ground, and is thriving, an interesting addition to the landscape.

Glen Moriston. This famous glen, renowned for its history and its beauty also, is on the very verge of the limits set for this volume, in describing the eastern side of Inverness-shire, since in character as well as situation it is almost as much a West Coast glen as is Glen Garry to the south; and its road is a well-known access to the West Highland seaboard. But it does open off the Great Glen a quarter of the way down Loch Ness-side; and its river is east-flowing. It has long been a lairdship of a branch of the Grant family; and anciently it was a separate parish, united with Urquhart to the north soon after the Reformation. The river is about 19 miles long, flowing from Loch Cluanie, which has been much enlarged by hydro-electric damming. The name has nothing to do with the town of Morris, as might be thought, but is a corruption of the Gaelic *Mor Essan*, the great waterfalls. It is not a heavily populated glen today, though once it was, having been a victim of the notorious Highland Clearances of the early 19th century. The road up the glen was engineered by English military from 1770 onwards, as part of the campaign to "pacify" the Highlands. This road was still unfinished when Dr. Johnson and Boswell passed here on their way to Glenelg in 1773. They stayed the night at the inn which was predecessor of the hotel, and Dr. Johnson presented the landlord's daughter with an arithmetic book. It is said that here they conceived the idea of the Tour of the Hebrides.

At the wooded mouth of the glen, where the A.82 has to make a major re-entrant inland, from Loch Ness-side, to cross the marshy flats of the River Moriston's outflow, is Invermoriston, a scattered community rather than a village. Here is the quite large hotel, Invermoriston House the laird's seat, the church, the school, the old graveyard, some cottages and modern forestry housing, and a recent chalet-development for visitors, all set pleasingly amongst steep slopes and old woodland.

Invermoriston House stands on the lower slopes below the road a little way north of the bridge, with a jetty at the lochside. The present mansion is modern, but the old house is still extant, with its steading behind, long, two-storeyed, whitewashed, dating from the late 18th century, with gables, coped chimneys and a hip-roofed pavilion extension at each end, a pleasingly dignified edifice, al-though now relegated to farming purposes. Traces of the old pine panelling and woodwork remain. The Grants, who happily still retain possession, descend from a son of the chief of the name, Grant of Freuchie, who gained this property in 1509, at the same time as his brother got Corrimony in Urquhart. There have been notable members of this family. Not far away, also below the road, is the ancient burial-ground, called Clachan an Inair—many such places are called clachans in the Highlands, meaning the villages of the dead. Here was the site of the original parish church, but this has wholly gone save for part of an old wall-memorial to one Peter Macleod, Piper to Glenmoriston, who died in 1848. There are many old and very rough grave-slabs here, and some table-stones. Also, of course the burial-place of the Grants. The present church stands on higher ground, above the road and near the hotel, an attractive whitewashed building with Gothic apertures and an unusual square battlemented tower. Internally it is pleasing, with panelled lower walls and stone above, and a high Gothic arch, built, as a tablet reveals, by a daughter of Grant of Glenmoriston in 1913 in memory of her husband. Another tablet commemorates her father, the 13th laird, who died in 1953 aged 93, having been laird for 84 years.

There was an interesting development at Invermoriston in 1785, when an Inverness man called Shaw set up a linen manufactory here, together with a school for teaching English to the Gaelic speakers. This was abandoned however, after a few years.

Lower Glen Moriston is very beautiful, heavily wooded, the vast Coille na Feinne, or Wood of the Warriors, clothing all the hillsides to the south for miles, right up to the tree-level above 1000 feet. About 2 miles up the A.887 glen road, near Bhlairaidh, is another chalet-development, blending quite well; and near by is the Livishie power-station and hydro-electric dam, with an attractive cascade at the roadside and a few timber houses at the bridge. The woodlands continue mile after mile, mainly planted forest, but with old pines and birch growing out of heather also. Seven miles up, near Dundreggan Lodge, is the Free church of Glen Moriston, with an empty belfry and one grave; and near by the old military bridge bypassed with a new one. A little further are the half-dozen houses of the Dundreggan forestry community. Another mile on is Torgyle Bridge, a fine three-arched structure, where the main road crosses to the south side of the river, and a lesser road continues on the north. Just before this is reached, is the site of the former inn of Torgyle, now a private house; also the little Catholic church, in the birch-woods.

The lesser road proceeds for about 3 miles, with a school on the right—and oddly enough, this little dead-end road is the most populous part of all the long glen today, with forestry houses, cottages and farms, and quite a hamlet at Dalchreichart. The prospects up the valley to the high hills are very fine. At the farm of Balintombuie 2 miles up, where a major burn comes rushing in, a track leads down to another lonely ancient graveyard, this one called Clachan Merechard, and still in use. There is no sign of a church amongst the old and modern tombstones, one old one having Grant heraldry.

Across the main road bridge, at Torgyle, a private road strikes back eastwards into Inverwick Forest, with the small farm of Inverwick. This was a focal point on a famous drove-road, which ran from Strathglass southwards over a vast wilderness of mountains, and crossed the Moriston at Boat of Inverwick, proceeding on up and over the lofty intervening ridge, through Inchnacardoch Forest and so down to Fort Augustus and the Great Glen. Up on the high ground to the south, near Fuaran Ruadh, the Red Cold Spring, a mineral well, a battle was fought between the Gordons and the Camerons, one of the few which both sides were prepared to call a draw. On the other, northern, side some 5 miles up into the empty heather, this drove-road passes the mile-long Loch na Beinne Baine, the Loch of the Milk Mountain, clearly the scene of a summer sheiling for cattle in the old clan days.

Two miles on from Torgyle Bridge is the large farm of Achlain, where a "coffin road" came down from the high ridges to the south, to bring back Glen Moriston dead, from Glen Garry and those parts, to the little Clachan Merechard across the river, which here could be forded. Cairns mark the line of this route right over the hills to Aldernaig in Garry, 8 miles, reaching 2000 feet on the way—and many are the stories of funeral mishaps *en route*. A military track also used approximately the same route.

Three miles beyond Achlain is Mackenzie Cairn, at the roadside. This marks the scene of the famous incident in 1746 when, after Culloden, Roderick Mackenzie, a Jacobite officer and son of an Edinburgh jeweller, was captured by government troops out searching for Prince Charlie—whom Mackenzie much resembled. His captors believed that they had found the much sought-for Prince, for whom a £30,000 reward had been offered by his appalling cousin, the Duke of Cumberland—and Mackenzie did not disillusion them, for his Prince's sake. They slew him there and then and sent his head to Cumberland—but were disappointed of their payment. Actually, the Prince was hiding quite near at hand, in a cave up in Corriedoe, guarded by the famous "Eight Men of Glenmoriston". The River Doe comes in to join the Moriston from the north-west, only half a mile from here.

This area is all part of the renowned Ceannacroc Forest, the large shooting-lodge for which is at the junction of Doe and Moriston. Ceannacroc Bridge carries the A.887 over to the north side again, but the old humpbacked three-arched structure, with cutwaters, is now disused, near the modern one. Soon thereafter the road is joined by the new A.87 which has come over the hills from Glen Garry and Tomdoun, by Glen Loyne, the main route up the west side of Highland Scotland. The River Loyne joins Moriston a mile west of Ceannacroc. Thereafter the new and broad highway follows the enlarged Loch Cluanie westwards, for Cluanie Inn and Glen Sheil, to salt-water at Kintail, amidst a welter of magnificent mountains which reach well over 3000 feet. It is bare of woodland up here, after the 20 miles of forests behind, but the vistas are superb. Climbers' country. The woodlands of Glen Moriston have always been renowned. In 1665 the then Lord Lovat built at Inverness a great ship with trees from here, said to have been the largest ever seen locally. Fir-spills from these Glen Moriston pines were much sought after as "candles".

Back at the mouth of the glen again, north of Invermoriston 3 miles or so, the Allt Saigh burn plunges over, from the lofty shelf of Craig nan Eun Forest, in a notable series of waterfalls, some drops as great as 100 feet. Not far away, at the side of A.82, is a memorial to John Cobb, the motoring and speed-boat racer, who was killed here on speed-trials in 1952.

Glen Urquhart and Drumnadrochit. Glen Urquhart is rather special amongst Highland glens, isolated but by no means remote, fertile, populous, picturesque, with an atmosphere of community about it which so many have lost, not long as glens go, and not leading anywhere, but a major feature nevertheless. It reminds the present writer of Balquhidder, in south-west Perthshire, in more ways than one. It strikes westwards, off the Great Glen, a third of the way up Loch Ness-side from Inverness, with Drumnadrochit, a sizeable community, at its mouth, only 15 miles from Inverness. The glen is approximately 10 miles long, threaded by the A.831, and with the quite large Loch Meiklie, an enlargement of the Enrick River, about half-way up. The valley comes to a dead end at Corrimony; but the road climbs on, over the low hills, 3 miles more to Strathglass, at Cannich. Urquhart is richly wooded, and dominated by the dome-shaped mountain of Mealfuarvonie—a name some folk find difficult, but more attractive than its English equivalent, "the lump of the cold moor".

Urquhart Bay, of Loch Ness, is a feature in itself, the greatest bay of the long loch, a mile wide and a mile deep, guarded by Strone Point on the south, whereon rises the famous Urquhart Castle. There has been a fort or castle on this important and strategic site from before recorded times; for, on the highest point of the headland, within the castle curtain-walling, are the remains of an early Iron Age vitrified fort. St. Columba baptised a Pictish chief here, one Emchath, and his son Virolec, in the 6th century; for how long before that the fort had existed there is no knowing. By Malcolm Canmore's time (1057–93) there was a castle of sorts. It was a royal castle by the reign of William the Lion, a century later, and given into the keeping of the great Durward family, the hereditary doorwards or custodians of the Scots kings. A century later still, English Edward besieged and captured it, in his domination of Scotland, and ordered the gatehouse to be strengthened thereafter. This was not the present gatehouse however, which appears to date from the early 16th century, like much else here. Bruce assailed and took Urquhart from Edward's Comyn keeper; and thereafter it continued to be a much sought-after prize in the stresses and strains which convulsed Highland Scotland. The Lord of the Isles seized it in 1395, and in 1411 his cousin the Earl of Mar, victor of Harlaw, got it instead. It passed through Gordon and Grant and Chisholm hands, and back to the Lords of the Isles. Eventually the Grants, with their nearby base of Glen Moriston, consolidated their hold. It was besieged by the early Jacobites, and partly blown up by government troops to deny it to the Stewart supporters. Gradually thereafter it sank into ruin. It is now handsomely cared for by the Department of the Environment, and a magnet for visitors.

The remains cover an extensive figure-of-eight site above the loch —which, it should be remembered, the Caledonian Canal construction raised by 6 feet—within a lengthy curtain-wall which has had four or five flanking-towers, the drum-tower gatehouse and an early and later keep. The latter, at the extreme north end, is the most complete portion, and still rises to parapet-walk level, although its roof has gone. This is 16th century work. There is an upper and a nether bailey, a circular doocot within the former and a chapel within the latter. The oldest work, whereon was the Norman motte, was to the south, the same higher portion where was the Pictish fort. The early keep here had walls 8 feet thick, but little of this remains. A water-gate faced the loch.

The opposite horn of Urquhart Bay, to the north, is not so prominent; but here too are features. This vicinity is called St. Ninians, and here was an establishment of the Knights Templar. The pier that projects below is still called Temple Pier. Grain was shipped from here direct to London as late as the 19th century. The site of the Templars' house above is marked by a standing-stone at the roadside (A.82), with near by a well with an arched stone canopy, St. Ninian's. When this was excavated during the road re-alignment, a hoard of ancient coins were found preserved in fat, and in shining condition. A stone from here, with a simple inscribed cross, is now enshrined in the altar of St. Ninians Episcopal Church, up the glen.

Drumnadrochit village lies at the junction of the A.82 and A.831, where the former highway makes a great loop round the flats of the Bay, and a bridge crosses the Enrick. Indeed, the name means the ridge of the bridge. There are a cluster of hotels here, shops and some modern housing. With neighbouring Lewiston, it has become something of a colony of artists and craftsmen. It is a very scattered place. The school lies half a mile to the east, on the wooded low ground, reached by a side-road; and off this, another lane leads to the parish church of Urquhart and Glenmoriston, a vast parish of 130,000 acres, united shortly after the Reformation. The earlier church, of 1630, was at Kilmore, almost another half-mile further to the east; and this present building was erected in 1836, small and whitewashed with a quite elaborate belfry. There are, naturally, no very old stones in this graveyard, although a lintel stone is inserted in the walling with a number of initials and the date 163?. The position is pleasingly sequestered amongst trees. The earlier site at Kilmore, retains a fragment of the ruined church, with a decayed watch-house against body-snatchers. Here are many old gravestones, including one for James Moray, master-mason, who repaired Urquhart Castle in 1623.

Immediately south of this, the little side-glen of Coiltie opens, with the quite large village of Lewiston in its entrance. This has a rather unusual V-formation, with the older houses strung along the eastern leg of the V for half a mile, and modern development on the western. The older part is attractive, with the cottages now largely restored and rehabilitated. Here is the fairly large Lewiston Arms Hotel. At the main road base of the village, opposite a rather unsightly modern store and filling-station is a monument to Bradley Martin of Balmacaan, a local benefactor who died in 1913.

Balmacaan estate lies up Glen Coiltie a little way. The mansion, of 1886, has recently been demolished, on its fine terraced woodland site, and a 50-bedroom hotel, with chalets, is planned for the property. It was a seat of the Grant Earls of Seafield. Two broken Pictish symbol-stones were brought here from Drumbuie, to the north, one with double-disc and a serpent and Z-rod, the other with two mirrors and comb symbols, plus the tail of a fish. The writer could not find these relics, amidst the demolishments, but they may have been removed to safety elsewhere. A small vaulted ice-house still survives in the bank, to the south. The Balmacaan deer-forest behind extends over a great area of the high ground to the south, dotted with innumerable small lochs.

Glen Coiltie probes deep into the deer-forest, wooded and very picturesque in its lower reaches, deep and steep. Almost 2 miles above Balmacaan is Divach Lodge, a romantically and astonishingly placed house, perched on a high ledge above the wooded ravine, like an eyrie. J. M. Barrie rented this lodge for a period, and it was a favourite with the artist John Philips R.A. Set against the walling is a well, now partly built over to prevent the recurrence of a child-drowning tragedy. The Falls of Divach cascade impressively over the great drop below the lodge, with a fall of perhaps 100 feet, highly dramatic.

A little further east on A.82, over the Coiltie River at Borlum Bridge—a corruption of Board-land, meaning the table-land or home farm, of Urquhart Castle—a small side-road strikes off, to climb swiftly and excitingly southwards, parallel with the Great Glen, by a series of zigzags, rising 800 feet in just over a mile, narrow and tricky but with excellent surface. This leads to the rather extraordinary scattered community of Bunloit, high above Loch Ness. Up here, on both sides of the Great Glen, at the 800–900 feet contour, is a lofty tableland, a sort of enormous raised beach area. On this side, once the ascent is made, it is all undulating heather and peat-bog, dotted with pines and birches, with a few crofts and small farms. There was a school up here until recently, now it is a private house. The road runs for about five miles at this level, and near its end, at Ancarraig, is an ambitious new development for visitors, a dozen luxury-type chalets for self-catering holidays. It is a bold venture. Beyond the road-end, the pointed, wooded hill of Dunscriben rises, with Mealfuarvonie behind, and on the former another early vitrified fort. Ruskich, or Ruisky Forest, which clothes the steep slopes below this, to Loch Ness, is famous for having many enormous trees, pine and birch, some of the latter 9 feet in girth.

Back at Drumnadrochit, the A.831 branches off westwards up Glen Urquhart proper. Half a mile up is another Established church for this end of the glen, without graveyard. And a little further is the attractive and quite large hamlet of Milton, on a loop road and slightly terraced site, facing south. Beyond it is the Free church, at the roadside, whitewashed, long and low, dated 1844, with the graves only of three former ministers. Here the A.833 turns off northwards, to climb out of the glen by another vigorous ascent of 700 feet in just over a mile; but this is a good, wide road, and the bends are not difficult. Where it begins to level off, on the right, is the track to the farm of Culnakirk, where is the Clach Mor, the Great Stone, a huge flattish boulder covered with cupmarks, allegedly 113 of them. It lies 200 yards east of the farmhouse. There are many small hill-farms at this high level on the north side of Glen Urquhart, keeping the heather at bay; and a number of former lime-kilns. This A.833 road goes on over the lonely hills, past a scatter of small lochs, 6 miles to Glen Convinth, and so on to Beauly and the A.9, a very pleasant and scenic route, especially for a round trip from Inverness.

Back in the glen, the A.831 continues westwards through heavily forested country, the valley being fairly broad. A little way on, between road and river, is the old mill of Tore, still retaining its wheel, prettily placed. This has been in the hands of a family of MacDonalds for 300 years. It is now being restored as a craft and agricultural museum.

Forestry predominates for the 3 miles up to Balnain, at the foot of Loch Meiklie, a scattered community with school, forestry houses and small farms. The loch is over a mile long and half that wide, very pleasant. Kilmartin estate flanks it on the north, and amongst the steeply rising woodlands here is another chalet development, quite a major one, the cedar buildings very pleasingly scattered and hidden amongst the birches. A little way beyond the mansion is the small Episcopal church of St. Ninians, aforementioned, a delightful little place by the loch-shore. As well as the Templar stone set in the altar, there is an aumbry with an ancient panelled door, and other interesting features. In the graveyard are a few tombs, and an old iron mort-safe. The church was built as an Established chapel-of-ease in 1840.

A mile further on, near the driveway to Sheuglie, is the Glen Urquhart post-office and shop, with a forestry hamlet across the river. Sheuglie, a whitewashed old house, now surrounded by planted forest, was the seat of an ancient lairdship.

Beyond this, a narrow side-road heads off at an angle north-westwards, to climb to the crofting area of Buntait. Where this road ends, up on the open heather, on the right is a little whin-clad knoll, and on this is a single standing-stone known as Char's Stone, with what looks like the remains of three small cairns stretching to the east. The present writer has not discovered the significance of the name Char's Stone—though perhaps there is a connection with St. Urodoin or Chairdean?

Level with this feature, but down in the valley-floor, the main A.831 bends north-westwards in turn, to climb out of the glen and over the heathery hills to Strathglass, 3 miles or so. But a side-road strikes off to the south here, crosses the Enrick by an old hump-backed bridge, and so enters the rather distinct area of Corrimony—which is, in fact, a sort of separate hanging valley at the head of

Urquhart, with its own character and history. Mony was a Norse prince, said to be a son of the King of Lochlann, or Norway, who invaded Scotland at Crinan, in Argyll, date unspecified, and worked his way up the Great Glen, to establish himself at Craig Mony, thought to be the site of Urquhart Castle. There is a farm called Achmony, the Field of Mony, down near the entrance of the glen. In time he was driven up Urquhart, and slain here at Corrimony, and buried at Mony's Stone. Or so says tradition. Just over the bridge is the little school, still in use; and across the road is the tiny and prettily placed church of Corrimony, amongst the birches, with no graveyard—this being further on. Less than a mile westwards, at the roadside, is a magnificent chambered cairn, now in the care of the Department of the Environment, in better state than most, with a domed central enclosure of heaped small stones, reached by an access passage only 3 feet high, and surrounded by ten monoliths. A cupmarked stone lies on the central heap. This burial cairn is thought to date from the period 3000–1800 B.C.

Corrimony House stands in trees, with its farmery, half a mile on, where the road ends, a mainly 18th century whitewashed house, not very large, but picturesque, across a graceful arched bridge. This was a Grant lairdship from 1509, founded by one son of Grant of Freuchie, chief of the name, while a brother founded the Glen Moriston line. Later Corrimony passed to the Ogilvie family. A larger and more modern mansion was built in parkland to the west, but this has been demolished. On the way to it, across a bridge, stands Mony's Stone, a single, simple monolith. And to the left, up the riverside amongst old trees, is the ancient graveyard of Kil-uraden. St. Uradain or Chairdean seems to have been one more Celtic missionary. There is no sign now of his cell or church, but the burial-ground is enclosed within a wall and well maintained. In the east wall is inset a bowl-like stone, almost certainly a holy-water stoup from the former church, called Clachantullan, with a Gaelic inscription relating to Uradain, dated 1890. Here are the graves of the Grants of Corrimony, their Ogilvie successors and other local folk.

Beyond this is roadless. The River Enrick swings southwards towards its source amongst the high hills of the deer-forest. A mile up is the Corrimony Falls, with near it a cave which once was used to shelter Jacobite refugees. A stalker's track leads on southwards for 6 miles, past innumerable small lochans, to end at the quite large Loch na Stac under lofty lonely mountains.

Inverness. There are a great many ancient towns in Scotland; but the royal burgh of Inverness can justly claim to be of greater antiquity than almost any other, since it was a recognised capital in the 6th century and earlier, when Saint Columba came here to convert its Pictish King Brude. For how long before that it had been an established centre there is no knowing; but since it is surrounded by prehistoric remains, of forts, cairns, stone-circles and artificial islands, it was clearly an important locality in the dark ages. This, of course, is readily accounted for by its vital position *vis-à-vis* the northern parts of Scotland, at the head (or foot) of the Great Glen, at the only crossing point between the deep-thrusting Moray Firth and the 23-mile long Loch Ness and at the heart of the fertile low-lying enclave of the North-Eastern Highlands, with its own seaport. Strategically, topographically, socially, historically, it is the focal point of a vast area, and has not been called the Capital of the Highlands for nothing.

Inverness has other claims to fame, of course. As well as being the county town for the largest county in Scotland—indeed in Britain, if Yorkshire's three counties are excepted—it is a very important communications hub, market town, shopping and business centre, and one of the best-known tourist meccas in the land, from which a great deal of the finest scenery in these islands is readily visited. It is set at the northern end of the famous Caledonian Canal. Also, it is a notorious bottleneck for traffic—though that is perhaps inevitable, with all roads having to lead here, in order to cross the River Ness.

Despite all this, Inverness is not a large town, by southern standards, although of recent years it has tended to sprawl badly to east and west, not all of these extensions sightly. Which is a great pity, since the situation itself is very fine. Its population is growing fast—in 1964, 29,000, in 1971, 33,000 with large new developments envisaged and indeed commenced, at Balloch 4 miles to the east (q.v.), and 60,000 the target figure. It is smaller than Perth, therefore; but nevertheless, it is the largest town north of Aberdeen.

It is a contradictory place in not a few respects. Despite its hoary antiquity it gives little impression of age today, having been notably ruthless throughout its long history in pulling down its ancient buildings. Although the centre of the town is cramped and awkwardly constricted, nor very distinguished architecturally, its suburbs sprawl widely; yet it has splendid parks and open spaces, and fine vistas in almost every direction. And certain of its residential areas are delightful. It is the headquarters of the Highlands and Islands Development Board, the Crofters' Commission, the North of Scotland Hydro-Electric Board, the North of Scotland Milk Marketing Board, and an important branch of the Scottish Tourist Board, An Comunn Gaidhealach, and other such institutions, with a large Tourist Information Office in Church Street; yet its north-eastern environs, at the mouth of the river in the Longman area, are an extended disaster—an area, moreover which, because of a desire to relieve the chronic traffic congestion, road-users are funnelled through, in an abomination of widespread litter, dumps and industrial detritus; while all around the views and prospects are magnificent. What the North Sea oil developments may do to Inverness, remains to be seen.

Historically the town has inevitably played an important role down the ages. Just where the Pictish citadel was sited is still argued over. Craig Phadraig, the prominent wooded hill-fort to the west, was long accepted as Brude's castle; but this is now contested. Torvean, another wooded eminence, is also claimed as its site. But most authorities now think that the original fortress was east of the river, not on the site of the present so-called castle, but on that part of the elevated Crown area called Auldcastle Road. Thereafter a medieval castle grew up on the Crown, whether on the same site, or elsewhere; and this was the fortress immortalised in Shakespeare's *Macbeth*, where King Duncan was alleged to have met his death— though this is now believed to have been at Bothgowan, near Elgin. After Macbeth's time, the timber castle, clay-covered, was burned, and a new stone-built citadel was erected on the mound now known as Castlehill, directly above the river, possibly by Malcolm Canmore. This remained a royal fortress for many centuries. It was demolished in part by Bruce, in his policy of denying fortified strengths to the invader, but rebuilt around 1412 by the Earl of Mar, victor of Red Harlaw—of whom more later. James the First stayed in it in 1427, when putting down Highland insurrection, and indeed held a parliament therein. Alexander of the Isles, pillaged the town and tried to capture the castle a year or so later, but failed. His successor, John of the Isles, was more successful, capturing and sacking both town and castle in 1455. James the Third was here in 1464, and his son James the Fourth in 1499. He conferred the hereditary keepership on the Earl of Huntly, and the Gordons held it until we read of the Duke of Gordon claiming £300 compensation at the abolition of the hereditary jurisdictions in 1751. By that time it was an office, rather than a duty, for the castle had fallen into ruin, been rebuilt by General Wade during the early Jacobite troubles and finally blown up by Prince Charlie in 1746. Wade had called it Fort George, after his monarch; and thereafter a great new fortress was built ten miles away at Ardersier, and called Fort George. Finally the present and unsuitably English-style of castellated building was erected on the site in 1835, to the design of William Burn, and here are now the Sheriff Court and County Police departments, their battlements dominating the town from the west, mellow-red and quite dramatic, but wholly sham and unauthentic. The old castle well, in the courtyard, was rediscovered, and is now a feature. And just to the south, on the grassy forecourt, is a statue of Flora Mac-Donald, for ever looking west and south for the Prince whom she helped to escape and who never returned.

David the First (1124–1153) constituted Inverness a royal burgh; and William the Lion fortified the town itself, with a fosse or ditch, and granted it the right of a weekly market. Shipbuilding was important here as early as 1249—with the great forests available for fine timber—and a large vessel was launched at Inverness that year, for a French nobleman, in which he accompanied his monarch St. Louis to the Crusades. And so on. Most of the stirring events which were endemic to this lovely and turbulent land affected Inverness, and this is no place to ennumerate or summarise them. But it should perhaps be mentioned that Mary Queen of Scots came here, in 1562, on her one and only expedition into the north of her kingdom, to put down the power of Gordon—and this was as far north as she attained. Being refused admission to the royal castle by its Gordon keeper, she had to take up residence, with her brother, Moray, in a comparatively modest house at the corner of Bridge Street and Bank Street—which was only recently demolished, to make way for the large modern building which houses the Highlands and Islands Development Board—development of a sort! When the castle finally surrendered, the Queen hanged the keeper. Montrose besieged it in 1644, but was called away before he could win it; though five years later some of his fellow Royalists did manage to capture it, one of them the ineffable Sir Thomas Urquhart of Cromarty who, as well as translating Rabelais, was proud to offer documentary proof of his entire descent from Adam! Four years later, again, Oliver Cromwell came to Inverness, and built a great new citadel, to house 1000 men and costing the then enormous sum of £80,000—some of the stones for which he actually bought from the Town Council, who demolished the Domican or Blackfriars Monastery to provide them. This fort was down near the river-mouth and harbour area, and was called, curiously, The Sconce—presumably as a reference to dousing out the light of "rebellion" in the North. In 1661, on the restoration of Charles the Second, the whole lot was demolished, however, save for the clock-tower, which still stands amidst the oil-storage tanks.

Enough of history, meantime—although inevitably more historical reference will occur in a more detailed description of the town, however superficially.

The centre of Inverness is made up of a sort of grid of close-packed and narrow streets—usually, sad to say, choked with traffic today. Of these, the High Street, plus its extensions of Bridge Street to the west and Eastgate at the other end, form the main axis, the A.9 highway running through them. But the most interesting street undoubtedly is Church Street, which strikes northwards at the junction of High and Bridge Streets, where rises the kenspeckle Town Steeple, a sort of tolbooth, consisting of a square tower with steeple surmounting, dating from 1791, rising 130 feet. Oddly enough it was badly twisted in 1816, by an earthquake, but straightened again. It has a clock and bells, and replaced an earlier tolbooth. Church Street is named after the High Church, about half-way down, which was the original parish kirk—at least, original in its tower. This stands on an eminence between street and river, called St. Michael's Hill—although the church seems always to have been dedicated to the Virgin Mary, not to St. Michael. The fairly plain but large cruciform building dates from 1772; but its square tower at the west end is much earlier, of various periods, with a balustraded parapet and a clock below a 17th century spire. This has a vaulted basement, once used as a prison, with a roll-moulded doorway, and above it a smaller one at first-floor level, only reachable by a ladder—a common defensive arrangement. The bell is alleged to have come from the cathedral at Fortrose. The kirkyard is well filled with old tombs, with many flat and table-stones; and there is a very ambitious burial-enclosure of the Robertson of Inshes family, near the street gate, dated 1660.

Churches proliferate around here, the tall-steepled St. Columba High, formerly Free and enlarged 1866, being just over the kirkyard wall to the south-west. And next door as it were, on the north down Church Street is the present Free Greyfriars, which was the Gaelic Church of St. Mary from 1649 to 1954, rebuilt 1793. There seems to be a certain amount of building switching amongst Inverness congregations. The pride of this latter used to be its famous Black Pulpit, of Dutch origin. Though changed denominationally, Gaelic services are still held here.

Just beyond is Friars Lane and Street, with a large new telephones building erected on part of the site of the former Blackfriars or Dominican Monastery. (There has been considerable confusion about the terms of Greyfriars and Blackfriars here; whether there was in fact a Greyfriars, or Franciscan, foundation in Inverness, is not certain—but the Dominicans were Black Friars.) Alexander the Second founded the Dominican Monastery here in 1233. As has been said, the stones of this establishment were sold to Cromwell by the Town Council; and all that remains is a single pillar in the centre of a small oblong of graveyard, reached from a gateway in Friars Street. This little place, although of so modest dimensions now, and filled with old tombstones, could and should be better known and cared for; indeed Inverness, so tourist-conscious, ought to make much of it. For it contains one very special grave, the recumbent effigy from which is now set upright in the south walling. This was the burial-place of a famous character in Scots history, Alexander Stewart, Earl of Mar, natural son of the Wolf of Badenoch (the Earl of Buchan, brother of Robert the Third). Mar was a scoundrel, but a gallant one, and victor of the great battle of Red Harlaw in 1411, where he defeated his cousin Donald of the Isles in a struggle which had a lasting effect on our country's story. Later he was made Justiciar of the North, with his headquarters in Inverness, rebuilt the castle, and died here in 1437. The effigy almost certainly represents the Earl, and though the head has been defaced, is a very fine one and unusual in two respects. The helmeted head rests on two tasselled cushions, not one as normal; and as well as the usual sword at the left side, there is a little dirk actually projecting on the right, still intact. With the graveyard tidied up, the grass mowed, and this effigy given pride-of-place, with an explanatory notice, this site could be an asset to Inverness, of great interest to visitors. It is notable that the river-bank below this area is still called Friars' Shot, and was where the monks shot their salmon nets.

Also in Church Street are other interesting buildings. Abertarff House, now the headquarters of An Comunn Gaidhealach, the Gaelic society and Highland centre, is a fine, late 16th century white-washed house, pleasingly restored by the National Trust in 1966, a typical L-shaped building with crowstepped gables and circular stair-tower, the latter corbelled out to the square at top to form a watch-chamber. It dates from 1593. The name Abertarff is misleading. It was the town-house of the Warrands of Warrandfield originally, passing only in 1801 to Colonel Archibald Fraser of Lovat, who held the Abertarff estate. It seems that he had previously built another house up on the Crown, also now called Abertarff. Across the street from here is the Dunbar Hospital, a fine, large 17th century house, with crowsteps, seven decorative dormer windows and some good interior woodwork, built in 1688 by Provost Alexander Dunbar, as an almshouse for the town's poor, and now in fact an Old People's Centre, with private flats above. The provost's arms remain over the doorway. It is a good example of authentic vernacular architecture, and at one time housed two schools, one the Grammar School. Just south of it across a little street is the restored Bow Court building, of slightly later date, highly attractive, now containing an art salon and private housing, with pend and little back court. The narrow street between is called School Lane, and in the walling here is a heraldic panel bearing the arms of Katherine Duff, Lady Drummuir, a famous lady, wife of Provost Alexander Duff, ancestor of the Earls of Fife, who had seized the town in the Jacobite interest in 1715. This, the house of his widow, was successively occupied by both Prince Charles Edward and the Duke of Cumberland, in 1746; and Lady Drummuir used to say that: ". . . she'd lodged twa kings' bairns, but ne'er wished to lodge any mair."

Up near the top of Church Street is the large and modern showrooms and office of the Tourist Information Centre, with arts and crafts exhibits. The well-known Caledonian and Cumming's Hotels are here also.

At the foot, Church Street and Academy Street merge, and here is a larger graveyard, called the Chapel Yard, where once was a chapel dedicated to the Virgin Mary—as was the High Kirk—even more neglected than that of the Friars, although still in use as a cemetery, overlooked by gasometers and the like. Amongst the crowded memorials is a cairnlike monument to the chiefly family of Chisholm, with other lairdly and magisterial graves. The large Forbes of Culloden enclosure is in a grievous state of neglect. A number of English officers who fought at Culloden are said to have been buried here.

Academy Street, as might be expected, once housed Inverness Royal Academy, a quite famous school now removed to a greatly enlarged site up on the Crown area to the south. Here also, until a comparatively recent period, was Farraline Park School, reached by a side-street. It was originally called Dr. Andrew Bell's School, and its very handsome classical buildings were erected in 1840. These are now used to house the Little Theatre, plus the Burgh Police courtroom, while its playground is turned into the town bus station. Near by is the former Volunteer Drill Hall, of 1873, quite architecturally ambitious. Also in Academy Street is the railway station, rather a famous one, and notably close to the town centre, with its large hotel. Almost opposite is the entrance to the interesting covered-in Market Arcade area, formerly an open market-place, where a great variety of permanent small shops and temporary stalls form a popular venue for the shopper. And further down the street are the premises of the well-known firm of A.1 Welders, which has made a name for itself.

Church and Academy Streets both end on the south at High Street. Most of the old houses and buildings of High Street have been swept away, but there are still some items of interest to more than shoppers. The Town House is here, on the south, towards the west end, a tall Gothic Victorian erection of 1882, over-ornate. At its front stands the Mercat Cross, rather undistinguished, and restored in 1900. Beside it, inset in a plinth, is a boulder called Clach na Cudainn, the Stone of the Tubs. It appears to have got its name from the housewives who used to rest their buckets thereon, on their way to and from the riverside, for water and washing, in the days before piped water; but its tradition is that it was the stance of an ancient seer who prophesied that so long as it was preserved, Inverness would flourish. The Town House still contains the municipal offices, and the meeting-place of the Town Council, with heraldic stained glass and a number of portraits. A Cabinet Meeting was held here in 1921, concerned with the Irish problem, allegedly the first ever held outside London—though this sounds improbable. Lloyd George presided, and amongst those signing the roll, retained in a frame, were Winston Churchill and Stanley Baldwin.

Near by, although actually in Bridge Street, an extension westwards of High Street, is the very modern and unlovely building which houses the Public Library, Art Gallery and Museum—all excellent features in themselves. The Museum is not large, but it contains many items of interest, including six fragments of different Pictish symbol-stones collected from various parts; two from Ardross, in Easter Ross, displaying a wolf and a horse's head, very spirited; one from Cullaird, Scaniport, showing the mirror and comb symbols; one from Torgorm in the Black Isle, with double disc and Z-rod; and two from other unnamed sources, one showing a bull, similar to but less dramatic than the Burghead bulls, and another with crescent and V-rod. There is a good collection of Highland weapons, targes and costume; also fossils, semi-precious stones, prehistoric remains and the like. An interesting series of water-colours of old Inverness buildings and streets lines the stairway. The small Art Gallery displays paintings ancient and modern. The Library is a good one.

Across the road, still in Bridge Street, and attached to the west side of the Town Steeple, is the Prudential offices, rather a good building of dignified Georgian character dating from 1794, with triangular pediments over the windows. Back in High Street, close by, is the pilastered classical yet highly ornate Bank of Scotland building, formerly the headquarters of the Caledonian Bank, with allegorical groups of figures. Many texts are cut into the masonry of a neighbouring building. The Custom House, in the High Street, is also a classical edifice, but less ornate. Westwards, the large, concrete box-type modern development is not to everyone's taste, especially on the south side, where Inverness surely might have insisted upon something, if not more handsome, at least less dully functional. Round the corner, in Bank Street, facing the river, the local newspaper, *The Inverness Courier* (founded in 1817) has gallantly resisted the heavy hand of "improvement", and retains its own gabled authentic building of the period.

Parallel with High Street, and lying between Church and Academy Streets, are a number of side streets, such as Union Street, Baron Taylor's Street and Queensgate, constituting the major merchandising area, Union Street perhaps the finest shopping venue, with many old established firms—for Inverness is one of the greatest retail vending centres in the North of Scotland. These streets are apt to be thronged with visitors from all over the world, for many months of the year. Another busy street is Castle Street, which climbs up towards the castle from the High Street, southwards, and which used to be called Domesdale, it being the route by which the condemned were led to their execution on the castle forecourt.

At the other end of High Street, Eastgate quickly deteriorates in character—which is a pity, for this is the main entrance to the town from east and south. Steep slantwise streets climb up to the Crown area on the south; and on the north the railway-yards and great cattle-pens of the auction-marts, spread over the low-lying reclaimed land of what was once Loch Gorm.

The Crown, actually a sort of plateau, or raised beach area, above the old town, is largely residential, laid out in pleasant wide streets and avenues, with large villas and gardens. Here are churches, schools and institutions also—the Royal Academy, the Youth Hostel, even the prison. Here, too, at 5 Culduthel Road, is the pilastered house known as Ardkean Tower, with dome, erected in 1842 as infant school and observatory. This Culduthel Road runs for a very long way, winding south-eastwards through mainly pleasant suburbs, Culduthel House itself, now a hospital, being more than 2 miles away. Out there the new housing schemes proliferate.

The River Ness, of course, wide and shallow here, forms a major barrier to the west. But there are old parts of the town on the far side also. The present Ness Bridge, at the foot of Bridge Street, is only the last in a succession—though the first road bridge across the centre of the Great Glen from Fort Augustus, 28 miles away. The original was a timber erection, described by one of Cromwell's officers as "the weakest that ever straddled over so strong a stream". It fell, under a crowd of 100, in 1664; and a seven-arched bridge was erected 21 years later, said to be the first stone bridge in the Highlands, though this is doubtful. Some of its landward arches were long used as a prison, a device used elsewhere. This was swept away in a flood in 1849, and the suspension-bridge, long a noted feature of the Inverness scene, succeeded it. This in turn has fairly recently given way to a wide modern bridge, much easing the traffic flow, if less picturesque. There is now another bridge, called the Waterloo, half a mile northwards, in the harbour area.

Across the Ness Bridge is a large and mainly residential area, principally of smaller streets and houses, with some industry. There is not a great deal that is characterful here; but Huntly Street, which follows the river-bank northwards, has some interesting features. There is a group of traditional houses and cottages at the top, one of the 17th century, L-shaped with crowstep gables. Near by is the large modern arcaded premises of an old-established kilt-making firm, and Highland outfitters. The Catholic church of St. Mary is here, with the West Parish church; and between them the house, 36 Huntly Street, of 1840, now the Red Cross headquarters, but built as a dispensary for the poor. Farther down, opposite St. Mark's Church of Scotland—Inverness is a great place for churches—is an impressive late 18th century mansion, Balnain House, now empty, boarded up and in a bad state—a pity, for restored it would make an excellent, commodious and dignified feature. Farther down still is the very modern but quite attractive Methodist church, much glass, with tower and needle-like spire. This street and its continuations, wind on down the riverside to the dock area of Capel Inch, past the yacht- and boat-building (formerly ship-building) yard and slipway of Thornbush, and on past the housing schemes to South Kessock, where is the ferry across to the Black Isle of Easter Ross, with its pier. Half a mile east is the low thrusting breakwater, at the very mouth of the Ness, which reaches out to the former artificial island, or crannog, of Cairn Airc, an early defensive feature, on which is now a navigational beacon. There is considerable industrial development hereabouts, on the coastal flats.

The main dock area, however, is across on the east bank, where is the true Inverness Harbour. This is reached from Shore Street, an extension of the united Church and Academy Streets. As with most docklands, it is hardly beautiful, but busy and with its own interest. Here is the Harbour Office, the towering modern Technical College, the Fire Station, and Northern Area headquarters, and the great oil-storage installations. These have all but engulfed the Citadel, Cromwell's mighty fort, of which only a green rampart or two remains, with the 30-foot-high and ogee-roofed Clock Tower aforementioned. Still further seawards, on the levels, lies the Longman Industrial Estate, not improved by the dumping processes which are being used to reclaim more land from the firth. At the very tip of the low and not very prominent headland, is the Longman's Grave, amongst whins—no doubt a Viking burial-place. A little further east, amongst the rubbish-tips is the low thrusting area known as Smith's Island, its barren and sordid reaches used meantime for stock-car racing. If the foreground is grim, however, the background is splendid indeed, on every hand. There is a moral here, surely?

Back on the west side of Ness Bridge, southwards, is an altogether different aspect of Inverness. Here are wider avenues, open spaces, guest-houses and hotels and so on, all under the wooded ridges of Craig Phadraig and the Leachkin. Dominating all hereabouts is the massive twin-towered Episcopal cathedral church of St. Andrew, a fine, rose-red, cruciform, Gothic-type building erected in 1869–74, the first cathedral in Great Britain to be wholly built and consecrated since the Reformation, as the seat of the combined bishopric of Moray, Ross and Caithness. It has many features, including eleven bells, most of them gifted, and rung by a team of talented experts. The great tenor bell weighs a ton. There is much stained glass and excellent woodwork, in the choir, rood-screen and stalls. Unusual are the series of stone masks of men's faces, ancient and modern, above the aisle pillars. There are five remarkable gold-engraved ikons, presented to Bishop Eden, the founder of the cathedral, by the Tzar of Russia in 1861. Also a 15th century painting of the Madonna and Child by Sano di Pietro. The font is a copy of the famous one by Thorwalden at Copenhagen, a kneeling angel holding a shell-like bowl, the angel's face in the likeness of that of General Learmonth's wife, the donor. All very fine.

Not far from the cathedral, in Ardross Street, is the park and offices of the Northern Meeting organisation, a very famous Highland institution, the venue for the annual Highland games, military tattoos and the like. The County Council offices are near by. Here too, in Bishop's Road, is the site of the proposed Eden Court Theatre complex, an ambitious scheme which has had many set-backs but with which the Town Council are determined to go ahead, despite escalating costs.

Farther up this west bank of the Ness is the great Royal Northern Infirmary, a well-known hospital, founded in 1804, with fine classical buildings as nucleus, and a pleasing riverside setting. And just to the south of this is the Bught Park sports ground, an extensive area with all sorts of playing fields and pitches, ice-rink, riding-stables, municipal caravan-park and other amenities. It was the 18th century Bught House until comparatively recently. This estate was formerly called Kilvean, from St. Bean. The nearby Torvean Hill has the same derivation—Bean being Baithene (536–600) the second abbot of Iona and a noted Celtic missionary. The mansion has been pulled down, but the walled garden remains. A Bught hydro-electric scheme and powerhouse lies immediately to the south, on a sort of mill-race of the Ness.

Level with the Bught area on this side, and the Drummond district on the east bank, is one of Inverness's great assets, the Ness Islands Park. This is a lengthy stretch of the riverside, on both banks, with a number of wooded islets in the centre, all linked by little bridges to form a quite delightful sylvan retreat amongst ancient trees, with walks and seats beside the fast-flowing Ness. On one of the larger islands, all but hidden in the trees, is a sports and open-air concert enclosure. And on the west bank at the south end, below Bught Road, is the General's Well, under a stone canopy in the bank, said to provide some of the best water in the district.

On the east bank, in this vicinity, is the Belfield Park, attractive, with paddling-pool, putting-green and children's playground, below the steep wooded bank of the high ground south of the Crown. Above is Godsman's Walk, named after an Englishman, Captain Godsman, factor to the Duke of Gordon, owner of the land, who in the early 19th century established this single access over the Duke's ground in place of numerous rights-of-way the citizens had previously used. On the other side of the park, flanking the river, is the Ladies' Walk, very pleasant also. The Forbes Fountain which used to stand outside the Town House has been re-erected here on Ness Bank. The entire district is delightful.

There is much of interest in the outer environs of Inverness—but little space left to deal with it here. Some of the outer suburbs are described under Bona, Culloden, Raigmore, etc. The extreme western districts however, have not been touched on, including the Merkinch area north-west of Huntly Street, and the Carse Industrial Estate. Near here, Telford Road leads to the Muirtown Bridge over the entrance of the Caledonian Canal. Flanking it are two different and old-established distilleries, the Glen Albyn and the Glen Mhor. The bridge leads over to the Muirtown and Clachnaharry districts, once distinct villages; and here is the basin of Thomas Telford's famous canal, built between 1803 and 1822, one of the greatest engineering feats in these islands. Including its constituent lochs, it covers 60 miles, connecting the North Sea and Atlantic, and cost £1,311,000, an enormous sum in those days—indeed three times the estimate.

It is still much used, especially by the east-coast fishing fleets travelling to western waters. Muirtown has now a motel, overlooking the locks and basin; and the former Duff mansion of the name stands behind, part 18th century. There is also an early 19th century toll-house here.

Clachnaharry, half a mile further on, at the extreme western outskirts of Inverness, was a fishing village once, and the part below the busy A.9 highway is still very pleasant and unspoiled, with its cottages and jetty-like sea-lock of the canal. Clachnaharry House is now the Canal Offices. The name attracts attention, *Clach-na-Faire*, meaning the Watchman's Stone. On the high knoll above the village is a masonry cairn, erected by a Duff laird to commemorate the battle, undated but allegedly in either 1333 or 1378, between the Clan Chatton and the Munroes of Foulis, with a Latin inscription. But James the Second is mentioned therein, and he reigned from 1437–60. It was on this knoll, now with modern houses creeping near, from the rear, that the Inverness magistrates kept a watchman stationed, to look out for Highland raiders from the north-east. This kind of sentry-duty was a permanent Inverness preoccupation in the old days; and it is rather amusing that other rather kenspeckle Inverness place-names are really only variations on the same theme,

Tomnahurich being claimed by some to be the Watchman's Hillock —although others claim it as Boat-Shaped Hillock—and Ballifeary being Watchman's Village. These two places lie to the south, still on the western perimeter, almost a mile and a half away. Ballifeary is now a district of residential streets; and Tomnahurich is perhaps the most spectacular cemetery in Scotland, being an abrupt wooded hill, covered with graves right to the topmost ridge, 220 feet up. The views from the summit are very fine. Horse races used to be run—by the magistrates, oddly—round the base. The Tomnahurich Bridge over the canal is near by, carrying the main A.82 highway down the Great Glen to Fort William. Torvean, another wooded ridge, now being quarried into, the Hill of St. Bean, lies another half-mile southwards, with a former fort and cairns on its crest. A fine double-link silver chain was found here in 1808. The Torvean 18-hole municipal golf course is here.

Still further to the west of the canal and A.82 the ground rises in green terraces to the high Leachkin and Craig Phadraig ridge. At the base of this area is the ancient estate of Kinmylies, once an important barony. Above lie the extensive grounds and buildings of two great mental institutions, the very modern Craig Phadraig Hospital for the mentally defective, at the Leachkin hamlet, and further south the Craig Dunain Psychiatric Hospital, large red-sandstone buildings in fine woodland grounds, both with magnificent prospects. The hamlet of Leachkin (pronounced approximately Larkin) is now much enlarged with staff houses and has a post-office and school. Behind and above rises the lofty ridge, scattered with high-set crofts amidst whinny knowes, a chambered cairn sited near a small lochan towards the south. At the north end Craig Phadraig itself, now under Forestry Commission planting, is crowned by a fort said to date from 300 B.C. This has been recently excavated, and found to have been burned, rather than vitrified—a pleasant object for a walk, with views. This entire ridge is interesting, with a remarkably remote atmosphere, with winding narrow roads, to be so near the town.

Back across canal and river, the south-eastern outskirts of Inverness reach in ever-lengthening tentacles down the axis of the Culduthel Road and the B.861 to Strathnairn, from the Crown area. The large Hilton housing district, with its geriatric hospital, is unusual in boasting the Jolly Drover public-house as something of a community centre, with dancing facilities. The Old Edinburgh Road, following the line of Wade's military road, also runs through this area.

Further east, and completing our circle of the town's outskirts back to the Culcabock area where the A.9 enters, the long and attractive Kingsmills Road is used as something of a bypass for traffic. Half-way along this is the Inverness Thistle football ground, and set into its west perimeter wall is a large flat boulder called the Broad Stone, with a socket cut for a post. This is said to have marked the boundary of the parish church lands. The original 18th

Glen Affric, one of the most beautiful glens in Scotland

Inverness Episcopal Cathedral, with the burial-hill of Tomnahurich in the background

century Kingsmills building is still there, by the side of the Mill Burn, but no longer a mill, being used as a wine-merchant's store. On one side is the large former mansion, now the Kingsmills Hotel; and on the other, the main Inverness 18-hole golf course, flanking the Mill Burn's valley. Further down this valley is the Fraser Park, with playing-fields, tennis and bowling facilities and a curling-pond. And on the higher ground to the east, the extensive barracks area of the Cameron Highlanders Depot. The burn reaches the sea soon after.

Inverness has another claim to fame as the site of the well-known high-security prison of Porterfield.

All this is admittedly a highly inadequate survey of a large, important, fascinating and historic town, with a deal of great interest inevitably left out. But perhaps it is enough to whet the prospective visitor's appetite to discover more of the Highland capital, with an atmosphere all its own—and even possibly to send its own residents searching, here and there.

Kilmorack, the Dhruim, Aigas and Balblair. Although Kilmorack is a tiny hamlet, it is also the name of one of the largest civil parishes even Inverness-shire can produce, covering 143,000 acres of some of the finest scenery in Scotland, including the beautiful glens of Affric, Cannich, Farrar and much of Glass. It also contains the little town of Beauly. But since it measures 36 miles in length, it would be ridiculous to try to describe it as a whole. The various constituent glens therefore are dealt with separately, as is Beauly. This article will describe only the parish centre; the Dhruim area which is the name given to the deep wooded defile of the Beauly River for about 3 miles west of the church; the district of Aigas at the west end thereof; and Balblair, which is a growing community and housing area at the east side, only a couple of miles from Beauly.

Approaching, as do most visitors, from the main A.9 highway at Lovat Bridge—where the A.9 crosses the Beauly by a fine five-span bridge, built in 1811 at the then huge cost of £10,000—A.831 strikes off on the left almost immediately, on its way up Strathglass and over to Glen Urquhart and Drumnadrochit. Near the road-end is the large sand-and-gravel works of the Natcon Company, with the parish war-memorial monument high above. A few hundred yards further is Balblair, rather a strange community, in that it is not really a village or hamlet, but more like a detached suburb, without shops and services but oddly enough having no fewer than three church buildings—although two of these are no longer churches. The remaining place of worship is a notably modern building amongst the new houses and off the main road, belonging to the Free Presbyterian persuasion, and replacing an earlier cottage-type kirk near by to the east. The other former church is at the roadside to the west, a two-storeyed edifice with small belfry, now used as a workshop. This was the Free church, a different foundation. A Pictish symbol-stone from Wester Balblair is now preserved at Beauly Priory.

A mile on, we come to Kilmorack proper, the parish church and

hamlet of the name, set at the east end of the Dhruim, where the
Beauly River suddenly emerges from its constricting gorge, and the
Falls of Kilmorack were a noted beauty-spot and salmon-leap before
the activities of the hydro-electric engineers, who have harnessed the
waterfall area with a dam and placed a power-station immediately
below. The position is still quite dramatic, with the kirkyard perched
high above river and dam. The present church is not in the graveyard but across the road to the north. Unfortunately it is not now in
regular use, no doubt Beauly being more convenient for the
majority of worshippers. The building dates from 1786, renewed
1835, and is a lowish whitewashed kirk, with belfry. Its predecessor
was across in the kirkyard, an ancient foundation, for the name commemorates the cell of St. Morok, who was Culdee abbot of Dunkeld.
The Vicar of Kilmorok is mentioned in 1437; and the lands of the
Kirkton were granted by the Bishop of Ross to Fraser of Lovat in
1521. The graveyard has many old and flat stones, one bearing an
unusual floreate calvary cross, plus sword, with the initials A.M. cut
later. Another rose-red and elaborate floreate design near by, much
worn and also re-used, might be a similar amplification in which the
cross symbol has been all but lost. The manse near by, its garden,
like the kirkyard, reaching down to the cliff-edge, dates from the
18th century.

There are a large number of duns, or early fortlets, amongst the
low hills to the north of Kilmorack, above a crofting area and near
the Ross boundary. Why there should be so many in this Farley
district, so close together, is not obvious. Most such duns, being the
seats of warlike chieftains, were kept well apart.

The Dhruim is an unlikely name for a wooded gorge, *druimm* or
drum normally meaning a back, hence a back-like ridge. The area
is heavily wooded, and it may be that a whale-back minor ridge
would be evident therein, somewhere, before the trees covered all.
The defile takes a great bend southwards over 3 miles, birch, pine,
oak and alder steeply flanking the rushing Beauly, which sweeps
over a red-stone bed in a series of cascades—all now somewhat
affected by the dam further down. This is a notable salmon river.

The Aigas area is really just an extension of the Dhruim. It takes
its name from Eilean Aigas, actually a high, rocky and wooded islet
in the river, formed by a divergence and then coming together
again, of the Beauly, amongst waterfalls, a spectacular place. It is
three-quarters of a mile long, and a quarter-mile wide, and has long
been famous. Here was the refuge of the Lord Lovat, on the run in
1697. It still belongs to Lovat, and is now crowned by a fine house,
reached by a bridge from the east. At one time this was the summer
retreat of Sir Robert Peel. It was a renowned place for roe deer, and
sometimes even red deer found their way to it. Crask of Aigas is
near by to the north, a small hamlet just off the main road, in the
jaws of the pass—*craos* meaning an enormous mouth. Aigas House,
on a terrace site further west, is now an Old Folks' Home, run by the
County Council. There was an Aigas Ferry below, and there is now

an Aigas Power Station. Aigas Forest on the north covers all the hillsides to Erchless, 5 miles on, described under Strathglass.

Kiltarlity, Convinth, Beaufort and Eskadale. Kiltarlity and Convinth is a huge civil parish extending to no less than 80,000 acres, or 124 square miles, and embracing the south side of Strathglass down to within 2 miles of the Beauly Firth. It has Kiltarlity village, sometimes also called Aultfearn, towards its northern end, near Beaufort Castle, seat of the Lords Lovat, whose great estate covers much of the parish. Convinth, the southern and mountainous end, was a separate parish once; indeed the original, Kiltarlity being formed out of it as early as 1226. Its ancient graveyard, site of the church, still exists up in sylvan Glen Convinth. Eskadale is a picturesque wooded area on the south bank of the River Beauly—so named after the confluence of the Rivers Glass and Farrar—4 miles west of Kiltarlity.

Kiltarlity—the name comes from the Celtic Saint Talarican, who died 616—is a pleasantly sited rural community, something of an estate village for Beaufort Castle which lies a mile to the north. It is situated on the sizeable Bruaich Burn, half a mile off the A.833 road —which links the A.82 Great Glen highway with A.9, through Glen Urquhart and Glen Convinth. There is considerable new housing here, with the post-office, war memorial and a Free Church standing isolated a little to the south. But the parish church itself is not here. It stands, with a quite large school and playing-fields, half a mile to the east, off a different side-road, surrounded by its graveyard. This is not the original site, either, for the first Kiltarlity church stood nearly three miles to the north, on the bank of the Beauly at the far side of Beaufort Castle estate. So it is all a little confusing, especially as the latter is often called Lovat Kirk, yet Lovat itself is almost 5 miles to the east. Of this, more later. The present church dates from 1829, on a foundation of 1763, and has a heraldic stone from the distant earlier building built into the gable—the Fraser arms, naturally, dated 1626. The church is typically plain externally, with a double belfry. It has a U-shaped gallery and a high pulpit. In the graveyard, with no very old stones, is a peculiar mound, shaped rather like a cottage loaf, with a tree growing from it. This is the medieval baronial seat of judgment, from which rises the hanging-tree.

A little north-east of the church, in a field of the Belladrum estate, is a chambered cairn within a stone-circle, one of a number hereabouts. The mansion-house of Belladrum, of 1838, has been demolished, but its fine balustraded terrace-site above a little wooded valley remains, flanked by attractive pavilions. Also in the estate is a ruinous oblong 17th century doocot, and a temple-like mausoleum of the Merry family, with grave slabs, on a knoll amongst trees near the walled garden. The property is a picturesque one, amongst undulating wooded foothills. A single large standing-stone is erected at the south entrance.

Beaufort Castle, over a mile to the north-west, is the seat of the

17th Lord Lovat, 22nd MacShimi, chief of the Clan Fraser of Lovat
—although not of all the Frasers. These Highland Frasers, long so
powerful in Inverness-shire, derive from a brother of the celebrated
Sir Alexander Fraser of Touch, in Stirlingshire, who married a sister
of the Bruce, was his companion in all his campaigns, and became
Chamberlain of Scotland. One of his brother's descendants married
the heiress of the Bissets of Lovat, and so moved up into the Highlands, his successors becoming more Gaelic than the Gaels. Simon,
11th Lord, famous in the Jacobite cause, was created Duke of Fraser
by the Old Chevalier, James the 8th and 3rd, but was beheaded in
London in 1747, the last peer of the realm to die by the axe. The
present chief was a distinguished Commando leader during the last
war; while his father, the 16th Lord, was a major-general who
formed the Lovat Scouts. Beaufort Castle is a strangely Anglified
name—like Beauly near by—to find in the Highlands; but it seems
to have been so called since the 12th century. The existing great red
stone Scottish Baronial building, rebuilt in 1937 after a disastrous
fire, is said to be the thirteenth erected on the site—but this seems
almost too much! It stands high on the south bank of the River
Beauly, in a fine position. There is apt to be some confusion between Beaufort and Lovat Castles; but they were quite distinct. The
site of the old Lovat Castle is about 4 miles to the north-east, beyond
Beauly town, at the farm of Wester Lovat, where the Beauly River
enters the Firth.

North-west of Beaufort Castle a mile, still on the left bank of the
river, are the ruins of the original church of Kiltarlity, sometimes
called Lovat Kirk, in its ancient graveyard, all rather attractive
although somewhat neglected. Oddly, it is only a few hundred yards
away from Kilmorack parish church—but the wide river intervenes.
The ruins are of a very rough and early edifice, in the prevailing red
sandstone, much delapidated and with large trees growing from the
walling. The graveyard is still in use, and there are modern as well
as ancient stones. It was from here that the heraldic stone was
removed to the present church. There is alleged to be a cup-marked
stone, but not found by the present writer. Near by, a fine modern
bridge now crosses the river.

Back on the A.833, to the south-east of the castle, where a side-
road forks right for Kiltarlity village near Belladrum, is the modern
Fraser Arms Hotel, at the junction, quite large. At the far, southern,
side of the village, near where one more side-road goes off to
Bruaich, is another chambered cairn, in the corner of a field, with
ten outer monoliths and a close-set ring of lesser stones. And beyond
this about half a mile to the north-west, on still another side-road, at
Culburnie, is a still finer cairn, with seven large uprights, now in a
cottage garden. Some of these stones are cupmarked.

This entire area is heavily wooded, quite heavily populated also,
and attractive.

The Convinth part of the parish is notably different, lying some
way to the south, up the quite deep valley of the Belladrum Burn.

A mile up from Belladrum is Glackbea, a tiny hamlet amongst fine old trees, with a caravan-park. The road, the A.833, is now climbing. On the west is the large Boblainy Forest, clothing the foothill country, and to the east Battan Forest. Two miles beyond Glackbea and on into Glen Convinth, is the site of the ancient church of Convinth in its burial-ground, a pleasant scene in its quiet, empty valley. There is only a fragment of ruin now, with many old gravestones; but unfortunately no sign of the cupmarked and sculptured stones, five of them, which used to be here, one of them Pictish. This ancient chapel was dedicated to St. Lawrence, its patron in 1221 being John Bisset Younger of Lovat. A side-road striking eastwards across the Belladrum Burn, eventually leads north to Moniack and the A.9 and south over the hills to Abriachan and Loch Ness. A mile from Glen Convinth, at the roadside, is a little corrugated-iron church, seemingly no longer used. And a little further, where the road forks, is the former Glenconvinth school, only recently closed. The oddly named little community of Foxhole is here.

The crofting area of Caiplich is partly in this parish, on the high ground to the east, but dealt with under Abriachan. In the north-east direction 3 miles on towards Moniack, is the site of Castle Spynie, on a ridge near Easter Clunes. This was a small vitrified fort, or possibly a broch, not a castle. Across country a mile to the north-west, on another ridge of Phoineas Hill, is another fort, called Dun Mor. The Phoineas area here was quite renowned in Clan Fraser history.

The western rim of the parish stretches for no less than 30 miles deep into the mountain massif; but most of this is best described under Strathglass and Guisachan. The stretch west of Kiltarlity, on the south side of the Beauly, from Lovat Kirk to Eskadale, belongs to this topographical area however. A side-road from the new bridge and old kirk vicinity leads south-westwards through a pleasant former crofting district called Fanellan, with the large Ruttle Wood covering the hillsides to the west, and the fort of Dun Fionn amongst its glades. This road joins the Culburnie one from Kiltarlity in 2 miles, and thereafter enters the Eskadale area, flanking the river, a picturesque district of old woodland, green braes and some population. This is really Lower Strathglass, and opposite the Aigas vicinity on the north side of the river. At its west end is the hamlet of Eskadale, where is the quite large Roman Catholic church of St. Mary, pleasingly set on a wooded knoll. The whitewashed building was erected in 1826 by the then Lord Lovat, and has a bright and attractive interior, quite ambitious for a country church, with two aisles, pillars and arches. The modern burial-place of the Lovat Frasers is in the graveyard here. Here too are the graves of the Sobieski Stuart brothers, John (1795–1872) and Charles (1797–1880) who claimed to be the grandsons of Prince Charles Edward, and called themselves the Counts d'Albany.

The views from Eskadale are very fine, looking up the river to the high hills.

So far as sheer acreage goes, the greater part of Kiltarlity and Convinth parish consists of mountain and moor and forest, stretching far to the south-west, a high tableland dotted with innumerable small lochs, roadless, empty. There is one quite large loch, however, called Bruaich, over a mile long, distinguished by having a crannog or artificial ancient island in a bay at the north-east end, formed out of logs of pine, oak and birch. The Earl of Arran, fugitive in 1596, came to live on this remote refuge; as did the Dowager Lady Lovat a year or two earlier.

Kincraig, Insh and Glen Feshie. This is mainly the north-eastern area of the vast joint parish of Kingussie and Insh, itself a huge tract of highly dramatic country. Kincraig, on the main A.9 highway, is a very scattered village, lying midway between Kingussie and Aviemore, actually in Alvie parish, its railway-station now closed. Insh is a former civil parish, now *quod sacra*, with a large and well-known loch, an ancient and notable church, and a pretty village. Glen Feshie is a major and renowned valley, fully 12 miles long, with a foaming river, forming the southern border of the Cairngorm Mountains. The east side of the glen is in Duthil and Rothiemurchus parish.

Kincraig is a community rather than a village, with three distinct portions. Two lie along the A.9, the third down on the lower ground near the outflow of the Spey from Loch Insh. Where the road to this leaves A.9 is what might be termed the centre of the area, comprising the well-known Suie fishing hotel, a former church and hall, the one-time railway-station, and a number of scattered houses, all attractively within birch and pine woodland. A golf course lies on the western side of the road, and some way back stands Kincraig House, a late 18th century tacksman's house of good lines, now a farm. The small conical outlier of the Monadh Liath Mountains, An Suie (The Snout), 1775 feet, rises behind. The second section of the community lies a little further north, along but off the main road, towards the school on its knoll, where there is a sizeable group of modern housing. A quarter-mile further is a rather gaunt former Free kirk, now disused, above the road. One feels that Kincraig has been over-churched. The third and most attractive area, down amongst the birch-knolls and meadows of the Spey, centres round the post-office and shop, houses dotted at random in the trees, with fine views eastwards across the mouth of Glen Feshie towards the high Monadh Ruadh or Cairngorm Mountains.

Loch Insh is deservedly famous, over a mile long and wide, with birch-lined banks and splendid vistas all around. Queen Victoria described it as: "lovely, not a wild lake, quite the contrary; no high rocks but woods and blue hills as a background". It takes its name from the Gaelic *innis*, or island, the lofty pine-clad mound at the north end, once an island, and which is crowned by the parish church. The loch, which is really only a great widening of Spey, is famed for its fishing, and nowadays there is a canoeing school and centre here. The bridge which carries the road thither was built over the outflow of the Spey, beside the church-mound, only in 1879, before which there was only a ferry; indeed the true name for the lower part of Kincraig is Boat of Insh.

The kirk, on its spectacular steep eminence, is a highly interesting as well as attractive place, standing in its ancient graveyard amongst the Caledonian pines. The hillock is called Tom Eunan, Eunan being the Gaelic form of Adamnan; and the church was founded by that famous biographer and companion of Columba. His typical Celtic hand-bell is still its most prized relic. This bell used to be credited with supernatural powers, and it is alleged that once, when stolen and carried off over the Pass of Drumochter, it detached itself from the thieves and flew back to Insh of its own accord, intoning the while "Tom Eonan, Tom Eonan!" The kirk is typically long, low and whitewashed, rebuilt in 1792 but incorporating much earlier work. It is sometimes claimed to be the only example of a Scots church still exactly on the site used from the 6th century—but this finds many contesters. The interior is very lovely, bright, with a timber ceiling and clear-glass windows framing delightful prospects which it would have been a shame to hide, the window in the gable engraved to represent a Celtic cross. Beside the bell is preserved a large pewter flagon, of 1828. In the entrance lobby is the stone pre-Reformation font. There are many old gravestones in the kirkyard, and the burial-place of the Macpherson-Grants of Ballindalloch and Invereshie. A lovelier place of worship would be hard to find.

Striking off this road, which flanks the north shore of the loch, is a drive to Invereshie House, an old Macpherson lairdship now merged by marriage with Grant of Ballindalloch, the house, mainly early 19th century but with an early 18th century rear, set as all else here-abouts amongst picturesque woodlands. The side-road joins the B.970, the "back-road" from Newtonmore to Rothiemurchus, just beyond the loch, and in the woods here are scattered a number of fairly modern houses, pleasingly placed. Near by is the former Insh Manse, now a guest-house, where the west-side Glen Feshie road strikes off. The long, pine-clad ridge of Craig Farletter closes the view to the south, and here is the Osprey Highland Timber Works and saw-mill, scarcely to be seen in the woods. The B.970 continues south-westwards for 2 miles, highly scenic, to reach Insh village. This dates from the late 18th century, its cottages lining the road amongst the juniper bushes, with open views after the forest. Many are now holiday-homes. At the north end is a most charming little church, created out of a cottage, tiny, seating about thirty, with one window delightfully formed in the shape of a Celtic cross, with mosaic glass, the interior bright and serene. It was rededicated in 1968. The former school is now a residence. Beyond this a couple of miles is Drumguish and Tromie Bridge, described under Kingussie. The wide meadows of Spey below Insh are very apt to flood, so that Loch Insh often appears to be twice its true size.

Two miles back at the former manse, the dead-end road branches off up the west side of Glen Feshie, splendidly scenic. It halts at a locked gate, at Tolvah, 3 miles up, whereafter is the private road to Glenfeshie Lodge and deer-forest—available for walkers, of course. The views up this side of the glen are magnificent. A signposted Forestry Walk branches to the right a mile above Inch Manse. There used to be a connecting road to the west, to Tromie Bridge and Drumguish, but this has deteriorated to a footpath. The upper reaches of Glen Feshie are quite superb, with the ancient Caledonian pines around the Lodge as colourful as they are characterful. For tough walkers only, the track goes on up the rushing Feshie, through the narrow jaws of the upper glen, to where the Eidart comes in through a great gorge from the Cairngorms, and so across the peat-hags and desolation of the Geldie watershed, a burn which long ago stole the headwaters of the Feshie and now flows eastwards to the Dee. The track reaches tarmacadam again at Linn o'Dee, about 23 rough miles from the locked gate at Tolvah. Landseer used to stay a lot at Glenfeshie Lodge and painted many of his Highland pictures here; until about 1930 traces of a fresco by him adorned one of the huts which used to dot the pine forest opposite the Lodge. Only one bothy remains, as shelter for the benighted or storm-bound traveller.

There is also a road, and a longer one, up the east side of the glen. This is reached from Feshie Bridge, another lovely spot. Where the road from Kincraig joins B.970, aforementioned, the left fork brings one to Feshie Bridge in a mile, and there makes an acute bend of it, where there is need for caution, the narrow, arched 18th century bridge having a steep, twisting hill to the east. It crosses the surging, splendid river at a rocky gorge amongst braes of pine and birch, and here there are a few houses. The east Glen Feshie road forks off through the forest, southwards, and after half a mile reaches open prospects at Lagganlia, a place of sheer charm. Here are two or three houses and a former school. Also the Lagganlia Centre for Outdoor Education run by Edinburgh Corporation, an excellent and quite ambitious establishment for the encouragement of youngsters in the adventurous recreations of hill-walking, mountain-eering, skiing, rock-climbing, camping, orienteering, canoeing and nature-study. The Centre is purpose-built, with five red-cedar buildings in an 8-acre site in sylvan surroundings, including two ski-lodges for family or corporate groups, which may be hired; and good hostel accommodation, drying-rooms, lecture and recreation facili-ties for the batches of Edinburgh pupils sent up here, all under the supervision of an experienced residential Principal. It is a venture highly to be commended—although the dangers inherent in any confrontation with the high Cairngorms are not to be blinked, as sad history has shown. An observation-point and seat, on a knoll to the east, commemorates the opening, by Prince Philip, in 1970.

Just beyond the Centre, at the farm of Blackmill with its level fields rather unexpected in this wild landscape, is another unexpected feature—an aircraft and gliding landing-strip, with wind-sock. This is a very useful facility, especially when mountain-rescue is the order of the day. Here commences the great National Nature Reserve, of the Nature Conservancy, which, by agreement with the landed proprietors, covers much of the eastern Cairngorms.

This east-side road runs for 5 miles up the glen, open to the public, and is the best access for walkers wishing to climb the eastern summits, including the Sgorans Dubh and Gaoith (3635 and 3658 feet) by the Carn Ban More stalker's track. This begins at the shepherd's house at Achlean, where the road ends. In the meantime the road has run pleasantly parallel with the river, under the frowning cliffs of Creags Mhigeachaidh, Ghiubhsachan and Leathan, with the hill-foots clad in old pines and the moorland in new-planted forestry. The zigzag track up Carn Ban More is a long haul, but the views make it very worthwhile; and the tremendous precipices on the east faces of the Sgorans are breathtaking; with sheer drops of 2000 feet to lonely and desolate Loch Einich, and the cliff-girt corries of Braeriach (4149 feet) opposite. An attractive waterfall at the foot of the track can console those who do not feel equal for the climb, in the old Caledonian wood of Badan Mosach where there is a 2-mile Nature Trail. Just over a mile further up the main glen, by footpath, is the mighty and impressive Coire Garbhlach, the Rough Corrie, a huge fissure in the side of the mountain and a notable feature of the east Cairngorm flanks, rocky and grim, with 1000-foot walls. Opposite is Glenfeshie Lodge.

Altogether, this is a magnificent glen, deserving to be better-known. Queen Victoria made it the object of "a delightful and successful expedition with Albert" in 1860. It may become almost too well-known hereafter, however, for there have long been plans to drive a highway through it, to link up with the Deeside road which stops at Linn o' Dee. This would be an enormous amenity of course, for travellers, for meantime there is no cross-Scotland road over the Grampians, save the road-about southern route by Pitlochry, Glen Shee and Braemar, or the taxing north-about route via high Tomintoul. Such a road, of about 25 miles, would link the east and west coasts at last, and be a great asset to all the North-East especially —with so many East Coast fishing-boats working out of West Coast harbours. And it would offer a notable round-trip for tourists and travellers. That it would in some measure spoil the inviolacy of upper Glen Feshie is the sad price that would have to be paid.

Beyond Feshie Bridge the attractive B.970 proceeds through the woodlands of Inshriach Forest, past Dalnavert, an old tacksman's house of character, with its tree-girt and hidden loch of Lochan Geal, to Inshriach House, the pleasant mansion where Jack Drake has created a renowned nursery for alpine and rock plants, sequestered amongst the birch glades and junipers, a popular venue. Thereafter the road enters the Rothiemurchus area, described separately.

On the south-west side of Kincraig, on the A.9, beyond the golf course, is the ancient estate of Dunachton, long a Mackintosh barony, passing to them from the MacNivens in 1500, indeed once the seat of the chiefs of the clan, who built a castle, destroyed by fire in 1689 and never rebuilt. The present mansion, on a terrace site with memorable views, is a Victorian baronial pile. Below the house, and easily seen from the road, is a ruined private chapel and burial-ground, built by Captain George Mackintosh, 60th Regiment of Foot, who died in 1780 and whose arms decorate the gateway. Dunachton is by no means preoccupied with the past, however, for here is now established a Highland Wildlife Park, where wolves, bears and other animals which used to inhabit these mountains and woodlands roam free in 136 acres of pine and birch forest and open hillside.

Kingussie and Glen Tromie. Kingussie, a small burgh of just over a thousand population, in lovely upper Strathspey, might be called the Capital of Badenoch. Its name is frequently mispronounced as Kin-gussie; it should be Kin-yousie, from *ceann-guibhsaich*, meaning the head of the pine wood. Kingussie is also the name of a vast civil parish of no less than 116,000 acres, or 180 square miles, which includes villages and districts such as Newtonmore, Dalwhinnie and also the former parish of Insh. It is more convenient to deal with these separately, however. This item will describe only the burgh and that part of the parish comparatively near by, with Glen Tromie, a long but almost unoccupied valley probing into the empty mountains to the south.

The little town lies along the grievously busy A.9 highway, and suffers in consequence the constant noise and disturbance of heavy traffic along its main street. This could quite easily be bypassed to the east; and this is the only drawback to a position otherwise pleasing, at the foot of the Monadh Liath mountains, in the haughlands of Spey, where the Gynack joins the greater river, with splendid views of the Glen Feshie flanks of the Cairngorm, or Monadh Ruadh, range. It is, of course, a community geared to the tourist and holiday-maker visiting this renowned scenic area, and is notably well provided with hotels, guest-houses and overnight accommodation, plus facilities for sporting activities, fishing, pony-trekking, shinty, sailing and canoeing, as well as the more normal golf, tennis, bowling and even open-air draughts. There is a local newspaper printed here, the *Strathspey and Badenoch Herald*. The town was, however, founded towards the end of the 18th century, by the Duke of Gordon, intended as a seat of woollen manufacture, though this project did not prosper. There is today a small but up-to-date precision engineering factory near the railway station; and of course there are excellent shopping facilities for a wide area.

Kingussie has a very long High Street, with climbing side-streets on the west side, where is most of the housing, the development to the east being to some extent restricted by the railway-line to Inverness. Also the Spey haughs are very liable to flooding; indeed Badenoch means the flooded land. A bridge carries the A.9 and High Street across the Gynack at the south end, and here is the large Duke of Gordon Hotel, with near by the substantially built Catholic church of Our Lady, of 1931. Many of the shops on the main street are particularly good, one sports emporium being also the Tourist Information Centre. Half-way along is the Court House, of 1806, recast later. Further northwards is the Drill Hall, housing the Army Adventure Training Centre, set in country so admirably suited to such activities. Not far away is the Badenoch Ski School. Just behind the Drill Hall, on a grassy knoll, is the parish church, dedicated to St. Columba, standing in a not ancient graveyard. The building dates from 1792, remodelled 1824, and after a destructive fire, rebuilt in 1926. It is high-ceiled and bright within, with a rear gallery, a war-memorial stained-glass window and finely carved Celtic style panels on the pulpit, worked by a pupil of the Misses Martineau, of Rothiemurchus, who taught this art locally. Here is a memorial to the oddly styled Count of Serra Largo, one Peter Mackenzie of Tarlogie (1856–1931) a local man who achieved distinction far from Kingussie. A cast-iron and unattractive fountain is also erected to his memory near the railway-station. This not being the original kirkyard, there are no very ancient stones.

The first St. Columba's church stood at the side of the Gynack, in a quite deep den west of the town, off what is now the short Mill Road, and here is the ancient graveyard, now sadly neglected. A pity, for it is a site which ought to be cherished. A panel in a Celtic decorated recess in the north walling declares, "Here is the hallowed site of the old church of Kingussie, dedicated to St. Columba and according to tradition planted by himself." Then follows a highly interesting statement in Gaelic, translated "My Druid is Christ the Son of God." This linking of the ancient pagan priesthood with the Christian one is typical of the attitude of the early Celtic Church, as exemplified in its adoption of the Pictish symbol-stones for cross-slabs and the siting of churches within stone-circles. This graveyard is terraced on the steep bank, and there are many very old and primitive stones—clearly many more hidden under the grass. Amongst the tombs which may still be identified is a stone to Macpherson lairds, one of the wives being a daughter of the famous Cluny Macpherson, chief of the clan during the Forty-five period. This hallowed spot, tidied and some of the gravestones cleared, would be an added attraction for this visitor-conscious town, as well as fulfilling a duty to its storied past.

A little further up Gynack, the old mill has been pleasingly converted to a dwelling-house. Thereafter the stream becomes wilder, and the den tree-grown. Off the Gynack Road which flanks it is the former large sanitorium, set on a terrace amongst the birch woods, now St. Vincent's R.C. Home. This road leads to and ends at the scenic 18-hole golf course, on the higher ground, and to the caravan-site. Just before this is reached is an attractive linn and waterfall, with a rustic footbridge spanning the little gorge, and a woodland walk. On the other side of the den a similar dead-end road climbs to a residential area, with modern housing and tennis-courts. Up here is the Youth Hostel. A landmark is the tall, battlemented

clock-tower, gifted to the town in 1925 by a native who had emi-
grated to New Zealand. The views from up here are superb.

Below the High Street, on the levels, is much of interest, with side-
streets leading to the parallel Spey Street. At the north end of this
is the famous Am Fasgadh Folk Museum founded by Dr. Isobel
Grant and now taken over by four Scottish universities, with financial aid from the Pilgrim and MacRobert Trusts. This is a fascinating establishment, consisting of two traditional houses of the 18th
century, a modern lengthy agricultural hall, a croft-house and a
reconstruction of a typical Lewis black-house, with a small, heather-
thatched water-mill alongside. The exhibits range from the prehistoric right up to the last stagecoach to ply in Britain, from Kingussie to Fort William, in 1914. As well as entire rooms furnished in
period, there are costumes, weapons, documents, implements,
grind-stones and querns, relics and so on. The black-house and its
internal arrangements is particularly interesting, with its beaten
earth floor, central chimney-less fireplace, sleeping and cattle compartments and furnishings. There are innumerable items here to
catch the attention—such as the excellent horse-hair fowler's rope
from St. Kilda, Pictish ball-stones, a local cup-and-ring prehistoric
stone, and a plaster-cast of one of the famous Burghead Pictish bull
stones. Am Fasgadh is not to be missed.

In Spey Street, opposite the post-office and a small public garden,
is the Town Hall, undistinguished. Also the defunct Episcopal
church of St. Columba. And in a connecting side-street is the
Established Church-house, with the Chapel of St. Andrew, centre
for meetings and activities. Still further south and below the main
road, the railway-station still functions. Here is the Free church, the
large and modern High School, a well-known educational centre;
also the auction and cattle markets, successors of the fairs held
for centuries, in the old droving days, half a mile to the south, at
Pitmain farm, where the herds were sold and assembled before
starting on their lengthy journey by hoof to the South. The lairdship
of Pitmain, an important Macpherson one, in fact lay over a mile to
the north-west, in Glen Gynack, above the present golf course and
near Loch Gynack. Macpherson of Pitmain still lives locally but no
longer owns this estate. Near Pitmain farm, on the main road, is the
site of a Roman camp, not to be distinguished, Badenoch being one
of the few places mentioned by Ptolemy in the North.

An equal distance out of town at the other, northern end, is the
war-memorial, a monument standing prominently on a knoll east of
the road, which was formerly the judgment seat, scene of at least one
witch-burning. When the monument was erected, calcified bones
were found here. The modern cemetery is opposite.

Not in the burgh of Kingussie, indeed just over the border into
Alvie civil parish, but less than a mile further, is Lynchat, an
attractive hamlet of 18th century cottages, with a pleasant back-
lane. Behind this, amongst the green braes, on a little ridge between
two clumps of woodland, is a most interesting and well-preserved

Pictish weem, or earth-house, of the usual horse-shoe shape, about 40 feet long by 8 feet wide and 6 feet high, wholly lined and ceiled with stone slabs. This tourist-conscious area should make more of this relic of our proto-history, at present used as shelter for sheep. More than Picts and sheep have used this souterrain. Local tradition tells how a gang of freebooters, called the Clann MacGilleonoidh, found good use for it as refuge and stronghold, building a house of sorts on top, and disappearing into the bowels of the earth when hard-pressed. Just beyond Lynchat on a wooded hillock on the west side of the A.9, is a private railed burial-ground for the Macphersons of Balavil, not ancient, with various graves round a handsome monument erected in memory of the famous "Ossian" Macpherson (1736–96) with a portrait in marble. The controversial James Macpherson was humbly born at Ruthven near by, and from being the parish schoolmaster rose to such heights as to be buried in the Poets' Corner of Westminster Abbey. Not here shall we enter into the controversy about the authenticity of the Ossianic poems; but at any rate Macpherson earned sufficient by his pen to buy the Balavil lairdship and build a fine house. His successors are still there. The old tacksman's house of Balavil, sometimes feebly called Belleville, stands beside its walled garden, attractive; while Ossian's large mansion stands terraced much higher, designed originally for him by Robert Adam, but twice destroyed by fire and rebuilt, scarcely in the best of taste, for the site. It stands near the site of Raitt's Castle, a Comyn stronghold, scene of a notable massacre in the clan-warfare days.

Ruthven, from which Macpherson came, was once a large community, centred round the spectacularly sited Ruthven Barracks, on their mound in the Spey haughs less than a mile east of the town. The present ruins, fine as they look, date only from 1718, in the government's "pacification" of the Highlands after the Rising of 1715. But they incorporate something of the 16th century ruined castle of the Gordons, which itself succeeded an ancient and very strong fortress here of the Wolf of Badenoch. From here the vast lands of that royal ruffian were ruled, rather than from his remote hide-out at Lochindorb Castle in Moray. In 1451 the lordship of Badenoch passed to the Gordon Earl of Huntly—and sometimes the Huntly regime was scarcely more kindly. Here were imprisoned in 1546 Lochiel and MacDonald of Keppoch, before execution at Elgin. Bonnie Dundee burned the castle in 1689, and so it remained ruinous until it became an anti-Jacobite barracks. After Culloden the defeated Jacobite forces reassembled here—but Prince Charles was in flight and the cause foundered. They burned it to prevent its use to their enemies, and so it has remained. It is interesting that the farms of Gordonhall and Killiehuntly near by still commemorate the Gordon overlordship.

The "back-road", B.970, from Newtonmore to Rothiemurchus, via Ruthven, Insh and Feshie Bridge, is a delight—especially compared with the deplorably overburdened A.9. Two miles along it

Glen Tromie opens to the south, amongst the pine and birch forests, the road making an acute dog's-leg bend at the attractive single-arch 18th century bridge, with the peat-brown waters rushing beneath through a rocky gorge. The road up Glen Tromie is private, leading no less than 11 miles to Gaick Lodge, a shooting and stalking property of vast dimensions. At the lower end of the glen, around Killiehuntly tacksman's house, it is pretty, with green braes and open birch-woods. But higher it becomes rocky and bare, with the hills rising to nearly 3000 feet. Loch-an-t-Seilich, just before Gaick Lodge, is over a mile long, and is a somewhat bleak prospect. Here there was a disastrous landslide in 1799, killing five deer-hunters, a tragedy long known as the Loss of Gaick. A right-of-way foot-track leads on past Gaick past Lochs Bhrodainn and An Duin, over the county boundary into Perthshire and southwards all the way to Dalnacardoch Lodge, on the A.9 again, a very tough route of about 25 miles from Tromie Bridge, used by Montrose on one of his spectacular cross-country marches in 1645. Another, and even longer foot-track route branches off Glen Tromie about 2 miles north of Loch-an-t-Seilich to follow up the Allt Bhran and cross the watershed southwards some 5 miles east of the aforementioned route, coming out eventually at Calvine, Struan in Atholl. This is the Minigaig track, nearly 30 miles out of sight of a road. Obviously only for the most experienced walkers, these routes. The Minigaig Pass reaches 2750 feet.

Less than a mile north of Tromie Bridge, but some way off the B.970 through the pine woods—actually on a now disused road through to Glen Feshie which has become only a footpath, is all that is left of the sequestered and pleasingly situated crofting community of Drumguish, on the edge of the heather moors. There are now only half a dozen houses, and some are holiday-homes. However, who knows, Drumguish may yet blossom again, after a fashion, for the long-projected Glen Feshie Road through to Deeside, may well eventually pass this way. The walk to Feshie from here is very pleasant, rising high through newly planted forest, with wide views, just over 4 miles. At Tom Fad, near the Allt Chomhraig crossing, out in the heather, are the remains of a stone kiln for drying grain. Glen Feshie is dealt with under Kincraig and Insh.

Kirkhill, Aird, Bunchrew and Lovat. This area lies directly west of Inverness for some miles along the coastal plain of the Beauly Firth, traversed by the main A.9 highway. Kirkhill is both a quite large village and a medium-sized parish of 13,000 acres, formed out of the ancient parishes of Wardlaw and Farnua, or Farnaway, in 1618. The Aird is a fertile and sylvan foothill district to the south, dotted with small farms and crofts, flanking the Moniack Burn, and containing the Fraser estates of Moniack and Reelig. Bunchrew is a firthside estate and hamlet, lying well to the east, only 2 miles from the Inverness boundary at Clachnaharry. And Lovat is the farming area in the estuarine flats at the mouth of the Beauly River between

Kirkhill and Beauly town. Though most of the parish is fairly level coastal plain, it rises inland to well over 1000 feet.

Kirkhill village itself stands to the west on a low ridge a mile north of A.9, served by a loop-road, B.9164. It is a scattered and growing place, with considerable modern housing. This ridge was called Cnoc Mhoir, or Mary's Hill, translated Kirkhill; but the extension of it northwards, where was the old parish church, is called Wardlaw. Here, within a moulded arched gateway is the ancient graveyard around the site of the church—this latter now the burial-place of the Frasers of Reelig. Prominent here is the extraordinary 17th century Lovat Mausoleum, erected as such in 1634. It has a highly unusual belfry contrived out of a cluster of pepper-box turrets, such as the writer has never seen elsewhere. The church itself has gone, save for the foundations; but its position is marked by an enclosure of fourteen yew trees. There are many old gravestones, mossgrown and part-covered by grass, one broken slab inscribed with an early Calvary cross. Near by is Wardlaw House, dating from 1840.

The present parish church stands in the village, a low stone building with a double belfry, dating from 1790 recast in 1892. It is bright and pleasing within, with a small end gallery. Near by, in a lane to the east, is the old post-office building, a long cottage dating from 1722, and used by the military in the Jacobite troubles.

Below the village, eastwards, on the loop-road, is Newton House, a small estate with a ruined late-17th century mansion adjoining the more modern whitewashed house. Also a circular doocot with conical roof, dated 1783. The ruined mansion has been E-shaped, with fairly large windows and no apparent defensive features—although it is so covered in ivy that details are difficult. Where B.9164 joins A.9 is Bogroy, a roadside hamlet, with Free church, hall, war-memorial, store and hotel. Behind, to the south and back from the road, is the little and older community of Drumchardine, on one of the many narrow side-roads which wander up into the Aird district.

This pleasant area of wooded foothills and green braes is usually entered from a better road a mile further west, at Easter Moniack. The Reelig estate lies here, on the east side of the Moniack Burn, with a mansion having a classical pink stone front and older work to the rear, a very pleasant house which has been in the hands of its Fraser lairds since the 16th century, the present owner being the 20th in succession. Behind the house are some enormous cedar trees, planted in 1780 by Edward Satchwell Fraser to celebrate his return from armed service in the American War of Independence. His present descendant has demonstrated his initiative by starting a quite extensive cedarwood-chalet and stone-cottage development for visitors amongst the delightful woodlands of Reelig Hill, on the 2000 acre estate, all fully equipped. The Forestry Commission has taken over Reelig Glen, and has laid out a forest-walk therein, with many interesting things to see. There are bridges, grottoes and follies, with many exotic plants and trees, amongst the more normal vegetation, largely the work of James Baillie Fraser (1789–1856) author and traveller, who spent many years in India and Persia.

Moniack Castle lies near by across the burn, a separate estate, also in the Fraser family. It is an unusual building, being based on an L-planned early 17th century fortified house which was greatly altered in 1830 and made to appear distinctly odd by lowering the roof-levels of the two wings while at the same time slightly heightening the stair-tower in the re-entrant. Nevertheless much charm remains, with some authentic features. The stair-tower is notably wide, and corbelled out to the square at the top, though now finished with an unsightly sham crenellated parapet. The spouts for draining the original tower roof project some way below. The walls are very thick, and iron grilles still bar two of the small windows. Moniack was, and remains, a house of the chiefly Frasers of Lovat. In front is a collection of stones brought from near and far to form a sort of rockery, some of them standing-stones. One inscribed with the figure of a kilted man, from Balblair, was not in evidence, though said to be here.

Behind Moniack the road climbs to the little foothill community of Cabrich, very attractive, with old cottages and modern houses scattered amongst birches. An ancient well, which never runs dry, is here. The large quarry near by is no longer functioning. The road climbs and winds south-westwards, eventually by Clunes to Glen Convinth, passing near the site known as Castle Spynie, probably a broch, in Kiltarlity parish.

The Aird district spreads eastwards along the green foothills, with the Lentran estate and railway-station hamlet of that name under the isolated Inchberry Hill. Two miles east of Lentran is Kirkton—more properly Kirkton of Farnaway. There is only a farm here now, but once this was the centre of the early parish of Farnua, sited pleasantly under the other side of Inchberry Hill. There is still an ancient graveyard, within a tall wall, actually in the farm-steading, overgrown with weeds but even so showing burials as late as 1949. The oldest readable stone is dated 1748. One narrow slab has a curious crossed spoons device. Most of the memorials are for Frasers. There were Barons Corbet of Farnaway, vassals of Lovat. Kirkton Muir lies behind, on higher ground, with two hill-forts and a cluster of burial-cairns. Also a little school and some fine wild country of heather, old scattered pines and scrub birch, with some small farms. Englishton Muir adjoins to the east, and the farm of Englishton, down near the main road, has an old house of some size and character. The well-doing Bunchrew Burn comes down to the shore hereabouts.

Bunchrew estate occupies a peninsular position north of the A.9, its red-stone turreted mansion belonging to various periods from the 17th century nucleus, although little of the old work is to be discerned externally. A fireplace lintel is dated 1621. Now a Fraser house, Bunchrew at one time belonged to the Forbes of Culloden family,

Inverness Castle. Only the site is ancient

Ruthven Barracks, near Kingussie, once the site of a castle of the Wolf of Badenoch

Part of the Highland Folk Museum, Kingussie

descended from the Tolquhon line in Aberdeenshire; indeed the famous Lord President Duncan Forbes was born here in 1685. There is a quite large caravan-park on the property. And near by, on the A.9, is a scattered hamlet, with post-office; also a small Established church standing isolated on the way to Phopachy, another former Fraser lairdship, now a farm, to the west. Offshore at Bunchrew, out in the Beauly Firth, is the artificial island of Cairn Dubh, rising 3 feet above a sandbank at low water, 170 by 135 feet in dimension, with massive bog-oak beams for base, though small stones have been piled on top. Presumably this was a defensive feature.

Back at the other, west side of Kirkhill, is the low-lying triangular territory where the Beauly River enters the firth, a place of wildfowl and reeds and reclaimed farmlands and meadows, where the name of Lovat comes from. Here are the farms of Easter and Wester Lovat, Fingask and Groam. It is on Wester Lovat farm that the site of the ancient Lovat Castle is to be found, seat of the great baronial family of Bisset, founded in 1230. It was by marrying the Bisset heiress that the Frasers gained a foothold in this northern land, James the First creating Hugh Fraser 1st Lord Lovat in 1458. The Bisset castle lay north of the present farmhouse, in the steading area, and on what then was a thrusting promontory in the marshlands. The river then came much closer than now, and the site would accordingly be a strong one. The present farmer, an antiquary and keenly interested, has dug up many ancient stones and foundations. Seldom can an important castle have so completely disappeared. The Frasers preferred the Beaufort site 4 miles to the south-west.

Laggan, Cluny and the Corrieyairack. These well-known names represent a huge area of country in South Inverness-shire, in the centre of Highland Scotland, Laggan parish alone covering 235 square miles, or over 150,000 acres. Yet it is probable that fewer than 500 people live therein, and there is no real village or sizeable community to it all. Laggan Bridge, on the main A.86 east–west Newtonmore to Spean Bridge road, is a roadside hamlet, with the parish church, shop and two or three houses, but probably the crofting township of Balgowan, on a small loop-road a mile to the east, at the start of the Cluny property, has more inhabitants, a pleasant and authentic strung-out scatter of crofts on a hillside terrace. The Cluny district extends for 4 or 5 miles eastwards, and Loch Laggan is almost 7 miles west of Laggan Bridge and is itself 7 miles long, with a large artificial dammed extension westwards for another 4 miles. Laggan parish extends southwards right to the Perthshire border far below Loch Ericht and the Ben Alder area. And the Corrieyairack is not really an entity at all, being a term often used to describe a vast tract some 12 miles into the Monadh Liath Mountains north-west of Laggan Bridge and Glen Shirra—really the basin of the upper Spey, culminating in the daunting Pass of Corrieyairack, through a lofty and remote range above the Fort Augustus district of the Great Glen. Amusingly enough, *Lagan* means a small hollow. Altogether, then, this is a difficult area to describe, with enormous distances involved. Yet it is a very interesting one, and of great historical significance.

The present parish church, on the main road, at Laggan Bridge, lies east of centre, successor of one 6 miles westwards near Loch Laggan. It dates from 1785, rebuilt 1842, a grey granite edifice somewhat gaunt within and without, high ceiled, with a dominant pulpit and unusual side-galleries. It stands on a mound by the Spey, in a graveyard wherein are some oldish stones and the burial-place of the Macnabs of Dalcholly. There is an interesting modern grave enclosed in a basket-work surround, filled with heaths and suitable plants. Mrs. Grant of Laggan, whose *Letters From the Mountains*, and other published works, achieved renown, was wife of the minister here from 1779 to 1803. There is a school and post-office near by. And not far away across Spey, what is left of another church, the prominent steeple of the former Free church, stands as a landmark. It was near here that General Sir John Cope made his celebrated about-turn in 1745.

Dalcholly, now a large farm, lies a mile away westwards, easily seen but less readily reached, the Spey intervening. It is served by difficult private roads, one by a small hump-backed Wade bridge over the River Mashie. A fine old tacksman's house of the 18th century, whitewashed and with stone slates, it was tenanted for generations by a family of Macnabs, under Gordon ownership. How they survived in the heart of the Macpherson country, and at permanent feud with the neighbouring Macphersons of Strath-mashie, is a wonder. Not only did they survive, however, but built a little chapel and graveyard almost a mile to the west, on a spur of the thrusting wooded hill of Black Craig, now represented only by five cypress trees and a few daffodils, above a little road-junction. The house of Dalcholly was one of those in which Cluny Macpherson took refuge in his hidings after Culloden.

Eastwards of Laggan Bridge, on the A.86 opposite Balgowan township, is Gaskmore House Hotel, a fairly modern converted mansion in a fine position in the wide valley. The war-memorial stands on a rocky outcrop not far away. A mile further and Cluny estate woodlands enclose the terrace site of the former Macpherson chiefs' castle. The present mansion, which can be glimpsed from the road, is not beautiful, successor of a true castle, and built after the original was plundered and burned by government troops. It is an Adam house, with feeble sham turrets, less than successful architecturally, but commodious and in a pleasant situation. Queen Victoria thought to buy it, but decided that the region was too wet, and went to Deeside. It no longer belongs to Cluny Macpherson. Many tales could be told of the Macpherson chiefs; but the Cluny of the Forty-five inevitably steals the limelight, owing to his remarkable survival for nine years as a fugitive on his own lands, with a price on his head—not quite so remarkable when the lands, their remoteness and distances are taken into account. His clansmen and tenants paid two sets of rent throughout, to maintain him. Various refuges, caves and "cages" are pointed out still, but more frequently, undoubtedly, he was able to lodge in the houses of his clansmen and friends. There is a small family burial-ground at the roadside at the west end of the policies. The hillsides grow very steep and rocky here, at the south end of the famous Macpherson hill of Creag Dubh, and high up amongst the crags is Cluny's Cave. Also, prominent on one of the lesser summits is a monument to Flora, wife of one of the Clunys— while away to the south-west, on Creag Ruadh, is a similar monument to her husband, 4 miles off but very visible. Below these features Lochan Uvie, a double loch, nestles picturesquely amongst the Glentruim woods. The Newtonmore area opens beyond.

Where the Free Church steeple rises south of Laggan Bridge, the A.86 sends off a branch, A.889, climbing due southwards out of Strathmashie to Dalwhinnie and the main A.9, 7 miles, by Catlodge. Here the cottages were once an inn, and a cairn commemorates one Calum Macpherson, a noted piper of Cluny's. Piping was taught here until comparatively recent times. The road rises to 1241 feet through the empty hills, with the quite large and little-known Loch Caoldair a mile away to the west, under craggy summits.

The River Spey has swung away due westwards towards the Corri-ayairack area, but the A.86 continues down what appears to be the main valley but which is in fact Strathmashie, the vale of a major Spey feeder, the Mashie. There is much woodland, Strathmashie Forest, some ancient, some replanted. Just beyond the former Macpherson mansion thereof there is another old military bridge alongside the modern one over the Mashie, and a waterfall just a little higher. Over a mile on, another river comes in from the south, and dramatically, the Pattack or Pataig, plunging down in a series of cascades from Loch Pattack high amongst the Ben Alder hills not far from Loch Ericht. The Pattack and the Mashie pursue similar and parallel courses only about 2 miles apart. Where Pattack reaches A.86 and turns sharply westwards to run into Loch Laggan, is a highly scenic tree-topped, rocky gorge with large waterfall, a favourite with visitors.

Just beyond is Inverpattack Lodge and the little school, hall, cottages and former lime-kiln of Kinlochlaggan, still half a mile from the loch-head. A little nearer, on the north side, is Aberarder Lodge, up a drive; and close to it is the ruined pre-Reformation church of St. Kenneth's or St. Killen's, a long narrow building, roofless but the walls still entire, in a weed-grown graveyard. There is a stone font built into the side of the entrance, and old gravestones within as well as in the yard, some very rudimentary. Beside the path is one thin, flat upright bearing a large incised cross and no other detail— apparently of very early date. The burial-place of the Macphersons of Strathmashie is here. There is a traditional story that the church was built by one Allan nan Creagh, a noted freebooter, in repentance for deeds done, at the behest of a witch in the shape of a cat—the cat, of course, being the emblem of the Macphersons, like other Clan Chattan tribes—with picturesque details about roasting another cat on a spit, while a concourse of sympathetic animals chanted "Bad treatment of a cat!" (Naturally, in Gaelic.) However, St. Kenneth's was built long before Allan's time.

The great loch of Laggan now opens south-westwards, 7 miles long and less than one mile broad, heavily wooded on the south side. At the head is the Lochlaggan Hotel, present post-office and shop, and a new development of timber chalets for visitors on the motel style, all in a pleasing position. All the long south side of the loch is private, the huge sporting estate of Ardverikie, one of the great deer-forests of the land. The huge castellated mansion 2 miles down, easily seen across the loch, was built only in 1840 by a Marquis of Abercorn, later burned and rebuilt. In 1847 it was occupied by Queen Victoria. But royalty had a much earlier connection, for the name is only a corruption of Ard Fergus, and a mound in the garden is said to be the grave of King Fergus—and some say three other early monarchs. There was a King Fergus of Dalriada died in A.D. 501, 14 generations before Kenneth MacAlpine who united Picts and Scots. In the loch near by are two islets, the Isles of Kings and of Dogs, assumed to have been the sites of Fergus's hunting-seat and of his kennels. The area around still abounds in game, and the loch itself is famous for its great trout, allegedly of up to 14 pounds. Not always realised is the fact that there is another loch here, little more than a mile behind that of Laggan, hidden by a narrow inter-vening range of hill, Lochan nan Earba, the Little Loch of the Roe-deer. Lochan and little are odd terms for a 4-mile long water, divided in the centre by a half-mile link. The mountains behind and to the south-west are particularly impressive and interesting, much appreciated by climbers in the know, a large group of rocky and spectacular peaks, with great cliffs and deep corries, the highest Beinn a' Chlachair (3569 feet) and Beinn Eibhinn (3611 feet). These reach towards the Ben Alder area. They make a dramatic skyline for South Laggan. There is a foot-track from Kinloch, within the Ardverikie estate, over into the valley of the Pattack, up past Loch Pattack, and on through the Ben Alder Forest to Loch Ericht, and along its north shore to Dalwhinnie, about 16 tough miles.

West of Loch Laggan and its overflow, with the dams, out of which rises the Spean, we are really in Lochaber of the West High-lands.

Back at Laggan Bridge again, an attractive but twisting side-road leads off due westwards along the north bank of Spey. In 2 miles is the Spey Dam, with a mile-long artificial loch behind it. At the head of this, at Shirrabeg, an old Wade bridge is rather oddly islanded out on the flats, where the line of the present road has diverged from the military one which from here probed its long and difficult way for the Corrieyairack and Fort Augustus. Glen Shirra branches off to the left just ahead, and Glenshirra Lodge has a picturesque wooded situation at the mouth, with a large sawmill and timber-yard behind. There is a loch called Crunachan, a mile long, hidden in Glen

Shirra, and a foot-track past it and over to Kinlochlaggan, about 4 miles.

Less than 2 miles further along the road Garvamore is reached, an estate-house now, in level but remote surroundings, which was once a barracks for troops building the road in 1732, later becoming an inn for cattle-drovers. Prince Charles Edward stopped here in 1745. In time it became a keeper's house. The long two-storeyed building is presently being restored, and the fine stone slates of its roofing cast down for modern replacement. There is said to be a good timber stairway within. A modern house adjoins. Half a mile on, the metalled road stops at Garva Bridge, another hump-backed, double-arched military bridge. Beyond its gate the state of the road notably deteriorates, and continues to do so as it rises to 1183 feet, and then on and on into the wilderness. By the time it reaches the summit of the Corrieyairack Pass, 8 miles from Garva, it is 2507 feet high, and a major engineering feat for the times—for it had to be passable for artillery—however disrepaired it has become today. It is a long, lonely road, and always was; a stout Land-Rover might cover it now, but you would be better afoot or on a garron. Hill Burton called it "the most truly Alpine road in the British dominions". It is a great pity that it should not have been maintained, for it would have made a wonderful and scenic tourist route. At Melgarve, 4 miles above Garva, the road trends slightly northwards to follow the Allt Yairack, while the Spey swings southwards a little for 3 miles to little lonely Loch Spey—a modest mother for so major an offspring. The watershed lies immediately behind, and within a few hundred yards of the Spey's headwaters those of the River Roy rise to flow to the Spean and the Atlantic. The surrounding Monadh Liath mountains are probably amongst the most lonely and unvisited in all Scotland.

Moy. The name of Moy is not uncommon in Scotland, being merely a corruption of *magh*, a plain. But this Moy in Central Inverness-shire is particularly renowned because of its connection with the chiefs of the great Clan Mackintosh—even though anything less like a plain would be hard to visualise. It is a fairly narrow glen area flanking the main A.9 highway, where the Monadh Liath Mountains come very close to those of Strathdearn and Strathnairn, 10 miles south of Inverness; and consists of a scattered community, a large estate, a loch and the huge conjoint civil parish of Moy and Dalarossie, the southern half of which is dealt with under Tomatin and Strathdearn.

Moy itself is a fairly clearly defined area. The Moy Burn rises in the lowish heather hills to the north-east, widens presently to the mile-long Loch Moy, amidst woodlands, in the fairly narrow throat of the mountains, which its shares with the highway and the main railway-line; and then proceeds on southwards, as the Funtack Burn, to join Findhorn in 2 more miles. There is no real village, but a few houses dotted at intervals, mainly connected with the estate, and the essentials of a community—small school, hall, post-office and parish church, all on the west side of the loch. Moy Hall, the Mackintosh seat, lies in woodland to the north-east of the loch-head; and the large planted Strathdearn Forest clothes the lower slopes for 3 miles on the east.

The loch is picturesque and interesting, half a mile across, with a sizeable wooded island of some 6 acres in the centre. On this are the remains of the 14th and 15th century Castle of Moy, inhabited until 1665. There is not a great deal left of this island stronghold, although it must have been large, capable of holding a garrison of 400 on one occasion. Two ovens were discovered in the ruin, wherein could be baked 150 lb of bread at a time. There was a little castleton on the island also, for a paved street was unearthed here—so it must have been a crowded spot, at times. It is said that Duncan, the 11th chief, who built the castle—presumably previously he had a mainland house—when he held his house-warming declared his relief that now he could sleep in peace from fear of Allan MacRuari 4th of Clanranald. Word of this pronouncement was quickly carried to Clanranald, who at once set out from Moidart for Moy. In curraghs, under cover of night, the MacDonalds crossed to the island, and surprising the sleeping Mackintosh, took him captive to Castle Tiorrim in Moidart, where he was kept for a year and a day, being then released with the admonition: "Never be free from the fear of MacDonald!" Many stories could be told of this castle and its picturesque lairds, including the one of the heroic breaching of the dam at the south end of the loch by a single Mackintosh clansman with an auger, to sweep away a host of besieging Cummings. A 70-foot obelisk now rises on the island, in memory of Sir Aeneas, the 23rd chief, who died in 1820. There is a smaller artificial islet near by, built of boulders, Eilean nan Clach, with a great stone on which prisoners were chained. There used to be a gallows here also.

Opposite, on the mainland, stands the parish church, small, plain and harled, dating from 1765 and repaired 1829, with five doors no less. It is simple and attractive within, and well lit. The Mackintosh chiefly pew is slightly elevated, at the other end from the pulpit. The graveyard is rather neglected and very full, with many old stones. On a knoll above the loch-shore is a tiny watch-house which has been two-storeyed. The former manse near by is now the post-office, with a small caravan-park.

The present Moy Hall is a squared, two-storeyed modern house of 1957, on the site of a huge mansion which had grown through successive generations, still the seat of The Mackintosh. Prince Charles Edward slept at Moy Hall in 1746, and the four-poster bed is still shown. There are many precious relics here. King George the Fifth was a frequent guest at Moy. Clan gatherings are held here at intervals.

The old military road to Inverness probes westwards from Moy through the hills to Strathnairn; and in this area, over a mile, is a pass through which Highland cattle-raiders used to drive their booty home from the rich lowlands around the Ness, provided a "collop" was duly paid to Mackintosh by way of toll. Here was the scene of the Rout of Moy, in 1746, when Prince Charlie was staying with the famous "Colonel Anne", Lady Mackintosh, and Lord Loudoun with government troops from Inverness sought to capture him. Four men manned the pass and in the darkness shouted to various supposed clans and groups to take the right flank and the left—and so alarmed the Hanoverians that the whole 1500 fled, not only back to Inverness but crossed the Kessock Ferry into Ross and safety. A circular hollow in the hill here, called Ciste Chraig an Eoin, was the dramatic place of concealment for Mackintosh women and children in time of trouble, accessible only through a very narrow opening.

South of the loch, Glen Moy opens out into the little strath of what is named the Funtack Burn; and a mile down this a small side-road branches off eastwards at the farm of Dalmagarry. In less than another mile this crosses the Funtack by an attractive, humped and single-arch bridge known as Moy Bridge, near Milton of Moy. The dead-end road follows the burn on the north side, which soon joins the River Findhorn in its wide valley, the river here spreading itself grievously over the flat meadows with great acres of stones. Past the lonely farm of Ruthven, the road begins to deteriorate as the valley narrows, and it ends at Shenachie 4 miles on from the A.9. Only a foot-track continues to follow the winding course of the Findhorn through the wild and lonely area known as The Streens, and soon into Nairnshire.

Nethy Bridge and Abernethy. The Nethy is a river which flows out of the eastern flank of Cairn Gorm itself, rising at 2700 feet at the col known as The Saddle—oddly enough only about quarter of a mile from Loch A'an and the source of the River Avon, but many hundred feet higher. It flows due northwards down Strath-nethy for 11 miles, where the major Dorback Burn joins it, the last 5 of this in the famous Abernethy pine forest. Then on a further 4 miles to join the Spey, half-way to which is the village of Nethy Bridge tucked into a re-entrant of the woodlands.

Nethy Bridge is one of those well-known Strathspey holiday resorts which have long and deservedly attracted discerning visitors, and of recent years undergone a notable advance over the boom in Cairngorm winter sports, plus the increase in popularity of such activities as pony-trekking, hill-walking, orienteering, canoeing and outdoor pursuits generally. The village, with a resident population of only about 400, is pleasingly situated on the B.970 south-side of Spey road to Grantown, 4 miles south-west therefrom, at its bridge over the rushing river and at a junction of side-roads. Most of the village is not on the main road at all, but up the two side-roads which flank the Nethy eastwards into the forest area, in picturesque fashion. The land to the west is more open, the level green haughs of Spey—but the Abernethy Forest in every other direction encloses Nethy

Bridge. Abernethy is a civil parish as well as a great forest, and has been since before the Reformation.

Nethy's bridge itself is quite attractive, of mid-19th century date, three-arched and slightly humped. Beside it is a rather ugly public fountain inscribed "Drink Hearty" but otherwise indecipherable. This main-road part of the village is rather dominated by the very large Nethy Bridge Hotel, on the north side near the former railway-station. Behind this lies the 9-hole golf course, with the war-memorial prominent near by. Close to the bridge are shops, and a ceramics studio making hand-painted pottery. Up the southern of the two riverside roads stands the present parish church in general use—although the old one is also used in summer, as described hereafter. This former Free church is very pleasantly situated amongst the trees of what is just a corner of the great forest. It is quite attractive within, also. The parish area now includes those of Advie and Cromdale also. The other side-road has more houses, leading up to the detached "suburb" of Causar, at a cross-roads, and passing on the way the site of an 18th century iron furnace, using charcoal made from the Caledonian pines. This road continues on for 5 miles eastwards, climbing from 700 to 1200 feet over the heather foothills, to meet the old military road (now A.939) from Grantown to Bridge of Brown and Tomintoul.

The hotels and guest-houses of Nethy Bridge have good facilities for transport to the Cairngorm ski-slopes, instruction in skiing, and so on. There is salmon fishing available on the Spey, and instruction courses in this also. Bowling is also catered for. And the Nethy Bridge Sheep-Dog Trials are well-known.

In a detached position almost a mile north of the village—although still on B.970—is the original parish church of Abernethy, an old whitewashed, many-windowed and crowstep-gabled building with a round belfry, quite large, remodelled in 1900, standing in its kirk-yard. It is roomy within, and bright, a preaching kirk with centrally placed pulpit, all refurbished—but owing to lack of artificial lighting is not used in winter. A large pre-Reformation font lies in the grave-yard; and there are many old flat stones, inscriptions mainly obliter-ated.

Just beyond the kirk is the interesting feature of Castle Roy. This is one of the simplest fortalices in the land—and one of the earliest, dating from the 13th century, a former stronghold of the Comyns. It consists merely of a lofty rectangular wall about 20 feet high, round which once would run a parapet and wall-walk. There is something of a rudimentary square tower at the north-west angle, a single arched doorway and an arched window (probably later) a garderobe in the south-west angle—and that is really all. No doubt there would originally be timber lean-to buildings within. It stands on a green knoll, and has remained remarkably complete considering its great age. Presumably it had an exciting history; but if so, none seems to be known.

Not far away, on the lower ground nearer Spey to the west, is the old tacksman's house of Coulnakyle, a rather handsome whitewashed building of the 18th century, with hipped roof and dormer windows, rather unusual, on another green knoll, once the seat of a branch of the Grants, now a farmhouse. The road running past it leads to the 16-span trestle-bridge over Spey at Broomhill.

East of kirk and Castle Roy another side-road curves away south and east back to Causar, passing a fine modern school for Nethy Bridge on the way. But before this is reached, a still lesser road strikes due eastwards, heading towards the great wood of Craigmore, which clothes the hill of Carn na Loinne, really a detached part of the Abernethy Forest, behind the large modern mansion of Aultmore on its fine terraced site. Below this, and nearer the road, is the House of Abernethy, an interesting establishment, a pleasant mansion grown out of the original manse, of 1760, and still with thick walling in parts. It stands in wooded grounds of 30 acres, with an old walled-garden, and is now the Abernethy Outdoor Centre. This embodies a new concept, combining a Christian-oriented holiday-home and outdoor activities centre for young people. There is accommodation for forty, and also cedar chalets for an overflow or family hire, with the former steading used for games and canteen facilities. Also additional premises at two cottages and the former railway-station, all run by the Abernethy Trust, from Glasgow, with a resident director—an interesting venture.

At the Causar crossroads, the right fork leads south-eastwards for a mile, to stop at Lettoch farm, another one-time Grant lairdship. Beyond this, foot-tracks radiate into the forest, or up to the Braes of Abernethy area where, flanking the Dorback Burn, many crofts and small farms sit amongst the knolls and foothills, below the mountains, an interesting district rather similar to that at the other, southern side of the forest, at Tulloch, described under Boat of Garten. Many paths for walkers may be explored hereabouts, some leading up into the high eastern Cairngorms.

At the west side of Nethy Bridge is the attractive E-planned laird's house of Rothiemoon, of the 18th century, nicely set amongst trees. And to the south stretches all the lovely fastnesses of the Abernethy Forest, a huge extent of natural pinewoods similar to those of Rothie-murchus and Glenmore, covering perhaps some dozen square miles, one of the great forests of Scotland. It climbs steadily towards the south, from 700 to over 1000 feet, threaded by many roads and tracks—quite easy to get lost in, for a while, even in a car, for there are no lengthy prospects. Here the pines, many of them ancient Caledonian giants, grow out of heather, blaeberries and junipers, deer roam, squirrels dart and capercailzie and blackcock abound. The forest sends off a major extension south-eastwards towards the high hills, round the eastern base of the Glenmore range, through which runs the River Nethy itself. Traversing it from Forest Lodge, near which cars can be taken, makes a magnificent walk, for all standards of walkers—from the stroller of a mile or two, to the determined strider. For this track, by Rynettin, the Memorial Stone (to a young man called Maxwell, killed at Ypres, who loved these hills) and the Ryvoan bothy, leads in fact, either right-handed through the Ryvoan pass to Glenmore, or straight on, up and up over the main Cairngorm range, by Bynack and the Lairig an Laiogh to Glens Derry and Lui and the eventual Dee, a mighty tramp. On the Nethy, not far from Rynettin, is one of the old log-floating dams, of the 18th–19th centuries, for sending the immense quantities of timber felled hereabouts surging down to Spey on artificial spates, there to be floated to Garmouth and Kingston ship-building yards.

The western section of Abernethy Forest, with the delightful Loch Garten and the osprey haunts, is described under Boat of Garten. A pity that this western approach to the area should be somewhat spoiled by the large, ugly and all-too-evident electricity station and pylon complex near one of the access-roads to Loch Garten.

Newtonmore, Glen Banchor and Glen Truim. Newtonmore, the well-known Badenoch holiday resort, is a large village flanking the main A.9 road, in the huge civil parish of Kingussie, picturesquely set where Truim and Calder join Spey, amongst pine and birch woods, at the foot of the Monadh Liath Mountains. Glen Banchor is the valley of the Calder River, which strikes north and then west for about 5 miles; and Glen Truim reaches southwards, threaded both by the railway-line and the A.9, towards Dalwhinnie and the Pass of Drumochter.

Newtonmore is an attractive place, full of character, and only spoiled by the incessant heavy traffic of the A.9 pounding through it, and which, like Kingussie, could easily be bypassed. It is a scattered community, the best bits of it back from the main street, with much open ground and trees everywhere. Very evidently it sets out to attract and cater for visitors, and there are many hotels, including the well-known Balavil Arms, whose far-seeing proprietor was almost the first to recognise the vast potentialities of this area in providing sporting facilities such as pony-trekking, deer-stalking, skiing, mountaineering and so on. Guest-houses and bed-and-breakfast accommodation also proliferate. The golf course is pleasantly situated along the haughs of Spey, and there are tennis, bowling, putting and shinty facilities. Newtonmore is a famed name in the Highland sport of shinty. The Newtonmore Highland Games are held here annually in August, with which are associated the Clan Macpherson Rally and March—for this is the "capital" of that great clan, and the Clan Museum is a feature not to be missed. It is housed on the main street, in a handsome, purpose-built edifice of 1970, and attractively laid out, with a rich collection of relics, portraits, weapons and papers, of interest to a far wider public than Macphersons or indeed other clansfolk. Here are displayed, for instance, the famous fiddle of James Macpherson, executed in 1700, who composed and played *Macpherson's Rant*, that renowned tune. He was the illegitimate son of a laird of Invereshie and a beautiful gipsy, and grew up a man of great stature, good looks and daring character—albeit a freebooter after the Rob Roy tradition. A talented musician, when eventually hanged for his crimes, he played the famous tune, offered his fiddle to anyone who would care for it, and when none responded, broke it over his knee. The pieces were picked up and brought to Cluny Macpherson, the chief. Here also is the blanket used in his wanderings by Prince Charles Edward, also other relics of the Prince. And the equally renowned Black Chanter or *Feadan Dubh*, a talisman of the clan, alleged to have fallen from heaven at the famous battle on the North Inch of Perth in 1396, described by Scott in *The Fair Maid*. There is an imposing candelabrum presented to Old Cluny, the 20th chief, 700 ounces of pure silver; the original MS of the *Memoirs of Chevalier Johnstone*, Prince Charlie's A.D.C., a notable account of the Forty-five Rising. And many more.

Newtonmore has a rather unusual church. Not being a civil parish, St. Brides is not in an old graveyard, and stands west of the main street, the exterior unimpressive and unconventional but the cruciform interior is very pleasing, well-lit with new woodwork and panelling. Four small stained-glass windows are in the choir, of good design and size. There is some old pewter communion plate from an earlier church. At this west side of the village is municipal housing as well as substantial stone villas, amongst the trees. There are no very ancient buildings, for this is not the original village. That stood to the south west, in Glen Banchor; but an English sporting gent bought the property in 1828 and, objecting to having the population on his doorstep, moved them down here. There are some oldish cottages on the main street, however, a public hall of 1913, and the very modern Highlander Motel. Also a small wood-girt loch with greenish water at the east side of the road, picturesque, with tennis-courts close by. The school is set back some way to the east, where the prospects open out, and hereabouts is considerable scattered housing, rather pleasant. Just beyond the last houses to the north is a grassy mound in trees, east of the road, which represents an ancient burial-cairn where bones were excavated.

The A.86 from the west, Fort William–Badenoch road, joins A.9 here, and a quarter-mile along this, beside the former Macpherson tacksman's house of Biallid is the site of a pre-Reformation chapel of St. Bride's, in an old graveyard, called Clad Bhryde. Nothing of the kirk remains, but the graveyard is still used, and extended. There are many old stones, and the burial-place of the Macphersons of Glenbanchor. The River Calder out of Glen Banchor flows past, and here is crossed by a graceful single-arch bridge built by Telford in 1820.

Glen Banchor is not very evident from Newtonmore, but is well worth a visit, particularly on foot—although a narrow driving road does go up it for over a mile, on the north side, climbing high above the river in the process. The valley takes a major bend to the south-west after a mile, and opens out to fine prospects of the Monadh Liath and into the four side-glens which join here. The long lofty

ridge of Creag Dubh, the famed Macpherson hill, forms the south
flank, grown with birch woods. Hill tracks lead off up the tributary
glens, that up the second-last to Loch Dubh in Coire nah Laogh,
the Calves' Corrie. Only one house now remains in Glen Banchor,
where formerly was a quite large community, a school and considerable fertile land.

The A.9 south of Newtonmore crosses Spey by a large modern
bridge, of quite attractive design, for once, and proceeds up Glen
Truim, Truim joining Spey 2 miles south of the village, directly
under the east face of Creag Dubh—the slogan of Clan Macpherson.
The hill is long, steep and rocky, and contains high on this south-
east face, above Loch Uvie, Cluny's Cave, where the clan chief hid
during his 9 years of hiding from government forces after Culloden.
Near by is a highly unusual waterfall, which only functions after
very wet weather—but when it does drops 500 feet in spectacular
fashion. Half-way along this eastern flank, on the A.86, at Biallid-
beg, is a small walled graveyard at the roadside, formed interestingly
around a former burial-cairn, containing the graves of Macphersons
of Biallid and others, some quite modern. At the far end of the hill
is Cluny Castle, once the seat of the chief, burned down after the
Forty-Five. This is dealt with under Laggan, however.

The lower part of Glen Truim is richly wooded. Glentruim House
has still a Macpherson laird. It is a castellated pile dating only from
1834, with a private burial-ground in the policies. An Ordnance
Survey point here shows the precise centre of Scotland between east
and west. The main A.9 continues up the glen on the east side of
the river, with a great gravel-works eating out the heather-clad
moraine near the road-fork at Raliabeg where the B.970 "back-road"
to Rothiemurchus strikes off eastwards. Ralia is another old Macpherson tacksman's property, now a shooting-lodge. Two miles
further up, Loch Etteridge lies hidden a short distance to the east,
and Etteridge Bridge, a single-arch Wade bridge, is near by. The
Falls of Truim are in this vicinity, in the wooded gorge, below road
and railway. Still further south is the disused double-arch early 19th
century bridge of Crubenmore, near Crubenmore Lodge, a former
shooting-lodge now a hotel. After this, upper Glen Truim widens
into a featureless and rather bleak open valley, between the heather
hills, for 4 miles, to Dalwhinnie, Strathspey and its woods and forests
being left behind.

Petty and Gollanfield. It is strange how little the name Petty
means today, when it was so important once. The names of Gollanfield and Dalcross have come to mean more, although mistakenly—
for Gollanfield is only a former railway-station, given the name of a
farming estate and hamlet, and the true Dalcross is not even in this
parish, though the Inverness Airport and its neighbouring Industrial
Estate have been so-called, for some reason, again no doubt connected with another former small railway-station. The railway age,
towards the close of last century, was a sad despoiler of place-names,

for the stations were often given the names of communities which they served but which might be a considerable distance away, and often these tended to supersede the originals; with so many stations now abandoned and derelict, the situation is the more absurd. Petty, formerly Petyn, is in fact a large parish of over 10,000 acres, lying along the Moray Firth coast 5 miles east of Inverness, comprising the pre-Reformation parishes of Petyn and Bracholy; and was for long a very powerful thanedom, lordship and barony. Today there is only the parish church of that name, and the farm and tiny hamlet of Newton—which should, of course, be Newton of Petty. There is another decayed hamlet at Fisherton, near the coast; and the larger hamlet of Tornagrain, central. But the castle of the lordship, now called Castle Stuart, still remains in good order, a fine place. A part of Culloden Moor and Forest comes into the parish.

Castle Stuart stands on the B.9039 road to Ardersier and Fort George, a mile north of the A.96, towards the west end of the parish and near the head of the shallow Petty Bay. It is a magnificent example of the early 17th century fortalince, with some rather unusual features. It was rebuilt in 1625 by the Stuart Earl of Moray, on the foundations of an earlier castle, on the L-plan, with two five-storey wings. These are really square towers, that to the west finishing in a flat roof and more modern crenellated parapet, with a stair-head caphouse topped by an open crown of masonry, also late work. The eastern tower is crowstep-gabled, and enhanced with three conical-roofed angle-turrets. Highly unusual are the two diagonally placed two-storeyed and gabled angle-turrets gracing the north-east and north-west corners of the main block. The windows are regularly placed, and there are many wide-splayed gunloops, also unusual in a house of this fairly late date in the defensive period —possibly relics of the earlier castle. The basement contains four vaulted chambers, with a great arched fireplace and oven in the kitchen to the west. The Hall on the first floor measures 37 by 24 feet, a fine apartment. There is a tradition that James the Fourth resided in the earlier castle, whether on this site or at Halhill is not clear. We read that, in 1624, Clan Chattan went to "ane house which the Earl of Moray hath now of late built in Pettie called Castel Stuart, they drive away his servants from thence and doe possess themselves of all the Earl of Moray his rents and of his handsome residence". This attack was by no means unusual, for the Mackintoshes of Clan Chattan had been the old Lords of Petyn, and presumably still reckoned that they retained some right to it. They continued to hold Dalcross Castle near by—and still do. There were "Herships of Pettie", harryings, in 1502 and 1513. Castle Stuart is also still the property of the Earl of Moray, although long let to a tenant. It stands, tall and impressive, quite close to the roadside. The original castle of the Thanedom of Petyn, at the former Halhill, is dealt with hereafter.

The parish church lies behind Castle Stuart to the north, on a little cul-de-sac, on higher ground above the bay. Unfortunately it is now unused and shut up; and certainly it is not conveniently placed for present-day worship. But it has a fine situation and is a place of character and interest. It dates from 1767 and 1839, but has a fragment of the ancient church, dedicated to St. Columba, at the east end, with pointed windows and doorway, the latter flanked by two large cast-iron cats holding the standards of Clan Chattan. This is the burial-place of the Mackintosh chiefs, the cat, of course, being the emblem of Clan Chattan. Here was brought, from Dalcross in 1704, the body of the 19th chief, escorted by 2000 clansmen, after it had lain in state for 40 days. The burial-enclosures of other chiefly families of Clan Chattan are also in the kirkyard. And here was interred the chief of the MacGillivrays of Dunmaglass, who fell at the Well of the Dead, at Culloden. There are many other old grave-stones, as well as modern ones, for the kirkyard is still in use; and there is a watch-house to guard against body-snatchers. Near by, to the west, are two whin-covered knolls, which are in fact ancient burial mounds and cairns. In the bay which they overlook is an interesting feature known as The Travelling Stone of Petty, a boulder of some 6 feet cubed, which used to mark the boundary between the properties of the Earl of Moray and Forbes of Culloden. In the severe winter of 1799, sea-ice in the bay moved this for over 250 yards to the west—no doubt to the Earl's satisfaction. West of Petty Bay projects for over a mile into the Moray Firth the triangular promontory of Alturlie Point, long called The Island, or Isle Inch-martin. There was a burial-ground, and presumably the site of St. Martin's chapel, at the tip.

Where the B.9039—the airfield road—joins the A.96, is Newton; and at the farm here is a stone-circle or ring-cairn, with concentric rings, near the railway-line. Another fragmentary circle lies at the south side of the A.96 a mile further west, but this is just over in Inverness parish, and dealt with under Culloden.

The present parish church of Petty, formerly the Free church of 1849, stands in a more convenient position at a road-junction on the A.96 2 miles east of Newton. Beside it is a parish hall built by the Earl of Moray in 1897. Also the war-memorial. Just opposite, in Tornagrain Wood, is the former ancient well, known as *Tobar na gul*, the boiling fountain, a spring which spouts up intermittently, and which for long was the water-supply for the hamlet of Tornagrain, a little to the south on a side-road, the name thought to be merely a corruption of the well's. This excellent spring was utilised to supply water piped to the war-time airfield, out of which Inverness Airport has developed; a concrete cistern and a small pumping-house now scarcely improve the aspect. The Airport lies to the north-east of Tornagrain Wood, a useful amenity which calls for no description. At the north-west end of it is the Dalcross Industrial Estate, of 43 acres, in a notably non-industrial setting of woods, farmland and shoreline, with eight factories at present occupied. It is a compara-tively small development—but much more is planned, in connection with the projected new town of Culloden, with its possible 20,000 population. The oil boom off the Moray Firth may make this ambitious scheme over-modest. The airfield and Industrial Estate are built on what were the lands of Connage. Connage and Petty were often bracketed together in the old days. There is still a farm of Connage, nearer Ardersier. It was an important place, the residence of the 7th Laird of Mackintosh in 1368, which passed to the Ogilvies of Findlater, and from them to the Earls of Moray.

North-west of the airfield area, reached by a short side-road from the B.9039, is the hamlet of Fisherton, now only a few cottages on a slight rise above the coast, with fine views both to north and south. It was once a fishing-village of some size, with twenty-four boats—but significantly, no harbour. Oysters were fostered here. Directly inland from Fisherton a mile is the Dalziel area, where is the school, and a level-crossing at the former Dalcross Station. In this vicinity is thought to have risen the former castle of Petyn, called Halhill. This was a very important stronghold, seat of the Thanes and later Lords; but it has completely disappeared. It was burned in the Hership of 1513, but rebuilt—although it is just possible that the rebuilding took place at what is now Castle Stuart.

The Gollanfield and Flemington area, the one-time Bracholy, lies at the east end of the parish, 4 miles from Castle Stuart. Gollanfield is a farming estate, with a hamlet of cottages and a public hall, set along a side-road from the former Gollanfield Station—which would have been better called Flemington, for it is nearer to Flemington House. This latter small estate was a Rose property, and its offices were said to have been built partly out of the stones of a stone-circle —although nothing of this is apparent now. Flemington Loch lies over a mile to the south, half a mile long, amongst whins and broom, near the Brackley, or Bracholy, cross-roads.

The pre-Reformation parish of Bracholy is now represented only by the old burial-ground and two farms, Brackley to the south and Milton of Braiklaich to the west. The graveyard is still in use, with stones ancient and modern, but there are no signs of the ancient church. A Culloden Pottery and Crafts establishment is near Brackley farm. General Wade's military road passes Flemington, Brackley and Gollanfield Station, on its way to Fort George.

Raigmore, Culcabock, Inshes and Leys. This area south and east of Inverness royal burgh, and almost suburban thereto, is part of the large and far-flung civil parish of Inverness and Bona, of 23,000 acres, spreading on either side of the River Ness and the Caledonian Canal. For descriptive purposes this not only falls to be dealt with apart from the urban area of Inverness, but itself is best divided up. Here we deal with the area between Culloden and Inverness town and the parish boundary with Dores on the south, an area of perhaps 9 square miles. Raigmore is a former estate and now the large and well-known hospital; Culcabock another former estate and village, site of the golf course and now the scene of much housing development;

Inshes is the district to the west of the A.9 at the foot of the long climb towards Drummossie Moor and Daviot; and Leys is a wide area to the south-west still comparatively free from "development".

The Raigmore Hospital is now very extensive and serves a vast area of the North, its many buildings dispersed over the former Mackintosh estate. To the north of the property is now a development of high flats amongst old trees, served by King Duncan's Road —this was Duncan the First, slain by Macbeth in 1040, who made a base of Inverness. Near by is the Red Cross House, a fine modern training-centre for handicapped young people. Still in the grounds of the hospital is a fragmentary ring-cairn stone-circle, a new hospital roadway realigned so as not to disturb it. To the east is Stonifield House, a pleasant small Georgian mansion of 1820, whitewashed, with pilastered entrance.

Culcabock is now a busy traffic hub, where the main A.9 highway approaches the town, just opposite the hospital, and the roads fork, B.853 branching off to the left, westwards, to provide a sort of awkward ring-road through the southern environs, passing the golf course first of all, and A.9 continues northwards on the old line, down the hill to the level of the old town. Little aspect of the former village remains, and modern housing prevails. Refugees from the Battle of Culloden hid in the cellars of Culcabock House in 1746, which still stands back from the road-junction. At the north side of the junction is the semi-subterranean feature known as King Duncan's Well, and across the road, beside the filling-station, a stone commemorates the supposed temporary burial-place of Duncan, after he was slain by Macbeth, and before the body was taken to Iona for permanent interment. Duncan's castle was, of course, near by on the Inverness Crown area.

The Inshes area lies south-eastwards along the A.9 a further mile or so from the town. This is a former old barony of the Mackintoshes and still a private estate, set in the skirts of the braes that rise to the high tableland of Drummossie Moor, down from which tumbles the Inshes Burn, with some pleasant cascades. The present mansion dates only from 1767, with Victorian additions, harled and with some good panelling. The older fortalice is now represented by only a doocot near by, but this has been in fact a flanking-tower of a court-yard castle, and is crowstepped and provided with gunloops. Dell of Inshes lies lower on the burn, and Balvonie of Inshes higher. Much of the sandstone used in the building of Inverness came from quarries here. The B.9006 to Culloden Moor strikes off the A.9 near Inshes, and a mile up this is the Muckovie area, with a scattering of houses blessed with magnificent views across the Firth. Here is what is sometimes called the Raigmore Tower, actually an early 19th century folly or gazebo, octagonal, whitewashed and now constituting part of a house, quite a prominent landmark. A similar distance up the A.9, southwards, is the large Drummossie Hotel, now being called the Royal Stuart Motor Hotel. The Daviot parish boundary is a mile on.

South-west of Inshes is Leys area, on the same green hill-skirts, centred round Leys Castle, a large modern castellated mansion in the Tudor style, surrounded by the farmlands of Milton, Wellton, Braeton and Balmore of Leys. The farm of Druidtemple stands a mile north-east of the castle, on slightly lower ground, and here, across a picturesque little ravine, in a grove of trees, is a very fine and large chambered cairn, its inner ring of close-set stones almost complete, with ten outer standing-stones, one 10 feet high. The views from here are notable. Below this is the large farm of Castle Heather, not however a castle.

A mile to the west, now all but engulfed in the ever-spreading housing schemes of Inverness, is Balloan farm, a late 18th century building with an older range to the rear, and an interesting lectern-type multi-faced sundial of the 18th century in the garden. Not far to the south-west is the large hospital at Culduthel, in a wooded estate; and to the south near by, in open ground, another chambered cairn. But a more notable feature stands near a fork of side-roads half a mile further to the south-west. This is the famous Boar Stone on Knocknagael farm, a massive Pictish monolith, of early type prior to the cross-slabs, depicting a magnificent and spirited representation of a wild boar, with mirror symbol above. It is about 7 feet high and now enclosed within a strong mesh fence to prevent further initialling by vandals. Obviously this hillskirts area near the mouth of the Ness has been a very important area for our prehistoric and proto-historic ancestors.

A little way to the west of this is Ness Castle, like Leys no true castle but a pavilion-type Georgian mansion of 1840, with portico, now a hotel, in a wooded park on the south bank of the River Ness and built to replace the older Fraser laird's-house of Torbreck. Torbreck farm, just to the south, has also a ring-cairn stone-circle, only the inner ring remaining, remotely set on the edge of woodland. Dores parish boundary runs alongside.

Rothiemurchus, Inverdruie and Loch an Eilean. Rothiemurchus is a place of superlatives, an area which it is almost impossible to over-praise or indeed to describe adequately. Of late years it has become, on its fringes at least, much better known than heretofore, owing to the dramatic development of nearby Aviemore and the road to the Cairngorm ski-slopes via Glenmore. But this, happily, has not really spoiled the great extent of this lovely place, the largest stretch of ancient natural-regeneration Caledonian pine forest in all Scotland.

A great extent is no mere figure of speech. The Rothiemurchus Forest covers a large area of the north-facing foothills of the Cairngorm or Monadh Ruadh range, an area not easy to delineate exactly, for what is casually described as Rothiemurchus tends to merge imperceptibly with the contiguous forested areas of Glenmore, Inshriach and Abernethy. It might be fair to describe as Rothiemurchus proper an area of about 20 square miles lying east and south-east of Aviemore. But there are other aspects of Rothiemurchus which may comprise rather different boundaries and conceptions—the ancient civil parish, now united with Duthil to the north, and the huge Grant landed estate of the name. Inverdruie is, not a village, but the only real community in the forest, and Loch an Eilean is the well-known beauty-spot, roughly central in the area, one of the most picturesque and famous in the land, with its Comyn's castle-island.

To most people Rothiemurchus undoubtedly means a pine forest —but a special kind of pine forest, which once clothed practically all Highland Scotland, and far higher up the hillsides than the present tree-level, here or elsewhere. Today there are only small patches of this forest left here and there, with quite a large stretch at the Black Wood of Rannoch, in Perthshire, and this Rothiemurchus, the greatest surviving entity. It is important to grasp how very different this kind of Caledonian forest is from the regular and disciplined conifer plantations which are becoming an ever-increasing feature of the Scottish scene, thanks to the Forestry Commission. First of all, the pines themselves are not the same. These are slow-maturing great trees, not the usual slender and pointed shape of conifers but with a rounded outline similar to deciduous trees. Their trunks and boughs are a rich red-brown and can grow to immense thickness, their needles bottle-green, beautiful and noble trees which reach ages to rival and outdo most ancient oaks. They grow normally fairly wide-scattered, certainly not in ranks and rows, rising out of a rich carpet of heather, blaeberries and juniper-bushes, to provide the most romantic and lovely glades and vistas anywhere to be seen, is this author's opinion, the open spacing giving light and colour and long prospects. This area of Speyside obviously ideally suits these fine trees. They are not, as it were, museum-pieces, carefully pre-served, but are, as they have long been, "cropped" regularly but judiciously by the estate—as distinct from the shameful wholesale clear-felling of the war years. Always the value of these pines has been realised—but not always in the right sense. In 1728 Sir James Grant sold 60,000 trees for £7000. The Rothiemurchus forest yielded its lairds enormous sums "the profit being sometimes about £20,000 in one year". A large Grant labour force was employed felling, dragging the logs to the rivers and floating them down Spey to Garmouth and Kingston on the Moray coast, where the ship-building yards built of them the clippers which sailed the Seven Seas. The turning of wood into charcoal for iron-smelting was also long an industry. Dams are still to be discerned here and there for gaining a sufficient head of water to float off the log convoys. But long before all that, the Vikings had been cutting down these pines for their long-ships, and burning the forests to smoke out the inhabit-ants—an activity followed by the Wolf of Badenoch and other marauding chiefs. The wonder is that any survive to delight us today. As well as the Grant estate, the Nature Conservancy now controls a large part of this area as a National Forest Park, so that the trees are at length safe. Except from fire. Frequently careless visitors cause the destruction of stretches of the forest, unhappily, and a few years ago a vast area was devastated before the fire could be brought under control, the scars of which will long remain.

Finer walking-ground than the innumerable paths of the Rothiemurchus Forest would be hard to imagine, either as an end in themselves or on the way to the hill-climbs, the Lairig Ghru, Glen Einich or Ryvoan and Loch Morlich. Deer, roe and stag, red squirrels, capercailzie and blackcock are often to be seen, and the pine-forest birds such as siskins, goldcrests, long-tailed tits and tree-creepers, are everywhere.

Turning off the main A.9 at Aviemore, a new broad road crosses Spey and leads through 7 or 8 miles of loveliness to Glenmore and the ski-grounds. A mile from Spey is Inverdruie, where the backroad, the B.970 from Feshiebridge, joins. This place has changed considerably of late. There is a large showroom, craft centre and tourist shop here now, and the old smiddy on a sort of central green gone. Dellmhor, modern housing but quite attractive, lies beyond the present parish church of St. Columba, small, in granite, its bell over the porch and rather dull within, with varnished woodwork. There is an interesting memorial to members of the talented Martineau family who did much for this neighbourhood. A little to the west is the more interesting Episcopal church of St. John the Baptist, a small but fine cruciform building, white-harled amongst the pines, bright, attractive and serene. The architect was Sir Ninian Comper. Some few graves flank it, and there is a modern consecration-cross beside the door, dated 1913–27. Across the road, behind the woodland tennis-courts, lies first the Tourist Information Bureau where even guides may be hired, and then Corrour, formerly a mansion of the estate and now a guest-house. Inverdruie House, belonging to Grant of Rothiemurchus, stands back a little to the south, a tall, grey plain house facing out over one of the most splendid prospects in all Scotland.

From Inverdruie the roads branch out. As well as the B.970 southwards, a mid-road leads directly into the forest for Loch an Eilean, by Blackpark and The Croft. Another short road goes northwards to the River Druie, here nearing its confluence with Spey. While the main leads on to Coylum Bridge a mile, and then forks. To deal with the last first, for a major road this one is quite delightful, traversing the open woodlands amongst the heather and junipers. On the left is the very large, modern Coylumbridge Hotel, of Messrs Rank, an attractive complex in lovely surroundings, with many extra facilities, such as an ice-rink and pony-trekking, unquestionably one of the finest sited of the hotels in Scotland. Half a mile further is Coylum Bridge itself, where the road crosses the scenic Druie, the B.970 going on northwards by Pityoulish to Nethybridge and Grantown, and the Glenmore access road swinging away due eastwards through the forest. There is one old-fashioned and one new craft-type shop at Coylum Bridge, a few houses and a popular camp-site delightfully set by the river. Also the gates to

Drumintoul Lodge, the seat of the present Grant of Rothiemurchus.

Just to the west of the camp-site a foot-track leads off through the pine glades, to fork presently, the left-hand path leading splendidly for 2 miles to the Cairngorm Club footbridge over the sparkling Bennaidh, a main Druie tributary coming out of Glen Einich, and on another mile or so to a renowned junction of paths well known to all walkers, often called Charing Cross, or just The Crossroads. In this picturesque spot various options are open. The main track continues, climbing now, to the famous Lairig Ghru pass to Deeside, another five quite strenuous miles to the summit thereof, leaving the tree-level in just over a mile, the views becoming superb. The Lairig is one of the toughest places in the land, even though called a pass, strewn with enormous fallen boulders for miles, which the walker has to clamber over, and reaching a height of 2733 feet—no place for the tyro unescorted, or the inadequately shod or clad. It is a long, long way further to what is called Deeside, even though the Pools of Dee are actually in the Lairig itself, and the description of "Public Footpath to Braemar" ought to be taken with a pinch of salt! A commanding officer of the Scots Greys omitted to do that, a number of years ago, and led a so-called recruiting march through from Braemar to Aviemore—having to shoot many horses with broken hocks in the process. But treated with proper respect the crossing of the Lairig Ghru is a wonderful experience. But be warned—it can manufacture its own climate, irrespective of what may prevail "outside", and the results can be lethal. Other routes from the crossroads take the walker to Loch Morlich, or to the Rothiemurchus Hut, or up on to the Cairngorm summits.

Back near Coylum Bridge, the right-hand fork leads on through the forest to another cross-roads in 2 miles, a more open one this, near Auchnagoichan, from which one can strike left to the metal footbridge again, right to Loch an Eilean, or carry on southwards into Glen Einich. This is a long glen, and it is almost 7 miles further to lonely Loch Einich at the head of the glen, under the frowning precipices of Sgoran Dubh and Braeriech—but well worth the tramp for good walkers. This is all part of the Rothiemurchus estate. The cliffs above the long, narrow loch have to be seen to be believed, 2000 feet high. Straight ahead, above the loch-head itself but higher by 1200 feet sheer, is an extraordinary place, a vast water-logged tableland of perhaps 8 square miles, called An Moine Mor, the Great Moss, lying between the mountains of Carn Ban More, Cairn Toul and Braeriach, playground of the mists and of the deer and the eagle, one of the wildest spots in these islands. Braeriach, with its magnificent scooped corries, at 4248 feet, is the third highest mountain in Britain, really a range in itself, and Cairntoul is only 7 feet lower.

Returning to Coylum Bridge and tarmacadam, the access road goes on eastwards flanking the Luineag now, another major feeder of the Druie, from Loch Morlich. It is a little difficult to assert where Rothiemurchus ends and Glenmore begins in this mighty forest, but

it is probably sensible to make the division at the west end of Loch
Morlich, over 3 miles on. Here is the estate boundary. On the way
there are few features to describe, but consistent beauty and grandeur backed by tremendous views of the Cairngorm giants on the
right and the four lesser but shapely summits of the Glenmore Hills
on the left. Loch Morlich and Glenmore are described separately.

From Coylum, the B.970 strikes over open moorland, some of it
war-felled forest again replanted, 2 miles to Pityoulish. This is a
pleasant spot, a green, birch-clad hill, a serenely beautiful loch half
a mile long, and an old estate with a small mansion and cottages.
Pityoulish Hill reaches only 1465 feet, but stands isolated. At its far,
northern, side is the pass known as The Slugan, or Throat, threaded
by a climbing track, now a forestry road, which leads through from
Glenmore to Abernethy, an ancient route. On the south side of
Pityoulish Hill lies the picturesque old Grant tacksman's house of
Achnahatnich, on the edge of the pine forest, with heart-catching
vistas, reached from the Glenmore access road.

As has been indicated, Loch an Eilean may be approached by
various routes. I personally prefer that from the Doune area, a mile
south-west of Inverdruie. This is reached via the B.970; and half-
way to the road-end is the site of a one-time boring-mill for water-
pipes. If this seems unlikely today, it must be remembered that metal
pipes are a comparatively modern development, and the Caledonian
pines provided ideal material for making long and long-lasting
wooden pipes; indeed much of London's piping once came from
Rothiemurchus. Nothing now remains of the mill, at a bend of the
road. Where the loch-road strikes off eastwards is a Celtic-decorated
column commemorating Dr. James Martineau, once Principal of
Manchester College, 1805–1900, who had a house locally, and much
advantaged the district; also tribute to his daughters, who taught
wood-carving hereabouts. From here to the loch is a short mile, by
a burnside under the steep wooded hill of Ord Ban (1404 feet.)

Loch an Eilean is deservedly one of the best-known and most-
photographed lakes in Scotland cradled in the pinewoods below
mighty mountains. It is irregularly shaped, almost a mile long and
less than half that in width, with the little island which gives it its
name towards the north end. The ruined castle, which occupies
almost every inch of the islet, is comparatively small and dates
probably from the 14th century. It is often claimed to have been
built by Alexander Stewart, Earl of Buchan, son of Robert the
Second, the notorious Wolf of Badenoch, who may have used it; but
it probably was a Comyn stronghold before that. It has been of the
courtyard type, a square keep with high curtain-walls and lesser
flanking-towers. An underwater zigzag causeway is alleged to extend
out to it—as was contrived elsewhere. Ospreys long nested here,
until comparatively recent times—and perhaps will come back
again, now that they are breeding near by at Loch Garten. There is
an excellent triple echo from the lochshore opposite the castle to the
west. A fine Nature Trail circumnavigates the loch, and there is a

Tourist Information Centre at the north end, with a former limekiln near by. A splendid walk may be taken by pushing on south-westwards beyond the head of the loch and past little Loch Gamhna, and so through a sort of forested pass into Glen Feshie and Inchriach Forest.

Back on the B.970, at the other side of the loch road-end, is the private drive down to The Doune, the former main Grant mansion of the Rothiemurchus estate, now unfortunately abandoned and derelict, although the estate is kept in good order. The original mound of the dun rises behind—seat of the early Thanes of Rothiemurchus. These were the chiefs of Clan Ay, or Shaw, who owned the lands until the Grants gained them in the 16th century. Alastair Ciar Shaw was Thane in 1469. The mansion was large, and dates from various periods, but the heraldic lintel from a moulded doorway built into the northern walling, came from Muckerach Castle near Dulnain Bridge. It shows the Grant arms, dated 1598, with the motto *In God is all my Trest*. The Doune is surrounded by pleasant parkland whereon Highland cattle graze. It seems a pity, amongst all the development in this area, that the fine house should not be used for something. It served as a hotel, at one time.

Not far away to the south, and easily accessible across a narrow crescent of field on the right side of the B.970, is the roofless church and still-used graveyard of the former parish, a lovely and peaceful place on a wooded bank above the Spey. The ruins, although on an ancient site, are not themselves very old, the church having been rebuilt more than once. There is a belfry, and, built into the west gable, a lintel of some age showing a 6-petalled flower. The kirkyard is highly interesting, however. Here is the famous grave of Seath Mor, a Shaw notable who distinguished himself at the great clan-fight before the King at the North Inch of Perth in 1396. Five oddly shaped stones stand loose on his grave-slab. The story is that the Shaws of Rothiemurchus had a familiar spirit, or brownie, known as the Bodach an Duin, the Old Man of the Dun. When the Grants gained the property, the Bodach allegedly left the Doune and came here to guard the Shaw tombs instead—and no one in the Highlands would dare to remove one of these five stones, easily enough moved as they are. Like the saint's bell at Insh Church, if taken, these stones come back on their own—but woe betide the taker! Near by, in this sequestered God's acre, the ranks of the Rothiemurchus Grants lie buried; the Bodach does not seem to resent them.

Less than a mile on, southwards, a foot-track leaves the B.970 to strike up and over, eastwards, through another little forested pass, to the south end of Loch an Eilean, a little-known and delightful walk. Here we are at the southern boundary of Rothiemurchus, moving into the Kincraig, Feshiebridge and Inchriach area, separately described.

Stratherrick, Foyers and Boleskine. Stratherrick shares with Strathnairn that long and fairly narrow stretch of country lying on the south side of the Great Glen, between Loch Ness and the Monadh Liath Mountains, and is the south-westerly and larger portion thereof. To be accurate, the actual lochside shelf of Ness is not part of the strath, since a low, narrow range of hill intervenes, and its character is dissimilar; but it is convenient here to describe this with Stratherrick, especially as Boleskine civil parish embraces both, with old Boleskine kirk in the one and the present parish church in the other. Although part of the parish of Dores is involved in the area, the major and inhabited portion of that parish, with Strath Dores, is a distinct entity to the north-east, and will be dealt with separately. Drawing dividing-lines here is difficult, and they must be arbitrary, with parish boundaries of little help. Strathnairn is also described separately.

Stratherrick presumably derives its name from the Errogie area on Loch Mor, part-way down its length, for there is no river of similar name: the suggestion that it might derive from the same source as Corrieyairack, some 15 miles to the south, seems improbable. For our purposes the strath could be said to start at Torness, on the north, and run south-westwards, threaded by the A.862, for some 15 miles, to the empty area around Loch Tarff, in Abertarff parish near the foot of Loch Ness. Boleskine civil parish, united with Abertarff in the 18th century, is partly in the Loch Ness "shelf" but mainly in Stratherrick. Foyers is a village and district in Boleskine about half-way down Ness-side.

From Inverness and Dores the A.862 to Fort Augustus climbs up over Ashie Moor to the foot of large Loch Duntelchaig, passes the smaller Loch Ceo Glais, and runs down into green Stratherrick at Torness, where it crosses the Farigaig River by a new bridge alongside the old narrow, hump-backed one. The area is attractive, with the river rushing through a small rocky gorge. There is a scattered community in the valley, with the school isolated rather oddly half a mile to the north on much higher ground. At Torness a dead-end side-road strikes off south-westwards down the Farigaig, in a most pleasing fertile vale called the Leud-Lainn, literally the broad cornland, wherein is the old Fraser lairdship of Ledclune about a mile down. This is now a picturesque whitewashed farmhouse, burned some years ago and restored. Here was the home of a family of Frasers, who came from Erchite on Ness-side a few miles to the north, descended from the second son of the first Lord Lovat. They were created baronets of Ledclune and Morar in 1806, and though long departed from Ledclune, the line continues. Beside the house is a red granite memorial stone to Sir James, 3rd baronet, who was a distinguished soldier who fought at Waterloo. A quarter-mile to the west, in a field, is a cattle-shed which marks the site of the ancient house of Balnain, seat of another line of Frasers.

Beyond Torness the A.862 crosses vacant moorland to join, in 2 miles, B.851 coming over from the head of Strathnairn. A mile further and the head of Loch Mor is reached. This is a 4-mile stretch of water in fine scenery, its name somewhat confusing. It is divided into two almost separate sections, the southern end called Loch Garth, while the northern end used to be called Loch Farraline, Loch Mor being a comparatively modern designation. The estate of Farraline lies on the south side, on a private road, the pleasing early 19th century Adam-type mansion having an older nucleus. It is easily seen across the water, and has a summerhouse with a turret, which may have been a doocot. It was another Fraser seat. Opposite Farraline, on the main road, is the lochside community of Errogie, a strung-out scattering of houses, with two churches almost side by side, one of corrugated-iron, tiny, a mission of the parish church, the other larger, in harled stone, the United Free. There are only three or four houses, one very modern. A side-road strikes due westwards for Inverfarigaig, with post-office at the junction.

Further, the lower end of the loch is flanked by a long series of crofts, many now abandoned, called Lochgarthside. Before these are reached there is another small side-road to the west, with a little Free Presbyterian church at the road-end and the local war-memorial on an isolated rock near by. Up the side-road, on a shelf overlooking the loch, is the old and historic house of Gorthlech. This late 17th century tacksman's house was where Prince Charles Edward first halted on his flight from Culloden in 1746, and was given refreshment by Fraser of Gorthlech before pressing on into the West. Gorthlech has long been a farmhouse, and though the old portion is no longer used, it remains intact and Prince Charlie's Room on the first floor, is still pointed out. The building is typical, not large, but still with pine panelling and wainscoting remaining, and the draw-bar still in its slot at the door.

At the loch-foot is a farm called Glebe, indicative of an early church here. The present parish church of Boleskine stands on a slight ridge a little to the west, beside the school, something of a landmark, a long, low granite building with a small belfry and windows only on the south side. The site, in its graveyard is rather bare but the views are fine. There are no very ancient gravestones for the church dates only from 1777 and this is not the original kirkyard. Indeed the parish church position here is rather strange, its predecessor being near Foyers 4 miles to the north—and that this is the real Boleskine is proved by the name, which means at the head of the great waterfall, aptly describing the Falls of Foyers, and does not at all apply at Lochgarthside. Presumably a shift of population, possibly the setting up of the Lochgarthside crofting community, obviously a planned development, brought the parish centre here. Ironic perhaps that the aluminium-works village of Foyers grew up thereafter on the old site, necessitating a replacement for the ruined church there. There is at present construction activity at this end of Loch Mor connected with the new hydro-electric developments linked with Foyers, of which more hereafter. A mile on, where the A.862 crosses the Foyers River by a new bridge replacing a pleasant double-arched one, the road from Foyers comes in, and here is the little Catholic church of the Immaculate Conception, yellow-washed and attractive in a garden with trees, its presbytery-house attached.

A mile still further south, with the road beginning to rise into emptier and rougher country, is the community of Whitebridge, the last such in Stratherrick before Fort Augustus 10 miles on. There is a high, old and narrow Wade bridge, of 1732 now disused, over the Fechlin River which comes out of Loch Killin hidden in the hills 4 miles to the south, the river here rocky and picturesque, all under the dominant regard of the fine rocky peak of Beinn Sgurrach. There is a hotel, successor of a military rest-house, then an inn, and a few houses at Whitebridge, with considerable woodland around about. Beyond this the road climbs to 1275 feet over the heather moors before sinking down past Loch Tarff to Glen Doe and the head of Loch Ness, where the rocky hills come close to Fort Augustus. There are a great many lochs in the 12-mile-long stretch of hilly land between the A.862 and Loch Ness, mostly small but one over a mile long, Loch Knockie. In all the thirteen or so miles of Loch Ness-side south of Foyers there is no road nor any house, the slopes being uniformly steep, though well-wooded. Many small waterfalls descend to the loch, one large cascade at Glen Doe at the southern end.

Back at Loch Mor, the Foyers road strikes northwards for 3 miles, dropping rapidly towards Ness-side. Foyers, which used to be called Fechlin, the original name of the river, is a complicated area to describe. It is scattered around the deep and dramatic wooded ravine which the river carves through the escarpment, and therein are the two Falls of Foyers. The upper, and smaller, is readily seen from the road, indeed a little and narrow stone bridge crosses just below it, with cottages near by. This one is only 40 feet high. The lower and more famous fall is of 165 feet, and has been called the most magnificent cataract in Britain—but that was before the aluminium company came. It is still a fine cascade set amongst the hanging woodlands, a footpath leading to it. Burns described it: "Among the heathy hills and rugged woods, the roaring Foyers pours his mossy floods." And one enthusiastic professor declared that it was worth walking a thousand miles to see. Upper Foyers village, above the falls area, is modern, with post-office and school, and quite pleasantly set on a wooded terrace site, around a quite large square green in which is a Victorian Jubilee fountain. Low Foyers, on a shelf above Loch Ness, is reached by a road which branches off the B.852 almost a mile to the north, because of the steepness of the descent, and crosses the deep wooded gorge diagonally. Down here is the former aluminium works now superseded, and its associated modern housing schemes, larger than Upper Foyers. A large pump-storage hydro-electric development is being created, to harness the waters of Loch Mor which, falling over 500 feet in 2 miles, will give a great head of power for the turbines, the water to be pumped up pipes again by its own generated power during the period when current is not required for the grid, so providing an endless chain reaction. This scheme is costing £12 million with the power-station hidden down amongst the lochside trees having a 400 million watts capacity. Foyers House, a one-time Fraser lairdship, used to stand to the south-west of the river and Foyers Bay, its farm-steading and stableyard now encroached upon by modern housing. In the grounds there is a pleasantly sequestered modern burial-ground for the community, reached by a woodland path.

Between Upper Foyers and the Lower road-end, the modern church stands high on a wooded eminence above the B.852 main road, small and rather dim internally, with stone walls and an elaborate timber ceiling. There is no graveyard around it. Foyers Hotel, at the roadside further north, is above the former steamboat jetty, and developed out of the building known as The General's Hut, a base of the famous road-making General Wade. A long row of fir trees, planted along the roadside by a local forester in 1933, with seed from Dunmaglass, the MacGillivray lands at the head of Strathnairn, has flourished splendidly. Half a mile north of the hotel is the site of the original parish church of Boleskine in its old graveyard just below the road. A small part of the ancient walling remains, with a little watch-house. Amongst the many old stones are some good 17th century heraldic panels relating to the Frasers, especially those of Ledclune. The 38th chief of the Lovat Frasers, so claimed—although some would say that the present Lovat was only the 22nd MacShimi—is buried here, son of the famous Lord Lovat of the Forty-five.

Above the road in the same vicinity, in a wooded estate, is Boleskine House, a very unusual but attractive smallish mansion of the late 18th century, with later alterations, long and low, with a sort of pillared cloister-like frontage and two large bow windows to the rear. Internally a fine pilastered corridor runs the length of the house. Another Fraser lairdship, this house gained notoriety for a time earlier this century as the home of Alister Crowley, the eccentric who went in for much-publicised witchcraft and dark doings generally.A group of artistic folk now live here.

Over a mile further on B.852 the Farigaig River comes in spectacularly through a deep wooded gorge to enter Loch Ness at Inverfarigaig. Here there is a pier built by Thomas Telford—who designed the Caledonian Canal. Above is a cottage said to have been an inn at the Forty-five period. The Pass of Farigaig is an exciting place, with lofty rock bluffs towering steeply over the narrow forested sides, a notable geological area—indeed where the famous geologist, Dr. James Bryce was killed in 1877. A tall grey monolith stands to his memory at the roadside just above the Forestry Centre. This last is an interesting establishment where, in a converted stable, has been set up an excellent exhibition of forestry and wild life features, with photographs, models, wood-samples and stuffed birds and animals, all admirably explained. There is also a sound programme of recorded bird and animal cries. Particularly interesting is the record of the Sika deer introduced into Loch Ness-side in 1899, a dark-coated species, larger than the roe and smaller than the red deer, which have flourished here. It is all an admirable development, and well worth a visit. There is also a Forestry Walk of about a mile, duly signposted and described. Above the deep gorge here rises the vitrified fort of Dun Dearduil, commanding extensive views of Loch Ness. Threaded by a road to Errogie on Loch Mor-side, the Pass of Farigaig climbs inland for 2 miles through wooded steeps, to emerge on to the open green hills at about 550 feet. It sends off a branch-glen south-westwards after a mile, with a forestry-road, called Gleann Liath, long and narrow, a curious geological formation.

The Farigaig Forest continues north-eastwards along Loch Ness-side for many miles, flanking the B.852—the line of Wade's road. Four miles on, below the hidden small farm of Whitefield, is a roadside memorial stone marking the spot where Dr. Samuel Johnson and his friend Boswell halted, on their peregrinations, in 1773. Thereafter is entered the Erchite area, still similar wooded hillsides, from which came the Frasers to Ledclune. Dores village and district lies ahead—but this is described separately.

Strathfarrar. This fine valley, often erroneously called Glen Strathfarrar—glen meaning a narrow valley and strath a wide one—lies off Strathglass, and is the northernmost of the trio, with Cannich and Affric. Its river, the Farrar, is a major one 27 miles long, flowing out of Loch Monar, far amongst the mountains of the watershed with the West, and near the heads of Strathconon and Glen Orrin. Although somewhat longer than either Cannich or Affric, its general altitude is lower, most of its course being around the 400-foot contour. Also it is more open, fertile, softer as to scenery—a strath indeed rather than a glen. Unfortunately the public road ends barely a mile up, at Leishmore, and a key to unlock the gates has to be obtained for further travel by car.

At Leishmore there is a farmery and a few houses, with open woodlands. The woodlands continue for some six miles, becoming extensive at Culligran Wood, with tree-covered hills rising out of them, the road winding through. There are falls on the river at Culligran. About 7 miles up from the locked gates the Farrar widens out to Loch Beanacharan, amidst meadows, 2 miles long but fairly narrow. Another mile beyond is Loch Mulie, or Mhulidh, half that length. The hillsides are now more craggy, but of no great height, and the valley still wide and open, with good pasture. This is a fine valley for cattle-raising—and always was, for it was quite heavily populated in the clan days, one of the best of the Chisholm glens, before it was cleared after the Jacobite troubles. There are still more houses here than in Affric or Cannich.

Towards the head of the strath the scenery becomes more dramatic, with steep rocky hills shouldering close, and the road winding through quite a pass to the foot of Loch Monar. The river here is called the Garbh-uisge, or Rough Water, which speaks for itself. Monar Lodge is near by. This was a drove-road, with many incoming tracks to it from outlying areas, in the old clan days of extensive cattle-rearing.

Loch Monar itself is 4 miles long, with the Inverness-shire–Ross county boundary crossing it three-quarters of the way up. There is no road along its rather bare sides, only a track, to Strathmore Lodge at the west end.

The area at the head of Strathfarrar is now much developed by the hydro-electric engineers, with new access-roads. There is a dam at the foot of Loch Monar. As a contrast, Ptolemy of Alexandria mentioned the Farrar in his writings.

Strathglass, Cannich and Tomich. Strathglass is one of those long and pronounced rift valleys which run north-east and south-west across the face of Highland Scotland, of which the Great Glen is the mightiest. Strathglass lies north and parallel to the Great Glen about a dozen miles, and is, overall, about 30 miles long. This falls to be divided up, however. If the actual valley of the River Glass is considered, this covers only about 12 miles, Strathglass proper. But at each end there are complicating factors, as far as description and delineation are concerned. For the River Glass is formed out of the Rivers Affric and Amhuinn Deabhas, and while Glen Affric is very much a separate entity, and dealt with as such, it could be argued that the valley of the Amhuinn Deabhas is really only the south-westwards extension of Strathglass into the great Guisachan Forest, another 8 miles or so. Moreover the River Glass ends when it is joined by the River Farrar, and becomes the River Beauly for the remaining 10 miles to salt water at the Beauly Firth. And this stretch of the valley is frequently called Lower Strathglass, and never Strathbeauly. It is in fact an integral part of the strath, despite the change in the river's name. But for the purposes of this work it is probably better described under Kilmorack on the north side, and Kiltarlity on the south, the respective parishes. Strathfarrar too, the tributary river's valley, is separately dealt with, as is Glen Cannich and Glen Affric.

Strathglass proper, then, is a fairly straight valley—although its river winds considerably in its floor—averaging just over half a mile in width, before fairly steep braesides rise for about 1000 feet, to not very lofty enclosing hills. It is not very heavily wooded at this stage, nor exciting in its scenery, but very pleasant. It was the patrimony of the Clan Chisholm.

It is convenient to commence a description at the north-east end, where most travellers reach it, having already traversed the more spectacular Lower Strathglass and Druimm area, from Kilmorack and Beauly. Three miles after the Aigas district is passed, on the A.831, the River Farrar comes in from the west, and the Beauly becomes the Glass. At once, in the level area of the confluence, are the Erchless Castle policies, former seat of The Chisholm. The castle still rises proudly in the midst of parkland, more like a Lowland house in a Lowland setting, despite its enclosing mountains.

The site would be marshy once, and so add a defensive dimension not obvious today. The building is a tall, L-planned fortalice of the late 16th and early 17th centuries, whitewashed, with crowstep gables and angle- and stair-turrets, very picturesque. There is later work to the north, and a later oriel window rather disfigures the west gable. The basement is vaulted and the walls are pierced by shot-holes. Erchless—a corruption of *airidh ghlais*, the shieling on the stream—was until 1368 a possession of a Celtic family which had adopted a Normanised name, called de l'Aird, the Aird being a foothill area in Kirkhill parish south of Beauly. The heiress of this family then married the son of Sir Robert Chisholm, a Lowland laird, who had been appointed keeper of the royal castle of Urquhart. Thus the Chisholms—Chisholm, or Cheeseholm, is in Roxburghshire in Borderland—came into the Highlands, and like the Lowland Frasers near by, in due course became a Highland clan indistinguishable from their Gaelic neighbours. Erchless was besieged by 500 of Bonnie Dundee's Jacobite troops in 1689, but by 1715 Roderick Chisholm was leading his clan, on the Jacobite side, to Sheriffmuir. And in 1746 the chief's son and 30 of his clansmen died at Culloden. The direct line ended in 1838, when the chiefship passed to descendants of the last laird's sister, who was famous for her efforts to counter the evictions of the clansfolk of Strathglass, during the unhappy Clearances period. The Chisholms no longer own Erchless, but the castle is still occupied and cared for.

A little way west of the castle is the hamlet of Struy, where the side-road strikes off up Strathfarrar. Here there is an Established church, built by The Chisholm just before the line ended. It must have been on an earlier site however, for in the graveyard is a stone dated 1722, and some of the chiefs are buried here. Another church near by, presumably a Free establishment, is now a barn. There is a school, post-office, inn and small scattered village. And on the hillside behind, to the north, the remains of an ancient dun, or fort. Struy Bridge is rather fine, slightly humped, with five spans, dating from 1809.

Strathfarrar is described separately.

Continuing south-westwards on the A.831, soon a side-road strikes off to the left, to cross the Glass and join the road from Kiltarlity and Eskadale, which follows the south side of the river. At the south bridge end is a house with, in its garden, a tall narrow upright stone inscribed W.C. and C.F. 1716, no doubt a Chisholm marriage-stone. There are two more duns, or forts, crowning the steep banks at the north side, hereabouts.

The A.831 continues through pleasant country without any particular features, some 5 miles to Glassburn, where a major burn descends in an impressive waterfall, quite close to the house. Half a mile before this is reached is the roadside well and shrine of St. Ignatius, topped by a cross inscribed A.M.C. and M.F.C. 1867. This was a holy well, reconstructed in 1880, further inscribed to honour various saints and also to commemorate the coronations of more recent monarchs. At the other side of the river, the lesser road is picturesque but without especial interest.

Three miles on from Glassburn, A.831 crosses the incoming Cannich River, and then bends sharply southwards, at Cannich village—more properly Invercannich—to cross the Glass next by a modern bridge and then strike back in an easterly direction, to climb over the hills to the head of Glen Urquhart and so down to the Great Glen at Drumnadrochit. Cannich is a quite large scattered community which has grown greatly in recent years on account of hydro-electric and forestry developments, and is scheduled to grow more as a tourist centre. Ambitious plans are in hand to make this the tourist hub of the five attractive glens of Affric, Cannich, Farrar, Glass and Urquhart, with facilities such as swimming-pool, gymnasium, squash-courts, motel, etc. The village itself is not notable in character or beauty, although its setting is fine. There is a small and fairly modern Established church on a pine-clad knoll above the hotel, and a larger Catholic church, built in 1866, on the lower ground near the river. Also a youth hostel. Comar House, now a farm, lies a little way to the west, with an allegedly 17th century core, and pine panelling within. Across the river from it is Clachan Comair, an ancient graveyard and remains of an early church, in the riverside haughland, enclosed within a wall. Here are very many old flat and primitive tombstones, largely overgrown with moss and grass. There is also a rough fontstone, known as St. Bean's Holy Water Stone, with an 8-inch diameter basin. There was said to be another of these stones formerly, but it is not now evident.

The road which continues on the north side of the river is no longer A.831, and leads eventually into Glen Affric, to end at the floor of Loch Beneveian, but this is described separately. Before that, however, about 2 miles on, another fork and bridge crosses the Glass to the south side. Here is a fairly large Free church on a knoll, quite impressive, with a modern burial-ground not attached but near by. Also here is the Fasnakyle Power Station of the hydro-electric Board. Fasnakyle Bridge is a graceful single arch over a picturesque rocky linn.

The strath, in its upper reaches, now becomes much more heavily wooded. Two miles beyond Fasnakyle Bridge, on the south side, and now really on the Amhuinn Deabhas is the village of Tomich, a former estate "model" hamlet for the great Guisachan House property. It is a place of grey substantial stone houses, a post-office and hotel, with a distinctly Victorian air about it, all built by the first Lord Tweedmouth, Sir John Marjorybanks M.P., between 1854–94. A fountain to the memory of Lord and Lady Tweedmouth is erected at the roadside, by his son and daughter, with bronze portrait plaques. His Guisachan estate extended over about 20,000 acres of mountain territory to the west, almost wholly empty, roadless deer-forest. Its mansion is now roofless. A modern Celtic-type cross commemorates the 2nd Lord's wife, Lady Fanny Spencer-Churchill, aunt of Sir Winston—who himself visited here in 1901.

Beyond Tomich, near the gates of Guisachan estate, is Knockfin Bridge, another quite high single arch. The Knockfin area takes its name from the Fionn, the legendary group of heroes gathered round Fingal—one of whose alleged graves is here in a field, beside the foundations of a chapel, with another baptismal font-stone. There is also a cairn, with standing-stones. The wooded hill above this area, to the north, is still called Larach Tigh nam Fionn, the Ruined Camp of the Fair-haired Strangers (Gaelicised Norseman), actually with an early fort. Forestry is now much in evidence in this upper Strathglass. The public road stops at Knockfin.

Strathnairn and Dunlichity. The area south of the Great Glen, between Loch Ness and the Monadh Liath Mountains, is interesting, a distinct entity roughly 30 miles long by 7 miles wide, very much a world unto itself. Something of a great shelf, around the 750-feet level, it is divided into two lengthy narrow sections by a central ridge of low rocky hills, Strathnairn to the south, Stratherrick to the north. Between them they make a fascinating and attractive area, less well known than it deserves, being not really on the road to anywhere —although Fort Augustus can be reached therefrom. It is convenient here to describe Strathnairn as the area south-west of the A.9 from Daviot—even though 3 or 4 miles north-eastwards therefrom could also be so described, but this is dealt with under Daviot itself. The huge and elongated civil parish of Daviot and Dunlichity is not really an entity. Dunlichity is a former parish, united with Daviot in 1618, but retaining its parish church 7 miles south-west of the other, approximately midway down Strathnairn. The Nairn rises about 12 miles further south, in a burn called the Allt Mor, on the side of Carn Chriogain (2637 feet) a Monadh Liath summit.

Strathnairn, so described, is some 13 miles long, fairly narrow, but fertile, an open smiling valley, with the B.851 road flanking the river on the south side, and the districts of Lairgs, Inverarnie, Tordarroch, Farr, Flichity and Brin, Croachy, Aberarder and Dunmaglass succeeding each other. After the last, the road climbs over a small watershed into the lower part of Stratherrick. It is convenient therefore to describe this elongated valley from north-east to south-west.

The Strathnairn passing-bay road leaves A.9 at the great hairpin-bend just below Daviot, 6 miles south of Inverness. A mile along is the graceful single-arch hump-backed Wade bridge at Faillie, where the old military road crosses the Nairn. Half a mile further, at Scatraig, a side-road heads a short distance southwards to Mid Lairgs, where there is now an enormous sand and gravel workings quarrying the terminal moraines. The farm of Mid Lairgs is now abandoned, and the former stone-circle thereon has disappeared amongst the sand-pits. One of its stones is said to have been incised with a rude cross. There is another old Wade bridge here, disused and shored-up. The hillsides are much planted by the Forestry Commission, part of the large Strathnairn Forest.

Further along the B.851, near Littlemill, is another hump-backed bridge, double-arch this time, and less old. And 2 miles on is the little road-junction community of Inverarnie, with shop and a scatter of houses, where the B.861 from Culduthel, Inverness, comes in. Up this B.861 a mile, on higher ground at Gask, is a particularly fine concentric ring-cairn, east of the road, notable for its huge, flat gable-like westernmost outlier, 10 feet high and as broad, highly unusual. There are ten large stones in the outer circle, and within the tightly set inner circle multiple chambered burial-sites. One of the flat stones is cup-marked.

The Farr area comes next up the strath, centred round an old Mackintosh estate, the mansion of which is being demolished, Victorian but with traces of earlier work, probably late 17th century. The modern house is near by, beside the walled garden. There is a small school at Farr, also a plain grey granite Free church amongst a curious area of widespread large stone outcrops. A narrow winding side-road strikes off northwards at the post-office for Tordarroch and Dunlichity, and a short distance up is the quite attractive little whitewashed Free Presbyterian church.

Shaw of Tordarroch is the chief of Clan Ay; and though the old house of Tordarroch has long disappeared, its succeeding farmhouse has recently been rebuilt into an attractive small mansion with a tower, by the present chief, Major Ian Shaw, descendant of the ancient owners of Rothiemurchus in Strathspey before the Grants. The Shaws are one of the clans making up the great Clan Chattan federation. To the east is another good ring-cairn, in a field amongst the outcrops, with seven stones still upright in the outer ring, one very tall; also a flat stone with a great many cupmarks. A graceful shallow single-arched hump-backed bridge crosses the Nairn here. At Tordarroch, in 1532, the Earl of Moray is said to have hanged 200 of the Clan Chattan in a barn, as reprisal for the Raid of Petty.

About 2 miles west of Tordarroch, still on the side-road, stands the Clachan of Dunlichity, under the thrusting rocky hill of that name (1196 feet). Dunlichity is said to be a corruption of Dun le Catti, the stronghold of the Pictish tribe of the Catti, thought to be the ancestors of the Clan Chattan, whose member clans take the wild cat as their emblem and crest. There was a fort and the Watching-Stone on the hill-top. Here is the parish church, attractive on the hillside, a small, long and low building with very thick walls, said to date from 1758 but obviously incorporating the ancient pre-Reformation kirk. There is a good two-storeyed watch-house in the graveyard, built 1820, and many old tombstones. Here are the burial-places of the Shaws of Tordarroch, and also the MacGillivrays of Dunmaglass, chiefs of another branch of Chattan, the latter having their wild cat, in wrought-iron, on the gates, dated 1968. At the angle of this walling is a stone much scored by sword-sharpening. There are many rock outcrops in the slanting kirkyard, one alleged to be cupmarked, but this could not be established. The original chapel here was dedicated to St. Finan (*circa* A.D. 575). In the vestry is an old communion-bell dated 1704. Outside the kirkyard, beside the start of the little winding road to Brin, and at the burnside, is said to be the former baptismal stone for the Episcopalians of Strathnairn, who were refused the facilities of the church by the Presbyterians—but which amongst the many outcrops it is uncertain. Just beyond Dunlichity, in delightful country, is the little Loch a Chlachain amongst the birchwoods and rocky hills, and this pretty road continues round the head of the 4-mile-long Loch Duntelchaig, now part of Inverness's water supply. But this is into the Stratherrick area.

Beyond Farr, back on the Strathnairn B.851, the Brin area lies north of the road with Flichity to the south, under the frown of the rocky Creag Dubh (1450 feet). Brin Rock is impressive, with below it a cave. Brin House is a trim modern mansion, near where the Brin River joins Nairn from the south. Flichity, across the road, is a pleasantly sited estate, with a large mansion of no great age which has grown over the years, its walled garden thought to be on the site of a former graveyard and possible chapel. This was once a property of the Davidsons, another of the Chattan branch clans.

Croachy lies a mile on, with a post-office and the Episcopal church of St. Paul, an ancient foundation, although the present small building dates only from 1817, rebuilt 1869. There is kept a list of Rectors from the Reformation period, 1560. Also preserved are Parson Duncan's spurs. This was the Reverend Duncan Mackenzie, born 1781, and a much beloved medico as well as priest, who travelled afar on errands of mercy. The west stained-glass rose-window is in his memory.

Two miles on, with the Nairn swinging away southwards towards its source in the hills, is Aberarder, a former Mackintosh property, with the modern shooting-lodge hiding a most interesting old laird's house at the back. This is a long, low, hall-house type of building, of rough masonry harled, dating from the mid-17th century, crow-stepped-gabled and with a particularly massive kitchen chimney-stack, a very unusual house.

In another mile Strathnairn ends, with the B.851 turning away westwards to climb over into Stratherrick, and the wide valley suddenly narrowing to the dead-end glen of Conagleann, through which runs the Farigaig River, not a tributary of the Nairn but flowing north into Loch Ness. Up the glen, reached by a very lengthy drive of over 2 miles, is Dunmaglass Lodge, former seat of the Mac-Gillivray chiefs, from about 1500. The present building is typical red granite Scots Baronial Victorian, but amongst fine old trees in a lovely setting. The Clan Chattan regiment at Culloden was commanded by Alexander MacGillivray of Dunmaglass, who died there. Down at the main road, Dunmaglass Bridge spans the Farigaig, single-arched and humped, rather unusual in having pointed finials at its ends.

Strathnairn is not really rich in lochs as is Stratherrick, with only Loch a Chlachain and Loch Farr of any size, but it could be said to share with Stratherrick, on its higher northern edges, parts of the larger lochs of Duntelchaig, Ruthven and Bunachton.

Tomatin, Strathdearn and Dalarossie. This is the southern section of the huge Central Inverness-shire parish of Moy and Dalarossie, which covers 112,000 acres, is 26 miles long and averages about 8 miles in width. The northern part is dealt with under Moy. Tomatin is a small village but larger community on the A.9 nine miles north of Carrbridge, where that highway crosses the Findhorn; Strathdearn is actually the upper basin and valley of the Findhorn; and Dalarossie is the kirkton of the old parish church, 3 miles up the strath south-westwards, on a long dead-end side-road, very attractive.

Travelling north from the Carrbridge area, after the Slochd pass and summit, the A.9 leaves Duthil parish and crosses bare open moorland for 3 miles, reaching 1333 feet before slanting down a series of long braes to the Findhorn valley. It crosses that swift river by a massively ugly modern concrete bridge, replacing one by Telford, ridiculously top-heavy of appearance, and no advertisement for our age in a land of graceful 18th century arched bridges. Just before this, a small plain Free church stands at the roadside, opposite an east-going side-road following a great loop of the river—of which more hereafter.

Tomatin village, a mile further on the A.9, is rather dominated by two high railway viaducts. Before reaching it, the monument marked on the Ordnance map is the war-memorial, surmounting an eminence in a field. The community covers quite a wide area but is basically in two parts, that flanking the main road where is the post-office, school and a modest little corrugated-iron church, with some cottages; and the Tomatin Distillery and its associated housing, a mile to the north-west on a short side-road, large but less attractive than some distilleries. Half a mile further on the A.9 is the Freeburn Hotel, standing isolated, formerly an inn, the golf course marked on the map near by gone—an unusual circumstance. Freeburn was once a more important place, with cattle and sheep fairs being held no fewer than five times a year. It is now a fishing hotel for Findhorn anglers.

Back at the Free church the aforementioned side-road winds eastwards pleasantly amongst birch-woods. In a mile is the sequestered hamlet of Raibeg, where there is a little school and a narrow wood-and-girder bridge across Findhorn, with beside it a memorial-cairn to a Reverend Brown from Eastbourne, who was shooting-tenant here for 20 years—an unusual testimonial for a clergyman. The road continues up what has become the small Glen Seileach, passing the modern mansion of Corrybrough, formerly the seat of the chiefs of the small Clan MacQueen, a branch of the great Clan Chattan. Further up the glen becomes somewhat bare, although there are some old trees around the large shooting-lodge of Balvaird. These grass-and-heather hills, the same ranges as enclose Lochindorb far to the east, are fairly gentle and unspectacular, but with their own attractions, only just reaching the 2000-foot level. The road across the girder bridge leads to Tomatin House, in a huge loop of the river, another modern mansion on an old property of the MacBeans, also Clan Chattan, with its own little loch, the estate richly wooded, one of the MacBeans having planted one and a half million larch and fir trees.

Although the term Strathdearn applies to all the upper section of the river-valley, what is generally meant by the word is the portion west by south of the main road, probing into the Monadh Liath Mountains for about 15 miles. A word about the name, which might have been expected to be Strathfindhorn. Originally this river was called the Earn. In 1224 Dalarossie is referred to as "Dalfergussyn in Stratherne". This name was amplified to *Fionn-Earn*, *fionn* meaning white, presumably in reference to its famed rushing spates, for this is the fastest-rising river in Britain. Findhorn is not a grievous corruption, but Strathdearn, for the valley, is more accurate. A good, though narrow, side-road penetrates Strathdearn for almost 10 miles, before becoming private to the remote shooting-lodge of Coignafearn. It commences just north of the modern Findhorn Bridge and runs through the Morile area under Craig Morile, where there are good wide and fertile fields in the valley floor. Two miles on is Kyllachy, modern Scottish Baronial replacing an old laird's house of the Mackintoshes. These were quite an important branch of their renowned clan. They no longer own Kyllachy but still have property in the strath.

Over a mile further, past the former school, now a private house, is the parish church of Dalarossie standing back from the road at the riverside. The name is pronounced with the accent on the second syllable, and was *Dail-a-Ferghais*, the field of Fergus. There is some debate as to whether this was a St. Fergus or the King Fergus of Dalriada after whom Ardverikie in Laggan was named. The church, dating from 1790, on the site of one much older, is tiny, with no belfry, attractive by the waterside, in an old graveyard. The interior is bright, with a coved ceiling, wainscotted walls, a high-backed pulpit and only seven rows of pews. The pre-Reformation Stone font is still there, mounted on a boulder, and there are memorials to various Mackintoshes of Kyllachy. Sir James thereof was a noted literary man of the early 19th century. On a gablet on the vestry chimney, very unusual, is a heraldic Mackintosh panel with initials. There are many old stones in the still-used kirkyard. All very pleasing. Glen Kyllachy comes in from the north almost a mile on, with its Lodge beyond, and here there is a small hump-backed bridge over the burn. A foot-track leads up the glen and over the hills into Strathnairn, 8 miles.

Strathdearn is highly attractive hereabouts, with the sparkling river, steep hillsides and both planted and natural forest. Glen Mazeron opens off northwards in another mile or so, its Lodge near the roadside, and the road continues good but narrow and now high above the river. It descends again at Coignascallan, 4 miles up, where there opens a wide amphitheatre of the hills, with three side-glens branching off. There are many ruined crofthouses scattered over all, but their fields are still cultivated by the one remaining larger farm. The surrounding hills have now grown bare and rocky, and wild goats may be seen. The main Findhorn valley continues a long way yet, no longer a smiling strath but a narrow glen, past Old Coignafearn, now deserted, to Coignafearn Lodge 4 miles further, and thereafter three more to where Findhorn finally splits up into its various headwaters, at 1550 feet, and the great watershed looms ahead—likewise the parish boundary. Coignafearn is one of the really large deer forests, in the very heart of the lonely Monadh Liaths, with literally scores of peaks around 2500 feet in a trackless wilderness.

MORAY

This is one of the most ancient and famous names in Scotland, and originally applied to a much larger area than the county of Elgin now called Moray. From the Pictish and early Celtic period, Moray, or Moravia, or again Muref, was one of the seven great provinces into which Scotland was divided, under the seven mormaors, later earls, and in those days its boundaries extended as far north as the River Beauly, where Inverness-shire now meets Ross, and reached as far west as Lochaber and as far south as Atholl. Gradually this vast area was reduced, however, with the limiting of the earldom and the bishopric thereof. Eventually Moray became more or less synonymous with the fertile Lowland plain lying between the mighty Monadh Ruadh, or Cairngorm Mountains, mass and the Moray Firth. It is from here, of course, that the well-known surname of Murray derives. The Moray-men were a distinct and much-envied folk in old Scotland, and consequently much-assailed by their less prosperous neighbours, on account of the noted fertility of their lands and the fatness of their cattle. "Morray land quhare all men take their prey," wrote Cameron of Locheil in 1645, as acceptable excuse for raiding therein.

Today Moray is a comparatively circumscribed territory, the county between Banffshire and Nairnshire, a triangular area with 30-mile sides, covering 304,000 acres, with a population of nearly 57,000, its county-town the old provincial capital of Elgin still. It is only three-quarters the size of neighbouring Banffshire, but its rateable value half as much again.

The Laigh, or coastal plain, of Moray is one of the most renowned districts of the land, sometimes called both the Granary and the Garden of Scotland, both on account of its magnificent soil and its famed sunny climate—alleged to have up to forty days more of summer than anywhere else in Scotland. This portion stretches from the Spey to beyond the Findhorn, a low-lying plain measuring perhaps 30 miles by an average of 5 miles—although geographically the Laigh really extends on westwards into Nairnshire and almost to Inverness. Inland from this there is a foothills area, not much more than another 5 miles in width, then the heather hills of the interior take over, and in fact cover the major area of the county. These hills, however, are not as the lofty mountains of Banffshire to the east, but lowish, rounded heathery ranges and extensive high moorland, never reaching 2000 feet save in the Hills of Cromdale in the far south, an empty wilderness, dotted with small and remote lochs, and known as Braemoray. But piercing this plateau area is the splendid wide and fair valley of Strathspey, its lower section in Moray, up to and including Grantown-on-Spey, a land very distinct from the Laigh, with its own fame and traditions. So the county can be divided into three; the Laigh, with Elgin at its heart; Strathspey, with Grantown; and Braemoray, which has no towns or even villages, brooded over by the isolated and prominent hill of Knock of Braemoray (1493 feet), near the famed but equally remote Lochindorb, where the Wolf of Badenoch had his most secure stronghold.

The first thing to be said about all this area, from the visitor's point of view, is that it is very lovely—even the bare moorlands around Dava and Lochindorb frequently having enormous prospects to far blue mountains, south and north, being a tableland with lower lands around it. Elsewhere the beauty is continuous and self-evident, for this is part of the most highly wooded area of the British Isles, both Strathspey and the Laigh foothills being richly covered in forest, both ancient and modern, deciduous and conifer. The great forests of Darnaway, Culbin, Altyre, Monaughty, Dallas, Lossie, Teindland and Speymouth are vast entities, but all over the land trees are the most prominent feature of the landscape, with innumerable woods of, say, 2 miles square, and copses, clumps, strips and isolated timber everywhere. Only in the green heart of the Laigh itself is the land too precious for trees, around Drainie, Duffus, Hopeman and Kinloss. It is perhaps ironical that just here, on this magnificent soil, government has seen fit to take over and make unproductive huge acreages, by the establishment of the well-known military airfields of Lossiemouth and Kinloss, the two largest in Scotland and only ten miles apart—although these, of course, have their own value for the local communities.

The industries are what would be expected—agriculture and fruit-growing, forestry and timber products, fishing and ancillary trades along the lengthy shore-line and distilling, very important. Moray gives place only to neighbouring Banffshire in the number and fame of its distilleries—Glen Rothes, Longmorn, Knockando, Miltonduff and Tormore are typically renowned names. Another industry which deserves special mention is the large and well-known Baxter's food and canning establishment at Fochabers, where a family grocery firm has grown, through initiative and flair to become a household word throughout the land. Fochabers, although with only 1200 of population, is also notable for another old family firm which has flourished into far beyond local fame—Christie's nurseries, covering over 200 acres, where amongst the flowers and shrubs six and a half million young trees are grown. Elgin and Forres both have their own industrial estates, of course, where a wide variety of goods are produced. Lossiemouth has the largest seine-net fishing-fleet in Scotland, as well as a boat-building yard. Burghead, so famous for things ancient, has also a great maltings, connected with the thriving distilling industry, well-known and standing out prominently above the low-lying plain of the Laigh. and the tourist industry is becoming ever more developed, with so much to offer—although Strathspey has always been prominent in this, with Grantown one of the most popular centres in the land for the discerning visitor.

Reference must be made to the ambitious Culbin Sands experiment, which after many set-backs has now become so successful. Here, covering a 7-mile stretch of the sandy coastline, is an area averaging 2 miles wide, overblown with sand disastrously in the 17th century, so as to bury a whole barony and become one of the largest deserts of the British Isles—although it had all once been part of the Granary of Scotland. The process of thatching the endless shifting sand-dunes, and planting Corsican pines, has at last paid off for the immense labour involved, and now the Culbin Forest is a vast and attractive monument to man's determination and initiative. It is quite possible to get lost amongst its quiet glades today, some 50 feet above the level where once men ploughed and dwelt.

Sport is well catered for throughout the county, with its angling pre-eminent on the Findhorn, Spey and Lossie rivers, some of its golf courses of championship quality, deer-stalking, shooting and pony-trekking available, and yachting highly popular, especially on the great sheltered basin of Findhorn Bay. There are long miles of sandy beaches, and ample facilities for hill-walking, cliff-scrambling and similar activities. Caravan- and camping-parks are sited all over the area.

In antiquities, of course, Moray is particularly rich. There are splendid monuments and relics dating from the earliest times. Burghead is unique in having a huge Pictish vitrified fort completely covering a long narrow peninsula thrusting into the Moray Firth, with an extraordinary underground well-chamber and rock-bath baptistry. Also the famous bull carvings, renowned wherever archaeologists and Celtic scholars exist, a type confined to this site. Sueno's Stone at Forres is another Pictish monolith, the tallest and most intensively carved there is, a magnificent feature. The so-called Rodney Stone at Brodie, is a particularly fine cross-slab, and there are other symbol-stones and relics of proto-history—as well, of course, as many stone-circles, standing-stones, burial-cairns, forts and so on, of a still earlier culture.

The medieval period is notably well represented also, ecclesiastical remains being exceptionally fine and plentiful—for the Bishopric of Moray was long one of the richest and most powerful in Scotland. Elgin Cathedral is still quite outstanding, a tremendous experience in stone, despite the vandalism of centuries, and once probably superior to any other ecclesiastical building in the land. Pluscarden Priory, deep in its peaceful and lovely dead-end valley, restored and reoccupied by its Benedictine monks, is a joy, a mellow and delightful place of pilgrimage for all, of any faith or none, who have any feeling for tradition and the enduring spirit of man. Kinloss Abbey is sadly ruinous and abandoned, but sufficient remains to indicate something of its former greatness. There was once a Priory of Urquhart also, but of this only the site remains. Spynie Palace, although in reality a castle, was the principal seat of the Bishops of Moray, and is a quite splendid structure, with some unique features, which deserves to be a lot better known. As for smaller establishments and churches, these are many and varied. The ancient 12th century nucleus of the parish church of Birnie, with its heavy Norman chancel arch, its handsome Celtic saint's bell and Pictish symbol-stone, is alleged to be the oldest church in continuous use in all Scotland—although similar claims *have* been made elsewhere. A most interesting little place of worship is the most modest St. Ninian's Catholic church in Bellie parish, at the extreme eastern edge of the county, the oldest post-Reformation R.C. church in Scotland, looking just like a row of cottages in a field—and deliberately so, that it might not arouse the crusading zeal of Reformers. The ruined St. Peter's Kirk of Duffus is another treasure, with its excellent groined-vaulted early 16th century porch and crypt, and its St. Peter's Cross, one of a group of rather special Moray mercat-crosses of unusual style and connected with churches rather than with burghs and baronial seats—an indication perhaps, of the power of the ancient church here.

The baronial establishments are no less numerous and splendid than the ecclesiastical, however, ruinous or otherwise. Duffus Castle, built on an older motte in the 14th century, is one of the finest examples of the motte-and-bailey type of stronghold in the land. Brodie Castle, still in the hands of the Brodies, who have been here since 1160, is a fine pile of the 16th and 17th centuries. Darnaway Castle, still the seat of the Earls of Moray, in its vast forest-kingdom, is a place which has seen much of the history of Scotland enacted, although it is now mainly a huge and symmetrical mansion of 1810, the ancient banqueting-hall with its fine arched oaken roof, is still incorporated. Castle Grant, now unfortunately abandoned to wind and weather, is not yet a ruin, and though scarcely beautiful, towers impressively, once called Freuchie Castle and seat of the Grant chiefs, now Earls of Seafield. Of lesser castles and fortalices, the little 17th century tower of Coxton, a gem indeed, might be singled out, but there are many, two particularly interesting being the twin castles of Burgie and Blervie, almost identical and only a couple of miles apart.

Gordonstoun is another old estate whose mansion and grounds have attained a new prominence in modern times, to house the famous school where were educated both the present Prince of Wales and his father, Prince Philip. This resounding and inspiriting educational venture, with its own fire-brigade, mountain-rescue, coast-guard and other teams, is an asset not only to Moray but to the whole country, and a more satisfactory place for young folk to grow up would be hard to imagine—and today, the young folk include girls also. The Outward Bound School, another related and unconventional enterprise, has its headquarters at Burghead only a few miles away.

For all this area Elgin is not only the county town and capital, but very much the centre and heart, a town—which proudly demands the title of city—vastly more important, distinctive and characterful than its population of a mere 16,000 would suggest. In appearance, atmosphere and architecture, as in history, this is a major municipality, with a "presence" many a great city would envy. It is much the largest town, with the bustling fishing burgh of Lossiemouth (6450 population) coming next. Forres has 4800 and Grantown only 1600, while Rothes, Burghead, Fochabers and Hopeman have each something over the thousand. But size is by no means the vital standard, here or anywhere. Moray is fortunate, too, in many of its villages, with Dyke, Garmouth, Urquhart, Llanbryde and Findhorn particularly pleasant.

The county is rich in fine scenery, despite having no major mountains or any large lochs save Lochindorb—wherein, on an island, is the Wolf of Badenoch's picturesque stronghold, scene of events stirring and grim. Heavily forested lands can quite frequently be monotonously sylvan, but Moray is largely hilly and undulating, and its woodland views lovely as they are varied. In late autumn especially, this is a wonderland of vivid colour. The coastal scenery between Covesea and Burghead is exciting, with cliffs and stacks and caves; and the wide vistas of Findhorn Bay, backed by the Culbin Forest, are memorable. Strathspey, of course, is renowned for beauty over almost all its length, but less generally known, though locally famous, are the beauty-spots of Bridge of Dulsie, Randolph's Leap, Daltulich Bridge and so on, along the strung-out gorges of the rushing Findhorn. The prospects from above Pluscarden looking down the Vale of St. Andrew are lovely indeed; and from almost anywhere on the north-facing foothill country the views across the Moray Firth to the Highlands of Ross, can be little short of breath-taking.

History has always been so much part of Moray-land that it is almost superfluous to refer to it here. Its rich fertility, though a source of constant invasion and friction, also made it a favoured haunt of the early Scots kings, who often preferred to live up here than in their southern domains. The Earldom of Moray was always so important that for long the Crown preferred to keep it in its own care, bestowing it only temporarily on very favoured relatives or entirely reliable supporters. Bruce gave it to his nephew and lieutenant Thomas Randolph, the first Regent Moray. The Wolf of Badenoch, Alexander Stewart, son of Robert the Second, Bruce's grandson, was never actually Earl of Moray—but as he was Earl of Buchan to the south, and in right of his wife, Earl of Ross to the north, he ruled here too, if rule is the word for his lawless tyranny. The Douglases in time gained Moray by marriage, ensuring more upheavals, until they were brought low by James the Second—who thereupon gave Moray to his infant son. James the Fourth bestowed it on *his* illegitimate son by Flaming Janet Kennedy, and used to visit her at Darnaway frequently, to get away from his unloved Queen, Margaret Tudor, sister of Henry the Eighth. Mary Queen of Scots granted the earldom to her eldest half-brother, James Stewart—who in time became the second Regent Moray, for his nephew James the Sixth. His daughter and heiress married another Stewart, who was the Bonnie Earl o' Moray of the ballad, slain by Huntly. And so on, down through the whole colourful cavalcade of Scottish history. The Stewarts were, in fact, never ousted from the earldom thereafter, and the present Earl, at Darnaway Castle, is the 19th. His uncle was the late Viscount Stuart of Findhorn, the well-known Secretary of State for Scotland.

Alves. This is a rural and much-forested civil parish of 9400 acres, with a village on the main A.96 road, lying west of Elgin. Part of the great Roseisle and Monachty Forests, also the large woods of Alves and Carden and Knock, apart from lesser woodlands, make the area very tree-conscious. There is, indeed, a Forestry Commission Tree Nursery at Newton, on the eastern boundary of the parish where the Burghead road strikes off.

Although today's population is mainly concentrated along the main road, where Crook of Alves has developed into a fair-sized modern village, it was not always so, and the parish centre formerly lay a mile to the northwards, where is still the Kirkton and abandoned former parish church. There is a rather fine war-memorial at the present village, rather like a miniature Elgin Muckle Cross. Also a modern school. The parish church here was formerly the Free church of 1878, classical but renewed, with a square tower, standing somewhat isolated to the south.

The old Kirkton, now only a farm, is situated on a side-road to Burghead, and here is the parish graveyard on a slight eminence, with the disused church, plain, harled, Georgian, with an empty belfry dated 1769. There is older work incorporated however, and built into the east gable is a good heraldic panel of the Innes family dated 1722 and initialled B.I. and I.F. In the kirkyard are many 18th century flat and table-stones, and an interesting deep stone coffin of earlier date. A burial enclosure of the Russell family is dated 1725.

Half a mile north-west of the Kirkton is Kirkhill farm, a place of wide prospects, where there is an interesting feature, the remains of a typical Mercat Cross, with plinth and truncated shaft, now at the back of the steading but formerly in the open field. Presumably an earlier and pre-Reformation kirk stood hereabouts, connected with a burgh of barony, and this cross, plus the name, is all that survives. The local tradition is that this was a resting-place for monks on their way between Kinloss Abbey and Pluscarden Priory. The farm of Coltfield near by used to be an old lairdship.

Two miles to the west, on the edge of the parish, is Milton Brodie, an interesting estate on the Kinloss Burn. The pleasing mansion, amongst old trees is typically Georgian to the front, with Ionic portico and good contemporary interior decoration. But at the back is earlier work, built on a nucleus of the house of the one-time Chantor of Moray, a cathedral dignitary. Little of pre-Reformation date appears to remain, but late 17th century work is evident. A former doocot is gone, but an unusual two-storeyed 18th century garden-house, octagonal with a chimney, remains to the south. This was a property of the Brodie and Innes families. Seaward is the Roseisle Forest and Burghead Bay.

At the extreme other end of the parish eastwards is Newton House, under the forested and conical Knock Hill (335 feet). This is a handsome and commodious mansion of 1792, in wooded grounds, near the tree-nursery, formerly belonging to the Forteath family, a name of very limited distribution. Prominent above, on the crest of the Knock, is the York Tower, erected by one of the Forteaths in 1827 to celebrate the visit of the then Duke of York, who, although intending to travel deep into the Highlands, decided that he had had enough when he got thus far. It is Gothic octagonal, three storeys with a parapet, and seven counties can be discerned therefrom. Knock Hill once boasted a Pictish fort of major size, with inner and outer ramparts. Here, too, is one of the places claimed for Macbeth's meeting with the famous witches. On the lower slopes is the Forteath early 19th century mausoleum, with subterranean burial-vault. Just to the west is the neighbouring Carden Hill, also richly wooded —indeed larches from here used to be felled to build fishing vessels at Buckie. Sandstone outcrops on the hill are liberally sprinkled with prehistoric cupmarks.

Between this succession of low summits, south of the A.96, and the much higher wooded ridge of the vast Monaughty Forest 2 miles further south, ran the line of the old military road. There are a succession of pleasantly placed large farms in this open vale with the wide prospects, from New Alves on the east, by Monaughty, to Asliesk on the west. At the latter are the remains of a small fortalice of the late 16th or early 17th century, in the stackyard. Only part of the west gable stands to any height, but this shows the base of an angle-turret, and is liberally provided with five splayed gunloops. The windows have chamfered edges. A small heraldic panel of the Innes lairds is built into a steading gable.

Archiestown, Knockando and Elchies. The large central Moray parish of Knockando, of 28,000 acres, in the main hill and moorland, lies along the north bank of Spey for almost 15 miles, opposite that of Aberlour in Banffshire. It is in the heart of the distillery country, with a fertile, woodland and fairly populous belt along the river, a cultivated terrace area above it, and the rest largely empty heather. Archiestown is quite a sizeable village midway along the said shelf or terrace, and Elchies, Wester and Easter, with the great Forest thereof are two former great Grant estates, which once divided all between them. Because of the booming distilling industry, plus the much-sought-after Spey salmon-fishing, the area is prosperous as well as scenic.

Archiestown is a planned village of the mid-18th century, on the usual rectangular lines, set on the open bare slopes of the Moor of Ballintomb, around the 700-foot contour, 2 miles up from the river, with splendid views to south and west. It was founded by Sir Archibald Grant of Monymusk in 1760, and was almost destroyed by fire in 1783, and rebuilt. It consists of a long main street, actually the B.9102 Rothes–Grantown road, with a square at the west end, and side-lanes leading to parallel lesser streets to south and north. The square is grassy and tree-planted, and here is the good hotel, popular with anglers, a war-memorial in form of a mercat cross, and near by the Speyside Weavers handloom establishment, making tweeds, rugs, scarves and so on. There is, too, a small abandoned Free church, of 1845, with belfry. It is curious that this conveniently placed church should be disused, whereas that inconveniently placed at the roadside, in isolation a mile to the east, rather similar in size and style, is still in use.

Neither of these, of course, is the parish church. That is situated, also in no very convenient spot, however attractive, 3 miles to the west, above the same B.9102 road, near Upper Knockando and the Cardow Distillery. This is an unusual style of building, in its old churchyard, long and narrow, first built in 1757 but much altered, now a fairly low harled edifice with a round, conical-roofed tower and weather-vane. Internally it is bright, having galleries on two sides, with shallow arches, and a stained-glass window. Built into the kirkyard wall between the two gates are three Pictish stones, now very weather-worn. On one can be discerned two crescents and V-rods, on another a serpent and mirror symbol. The third is now blank to ordinary eyes, but is alleged to bear runes. Also in the graveyard, an ancient standing-stone has been utilised as memorial in the Grant of Wester Elchies tomb—possibly from an alleged stone-circle at Ballintomb. There are a number of old gravestones, many of Grants. The manse stands close by, and not far away is the little school, like the church, on the edge of a steep wooded drop.

At the other side of Cardow Distillery with its associated housing, almost a mile eastwards, Knockando House stands on a delightful terraced site above a den, in old trees, facing south over wide Strathspey, an attractive small mansion of the Grants of Carron, built in 1732, with later additions, L-planned with typical crowstepped-gables, chimney copes and steep roofs. An 18th century doocot adjoins.

Knockando Distillery lies a mile to the south-west, at Lower Knockando, down at the riverside in the woodland, with quite close to it another distillery, Tamdhu. Because of the trees and deep winding dens leading down to Spey, neither establishment can be seen from any distance. Near by also, at Nether Tomdow, is the highly interesting and picturesque little woollen-mill of Knockando, where the Smith family have been spinning and weaving tweeds and blankets for almost 200 years. This is a fascinating family business, in a farmery and gardens, with its spinning-jenny of 1870 still in action, and real teasles used to fluff out the woven cloth. The entire process from fleeces to finished article may be seen here, and fine suitings and blankets purchased.

Above this, almost a mile, and below the parish church, is the Poolflasgan Bridge, of the 19th century, now replaced by a modern one, and with a small waterfall in the wooded den. Upper Knockando hamlet, with its post-office, is on B.9102 half a mile on, westwards, a pleasant spot, and here a side-road strikes off northwards to cross the heather hills to Dallas and Forres, a lonely 8 miles or so, rising to 1000 feet. The hill called Cross of Knockando (1221 feet) flanks it at the parish boundary. There are a number of hill-farms up here. A mile beyond Upper Knockando, on the B.9102, is Bridge of Cally, another 18th century high arch, formerly without parapet, over a deep narrow ravine with tall trees. And at Pitchroy, on the lower ground 2 miles on, with the woodlands of Scootmore Forest above and the Spey at Blackboat Bridge below, are two standing-stones in a field at the roadside, one fallen. A mile on is the western parish boundary.

Returning eastwards, the small village of Carron lies at a bend of Spey, again in woodland, 3 miles along the great river's windings from Lower Knockando, with a distillery and a former railway-station—a modern development, for Carron House, of the Grants, and the Burn and Daugh of Carron all are on the other, Banffshire, side of Spey. Laggan House, a red Scots Baronial mansion of 1861, stands on a fine terraced position on the Moray side, to the east.

Another 2 miles down river is the former great estate of Wester Elchies, now fallen on hard times indeed. Like all else hereabouts it was a Grant property, and Charles Grant thereof founded Charles-town of Aberlour burgh in 1812. Their large mansion, now aban-doned in a bad state of repair, developed from a plain L-shaped tower-house of the early 17th century, extended later the same cen-tury to the Z-plan—though there may have been an earlier fortalice incorporated, for the east wall of the tower-house is very thick, with a curious buttress-like projection. The gables are crowstepped, there is a circular stair-tower, the basement is vaulted and a shot-hole is covered by harling. An old Grant heraldic panel is built in above the arched entrance of the great later portion. In 1565 Wester Elchies was held by James Grant, a cadet of Freuchie, from the Bishopric of Moray. It passed in the 18th century to another branch, the Grants of Ballindalloch. An observatory was built near the house in 1851, and a number of Hindu stones, brought from India, placed about the estate. The cave of Dellagyle, at the riverside below, was the refuge of the noted cateran, James-an-Tuim, one of the Grants of Carron.

The neighbouring estate of Easter Elchies lies 2 miles further east. Here is as great a transformation. The large Macallan Distillery now rises at the back of the former mansion, high above Spey, with its housing development. The old house still stands, abandoned. One would have thought that the distillers could have made good use of it, when building so many new houses. It is a T-shaped fortalice on a splendid site, of the early 17th century, partly rebuilt 1857, typically tall with crowstepped gables and a circular turret corbelled out above first floor level, the chimneys with large copes. There is a panel, dated 1700, with weather-worn initials. Easter Elchies was another Grant lairdship, the first recorded being Patrick, second son of the 15th Laird of Grant (or Freuchie). A descendant was the famous Lord Elchies, of Session (1690–1754). Below the house south-wards is the graveyard of the former parish of Macallan—alleged to refer to St. Colin—which was united with Knockando in 1646. A fragment of the ancient church walling remains, with many old table-stones. The Grant of Easter Elchies mausoleum, of 1715, is also ruinous but has been impressive. A highly self-satisfied memorial commemorates Lord Elchies—who would undoubtedly be much affronted by the prevailing neglect and ruin. Behind rise the empty heathery and lumpish hills of the Elchies Forest.

Less than a mile on is the parish boundary, and the Moray end of Telford's Craigellachie Bridge, of 1814, superseded by a modern erection.

Bellie and Spey Bay. The civil parish of Bellie, lying at the extreme eastern end of Moray, extends to 13,200 acres, fully half of which is covered by the planted glades of the great Speymouth Forest and Wood of Ordiequish. It is roughly an oblong, some 7 miles by 4 miles, between the Banffshire border and the Spey with the sea as its northern boundary. Fochabers town lies in this parish, but is dealt with separately. There are no fewer than six villages or hamlets squeezed into the northern half of the area, low-lying moorish ground around a disused airfield. The rest comprises the great estate of Gordon Castle, and the vast woodlands. The ground rises from the sands and shingle and coastal plain to the wooded summits of Whiteash Hill (866 feet) and Scotch Hill, Ordiequish (717) near the southern border.

Before the rise of modern Fochabers, the parish centre used to lie between Gordon Castle (formerly Bog o' Gight) and the old church of Bellie. The castle and estate are described under Fochabers. Therein also is the more modern parish church. The old graveyard of Bellie is still extant, however, with the very scanty fragments of the original church of St. Ninians, just off the B.9104 road to Spey Bay, a mile north of the castle, easily accessible and still in use. It occupies a grassy slope, facing west, and at the summit is a classical temple-like mausoleum with twelve pillars dated 1825, where are buried Jane Duchess of Gordon, second wife of the 4th Duke, and her children. A village girl, he had married her after the death of the more famous Duchess, also Jane. Also buried here, amongst the many old and tumbled table-stones, was the 15-year-old Earl of Kincardine, or Lord Graham, son and heir of the great Marquis of Montrose, who died at Bog o' Gight Castle in 1645, while campaign-ing for King Charles with his father. The stone sometimes pointed out as his, built into a fragment of the old kirk-walling, although weatherworn, seems to represent the Dunbar family, and certainly is not the Graham arms. This church was originally attached to Urquhart Priory.

A mile further north is the Romancamp Gate, a pleasant house in woodland. Whether in fact the camp here, visible still in 1780, was Roman, Danish or Pictish, is not certain; at any rate, nothing now remains to be seen, on the level farmlands a little way to the south-west.

Beyond Romancamp half a mile are two of the aforementioned villages with which this plain is dotted, in highly unusual fashion—Upper Dallachy and Bogmuir, within a quarter-mile of each other. The former is the prettier, with some old houses; Bogmuir is the larger, and more scattered. Half a mile east of Upper Dallachy, on the farm of Cowiemuir and near a road-junction, is a stone-circle, now consisting only of three lumpish conglomerate boulders. It has been a cairn-circle, with burial-place in the centre. To north and east of these villages stretch the many disused runways of an abandoned airfield.

At the northern end of the airfield is Nether Dallachy, another attractive small village now surrounded by young plantations. The reason for this concentration of small communities in what does not appear to be very fertile country, largely whins and moorland, is not clear; perhaps they represent planned settlements of the Dukes of Gordon. The next one is more readily explained, Spey Bay, for it lies on the shore and has been a fishing community, although now its cottages are largely holiday-homes and there is a caravan-site. It boasts a small hotel, a public hall near the disused railway-station, and the quite well-known golf course stretching eastwards along the links. The shore is not enhanced by a high shingle-bank of stones brought down by the Spey, which here finds its way to the sea through marshland in ever-changing channels. The farm of Tugness is the end of the road, directly opposite Kingston on the west shore, and here are three semi-subterranean vaulted ice-houses, for the preservation of fish, still used in the salmon season.

There are two more hamlets in this populous parish—Auchenhalrig, on the edge of the forest a mile east of Romancamp, and Bridge of Tynet another mile south-eastwards, where the main A.96 crosses the Burn of Tynet into Banffshire. This last has been a milling hamlet. Near by, at Newlands to the south-west, is a most interesting feature. This is the little Catholic church of St. Ninians, the oldest post-Reformation R.C. church in Scotland allegedly. None would think it a church at first sight—a deliberate precaution—for it looks like a long whitewashed cottage, with chimney-stack and square windows, set down in a field. It was indeed an old woman's cottage, with additional premises for sheep, when the laird of Tynet granted it to the churchless Catholic community of Enzie (just over the burn, in Banffshire) in 1755. The strong Catholic community here suffered much after the Jacobite risings, despite the traditionally Catholic overlordship of the Gordons, but the Enzie area was stout in its faith, and indeed produced no fewer than eleven bishops and over fifty priests. The little church is quite delightful with two doors on the south side, a vestry to the east and a baptistry to the west of the long low range. There are a number of good features. The building appears to be temporarily out of use. It is to be hoped that this gallant little shrine is not allowed to fall into decay.

The great forested area to the south, threaded by the A.96 and innumerable paths, requires little description but offers many delightful walks. There is a monument in the form of a cairn, near the summit of Whiteash Hill, to Frances, Duchess of Richmond and Gordon, dated 1887.

Birnie and Thomshill. Birnie is a rural civil parish of 6750 acres in foothill country immediately to the south of Elgin, with no real village but a distillery hamlet at Thomshill on the way to the lofty hill area of Glen Latterach to the south, the land level rising from a mere 120 feet to ten times that. It was anciently called Brenuth or Brennack.

The parish church is of great interest, one of the most ancient in the North-East, indeed said by some to be the oldest church in continuous use in all Scotland—although this claim has been made for others. Dedicated to St. Brandan, it stands isolated on a knoll off a side-road, at Paddockhaugh, near the east bank of the Lossie 2 miles due south of Elgin, in its old kirkyard and with a good early 18th century manse near by. It is a long, low, sturdy building, actually shortened in 1734 when the belfry was added, with a sundial on the south walling, much weatherworn. It was built in 1140 on the site of the Celtic foundation of St. Brandan the Navigator, who flourished in the 6th century. The stone-walled interior, although much modernised in 1891, is still fine, with a splendid Norman chancel arch, and many special features of interest. There is an ancient font, said to be one of the oldest in the land. The Coronach Bell is preserved, a typical "deid bell"; also the Hairy Bible, bound in undressed calfskin and dated 1773. There is a handsome heraldic memorial of 1670 to Master William Sanders, then minister; also a small but good stained-glass window to St. Brandan.

But perhaps the two greatest treasures of Birnie are outside. The famous Ronnel Bell is kept at the manse for security, a notable tall Celtic saint's bell 13 inches high, in typical cowbell shape. And built into the kirkyard wall on the right, or west, side, is the Birnie Stone, a Pictish symbol-stone, the carvings now very weatherworn and unclear, but representing the eagle and rectangle, with Z-rod symbols. There are said to be other fragments, from a stone-circle, built in elsewhere, but these were not evident to the writer. This little church, strangely enough, was once for a time the seat of the great Bishopric of Moray, before Elgin Cathedral was built, and Simon de Tonci, 4th Bishop, was buried here in 1184.

There is no hamlet near the church. Thomshill lies on another side-road, a mile to the south, a thriving distilling community, where, in a quite narrow valley, are two large distilleries side by side—John Haig's Glen Lossie, and also the fine new D.C.L. Mannochmore, which cost £800,000, with an annual capacity of a million proof gallons. There is also a by-products recovery plant. When the author visited this distillery, it was proudly displaying a sign declaring that it had gone 278 days without an accident—

The so-called Rodney Stone, Brodie, a fine example of Pictish cross-slab, with the strange and typical but still unexplained symbols in high relief

The so-called Roman Well, Burghead. Actually a Pictish bath-chamber cut in solid rock underground

evidently a noteworthy accomplishment. Thomshill, an isolated community, although not very far from the distilleries of Longmorn and Whitewreath in Elgin parish, has its own school.

The parish is long and wedge-shaped, with the greater southern section of it empty hills and moors around the Moss of Birnie, Glen Latterach marking its westernmost boundary to the south, the Lossie to the north. Much of Glen Latterach has been flooded by the building of a great dam by the North-East Scotland Water Board, to form a reservoir, much of the stone therefore coming from the demolished part of Gordon Castle, Fochabers. The Ess of Glen-latterach, a fine waterfall, still survives however. In this bare area, the Bardon Burn runs in a parallel valley to the east, and near Bardon is said to be a Roman camp, with trenches—although the present author could not find the site. There is, however, another alleged camp, said to be Danish this time, near the large farm of Shougle, on a side-road, a short distance to the north, again indeter-minate as to site—and there may be confusion in the matter. There are large sand and gravel workings in this area of moraines.

Burghead and Cummingstown. It is to be feared that many travellers to Moray will tend to miss Burghead as a place to visit—which would be a pity, for it is of great interest and antiquity. Also it occupies an extraordinary position, jutting out on a narrow, thrusting rocky peninsula for exactly half a mile into the Moray Firth, on the east side of the wide Burghead Bay, which stretches for 4 miles to Findhorn. Very much on the road to nowhere, it is a self-contained former fishing community and small port, a little town of some 1400 people, in the parish of Duffus—not a burgh of its own, perhaps unfortunately. From a distance it seems to be dominated by a huge modern tower of a maltings establishment—but this is not so evident on the spot. Cummingstown is a small road-side village, on the seaward side of Clarkly Hill, to the east.

Burghead's name refers to the borg, or early fortress of a Norse Yarl, Sigurd of Orkney, established here in 889, but the vitrified stonework and ramparts he made use of had been there for long, a Pictish fort of great importance, which remains are still very evident crowning the seaward tip of the peninsula, a strategic site of obvious strength, dominating the levels of the Moray coast, the Alata Castra of Ptolemy. Much used to be made of a brief Roman presence here, by last century's archaeologists, but much more important was the native Pictish connection, for this is thought to have been a Pictish capital, and it is even suggested that the famous if hard-to-place Battle of Mons Graupius was fought in the fertile Moray plain near by. Be that as it may, Burghead was highly significant to the Picts, and they have left certain very special signatures in the shape of the famous bull carvings and the notable well. The spirited and attractive representations of bulls do not occur elsewhere, but seemed to proliferate here, for some reason. Only two remain at Burghead, in the Harbour-master's office, but two more, fragmentary, are in

Elgin Museum, with a plaster-cast of a magnificent specimen now in the British Museum, London. Another is at Edinburgh Museum of Antiquities. For some time it was believed that these bulls were of Roman origin, or at least relics of Mediterranean bull-worship introduced by the Romans; but this is now discounted. The bulls are purely native Pictish—but the reason for them here is as little known as with most other Pictish symbols.

Something which *cannot* be taken away to museums elsewhere, and is equally dramatic and significant, is the quite extraordinary feature, long thought also as Roman, and a bath, but now known to be a Pictish well-chamber. It is a magnificent pool, 10 feet square by 4 feet deep, cut out of the solid rock, near the extremity of Burghead Point, in a subterranean artificial cavern with vaulted ceiling. It is all on a large scale and highly impressive, a long flight of steps leading down. It is now thought to have been a baptistry of the early Christianised Picts, a sunk tank fed by a spring in the living rock. Discovered in 1809, it is now in the care of the Department of the Environment, and one of the sights no visitor should miss in the North-East. The set of three ramparts at the fort near by, each 800 feet in length, is also of great importance, for no similar work exists in Britain, although some in France is of this quality. Unfortunately much of the fort was swept away by an enthusiastic contractor in 1807, when the town was being developed, who indeed left a record of "a contract for the removal of 20,000 yards of rampart".

Also out at this point of the long narrow peninsula, where the views to the north especially are magnificent in clear weather, is the coastguard station above the good and large harbour, begun in 1807. It is quite a busy haven, with coastal trade, largely connected with Moray's distilleries, animal feeding-stuffs, timber, etcetera, as well as a few fishing-boats and pleasure craft. Here is also the Boat Centre connected with the well-known Outward Bound School, which has its main establishment at the south end of the town, so that much inspiriting activities of youngsters is apt to be evident here. There is coastguard rescue equipment. At the aforementioned Harbour-master's office is a little museum of locally collected items, including Pictish stones, one showing a stag being attacked by wild animals. Above the harbour, surrounded by the streets of fisher cottages, is a small, overgrown and disused graveyard and site of an early church, presumably once dedicated to St. Aethan, the local patron. Here is the feature known as the Cradle Stone, a small upright with a scooped-out hollow in the face of it, and the initials A.E.—although these are probably an addition. Various local explanations, for the name, are given, none very convincing. I have seen a similar upright with central hollow in Wigtownshire, where it is called the Devil's Stone. Fairly recently a deep cylindrical well, stone-lined and obviously medieval, has been discovered down near the shore to the south-west, and provided with a new stone parapet.

Burghead town is hardly beautiful, consisting of long straight streets of grey stone cottages stretching along the peninsula, with cross-lanes, all very symmetrical, typical of early 19th century development. Here is the *quod sacra* parish church of 1830, undistinguished as to appearance, founded as a chapel-of-ease from Duffus. The school is near by. Opposite is the war-memorial in the mercat-cross form, and a drinking fountain. The great maltings, connected with the innumerable distilleries of the area, rises at this southern end and provides considerable and necessary employment, if little amenity. A former manure-works and boat-building yard are now gone.

No description of Burghead must omit to mention the annual celebration, carried out on 12th January, of The Burning of the Clavie, an interesting relic of fire-worship, presumably from Pictish pre-Christian times, or perhaps a Norse insertion, where a blazing tar-barrel is paraded and rolled down Dorrie Hill, allegedly to warn off evil spirits.

Rather dominating the area to the south, in opposition to the maltings, is the 500-feet high B.B.C. transmitting mast, erected in 1936, on the side of Clarkly Hill. East of this, on the Hopeman road, is the village of Cummingstown—not to be confused with Cuminestown in Aberdeenshire—long and narrow, stretching along the road for half a mile between the two small towns. There are no particular features. To the west stretch the vast green levels of the planted Roseisle Forest flanking Burghead Bay, in which an ancient cairn is located.

Cromdale and Advie. Cromdale is a large civil parish which, with Advie and Inverallan, spread over 64,000 acres of Strathspey, at various times partly in Moray, Inverness and Banff shires—for the county boundaries hereabouts have been much altered. Inverallan however can now be identified largely with Grantown, and this item deals with Cromdale and Advie district proper, almost wholly south of the Spey, still partly in three counties—and large enough, in all conscience, but mostly consisting of the heather heights of the Hills of Cromdale.

The area is served by three main roads, B.970 from Nethy Bridge A.95 Grantown to Keith, and A.939 Grantown to Tomintoul, the first two following the Spey valley, the third climbing across the hills southwards by Bridge of Brown. There is a small loop-road through the Haughs of Cromdale, from A.95, to the north-east.

Cromdale village is situated on A.95 where this loop-road starts, 4 miles north-east of Grantown, a not particularly attractive place although in very pleasant wooded country. It is really a distilling village, serving the large Balmenach–Glenlivet Distillery a mile away up a side-road to the south. There is also a timber-yard and saw-mill and a broken-down meal-mill, with cottages, council houses and some new housing of character. There is a shop, village hall, and the former school converted into an Outdoor Centre by the Moray–Nairn education authority. The parish church lies half a mile away, in an isolated position on the bank of Spey at what was the site of the former village, Boat of Cromdale, once a ferry-town, where is now a fairly modern girder-bridge, replacing an 18th century structure. The former ferryman's house still stands on the north bank. The church, of granite, dates from 1809, although it has a stone from its predecessor built into the walling, dated 1602 with Grant initials. It is fairly plain, quite large, with a belfry, wide and substantial, and bright within, having a timber ceiling and rear gallery. The Grants of Congash have a memorial tablet and there is an oil portrait of a parish minister, James Chapman (1702–37), hanging in the vestibule. There are a great many old flat gravestones in the kirkyard, and two notable ancient beech trees of great size. The situation by the riverside is very pleasant. The fine Georgian manse stands near by.

Congash, actually in Abernethy parish but better dealt with here, lies 2 miles further west, an old Grant lairdship now a farm, the interesting and characterful long, low tacksman's house distinctly neglected. There is a very interesting feature near by in the fields to the south, a very large cairn-circle, in a bad state of repair. There was said to be several Pictish symbol-stones somewhere here, amongst the great mass. One was fairly readily discovered, upright to the west of the circle, with double-disc and Z-rod, and below, partly buried, a curious symbol with what might have been a circle with a sort of cross within, or perhaps a crescent with decoration. After search, we discovered another, only a yard away, again partly buried, displaying the horseshoe symbol. A proper and careful scrutiny might well discover others. It is ridiculous that such an important monument to our early forefathers should be so utterly neglected.

A mile west of Congash the A.95 crosses Spey by a modern bridge to Grantown, the Old Spey Bridge of 1754 slightly downstream, three-arched with cutwaters and very picturesque, built by the military and now open only to walkers. B.970 heads on southwards towards Nethy Bridge and Rothiemurchus. Almost 2 miles along this is the attractive old laird's house of Auchernack, on a green mound with old pines around, now a farm. This stretch of country between the Spey and the hills is consistently pleasant.

At the other, eastern, side of Cromdale village the aforementioned loop-road curves off south-eastwards for 5 or 6 miles, through the foot-hill area known as the Haughs of Cromdale, dotted with small farms and with many burns flowing down out of the Cromdale Hills above. Here was fought, in 1690, soon after Killiecrankie, the Battle of Crom-dale, in the early stages of the Jacobite struggles, when a party of dragoons surprised Buchan's sleeping Highlanders killing over 300 of the 800 engaged. There is a Piper's Stone, *Clach nan Piobair*, mark-ing the approximate site, south of the road about half-way along. Nearer Cromdale is Lethendry Castle, now only a vaulted basement and some walling with traces of an angle-turret, in the farm-steading. A Grant place, some of the fugitives hid here after the battle.

Where the loop-road rejoins the A.95, 4 miles on from Cromdale

village, past the lengthy Tom an Uird Wood, is Dalvey, the 18th
century small laird's house thereof now a farm, whitewashed on a
knoll by the roadside. The Grants of Dalvey removed to Grangehill
in Dyke and Moy parish of Moray, from here, and changed the
name of that property to Dalvey. A mile on, three ancient burial-
cairns cluster near a burnside on the same side of the road, not now
readily distinguished. Another mile and Advie is reached, a scattered community rather than a village, near another crossing of
Spey. A prominent war-memorial pillar at a road-fork marks the
start of it, and a little way along the main road is the church, now
linked with Nethy Bridge and Cromdale, but still in use, a rather
fine Gothic building of 1874 with a square pinnacled tower and
much good stained glass. Built into the vestry wall externally is a
Pictish symbol-stone, much weathered, showing crescent and V-rod,
and part of a double-disc. The position is pleasant, on sloping woodlands above the river levels. Two miles beyond this we run into the
Ballindalloch area of Banffshire, with just before the boundary, the
large and handsome modern Tormore Distillery, making "Long
John" whisky.

Most of the community of Advie lies down the lesser road, from
the war-memorial. Here is the former school, a village hall, post-
office and a scattering of houses. At the river is the fairly narrow
modern concrete Bridge of Advie, 1922, replacing a high 18th
century structure. It is probably sensible to deal here with the area
immediately at the other side of Spey, for it is too far east to be
included conveniently with Grantown, and certainly cannot come
under Knockando in Moray, eastwards. Moreover this Tulchan
district was a companion barony with Advie, and together they
formed the old Advie parish. They were both anciently in the
possession of the early Earls of Fife, passing in the 15th century to
the Ballindallochs of that Ilk, before eventually coming to the Grants.
Just a little north of the bridge-end Glen Tulchan opens off, under
the large hillside wood of Straan, and probes northwards into the
empty hills, which come very close here, for 4 miles. Tulchan estate
itself is a mile further along the B.9102 towards Knockando. At
the westwards side of the bridge-end the road climbs to the little pass
in the wood of Old Tulchan, in a mile, where is a quite impressive
and steep tree-lined ravine. Beyond it the land opens out again, at
Lettoch, where there is a small monolith at the roadside on the north
in a dip of this very pleasant road. There is a small community at
Delliefure another mile on, and still further between the road and the
farm of Upper Port is a single standing-stone in a field on the left.
We are here almost back at Boat of Cromdale bridge.

Something should be said of the Hills of Cromdale, the fairly
distinct range of about ten summits, averaging around 2200 feet,
separated from both the main Eastern Cairngorms and the Glenlivet
hills by the valley of the Avon. They extend north-eastwards and
south-westwards, roughly parallel with Spey, for perhaps 9 miles,
their highest point Creggan a' Chaise (2267 feet) whereon is a large

cairn commemorating Queen Victoria's Jubilee in 1887. They are not an exciting range, rounded and heathery, but make a fine background. Four main foot-tracks cross them from the Haughs district, and the A.937 Grantown–Tomintoul road climbs round their southern perimeter, over bare terrain with magnificent views backwards over the Braes of Abernethy to the high Cairngorms—which some have claimed to be amongst the finest prospects in Scotland, much photographed and painted by artists. On the route of the military road this reached 1424 feet 6 miles south-east of Grantown. Two miles further it drops suddenly and dramatically, by zigzags, to the picturesque single-arch Bridge of Brown, in Glen Brown (formerly Bruan) where there is a tiny and remote hamlet. Here is the county boundary between Banff and Inverness-shires. There is a fine linn, or waterfall, just a stone's throw from the bridge. 2 miles more, this road is joined by the B.9008 Ballindalloch–Tomintoul route up the Avon valley, which offers the motorist a most satisfying return journey to Speyside.

Dallas and Kellas. The River Lossie rises in the rather feature-less welter of lowish hills of upland Moray, about 17 miles south-west of Elgin, in Dallas parish. As with most hill parishes, Dallas is of large extent, but principally empty heather and moor, covering 22,000 acres. Of this great area only the northern and lower-lying parts, in the Lossie valley, are of much significance—to any save sheep, grouse and the North-East Scotland Water Board. There is a sizeable village of Dallas, nestling under the wooded Hill of the Wangie, and 3 miles or so to the east, in the same valley, the populous farming area of Kellas.

Dallas community consists of two parts—the fairly compact village flanking the road for half a mile, in the open haugh of the Lossie; and the detached area half a mile to the south known as Bridge of Lossie, where is the parish church and large manse, and a former mill beside the bridge. The parish church, secluded in a wooded den, in its old graveyard, is attractive, dating from 1793, a long stone building with an open belfry and a pleasant pilastered doorway, successor of a former heather-thatched edifice dedicated to St. Michael. It is plain and bright within, with a coved ceiling and small gallery, to which there is an outside forestair, not now in use. In the kirkyard is the old Dallas Cross, a fairly typical Mercat Cross, 12 feet tall, on a square plinth, its shaft topped by a broken fleur-de-lis finial. There is a watch-house, against body-snatchers, at the gate, and amongst the old gravestones is one very small, only 18 inches high now, bearing the Hay arms impaled with those of Dunbar, and the initials R.H. and E.D.

The old Bridge of Lossie near by has recently been replaced by a modern structure, and in the process the ancient St. Michael's Well has been covered up. The picturesque old mill buildings here, at the Lossie-side, amidst pleasant gardens, represents a former woollen mill. A mark on the walling, up near the eaves, dated 1829, tradi-

tionally shows the height to which the river rose during the disastrous
Moray flood of that year.

The main village of Dallas slightly to the north-west is not particularly interesting or attractive, although the surroundings are pleasing.
There is a population of under 500, a long straight street, and an
Institute erected by the Houldsworth family of Dallas Lodge, in
thankful memory for the safe return of Dallas men in the 1914–18
war—an unusual and suitable thank-offering gesture. Just to the
north, near the road-junction with B.9010, in the open haugh, stands
the single gaunt fang of masonry which is all that remains of Tor
Castle, a former stronghold of the Comyn or Cumming family,
allegedly built in 1400 by a Sir Thomas thereof, of Altyre. Although
today it does not seem a strong position, formerly it would be guarded
by the surrounding marshland and moat.

Dallas Lodge lies a mile to the west, on a side-road, under the
wooded Hill of Mulundy—on which are a cluster of early burial
cairns to the north. The Lodge is interesting in having a late 17th
century Round Square, as stableyard, similar to that at Gordonstoun, indeed a copy, designed by the same Gordon laird. It is a
pleasing structure, with crowstepping, stone-slates, dormer-windows
and other features of the period. The old nucleus in the mansion
itself is overlaid by 19th century work. There is much moorland
around here, with some new-planted forest; but to the north-east
rises the large Dallas Forest clothing the 1046-feet-high Hill of the
Wangie, beyond which lies Pluscarden. These woodlands are very
attractive, above the B.9010 road to Elgin which follows the Lossie
for 3 miles, with much of oak. At the eastern end of the woodlands
is the Kellas area, of many scattered small farms. There is a roadside
hamlet, with war-memorial, and a modern mansion. The heather
hills rise in swelling waves, to the south.

This large heathery section of the parish, from which issues the
infant Lossie, stretches into the upland wilderness, which prevails
southwards and westwards right to the Speyside and Lochindorb
districts, largely waterlogged moors, with a great many small lochs
—but some of a fair size, Loch Dallas itself being half a mile long.
The fishing is good. A feature up near the head of the Lossie, where
it comes out of little Loch Trevie, is the Seven Sisters' Springs. The
names up here have a boggy and watery ring to them—Moss of
Bednawinny, Lochs of Bogmussach, Lochs of Little Benshalag, Eass
of Auchness—a waterfall. Glen Latterach forms the parish boundary
to the east, with its large Water Board reservoir.

Duffus, Hopeman and Roseisle. Duffus is a large coastal
parish, with village, of the Laigh of Moray, extending to nearly
10,000 acres, north-east of Elgin, and Hopeman a large planned
village, with harbour, while Roseisle is a purely rural area now,
with a huge planted forest to the west. The small town of Burghead
is also in Duffus parish, but, with the nearby village of Cummingstown, is more conveniently dealt with separately. There is a coast-

line of 7 miles, sandy to the west but elsewhere rocky, with cliffs and caves, formerly a great haunt of smugglers. Much of the parish used to be under water, partly from an arm of the sea stretching inland eastwards from the Roseisle area, partly from the great Loch of Spynie. A mighty sand-blow, of the Culbin variety, cut off the arm of the sea in the late 17th century, and subsequent reclamation, with the draining of the loch by the Spynie Canal, leaves this now a most fertile expanse. The name Duffus means the Black Water.

Duffus rose to prominence because of its great castle, built in the reign of David the Second, Bruce's son, on what would then be an island in the waterlogged area, a green eminence, largely artificial, with surrounding moat. The first motte-and-bailey castle was of timber harled with clay—we read of Sir Reginald Cheyne, who married the heiress in 1286, petitioning the all-conquering Edward of England in 1305 for permission to fell 200 oak trees "to build his manor of Duffus"—galling indeed to have had to win English permission to fell his own trees. This stronghold was replaced in due course by a stone keep and surrounding curtain-walling, the remains of which dominate the flat lands today as a noted landmark, and are in the care of the Department of the Environment. The property was granted to the progenitor of the great Moray or Murray family, the famous Freskin, in 1150, but passed, through the marriages of heiresses, first to the Cheynes and then to the Sutherlands, in 1350— these Sutherlands however being of the same Moray stock. The 10th Sutherland laird was created first Lord Duffus in 1651, for aiding King Charles the Second, and the line survived until 1843, when the title fell dormant for lack of accepted heirs. Long before that, however, Duffus Castle had ceased to be occupied.

It does not appear to have featured largely in history, despite its size and strength, covering no less than 8 acres within its 25-feet-wide ditch, with outer and inner baileys, drawbridges and 10-feet-thick walling, honeycombed with mural chambers. This stone castle was built well on in the 14th century, and it is interesting to note that the keep, although wide, was not vaulted as was usual, but provided with timber floors—a testimony to the great oaks which grew in this tree-growing Laigh of Moray, to make such timbering possible. A small chapel, or oratory, was contrived in the thickness of the walling. Large sections of the masonry have sagged or collapsed, because of the sandy soil of the hillock, but it is notable how the mortar has not given way, and substantial lengths of walling lean at odd angles. Much of the curtain-walling remains, and the whole gives an excellent impression of the lay-out of a typical motte-and-bailey castle, but little altered.

Duffus village, old church and later mansion, lie over a mile to the north, on slightly rising ground. The village, once called New Duffus, is pleasantly situated, and fairly compact, although it has increased largely in recent years with modern housing. Here, at the roadside, is the present parish church, dating from 1868, quite large and handsome, with a tall spire and a fairly recent graveyard. There are still some old village houses. This was not the site of the original church, which stood half a mile to the east, near Duffus House, and is now a roofless but well-preserved ruin, known as St. Peter's Kirk, with its ancient kirkyard surrounding. It is a pleasant place, amongst old trees, well cared for. The present walls are mainly 18th century, but with much older work included, and a most excellent early 16th century porch, complete with groined vaulted roof. There is also a barrel-vaulted Sutherland of Duffus crypt, or aisle, to the west, which was the basement of the original tower. Here is some heraldry and a Sutherland grave dated 1626. There is a holy-water stoup just inside the main doorway, and a graveslab with an early calvary cross on the floor of the church, with many other old slabs used as paving. On the outside east gable is inserted a Latin tablet dated 1616. There are two outside forestairs to what has been a timber-floored loft, and an empty belfry. High on the south front is a stone cherub built in, and on the north walling also part of a very ancient gravestone showing a two-handed sword, plus other built-in fragments. In the kirkyard rises the Duffus or St. Peter's Cross, a typical medieval Mercat Cross, a tall slender column on a plinth, similar to that at the Michael Kirk, Gordonstoun, near by. The former holy well lay at the roadside just to the north, but is now barely discernible.

Duffus House, now a boarding-house of Gordonstoun School, is a large whitewashed mansion standing in its grounds to the south, mainly Victorian but with very early 18th century nucleus and some good painted heraldry in the vestibule. It belonged to the baronet family of Dunbar of Northfield, and used to be called Thunderton; their town-house in Elgin still survives, although converted into a hotel.

A mile west of Duffus village is the farming estate of Inverugie, which once belonged to the Keith Marischal family, who named the property after their great lands on the Ugie in Buchan. There was a small castle or fortalice near the present rather pleasant mansion. To the south, in the park, is a large, rough weatherworn and cracked boulder, six-and-a-half feet high, known as the Camus Stone, and alleged, like other stones so called, to mark the scene of the death of an evidently very fierce Danish invading leader named Camus. It was formerly at Kaim of Duffus, to the south.

The village, or small town, of Hopeman, lies a mile to the north, on a gentle ridge sloping down to the sea. It was founded as a fishing community only in 1805, and was much enlarged and the harbour improved by Admiral Duff of Drummuir who bought the lands in 1837. It has a rather bare aspect, lacking trees in a countryside so rich in timber, but compact, its streets laid out at right angles. Quite large, with a population of over 1000, it lays itself out to attract holiday-makers. But its two dozen seine-net fishing-boats still constitute its basic industry—although 120 boats once fished from here. Its harbour is also much used by pleasure-craft, but unfortunately suffers from sand-silting. There is an old ice-house, with the usual vaulted roof, for the storing of fish. At the top of the little town is the *quod sacra* church, which was the Duffus Free church originally, of 1854, with a tall clock-tower and noted landmark added in 1923 as a gift from an Elgin distiller who worshipped here. The church is large, with a gallery round three sides, but no graveyard. The village has many stone cottages of traditional fisher style, considerable modern housing, a caravan-site, playing fields, other sporting facilities including a 9-hole golf course, and a Tourist Association, all above a rocky coast with one or two beaches. The renowned Covesea caves, one with Pictish roof-carvings, are usually approached from Hopeman, and the cliff-walk very scenic.

Roseisle, as its name suggests, was once another island in the great formerly waterlogged area of Duffus and Drainie parishes. A ridge of hill there rises to 280 feet—no great altitude, but notable indeed in an area where the height above sea-level averages around 20 feet. To the west of this hill the vast planted Roseisle Forest extends along the coastal plain for nearly 5 miles, with the parish boundary more than half-way. For the rest there are only farms, and the tiny cross-roads hamlet of College of Roseisle. This ambitiously named little group of cottages stands on the site of what was a quite important community of the Celtic Church, planted here in the early days of Christianity in Scotland.

Cummingstown, a village of the parish north of Roseisle and west of Hopeman, is dealt with under Burghead.

A Pictish symbol-stone from Easterton of Roseisle, depicting goose and fish sculpturing, was taken to the Museum of Antiquities, Edinburgh in 1932.

Dyke, Moy, Brodie and Darnaway. Dyke and Moy are two rural parishes at the extreme west end of the county of Moray, united in 1618, and situated in the level Laigh just north-west of Forres—the Moy not to be confused with the better-known Highland Moy on the A.9 south of Inverness. The conjoint parishes form a pleasing and mainly sequestered area of 15,500 acres, admittedly threaded by the busy A.96 Elgin–Inverness road, but elsewhere with a distinctly off-the-beaten-track atmosphere about it, both northwards over the flat Findhorn plain to the vast modern forests of the Culbin Sands area, and southwards amongst the rising old woodlands of the great Darnaway estate of the Earl of Moray. In the centre is Brodie Castle, an ancient and interesting lairdship, where the Brodies of that Ilk have been settled since time immemorial. There is a sizeable and attractive village at Dyke, a fishing hamlet at Broom of Moy, a farming hamlet of Kintessack to the north, and the estate community of Newton of Darnaway amongst the woods to the south.

Dyke village, where is the parish church, is situated on a slight eminence amongst the levels, near the Muckle Burn—which flows parallel with the Findhorn and joins it near its mouth—3 miles west of Forres. It is a most pleasing place, full of character. It centres round the church, on its mound, a most interesting building of 1781, fairly plainly Georgian as to exterior, but with a much older nucleus, including an ancient aisle to the east, possibly 15th century, now used as vestry, over the Brodie burial crypt. Here, in the walling, is a calvary-cross slab of early date, with Latin inscription. The church interior is attractive, small, with tall slender windows on the south side only, with light woodwork, an almost semi-circular gallery and three-decker central pulpit all under an excellent timber roof. Enormous locks guard the doors; and in the porch is a heraldic stone dated 1613 and initialled W.K. and E.I., inscribed: "Valter Kinnard, Elizabeth Innes. The bvuildars of this bed of stane. Ar Laird and Ladye of Covbine's quhilk tva and thair scvhaine braithe is gane; Pleis God vil sleip this bed vithin." This was the second-last laird of Culbin, the estate lost under the famous and dire sand-blow of the 17th century. There are many old tombstones in the kirkyard, one dated 1681. And a good war-memorial gateway thereto. Altogether a place worth visiting. In 1780 a hoard of silver coins was dug up here, of the reign of William the Lion.

The village climbs some little braes and has a pleasant old-world air. There is an old-established nursery here, growing carnations under glass in a big way. The old schoolhouse is interesting. The former Free church to the north is now a store, and there is a hollow to the west, locally known as The Forty-five, with Jacobite associations.

Brodie Castle and estate lies a mile to the south-west, in fine old trees planted in the 1650–80 period. The lands have never, in recorded time, been held by any other family than the Brodies—a notable claim even in Scotland where old families cling tenaciously. The Brodies can trace their holding here from 1160, but the oldest part of the present castle appears to date from the 16th and 17th centuries, although there may be an older nucleus. The major part of the large building is comparatively modern, but the old L-planned tower, with its parapet and wall-walk, still dominates from the south-west corner. This rises four storeys, with a garret within the parapet, and a tall, slender stair-tower in the re-entrant angle. The parapet is drained by the usual cannon-like spouts, and there are open rounds. The basement is vaulted, lit only by arrow-slit windows. The eastern gabled addition is probably 17th century and a storey lower, and, like the north-western wing of the L, decorated with a stringcourse.

Internally the castle is full of interest, although inevitably there has been much alteration down the centuries. The old kitchen retains its enormous arched fireplace, with bread oven; and the vaulted hall on the first floor has decorative plaster-work featuring the Tudor Rose amongst other symbols—so that it probably dated from 1603 or soon thereafter, celebrating the Union of the Crowns. The house is full of treasures—although recently it has lost a 10th century bishop's pontifical, found in a coachhouse and sold for £14,000 to the British Museum.

Malcolm the Fourth confirmed the Brodies in these lands in 1160, and there was a Malcolm, Thane of Brodie, in Alexander the Third's reign. Thane Michael had a charter from Bruce in 1311. Alexander the 9th laird died in 1627, leaving six sons, who acquired considerable lairdships in Moray. The castle was burned by the young Lord Lewis Gordon in 1645, during the Montrose campaigns.

In the estate, near the east gate and at the side of the drive, is a notable relic, foolishly named the Rodney Stone. It is in fact one of the finest of Pictish symbol-stones, protected by a canopy, the decoration and symbols in high relief and excellent preservation. There are also ogham characters. The slab is 6 feet tall, and as well as the usual cross with Celtic ornament, displays dolphin-headed serpents, the typical Celtic beast or elephant, double-disc and Z-rod symbols. The oghams are said to refer to one Eddernon, presumably St. Ethernan, and may be linked with the Burghead Pictish remains. It was found in 1781, and used the year later to commemorate Admiral Rodney's victory at Dominica—but fortunately only little spoiled.

The Nairnshire, as well as the parish, boundary, lies only a mile to the west, at Hard Muir, where Shakespeare made Macbeth meet the Weird Sisters.

East and north of Dyke a network of minor roads serve the level lands between the A.96 and the great Culbin Forest. A mile to the east, at a complicated bend of the Muckle Burn, is the estate now called Dalvey, once the barony of Grangehill, with an old castle, now gone. The present mansion is substantial and dignified, dating from 1750, when it was built by Sir Alexander Grant of Dalvey, 5th Baronet. The real Dalvey was, and is, on Speyside, in Advie parish, 20 miles to the south as the crow flies, but the Grants thereof came here and changed the name of Grangehill. A square crowstepped-gabled doocot of the 17th century, with a walled garden, is all that survives of the earlier establishment of the Dunbars. An attractive private bridge carries the driveway fairly high over the burn.

Another mile to the east, beside the Findhorn itself and 2 miles from its mouth, is the hamlet of Broom of Moy, a charming and secluded community of small fishermen's cottages, amongst whins and greens for the drying of nets. A modern footbridge links it with the Greeship suburb of Forres across the river. This was a salmon fishers' village, and is still a fishing-station although none of the cottages are now occupied by fishermen. It was, and is, a bad place for flooding, the Findhorn rising as much as 14 feet above normal, on occasion:

> *Says Divie to Dorback, whar shall we sweep?*
> *Through the middle o' Moy, when all men sleep.*

Although the sea is not far away, no trace or feeling of it is perceptible here.

Half a mile to the north is Moy House, substantial and of Georgian aspect but with a 16th and 17th century nucleus, including a vaulted basement and moulded and chamfered window surrounds. The two earlier wings project to the rear. Internally there is some good woodwork and panelling. The older house was rebuilt by Major George

Grant, of the Glenmoriston family, who was cashiered from the Hanoverian army for surrendering Inverness too hastily to Prince Charles Edward in 1745.

A mile north of Moy is Kincorth House, dating from 1797, but greatly altered. It was another Grant estate, and the first attempt to plant trees on the Culbin sandhills was made by the Kincorth laird in 1846. It was not very successful, but later efforts succeeded with Corsican pines. Binsness, another Findhorn lairdship of the incoming Grants, at the extreme end of this road, on the Bay shore, is now a Forestry Commission property. The so-called Lake of Moy, merely an arm of the estuary, is passed on the way.

Back south-westwards 3 miles, on the way to Dyke again, is Kintessack, a hamlet built on the edge of the great planted forest, a quietly secluded place. Culbin could be described at length, for few places have changed character so greatly as this stretch of the Moray Firth coast. The ancient barony of Culbin, of the Kinnairds, covered almost 10,000 acres of some of the finest land in Moray, with farms, village and a church. In 1670 the sand began to take over, both blowing from the sea sand-bars and through injudicious uprooting of juniper and broom bushes, which had held the dunes in check. It was not all covered in a night, as tales declare, but the entire area, sometimes called the Granary of Moray, was eventually overwhelmed, the sand in places lying as deep as 100 feet. The sands used to shift and drift with the wind, and sometimes skeleton trees and even the tip of the church tower are said to have appeared now and again, always to vanish again. Then in the 1920s, at last, "thatching" with brushwood and the vast task of planting with Corsican pine was commenced in earnest, and today there are mature woodlands stretching for 7 miles along the coast, and 2 miles inland, threaded by rides and tracks—but very easy to be lost in. It must be one of the greatest forestry achievements in Britain.

All which has been described so far has been north of the A.96. To the south is a somewhat smaller section of the conjoint parish, but with a special atmosphere of its own—part of the vast Darnaway estate and forest, a huge tract of land of ancient woodlands, with Darnaway Castle, the seat of the Earls of Moray, in the midst. The lands and forest stretch far beyond the Dyke and Moy parish, but are conveniently described here. The castle, like the property, is vast, but although on an ancient site and incorporating the great banqueting-hall of the original building, the present house dates only from 1810, an impressive rather than a beautiful or characterful edifice externally. The banqueting-hall, which with its gabled roof is easily distinguished from the rest, especially from the west, is famous for its splendid arched oaken roof, similar to that of Parliament House, Edinburgh. Like Brodie, the castle is full of treasures. Bruce's friend and nephew, Randolph, Earl of Moray, given these Comyn lands, founded the original castle, and very important it was through the centuries, the earldom being almost a royal fief. James the Fourth conferred it on his illegitimate son by Flaming Janet Kennedy, and frequently visited here to see both mother and child—and to get away from Margaret Tudor, his wife. Mary Queen of Scots, in her turn, conferred Darnaway on her illegitimate eldest brother, James Stewart, the famous Regent Moray, in 1560, and from him the present line descends or, more accurately, from his daughter and son-in-law another James Stewart, Lord Doune, who gained the earldom in his wife's right—the Bonnie Earl o' Moray of the ballad. The present Earl is the 19th.

The estate is a small kingdom on its own, covering a score of thousand acres, with villages, farms, sawmills, lochs, and threaded by a network of roads. Ten million trees were planted here towards the end of the 18th century, and for mature hardwood timber, Darnaway must be difficult to beat in all Scotland. No brief description can do justice to Darnaway. Happily for visitors, many of the roads which traverse these lovely woodlands are now public ones, moreover, because the land is far from flat, all hills and valleys and indeed lifting up to the heather summits of Braemoray, the far prospects and vistas are frequently as fine as those close at hand. The Golden Gates, as they are called, wrought-iron with gilded coronets and decoration, are to the north in the Tearie area, just south of Brodie, and date from 1868. There is an estate hamlet at Whitemire, with a large farm, about a mile west of the castle, and a larger community, hidden away amongst the woods, at Conicavel, or Newton of Darnaway, another mile to the south-east, with school, post-office, store and many old stone cottages, some being replaced by fine modern estate housing—all most attractive. Most of the southern section of the estate is in Edinkillie parish, and some of its features are described thereunder.

Edinkillie, Logie, Dunphail and Dava. Edinkillie is the largest civil parish of Moray, 33,000 acres, but it boasts no real village— although the large estate hamlet of Conicavel, on the Darnaway property, is included, described, with the rest of that great estate, under Dyke and Moy. Logie and Dunphail are ancient estates in the picturesque valleys of the Findhorn and Divie, and Dava is the lonely hamlet far out on the Braemoray moors to the south, on the way to Grantown.

The parish stretches for no less than 14 miles, from Lochindorb on the south to within 2 miles of Forres on the north, with Nairnshire county boundary as its western flank. The valleys of the Dorback, flowing out of Lochindorb, and Divie, are almost wholly in Edinkillie, as is about 7 miles of the Findhorn. The two former join the Findhorn just a mile below the parish centre, near Dunphail, at a noted beauty spot, known as the Meeting of the Waters. All the southern part of the parish, indeed most of its area, is heather upland and hill, with the isolated and prominent Knock of Braemoray (1493 feet) dominating. Braemoray now refers to this specific upland area, with little Dava at its lonely heart, but once Braemoray was the name for all the Highland area of the great province of Moray, as distinct from the Laigh, or lowland part, flanking the Moray Firth. The central and northern lower-lying parts of Edinkillie are heavily wooded with old forest as well as more recent planting; indeed the area is one of the most densely wooded in the land. Also highly picturesque, for the three rivers cut deep and dramatic gorges and ravines, providing much fine rock scenery, with falls, cauldrons and rapids, some of them renowned in picture and song. Many of the bridges crossing these gorges are themselves of great interest.

The parish centre, at Edinkillie itself, where the A.940 crosses the Divie a mile above the Meeting of Waters, contains only the parish church, with manse and a couple of other houses, the tall, seven-arched viaduct of the former Highland Railway prominent to the east. The church dates from 1741, long, harled and cream-washed, in an old graveyard, with a six-sided watch-house against the southern kirkyard-wall. There is a central pulpit, lofts or galleries on three sides, and a large old bell in a renewed belfry. The former mort-bell of 1698 has disappeared. There are some old gravestones, and a memorial in the west gable to one Alexander Wilson, died 1827, erected by no fewer than five local lairds in appreciation for his management of their estates. The well at the roadside to the north has been renewed as a war-memorial. The manse is a fine house. A stone-circle, which used to stand on the farm of Dallas-broughty a mile to the east, has now gone. North of this farm over a mile, on the Divie, are the Falls of Feakirk.

The A.940 climbs southwards up the Dorback valley and over the western shoulder of Knock of Braemoray, to join the A.939 to Grantown at Dava, 6 miles on, passing Glenerney and Braemoray Lodge, the latter attractive, small and whitewashed. The views up here, as the road crosses miles of rolling heather ridges, are magnificent. Dava, remote amidst the empty brown moors near the 1000-feet contour, has a "former" air about it, former railway-station, school, etcetera, but it is an important highways junction still although with only two or three houses, the roads to Nairn, Forres, Grantown and Lochindorb meeting here. A bleaker spot on a grey winter's day would be hard to imagine. The boundary with Cromdale parish is here, Lochindorb, 2 miles to the south-west, being dealt with under Grantown-on-Spey. The smaller loch of Allan, with many another lochan, lies amongst the peat-hags and heather north and west of Dava.

Just north of Edinkillie kirkton is the old estate of Dunphail, formerly sometimes spelt Duniphail. The mansion, like the entire property, is very fine, and meticulously maintained, Italianate in style, built in 1829 and 1841 to designs of Playfair, and extended in 1871, on a terrace above the Divie. There are delightful gardens. Along with the neighbouring estates of Logie and Relugas, Dunphail was purchased by Sir Alexander Grant, first Baronet of Logie, the well-known biscuit-manufacturer, philanthropist and friend of Ramsay MacDonald, all now being in the possession of his descendants. To the north of the house are the remains of Dunphail Castle, crowning a dramatic conical rocky bluff, surrounded by a former moat. Not a great deal of the ruins remain, consisting of three vaulted basements and parts of two gables, and though the original castle was ancient, a seat of the Comyns, and indeed was besieged by Randolph, Earl of Moray in 1330, nothing now remains that is apparently older than the late 16th or early 17th century, the walling comparatively thin. It is all notably picturesque, however. It passed from the Comyns to the Dunbars.

The aforementioned Randolph is commemorated by Randolph's Leap, a noted beauty spot a mile to the west, but on the B.9007 across Divie on the Relugas estate. It is readily accessible from the road and a favoured haunt of visitors. Here, in a rocky gorge, the rushing Findhorn narrows, and across the gap leaped, not Randolph but Alastair Ban Comyn, or Cumming of Dunphail, with the Comyn standard, to escape—his father and five brothers allegedly having been executed by Randolph, though this is very doubtful. At any rate, whatever the cause, it is a feat few would wish to emulate. This whole Meeting of the Waters area is quite delightful, in the old woodlands. There is a stone here to mark the great height reached by the flood-waters in 1829, half-way up to the road. Close by, to the north, near the bridge carrying the B.9007, in more forest, is the Doune of Relugas, site of a former Pictish vitrified fort, 160 by 100 feet, with ditch and rampart. Relugas House has now been demolished. There is a small hamlet on this very lovely road above the former entrance, with Relugas Mains skied high above all, with splendid vistas, reached by a hairpin-bend track. The Nairnshire boundary is to the south and west, and Daltulich Bridge crosses Findhorn there, a high single arch of 1800, above a deep ravine of dark and rushing waters.

Just north of the meeting of A.940 and B.9007 is Logie estate, with a fine and large whitewashed mansion in Scottish Baronial style, on the site of a 17th century fortalice, and perhaps containing a nucleus thereof. It was another Comyn or Cumming stronghold. The estate is again richly wooded and finely maintained. Near by, on the A.940, is the farm of Presley, now the estate-office, but until fairly recently occupied by a long succession of Calder farmers, here since the 17th century, and including many noted men. A descendant still lives in a house across the road.

Logie marches with the vast Darnaway estate to the west, across Findhorn, and here follows a notable series of riverside scenes amongst the woodlands, in the Sluie and Meads of St. John area, for almost 5 miles. A famous heronry used to subsist here, and in the great Pool of Sluie 1300 salmon are said to have been taken in one night in 1648.

The parish ends in a point, at Mundole, down near the main A.96 and Forres.

Elgin. The city and royal burgh of Elgin is a famous place, and deservedly so, despite the fact that its population is only 16,400—

A memorial stone within the Cathedral

Elgin Cathedral

The Bishop's House, Elgin. Note the ecclesiastical-type gabled crowsteps of the roofs

small to maintain the status and dignity of a major municipality. Yet it has an undoubted "presence", the air of a place of distinction and importance, with many excellent and outstanding buildings, both ancient and later. Elgin is more than merely the county town of Moray, by any standards.

Its history, naturally, is of long standing. Some say the name derives from one Helgyn, a general of the Norse army of Siward, Earl of Orkney, who invaded mainland Scotland in 927, and is alleged to have camped hereabouts—the camp site at Romancamp Gate, near Fochabers, is by some thought to have been Norse, or Danish, not Roman. The name Helgyn is incorporated in the city's seal. Be that as it may, Moray as a whole was one of the most important provinces of Scotland from earliest times—although it then extended much more widely than today, indeed from sea to sea, and Elgin necessarily was a place of great influence, especially as its surrounding forests and rich plains were favourite hunting-grounds of the early monarchs. It was created a royal burgh of David the First—although the earliest charter still extant is that of Alexander the Second. About this same period (1224) Bishop Andrew de Moravia established his episcopal seat here—prior to which it had been at Birnie 3 miles to the south. So arose the magnificent cathedral which became the architectural pride of Scotland—before becoming its shame. Thereafter, history and the centuries seldom failed to leave their mark on Elgin, for this Moray was the Garden and Granary of Scotland, and the inevitable target for invaders, high-born brigands and strategy-conscious generals. It was occupied by Edward of England in 1296, burned by Alexander Stewart, Wolf of Badenoch in 1390, raided by Alexander of the Isles in 1402, half-burned by Huntly in 1452, damaged by the Reformers, involved in the Montrose campaigns, occupied by Cromwell's troops, mixed up in the Jacobite struggles and visited by both Charles Edward and Cumberland before Culloden. The wonder is that anything at all survived.

The city lies along a low ridge, on an east–west axis, with the River Lossie making a great bend around it to west and north. For long the walled town was enclosed within these limits, but it has now spread greatly to north and east.

The High Street follows the line of ridge for over half a mile, with the Cathedral at the east end and the castle ruins on Lady Hill at the west. The wide tree-girt stretches of Cooper Park, between High Street and Cathedral, and the grassy heights of Lady Hill, add much to the attractions of this central part of the town.

The ruined Cathedral of the Holy Trinity is, of course, Elgin's most renowned feature, and one of the most impressive relics in the land, long known as the Lantern of the North. It should be dealt with first. Built in mellow brown stone it has a distinct resemblance to that of St. Andrews. Experts have claimed, however, that "in extent, in loftiness and in impressive magnificence, Elgin was manifestly superior to any other ecclesiastical building in Scotland". Enough remains to delight and impress the visitor, but in its prime it must have deserved all that has been claimed for it. 289 feet in length, it is shorter than St. Andrews, but its central tower was probably higher, at 198 feet. It is the only ancient British cathedral with double aisles to the nave, and its three great towers, splendid western doorway, magnificent eastern window-complex and superb, high-roofed octagonal chapter-house, give it a distinction which even Melrose cannot rival. This is no place for any detailed description. Let it be said, however, that when folk talk of Scotland as anciently a poor, backward and even semi-barbarous land in the Middle Ages, they ought to remember Elgin Cathedral, which authorities admit to be inferior to few in all Europe.

Commenced by Bishop Andrew, in 1224, the first building was burned in 1270, whether by accident or maliciously is not certain, so that most of today's remains date from the rebuilding then. Unhappily it was again burned, in 1390, by Robert the Second's graceless son, the Wolf of Badenoch. But once more it rose anew, Bishop Bur, although very old, pressing on energetically. The next major despoiling, however, was not the work of freebooting vandals but of lawful authority, for in 1568 the Privy Council, now Reformed of course, ordered the Earl of Huntly to take the lead off the roof and sell it, for the maintenance of the Regent Moray's soldiers. It was ironic that the ship loaded with the lead should sink just outside Aberdeen harbour on her way to Holland, and all was lost. After that, Elgin Cathedral was left to wind and weather and less ambitious spoilers and quarriers—although in 1640 the minister of Elgin, with the help of the young Laird of Innes, ardent Covenanters, hacked down and destroyed all the splendid carved work and screens; it is recounted that they tried their hardest to burn the offending woodwork thereafter, but the flames always expired. The foundations of the great central tower gave way in 1711, the crash destroying all that was left of the nave and transepts. In all this tale of folly and hate, it is good to remember the devoted love of one humble man, John Shanks, shoemaker, who for many years alone cherished the noble ruin, clearing and tidying the rubble and carting away more than 3000 barrowloads of debris, before dying, in 1841, aged 83. A stone in the churchyard surrounding the Cathedral commemorates his labours of love. Today the Department of the Environment is replacing some of the stonework, especially the splendid window-mullions.

There are many interesting features within the ruins and in the graveyard. Pride of place must be given to the fine Pictish granite cross-slab in what was the nave, a handsome example, over 6 feet high, depicting a cross with angels and priests and intertwined serpents on one side, and on the other a spirited hunting scene, with a mounted hawker and other horsemen, deer and hounds, below typical double disc and Z-rod and crescent and V-rod symbols. There are many recumbent effigies of bishops and lairds, including the first Earl of Huntly, and some excellent heraldic stones, particularly that of the Innes tomb. A stone coffin here is alleged to have contained the body of Duncan the First before it was removed to Iona for permanent burial.

Grouped around the Cathedral are numerous items of interest. The finest is probably what is called the Bishop's House, just to the west, a comparatively small but tall L-planned fortified house of the 15th and 16th centuries, with little ecclesiastical about it save for the gableted crowsteps. It is somewhat reduced in size now, but still entire, with a vaulted basement, stair-tower and corbelled-out turret, plus a number of good heraldic panels relating to Bishops Innes, Stewart and Hepburn, and the Earl of Mar, victor of Harlaw and son of the aforementioned Wolf of Badenoch. Not far from this, to the north, and standing in its own grounds as a private mansion, is the North College, which was the Dean's Manse, an attractive whitewashed and crowstepped dwelling of some size, with some 16th and 17th century features remaining. Much less is left of the old South College, or Archdeacon's Manse, rebuilt as a mansion in the 19th century but incorporating the 16th century vaulted basement. There were originally many manses around the Cathedral chanonry to house some of the twenty-two canons of the chapter and other dignitaries. Near by also are two remaining gates of the walled city. The Panns Port is to the east, slotted for portcullis, which admitted to the Cathedral precincts. Here, with their lazar-house near by in Lazarus Lane, the local lepers were wont to be given bread by the churchmen—hence the name. This is thought to have been an establishment of the ancient but still existing Military and Hospitaller Order of St. Lazarus of Jerusalem. The North Gate, into the city itself, lies further to the west, within Cooper Park, beside some quite spectacular modern flats.

Cooper Park is a great asset to the town, a 40-acre pleasance gifted to Elgin in 1903 by Sir George Cooper, Baronet, a native and well-known philanthropist. It contains a large and picturesque boating-lake, cricket, football, tennis, bowling and putting facilities and a children's playground, amidst gardens and tree-shaded parkland. Its former mansionhouse, Grant Lodge, is now the public library, a fine Georgian house.

The east end of the High Street starts near by, enhanced by what is known as the Little Cross, a 17th century cylindrical shafted mercat cross on a four-step circular plinth, topped by a sundial finial. This stands in the centre of the busy road where North and South College Streets fork from High Street. Beside it is Elgin Museum, a quite massive Grecian-style building of 1842, the museum run by the private Elgin Society, an excellent body which has done much to safeguard the natural beauty and historic heritage of the town. Here are many notable relics. Pictish stones and fragments thereof include two of the famous bulls from Burghead and a plaster-cast of that in the British Museum, also some from Kineddar, one showing men on horses, others with typical Celtic design. There is a jet necklace 4000 years old found in a stone-cist at Burgie near by in 1913, and the skulls and bones of enormous prehistoric bears and deer, also local. A dug-out canoe found at Gordon Castle loch, 16 feet long, is probably unique, and a currach, or coracle from Advie, made of ox-hide and wicker-work, 4½ feet in diameter, is thought to be the only remaining Scottish example. These, and many other important items and collections make this a fascinating place.

There are a number of 17th and 18th century houses remaining in North and South College Streets. The Bede or almshouse at the east end of the latter, is a fairly small, single-storeyed, crowstepped-gabled building of 1624, rebuilt 1846. Across the road, standing in its grounds, is the impressive present-day refuge for old folk, Anderson's or Elgin Institute, inscribed as such "For the Support of Old Age and the Education of Youth". It is a large Grecian building endowed by one General Anderson, an East India nabob, at a cost of £70,000 in 1832.

The High Street also retains many relics of the days when Elgin was full of the town-houses of Moray's landed gentry, and the arcaded premises of prosperous merchants of the 16th and 17th centuries— though all too many have been swept away. Closes lead off, reached by low-browed pends, many of them attractive as they are intriguing. Near the Museum and Little Cross is Braco's Banking House, 7 High Street, an arcaded building of 1694, where Duff of Braco, progenitor of the soaring Earls and Dukes of Fife family, had his place of business from which so much stemmed. Unfortunately it is not now in a good state. The close behind, with its cobbled entry, is pleasing. Almost next door, at 15–19 High Street, is the Masonic Lodge building of 1728, now restored and very fine, used as the Tourist Information Centre. The large classical building opposite is the 19th century Sheriff Court-house.

Proceeding westwards there is the excellent arcaded former Red Lion Inn of 1688, 42–6 High Street, again in poor condition but scheduled for restoration. It has a five-arched piazza. Here Boswell and Dr. Johnson dined, in 1773, on "a vile dinner". Happily an Elgin Fund has been organised, to promote the preservation of such meritorious old properties, not as museums but as integrated into modern requirements, hotels, shopping developments and so on. Pleasingly, there are some modern shop buildings arcaded in the old style.

In the centre of the High Street, in both senses, rears the town's main church—which is also the church of Elgin parish—St. Giles, or the Muckle Kirk. It is a fine building, of 1828, on plans by the famous Archibald Simpson, in typical Greek Revival style, with a tower 112 feet high, a prominent landmark. It was then thought to be "one of the most elegant in Northern Scotland". It is large, to seat 2000, and boasts a minister's bell of great age. The real Muckle Kirk, on the same site, was a famous foundation, older than the Cathedral itself, and had altars belonging to the six Incorporated Trades of Elgin—Hammermen, Glovers, Tailors, Shoemakers, Weavers and Square-wrights. It was rebuilt in 1684, but was finally demolished about 1800. To the east, on the same island site amongst the endless traffic, is the Muckle Cross, the main city mercat cross, rising, like Edinburgh's, from a pulpit-like base. Its present 12-foot high marble shaft dates only from 1888, but its Lion Rampant finial is 17th century, with Charles the Second's initials. At the other, west end of the same island site, is an impressive war-memorial, in bronze. And, just across the street on the north side, projects the fine circular stair-tower of the Tower Hotel, dated 1634, and corbelled out to the square at top to form a gabled watch-chamber. The remainder of the building, which was the town-house of the Leslies of Glenrothes, was unfortunately wholly remodelled in 1860, although certain internal items and heraldry of the 17th century remain. Near by are the offices of the local newspaper, *The Northern Scot & Moray and Nairn Express*.

Thunderton House, now another hotel, lies on the south side of the street further west. This was a major building of the 17th century, erected as a town-house by the first Lord Duffus, and sold in 1707 to the Dunbars of Thunderton. Much of it is still basically intact, despite great alterations, especially to the upper storeys, which destroys the original aspect, and the tower was demolished in 1822. Prince Charles Edward stayed here in March 1746. Many heraldic dormer pediments are built into the walling, and a row of dormers still remain on the south front. The chimneys are coped, and there is a very massive heraldic panel in a low wall at the former courtyard entrance. Two stone savages from here are preserved in the Elgin Museum. There are other altered 17th and 18th century buildings in this long High Street.

A gap occurs on the north side two-thirds of the way westwards, where is the entry enclosure and lodge for the Lady Hill park, rather attractive. The hill rises steeply, though to no great height, and is crowned by the grass-grown ruins of the ancient Elgin Castle of the early kings, with traces of outerworks. This castle existed in 1160 and was probably the site of the fortress of the old Mormaors of Moray. Edward of England resided here, and described it as a "bon chastell et bonne ville". A local legend accounts for the odd shape of the hill thus: an earlier castle stood at a lower level, and so much iniquity stemmed therefrom that, in due course, God sent a plague, in the form of a blue cloud, to hang over it and finally settle on it— whereafter the people of Elgin covered the castle and all its inmates under a great mound of fresh earth, which now represents the upper part of the hill.

The castle in a single night, with all its inmates sunk out of sight;
  There at midnight hour is heard the sound, of voices talking underground
The rock of cradles—wailing infants' cries, and nurses singing lullabies

Near by soars the 80-foot Tuscan column of 1839 and 1855, to the last Duke of Gordon. There are splendid views of the town and countryside from this hill top, particularly noticeable being the modern spread of the city northwards. On the south-west flank is Lady Hill House, once again converted into a hotel, a pleasing whitewashed house mainly of 1811. Built into a loggia here are a great many carved and inscribed stones, obviously gathered lovingly from various demolished buildings, mainly of the 17th century, dormer pediments, corbels and heraldry. Over the entrance gateway to the house a lintel is dated 1623. The level ground to the north, at the riverside, is known as the Blackfriars Haugh, and was the site of the first Dominican monastery introduced by Alexander the Second into Scotland. And to the south, on High Street opposite, is the large and highly modern post-office complex.

The western end of High Street is dominated by the great bulk and lofty dome of Gray's Hospital and Bilbo Hall, occupying a mound between the forking Inverness and Pluscarden roads. It was erected from an endowment of another East India nabob, Dr. Alexander Gray (1751–1808), who left £26,000 for the relief of the sick poor of the neighbourhood, to the designs of the famous Gillespie Graham. Today it is a modern hospital, with the Mental Hospital adjoining. Thereafter the Lossie quickly limits development, and fields and woods resume. The Maryhill Maternity Hospital stands in trees between Lady Hill and Gray's.

Somewhat higher on the ridge axis, South Street parallels High Street, and on this line also are places of interest. At the west end is the large, functional and modernistic North Caledonian headquarters of the Hydro Board, and near by, the more pleasing Georgian house of Northfield, which now houses the city chambers. This was the later town-house of the Dunbars, who had changed their Moray estate from Thunderton to Northfield. In this vicinity used to be the well-known Elgin Academy, dating from a foundation in 1489 and another in 1585. The buildings are still there and still used for educational purposes, but the Academy itself has moved half a mile to the north to the Morriston area beyond the river, where an enormous glass, steel and concrete tower-block and assorted buildings rise in open grounds above the Lossie. The Academy premises developed in three stages; the first smaller building in Academy Street being now the Girls' Technical College, the second, larger and rather fine classical range of 1800, with later additions to the back, now the Boys' Technical. A bell from the original school is hung in an arch erected in the grassy lawns of the latter. The very modern and extensive police-station building stands opposite, unusual both in appearance and situation. The tall Free church is not far away.

To north and south, cross streets and lanes branch off South Street, often very pleasant, with villas and large houses amongst trees and gardens, a fine residential area yet very near the centre of the town. Here are St. Sylvester's Catholic, the South and the Baptist churches. Also hotels and guest-houses of the more residential sort, in streets running down to the southern ring-road. Towards the east of this area, the names Greyfriars Street, Abbey Street and Maisondieu Road indicate early ecclesiastical development, and sure enough, here still flourishes a religious house, the Convent of Mercy. It is a Catholic girls' school, run by the Sisters of Mercy, which came to the old Greyfriars monastery here in 1895—although established in smaller premises near by 25 years earlier. The well-known philanthropist, the 3rd Marquis of Bute, bought Greyfriars for them, and restored and rebuilt the monastery magnificently. The convent is both a boarding and day school, and has a school of music and one for commercial subjects. The monastic buildings today are delightful, grouped round a cloister and green quadrangle, with a deep and ancient central well. The chapel, which forms the north side of the complex, is very ancient, supposed to have been founded by Bishop Innes in 1409. It was a roofless ruin when taken in hand by the Marquis, but many of the original features survive to form a most noble church. The great central rood-screen is modern, and of fine workmanship, and the stained-glass is of a high order. The plain white walls set off the very ornate high altar, and the ancient sacrament-house on the north side, beautifully gilded and canopied as it originally would be, is notable. A leper's squint window, from a little mural chamber 15 feet up is unusual. Also unusual are the duplicate set of aumbry and piscina *below* the screens, ancient also— giving the impression that the church was once divided into two. Little remains of ancient work in the restored and rebuilt monastic wings, but traces of tempera paintwork may be seen in beams in the nuns' refectory.

In Abbey Street also, across from the Convent, is an unusual commercial establishment—a cod-liver-oil cream factory. An ancient malt-kiln which used to stand near the top of the street, has recently been demolished.

On the north side of the High Street there is much less to be detailed, largely because of the extensive Cooper Park, and also in that this was once low marshy ground near the river-bank. Here, on North Street, the busy road which leads to the Bishopmill suburb and on to Lossiemouth, is the new Town Hall, very modern in concrete and glass, facing across the open parkland, with a large wrought-iron representation of the city arms, and another wrought-iron effigy of St. Giles, the patron saint, at a rather good fountain. In the vestibule is a large circular stone panel from the former Town Hall, destroyed by fire in 1939, again portraying St. Giles. The hall facilities here are excellent. Near by to the west is the Munro swimming-bath building, reconstructed and splendidly equipped. Across the road is the Episcopal church of the Holy Trinity, cruciform and bright within, with white walling. Behind rises the Scottish Malt distillers' headquarters, again very modern—Elgin is ringed around with distilleries, many of them famous. And close by is the highly ambitious Community Centre, in a fine new edifice, with facilities for all ages. Elgin, although proud of its antiquity and ancient buildings, is very go-ahead, with many fine modern structures, as befits a municipality which has grown strikingly in recent years and has erected almost 2500 houses since the last war. The proximity of the two great service airfields of Lossiemouth and Kinloss have helped to make this necessary.

The outskirts of the town have their own interests. At the eastern extremity, where the A.96 enters Elgin, is the Pinefield Industrial Estate, at the former army-camp area. Near here, beside the railway-line is the site of the Order Pot, more properly Ordeal Pot, where unfortunate women branded as witches were drowned. It was a pool, now gone, not part of the Lossie but said to rise and fall with the river. At the Newmill bridge to the north, near the Cathedral, the old King's Mills have been tastefully renewed as public-house premises. There is a pleasant riverside walk here.

The Bishopmill industrial suburb on the higher ground across the Lossie to the north is large and busy, and here the main housing development has taken place. At its head is the large Craig Moray Geriatric Hospital, and some way to the west, on the Burghead road, the Infectious Diseases Hospital. Morriston Road, here, leads down through a modern residential area, past the new Acadamy, to join the main Inverness highway, but sends off a branch across the old Bow Bridge of 1630-6, the first stone bridge over the Lossie. The Ladies' Walk skirts the river here. Across the bridge is Oldmills Road, and the Old Mills and picturesque mansion lie a quarter of a mile nearer the town across the meadows, and make an attractive group, with the mill-wheel still *in situ*.

At the southern side of the town, the aforementioned temporary ring-road carries some of the through-traffic, past the railway-station (which still functions on the Aberdeen–Inverness line), the auction-marts and another residential area. From this the A.941 highway strikes off southwards across the railway into the suburb of New Elgin, formerly a separate village outside the municipal boundaries, with its own school and other features—including a fine beehive-shaped 17th century doocot. Beyond this, on rising ground, is the popular 18-hole Elgin golf club's course, at Hardhillock.

Elgin City Football Club is a quite famous entity, known far beyond Moray. Its grounds lie within a loop of the Lossie north of the town-centre, off Burgh Briggs Road. The controversial issue of the proposed bypass-road is as yet unresolved. There are vehement arguments for and against various routes, which might spoil this or that area, even part of the Cooper Park—and very valid doubts these represent. But the enormous weight of traffic grinding through the narrow centre of this ancient city, on the A.96, is quite insupport-able, and threatens to destroy the entire character and charm of the place—as it does in so many another. This is a nettle which *must* be grasped firmly, here as elsewhere, whatever the cost.

Elgin is a quite large civil parish as well as a city and royal burgh, extending to no loss than 19,000 acres—and in a most fertile land. Most of this lies south and west of the town, in the valley of the Lossie, although it is oddly shaped, with a detached portion thrusting east-wards. Pluscarden lies in Elgin parish, to the south-west, but, with its surrounding area, is better dealt with separately.

West of New Elgin and the golf course one mile is the old estate of Mayne, its mansion mainly modern but with a late 17th century core, and with old Grant heraldry built into the front walling. Across the Lossie another mile, is the bridge and milling hamlet of Pittendreich, the mills still intact but no longer working. The 18th century bridge is a single and shallow arch over the Black Burn which flows down its own valley from Pluscarden. On the west side there is an excellent and unusual 16th century square, gabled and stone-slab-roofed doocot, in the farm-steading, unfortunately beginning to fall into disrepair.

Another mile south-westwards along the same burn lies Muir of Miltonduff, a scattered rural hamlet with school and hall, rather pleasant. Also another doocot, lean-to and early 18th century this time, standing in a field near the distillery. This is Ballantyne's Miltonduff–Glenlivet establishment, and less beautiful than some. Two miles due south of Miltonduff, at the end of a very long and bumpy farm-road, is Upper Manbeen, amongst low foothills. Two hundred yards north-west of the farmhouse in a field is a single Pictish standing-stone, much weatherworn and marred by initial-scratchers, which however still faintly reveals the fish and mirror-and-comb symbols. There are many old wells on this farm, not in use, one named the Butter Well. The Manbeen area is also notable for itss and-and-gravel workings.

In the detached eastern portion of the parish, sandwiched between St. Andrews–Lhanbryde and Birnie parishes, are a group of distilleries in the Longmorn and Whitewreath areas just off the main A.941, on the way to Glen Rothes. Longmorn is a famous name in whisky-distilling. Here also are the Benriach–Glenlivet and Glen Elgin establishments. Whitewreath is a hamlet in pretty foothill country just east of the main road. From here another and very lovely side-road strikes off south-westwards to Shougle and more distilleries in the Glen Latterach and Mannochmore area in the Lossie valley—but that is in Birnie parish, and dealt with there.

Half a mile east of Whitewreath is the estate and loch of Millbuies, 140 acres gifted to the town, with the fishing, by G. Boyd Anderson, of Lossiemouth, in 1958.

Fochabers. Oddly enough, the town of Fochabers, at the very eastern rim of Moray, is not a burgh, although it has almost all the attributes of such an integrated and independent community—and is larger than some. It was a burgh of barony once, in the old days of ducal Gordon rule, when the township clustered around Gordon Castle, within the estate, a mile north of its present site. Like many another, it was shifted to give its lord privacy and increase his policies, in the late 18th century. Today it is a thriving and attractive place, unfortunately perhaps threaded by the busy A.96 Aberdeen–Inverness road, 8 miles east of Elgin, on the Spey 4 miles from its mouth, and within the civil parish of Bellie—which is dealt with separately.

The town stands on a sort of terrace on the wooded east bank of Spey, and was built on regular and planned lines, about 1790 and later. It makes a fairly compact rectangle, half a mile long by half that wide, although there are some modern extensions now to east and south. The main street—which is A.96—widens to a central square, tree-grown and comely, and the parallel side-streets to north and south, with their communicating lanes, are attractive—especially South Street, with its south-facing prospects. The population is about 1200, and there are some good buildings. The surroundings, like most of Moray, are richly wooded, with the huge Speymouth Forest, and the large Gordon Castle estate, providing amenities, and the atmosphere of the place is very pleasing—save for the incessant traffic which spoils so many of our excellent communities today.

The parish church—that of Bellie—stands centrally on the south side of the square, a handsome, commodious building of 1798, with portico, spire and clock. Internally it has very classical lines, bright, with central pulpit of a "preaching-kirk", and pillared galleries. It is flanked by two dignified and almost identical houses, built in 1800, Darnley House to the west, now the Manse, and the Crown Estate Office to the east. The grassy square is enhanced by a fountain, erected by the inhabitants in gratitude for the generosity of the 6th Duke of Richmond and Gordon in supplying the town with water.

Towards the east end of the main street is the impressive and rather fine Milne's Free School, a large Tudor-style building in its own grounds erected in 1846 with the bequest of one, Alexander Milne (1742–1839) who, in the ducal employ, refused to get his hair cut, was dismissed, and went to Louisiana and made a fortune. The more modern buildings of the High School adjoin. Not far along the street is the Public Institute, of 1905, with hall, reading-room and other facilities.

The Episcopal and R.C. churches are at the north and south sides of the little town respectively. The former, the Gordon Chapel, can be seen from the square, is unusual in that it comprises the rector's house on the ground floor, with the church proper above. It is a Gothic edifice of medium size but some style, designed by the famous Archibald Simpson and erected by the then Duchess of Gordon in 1832, renewed in 1874. The Catholic church of St. Mary is situated in South Street, the terrace with the fine prospects, and is quite attractive, not large, Gothic again, and dating from 1828. The playing-fields are near by, with some modern housing development at a lower level, which does not greatly spoil the aspect. This area was formerly the Market Green, where were held renowned cattle sales.

The west end of the main street is made picturesque by the pleasing, whitewashed Gordon Arms Hotel, of 1800, and then by the entrance-gates of Gordon Castle estate, with their fine grassy approach and twin lodges of the late 18th century. The classical column monument in the centre of the greensward is the town's war-memorial, with opposite it a fountain in memory of a Boer War hero. Gordon Castle estate, once called Bog o' Gight, is very large and occupies a sizeable part of Bellie parish, but its house and history being inseparable from Fochaber's it is described here. The formerly

huge castle and added mansion—568 feet long—was largely demolished in 1955, leaving two flanking pavilions and the very tall and
slender central stair-tower, six storeys and 84 feet in height above a
vaulted basement—which looks rather odd and out-of-proportion
now. This tower probably dates from the very early 16th century,
and is kept in good order. Indeed its immediate surroundings have
recently been built up in the form of a courtyard with curtail-walls
and round tower, modern but harled—which much helps the appearance. The two remaining portions, on the flanks, are of much later
date, that on the left now forming the house of the Gordon-Lennox
family, who are still in possession; that on the right serves as farm
premises. Bog of Gight came to the Gordons of Huntly by marriage
about 1490, and from it the subsequent chiefs of Clan Gordon took
their odd but quite proud title of Gudeman o' the Bog, to add to
Cock o' the North. In due course the Earls and Marquises of Huntly
became Dukes of Gordon, which dukedom expired with the fifth
holder in 1836, when these estates went to his maternal nephew the
5th Duke of Richmond and Lennox, the Gordon dukedom being
revived for his son in 1876. Much of the estate has been sold to the
Crown. Here, in 1645, died the 15-year-old son and heir of the great
Marquis of Montrose, on campaign with his father in the King's
cause. He was John Graham, usually called Lord Graham, though
by then actually Earl of Kincardine. It was a sad blow for his much
tried hero-father. The boy was buried in Bellie kirkyard. The
policies of this great house formerly covered 1300 acres.

Within the grounds are certain items of interest. A picturesque
tree-girt loch lies between town and castle, with a pleasant walk
flanking it, leading to the walled garden. Here, in front of two
garden-houses, stands the former Mercat Cross of the burgh of
barony, unusual in being merely a Doric column, and obviously of
no very early date. Iron jougs hang on a chain therefrom. This was
the site of the original Fochabers. A large dug-out canoe 16 feet
long extracted from the loch here, and is now preserved in Elgin
Museum. Many fine trees adorn the grounds. There was a Gordon
Castle Highland Gathering held here annually until 1938, with the
Duke its chieftain.

Fochabers is by no means wholly concerned with things of the
past, needless to say. The well-known foodstuffs firm of Baxter has
made the name renowned of recent years, developed by an old-
established grocery family in the town. The original George Baxter
made famous jam, and his son William sold it round the neighbourhood on a bicycle. From such humble beginnings came the great
modern factory, not actually in Fochabers itself but across the Spey
to the west, in Speymouth parish, more of an extension of the long
roadside village of Mosstodloch. The A.96 formerly crossed the river
here by a lengthy, three-arched bridge, which was partly swept
away by the great flood of 1829. Repaired then, it has just recently
been replaced by a wider modern structure, but remains alongside.
Another well-known and old-established Fochaber firm is Chris-

tie's Nurseries, at the east end of the town, extensive on pleasingly sloping 200 acres. Here 6½ million trees are grown annually. The firm was founded in 1820. It has a small museum of carts and carriages. Until very recently a large Fochabers bakery used to supply a great area of the North-East, but this has been taken over by an Inverness company, and is now only a distribution centre—to the town's loss.

Forestry lands surround Fochabers and timber production has always been important hereabouts. The Forestry Commission local base used to be in Fochabers, but has recently been removed a mile off to Mosstodloch. Picnic furniture is made there. Many attractive walks are provided in the forests, with paths leading to places with names such as The Peeps, Slorach's Wood and Jean Kerr's Stone.

There are the usual recreational facilities, with Spey fishing prominent. A caravan site lies to the east of the town, and the well-known Spey Bay Golf Course stretches along the shore links to the north, 4 miles away.

Forres. This famous, although not large, town of great antiquity, is a royal burgh whose earliest charters have been lost, so that no dates and proofs can be given, other than a *novo damus* renewal by James the Fourth in 1496. But Forres was renowned long before King Duncan held his Court here and Macbeth rebelled against him; indeed King Dubh, or Duffus, is reputed to have been murdered in Forres Castle in 967. Also some claim it to have been the Varris of Ptolemy; and the admittedly unreliable Boece claims that, as early as 535, some of its merchants were executed for some offence. So its antiquity is not in doubt. Today it has a population of just under 5000. Forres is also a civil parish of 5400 acres, of very irregular shape, in the Laigh of Moray south of Findhorn Bay.

The town lies along the busy A.96 Elgin–Inverness road, which has its disadvantages on the score of amenity, but it is a pleasant place, backed on one side by wooded hills, and a favoured holiday resort, with a great many large and substantial villas in their own grounds, some now turned into hotels and guest-houses. There is some industry also. The High Street coincides with A.96 for almost a mile, and two other main roads, A.940 and B.9010, strike off southwards, while B.9011 goes northwards to Kinloss and Findhorn.

St. Lawrence is the patron saint, his representation appearing on the burgh seal, with gridiron, and St. Lawrence's is the parish church, a fine and impressive edifice dating variously from 1775, 1839 and 1860, in an old kirkyard at the north side of the High Street towards the west end. It now approximates towards the Gothic style, with a steeple, and internally is large, seated for 1000, with an L-shaped gallery, on only two sides, plus an aisle and much excellent stained-glass, the gift of Sir Alexander Grant, Baronet, the Moray philanthropist and friend of Ramsay MacDonald, in 1939. There is an attractive baptistry. In the kirkyard are many oldish stones. Near by is a good 17th century L-planned house, at the corner of Gordon and High Streets, with crowsteps, dormers and coped chimneys, the ground floor a shop. Still further west is Achernack Eventide Home, rather unusually placed in the High Street. And opposite, on the south side, is the small park of Castlehill, the site of the ancient castle of Forres, so important to Scotland's early monarchs, and now completely gone. A tall obelisk of polished red granite rises there, to a height of 65 feet, in memory of Assistant Surgeon James Thomson, born 1823 and died a Crimean War hero 31 years later.

East of the parish church are various features in the High Street. The Mercat Cross, in the carriageway, is of unusual type, built in 1844 in imitation of 'foreign' town crosses, in rather wedding-cake style. Near by is the Town House of 1838, in Tudor-style Gothic, over-ornate, with a tall clock-tower, built on the site of the Old Tolbooth of 1700, and jutting into the street. In Tolboth Street near by, the beginning of the B.9010 road to Rafford, etc., is the Falconer Museum, of 1870, in Italianate style, with a renowned local collection of fossils especially. The Mechanics Institute and Town Hall are a little further east, in classical style, and were originally the St. Lawrence Masonic Lodge, erected 1823, with an Archibald Simpson extension of 1829, refronted in 1901. The building was used as an auxiliary hospital in the 1939–45 war. Next door is the large Established church of St. Leonards, again perhaps over-ornate in architecture.

There are many rather intriguing closes opening off the High Street, with some 18th century houses remaining. Attractive is Milne's Wynd, with its through pend. The row of houses tucked therein has as its first the suitably named "No Vu".

At the extreme east end of the High Street proper, standing back to the south, is the Anderson Institute for the Education of Children, now the primary school, a good Grecian building of 1823, funds for its erection being provided by one Jonathan Anderson, a native who made a fortune in Glasgow and made over the lands of Cowlairs, now a railway junction, to provide education for the necessitous children of Forres, Rafford and Kinloss parishes.

The extension eastwards along A.96, although hardly any more the High Street, has some features. The fine Cluny Hills Park is on the south side, reaching up to a wooded ridge on which is a 70-foot three-storeyed Gothic tower, monument to Admiral Nelson, erected 1808. There are excellent recreational grounds here. From this hill, sadly, witches used to be crammed into barrels and sent rolling down the steep brae—and where the barrels came to a halt, they were burned. The last unfortunate so dealt with was an old woman called Dorothy Calder, and we read that 15 cart-loads of peat were used to "justify" her—and this only at the end of the 18th century. The Witches' Stone, which is used to mark the spot where most of the rolling and burning took place, is still at the roadside here, near the large modern police-station. Almost opposite is the cruciform and Grecian-type Episcopal church of St. John the Evangelist, of 1840, bright within and enhanced with three fine mural paintings. There is also a small and rather nice St. Margaret's R.C. church near by. Large villas and hotels line the road eastwards, and, where B.9011 strikes off northwards for Kinloss, and a little way along it, rises the famous Sueno's Stone, a notably tall Pictish inscribed stone, unique, 23 feet high and covered with intricate and spirited carving. It displays a cross and Celtic decoration, but also headless bodies, horsemen, spearmen, women captives and a Pictish broch. It was the enthusiastic but rash Boece who named this lofty monolith Sueno's Stone, associating it with a victory won by Sueno, son of Harald of Denmark, over the Scots hereabouts in 1008. It is of course Pictish and 9th century, probably a cenotaph for a much earlier battle.

Away from the centre of the town in other directions is much of interest. To the south, at the other, west side of Cluny Hill, is a pleasant residential area, and on a wooded terrace looking south is the large Cluny Hills Hotel, formerly the Hydropathic. Not far away is the well-known Leanchoil Hospital, founded by Lord Strathcona, pioneer of the Canadian Pacific railway, in 1892, in a pleasant sylvan setting. Between them is the golf course. And a little further out, on the way to Califer Hill, are the Cathay Woods, with woodland walks. Forres has very extensive common lands in this direction, and the parish boundary has been oddly extended deeply south-eastwards into Rafford in order to include the Califer Hill and Moss area more than 3 miles from the town. Up here is the Califer Stone, at 700 feet, a boundary-mark for the 15-mile march-riding perambulations. Gloriously extensive views are to be had.

In the south-west environs are the large modern buildings of Forres Academy. There is much recent housing hereabouts. Industry tends to be sited at the west end of the town, with a small industrial estate on the outskirts. And to the north is the Benromach Distillery, near a pleasant waterside park. Still further west, at the parish boundary, is the Mundole Caravan Park, beside the high modern bridge over the Findhorn, built in 1938. The former toll Chain Bridge, designed in 1831 by Sir Samuel Brown R.N., rejoiced in "elegant Gothic arches of iron".

The heavily wooded nature of the area has ensured that Forres was always concerned in the timber and saw-milling trades. Indeed, the wooden blocks which used to go for paving London's streets, were supplied from here. Auction-marts and agricultural shows and supplies are also important. An interesting modern development is a glass-engraving establishment by an expert craftsman.

In the parish area to the north are a group of small old estates and farms occupying the levels which lead to the great basin of Findhorn Bay, an area which has suffered much from flooding—the turbulent River Findhorn being the parish boundary to the west. Amongst these are the properties of Greeshop or Grievship, of the 18th century, and Invererne House, which used to be named Tannochy, dating from 1818, with a doocot at the home-farm. This was once the home of Charles St. John, the famous naturalist. Sanquhar

House, to the south of the town, also changed its name in the 19th century, from Burdsyards.

No even brief description of Forres can end without at least some mention of Shakespeare's *Macbeth*, of which this area is the principal setting—although how much fact is involved in the play is debatable. Macbeth allegedly met the Weird Sisters on Hard Muir, in Dyke parish just to the north-west, and asked "How far is't called to Forres?" But, of course, some declare that the famous Witches in fact operated far away to the south, in Perthshire, near Dunsinane, where the Witches Stone is still pointed out. No one expects topographical and historical accuracy from playwrights—so one can take one's choice.

Gordonstoun and Drainie. The coastal parish of Drainie covers 7250 acres of the fertile Laigh of Moray north of Elgin and Spynie, but quite a large proportion of its acreage is now taken up by the great Lossiemouth Air Station, and the burgh of Lossiemouth, with Branderburgh, it is convenient here to deal with separately. So that the parish now to be described is much reduced and does not rise to a single village, or even a parish church. But it does include the famous public school and ancient estate of Gordonstoun, a feature of much interest and significance. And there are other items of interest.

The parish extends westwards from the River Lossie almost to Duffus village, a length of 5 miles, half that in breadth. Much of it was once under water, for the now quite modest Loch of Spynie was originally of great extent, and indeed almost an arm of the sea, connecting with salt-water another 5 miles westwards at Roseisle near Burghead in Duffus parish, so that a great part of this low-lying and fertile vale was tidal, and there was a port at Spynie, now 3 miles inland. The conversion of this great area to rich farmlands was partly natural, the result of the alarming sand-blows of the late 17th century, when Culbin near by was buried, and which cut off Spynie Loch from the sea; and partly by drainage by landowners over the subsequent years, most notably by the Spynie Canal designed by Thomas Telford in 1808, but destroyed in the great Moray flood of 1829 and rebuilt in 1860. As the loch was 5 miles long in 1779, the lack of early features in the terrain is understandable. The parish was formed in 1669, out of the medieval parishes of Kinneddar, to the east, and Ogstoun to the west, but the united parish church of 1823, was demolished to make way for the airfield, leaving only a foundation, so that the parish's principal place of worship is now at Lossiemouth. The scanty remains of Kinneddar's early parish church, and its castle, are described under Lossiemouth.

It is interesting that, despite this low-lying vale, the coast of Drainie parish is, in fact, lofty, rock-girt and dramatic, for the land slopes up again to the north, to culminate in whin-and-heather moorland and then the exciting cliff and caves of the Covesea coast, between Hopeman and Lossiemouth.

Gordonstoun lies in what was a sort of green isle in the water-logged lands, less than a mile east of the similar "island" of Duffus, and so at the western edge of the parish. It was originally the property of the Ogstouns of that Ilk, and went under the name of Bog of Plewlands. The first recorded Ogstoun, Simon, died in 1240. The site of the original barony and parish church of Ogstoun is to the east of the Gordonstoun grounds, and is now known as the Michael Kirk. The Ogstouns sold out to the Innes family in 1473, and there followed seven generations of Inneses at Bog of Plewlands, until it was bought by the Marquis of Huntly in 1616. By 1642 the name was changed, and the property erected into a barony of Gordonstoun for Sir Robert Gordon, a son of the 11th Earl of Sutherland, and the premier Scottish baronet. A succession of Sir Robert Gordons followed, his grandson being the famous Sir Robert the Warlock—really a fairly inoffensive scientific experimenter who invented an effective sea-pump and other items, but this was forgotten, and he was branded wizard, largely it seems because he preferred to sleep by day and walk by night. The Devil, of course, was alleged to have got him in the end, with grisly details. *His* grandson was the Sir Robert of the Jacobite period, who seems to have been more of a smuggler than a campaigner, with Gordonstoun a noted depot for contraband. He found, in troubled times, that the inaccessible Covesea caves were as good a place to hide his horses from requisitioners on one side or the other, as for duty-free imports, and one of these is still called Sir Robert's Stables. He left no son, and the estates passed to the Gordon-Cumming family of Altyre, who retained them until modern times. The present house was largely built by the first Marquis of Huntly, in 1616, and at first it consisted of a tall tower between slightly later 17th century wings, with angle-turrets and unusual hipped roofs, such as I have seen nowhere else. The tower was replaced by a massive, oblong balustraded block in 1729, much more commodious but hardly in style, while the wings remain. Some interesting features are retained here, although the building suffered a serious fire during the late war. These include the Priest's Hole, under the floor of the Founder's Room, reachable by a secret stair—the Gordons, of course, being a staunchly Catholic family. The ill Sir Robert, son of the Wizard, is said to have locked up his unpopular wife herein. Highly interesting near by to the west is the 17th century Round Square, built as a farmery and stable-block by the Wizard around 1690, but in circular form and of allegedly magical proportions as "a scientific sanctuary for his soul". It is now utilised for scholastic, recreational and library purposes.

Gordonstoun was taken over for a new type of residential educational experiment by the renowned Dr. Kurt Hahn, from Germany, in 1934, and its fame is too well-known for elaboration here, with both the Duke of Edinburgh and the Prince of Wales amongst its many distinguished former pupils. Just recently it has started a co-educational development and there are now a number of girls in

Sueno's Stone, Forres. A unique Pictish monolith, displaying, as well as early
Christian symbols, spirited carving of horsemen, spearmen, women captives
headless bodies and a Pictish broch or fortlet

Grantown-on-Spey: Castle Grant

residence and evidently enjoying themselves. Many new buildings have been erected in and around the ancient nucleus, in the spacious grounds, and altogether a more splendid and characterful educational establishment scarcely could be conceived.

There are numerous features of interest beyond the house and Round Square. The Plewlands Bog was drained around 1660 by Sir Ludovick, and now forms a picturesque, long and tree-girt loch, just south of the house, and much appreciated by the youngsters. The ill Sir Robert seems to have been an ill husband also, and was determined to get rid of his wife; he believed apparently in the adage that if you build a doocot there will be a subsequent death in the family—so he built four. One, beehive-shaped occupies an artificial mound to the south, and another, taller but also cylindrical, was converted out of the base of a former windmill to the east. Also south of the house in the very ambitious modern St. Christopher's Chapel, built on the cantilever principal, with dome, in 1965, at a cost of £80,000 provided out of the estate of Lady MacRobert of Douneside, in memory of her husband and three sons. It seats 600, and its curving walls provide an ambulatory as well as music-school and playing rooms. Unfortunately the acoustics are imperfect. The foundation-stone was brought from the demolished Kirk of Drainie, in the airfield.

Other notable buildings house a splendid swimming-pool, gymnasium and squashcourts, also Mountain Rescue and Coastguard facilities; even a Fire Brigade, manned by the boys, which actually attends fires outside the school area. Gordonstoun is famed, of course, for the practical and adventure side of its educational scope.

The Michael Kirk lies within the estate half a mile to the east, and makes an attractive sanctuary. It was built on the site of the original pre-Reformation parish church of Ogstoun in 1705, by the widow of the Wizard, as a memorial—so that they were on rather better terms than her son and daughter-in-law. The old graveyard still surrounds it and is in use, with many old recumbent stones and many modern, some connected with the school. In the centre rises the Mercat Cross of the burgh of barony, with an unusual five-pointed cross surmounting a tall shaft on a solid plinth, having small incised designs of cross and what look like hammers—also unusual. Elgin tried to have the markets here suppressed in 1599. The actual chapel building is not large, and has been altered twice, in 1900 and 1959, when it was reroofed and brightened. There are some notable features internally, with two beautiful stained-glass windows of 1900, and an elaborate genealogical panel in yellow sandstone detailing the descent of the Gordon lairds. There is also a handsome sculptured statue of St. Michael in armour slaying the dragon of evil. The school hold occasional services here.

The only other features of this parish to note are along the Covesea coast about a mile and a half to the north. This is a very interesting cliff-girt seaboard, the rocks carved into fantastic shapes by the waves, stacks, arches and fissures, with many caverns. The most famous is the Sculptured Cave, where rock-carvings of the Picts decorate the roof with symbols. In another many pre-historic relics have been unearthed. A third is the aforementioned Laird's Stables. They are all fairly inaccessible, especially at high tide. There was a village of Causea—the original name—once. The cliff-top area is wild, and given over to whins and rabbits and gulls, but an exhilarating path threads it for miles. Half-way along, between the soaring white Covesea Lighthouse (Alan Stevenson, 1844) and Hopeman, is a modern white look-out tower with gallery, erected by Gordonstoun School for its coastguard activities, opened by the Duke of Edinburgh in 1955. A Ministry of Defence radio-station rises just inland. An interesting though ominous feature of this coast is its parallel line of skerries and reefs offshore, scene of many wrecks.

Fifteen fragments of Pictish stones from Drainie parish are preserved in Elgin Museum.

Grantown-on-Spey, Inverallan and Lochindorb. Long renowned as one of the most popular holiday-places for the discerning in the North East of Scotland, the burgh of Grantown lies delightfully in mid-Strathspey, amongst pine woods and between the Hills of Cromdale and the lofty heather moors of the Lochindorb ranges, with the great Cairngorm massif only a dozen miles to the south. The former civil parish of Inverallan, now joined to Cromdale on the south, encloses it to the north, and the parish church of Inverallan is now the principal burgh church, its predecessor, within its old graveyard, down at the riverside to the south-west. Grantown has a population of 1500, is notably well supplied with fine hotels and guest-houses, and forms a splendid centre for visitors for a large area of delightful country, with excellent shopping, sporting and recreational facilities.

The existing burgh is not really very old, having been founded in 1766 to replace the old Castleton of Freuchie, which lay too close to the great Castle Grant for 18th century tastes, however natural and convenient for earlier clan chiefs, and which had been in existence from at least 1553. In 1694 the then Laird of Grant obtained a charter erecting "the town formerly called Castleton of Freuchie now and in all time to be called the Town and Burgh of Grant, and to be the principal burgh of regality, a market cross to be erected therein and proclamations to be made thereat". Despite this flourish of a start, Old Grantown was presently removed over a mile southwards to the present site near the river, and methodically planned and laid out in long parallel streets and linking cross-lanes, with a square towards the north end. Its site was then said to be a barren moor, but tree-planting altered all that, and it has now notably fine woodland environs. In those early days it was a centre of the linen industry, with a factory on the north side of the Square, but, as elsewhere, this trade declined as that of cotton grew in the South, and for long Grantown has depended on its visitors, its Spey fishing and its situation as a shopping and service centre for a very wide area—although there is a small knitwear factory and showroom, producing Schooner Brand goods. No comparable town is sited for over 20 miles in any direction. Here are all the necessary facilities and amenities for the important Strathspey vicinity—hospitals, old folks' home, secondary schools, fire-services, banks, newspaper-office, Tourist Association and so on. And here are held agricultural shows, gatherings, curling bonspiels and other and famed annual events. The Cairngorm winter-sports development, of course, has produced a new dimension and greatly added to Grantown's popularity, and there are two ski-schools.

The Square is the obvious place to commence any exploration. There is a handsome granite column war-memorial in the centre, the old trees greatly enhancing the scene, and grassy lawns now covering the former market-place. On the east is the Orphanage of 1824, Speyside House, endowed by Lady Grant of Monymusk, architecturally attractive in granite—as is most else in Grantown—with an octagonal clock-tower and ogee roof. It is interesting that the clock was paid for out of moneys collected for comforts for soldiers in the Napoleonic Wars, but, on victory, no longer required for that purpose. Next to this is the large Grants Arms Hotel, in mid-19th century Scots Baronial. Victoria and Albert came here in 1860, when, according to the Queen's Journal, not having slept well they got up early, and had to wait for a considerable time in the drawing-room until breakfast was ready—and were then regaled only with porridge, tea and bread and butter. Things have changed since then in this four-star establishment. Near by is the Court House, now the police-station, and in this vicinity are most of the remaining 18th and early 19th century buildings. The town's principal church stands on the east, down the short Church Avenue, successor of the old Inverallan Kirk at the riverside, a large Gothic edifice built by the Countess of Seafield in 1886 in memory of her husband and son, the 7th and 8th Earls, who died within three years of each other. Not particularly distinguished externally it is large and lofty within, cruciform, with pale stone walls and timbered ceiling. Moreover, it contains some of the finest wood-carved work in Scotland, installed here from Castle Grant and Cullen House. At the rear is a screen composed of eight dark oak finely worked panels, displaying heraldry and quotations from the Psalms, and the pulpit is formed out of panels pieced together, elaborately, indeed luxuriantly carved, dated 1639, oddly enough including a horned and leering Devil. There is an old clock here too—which would have had its uses at sermon-time. There is no graveyard. The immediate predecessor of this church, built in 1803 (on abandoning the old kirk by the river), is used for hall purposes.

The main business centre of the town, High Street, stretches southwards from the Square for a considerable distance, with notably good shops, sending off side-streets right and left, and with the quietly pleasant South Street running parallel. The main public buildings tend to be in the other direction, northwards, but on the High Street is the rather ornate Baptist church, one of whose ministers was the Rev. Peter Grant, famous as a Gaelic hymn-writer and preacher. Opposite is the Victoria Christian Institute and hall, scene of many a concert, of 1897, with the Moray–Nairn county library next to it. The High Street runs out eventually into Woodlands Crescent— which still carries the main A.95 highway—and here is the small Episcopal church of St. Columba, comparatively modern, with council housing behind, some of it rather pleasing. There is a Catholic church in Forest Road.

At the north end of the town are many features. The Grammar School, of some fame, the new secondary school in highly modern premises, the primary school, the quite large Ian Charles Hospital— on the outskirts this, and called after the 8th Earl of Seafield—the Grant House modern old folk's home, and many others. Near here is the fine 18-hole golf course, of tournament standard, with splendid views to the distant Cairngorms. Putting, bowling and tennis facili- ties are also available, the last with eight good hard-courts where tournaments are held likewise. There is a children's playground with paddling-pool, to the west. Pony-trekking and riding are catered for. The Curling Club, over a century old, must be mentioned, for Grantown in winter has a most bracing cold but dry climate, and more outdoor curling is enjoyed here than anywhere else in the land. Floodlit, these winter bonspiels are exciting occasions. Fishing, of course, is perhaps the place's speciality, especially the angling on the 13 miles of one of the finest salmon-rivers of the world. Sea-trout, brown trout and finnock are also fished for—and there are many other rivers and lochs available besides Spey. As well as the many hotels, guest-houses and bed-and-breakfast establishments, campers and caravanners are well catered for. The main caravan and camp site, of 14 acres, lies quite centrally, behind the parish church area. At what is now the Garth Hotel, Marie Corelli the novelist once lived for a while.

The walks in and around Grantown are particularly attractive, especially for such as are not ambitious for major tramping—though these have plenty of scope likewise. The woodlands which surround the town are very fine and one can wander at will. Especially pleas- ing are the riverside walks, where the anglers can be watched at their casting amidst sylvan scenery. Down here, half a mile south-east of the town, is the old kirkyard of Inverallan, where the Glenbeg Burn enters Spey through a picturesque and secluded little glen of birch trees. The last remains of St. Figgat's kirk itself have gone, but much of interest survives. In especial, a Pictish symbol-stone is built into the north walling, displaying crescent and V-rod, and "tuning-fork" and Z-rod symbols. The original stone font stands on a modern plinth in a corner. In mid-kirkyard is the Priest's Stone, a weather- worn slab inscribed with a simple Celtic cross of possibly the 9th or 10th century. It may represent the burial-place of the little-known Celtic missionary Figgat, whose well is still pointed out some 600 yards to the north. A Figgat's Fair used to be held here. There are many old stones in the graveyard, which is still in use, a pleasant place by the lovely river.

Further north along this riverside road half a mile is the New Bridge of Spey, carrying the A.95. This was built in 1931, then the longest single-span concrete bridge in the country, a fine piece of engineering with excellent lines. A little way down a pleasant residential road with attractive houses on one side, is the Old Bridge, built in 1754 by Caulfield and the 33rd Regiment of Foot under Lord Charles Hay, three-arched, narrow, with walkers' bays and cut-waters, and on a distinct slant, now open only to foot-passengers, a much photographed feature. The approach to the town, through the pine woods, from these bridges is most picturesque. A gravel road striking off on the left represents part of the old military road between Perth and Fort George.

The Inverallan part of the joint Cromdale parish lying north of Grantown—the southern part across the Spey is dealt with separately—has its own interests. Beyond the hospital the A.939 heads directly north for Nairn, climbing to 1100 feet in the process. A mile up here the railway-line crosses the road and goes on through the Castle Grant policies on the right. To show appreciation of the Seafields' permission for this—or perhaps the price therefor—the Highland Railway Company built here a most handsome gatehouse, bridge and private railway-station for the estate. Those were the days. The private drive through the very extensive grounds passes the site of the former town, and presently emerges at Castle Grant itself—something of a shock. For this huge and historic castle in the midst of its boundless and well-kept grounds is itself a fairly recently abandoned wreck, a strange fate for so notable a seat of a powerful family, home of the great Clan Grant. It was once one of the most noted treasure houses in Scotland. This was the original Castle of Freuchie, an L-planned 15th and 16th century tower-house of fairly modest dimensions grown into a vast E-shaped lofty mansion, mainly of 1750 and later, not in fact very beautiful though designed by the brothers Adam—Victoria baldly describing it as like a factory! But it is certainly impressive in its sheer size and position, and had this later and ugly extension been pulled down, when no longer needed, and the ancient parapeted tower left to stand alone, as originally, it could have looked very fine and provided a convenient house for these days. This, of course, could still be done. The tower rises four storeys to its corbelled parapet, and two storeys above to its gabled watch-chamber—though the top one is a 16th century heightening. A tall, slender stair-turret rises in the re-entrant, ending in a circular caphouse. The basement is vaulted, and the Hall, on the first floor, was enlarged in Georgian times to form a large dining-room 50 by 30 feet. The Grants, some say descended from Gregor, son of Kenneth MacAlpine (and so of the same stock as the MacGregors) and some say of French origin, Le Grands, were early settled in Stratherrick to the north-west, and came to Strathspey on the collapse of the Comyns, who took the wrong side in the Wars of Independence.

The first of Freuchie was Sir Duncan Grant of Inverallan, whose father was chief of the clan in 1434. It was John, 5th of Freuchie who, when offered the title of Lord Strathspey by James the Sixth asked "Wha then would be Laird o' Grant?" His grandson was to have been created Earl of Strathspey by Charles the Second in 1663, but died before the patent was signed. It was the 8th Laird who got the lands erected into the Regality of Grant, and the old name of Freuchie was discontinued. Sir Ludovick (1743–73) was the builder of the ugly extensions. He married the heiress of the Ogilvie Earl of Findlater and Seafield, and his grandson in 1816 succeeded as 5th Earl of Seafield—but not of Findlater, a male fief. Since when the family have called themselves Ogilvie-Grant. The present 13th Earl lives at Cullen House near Banff. This great estate is one of the most heavily forested in the land.

Beyond the castle policies the A.939 begins to climb, and in 2 miles squeezes through a rocky, wooded pass, wherein is sited Huntly's Cave, refuge of one of the Gordon chiefs. Then it emerges out on to the open heather moors, the country, at about 1100 feet, quickly becoming very bare and windswept, with a surprising lack of trees after the richly wooded Strathspey, so near. Snow poles mark the line of the road. Four miles of this and the road forks at Dava, A.940 continuing straight on for Forres (13 miles) and A.939 swinging westwards for Nairn (15 miles). Dava is almost as lonely and bleakly sited a community as you will find south of Caithness, just two or three cottages and a former small school now merely the county library branch, islanded in the midst of endless brown heather moors. There is a good single-arch 18th century bridge over the Dorback Burn here, and the small Loch Allan lies half a mile to the west, with a few wind-blown trees, but otherwise all is bare. There are quite a number of small lochans scattered over the moors.

Just before Dava is reached a side-road strikes off westwards 2 miles to Lochindorb. This, of course, is a famous place, set like an island in the brown wilderness, and given added renown through Maurice Walsh's novels. The loch is fish-shaped and 2 miles long, under Aitnoch Hill (1351 feet) on the north, and Craig Tiribeg (1586) on the south. There are trees here, but it is not a beautiful loch to compare with Morlich, Insh or Loch an Eilean. There is a slightly glooming atmosphere—indeed the name means Loch of Trouble. Its fame, or notoriety, stems of course from its connection with that princely scoundrel the Wolf of Badenoch, whose ruined castle occupies the little island, said to be artificial, towards the north end of the loch. The castle was here long before the Wolf's day, however, for it was captured by Edward the First in 1303— for the ancient highway between Findhorn and Spey came this way. The castle is a simple rectangle of curtain-walls, with low round towers at each angle, 180 by 126 feet, with a square keep and traces of a chapel. The portcullis is now at Cawdor Castle, near Nairn. Probably most of the building was in fact erected by English Edward himself, after he had taken the much smaller Comyn's hunting-seat. It remained a royal castle thereafter until in 1372 Robert the Second gave it to his third son, Alexander Stewart, Earl of Buchan and Lord of Badenoch, the Wolf. This prince had, and took, other seats in plenty, but he seems to have found Lochindorb peculiarly to his taste—and certainly it made a highly secure refuge. During his weak brother's reign (Robert the Third) he was his Lieutenant of the North, and held the entire North-East of Scotland under his barbarous sway. His tyrannies and colourful sins are not for recounting here. Suffice to say that from Lochindorb he swooped down on all the settled lands, burning and slaying at will, laughing at protests from the highest in church and state.

Lochindorb is only 6 miles, as the crow flies, from Grantown, yet it seems to be in another world. The side-road continues on south of the loch, and then bends away westwards to join the lonely Duthil–Glenferness road, B.9007, dealt with under Carrbridge.

Kinloss and Findhorn. Kinloss is a well-known name, because of the great R.A.F. Station long established there, and the all-too-busy Mountain Rescue unit which operates therefrom. It is a medium-sized civil parish also, of some 6250 acres, in the Laigh of Moray, north-east of Forres, and site of an ancient ruined abbey. Findhorn is a large coastal village and holiday resort to the north, at the mouth of the great basin of Findhorn Bay, where that river reaches the Moray Firth.

The parish, flat and low-lying, inevitably is now dominated by the airfield and the large and very permanent community, which it is ridiculous to call a camp, attached thereto, a busy, far-flung but self-contained place, with its own amenities, housing schemes, garrison church, school, halls and so on, in addition to the base installations. The older parish facilities seem merely an attachment thereto nowadays, for the base is set down contiguous to the kirk and kirkton, with the abbey close by.

Kinloss Abbey, a Cistercian establishment, was founded in 1159 by David the First, like so many others. But this one was rather special, for the King actually marked out the area the abbey was to occupy with his own sword, in gratitude for an allegedly miraculous white dove which guided him to an open glade in the wild scrub forest when he was lost, out hunting from Forres. He himself spent the following summer at Duffus Castle, near by, superintending the work of building, so that it was very much a royal foundation. Later kings enriched it extensively, and its mitred abbots were important men in old Scotland, with a seat in parliament. After the Reformation the lands were granted to Sir Edward Bruce of Clackmannan, who was created Lord Bruce of Kinloss, and whose son was the first Earl of Elgin. The property was later sold to the Brodies—and the new Brodie laird sold much of the masonry to Cromwell, to build his fort at Inverness. Very little of the former extensive monastic buildings remain therefore, and in fact, the tall gable and round stair-tower which make a prominent feature of the landscape, were part of a secular fortalice erected by the Bruces out of the former Abbot's House, of 1530. Only the foundations of the abbey church remain, which boasted a lofty central tower at the crossing of transepts and nave. There is a relic of the monastic buildings to the east where two rib-vaulted chambers remain in a poor state, and to the west is part of the Cloister Garth, a high wall with two fine "Saxon" arches. All is in a neglected condition. A parish graveyard surrounds the ruins, for part of the premises were long used as the parish church, and herein are many old stones—but also a great many modern graves of R.A.F. personnel killed during the late war and afterwards, with a simple, dignified and telling monument. The graves of so many young men, aircrew who died so early in their lives, gives the visitor cause for contemplation.

Near the abbey, the B.9089 joins the B.9011 Forres to Findhorn, and here is the kirkton hamlet, with shop, garage and so on. The present parish church stands just a little down the Findhorn road, the pleasant building of 1765 and tower of 1830, its bell however being Elgin-cast of 1688. Near at hand is the former Seapark estate of the Dunbars. And to the south, the more ancient Grange Hall property, where there is an 18th century hexagonal doocot with weathervane, rather fine, and a large and commodious mansion of the early 19th century, of the Grant-Peterkin family, with Doric columns.

The B.9011 runs from Kinloss northwards along the flat shore of Findhorn Bay for almost 3 miles, with the airfield on the right. A large caravan-park is sited here. Findhorn itself is an interesting, long and narrow village of much character, on a very open site, with many 18th century houses. This is, however, the third Findhorn village, its earlier predecessors having been swept away by either the shifting Culbin sands, across the estuary, or changes in the course of the Findhorn River. The original burgh of barony was almost 2 miles to the west. At one time it was a prosperous port, enjoying a good trade with the Continent, building its own ships with good Moray oak. Even as late as 1880 no fewer than 470 fishing-boats worked out from the district. Today salmon fishing is still engaged in by two companies, and a group of semi-subterranean ice-houses, for the storage of fish, remains in use to the north. But pleasure-craft have now largely taken over the harbour—rebuilt 1840—and the anchorage, for the great Findhorn basin makes an admirable sheltered waterway for yachtsmen, and the near presence of the air base, as well as that of Forres and Elgin, ensures a ready supply of enthusiasts. Moreover a great many of the houses and cottages have been taken over and renovated as holiday-homes, there being magnificent sands stretching for miles eastwards round Burghead Bay, and at Findhorn Point itself. There are hotels and guest-houses, and holiday-chalets are going up near the beach, with craft-shops and the like. A boat-yard, water-ski club and sailing-centre back the harbour area. The Royal Findhorn Yacht Club occupies an attractive range of renovated 18th and 19th century houses overlooking the Bay.

Other interesting buildings are the whitewashed Crown Inn, of 1739, the Kimberley, of 1777, and Quay Lodge, 1775; the James Milne Institute, with clock above, is near the harbour. The church, formerly a Free kirk, dates from 1843. There is a library, and considerable modern housing.

An unusual and interesting feature is the Findhorn Trust, a religious community venture, established here of recent years, which has received nation-wide publicity.

Lossiemouth, Branderburgh, Stotfield and Kinneddar.

The well-known fishing-port and seaside resort of Lossiemouth, with its constituent entities of Branderburgh and Stotfield, and the scanty remains of the ancient community of Kinneddar to the south, are all part of the civil parish of Drainie, but it is convenient to describe them separately. Lossiemouth is famed as the birthplace and home of the first Socialist Prime Minister, James Ramsay MacDonald, and because of its great airfield near by. But it is a characterful, thriving, self-contained and rather unusual burgh in its own right, with a population of some 6500, having a peninsular setting and the largest seine-net fishing-fleet in Scotland. It lies 5 miles north of Elgin, for which it was founded as a port in 1698, when Spynie became useless through sand-drift in the green Laigh of Moray, occupying a blunt headland thrusting into the Moray Firth—indeed the most northerly point of that 80-mile-long seaboard—just to the west of the River Lossie's sandy estuary. Flanked by great sands, the 5-mile-long Lossie Forest, and the dramatic cliff-and-cave coast of Covesea, it occupies a wide, open and isolated position, very much dominated by salt-water, and, on the road to nowhere, as it were, it is visited only by those who elect to go there. Inevitably it is an independent sort of place—which claims to have the lowest rainfall in the British Isles, as well as many other attractions.

The burgh consists of the three distinct entities, the old Seatown of Lossiemouth, at the original harbour within the mouth of the river, the planned village and later and larger harbour of Branderburgh, founded by Laird Brander of Pitgavenny, some miles inland, around 1830, and the residential suburb of Stotfield to the west, quite different in character. Kinneddar is now only a farm-hamlet with an ancient graveyard, a mile to the south.

The old Seatown, lying to the east, is fairly picturesque, unplanned and low-lying, with traditional fishermen's cottages, but also much modern housing near by, centred round a grassy green wherein rises the Mercat Cross of 1700, a slender shaft on a four-stepped rounded plinth, lacking its finial. There is an esplanade here. The fishertown lies across the outflow of the Spynie Canal of 1808, on a sort of island site with the Lossie beyond. The regularly designed crisscross of modern streets and avenues lies westwards, and here, in Moray Street, is The Hillocks, Ramsay MacDonald's house, still occupied by members of his family. Across the Lossie are the very evident sandhills, reached by a long timber footbridge. This East

Beach encloses the long shallow lagoon of the river's estuary, and is just the beginning of a 7-mile sandy shore backed by the planted conifers of the Lossie Forest, extending all the way to Kingston and Speymouth.

The Branderburgh harbour to the north at Haliman Head, cut out of the solid rocks, was necessary to avoid the constant sand-choking to which the old harbour had been liable. It is an extremely active fishing-port, but handles coastal trade likewise. Seventy or eighty seine-net boats operate from here, and it is a great sight to see the whole fleet leave for the fishing-grounds of an early Monday morning. There is a busy fish-market, and all the usual features of merchants' stores, chandlers' premises, cold-storage and the like. Also there is a boat-building yard and slipway at the Stotfield end of the harbour complex.

The main town rises on terraces inland from the harbour and Shore Street, in a regular, planned network of quite broad streets, to surround a wide green central St. James Square, not a cramped or huddled place. The High Street runs north and south at the east end of it all, with shops, and the large Victorian Town Hall and Public Library edifice near its head, opposite the very modern post-office and governmental building. There are few architectural gems here, but the town is neat, clean and open. There is the Queen Elizabeth the Queen Mother Institute and Royal National Mission for Deep Sea Fishermen establishment down near the harbour, a club, café, television and social centre.

The civil parish is Drainie, but there is a *quod sacra* parish church of St. Gerardine, in St. Gerardine's Road away to the south-west and scarcely central, succeeding a chapel-of-ease which, we read, was in 1792 in the happy position of having to cater for "no lawyer, writer, attorney, physician, surgeon, apothecary, Negro, Jew, gipsy, Englishman, Irishman, foreigner of any description, nor family of any religious sect or denomination except the Established Church". Could the Kirk's stout representative say fairer? St. Gerardine, which sounds feminine, was really Gernadius, a Celtic missionary, who came to Christianise the Picts, and lived in a 12-foot-square cave where is now the escarpment above the esplanade, long demolished by quarrying. Here he used to keep a light burning of a winter night, to guide local fishermen in over the treacherous sandbanks. They loved him, and called him the Haly Man, and Haliman Point and Skerries are still so named, with the saint appearing on the town seal. There are also Free, Baptist and Episcopal churches here.

Lossiemouth is well served with hotels, large and small, for it is a popular holiday-place, and its fine 18-hole Moray Golf Club's course, stretching westward along the coastal links towards Covesea, is famed, and sometimes a championship venue. The extensive sands are ideal for bathing, and the cliff-walks exhilarating. There is a large Silver Sands Holiday Park and caravan-site, over a mile to the west, with its own shopping facilities, reached by a road through whinny moorland. Directly behind rises the tall Covesea Light-house, designed by Alan Stevenson in 1844. Most of Lossiemouth's hotels and guest-houses are in the Stotfield suburb, overlooking the golf club-house and West Beach, with its sand-dunes. In this area were formerly lead-mines, and long before that prehistoric kitchen-middens and great shell-mounds. On the Stotfield sea-front also is an interesting establishment, the Order of St. John of Jerusalem's Convalescent Resthouse for old people. Here also is the Marine Park, with bowling, tennis and other facilities. Playing-fields lie to the south.

It is perhaps interesting to recall that, after the First World War, one John Campbell here designed the first modern seine-net fishing-boat, incorporating Scandinavian principles, in the *Marigold* proto-type. From this has so much arisen.

Kinneddar lies inland a mile, on a side-road. Little remains of its former importance, but it was once a parish of its own—combining with Ogstoun, to form the present Drainie parish—and the barony from which Lossiemouth sprang. Its castle was the occasional resi-dence of the powerful Bishops of Moray, and stood in what is now a field to the north of the graveyard, the site marked by a modern cairn built out of some of its masonry, some more of which is in-corporated in the kirkyard walling. The old Mercat Cross of the burgh of barony still stands within the churchyard, an octagonal shaft on three steps, which like so many has lost its finial—possibly a cross hewn off at the Reformation as being "Papistical". A slender iron weather-vane has been put on, instead. The scanty foundations of the old church are still discernible on a slight mound, and there are many old gravestones. The pleasant former manse is opposite, and a farmery near by.

The great and busy Lossiemouth Airfield lies immediately west of Kinneddar, covering a large area of the level Moray plain. It was for long famous as a Royal Naval Air Station, and its staff added much to the liveliness of Elgin, Lossiemouth and district. It has fairly recently changed over to the Royal Air Force.

Pluscarden. Pluscarden—with the accent on the plus—is a well-known name, and justly so, for the renowned Priory is one of the most interesting and inspiring features of the North-East. But it is also a district, some 4 miles long by 2 miles broad, a wide and smiling upland valley, actually part of Elgin parish, which it is con-venient to describe here separately. The vale, or strath, which once was called the Vale of St. Andrew, and later Kail Glen, which was but a Scots corruption of the Latin Vallis Caulium, the abbey of which, in France, was the parent-house of the Valliscaulian Order priory established here by the Cistercians in 1230. It lies between the long ridges of Heldun Hill (767 feet), clothed by the vast Monaughty Forest, on the north, and the Hill of the Wangie (1046 feet) also largely wooded by Dallas Forest, on the south, the gentle valley between being threaded by the Black Burn, a major tributary of the Lossie, and dotted with farms. This sequestered strath comes to a head at the Elgin parish boundary, at 540 feet. And half-way up the 4-mile peaceful tract is the great Priory of Pluscarden.

There are many abbeys and priories in Scotland, almost all the ancient ones in ruins, and there are a few monastic establishments, modern though perhaps bearing ancient names. But here is one of the most ancient, yet very much a going concern again, after the inevitable post-Reformation hiatus. The building itself is both impressive and a delight, the area and atmosphere most attractive, and the entire monastic venture contained therein admirable and quietly challenging—all calculated to lift the heart of the visitor, Catholic and otherwise.

The first sight of the Priory, with its tall and massive parapeted square tower and steep gables, rising in mellow golden masonry above ancient trees, and under the forested hillsides, is a worthy foretaste of what closer inspection reveals. The old precinct walls, enclosing 10 acres of gardens and lawns, lead up to the great cruciform church, which presides genially over, rather than dominates, the handsome gabled and dormered ranges of monastic wings, where reconstruction and wholly modern building blend in satisfyingly with the ancient stonework. There is much yet to do, and work goes on with a gentle persistence, but one feels here a timeless and serene confidence and lack of haste, salutary as it is refreshing in these days of inevitable hurry and bustle, with quality almost a forgotten objective. The Benedictine brothers here at work and prayer are, one senses, concerned with eternity rather than tomorrow.

Pluscarden, despite its air of settled peace and quiet assurance, has seen its days of declension and violence. Founded by Alexander the Second, on the site of a Celtic missionary's cell dedicated to St. Andrew, the Priory grew in quiet isolation, away from the turbulent main stream of political and ecclesiastical development and upheaval. Nevertheless it suffered damage in 1303, from the invading armies of England, in the Wars of Independence, when the Church was so much on Bruce's side, and again, by that scourge of the North, the Wolf of Badenoch, in 1390. Then in 1454, the Priory was united with that of Urquhart, 10 miles to the east, and the white-habited Valliscaulians were replaced by the then black friars of St. Benedict—the Order which still reigns here. There had been eleven Valliscaulian priors, and there followed seven Benedictines, before the Reformation—important men, ranking with mitred abbots and having a seat in the Scots parliament. The last was a local man, Prior Alexander Dunbar, insinuated into his position, like so many another, so that, foreseeing the coming dispersal of the Church lands, he might ensure that a large portion went to his own family and nominees. Thereafter, under the new secular policy, the remaining property was granted to Alexander Seton, son of Lord Seton, who became successively "of Pluscarden" Lord Urquhart, Lord Fyvie and Earl of Dunfermline, a notable man and Chancellor of Scotland. Later Pluscarden passed to the Mackenzies, Brodies and Duffs. The

Priory itself fell into ruin—but, no doubt because of its comparative isolation, was not forcibly demolished and used as a quarry, like most.

It was not until 1943 that the Benedictines came back, from Prinknash in England. The well-known Catholic philanthropist, the 3rd Marquis of Bute, bought the property, and contributed generously to the work of restoration. Building started, and by 1948 the great central tower was reroofed, monastery bells sounded again amongst the wooded hills and the community took up prayerful but active residence. They are still labouring as well as praying, with much rebuilding still to do—but also working at other things, stained-glass (for which they are becoming renowned suppliers) wood-carving, gardening and so on.

The monks have concentrated on restoring the huge cruciform church first, and though it is not yet fully completed, it makes a magnificent place of worship. The Choir, to the east, is still only a lofty roofless shell, but the transepts to north and south are reroofed and in use, and the projecting features of the Lady Chapel, with Prior's Chapel above, the Chapter House, Slype (now used as library) and Calefactory (now refectory and kitchens), also the groined vaulted Dunbar Sacristy on the north, with its graveslab lintel, possibly 13th century and the oldest stonework in the building. Here is no place to attempt to describe all the features and excellences of this great complex, but at least reference must be made to the fine ancient Lady Chapel, now used as the monastic church, and the splendid Chapter House doorway. The roomy Cloister lies to the south-west, and much reconstruction and additional work proceeds around it. Throughout, of course, there are many items of especial interest, windows, aumbries, consecration-crosses, memorial stones and the like. There are traces of original tempera-painted frescoes around the Chancel Arch.

Altogether, Pluscarden Priory, with its now white-robed Benedictine monks, is a place not to be missed.

There is a small village near by to the south, with some modern housing, and a local school. Scattered farms cover the valley-floor and slantwise fields to east and west. The great wooded ridges of Monaughty and The Wangie enclose all, and in the former forest are many fine woodland walks, with a picnic area and access provided, at the roadside 2 miles east of the Priory. The road westwards and upwards, over the high ground towards Rafford, and to the north and A.96, is particularly lovely, with fine views, natural open birchwood, heather and bracken, as well as the planted conifers.

At the other, eastern end of the Vale of St. Andrew, where it opens on to the wider valley of the Lossie, in the Miltonduff area, are sundry features of interest, but these are dealt with under Elgin.

Rafford and Altyre. The Moray parish of Rafford, to which was added the pre-Reformation parish of Altyre in 1659, covers 12,500 acres of foothill country, heavily wooded, south of Forres, and

contains the straggling village community of Rafford itself, the huge
ancient estate of Altyre to the west, and the Burgie and Blervie areas
to the east, coming very close to Forres town at two points.

The village consists of the kirkton district to the north, near the
parish church, and half a mile to the south, on the higher ground of
Moor of Granary, the upper village, all under the ridge of Blervie,
with its prominent castle ruin. The present parish church stands on
a wooded bank to the east, an ambitious Gillespie Graham Gothic
Revival edifice of 1826, with a lofty pinnacled tower, improved by
its pinewood surroundings. The old kirk lay in the low ground not
far away, where is still the kirkyard with many old graves. In the
centre are the scanty remains of the earlier building, with a square
moulded doorway and worn monogrammed panel dated 1640 and
initialled R.D. and I.G. for the Dunbars of Grange—now a burial-
enclosure. A watch-house in the midst has been part of the old
church likewise. It is all rather neglected today. There is some
modern housing near by, and a scheme on the hillside, near the
later church.

Upper Rafford has more housing, and the former Free church, in
more open country.

Blervie Castle's single tall tower dominates the landscape from its
ridge, the later Georgian farmhouse near by. The square keep-like
five-storey block, with its slender circular stair-tower, at a distance
gives the impression of a free-standing tower, but it is in fact only the
remaining wing of a large Z-planned fortalice of the late 16th century. From its broken parapet seven counties may be seen. It is odd
that this remaining portion is so entire, when all else is gone—but
the rest was deliberately demolished to provide masonry for the
modern Blervie House a mile to the south. The handsome Hall fireplace survives, now on an outer wall, with its weatherworn heraldic
lintel of the Dunbar lairds, dated 1598. The wing, although semi-
ruinous, is excellently built and provided with many shot-holes and
gun-loops. The basement, first floor and top storey are all vaulted—the
last to provide a platform roof for the use of artillery. The similarity
with Burgie Castle near by is very pronounced. Originally Comyn
lands these fell to the Dunbars, descending from the ancient stock of
the Cospatrick Earls of March and Dunbar. Just behind the castle
to the south, is the small abandoned farm-steading of Templestone,
its name significant, and sure enough, in whins near by, are the
remains of a stone-circle, with only one stone remaining upright.

Burgie estate lies to the east of Blervie, and was also a Dunbar
lairdship, with a castle so similar in state and appearance as to be
uncanny. Its position is not so dominant however, occupying only a
small mound in woodland. Even the Hall fireplace again remains
visible on the outer wall of the remaining single wing of the Z,
although its carved lintel is less weatherworn, bearing the Dunbar
arms again, a defaced motto, and the date 1602. The tower is six
storeys high and here the parapet is still entire. The massive iron
yett is still in position outside the vaulted basement. The castle rises

within a fine pleasance wall, and there is a lean-to doocot of the period. The remainder of the building was demolished in 1802 to erect the nearby large mansion of Burgie House, which was again rebuilt in 1912. Burgie lands belonged to the great Bishopric of Moray, and the transfer to the Dunbars is typical of the unsavoury manoeuvrings of the Reformation period. The Dean of Moray and Prior of Pluscarden was Alexander Dunbar, himself an illegitimate son of the former Dean, and embracing Protestantism and marrying the daughter of Robert Reid, Abbot of Kinloss and Bishop of Moray, he managed to acquire large portions of the Church lands, including Burgie and Grange. Burgie Castle defied Montrose in 1645.

Burgie Distillery lies half a mile to the north, attractively laid out by a burnside, amongst mown lawns and trees, with associated housing. Not far to the north again, just across the busy A.96 highway, is a huge erratic boulder of conglomerate, in a field, with a smaller one near by—whether part of a stone-circle or not is not clear. Sueno's Stone, the famous Pictish monolith, is just within this parish, but is more suitably described under Forres.

The great wooded estate of the Gordon-Cummings, at Altyre, covers all the western side of the parish, and was itself formerly a parish, with its old ruined kirk, dating from the 13th century, still standing within the policies. These cover an area of about 6 square miles, and include many features of interest. The former large, Italianate mansion of the 18th century, with additions, has been demolished, but Sir William Gordon-Cumming, 6th Baronet, is still the laird, and lives in what was Blairs, a dower-house. The aforementioned church, a small First Pointed structure, but with not much of the 13th century about it remaining, is interesting, standing on a slight eminence south of the lovely, wooded Loch of Blairs, roofless but its walls entire, with buttresses, lancet windows and steep gables. A draw-bar with slot has guarded the arched doorway on the north side, and the window in the west gable has an empty moulded panel-space above. There are a few gravestones still to be found amongst the weeds.

Not far away across the parkland to the east is a tall Pictish cross-slab, 11 feet high, with faint traces of the Celtic cross on one side and indeterminate symbols on the other. The main driveway passes near by. This stone was removed here from Duffus. A prehistoric grave, a stone cist, was discovered not far away in 1931.

These Gordon-Cummings, of the same family as formerly were at Gordonstoun and Dallas, are the descendants of the ancient Comyn Earls of Buchan and Lords of Badenoch, who suffered declension for opposing the Bruce during the Wars of Independence. They were originally Anglo-Normans who came to Scotland with David the First, and married into the Celtic aristocracy, at one time having three earldoms and innumerable baronies and lairdships. There are few Comyn or Cumming lairds left. Sir William is head of the name —the Gordon of Gordonstoun connection is through the female line —and there are still Cummings long settled at Rattray, in Buchan.

Just outside the north gate of the Altyre estate, and really in Forres parish, at Manochy, is the Dallas Dhu Distillery.

Of Rafford's entire area, more than half is wooded, with Altyre and Burgie Woods, Newtyle Forest and part of Monaughty Forest, along with lesser woodlands covering thousands of acres.

Rothes and Orton. Rothes is a well-known name in Scots history, the Leslie family, which took its title from here, eventually reaching the status of duke. But it is, in fact, only a very small Speyside burgh of just over a thousand population, with its own parish of 20,000 acres—although most of this is empty hills and moors. Orton is the north-eastern corner thereof along the riverside, a district with a large estate and a former railway-station.

The little town of Rothes, nearly 10 miles south-east of Elgin, is very much a distilling centre. There are, in fact, no fewer than five distilleries in the burgh, every side-street seeming to contain one. The place is essentially one very long main street, with a bridge over the Burn of Rothes in the centre, and a widening just to the south, called Seafield Square, really the start of a dead-end thoroughfare which probes north-eastwards down towards Spey. Other side-streets are mere lanes. Over all, the remains of the Leslie's Rothes Castle presides, a lofty and massive stretch of curtain-walling all that remains, crowning a green bank to the west. The town is scarcely beautiful, its architecture undistinguished, but the surroundings are very pleasing.

The present parish church stands at the Square, a plain building of no great size, 1781, renewed of 1868, with a clock-tower, its aspect and position not impressive. It superseded the old pre-Reformation church of St. Lawrence, which stood across the burn, to the west, up Burnside, between two distilleries. Here there is still the old kirk-yard, with fragments of the former church used as a burial-aisle, having a rather fine heraldic stone dated 1576, with the Leslie arms and initials M.I.L. This was the first Presbyterian clergyman after the Reformation, James Leslie, brother of George, Earl of Rothes. There are other Leslie stones including one which states: "This Tomb in East End of the First Church of Rothes Built by Alexander Leslie of Balnageith." There are many old gravestones here.

The distilleries naturally form a very important feature of the scene, and are the main employers of labour. But, as is usually the way, they do not greatly obtrude or spoil the amenity as factories so frequently do. Perhaps this is a psychological reaction? Most of them, of course, here as elsewhere, tuck themselves into deep dens of burns, the water-supply being of prime importance. At Rothes an ancient well up the Back Burn, at the north end of the town, has been utilised as a copious water-supply for one distillery, the woodland path thereto picturesque.

Rothes was created a police burgh in 1884. It suffered grievously in the great Spey floods of 1829. The war-memorial is at the north end of North Street, in the form of a mercat-cross. Also in North

Street is the heavily ornate Victorian Drill Hall. There is considerable modern housing at the south end. Rothes has a recreation-
ground, and tennis, bowling and football facilities; also pony-
trekking. The wide haugh to the east, at a bend of Spey, was laid
out as a rifle-range.

The ruins on Castlehill are of a probably 15th century stronghold,
not old enough to have housed Edward the First on his punitive
expedition up here in 1296. Originally the barony belonged to a
family named Pollock, but passed to the Leslies in 1390, when a
younger son of Leslie of Balquhain wed the heiress. George Leslie
was created Earl of Rothes in 1457 by James the Second, and his
successors took their full part in Scotland's story, one falling at
Flodden. The 7th Earl carried the Sword of State at the coronation
of Charles the Second at Scone. He was created Duke of Rothes in
1680, but left only a daughter, who did not succeed to the dukedom.
Her elder son by the Earl of Haddington became Earl of Rothes, her
second son in due course Earl of Haddington. The present Earl of
Rothes still owns the Castlehill, as nucleus of the ancient barony.
Apart from the stretch of curtain-wall, only traces of ditch and
foundations remain.

The road forks at the north end of the burgh, the A.941 going on
north-westwards through Glen Rothes and the hills to Elgin, and
the B.9015 striking north-eastwards along Speyside to Speymouth.
The Rothes Glen Hotel, a large and renowned establishment stands
3 miles along the former road not far from the parish boundary. To
the west lies a great mass of empty hills and mosses, of no notable
height and few features of interest.

Along the B.9015 a mile the road comes very close to a great bend
of Spey, with fine views across the river to Ben Aigen's wooded
slopes, and the site of the ancient castle of Aikenway, sometimes
called Oakenwalls (which is still in Moray though across Spey) at
the tip of the river-bend. Little is known of this very early fortress.
Half a mile further is the site of the roofless old church and kirkyard
of Dundurcas, in a lovely setting down in the haugh. This was once
a parish of its own, suppressed in 1788, very soon after being largely
rebuilt about 1760. Traces of older work remain. Part of the parish
was assigned to Boharm in Banffshire, part to Rothes. The Vale of
Dundurcas is very attractive.

Two miles on along this pleasant road, beyond the B.9103 road
which heads eastwards to cross Spey by Boat o' Brig for Keith, is
Orton, a large area covering the haughland for 3 miles, consisting
of the various ramifications of the estate of the Wharton-Duffs, interesting as still demonstrating the ambitious and far-seeing methods
of the Fife family. The lands, purchased by the first Earl of Fife for
a son, in the late 18th century, were built up into this great property,
and still belong to descendants. The four-storey Georgian mansion,
handsome, with some good heraldry, dated 1786 and reconditioned
1848, is now empty and abandoned, the present owners preferring
to live in the smaller 18th and 19th century home-farm of the

Mains. A circular 18th century doocot still stands in the haugh below the road, and there is an interesting icehouse, for the preservation of fish, game and meat, vaulted and built into a steep bank near by. At the north end of the property, in the extensive haughlands, is the picturesque St. Mary's area, centring round a pre-Reformation chapel and burial-ground, with saint's well, to which crowds used to flock in May. This latter is still in the walling of the chapel enclosure, with a stone canopy incorporating what looks like the old font. The chapel was rebuilt in Gothic style in 1844 as a family mausoleum, with a number of Wharton-Duff graves in the walled enclosure, and a fine heraldic panel above the doorway. The farmhouse of St. Mary's near by is a pleasing place. The estate is well cared-for and with much planting and improvement. There is no actual village of Orton, but a post-office and community at Inchberry here, at the parish boundary.

St. Andrews-Lhanbryde. This parish of 9400 acres is situated directly to the east of Elgin, in the fertile Laigh of Moray, inland from the sea 4 miles, and threaded by the main A.96 highway. It was formed in 1781 out of the two former parishes of those names, when the churches were demolished. The civil parish has a most irregular outline and contorted shape, with much of it really suburban Elgin and better described thereunder. Indeed proximity to Elgin has the inevitable effect of draining away much of the area's life and character.

There is only the one village, Lhanbryde—which means the church of Bride or Bridget, situated on the main road at the eastern extremity. It would be quite a pleasant place were it not for the busy traffic of the highway. The older part, which lies up a slope on the north side, is attractive in an old-world way, amongst trees, with the cottages, many of them restored, linked by unpaved lanes. Up here is the graveyard and site of old Lhanbryde church, now unfortunately neglected, though picturesque. Here are many old tablestones and a highly interesting recumbent effigy of an armoured knight, Innes of Coxton, feet on lion, sword at side, in a pointed recess—which ought to be better cared-for. There are also heraldic slabs to the same family, and to the Gordons, of the 17th and 18th centuries. There is much modern housing to the east of the village.

The present parish church stands over a mile to the north-west, in a somewhat isolated position on the B.9103 road to Lossiemouth, fairly modern, a quite pleasing edifice replacing one of 1796, with belfry and porch. The school is near by. At a crossroads in woodland to the east is a large sawmilling centre, with a bowling-green and pavilion rather strangely sited in this Crooked Wood. The site of the early church of St. Andrew's lay to the east of the present parish church, but across Lossie, at what is now the farm of Kirkhill. The kirk is wholly gone, but there are remains of the graveyard.

The Coxton area lies to the south of the main road, and Coxton Tower is readily seen therefrom on slightly higher ground. It is a most notable and attractive small tower-house of the 17th century, tall and square, with two circular angle-turrets and an unusual square open bartisan at another corner, crowstepped gables, and small windows still retaining their iron yetts or grilles. It is four storeys in height, and very unusual in that all four are vaulted, making the house entirely fireproof. The Innes arms and the date 1644 are displayed. The building is not now occupied, but is still roofed, with a small mansion close by. Like other Innes lands, Coxton was sold to the Duffs. In 1635 the Privy Council ordered Innes of Leuchars and others of the clan, to restore the property of "umquhal Mr. John Innes of Coxtoun . . . and the charter kists of Coxtoun and Balvenie as well as pay 1,000 merks for the wrong and insolence committed in taking the place of Coxtoun". Leuchars was in fact brother to the new Laird of Coxton. Another brother, James "undeutifully coupled himselff in marriage with Mariory Innes, dochter to Alexander Innes of Cotts", much to the fury of father and brothers. An awkward family.

The north-west corner of the parish stretches out towards Lossie-mouth. At Calcotts, where was a railway-station, is a graceful 18th century bridge of two shallow arches with a slight hump, narrow and with originally no parapet, now a metal one. Near by is a very attractive long, low farmery, at Lossie-side. The mansion and estate of Pitgavenny lies a mile more north-westwards, near the Spynie Loch and Canal, a late 18th century Georgian house with a Portuguese flavour, built by James Brander, a Lisbon merchant and notable improver, in 1765, whose name is perpetuated in Branderburgh, the northern part of Lossiemouth not far away. The Brander-Dunbar family still own the property. There is also an 18th century doocot. The Loch of Spynie, once so much larger, is in this parish, but is better described when dealing with Spynie parish.

To the south-east of Lhanbryde village is a heavily wooded area enclosing five small lochs, the largest, Loch na Bo, half a mile long, with good fishing. The Cranloch and Teindland portions of the parish, almost detached, lie to the south.

Speymouth and Mosstodloch. Speymouth is a comparatively small parish of 6350 acres, formed only in 1731 out of a union of the old parishes of Dipple and Essil, lying along the west bank of Spey to near its mouth—although, oddly enough, it does not include the actual mouths of the great river, which are at Garmouth and Kingston in Urquhart parish. Mosstodloch is not quite a village, more of an elongated community stretched along the A.96 main Elgin–Banff road, really nowadays a suburb of Fochabers across the Spey.

The parish is most clearly divided into the Dipple sector south of the main road, and the Essil sector north of it, with the present parish church in the latter area. Dipple became famous as the house of Duff of Dipple, bought by William Duff in 1684, who later inherited Braco and was the founder of the family fortunes, father of

249

the first Earl of Fife. The farmhouse is very pleasant, dating from
1672 and built by Sir James Innes of that Ilk, but largely rebuilt.
The prosperous farmery is well-kept and enhanced with a pretty
duck-pond. The old church of Dipple, now gone, was dedicated to
the Holy Ghost, an unusual dedication in Scotland, and at its former
lych-gate is said to have been a small building known as the House
of the Holy Ghost. Round this, following the course of the sun,
funeral parties always bore their corpses. In the area to the south of
Dipple is the farming estate of Orbliston, with a small community,
picturesque in undulating, whinny-knowed country, the cottages
bearing the Duff arms.

Mosstodloch is a strange place, the houses detached and stretching
on either side of the busy main highway, straight and bare, for over a
mile, in flat country, with no atmosphere of a village. There is a
central crossroads where the B.9015 crosses the A.96 on its way to
Garmouth. The place is, however, developing as is Fochabers
near by, with modern housing. There is a large sawmill here—a link
with the past, for this area was notable as a centre of the timber
trade, the logs being floated down Spey from the great Strathspey
forests. There is also a Forestry Commission Headquarters and
workshop at the east end of Mosstodloch; and this side of Spey, is the
large and now renowned food factory of Messrs Baxter, of Fochabers.
Though this is in Speymouth parish it is better dealt with under
Fochabers. The Spey Bridge here, an iron replacement of 1829, is
now itself replaced by a modern one.

Down a side-road northwards from Mosstodloch, not the B.9015
but parallel to it, on the east, under a mile, is the handsome bonnet-
laird's house of Stynie, of the 18th century, with its farmery. Near
this is the parish church, known as the Red Kirk, and unusual in
being harled a reddish colour. It is a Georgian building with a
"bird-cage" belfry dated 1733, and a well against the belfry gable
encasing an old stone. There is also a sundial on the south wall.
The graveyard is not here. The church has within it a pew-back
from the old Dipple church, date 1634. The manse is not far away,
to the north, large, whitewashed and attractive, and here were great
goings-on in 1746, when, before Culloden, Prince Charles's army
arrived, this portion under the Duke of Perth, who stayed in the
manse, and with him many other notables, including the Earl of
Kilmarnock and the Lords Elcho, Ogilvy, Strathallan, Balmerino
and Mr. Secretary Murray of Broughton. "Although this was very
expensive for the minister, they used him very civilly and gave him
no disturbance on point of principle, but there was no public worship
during their stay." A week or two later, however, it was the Duke
of Cumberland's turn, who forded Spey in the same place ". . . with
the loss of one man only drowned, and encamped from Redhall to
Speymouth Manse, where he sleeped". Long before 1746 this ford
of Spey had been bringing travellers here, military and otherwise,
Malcolm Canmore in 1087, Edward the First in 1296 and 1303,
Montrose in 1645 and Cromwell five years later.

The old church of Essil stood over a mile further down this road, on a bank above Spey, here beginning to widen, only a mile from the sea. Here is still the graveyard, old and crowded, with a modern extension. Fragments of the early kirk survive, with memorials to former ministers. There are many table-stones. Garmouth village lies only half a mile to the north, but is in Urquhart parish.

Spynie. This is a comparatively small civil parish of some 6000 acres lying immediately to the north and west of Elgin, in the Laigh of Moray, wholly rural and without even a village. It has its own claims to fame, however, mainly on account of its great castle, the former palace of the Bishops of Moray. There is a Loch of Spynie at its eastern end, and this used to cover a large part of the parish, but has been drained and confined to less than a mile long by a quarter wide.

The main A.96 to Inverness, on leaving Elgin, crosses the Lossie into Spynie parish, and, passing the Riverside Caravan-Park, runs for 2 miles through the picturesque glades of the great Quarry Wood, old deciduous forest, not planted conifers. In the midst of the woodland, pleasingly set at the roadside, is the Oakwood Motel—although the prevailing trees are beeches not oaks. The quarry which gives name to the wood and to the hill it covers, rising to 418 feet, was an ancient one. On the hillside near by is also the site of a Pictish fort.

Quarrywood is also the name of the parish's only hamlet, situated on the north side of the hill and reached by a side-road striking north-eastwards. This is only a tiny community, attractively placed on a terrace with fine views out over the Moray plain. Here is the parish church, set in a garden not a graveyard, a fairly plain T-shaped Georgian edifice, coomb-ceiled within, having two lofts and some box-pews, and a square aumbry in the east wall. The belfry is dated 1736, and between the two doors is a sundial inscribed "Johannes Dugall fecit 1740". This church superseded that of the Holy Trinity, which stood near the palace, in its burial-ground, and was demolished. There is a fine ex-manse near by, and a large parish-hall, a deserted school and a farmhouse with cottages. A rectangular doocot of the 16th century, with stone-slabbed roof and crowstepped gables stands in the field near by, relic of the castle or fortalice, of Quarrywood, of which no trace remains. It is all very pleasing.

A mile further along the same side-road north-eastwards is Findrassie, an old lairdship, where was once another fortalice, the doocot again surviving down near the remains of a large old walled-garden at the farmery. This doocot is of the lean-to variety, dated 1631, with an empty panel-space, above the door. Unfortunately it is falling into ruin. The present mansion is rather fine dating from 1780, enlarged 1830, dignified amongst old trees, with the rather unusual feature of three underground cellars in the garden at the rear, not apparently of any great age and presumably wine-cellars. The castle is wholly gone. It was a Leslie place.

Two miles still further north-eastwards rises the slight Hill of Spynie, in the plain, crowned by a large farmery. Sharing the gentle eminence is the parish graveyard and site of the old church, a somewhat remote situation which would be almost an island when the loch was undrained. Here are many old flat memorials and table-stones, and the burial enclosure of the Leslies of Findrassie. Within the latter are some interesting stones, one with a cross-crosslet incised, another with a two-handed sword. Leaning against the outside wall are four early cross-stones, now unfortunately very weatherworn and indecipherable. The finial of an ancient cross, on a later base, marks the eastern end of the former Holy Trinity parish church, wherein was buried an early 13th century Bishop of Moray and which at times had to serve as cathedral of his see, before Elgin was built. Also buried in this kirkyard is the former Prime Minister, James Ramsay MacDonald, who died in 1937. Also members of his family.

The progress north-eastwards continuing, across what was formerly loch half a mile, rises on a one-time island site the great castle and palace of Spynie, today a highly impressive ruin amongst old trees. This is a magnificent feature which ought to be made much of, and kept tidy and preserved, for Spynie was one of the finest 15th century castles in the land, a testimony to the wealth, power and taste of the Bishops of Moray—if scarcely to their piety. The building dates from various periods, but the great keep dominates, six storeys and 70 feet high, still complete to the parapet, although the inner floors have gone, with walling 10 feet thick. An interesting feature is the series of five vaulted chambers in the thickness of the walling, one above another, just large enough for sleeping accommodation. On the south front are three large heraldic panels, one empty but two containing the arms of Bishop David Stewart, the builder (1461–75) and Bishop Patrick Hepburn, a notorious character and last pre-Reformation prelate. Notable are the enormous gun-ports, the largest I have seen on other than a military fortress. Bishop Stewart erected this great tower in answer to the then Earl of Huntly, whom he had excommunicated for part-burning Elgin, and who had threatened in consequence "to pull the Bishop out of his pigeon-holes at Spynie". This implies that there was already a less strong castle at Spynie, and in fact the surrounding courtyard, with its flanking towers, is unusual in being in some parts older than the keep, the splendid gatehouse complex to the east, almost unique in Scotland, bearing the arms of Bishop Innes, consecrated in 1406. This was defended by a portcullis. A chapel was erected against the south curtain-wall.

At the Reformation the lands were granted to Alexander Lindsay, a son of the Earl of Crawford, who was created Lord Spynie. King James prevailed on him to resign the property later, to be restored to the Protestant bishops. Spynie was frequently the scene of conflict thereafter, especially in the Covenant and Montrose wars. The last resident Episcopalean bishop died there in 1686.

North-east once more from the castle lies Spynie Loch, all that was left after the drainage scheme represented by the Spynie Canal, begun by Telford in 1808, destroyed by the great flood of 1829 and rebuilt 1860. The canal is 3 miles long and reaches the sea at Lossiemouth. It is interesting that it should be 3 miles from Spynie to salt water today, for once, before the drainage and the great sandblows of the 17th century, Spynie was a harbour and port, mentioned in 1397 and 1451, a shallow arm of the sea reaching in from Burghead and Roseisle. At the north-western end of the parish, near Duffus, are three farms bearing the name of Kintrae, which means the head of the shore. In this area there was a Celtic or Culdee church, referred to in the early 13th century as *veterem ecclesiam de Kyntra*. Its grave-yard used to be distinguishable in the Chapel-field of the farm of Westfield.

Urquhart, Garmouth and Kingston. There are three Urquhart parishes in Scotland, the name meaning merely a long coastal strip. This one certainly has that, between the mouths of Spey and Lossie, 7 miles of mainly sandy shore backed by dunes, these last now planted in a big way with the conifers of the Lossie Forest. The parish, of 13,600 acres, stretches inland in triangular shape, between Elgin and Speymouth parishes, to a point 5 miles from the coast near the former Orbliston railway-station. There are three villages, Urquhart itself, roughly central, and Garmouth and Kingston close together at the mouth of Spey, both particularly interesting. There is also the great estate of Innes, and a community at Leuchars, at the western end, part hutments, part caravans, connected with the naval airfield at Milltown. All in the fertile Laigh of Moray.

Urquhart village lies east and west along a slight ridge, a pleasant, small, rural place, sequestered on side-roads, with the former parish church and graveyard at the foot, and the attractive whitewashed manse of 1822 at the top. There are some old cottages, long and low, in their gardens. The original church at the east end was demolished, to build the Free church—which in turn is now a garage—and the present parish kirk stands in an isolated position half a mile to the north. The old graveyard remains, however, and in it are some burial enclosures, one to an Alexander Gadderer dated 1688. There is also a pretentious tall monument with heraldry, including a clerical hat, referring to a family called Cooper. The important relic here, however, is not in the kirkyard at all, but built into the interior wall of the church-hall alongside, above the fire-place—a small, ancient wheel-cross, 2 feet by 1 foot, in a panel with a decorative edge. It has been used as an ordinary building stone in the Free church, and came from the original parish church—but almost certainly brought to that from the one-time Priory of Urquhart, a foundation of David the First here, in 1125, and which was demolished after the Reformation, in 1654. It was a Benedictine cell under Dunfermline Abbey richly endowed, and at the Reformation lands carve-up this property went to Alexander Seton, who was created Earl of Dunfermline, the famous Lord Chancellor of Scotland, who built Pinkie House, part of Fyvie Castle and other great houses. The early wheel-cross belongs to a still earlier Celtic Church period, of course.

Another relic of the Priory is to be found in the manse-garden. Here is a lintel-stone from a former doorway, which the present minister has found and lovingly preserved, amongst other old stone fragments. It bears the sacred monogram I.H.S., but when used, like so many of the Priory stones, in the building of Garmouth, was put in upside down over the inn-door, and the date 1708 added, much more crudely. Amongst the fragments is a deep egg-shaped bowl, not quite like a font. Also in the manse-garden is an interesting small, square doocot of unusual type.

The present parish church is pleasingly if inconveniently sited on a wooded knoll to the north, a large Gothic building of some style, of 1844. It has a square battlemented tower and a galleried interior.

North-east half a mile, in a corner of a field at cross-roads, is a stone-circle, with five upright stones, three very massive, and another three fallen. This is in the Innes vicinity, and Innes House in its extensive wooded policies rises a mile to the north-west. This is a most handsome and interesting mansion of the 17th century, yellow-washed, tall and impressive, basically a fortified house of that period, L-planned with a square stair-tower in the re-entrant, dormer windows, stringcourses and a profusion of dressed stonework, particularly Renaissance window-pediments. The turned chimneys are also highly unusual, although like those of Winton House and George Heriot's School—not to be wondered at, since the Laird of Innes employed the same famous master-mason, William Aytoun. The house was built between 1640 and 1653. The Innes family derived from one Berowald, allegedly a Fleming, to whom Malcolm the Fourth granted these lands in 1160 for aid in his fight against the rebellious Mormaor of Moray. The 12th Laird entertained James the Third at this house's predecessor, the 15th was a great Reformer and the 17th resigned the chiefship of the name to a kinsman, Innes of Crombie—which led to a disastrous feud. The 20th, who built the house now seen, was created a baronet, and welcomed Charles the Second to Garmouth in 1650, not entirely kindly. A descendant succeeded to the Dukedom of Roxburghe in 1805. By then Innes House had been sold to the Duff 2nd Earl of Fife. The present owners frequently entertain royalty here.

Just over a mile westwards is another and smaller mansion, Leuchars, beside which is the aforementioned naval airfield and camp. This was also an Innes house, and a heraldic stone with their arms and the date 1583 is built into the walling of the Regency front of the mansion. This property was interesting in possessing one of the two very unusual type of doocots, of the late 16th century, circular at base but corbelled-out to the square and gabled above—the other being at Auchmacoy in Buchan. Unfortunately this has recently been destroyed by vandals, to the owner's great regret.

This is at the western parish boundary. To the south is the Moss of Meft, and on the farm here, in 1870, was discovered a particularly large and interesting hoard of flint implements and fragments, evidently a neolithic manufactory. Also a burial-mound with urns and burned bones. Just south again is Longhill Mill, an early 19th century water-mill, with wheel, still grinding oatmeal.

At the other side of Urquhart village is West Clockeasy farm, and in a field at the roadside is a large granite stone, possibly only an erratic, but no doubt where the *clach* in the name comes from. There is a great deal of planted woodland hereabouts, Sleepieshill Wood covering a large acreage to the south. At the farm of Finfan was established in the early 19th century, by the new Duff proprietors of Innes, a medicinal well and spa, on a small scale.

The interesting village of Garmouth lies a mile to the east, quite a large place quaint with narrow winding streets and houses set down haphazardly. It was founded to exploit the timber floated down the Spey in great rafts from the huge pine forests of Rothiemurchus, Glenmore and Strathspey, a thriving and exciting trade which went on for centuries, to the enrichment of the lairds and development of this whole area. Timber working is still to the fore here, and the large sawmill at Mosstodloch near by is in the same tradition—though today the forests are much nearer at hand, the planted Forestry Commission woodlands of Speymouth, Lossie and Culbin. Garmouth was created a burgh of barony for the 19th Laird of Innes in 1587, but has long resiled from that status, an old-fashioned place with some good houses, a particularly fine one of the 18th century standing down beside the play-park. On Brae House wall near by is a plaque, on the site of the house where Charles the Second was forced to sign the Solemn League and Covenant, proposing to impose Scots-style Presbyterianism on England, on his landing from exile in 1650, after Montrose's execution. There is a long, white-washed 18th century inn, and a rather fine later school building. The church, however, formerly a Free kirk, is ugly, with a heavy frontage dated 1844 and a cylindrical belfry. Garmouth was a port in the old days, but the temperamental Spey has changed the position of its mouth, and left the village high and dry. A 9-hole golf course is on the site of the former harbour, reached by a footbridge across a channel. A curious circular water-tower in stone, not unpleasing, forms a landmark on a mound to the north. The Maggie Fair is held here in June, recalling one Lady Margaret Kerr, a 17th century royalist, heiress of the Duke of Roxburghe, who married Sir James Innes and brought the dukedom to that family.

Only half a mile north of Garmouth, at the sea's stony edge, is another large village, Kingston, with its own fascinating story. For this, as its name gives clue, was founded by a little group of Englishmen, shipwrights from Kingston-on-Hull, who came here in 1784 to build ships from the fine timber available from the Spey forests. They did so well at it that Kingston-on-Spey grew famous, and here were built hundreds of ships—allegedly 300—in seven yards, some of them world-famous clippers and Cape-Horners—indeed the records indicate that many were wrecked on that dangerous passage so important in the 19th century. It is hard to realise that this could be possible, now, with acres of stones and pebbles brought down by the Spey spates where once were the shipyards. Yet it is all fact, and some of the best-known names in Scottish mercantile shipping came from here, ships of up to 800 tons, large in the days of sail and timber. Owners were here also, John Duncan of Garmouth, for instance, one of the leading shipowners of Scotland in the mid 19th century. Today Kingston is a village of long parallel streets of low-browed cottages, with a few villas, and a very stony beach. At one end is the very attractive Dunfermline House, large, long and whitewashed, basically of the late 18th century but with a much older, thick-walled nucleus representing probably a change-house of Urquhart Priory which Lord Dunfermline would utilise in his ambitious plans for his new property. It was afterwards called Red Corf House for a time, just why is not apparent. A corf or corb was a basket, usually of iron. Here John Duncan had his shipyard-office. At the west end of the village, is a large pre-cast concrete works, unsightly but providing valuable employment, the lorries for which do not add to the amenity of Garmouth's narrow lanes, which they must traverse—the price of progress.

NAIRNSHIRE

This is one of the smallest counties of Scotland, with an area of only 104,000 acres, five parishes and a population of but 8000, only Kinross-shire having fewer people. For the North of Scotland, it is tiny, and makes one wonder, perhaps, why, with Moray (304,000 acres) and vast Inverness-shire (2,695,000 acres) flanking it, it should ever have been made a county. The answer lies in the power of great lords, in this case the Thanes of Cawdor. It was separated from Inverness-shire in the second half of the 13th century, within the great ancient Province of Moray. The Thanes of Calder or Cawdor, important Celtic lords under the Mormaors of Moray, owned most of the lands here—and were so influential that they managed to get no fewer than five detached portions of their property included in the county of Nairn as early as 1476, three in Moray (one patch in fact no larger than 43 acres), one in Inverness-shire and one actually across the Moray Firth in the Black Isle of Ross. This was the Barony of Ferintosh, south-east of Dingwall, famous for its whisky. These detached portions remained part of the county until modern times. The Thanes of Cawdor persist too, at Cawdor Castle, although they have long changed their title to earl, and are still the largest landowners in the county.

When it is recognised that, of Nairnshire's total acreage, by far the largest proportion consists of moorland wastes and empty heather hills, in the Cawdor and Ardclach parishes that reach far inland, touching Lochindorb, and on to within 4 miles of Carrbridge on the A.9 in Inverness-shire, 17 miles from the Moray Firth, it will be understood how small is the populated area. In these days of elaborate and expensive county and regional services, this tiny area and population is just not practicable for administrative and funding purposes, and so Nairnshire has now been combined administratively with neighbouring Moray, a reasonable arrangement.

The county has only the one town, the renowned royal burgh and holiday resort of Nairn itself, at the mouth of the River Nairn. With a population of about 5000, this leaves only 3000 for the rest of the county. The best land is stretched along the fair and shallow vale of Strathnairn, for some 9 miles, and here are the great old estates of Cawdor and Kilravock. There are villages only at Auldearn and Cawdor, with Croy's parish partly in the county but the village itself in Inverness-shire. Hamlets are at Blairmore, Clunas, Culcharry, Clephanton, Geddes, Glenferness and Littlemill.

The coastal plain, really an extension of the Laigh of Moray westwards, is not so fertile and broad as the Moray portion, so famed as the Granary of Scotland. It is more sandy and heathlike, and on the east includes a couple of miles of the great Culbin Forest. The coastline itself is uniformly flat and sandy, with no cliffs and little of rock, fine for picnickers and bathers. At both ends of the county's sea-board, peculiar long sand-bars extend, although there is no real bay as is usual in such cases, that to the east, off Culbin, over 2 miles long and wholly detached from the shore, that to the west 2 miles like-wise, but a very narrow peninsula known as Whiteness Head, reach-ing out from the Carse of Delnies. At the base of this, today, industrial developments connected with the North Sea oil boom are taking place. Save at Nairn town itself, no road runs along the 10-mile coastline, and unlike the rest of the Moray Firth seaboard, there are no fishing villages.

Nairnshire is not rich in lochs, but there is one, a mile long though very narrow, at Lochloy, at the west end of the Culbin Forest, only half a mile in from the coast. And the Cran Loch, smaller, a short distance east of it. The county boundary passes through the middle of Flemington Loch to the west, about half a mile long, and the Loch of Boath, is not at Boath, near Auldearn, but inland 8 miles in the Ardclach foothills, a tiny stretch of water. None of the famous Lochindorb is actually in the county, though the boundary touches it.

From the foothills to the sea Nairnshire is well wooded, with the Forests of Assich, Laiken and part of Darnaway, and the Woods of Cawdor, Kilravock, Dallaschyle, Carse, Delnies, Urchany, Lethen, Inchoch, Shaw and Glenferness. There is no particularly spectacular scenery, but a great deal of sylvan beauty and charm—and the vistas across the Moray Firth from the higher grounds are, like Moray's, superb.

Although the county can boast no ancient abbeys and priories, there are some interesting churches—notably the major ruined former parish church of Barevan, possibly of the 14th century, and abandoned since 1619—which ought to be better known. It lies 2 miles south-west of Cawdor, within a neglected graveyard packed with interesting stones and memorials. The present parish church of Cawdor itself is interesting, erected by Thane John Roy Campbell in 1619, with a highly unusual tower and curious angled vaulted porch. Little is left of the Chapel of St. Mary of Rait, again of the 14th century; likewise only a part of the ancient kirk of Auldearn survives. Ardclach is famous for its almost unique bell-tower, a small, whitewashed and gabled free-standing tower, set remotely on a hillside high above the old parish church deep in the valley, where its bell might be heard from much further afield, both to summon worshippers and to warn of invasion from Highland caterans.

For its size Nairnshire is quite rich in castles. Cawdor, of course, is renowned, one of the finest and least spoiled fortified strengths in the land, picturesque above its wooded ravine. Kilravock, of the Roses, is almost as well-known, dating from the 15th and 17th cen-turies, still also in the hands of its original family. Ruined Rait Castle is almost the only one of its kind in Scotland, English in aspect—perhaps because its Cheyne builders were noted supporters of Edward the First. Inchoch is now very delapidated, but has been a fine place of the late 16th century, seat of the ancient Hay barony of Lochloy. There was a royal castle at Nairn itself, now gone, and the site of another at Auldearn, now crowned by the well-known Boath Doocot. Other ancient houses, not fortified, are at Lethen, Clunas, Coulmony, Brightmony, Balblair, Kildrummie and House-hill.

Prehistoric and proto-historic monuments are not lacking, although there is nothing of outstanding importance. There are stone-circles and cairn-circles at Auldearn, Balanrait, Wester Urchany and elsewhere, one or two forts, and Pictish symbol-stones at Glenferness, Carse of Delnies and Cawdor. A later feature which deserves mention is the number of notable bridges, over the Find-horn and Nairn Rivers and the Muckle Burn—Dulsie, Daltulich, Ferness, Highland Boath, Barevan, Kilravock (White), Cantray and others, mainly of the late 18th century.

Nairnshire's history is very largely the story of two great families, those of Cawdor and Rose—although, on a national scale, Mon-trose's resounding Battle of Auldearn was fought within the county in 1645, and Culloden, taking place just beyond the western boundary in 1746, greatly affected the area. The origins of the Celtic Thanes of Calder, or Cawdor, is lost in antiquity. The famous MacBeth himself was Thane of Cawdor, resigning the thanedom to his brother on assuming the Crown. How long they had been at Cawdor before that is not known. By the 14th century, the office of Constable of the royal castle of Nairn, and Sheriff of the county, had become hereditary in the Cawdor family. In 1498, the 7th Thane produced only a child heiress, Muriella Calder, who was kidnapped at the instigation of the Earl of Argyll, and married to his 3rd son, Sir John Campbell. The Campbells continued to use the title of thane long after it had died out elsewhere in Scotland—it was still being used in the 17th century when the then Thane fell from his horse, allegedly by witchcraft, and died. The 10th of the Campbell line changed the title, he being created Lord Cawdor in 1796 and Earl Cawdor in 1829. Campbells have always been good at hanging on to their lands—and, some would say, to others!

In this respect the Roses of Kilravock are scarcely their inferiors. The mother of the heiress Muriella Calder was herself a Rose of Kilravock, and Kilravock meant the girl to be bride for his son— hence the initiative of the Campbell kidnapping. The Roses seem to have started many more lairdly houses in the area, so that a large number of the estates of Nairnshire, and the flanking parts of Moray and Inverness-shire, have had Rose proprietors. Whether they too were of Celtic origin, or later Norman, is not clear, but they were long settled at Geddes in this county, before acquiring Kilravock by marriage early in the 13th century. The present laird, Miss Rose, is the 25th of her line, whereas the present Earl Cawdor appears to be 23rd. Of the forty-six Provosts of Nairn between 1450 and 1777, forty-five were Roses, and the 46th was a brother-in-law stop-gap! They were involved in most of the excitements of the North-East, and yet, oddly enough, were quite renowned at times as peace-makers—which, with Inneses and Dunbars, Brodies and Mackin-toshes living around them, was a much-needed but thankless role. It was the same reasonable state of mind, no doubt, which prompted Hugh, 16th baron, to entertain the Duke of Cumberland before Culloden, in his town-house in Nairn, on 14th April, and Prince Charles Edward at Kilravock itself on the 15th.

Nairnshire was notorious for its witches and witch-trials, a sorry chapter.

From what has been said, it will be apparent that the county is not a hub of industry. But agriculture is well-developed in the strath and on the coastal plain, sheep-farming preoccupies the up-lands, and forestry is pursued everywhere. Tourism becomes ever more important, and with justice, and Nairn lays itself out to cater for all tastes. With continuing oil development in the North Sea off this Moray Firth coast, who knows what impacts there may be on this little county? Let us hope that, whatever the future may hold, the authorities will never allow the essential character of Nairnshire to be changed, even under the new local government reorganisation.

Ardclach, Glenferness and Dulsie. Ardclach is a huge civil parish in a small county, covering 40,000 acres of the total 104,000. Yet it has no real village, only the estate hamlet of Glenferness. Not that it is so very remote in position, for its northern tip comes within 3 miles of Nairn town. It is set partly in foothill country, but the main acreage is empty heather hillside and moorland, this reaching far to the south, to march eventually with Duthill in Inverness-shire, only 3 miles from Carrbridge. The parish is 14 miles long, of varying widths, and is threaded for much of its length by the lovely and serpentine River Findhorn. Much of the lower area is very scenic, and included are the well-known beauty-spots of Dulsie Bridge, Daltulich Bridge and the Ardclach bell-tower valley. These areas are heavily wooded.

The parish centre, at Ardclach itself, is not even a hamlet, within a deep bend of the Findhorn, near the crossing of A.939 and B.9007, 10 miles south-west of Forres. It is a highly picturesque vicinity, with the very inconveniently placed former parish church now abandoned, down in a lovely wooded amphitheatre at the riverside, the present church, formerly a Free kirk, on higher ground almost a mile to the north-east, and the famous bell-tower high on an emi-nence between. There is a scattering of farms, cottages and the manse, but no recognisable community.

The old church, in its ancient graveyard, is of most pleasing appearance, rebuilt in 1762 and enlarged in 1839. It is now stripped internally—although the kirkyard is still in use—and has had two galleries and a coved ceiling. There are many old stones in the yard, mainly 18th century table-stones, but one flat slab is dated 1670. The steep road down must be a hazard for winter funerals.

The 17th century bell-tower, almost unique in Scotland, is interesting, built high above the amphitheatre, both as a watch-tower for defence purposes and to house the church-bell so that it could be heard far and wide. Square, with a gabled roof and belfry, two storeys in height and whitewashed, it has something of the appearance of a small fortalice-tower, and it commands a wide prospect over the surrounding foothill country. The tower is 14 feet square, with a vaulted basement and mural garderobe, the door being only 3 feet 9 inches high. A straight stair ascends to the first floor, where there is a room with a fireplace, the lintel carved with a monogram M.G.B. There are small windows and a shot-hole. The belfry crowns the south gable, and below, on the external wall, is the date 1655. The initials probably refer to a parish minister of the Brodie of Lethen family, on whose lands the tower stands. It all makes a most picturesque and unusual feature. At the approach thereto is a small monument to the Rev. Donald Mitchell, born 1792, died 1823, son of the parish minister, and Scotland's first missionary to India allegedly, whose church is in the Leprosarium now maintained by the Church of Scotland.

The present parish church stands a further half-mile to the west, at a junction of side-roads, a pleasant small edifice of the 19th century, low-roofed, with belfry, bright within and having a high pulpit. A mile to the north is the woodland-girt Loch of Belivat, odd in having no evident outlet, although half a mile long.

Not very far south of Ardclach as the crow flies, but quite a long way by road, via Ferness Bridge over the Findhorn and the B.9007, is Glenferness, a large wooded estate on the east bank of the winding river, lifting up to the heather moors—indeed the heather coming down to flank the driveway. It is the seat of the Earl of Leven and Melville, Lord Lieutenant of the County of Nairn. The long and rather rambling mansion, with colonnaded porch, dates from 1844, with later additions, and is most pleasantly sited, having many treasures within, including the saddle and boots of the first Earl of Leven, the famous Covenanting general, Sandy Leslie. Three hundred yards to the south, on the wooded bank of Findhorn, is the Princess Stone, a fine Pictish cross-slab, $4\frac{1}{2}$ feet high, showing the Celtic beast, double-disc and Z-rod and crescent and V-rod symbols, with two figures apparently embracing, within a rectangle, plus the usual Celtic decoration. It is often alleged that this commemorates the death of a Pictish princess, eloping with her Danish lover, who both leapt into the river to avoid capture, the cross being erected where their still-embracing bodies were washed up, but this is very likely a typical romantic invention to explain the embracing figures, which much more probably have a purely religious significance. The stone was moved to its present position in 1960, when the river undermined its previous site.

Glenferness has a "planned" hamlet, on one side of the road at a steep bank a mile or so to the north-east, with post-office and greystone cottages. Ferness, or Logie, Bridge to the north, carrying A.939 over Findhorn on three arches, was built by Thomas Telford in 1805, and survived the great flood of 1829, when many another did not.

Dulsie Bridge was another survivor—less surprising, for it is a very lofty single arch built over a deep dark gorge of the rocky river, in a highly spectacular situation, a steep descent by road on either side. It was erected in 1750 to carry Wade's military road from Grantown to Fort George, long and narrow and graceful, with a distinct upward slant. It is a favourite venue for visitors, and understandably, for the river scenery here is very fine. To the north-west, the military road rises through scattered pine forest, to cross another smaller hump-backed bridge over a burn, and on over the open heather hillside, near the 800-foot contour, to Highland Boath and the Clunas area. At the former there is a slightly later bridge, of 1764, near Whitefold farm, over the Muckle Burn, graceful and single-arched again, but harled, which is less usual. The vistas from this moorland road, over the Laigh and the Moray Firth to the Northern Highlands, are magnificent.

South of Glenferness and Dulsie the wilderness takes over almost completely, B.9007 climbing the empty moors to the 1229-foot summit, a dozen miles of lonely mountain road almost to Carrbridge on the A.9, double-width in Nairn and Moray, then passing-bay in Inverness-shire. The prospect, when the Cairngorm Mountains burst into view beyond the small bealach or pass at the Inverness county boundary, can be breathtaking.

North of Ardclach, on the west bank of Findhorn, is Coulmony House, a delightful mansion, formerly delapidated but now tastefully restored to its original 1750 proportions, on an open terraced site. It was a Rose of Kilravock property, passing to the Brodies of Lethen. The date 1750, and a weatherworn inscription, are above the door. A mile north-east is Daltulich Bridge, on the Edinkillie (Moray) boundary, another very pleasing high, single-arch structure over a fine stretch of the rocky Findhorn. It is related of this bridge, erected in 1800, that it fell at the first building, and the contractor had to rebuild it at his own cost. He mentioned, philosophically however, that: "It would have been waur if I hadna estimated enough to gie me a profit on twa brigs!" The side-road northwards through the Darnaway Forest from here is a prolonged delight, to Conicavel and the Forres vicinity. It was at Daltulich that the seven sons of Campbell of Inverliver died in the rearguard action during the kidnapping of the Cawdor heiress Muriella.

Auldearn. Auldearn is quite a famous name in history, thanks to the great battle fought there in 1645, when Montrose won his brilliant victory over the government and Covenanting forces. But it is also a large Nairnshire parish of 14,000 acres, a sizeable village, and once a burgh of barony. The village lies only 2 miles east of Nairn, with most of its parish extending eastwards and southwards, much of it flanking the county boundary with Moray. There is no other village or real hamlet, but a number of ancient estates and other features. The Hard Muir where Shakespeare made MacBeth meet the Wierd Sisters is partly in this parish.

The village is set on and around a rather curious semi-circular formation of green banks and braes—which had a vital effect on Montrose's tactics at the battle. The lower ground has now, of course, been drained, but in 1645 it would be very marshy and impossible terrain for cavalry. Housing now extends into a part of this; indeed the A.96 and B.9101 roads traverse it, but the old village remains up on the higher ground, a fairly compact place. Kirk and village were involved in the battle—although little of the present buildings.

The oldest edifice here today is the well-known Boath doocot, a 17th century circular and drum-shaped building with a conical roof, whitewashed and enhanced with stringcourses, having a slightly unusual entry-place for the birds. This, now in the care of the National Trust for Scotland, stands at a high point of the crescent-shaped eminence, which was the site of the former early castle of Eren, a royal stronghold from which, it is thought, William the Lion issued the second of his charters for Inverness. Why there should have been another royal castle so close to that of Nairn is not explained, but the grassy mounds and foundations surrounding the doocot are very evident. Modern housing comes close on the east.

The church crowns another eminence, eastwards, a not very attractive building of 1757, renewed in 1900, erected to replace an early chapel dedicated to St. Colm. Fortunately part of the old kirk still remains at the east gable. Here are many ancient tombs, one panel relating to a Hay of Lochloy who died in 1563, another a replica of 1883, commemorating the deaths at the Battle of Auldearn of Sir John and Maister Gideon Murray. Others of General Hurry's army were buried here, for the Covenanting casualties ranged between 1000 and 3000, according to various accounts, while Montrose's were said to number from 15 to 200. The Dunbars of Boath and the Brodies of Lethen have their burial enclosures here. One of the Brodie tombs is extraordinarily massive. There is an 18th century pedestal sundial.

The village is grouped around these two features, and partly along the busy A.96 highway below. Here there is quite a large hotel, developed from the old Lion Inn. A number of roads open off the main street, with difficult entrances and exits.

Just to the north of Auldearn lies Boath House, in its policies, an ancient estate of the Dunbars, with a Georgian mansion of 1825 to designs of Archibald Simpson, built over the vaults of the older house which the doocot served. The Dunbars, descended from the old Earls of Dunbar and Moray, gained these lands in 1555, the 9th laird being given a baronetcy of Boath in 1814. The family took a large part in the life of Nairn, especially the sporting side latterly, and the Dunbar Golf Course there was gifted by Sir Alexander. Sir Frederick, the 5th baronet, was a great cricketer, and is reputed to have been the last man in the North to bowl underarm in serious cricket. The Auldearn cricket team was unique in cricketing annals in Scotland. The Dunbars remained here until 1925.

An equal distance east of the village, at a side-road fork beside the war-memorial, is Kinsteary Cottage, in the garden are two small standing-stones, the remains of a stone-circle. Another circle has stood to the right of the side-road almost a mile further south-east, three uprights of red granite amongst the scrub.

To the north and east of Auldearn is the wide coastal plain, ending at the long sandy shore which stretches east of Nairn to Culbin. This is the area of Lochloy, once a powerful barony. There is still a loch of the name, long and narrow but only a shadow of its former un-drained extent. The Hay barons of Lochloy were amongst the prin-cipal cadets of the chiefly house of Erroll, and were settled here from an early date. Their castle stood at Inchoch a little way to the south. There is only a farm called Lochloy today, though once there was a village, with another at Maviston a mile to the east. Inchoch Castle is still an impressive ruin, standing in a farm-steading on a slight eminence among the flat lands. It has been a fine late 16th century fortalice on the Z-plan, with a 17th century addition. The main block has two circular towers projecting diagonally to north-west and south-east, the former containing small square-shaped rooms, the latter the main stair. The basement was vaulted, and stair-turrets in the re-entrants carried the ascent above main floor-level. All is now badly shattered and broken, but enough remains to show that it has been a place of some style. A heraldic panel display-ing the Hay arms is built into the gable of the adjoining farmhouse. The effigy, in armour, of Sir William Hay of Lochloy, died 1421, lies in Elgin Cathedral; and from this line descend various junior branches, including the Barons Haij of Sweden. The Hays remained at Inchoch until 1695, when the Brodies took over.

The south side of the parish has its own interest. It is heavily wooded, and here are the estates of Kinsteary and Lethen, and the old property of Moyness. Kinsteary, only a mile south of Auldearn, is an old Rose property, still held by descendants, although the mansion is not ancient. Older is the large farmhouse of Brightmony, once a small independent lairdship, later linked with Lethen as a dower-house. It has a fine substantial and traditional building of 1706, long, crowstepped and harled, on a ridge site with fine vistas. Near by in a field are two enormous erratic boulders of conglomer-ate.

Lethen is an interesting place, a large estate lying a mile further south, its mansion on the south-facing bank of the wide valley of the Muckle Burn. The Brodies came here in 1634 in the person of Alexander, second son of the then Brodie of that Ilk. They are still here. His fortalice was burned down in 1680, and the present house built thereafter a little to the north. It has been considerably altered, added to and then reduced, since then, but makes a handsome house still. Near by to the east is an unusual feature, a 17th century granary, attractive with crowstepped gables and a central gablet. It is now used as a laundry. At the other side, in a field, is an 18th century lean-to type doocot. There are important fossil-beds on the property. The Lethen Brodies played a considerable part in the affairs of the North-East. A mile or so to the east, down the Muckle Burn, is the farming area of Moyness, with a few houses at Milton, near the county boundary. From Broomton of Moyness in 1870 the Moyness Stone, removed from a demolished stone-circle, was taken to Cawdor Castle.

South-west of Lethen 2 miles, and actually just over into Ardclach parish, is the hamlet of Littlemill, where the A.939 crosses the Muckle Burn, a tiny place. Near by, overlooking the valley on the east is what is called the Shian Hillock, a distinctly pointed green mound, which looks as though it might have been artificial and defensive. It is locally known as the Fairies' Hillock, however—and, of course, Shian is near enough to the Gaelic for fairies. A little further along the A.939 eastwards is the house called Campbell's School. It was indeed once a small private school established by the Campbells of Cawdor.

There are large gravel quarries and workings situated at Park, 3 miles nearer Nairn on the A.939, on the side of the low hill covered by the Laiken Forest.

Mention must be made of the famous witch-trial of Isobel Goudie of Auldearn, in 1662. No doubt under torture, this poor half-crazed woman made a lengthy statement, believed by all and sundry declaring that the local association of witches was so large that it had to be divided into troops under officers, known as the Maidens of the Covine, young girls usually, who assembled their covens to dig up graves and make charms from the bones. They turned themselves into hares, cats and crows, and shot elf-arrows, to the danger of the lieges. Satan she said was a hard taskmaster, scourging and beating them—but evidently not so hard as her fellow Christians and judges, who preferred to burn their witches.

Cawdor, Barevan and Clunas. Most literate folk have probably heard of Cawdor, if only in connection with the Thane thereof in *Macbeth*. It has been a famous name in Scotland's story down the ages. It is also an earldom and a very large civil parish, of 29,000 acres, with a sizeable village of the same name, situated 5 miles south-west of Nairn. Strange, therefore, that the name should now universally be accepted as Cawdor—which is only the way it is *pronounced* locally—when it truly should be Calder. The original lands were called Calder, and the important family thereof, the Calders of that Ilk, descended from the brother of MacBeth himself, Mormaor of Moray—to whom, on his assumption of the crown he resigned the Thanedom. The fact that Shakespeare called the name Cawdor in his play, is highly interesting, possibly lending support to the theory, held by some knowledgeable scholars, that the great English playwright himself *visited* Scotland, on James the Sixth and First's urging, to gain material for this first play in which the Scots image was treated seriously and with dignity, and so picked up the local pronunciation of Cawdor, rather than having merely seen the name written as Calder. No doubt it is largely because of Shakespeare that the Cawdor spelling has become accepted universally.

Be that as it may, Cawdor itself is a most interesting and attractive place. Like the neighbouring large parish of Ardclach, to the east, at least two-thirds of its area is heather hill and lofty moorland, roadless and unpopulated. The rest, to the north, is either wooded foothill country, or the narrow belt of level farmlands flanking the River Nairn. It has an extreme length of 14 miles, from a base of 7 miles, rather in the shape of a very elongated triangle. Barevan is the former parish name, and a farming district to the south-west, with the more ancient church, long ruined. And Clunas another farming area to the south-east, in the skirts of the uplands, with an old lairdship, hamlet and post-office.

Cawdor Castle, with the village and parish church near by, is set amongst old woodlands just south of the B.9090 road from Nairn. The castle is renowned as one of the finest and most unspoiled in the North-East, more authentic in character than many in that it retains its deep dry moat and drawbridge entrance, along with other original features. It is very large and impressive, as well as picturesque, worthy seat of a long line of ancient lords—even though the present peerage of the Campbell earls dates from only 1796 and 1827, when the then laird, an M.P. and descended from the 15th century Earl of Argyll, was ennobled. The Campbells gained the property, far from their native Argyll, in 1499, by kidnapping, on the orders of Argyll himself, who had gained her wardship from the Crown, the child heiress of the 7th Thane of Cawdor, Muriel Calder, and abducted her across Scotland to their own country—at the cost of six of Campbell of Inverliver's sons, who died holding up the pursuit. Whether indeed the delicate little red-haired girl survived this rough handling is not to be known, but the Campbells have long had a proverb which claims that so long as there is a red-headed lassie on either bank of Loch Awe, Cawdor will never lack an heiress!

The present castle is very extensive, and largely of Campbell building. But the great central keep is said to date from 1396, although the upper works were added in 1454, when there was a special licence to fortify, granted by James the Second. The later and lower accommodation extending all round the keep was added in the 16th and 17th centuries—and there is nothing of later date. Intriguing is the story of the original building here. The late 14th century Thane—a royal officer responsible for the keeping of the official Nairn Castle—was minded to build a private stronghold on his Calder lands. He selected a site nearer the sea, but in a dream he was guided to load a donkey with a coffer of gold and let the beast go. It would stop to graze under one hawthorn tree, rest under a second and actually lie down under a third. Where it did this, the Thane was to build his castle, and his line would prosper there.

Calder obeyed his dream, so literally, that he actually erected his keep round the tree, without felling it. And today visitors can see the ancient hawthorn, long dead but still upright, rising out of the earthen floor of the basement and disappearing up through the vaulted ceiling, obviously built to receive it—a unique confirmation of an ancient story.

The keep is four storeys high to the parapet and wall-walk, two storeys being vaulted, and is unusual in that the formerly open rounds at the corners of the parapet were given conical slated roofs in the 17th century. There is a garret storey above. The walls are very thick, and contain many mural chambers. Curiously enough, the original kitchen appears to have been *above* the Hall on the first floor, not below as usual. Elsewhere, in the lower wings, there are a great many features of interest, with angle-turrets, dormer windows and crowstepped gables. One particularly fine fireplace lintel is carved with a fox smoking a pipe, a monkey blowing a horn, a cat playing a fiddle and a mermaid strumming a harp. The date 1511 has been recut—a fraud, for this was before the discovery of tobacco. The lintel is in fact of the 17th century, but set up to commemorate the marriage, in 1511, of the aforementioned ill-used heiress Muriel and Sir John Campbell, a son of Argyll. Interesting, too, is the great iron yett, or gate, under a belfry, which admits from the drawbridge into the outer courtyard; this was brought from Lochindorb Castle in upland Moray, which an early Thane was ordered to destroy. The castle is a treasure-house of portraits, tapestries, furnishings, etc. The gardens surrounding are a delight, including a wooded ravine of the Cawdor Burn. At the south side of the pleasance wall lies a large stone slab, now entirely weatherworn on its upper face, thought to be the Moyness Stone, cup-marked and curiously grooved, brought here in 1870 from Broomston of Moyness when a stone-circle there was removed.

The present Earl Cawdor is the 6th, but the 23rd Laird.

The village of Cawdor is suitably picturesque also, in old trees, scattered over almost half a mile, across the Burn from the Castle. Here is the school, almshouses of 1881, a hall, shop and a former 18th and 19th century change-house to the east, now used for estate administration. Also, of course, the parish church, an unusual T-planned building, erected by Thane John Roy Campbell in 1619 allegedly to fulfil a vow made when in danger of shipwreck, and enlarged 1830. He it was who changed the parish name from Barevan to Cawdor. The building has crowstepped gables, one of these surmounted by a tall and slender crenellated belfry-tower, highly unusual. Also a most interesting entrance, with a vaulted arch across an angle, the iron jougs of the burgh of barony hanging therein. Internally there are three galleries and a high pulpit, with a coved ceiling, and on display is an old pewter collection-plate inscribed "Kirk of Calder". There are a great many old gravestones in the kirkyard.

Barevan, and the former parish church, is less known, but

extremely interesting for all that. The Cawdor Burn forks half a mile above the castle, into the Allt Dearg, a truly Highland name, and the Riereach Burn, both quite major streams, flowing through the great Wood of Cawdor. On the former, 2 miles up, is Barevan, once the pre-Reformation parish centre, now only two farms and a bridge of that name, and the ruined church at the farm of Kirkton of Barevan. This ancient building in its graveyard, disused since 1619, and much neglected, deserves to be a lot better known. There is quite a lot left of the church, and the gravestones make a fascinating study. Indeed, here is quite a rich field for some archaeological body to explore and record, for there are scores of very early stones, some undoubtedly of much interest, many almost completely moss-covered and more hidden beneath the turf. The floor of the church is quite covered with them, used as slabbing, some bearing pre-historic cup-marks, and two at least showing calvary crosses, of considerable antiquity. A number have an unusual device of a circle inscribed at the foot, with dots for eyes and mouth, and what look like crossed batons beneath—an early manifestation of the popular skull-and-crossbones motif. Who knows what curious relics might be discovered from a proper inspection of this abandoned site? Here were buried the early Thanes of Calder.

The church itself has been quite large for a country parish, with rather good pointed windows, splayed internally, and two pointed arched doorways to the south, one with a draw-bar socket. There is a piscina, with unusual double basins and drains. In the kirkyard, amongst other items, are two of especial interest. One is a stone coffin, for use as penance and punishment, the unfortunate offender being laid in it, with a heavy stone slab on top to cover all but the eyes, and being left therein for many hours to repent—overnight in a kirkyard, in superstitious times, a grim experience. Beside this is a curious almost round ball of smooth pink granite, 17 inches in diameter and weighing 18 stones, allegedly. What this was for is not recorded—but it may have been used to roll on top of the said slab on the coffin, to help keep the offender down. This interesting old church was dedicated to St. Evan, a Celtic missionary. Just to the north is a rocky scarp, with scrub, the site of a former Pictish vitrified fort known as Dunevan. The bridge over the Allt Dearg near by dates from the 18th century, probably part of the military road to Fort George, hump-backed with a single arch. The extensive Assich Forest stretches westwards beyond.

North-east of Barevan another side-road leads eastwards to cross, after a mile, the aforementioned Riereach Burn by another small old bridge, spanning a deep and narrow gorge and cauldron. The road then enters the Urchany area, where a hill and a number of farms incorporate the name. At Wester, or Little Urchany, there is a large cairn-circle about 300 yards south-west of the steading, with three upright standing-stones remaining and many recumbent. And another 250 yards to the north of this, in a corner of the field, is the site of a former chapel and graveyard, now merely grassgrown foundations and loose stones. The writer has been unable to discover anything of the history of this church.

Higher into the foothills country, 2 miles to the south, is Clunas. The hamlet is pleasantly set, in woodland, with a former school, post-office and hall. Near by to the west is the farm now called Mains of Clunas, and here has been an old lairdship of the Clunas of that Ilk family. Part of the present farmhouse is ancient, probably late 17th century, a wing with crowstepped gables, coped chimneys and chamfered windows projecting westwards. The wing opposite, now a barn, also appears to have an old nucleus, but has been much altered. Joining the two wings on the west, to enclose a courtyard, is an interesting range of high walling, which appears to be one side of a non-existent house, probably of the early 18th century, having a good doorway with fluted moulding and a decorative empty panel-space above; also four built-up window apertures and peculiar stone drainage gutters at eaves-level at either side. A story to account for this is that a young laird hereof was building a new wing to the house, intending marriage, when he went off to the Jacobite campaign of 1715, and did not return, the building never being finished.

The boundary with Ardclach parish adjoins. To the south for many long miles stretch only the heather hills. Penetrating this great upland wilderness is that part of the Findhorn valley known as The Streens, with the remote Drynachan Lodge at its foot. The name is a corruption of the Gaelic *srian*, a bridle, and at best only a bridle-path follows the great river up here towards its birthplace in the Inverness-shire mountains of Strathdearn.

To the east of Cawdor village are one or two features. Half a mile along the B.9090 is the farm of Balnaroid, or Balanrait, where a single standing-stone, easily seen in a field, is all that is left of a stone-circle. Behind, on higher ground, is the prettily placed hamlet of Culcharry, with a Free church at the crossroads, and cottages on the braeside, backed by trees. Half a mile to the north-east is Blairmore, a quite large and growing residential community of housing, cottages, modern private and council, on the brae back from the B.9090, only 3 miles from Nairn and therefore suitable for commuters. Just below it, on the larger road, is Brackla Distillery, large and modern, with its associated housing.

Croy and Kilravock. The large and conjoint parish of Croy and Dalcross is a difficult one to delineate, for it is part in Nairn county and part in Inverness, yet not conveniently Croy in the former and Dalcross in the latter. Moreover, much of the great and distinctive Culloden district comes into it, but not all, and this is much better described separately. For the sake of simplicity of reference, therefore, I shall divide up the parish, and deal with Croy under Nairnshire and Dalcross and Culloden as separate items under Invernessshire. Actually, the county boundary runs right through the centre of Croy village—so this division is by no means accurate. Why this peculiar situation has come about is not clear. The parishes were united in the 15th century, so it is the modern county boundaries which are at fault. The total area is 22,700 acres, much of it in the very attractive Strathnairn. The fact that the western part was once in the powerful Lordship of Petty, very much an Inverness-shire entity, may have something to do with it.

The village of Croy is very picturesque, lying in undulating and wooded country just above the Moray Firth plain, 3 miles west of Cawdor and almost equidistant between Nairn and Inverness. It is a scattered community, with an old-fashioned air. The parish church stands on a slight eminence, in its old graveyard beside a farm-steading. It dates from 1767, renewed 1829, and is small and plain outside but brightly pleasant within, with a small gallery to the rear, and many memorials of the Rose of Kilravock family. The usual multitude of table and flat gravestones are ranked in the kirk-yard, and there is a watch-house. A hoard of silver Celtic brooches and coins were found at the farm here, Mains of Croy, in 1875. Not far to the west of the village, in a field on the right of the B.9006 road to Culloden, is a large and rough monolith known as Clach na Seanaish, or the Whispering Stone. Some prefer the Listening Stone. Almost a mile on westwards, at a crossroads, stands the Free church, of 1852.

The River Nairn bisects the parish to the south, and on its north bank are two ancient Rose estates—Kilravock, the famous seat of the chiefs of the name, and Holme Rose to the south-west. This renowned family have been settled here from very early times. There is some doubt as to whether they derive from the old Celtic Earls of Ross, or the Norman de Roos family, but it is perhaps significant that they bear a boar's head between boujets on their arms, not the lion of Ross. At any rate, they have been at Kilravock since the 13th century, when they came from Geddes, in Nairn parish a few miles to the east. There have been at least seventeen lairds of the name of Hugh, or Hutcheon, Rose of Kilravock, so that distinguishing between them is not easy. Of the forty-six Provosts of Nairn prior to 1777, forty-five were Roses. The family has taken a prominent part in most of the alarums and excitements of the North-East—although they often seem to have sought to play the part of peacemakers also. One Hugh Rose, the 10th, sought to soothe two quarrelling neighbours, and signed himself "Hutcheon Rose of Kilravock, an honest man illguided between you baith!". Incidentally, the pronunciation is Kil*rock*.

The castle is very interesting, an impressive and composite building of great extent, built on quite sharply rising ground above the Nairn's meadows. The old square keep of 1460 rises to the east, simple and lofty, with five storeys to the parapet and walk, and a garret storey above. This is the fortalice for which the 7th baron gained a licence "to fund, big ande upmak a toure of fens with Barmekin ande bataling upon quhat place of strynth him best likis within the Barony of Kylrawok". To this was attached, at more than one period in the 17th century, the large and commodious five-storey, gabled house with its stair-turrets and dormer windows. The basements of both sections are vaulted, and the building is well supplied with gunloops and shot-holes. Owing to the steep rise in ground-level, it appears much higher from the south. The castle stands in a large estate. Here have visited many prominent folk—including James the Third's parvenue favourite Cochrane, Earl of Mar, who tried to destroy what was then the newly built keep; he was, in due course, hanged over Lauder Brig by the outraged nobles. Here came Mary Queen of Scots, in 1562; and here was entertained her descendant Bonnie Prince Charlie, just before his defeat at Culloden, while Cumberland was occupying the Roses' town-house in Nairn. Robert Burns was here in 1787.

At Milton of Kilravock farm, 2 miles to the east, is an interesting small 17th century mill, with crowstepped gabling, fleur-de-lis finials and a drying-kiln. It bears panels inscribed 1641 H.R. and M.F.; and 1733 H.R. and I.R. A mile to the west is the hamlet of Clephanton, at a crossroads on the B.9091, with a good 18th century house of substance amongst some cottages. The name is interesting, for it is called after the 46th Provost of Nairn, Major Clephane, who broke the succession of Rose chief magistrates—although he himself was married to a Rose.

Holme Rose lies a mile further up the Nairn valley from Kilravock, the home of the present Secretary of State for Scotland. The Roses came here in 1541, and although nothing so old as that remains visible, there is 17th and 18th century work behind the typical Georgian façade, and an intriguing little central courtyard, with pillars, unsuspected from outside. The house is altogether a pleasing one, on a terraced site, attractive in mellow pink stone, with a pillared portico and some fine interiors. Holm means a small island, so it may perhaps be presumed that an earlier house has been sited down in the valley floor. The county boundary adjoins at Cantray Mill, to the west.

The northern part of the Nairnshire section of the parish is level open farmland which was formerly moor and swampy loch, still known as the Moor of the Clans, and containing the now tiny Loch of the Clans. These names refer to the night before the fatal Battle of Culloden, when an abortive night attack was started by the Jacobite army, on Nairn, where Cumberland was celebrating his 25th birthday. Unfortunately the assault was ill-planned, ill-led and started too late so that it had to be abandoned, and a retreat was made over this ground without ever coming to grips with the enemy —which meant weary and hungry troops to face the Hanoverian army on the morrow, with disastrous results.

Geddes and Rait. These two places are in Nairn parish, but it is convenient to describe them separately since they lie in a corner of the parish 3 or 4 miles south of the town, on the far side of the River Nairn, and have a detached entity of their own. Geddes was probably its own pre-Reformation parish, and Rait was a barony and ancient thanedom of once great importance. Both have given quite well-known surnames to Scotland, both producing famous literary men.

Geddes House lies just south of the B.9101 Auldearn to Cawdor road, at the beginning of the foothill country, a Georgian mansion of 1805 replacing a much earlier house of the Rose family. The lands were sold in 1800 to an Indian "nabob" named William Mackintosh, who built the mansion. John Mackintosh, "The Earnest Student" (1822–51) was of this family. Presumably there were Geddes of that Ilk proprietors before the Roses gained the lands, for this is the only Geddes in Scotland.

The burial-ground and former chapel of Geddes, dedicated to the Blessed Virgin Mary, stands on a climbing site, rather picturesque on a narrow side-road half a mile to the east, crowning a low eminence. There are many old gravestones here, a particularly good one, dated 1667, relating to the Roses of Bellivat. But this is nevertheless comparatively late in the place's history, for there is said to have been a church here from 1200, and for it to have been the burial-place of the Rose of Kilravock family, chief of the name, since that period. Certainly the church was further endowed by Hugh Rose, 7th of Kilravock, in 1473. Only part of the walling of the ancient church remains, with the Kilravock memorials within. This establishment, which is probably the chapel referred to also, in 1343, in "the hermit of the Chapel of St. Mary of Rait" was highly thought of for sanctity, for in 1475 Pope Sextus IV granted relief of one hundred days' penance to all who made pilgrimage to it or contributed a certain amount to its rebuilding. It seems also, at some time, to have been called St. Warn's Chapel.

The hamlet of Geddes, or Righoul, stands on a slight ridge amongst the foothills on another side-road, over a mile to the south, a tiny place but with fine northward views, with a former school and a few cottages. Near by, across a little valley, is the site of an early Pictish fort, called Castle Finlay, lost amongst broom and bracken. The extensive woodlands of Hill of Urchany and The Ord, climb to the south.

Behind Geddes burial-ground, on the same unclassified side-road half a mile, is Rait Castle, at the road-end. This is a highly interesting and important ruin, almost unique in Scotland. The remains now rise only to the second storey, and represent a fairly small oblong fortalice with a single projecting round tower, dating probably from the 14th century, but with many unusual features and quite elaborate masonry, indeed a distinctly English rather than Scots character. This might be because the Raits of that Ilk were strongly pro-Edward in the Wars of Independence, Sir Gervaise and Sir Andrew de Rait fighting actively in support of the English. This however was some time before the seeming date of the present remains, although they might conceivably have then been young men, suffered banishment to England, and come back later to rebuild their house. Be that as it may, Rait is unusual. The single round tower is certainly so, and oddly, is vaulted only above its first-floor chamber, a fine dome vault, and this is the only vaulting in the building, when Scots basements were always so ceiled, for security against fire. The basement is lighted only by small square windows like port-holes, again very unusual. And even more so are the series of fine pointed arched windows lighting the first floor, some of them actually mullioned, and the arched doorway there, the only one for the building, grooved for a portcullis, and reachable only by a removable gangway. The building is now roofless and gapped, but the remaining features are most interesting. It has had a courtyard on three sides. The place was important enough to rank as the Thanedom of Rait, so listed in 1238, when it was held by a Mackintosh family. The clan was very strong hereabouts in those days, their chiefs holding the great Lordship of Petty further west. The de Rait family, who seem to have succeeded them, were probably Comyns. The last of the line fled from Moray for slaying the Thane of Calder in 1404, and is said to have founded the family of Rait of Hallgreen, in Kincardineshire. The lands passed to the injured Calder or Cawdor family. There is said to have been a massacre of Comyns by Mackintoshes at Rait Castle, just when is unclear.

Nairn. The royal burgh of Nairn, although so near that of Forres, ten miles to the east in Moray, and of almost exactly the same size, with a population of 5250, is extraordinarily different in aspect, atmosphere and character. The fact that it is a seaside town is only partly responsible—for the sea and coastline do not make themselves very evident in the main part of the town. Both are holiday resorts and both are ancient, but there the similarity seems to end. Oddly enough, Nairn seems to reckon itself almost Highland, in a way Forres does not. Indeed it is claimed that the dividing line between Highlands and Lowlands intersects the High Street of Nairn about Rose Street! The name used to be Invernairn, Gaelic for the town at the mouth of the river of alders, and the Gaelic language lingered long in Nairn.

One of the first impressions the visitor is apt to get is that, despite its very real antiquity, ancient buildings are conspicuous by their absence—which is a pity. On the other hand, Nairn has had the good sense to channel the heavy through-traffic of the A.96 Aberdeen–Inverness highway round much of the town to the north, and has not allowed it to plough through the centre, as at neighbouring Forres, Elgin and Fochabers—a notable advantage. Another feature unlikely to escape notice is the great number of hotels, guest-houses and other offerers of accommodation—for this is a holiday town *par excellence*, with two splendid sandy beaches of great length, two famous golf courses, a notably large and convenient caravan-site, promenade, boat-harbour, fine parks, heated indoor swimming-pool and other attractions. And Nairn is very proud of its renowned dry and sunny climate. It is, of course, the county town of Nairnshire, but as well as having a rural parish of its own, is identified with the landward area in a way few county towns are, for the county is comparatively small (104,000 acres) with only four other parishes, and two-thirds of the total population lives in the royal burgh—which is, moreover, the only town. So Nairn and Nairnshire are very much an entity.

The town was old in William the Lion's time. Fairly recently discoveries of a prehistoric site at Kingsteps, to the east of the town, indicate a very early settlement, and the 4th century St. Ninian seems to have come here long before the more general tide of Celtic missionaries crossed from Ireland, the Brethren of Columba, in the 6th century, for they are said to have found a Christian cell here already established. Indeed the town seal depicts St. Ninian, open bible in hand. The original charter of the burgh is thought to have been granted by Alexander the First (1107–1124) and his grandson William the Lion built a royal castle here, between the river and the present High Street, on the site of what is now called the Constabulary Garden, the Sheriffs of Nairn being appointed constables thereof, an office which became hereditary in the Thanes of Calder or Cawdor, and remained with the Cawdor lords, though they became Campbells in the 15th century, until the abolition of the hereditary jurisdictions in 1747. It is interesting to note that the large house in Constabulary Garden is still the dower-house and office of the Cawdor family—surely one of the longest tenures of municipal property anywhere! Because of its position on the verge of Highlands and Laigh of Moray, moreover just south of Inverness and the first crossing-place by bridge at the head of the huge Moray Firth, Nairn has always been strategically important. Near by were fought many early battles. Two in later times took place very close by—Auldearn, 2 miles to the east, where Montrose defeated Hurry and the Covenanters in 1645, and Culloden, 10 miles to the south-west, in 1746, when the Duke of Cumberland spent the two previous nights in Nairn.

The town still centres round the mouth of the River Nairn, with the harbour and old fishertown on the west side of the river, north of the A.96, and the High Street striking southwards opposite, the Constabulary Garden site being almost immediately on the left at the north end of the High Street. The house here is large, commodious and dignified, although not ancient, with much Campbell and Cawdor heraldry. As has been said, no ancient buildings survive in Nairn, and there are few architectural gems of any period. The High Street, a notable shopping centre, with many quality shops, can boast little of interest in its buildings. There is a not very impressive Mercat Cross, removed from its original position, and renovated 1757, with slim cylindrical shaft and square top, which has lost its finial. This stands outside the Town and County building, an edifice of 1818 much altered in 1870, with an over-fancy clock-tower and spire, wherein is the Town Hall as well as offices. Near by, a plaque on the wall of MacGillivray's Building, on the north side of the street, commemorates the Rose of Kilravock town-house here, in which Cumberland slept before Culloden—while his opponent Prince Charles was himself being entertained at the said Rose's castle of Kilravock 6 miles to the west. The Roses feature very notably in Nairn's story; indeed between 1450 and 1777 there were forty-six Provosts of Nairn, and forty-five of them were Roses, the 46th, Major Clephane, being a Rose brother-in-law! And when Henry Mackenzie, author of *The Man of Feeling*, was Provost in 1785, *his* mother was a Rose.

The High Street has a number of narrow pends and closes opening off it, on each side. On the south, larger than these, is Church Street, leading down to the riverside. And here, at the end of a lane, is the abandoned kirkyard and site of the former parish church. All that is left of the kirk now are low walls with, in the west gable, a heraldic stone above the doorway, relating to David Dunbar and Margaret Hay. This is from the church of 1658, which was in use until 1808, when the gallery all but gave way during service, and there was an understandable panic, with worshippers jumping through windows and sustaining injuries. The church was rebuilt, but in no magnificent style, the resultant edifice looking more like a barn, with hipped roof, pictures of which still exist. A wooden floor and heating system were not added until 40 years later! A completely new parish church was built in 1897 some distance off. The kirkyard has many old stones, overgrown and tumbled, but the site is attractive enough, above the river, and the place could be an asset to the town if tidied up and cared for.

The present parish church is large and handsome, a Gothic building with a square crenellated tower 90 feet high, of Nairn sandstone. The interior is pleasing, with a deep U-shaped gallery and very high beamed ceiling. There is some good stained-glass, some of it by Strachan, and likewise good woodwork. It stands in an open site on Academy Street. Not far away, on Cawdor Street, is the very tall-spired High Church, built as a Free kirk in 1882, large and seating 1200. It succeeded the former Free church in King Street, now the very fine Community Centre, which is claimed to have been the first Free church, built as such, in the land. The smaller St. Mary's Catholic church, of 1864, is near the parish church, long and narrow but bright and agreeable within. The Episcopal church of St. Columba is also small, and dates from 1857, in Millbank Crescent.

These churches are all in the same general area, the residential district beyond the west end of High Street. Here also is Nairn Academy, in fine and extensive modern buildings, formerly Rose's Academical Institution. Close by, where High Street forks into Cawdor Street and Lodgehill Road, at the junction stands a monument of 1815, erected by his old pupils, to one John Straith, for 40 years parochial schoolmaster.

More recent buildings in the central area are the very up-to-date police station complex, near the large bus station, and the modern Seaforth Highlanders' Club in Gordon Street.

Nairn Bridge, which carries the A.96 out of the town eastwards across the river, on three arches, was originally built by Rose of Clava in 1632, but was renewed in 1782, 1829 and later. To the north and west of the bridge lies the fishertown, an area very different from the rest of Nairn, its narrow streets of former fishermen's cottages crowded haphazard. The fishing has died a death at Nairn, moving away to larger and more convenient havens down the firth, such as Lossiemouth and Buckie. But the fishertown is by no means neglected, and now caters for visitors in a big way. Here are shows, arcades, eating-places and so on. It is perhaps interesting to note that these fisherfolk were largely of Norse extraction, and, as fishing communities do, kept themselves pretty much to themselves; indeed there are still said to be many families here with the names of Main and Ralph, corruptions of Magnus and Hrolf. They had little to do with the Gaelic-speaking folk of Highland extraction in the upper town. Even King James the Sixth knew about this, and used to boast, when he went to London in 1603, that he had a town in his northern domains "sae lang that the inhabitants at one end didna understand the language spoken at the other!" Dr. Johnson claimed that he first heard Erse spoken here, and saw a peat-fire.

The harbour was designed by Thomas Telford, in 1820, but great damage was done by the flood of 1829. In 1882 there were 91 boats here, employing 250 resident fishermen. Also coastal trading flourished. Today there is little commercial fishing but many pleasure-boats. To the east, across the Bailey Bridge, is the extensive municipal caravan-park and camping-site, backing the East Beach. This fine sandy strand extends for miles, eventually reaching the Culbin Sands area. The Dunbar golf course also extends eastwards along these links, on land gifted to the town by Sir Alexander Dunbar of Boath, an 18-hole course of high standard.

To the west of the river-mouth there extends a comparable splendid beach, reaching away to the Carse of Delnies, and backed by the Nairn Golf Club's championship course, a mecca for golfers. Here the Nairn Open Tournament is held each August. There is also a 9-hole Newton course inland a little. Newton Hotel, 4-star and very large, incorporates an 18th century mansion greatly extended in Scottish Baronial style in the late 19th century. But before this is reached, is a pleasant residential area of the town, with parkland, open grassy links, with trees and gardens and fine seaward views to Easter Ross. Here is the first-class indoor, heated salt-water swimming-pool, at West Links. There are many large houses and hotels, quiet avenues of high amenity. In one of these, Viewfield Avenue, is the Nairn Pottery, where work of fine craftsmanship is produced. Near by is Viewfield House, standing in a spacious park. The former mansion of the Grant family now houses the county library, a small museum and offices. At its entrance is a statue to Dr. John Grigor (1814–86), a Scots medico with a practice in Rome who, recognising the health-giving properties of Nairn with its salubrious climate, came to settle here himself and urged his wealthy patients to do likewise, and so largely was responsible for the rise of the town as a health resort.

Nairn is well provided with sporting facilities. There are tennis-courts, bowling- and putting-greens, a children's playground. Mention must be made of Nairn's especial love of cricket—unusual in Scotland and the Highlands. It is played on the Links, and the Nairn County Cricket Club is renowned. Football and curling also have their devotees. The famed Nairn Highland Games are held here in August, attended by up to 20,000 spectators. Also in busy August is the Farmers' Show, with cattle-judging, show-jumping and the like.

On the southern outskirts, across the railway line, are Boath Park to the east and Queen's Park to the west, with the Riverside Walk between. Past the railway-station, on the B.9090, is the Town and County Hospital, small but pleasingly situated. A little further out, on the B.9091 stands the large old gabled mansion of Balblair, now a rather gaunt Eventide Home but once quite an important Rose lairdship. It was much altered in the late 17th century and mainly dates from that period and later. Here Cumberland's army camped, his officers in the house, and here the Duke joined them from the Rose town-house in the High Street. Near by is a large timber-yard and factory, at a former meal-mill.

This is out in Nairn parish, a highly irregular area covering almost 10,000 acres, mainly south and west of the town, and including the Delnies, Kildrummie Geddes and Rait districts. It is convenient to deal with Geddes and Rait, across the River Nairn, separately.

Delnies lies along the coastal plain to the west, and is wide open carse-land with a few farms. It extends to the "root" of that extraordinary sandspit-like peninsula of Whiteness Head, stretching for over 2 miles, long and narrow, into the Moray Firth, its highest point only 17 feet above sea-level. In this vicinity today large North Sea oil developments are taking place. Inland a mile, beside a gamekeeper's cottage at the roadside, stands the Kebach Stone. This is a broad Pictish cross-slab, its details and symbols however now so weatherworn as to be almost indecipherable. To the west stretches the extensive Carse Wood, a pleasant area of planted forest 2 miles long, but mainly in Inverness-shire's Ardersier parish, with an ancient earthworks hidden in its midst.

Inland, across the B.9092 and A.96 southwards, still in level lands, is the farming area of Kildrummie. Meikle Kildrummie is a charming laird's house of the early 18th century, whitewashed, with crow-stepped gables, coped chimneys and a drip stone over the front door. It is at present being pleasingly renewed. This was another Rose house, and here Robert Burns visited in 1787. A mile north-west of this is Drumdivan farm, on the edge of woodland, where, in the 17th century, a Campbell Thane of Cawdor fell from his horse and died. Witchcraft was immediately suspected. An old woman was duly found who "looked not like an inhabitant of this earth"—

and she did not remain so for much longer, being burned for the deed.

At the east end of the parish, and only a mile south of the town, is the estate of Househill, with its rather handsome tall mansion on a wooded eminence. The central part of the house appears to belong to the early 18th century, with an interesting stairway and some good woodwork. Later additions date from 1860. The lands were bought by the famous Colonel James Grant, C.B., born 1827, and son of a Nairn parish minister. With Speke he discovered the source of the Nile, in 1863, and wrote a book of the expedition entitled *Walk Across Africa*.

ROSS, EASTER

Arbitrarily to divide a great county down the middle, as the writer has had to do in this volume, with Inverness-shire and Ross, for purposes of convenience in space and presentation, is apt to be an awkward and unsatisfactory device. But in the case of Ross it is not really so, for there is a very great contrast and distinction, geographically, historically, even climatically, between Easter and Wester Ross, which is obvious to the least perceptive. Easter Ross is in the main green, low-lying, fertile, populous, settled—and now becoming dramatically industrialised, at least in part. Wester Ross is mountainous, beautiful—probably the most beautiful area in all Britain—very sparsely populated, completely Highland. So the division in this volume is not difficult, less artificial than the line which had to be drawn down the centre of Inverness-shire. The writer has sought, for consistency's sake, to draw it at approximately the same line of longitude as the other, from a little west of Garve, in the south, to Oykell Bridge area in the north. Some of the territory to the east of this is, in fact Highland, with mighty Ben Wyvis towering over all, but in the main the resultant area is fairly typically Easter Ross, the low-lying country of the Beauly, Cromarty and Dornoch Firths, with the great peninsula of the Black Isle to the south-east and the lesser one of Nigg–Fearn–Tarbat to the northeast. This district includes 22 parishes, and an area of perhaps 850 square miles. The former county of Cromarty is included; it has long been a component part of the shire of Ross and Cromarty.

There are no large towns in the area, Dingwall the county capital having a population of just over 4000, Invergordon and Tain each half of that, Strathpeffer about 1000, Fortrose and Rosemarkie, and Cromarty itself less—and the former village of Alness growing hugely. Today, Easter Ross is probably synonymous with industrial development of a sort, in many minds, with North Sea oil, deepwater anchorages, and the availability of vast hydro-electric power, changing the face of the land and altering all population statistics. Alness, which is scheduled to be the main residential area, may grow to four times the size of Dingwall, and is already bursting at the seams. Inevitably not all the changes will be for the good, and how much of Ross can survive as it has been is debatable. But the planners are very busy, and at least development will not be utterly uncontrolled and haphazard.

The main reasons for it all, of course, are the magnificent facilities of deep-water anchorage and sheltered harbourage, in the Cromarty Firth, with level ground around it for works and buildings. The firth is an almost land-locked loch 15 miles long, with sufficient deep water to anchor the entire Grand Fleet during the First World War —and that deep water coming very close to the shore at a number of points, so that the largest ocean-going ships can tie up at jetties. For bulk-carriers, whether of alumina or other ores, or of oil, the transport benefits are obvious, especially with cheap current from the many hydro-electric schemes in the mountains to the west readily available, and for oil-rig building-yards and service depots, so comparatively near to the North Sea fields what could be more convenient?

Easter Ross divides naturally into three sections—the Black Isle, the "mainland" portion from Muir of Ord to Invergordon, and the northern area, including the Nigg–Tarbat peninsula—all somewhat distinct in character. The Black Isle, or Ardmeanach to give it its ancient and true name, is a fascinating entity indeed, and although no island has many of the attributes of such, being a long and quite broad peninsula with a coastline of some 45 miles, only joined to the mainland by a neck of 5 miles. The old name means The Height Between, which is fairly descriptive, for the peninsula has a lofty whaleback culminating in the long spine of the Millbuie ridge running almost the entire length, and this is very prominent from the level lands around which flank the Beauly–Inverness–Moray Firths on the south and the Cromarty Firth on the north. To account for the term Black Isle is more difficult, for there is nothing very dark about it at all, indeed greens are the prevailing colour, a fertile, verdant, sunny place. Numerous alleged explanations have been put forward, few convincing—that it was once covered in black peat-bog, that when the rest of Ross was covered in snow, this area was apt to remain snow-free and therefore dark, and so on. More likely is that it got its appellation from being called Eilean Dhubhaich, or St. Duthac's Isle, and this got shortened to Eilean Dubh, which means dark or black. Be that as it may, the Black Isle has been so called all over Scotland for a long time. It is a place worth visiting, and visiting again, with a character and delight all its own. Although not Highland itself, it is hilly and with magnificent prospects of the Highland mountains to both north and south, all seen across blue, gleaming firths. The sun does not always shine in the Black Isle, admittedly, but it has an enviable climatic record. Moreover it is, by North Scotland standards, a populous land of age-old settlement, especially on its south-eastern side, where there is a fertile coastal plain of some width, and fine beaches. Here are small ancient towns and villages like Fortrose and Rosemarkie, Avoch, Munlochy and Kessock, all with great character and long stories. Cromarty, right out at the tip of the peninsula, is rather different, a little remote burgh, which was once on the road to somewhere—and will be again —and which gave its name to a whole county and an earldom and sheriffdom, sank back as it were to sleep, as though the effort had all been too much for it—and has now begun to wake up again, with the burgeoning oil and industrial developments taking place so dramatically just across the firth from it a mile away. The north-western side of the peninsula is less populous, with no large villages but many old estates and much that is attractive, including that strange and ancient barony of Ferintosh with its former unique privileges. The central spine, rising to 800 feet or so, is now almost wholly given over to forestry, the huge Kilcoy, Findon and Millbuie Forests running together to form a stretch of woodland a dozen miles long and averaging nearly 2 miles wide, lost in which are many cairns and duns and other relics of the ancients.

Prehistory, proto-history and recorded history are never far below the surface in the Black Isle, for it seems always to have been a place which coaxed men to come and to settle. The number of cairns, particularly chambered cairns, as the burial-places of important men always indicative of a high population, is remarkable. Earthworks, forts, duns and symbol-stones are represented. From the medieval period are many saints' wells, ancient churches including the remains of the Cathedral of Ross, at Fortrose, many castles and historic mansions. Older even than these, the geology of the area is highly interesting, and has had the advantage of rearing its own expert, in Hugh Miller, of Cromarty, to expound it. Modern development has not yet hit the Black Isle seriously—although with the advent of the scheduled bridge across the Inverness Firth at Kessock, undoubtedly added pressures will accumulate. Not that it is any sort of sleepy backwater; its farming methods are as up-to-date as anywhere in Scotland—and is primarily an agricultural and forestry area; indeed, for instance, a large cold-storage establishment for agricultural products has grown up here on local initiative. Catering for the visitor and the holiday-maker, moreover, as an important and well-developed industry, for there is much to entice—sandy beaches, fishing-harbours, cliffs, caves, fishing, bird-watching, fine golf courses, yachting and good walking country everywhere, including the great extent of forests, without the bugbear of rushing through-traffic. And always those splendid vistas. The Black Isle is the sort of place to which the visitor returns—and fortunately it is well provided with hotels, guest-houses, bed-and-breakfast facilities and caravan and camping places.

The Mid-Ross area has the greater diversity of scenery and conditions, for it includes the busy, low-lying districts of Muir of Ord, Dingwall, Evanton, Alness and Invergordon, the holiday areas of Strathpeffer, Contin and Garve, and the empty mountain tracts of Strathconon, Glen Orrin, Strathbran, Ben Wyvis and Kildermorie. So that, although publicity today emphasises industrial expansion on a dramatic scale, there is really, even in this central section, a vast area untouched by development. The overburdened A.9 highway, threading through, carries its own noisy and distracting influence admittedly—and unfortunately most of the larger communities lie thereon, as is to be expected. But since such are the arteries for the life's blood of the age, they fall to be accepted—although bypasses round towns and villages ought to have been a priority for long, and a modernising of the road itself was grievously overdue, even before all the industrialisation. But once off the A.9, the countryside is consistently and variously attractive. The coastal plain is comparatively narrow, with the mountain mass to the west ever evident, and the straths probing deeply into it. At Muir of Ord is the great parting of the ways—just as it once was the great assembly point for the drove-roads of the North, for the cattle—for here the A.832 leaves A.9 to head for the West, by Contin and Garve, for far Kyle of Lochalsh and Skye, for Torridon and Gairloch, for Ullapool and all that wonderland of colour and beauty. Not that Muir of Ord itself is the most lovely of gateways to loveliness—but its humdrum utilitarianism is confined to the main highway, and the surrounding area is pleasant.

Strathpeffer, one of the most famous holiday-centres in Scotland, lies off both these main roads, and therefore does not suffer from much passing traffic. Indeed one has to be going to Strathpeffer to reach Strathpeffer, as it were—which is perhaps no bad thing. It is fairly restrained in its catering for the holiday-maker, save perhaps in the size and number of its hotels which are remarkable for its population of little more than one thousand. But it gives its devotees what they want, peace, quiet, lovely surroundings, golf, fishing and walks of all types and lengths. No vulgarity, it will be understood. Its surroundings are rather unusual for a spa, at the head of a sylvan and quite deep valley, under the foothills of Ben Wyvis, with the interesting archaeological, historical and scenic plateau area of Knock Farrel and Loch Ussie high on the other side. It was discovered as a spa by an early 19th century Aberdeen doctor, but its "patron saint", if it had one, would not be Dr. Morrison so much as the Brahan Seer, whose vivid if slightly contradictory presence seems to haunt the neighbourhood.

Dingwall, the county town, suffers from traffic thrombosis on the A.9, but once the Kessock bridge is built and the projected causeway at the north side of the Black Isle, a great deal of the heavy through-traffic will be channelled away, and the town will have a chance to revert to a less noisy and fume-ridden existence. It will come as quite a surprise to many a traveller to realise that Dingwall is in fact a pleasant place, pleasantly sited, and on the coast, too, however little evident.

The Evanton–Alness–Invergordon area, further north, is of course the scene of most of the current excitements, although their influence extends ever further afield. Clearly this development is going to grow and grow, offering a challenge and test to the county and the indigenous community. The total population of Ross and Cromarty in 1961 was only 57,000, of which Easter Ross would contribute perhaps 35,000. So, when it is planned that Alness district alone may house 20,000 people in a few years time, something of the impact on an essentially rural community will be recognised. Inevitably a large proportion of the population of Easter Ross will be incomers, by 1980—already that is becoming evident, and incomers not only from Scotland, or even England. This, in the long term, may even be a good thing for the area—who knows? But the transition period will abound with problems.

A feature of this Mid-Ross district insufficiently recognised is the existence of fine straths and glens which probe westwards into the mountains, and which are, compared with such as Glens Affric and Cannich and Straths Glass and Farrar, not far to the south in Inverness-shire, very little known. They do not have the spectacular beauty and grandeur of Affric and Cannich perhaps, but they are highly attractive nevertheless, and deserve much greater esteem. They will get it, no doubt, when the population hereabouts explodes still further, but meantime such mountain valleys as Strathconon, Glen Orrin, Strath Sgitheach or Skaith, Glen Glass, Glen Averon, Strath Rusdale and Strath Rory are under-valued. There is another feature hereabouts, rather better known, though related, since the water from these valleys, with their quite large lochs, plays an essential part—that is, the prevalence of distilleries, most of them old-established. Hydro-electric dams and power-stations also pro-liferate, in the hills, but are generally tucked away in deep valleys, so that large and important as they are, they do not obtrude.

The northern section of Easter Ross has its own very distinctive character, for though a large part of it is another extensive peninsula, no one would ever confuse that of Tarbat–Fearn–Nigg with the Black Isle. This rather strange tract of land, whose seaboard for some 15 miles forms the northern shore of the Moray Firth, is an anvil-shaped and in the main low-lying territory—although its southern horn is the 666-feet-high Hill of Nigg, with the North Sutor of Cromarty—having no town or even large village, but quite highly populated, fertile and with a very definite and pleasing ethos, a very green land where the sea is always evident and the sun shines more frequently than in most parts of these islands. The remainder of the area, to west and north, seems rather to turn its back on the rest of Ross, in self-sufficiency, to face north to the Dornoch Firth and Sutherland, very much part of the North, and Highland in its aura —as well it might be, historically, for this was the cradle, rearing-ground and home of the great Clan Ross, as distinct from the ancient Celtic earldom, with Tain its capital, and having more of the aspect of a capital still, than has Dingwall. Though Tain is only a dozen miles north of Invergordon, it feels somehow entirely isolated, different, on its own—and quietly assured of the fact, a fine town with a character rather extraordinary considering its only 2000 population. By the time that the Dornoch Firth has contracted to the Kyle of Sutherland, the Highlands have taken over entirely— though we are still in Easter Ross, and will be right up to the head of long Strath Oykell, where this volume comes to an end.

For how long can this unspoiled and so distinctive part of Ross retain its essential individuality? So far, all the industrial develop-ment has been confined to the Nigg Bay area of the extreme south, where the Cromarty Firth's deep water is the magnet; the Dornoch Firth is more renowned for its mussel-beds and wrecking sandbanks than for anchorages. But development always brings its ever-widening echoes, like a stone dropped into formerly calm waters,

283

and already the royal burgh of Tain is beginning to feel the effects. In fact, Highland Fabricators Ltd., the rig-building consortium of Brown & Root and Wimpey, has taken over the old Tain Royal Academy building for its offices, and here is an obviously superior locality for executives and the higher-paid employees to seek housing, with desired facilities expanding under the impact. The bombing-range versus nature-reserve controversy for that especial tract, the Morrich More, is another issue for decision. Even the delightful fishing-villages of Portmahomack and Balintore, etc., are poised for expansion.

The clock is not to be put back.

Historically Easter Ross was a recognised and important entity from very early times. St. Duthac or Duthus established his head-quarters here at Tain, obviously because it was already an important Pictish area—and Pictish stones are notable hereabouts. Dingwall was the seat of the principal castle and assembly-place of the old Celtic Mormaors and then Earls of Ross. The Romish Church developed the Chanonry of Ross at Fortrose in the Black Isle, where the Bishops of Ross came to hold almost princely sway. William the Lion built a string of royal castles on this seaboard in his efforts to restrain the terrible incursions of the Norsemen. Bruce's wife and daughter and brother were betrayed and captured at Tain, and James the Fourth made yearly pilgrimages to St. Duthac's shrine here. And the great Montrose suffered his very final defeat at Carbisdale, on Oykell. The Mackenzie House of Seaforth domin-ated the south and west of the area, with their Brahan Seer prophesy-ing no doubt well-merited doom, the Munroes kept the central parts in a warlike stir, their martial predilections enabling them largely to officer Gustavus Adolphus's Swedish army when they could find in-sufficient military employment at home. And the Rosses themselves made sure that, unless your name was Ross, in that northern area, you might as well not have been born—to the extent that even today the majority of the population of Tain seem to be surnamed Ross. Cromarty produced one of the great eccentrics of all time, the Cavalier Sir Thomas Urquhart, inventor, linguist, genealogist, wit and *bon viveur*, who asserted that he could trace his entire descent from Adam, translated Rabelais, left 128½ folio quires of manuscript, concocted a universal language, fought at the Battle of Worcester and died laughing for joy at the news of the Restoration.

So much for the past and present, but what does the future hold for Easter Ross?

Alness and Ardross. Alness is somewhat like a comfortably settled, middle-aged lady who has unexpectedly come into a fortune —and rather wishes that she had not. For long it has been a large village or small town, with its civil parish and river of the same name, near the latter's entry into the Cromarty Firth, not remote but reasonably quiet and peaceable, with its own identity, interested in catering for holiday-makers and having agricultural fairs, nine of them no less at one period. Now all is suddenly changed. The great industrial expansion just to the north, at Invergordon and Nigg, has involved Alness willy-nilly, for the planners have decided that this is where the housing and residential facilities for the new development should be sited, and Alness is in the throes of major growing-pains, bursting at the seams—and not altogether enjoying it. Moreover, not being a burgh itself, it has no real control over the process. Ten years ago its population was 1177. Now it is more than three times that, and scheduled to double that again. Which, of course, in one way, is inspiriting, even exciting; in another, upsetting and disquieting, especially for the original inhabitants.

The village, which certainly by North of Scotland standards ought to be a burgh, with control of its own destiny, lies astride the A.9 some 10 miles north of Dingwall, but the busyness of that rather notorious highway was, in Alness's case, happily ameliorated by the fact that the Struie Hill "bypass", the A.836, strikes off over a mile south of the village, carrying most of the through traffic to the north. But now, of course, the enormous and ever-growing weight of industrial transport ploughs its way through the long, narrow town in an unending noisy stream—and presumably will continue to do so.

As well as not being the burgh it ought to be—and as Invergordon is, 3 miles away—Alness has another administrative problem, for it subsists in two civil parishes. Alness proper lies west of the Alness River, in Alness parish, but Alness Bridgend, now the greater part of the town, lies in Rosskeen parish to the east, the river being the parish boundary. For the purposes of description, naturally, the parish boundary will be ignored. Alness parish itself, on the other side, reaches to Evanton village, 4 miles to the west, where the River Glass or Allt Grannda is the boundary. It stretches inland into the hills for almost 20 miles, in a north-westerly direction, where it embosoms two large lochs and many small ones, with the quite major glen of Strath Rusdale, and the large estate and hamlet of Ardross midway. The hills come quite close to salt water in this area, with the coastal plain only about a mile wide.

To deal first with old Alness, on the west side of the river. Here stood the original parish church, now bypassed in more ways than one, for it has been abandoned as the place of worship, although the graveyard is still in use. The building is roofless but the walls entire, and it is somewhat complicated architecturally, quite large, and standing on a mound above a burn's ravine. Although said to have been built in 1780, it has a much older nucleus, evidence of the earlier work being apparent. Indeed the belfry is inset with the date 1625, with heraldic decoration of that period on the gable skews. The door to the earlier building, now within a later extension, has a lintel with Latin inscription dated 1672, and the initials W.M.L. and I.M.T., and at the east gable is another extension, enclosing the burial-place of the Munro family, dated 1671, above a moulded lintel. There is also a weatherworn Latin memorial to the Rev. John Fraser, dated 1712. Many old flat tombstones and table-stones litter the grass, mainly moss-grown, and below the west gable is a large rounded boulder, left here for some reason. The present parish church, in red sandstone with a tower, dates from 1843 and was formerly the Free church. It stands at the same bypassed road-side 400 yards to the east, now encircled by the spreading modern housing of Kirkside, one of the five new housing schemes and de-velopments which are transforming the face of Alness—the others at Teaninich, Culcraggie, Obsdale and Struie, each planned to have a population of 2500–4000, more or less self-contained localities, with the Georgian Coul Cottage, on higher ground, directly north of the church, to be the centre-piece of the schemes. Whether this will all transpire remains to be seen, but the planners so plan.

Below the main road here, nearer the firth, is Teaninich, with its own side-road leading down to Alness Point. Here is a large dis-tillery of that name, with the mansion near by, Georgian, and formerly a Munro seat, like most other lairdships hereabouts. Nearer salt water, on what was formerly an airfield, is now the headquarters of the R.A.F. Air–Sea Rescue establishment. At the shore is a tall old grain store of some antiquity, rather gaunt. The Alness Point area is still used for salmon-fishing on a commercial basis; and the old ice-house for the storage of the fish, before refrigeration days, is at the roadside, and very large, with three lofty vaulted semi-subterranean cellars.

Across the bridge, which carries the A.9 over the river, is the larger portion of the town. The river, which should be called the Averon, is highly picturesque over most of its course, a major asset scenically. Here, at the waterside, rises one of the benefits of all the expansion, a fine modern leisure centre and complex, opened in 1973, consisting of an excellent public library, well laid out, a com-munity hall with dance-floor, sports facilities, coffee-bar and so on, with the accent on youth, all set in an attractive position. The cost was at least £140,000, of which the British Aluminium Company at Invergordon gave £45,000. The bridge is single-arched, and narrow to carry the A.9, but provided with a pedestrian gangway. The taller railway-bridge crosses the river close by. Across the main street at this end are such adjuncts of modern urban living as a supermarket and a launderette, hardly typical of Easter Ross. Large numbers of shops, offices and businesses of various sorts, with a couple of hotels, stretch for almost a mile, to the top of the town, where the road forks, the A.9 going right, to follow the coast to Invergordon, the B.817 continuing straight on for Tain. At the junction is the Celtic-cross war-memorial, and near by, the Perrins Centre, another community centre of older vintage, with hall and associated facilities, bowling-green at the back. There are no fewer than thirty local organisations and associations, so such premises are in great demand.

On the higher ground to the north of the main street are two parallel residential avenues, with connecting lanes. Above these, at the west end, is the large and very modern Bridgend school. Up one of the avenues is another Established church, for Rosskeen parish, quite large and bright within, not old. The ancient Rosskeen parish church lies 2 miles to the east, near Invergordon, now abandoned. Just across the street here is the Free church public hall, more convenient for most people than the Rosskeen Free church itself, which also stands isolated to the east, over a mile away. These changes of population pose great problems for the churches.

At the east end of the town is the large housing development of Obsdale, an old name. At Obsdale House, in 1675, was a famous "illegal" celebration of communion by outed ministers, during the sad religious "killing-times", as a consequence of which the Rev. Mr. Mackilligen, of Alness parish, was sent to the Bass Rock as prisoner, there to die. The mansion, where the Dowager Lady Munro of Foulis lived, is now gone, but a red granite monument stands by the roadside on A.9, to commemorate the occasion. At the edge of the housing development, in a field between the two roads, and reached from Salvesen Crescent, is a fine chambered cairn, called Carn Liath, in a circle of trees. It is about 30 feet in diameter, within a retaining wall, and in the centre the burial cist still remains, with its massive stone lid. A quarter-mile down the A.9 here, past the aforementioned monument to the communion service, opens the drive of Dalmore House, now a Church of Scotland eventide-home, a former Scottish Baronial mansion in large policies. Near by, at the firth-shore, is Dalmore Distillery, with its associated hamlet. This was established in 1839, and is still in private hands, though now semi-automated and with increasing production. There is an old tradition of whisky-distilling here—in fact illicit stills used to be much to the fore. There was a little seaport formerly at the disused pier of Belleport, where large quantities of timber and grain were exported. Near the distillery, in 1875, many Bronze Age burials were discovered and excavated.

Behind Alness to the north, a side-road follows the course of the Averon or Alness River upwards, but high above it on the east. Up here is the golf course of 9 holes, in pleasing surroundings. The countryside is very attractive, with ever-widening vistas across the firth and to the Black Isle. Less than a mile up, a lesser side-road strikes off to the east, to the Nonakiln area. Another chambered cairn can be seen on the hillside to the left, in trees. And at Nonakiln farm, almost a mile north-east, is the former church and graveyard of St. Ninian (the name is a corruption of Ninian's cell). This was a pre-Reformation parish, incorporated in Rosskeen. In the neglected graveyard behind the farm is the gable of the old church, with very thick walling and a pointed window and doorway, this opening into a burial enclosure, itself not old. There is another burial-enclosure, for the family, important locally, of Aird of Heathfield or Calruchie. Many old tombstones are now unreadable. One is dated 1705, but others are obviously older. There is a plaster-cast of a Pictish stone from here in the Museum of Antiquities, Edinburgh, the original being lost.

A mile further to the north-east is the estate of Newmore. There is a fairly late mansion on one side of the road, and across, in its walled garden where there is a modern house, rise the ruins of New-more Castle, attractively set, part of a circular stair-tower and a vaulted basement of the main block remaining, with chamfered windows, a panel-space and shot-holes, all seemingly of the early 17th century. The Mackintosh lairds, who succeeded the original Munroes, were a sept of those of Balnespick, in Badenoch, and two brothers of the line became famous, one as a great traveller, the other as a Glasgow industrialist who introduced turkey-red into this country. The latter's son Charles was the inventor of the renowned waterproof.

Back on the road which runs up the Averon valley, this presently reaches the A.836 Struie Hill highway. Turning down it, south-wards, a steep hill is descended into the very picturesque wooded valley of the Averon, with meadows in its foot and an old mill. There is a high single-arch bridge across the river here. A mile further, uphill again, a side-road strikes off north-westwards, eventually to reach Loch Morie. This is a very attractive road, scenically, climbing from 250 to almost 800 feet, and passing in its early stages through the large Dalreoch Wood, where on each side burial-cairns are lost in the natural woodland and plantings. Two miles up is the former Munro estate of Lealty, now only a farm. Here iron deposits were discovered about 1840, yielding 75 lb per hundredweight—but these do not seem to have been worked. Beyond this the country opens out into the wide upland valley of the Averon, with splendid views. Houses are few and far between, though there is a telephone-kiosk at the former school building beyond Wester Lealty. At Acharn, half a mile more, there is a cluster of seven cairns, in rough pasture near the road. Two miles further and the foot of Loch Morie is reached, the Averon emerging therefrom. The loch is over 2 miles long, and steep-sided, the hills on the south rising over the 2000-foot contour. The road is private here-after, going up the east side and on to Kildermorie Lodge at the head. Up here are the remains of the chapel and graveyard which give the loch its name, Kil Mhuire, the cell of Mary. There is a former holy well, at which offerings of cloth were made.

Strath Rusdale opens across the river from the foot of the loch, but the public road to it is a long way off. It is necessary to return to the A.836 and go back northwards for 2 miles, to a cross-roads. Half a mile before this is reached, in trees on the right, is the site of another former chapel and well, dedicated to St. Columba, only the faintest traces remaining, beside a pylon. At the top of the same field is a circular walled enclosure wherein is a chambered cairn with small standing-stones. The Ardross cross-roads is just beyond, and here is the school for this scattered community. The large Ardross estate covers most of this side of the Averon valley, with its enormous Victorian Scottish Baronial castle, largely rebuilt in 1881, almost 2 miles up. This was a seat of the Rosses and Sutherlands, but passed to Sir Alexander Matheson in mid 19th century, descendant of the

Lochalsh MacMaths. There are some fine old trees. There is a story that the plague was buried here under a stone, caught in the form of a cloud—but this tradition is told of other places. Outside the castle gates is the estate hamlet, with post-office and church, and rows of quite attractive cottages on the wooded hillside. The church was built as a chapel of ease in 1899 by Captain Perrins of Ardross, who had succeeded the Mathesons, as a thank-offering for the recovery of his wife from a serious illness. Beyond the castle and this populated district, the road runs on very straight through planted forest, and finally bends north-westwards into Strath Rusdale, a rather bare valley, roughly parallel to that of Loch Morie. The public road stops in another 3 miles, whereafter a private road strikes westwards to Kildermorie and the loch, and another estate track continues northwards into the empty hills of the deer-forest for many more miles.

Pictish symbol stones from Ardross are now in the Inverness Museum, one displaying a horse's head and another a wolf.

Back at the Ardross cross-roads, a mile further up the A.836, on the left, is the Stittenham Drove Stance, which in the old clan days when cattle were the mainstay of the Highland economy, used to be a renowned penning-place and halt for the great droves on their way south to the Lowland markets. There is a cairn at the other side of the road from Stittenham itself. If, instead of turning northwards at the cross-roads, the road going directly eastwards is taken, it leads along the foothills through attractive country. Just over a mile along, the small secluded Loch Achnacloich is passed, and to the east of this, below the loftily placed farm of the name, is only the site of a former castle. Still further is the Priest's Well. There are more evident prehistoric remains along here, however, for the lofty ridge of Kinrive, on the left, is dotted with cairns, chambered and long, some very large. On the south side of this long stretch of quiet road is the great Newmore Wood, with Cnoc Navie rising out of it. Here is another chambered cairn, called Carn na Croich, of the Gibbet, where certain marauders were hanged out-of-hand by a laird in the good old days. The Rosskeen parish boundary, with Kilmuir Easter, lies some 4 miles along this road.

To the south-west of Alness is a large section of its parish, stretching far up Glen Glass, half of Loch Glass being in this parish, a loch credited with a monster or water-horse long before Loch Ness became famous for its denizens. But this area is best described under Evanton and Kiltearn. Nearer Alness however, on the lower ground near the coast, are the former Munro estates of Fyrish and Novar. Although it is inept to call Fyrish a low-ground place, for the mansion itself occupies a magnificent terrace site high on the side of wooded Cnoc Fyrish (1483 feet), with superb vistas. The house itself is very attractive, and dates largely from 1672, long and low, though there has been an older house still, for Hugh Munro of Fyrish was a great-grandson of the chief of Foulis who fell at the Battle of Pinkie in 1547. On the top of Fyrish Hill is an extraordinary landmark familiar to all who visit these parts. It is a huge replica of the gate of the city of Negapatam, in India, built here in 1782 by General Sir Hector Munro of Novar (who had distinguished himself at the relief of Negapatam) to provide work for the area then hard hit by unemployment and poverty. Novar House is larger, and lies on the lower ground amidst woodlands, near the A.9, the name better known as providing the title for the Munro Viscount Novar. The family is now Munro-Ferguson. The mansion is handsome, in the main of early Georgian period, with balustraded parapet, hipped roofing and pavilions.

Most of Rosskeen parish, as well as that of Alness, has been described here, although the burgh of Invergordon and Rosskeen former parish church, with House of Rosskeen, are dealt with separately, all being close together at the south-east corner of that parish.

Ardgay, Kincardine, Strathcarron and Strathoykell. Kin-

cardine, as well as being the most northerly and final parish of this volume, is the largest in Easter Ross, covering no less than 153,000 acres, almost empty mountain and moorland for the greater part, into which the long straths of Carron and Oykell probe deeply—although the north side of Oykell is in Sutherland and not dealt with here. Ardgay, at the mouth of Strathcarron, is the quite large village, and Culrain, up the Oykell, is a smaller one. These are both down near the Dornoch Firth coast and Kyle of Sutherland, for the rest, only tiny and scattered communities, shooting-lodges and deer-forests.

The original parish church of Kincardine is at the very south-east corner of the vast territory, no less than 34 miles from the western extremity, on the A.9 a mile south of Bonar Bridge Station and Ardgay. This is on a quite scenic stretch of road, 2 miles on from where the A.836 rejoins the A.9 after Struie Hill. The church is old and now disused, long, low, with an empty belfry, and though said to date from 1799, almost certainly contains much older work. Over its locked door is the date 1799 and the initials M.A.G., for Master Andrew Gallie, parish minister for 29 years. Amongst the many old and simple stones of the kirkyard is one of exceptional interest and importance, a recumbent 5-foot-long Pictish stone of very unusual type, with two rectangular cavities, of 3 and 1 foot wide. The relief carvings are on one side and the end only, and are now very weather-worn; moreover, unfortunately, the stone is upside-down, and this makes identification even more difficult. The side is divided into three panels, one showing a man on horseback, another a tree with animals and the third indecipherable. The end appears to represent two angels. This almost unique stone—the only other examples that occur to me are at the museums of Meigle and St. Vigeans—ought to be put right side up, and cherished. Near by is the burial-place of the later Rosses of Balnagown, up to and including the last of the Lockhart-Ross baronets, died 1942. Also that of the Mathesons of Lochalsh, who owned Gledfield hereabouts for a time.

The site of an ancient castle of the Earls of Ross lay between the church and the firth, with the Lady Well at the coast itself.

Ardgay village and Bonar Bridge Station lie a mile to the north, where the A.9 bends left for the bridge over the Kyle of Sutherland, a mile away—this built of cast-iron and stone, in 1812, and now being replaced by a suspension bridge. Ardgay is a strung-out place, for it includes the old village proper, the station vicinity, and a separate "suburb" of Lower Gledfield half a mile to the north-west. The part most travellers see is that on A.9, at the road-junction and station, which is modern and not particularly attractive. Few take the left-hand fork, for this leads only to dead-end roads, even though they go a long way. The village boasts a modern road-house and older inn, a bank, shops and a public hall, with some modern housing. It was actually created a burgh of barony by an Act of the Scottish Parliament in 1686, to be called Bonarness, in favour of the Laird of Balnagown, with instructions to build a tolbooth and erect a mercat cross. The name Bonarness is interesting, so long before the bridge, for Bonar Bridge village of course is on the *north* side of the Kyle, in Sutherland, but presumably the Bonar name came from this side. The burgh conception was never proceeded with, except for an annual November market, quite famous in the North, known as the Feille Edeichan, held at the White Stone of Kincardine, a quartz boulder, in lieu of the mercat cross, standing in what might be called the market-place, and formerly built into the walling of an inn. Elteag means white pebble or stone and may relate. The present parish church stands in a slightly isolated position mid-way to Lower Gledfield, back from the road, medium-sized and fairly modern, rather pleasing. Its car-park at the road-side rejoices in wrought-iron gates spelling out O ENTER YE HIS GATES —which may raise an eyebrow or two. Further along is the larger Free church. The road forks at Lower Gledfield, one fork to cross the River Carron, and the other to proceed up the south bank of that river.

Gledfield itself, formerly Gladefield, is a very large mansion in a wooded estate on the south road, a mile. It originally belonged to the Rosses and later passed through various hands including those of the Dukes of Sutherland. In a part of the mansion is the interesting small quality hand-weaving and designing establishment of Inverhouse, creating very beautiful if expensive materials, clothes and soft furnishings, to which visitors are welcome. There is a small lochan in the grounds, and an older, tacksman's type farmhouse to the west. A broch or dun is at the riverside half a mile on. The road continues fairly close to the river, up Strathcarron for 4 miles to Gruinards or Greenyards Lodge, a large Victorian mansion in woodland, formerly another Ross lairdship. The river is attractive hereabouts, with fine rocky stretches and rapids. A mile or so on, the little school is still in use, the country becoming bare but pleasant enough and the hills drawing close, with high mountains beginning to show ahead. In just over another mile the road crosses the river to rejoin the north-side road, just before the confluence of the Black Water with the Carron. It is up the former that the public road continues. Another mile on, and the tiny community of The Craigs is reached. Here is a small church, absolutely plain on a knoll, a minuscule corrugated-iron hall, and a telephone-kiosk, near the modern bridge which leads across to Amat Lodge, Glencalvie Lodge, Alladale Lodge and Diebi-dale Lodge, all shooting and stalking estates with their great deer forests and grouse moors, where the River Carron comes out of a number of tributary glens in the empty mountains. Amat, the first and lowest set of this group, which together cover perhaps 100,000 acres, is richly wooded in the valley-floor, and an old Ross lairdship, belonging to the Pitcalnie branch who became chiefs of the clan. It is interesting to note that in 1765 lands here were known as Amat-ni-Eglise. Whether the church referred to is the predecessor of that at The Craigs, or the one now called Croick, further up, is not clear —but it was a separate property from Amat proper.

Croick lies in the somewhat bare and straight tributary valley of the Black Water, called Strath Cuileannach, over a mile on, where the public road stops. It is no more than a small church in its grave-yard, seat of a *quod sacra* parish of 1817, a so-called "government church" established here 13 miles from the parish church proper. The church is now used only once a year, and the manse is a keeper's house, for the area no longer supports a congregation—though, when it was built, the church had 450 parishioners. This district was a late example of the shameful Highland Clearances, Glen Calvie being cleared as late as 1843—when even the London *Times* made protest. Many of the evicted, with the minister's sympathy, came to take refuge in the kirkyard, and some have left their sad memorials scratched on the church windows—but from the outside, for they were not allowed inside. The little building is now kept in good order, plain, with box-pews and a high pulpit with sounding-board, a small bell still in the belfry. There are a few mid-19th century table-stones in the graveyard, and a rather fine modern pillar-stone with Celtic carving, to a laird of Amat of recent times. At Croick in 1727 was born the oddity, Janet Macleod, known as "the fasting woman", who, despite refusing to eat more than a two-year-old child all her life, lived to the age of 70. Only a rough track now continues up Strath Cuileannach for another 5 miles, though a foot-path thereafter crosses the hills to the north-west, to upper Strath-oykell, which it reaches at another Amat, near Oykell Bridge, rather confusing.

Taking the road back down the north side of the Carron, through empty country, just over 3 miles from The Craigs is the large Brae-langwell Lodge, a pleasant whitewashed mansion opposite Green-yards, amongst woodlands, one more former Ross lairdship, a branch from Invercharron, which gained these lands in 1661. There is another Braelangwell in Easter Ross with a distillery, near Inver-gordon. From here on, down to the Gledfield area, the land is gentler, much forested, with quite good arable at the riverside levels and a number of small farms.

Instead of crossing the bridge back to Lower Gledfield and Ardgay, a fork here turns away north-eastwards, the road up the south side of Strathoykell. For a mile it follows the north bank of the Carron, to near its confluence with the Kyle of Sutherland, and here is the pleasant estate of Invercharron, noted in history as where the preliminary skirmishes of the Battle of Carbisdale were fought. The house is a delightful one, in a lovely setting, quite large and dating from at least the early 18th century, but probably with older nucleus. There are extensions, but in the same style of architecture. A stone dated 1732 is built into the walling. There is some good panelling and interesting plaster ceilings. Also two fine rooms in the grand manner built by Lord Ankerville, one of the Ross lairds and a Lord of Session, in the later 18th century. He died in 1805. Invercharron was owned by a senior branch of the great Clan Ross, the first of the line being William, second son of Sir David, 7th of Balnagown, who gained these lands in 1528. There were ten of that line, before the estate passed to the Ankerville Rosses.

Soon after Invercharron the road bends sharply to the north-west, to proceed up Strathoykell, following first the south side of the Kyle, then the Oykell River. Almost 3 miles up is Culrain, where there is a small village, with school but no church, tucked into a small side valley, rather attractive. Culrain was a lairdship of the Munro family, closely related to the chiefs of Foulis. Indeed George Munro of Culrain was brother of Sir Robert, the 27th chief, who fell at Falkirk, fighting against Prince Charlie, and who himself was shot a few months later at Loch Arkaig, in mistake for another government officer who had slain one of the Jacobites in cold blood. A son of the laird of Culrain who died in 1849 eventually inherited the Foulis baronetcy and chiefship. At Carbisdale farm here is an interesting establishment curing and dressing deer, sheep and other animal skins, for the commercial market, a recent and very worth while venture. This area was, of course, the site of the famous battle, of 1650, which marked the end of the brilliant career of James Graham, Marquis of Montrose. After returning from exile on the Continent, with a small force of inexperienced Orkneymen and some mercenary levies, and awaiting reinforcement from Mackenzies and Mackays, he was trapped here and defeated by Strachan's dragoons, and escaped, only to be captured at Assynt and sent South to his execution. Carbisdale Castle, a huge Scottish Baronial mansion, built allegedly by a Duchess of Sutherland just across from Sutherland lands, in spite, is now a youth hostel. It stands, highly spectacular and seeming to dominate the strath, on a knoll half a mile north of Culrain, its lands now planted forest.

North of Culrain this road winds on up the strath for another dozen miles, before coming to an abrupt end at the little community of Oape, just past Inveroykell Lodge. There has long been agitation to have a bridge built here—for the main A.837 leading to the West

Coast, by Inchnadamph is only a quarter-mile across the Oykell, and it would make an enormous difference to the dwindling communities here up this long dead-end road. It would also open up a very attractive area for the visitor. But so far the authorities have turned a deaf ear, and a difficult ford is now the only way out. The Kilmachalmack Burn, in its quite large valley, comes in about halfway up, in the Achnahanat vicinity, where there is another small community. Presumably once there was a Celtic church here, a foundation of Colmac, as at Portmahomack. There is no church now, though there was an 18th century mission-house at Ochtow a little further on. Depopulation is the rule hereabouts, unfortunately, and it seems to be nobody's business to do anything about it. Yet not far away boom conditions prevail, with land and houses at a premium.

The Oykell is a very famous salmon-river, and was mentioned as such as early as 1370.

Avoch and Rosehaugh. Avoch is a smallish but fairly regularly shaped civil parish, of 6000 acres, with a large fishing-village or small town, on the south Black Isle coast between Munlochy Bay and Chanonry Point, the name being pronounced "Och". There is no other village or hamlet, though there is a small community around Killen on the high ground of the Millbuie ridge to the north. Rosehaugh is the large estate to the west, famed as the seat of "Bloody Mackenzie", Sir George Mackenzie of Rosehaugh, noted Lord Advocate and founder of the Advocates' Library, Edinburgh.

Avoch is quite attractive, with a population of 1200, situated in a hollow where the Killen Burn enters Avoch Bay, the ground rising steeply behind. The major part of the little town lies in this hollow, with the harbour at the north end, and a fishertown stretching along the shore southwards. Two churches seem to dominate Avoch, perched on heights; the most prominent, now a hall, being the former rather gaunt Free church, to the south, in the Gallow Hill vicinity, less than beautiful. The other, in trees and less prominent, on the Braehead at the other side of the Burn, is the parish kirk, dating from 1670, enlarged in 1792 and 1833. It stands in a pleasant graveyard, has a lofty steeple, and a bell with a notable history. This was one of the Fortrose Cathedral bells, taken by Cromwell, along with much of the masonry, for the building of his citadel at Inverness. On the stormy voyage across the Firth, however, the bell was washed overboard, and about a century ago was dredged up by a fisherman, and appropriated by the parish kirk. Also notable here is the grave of Sir Alexander Mackenzie of Avoch, who died in 1820, the great explorer of the North West Territories in Canada, who gave his name to the Mackenzie River. There are many old flat stones here, also the burial-place of the Fletchers of Rosehaugh—of whom more anon. This Braehead residential area, on a sort of intermediate shelf of the hillside, is pleasant.

Down in the town, with little streets named after members of the

Randolph's Leap, near Relugas, Moray, where Alastair Ban Comyn leapt the Findhorn to escape from Thomas Randolph, Earl of Moray, Bruce's nephew

Cawdor Castle

Barevan Churchyard, near Auchindown. The most interesting pre-Reformation church in Nairnshire

Mackenzie family, there are hotels, guest-houses, shops, a bank and the usual offices. Also the Norscot Visitors' Centre, which combines ship and yacht chandlery with accommodation and eating facilities. There is one little establishment intriguingly entitled The Other Shop, with handicrafts. The harbour, unlike so many today which are devoted only to pleasure-craft, is busy, with many fishing-boats. These are apt to sail away to far-off fishing-grounds in the West and South. Yachting, however, is also to the fore. A feature of this whole area is the prevalent festooning of the roadside fences with the nets of the Avoch fishermen, hung out to dry. These fisherfolk are alleged to be descendants of survivors from a wrecked galleon of the Spanish Armada—though some give other derivations. Certainly rather odd names survive. The cottages of the fishertown are many of them gable-end to the street, and reminiscent of Buchan and Moray rather than the Black Isle.

The side-road, which crosses the Killen Burn and continues south-wards along the shore, at length climbs over the higher ground to Bennetsfield and back to the main road near Suddie. On the way it passes the farm of Castleton, and this refers to the former famous and important castle of Ormond, which occupied a commanding site on the high headland of Lady Hill here, overlooking Munlochy Bay on the north. Only green banks remain, amongst planted forest, but its name has been preserved in Scottish history. For this was the home of the famous Regent Sir Andrew Moray, patriot. The Douglases got it, and from it a brother of the murdered 8th Earl took the title of Earl of Ormond. Thereafter the Crown annexed it, and James the Third created his second son Duke of Ross, Marquis of Ormond and Earl of Edirdale—Edradour, an old name for the Black Isle. The castle was originally of 12th century construction and large, measuring no less overall than 450 by 150 feet.

To the north-west of Ormond is Chapelhead and Ballone. Near here is a famous wishing-well called Craigie or Craigock, similar to that near Munlochy, where on the first Sunday in May, many come to make wishes and offer a gift of cloth. No doubt it was a holy well, and the chapel therefor commemorated in the name only. Above Chapelhead, on a bank, is a single standing-stone, on which have been carved initials of the Matheson and Mackenzie families. These refer to the former estate of Bennetsfield, now a farm behind—or Benuatsfield, as once spelt—held by Mathesons who descended from the old chiefs of that clan, called MacMath. The stone for building Fort George largely came from quarries here.

Where this side-road rejoins the A.832, at the Avoch parish boundary, is one of the entrances to the large estate of Rosehaugh. This famous property has had an interesting history. Long held by the Mackenzies, it represents one of the prophesies of the Brahan Seer, who foretold, in the 17th century, that it would fall under the control of fishermen from Avoch—a highly unlikely fate for a great estate of the mighty Clan Mackenzie chieftains. But in 1864 Sir James Mackenzie of Rosehaugh sold it to a Mr. James Fletcher, for

£145,000. This Mr. Fletcher was actually the son of a William Jack, a former Avoch fisherman who had married Isobel Fletcher, an heiress, and assumed the name of Fletcher. The Fletchers pulled down the old mansion and built a great Victorian house on the splendid wooded and terraced site. This, in turn, has been demolished, and the estate is now an investment of the Eagle Star Insurance Company. Sir George Mackenzie first made this property famous. He was notorious for his activities, as Lord Advocate, against the Covenanters of the late 17th century, but he had his virtues, and many other claims to fame, a noted wit and much-cultured character, who, i is sometimes claimed, was the writer of the first novel actually printed and published in Scotland.

On the same terrace formation above the valley of the Killen Burn, but much nearer the town, is the modern Avoch House. Its predecessor was burned down in 1833, the seat of another branch of the Mackenzies, of which came the explorer. And high above this, but reached by a climbing side-road in over a mile, is Arkendeith, now a farm set on the edge of the 300-foot contour, with the land dropping steeply below and glorious views. In the garden are the scanty remains of Arkendeith Tower, a formerly small, L-shaped fortalice evidently of the early 17th century, only part of one vaulted wing remaining, with chamfered windows and doorway, the latter still provided with its deep draw-bar socket. It was sometimes referred to as Black John's Ark, and belonged to the Bruces of Kinloss, ancestors of the Earls of Elgin.

Still up on this high ground, but higher and 2 miles to the northwest, just below the great ridge forest of Findon and Millbuie, is the Bishop's Well. It is situated in a field, to the south of the side-road from Munlochy to Killen, below the farm of Auchterflow, and is exactly under a line of electricity pylons, a fenced-in enclosure with a bubbling spring. Which bishop, presumably of Ross, this refers to, is not clear. The Bog of Auchterflow is noted for its wild flowers, especially its orchids. There are also famed fossil-beds in this Killen area.

Conon Bridge, Maryburgh and Kinkell. The village of Conon Bridge and the district of Kinkell are in the civil parish of Urquhart and Logie-Wester, whereas Maryburgh is just across the Conon from the former, but in the parish of Fodderty. It would be ridiculous, however, to describe them separately. Also it would be inconvenient to deal with Conon Bridge under the large Urquhart parish, parts of which are as much as 9 miles away.

The River Conon enters the Cromarty Firth just south of Dingwall, the Ross capital, and 2 miles up from its estuary it became narrow enough to be bridged, in 1809, by the famous Telford. Here a quite large village has grown up, 300 persons in 1840, considerably more today, with the busy A.9 highway grinding through. Telford's fine five-arch bridge became inadequate for the traffic, and now a wide modern bridge replaces it. But the old toll-house remains on the northern, Maryburgh side. Maryburgh may now seem just an extension of Conon Bridge, but it is in fact an entity in its own right, having developed separately. Kinkell area lies to the south-east, just into the Black Isle peninsula, on rising ground, above the Muir of Conon, and includes the restored castle of Kinkell and the districts of Bishop's and Easter Kinkell.

Conon Bridge, naturally, shows little aspect of age, with indeed some very modern features, including the large cold-storage depot recently established at the bridge-end, grown out of the Allanbank project near Munlochy. The Established church is not old, nor very large, but calls itself the parish church of Ferintosh, thus keeping an old name alive. The public hall is dated 1906. There is a curling-pond near by. Opposite is the quite attractive and quite large Conon Hotel famed for its fishing. The school is at the southern and higher end of the village, and there are guest-houses, post-office, shops and offices.

Maryburgh across the river has much modern housing, yet, behind it all, rather more appearance of age, the part to the west of the busy main road being pleasant, open and quiet. Here is a large Established church, rather gaunt, a sizeable school and playing-fields, and more modern housing. The ground rises quickly, and on the heights, in a ring of trees, is a prehistoric burial-chamber. Below it, at Bakerhill, is the pleasantly situated county council home for backward children, established as a sanatorium by the German wife of one of the Seaforth lairds from Brahan Castle.

At the other, south side of Conon Bridge, one mile, lies the fine wooded estate of Conon House, at the riverside, where is an attractive large whitewashed mansion of 1758, with a high, hipped-roofed central block and wings, on the work of which the famous Hugh Miller was employed as a mason. Some of the interior features are most excellent. This has remained a Mackenzie house, of the Gairloch family. There is an octagonal doocot at the stableyard and farmery buildings near by. Across the A.9 from Conon is the smaller estate of Balevil, formerly another Mackenzie property, of which came General John Mackenzie, of some fame. The mansion is now demolished. The former church of the old pre-Reformation parish of Logie-Wester used to be near the river hereabouts. Hidden amongst woodland above the main road and railway, just south of Balevil, is the feature known as David's Fort, a late example of a well-engineered earth-fort, with moat.

The Kinkell district is widespread, covering the long gentle slopes eastwards of the A.9, rising from 80 to 350 feet and extending some 3 miles into the Black Isle along the Millbuie ridge, its higher levels former moorland with small farms and crofts—indeed called Muir of Conon, Muir of Highfield, Muir of Allanbank, and so on. This is an area of chambered cairns. Bishop's Kinkell lies closest to the main road, no doubt representing lands originally owned by the See of Ross. Modern housing is now springing up on this attractive tree-girt site above the Conon valley. Higher and eastwards, past a croft with a chambered cairn, where the side-road joins the B.9169 which heads eastwards up the Black Isle to Cromarty, is Millbuie school and public hall. Opposite is a tall cylindrical monument in memory of Major-General Sir Hector A. MacDonald, born at Rootfield here in 1833, entered the army as a private soldier, and died a knighted general in 1903. There is another and even loftier monument to him at the cemetery above Dingwall.

At the next cross-roads north-eastwards, on the way to Easter Kinkell—where is the school of Ferintosh—the left-hand road, the B.9162 from Tore, to be upgraded as part of a major highway scheme, leads down past the entrance to Kinkell Castle. This is a most interesting building, long ruinous but now most excellently restored by its new artist and sculptor owner, its features brought back to prominence, a fine example of what can be done to save our valuable heritage of stone, with enthusiasm allied to good taste. It is a Z-plan fortalice of the late 16th century, on a small scale, with a circular stair-tower at one angle of the main block and a tall, slender stair-turret at the opposite corner. A later wing of the same height was added to the east, probably in the late 17th century, but this has now been removed, to the advantage of the aspect and proportions. The castle rises tall and whitewashed, guarded by gun-loops and shot-holes, above a basement plinth. The ground floor is vaulted, and the Hall fireplace on the first floor is dated 1594. Kinkell was one more of the Mackenzie of Gairloch strongholds. Smaller and simpler than nearby Kilcoy Castle, in Killearnan parish, it is equally attractive.

The Millbuie or Ardmeanach ridge which starts here, and forms the broad backbone of the Black Isle for so many miles, is now largely forested, but used to be common grazing for the entire community. Dotted with chambered cairns and other prehistoric relics, it obviously was an important area in early times.

Contin, Strathconon and Garve. Contin is a huge civil parish and small village of South Ross, the former extending to 23 miles along the valley of the River Conon, the latter very much at the east end thereof, 7 miles north-west of Muir of Ord, on the A.832 highway to Wester Ross, by Garve, from which it is about the same distance southwards. Strathconon sounds as though it ought to be the valley of the River Conon, but there is a difficulty here, and some confusion amongst authorities as to which *is* the Conon. Some indicate that the very long river that flows down Strathconon is indeed the Conon, although it is called the Meig for most of its way. But the Ordnance map shows the Conon as much shorter and rising in a different valley to the north, where it flows out of Loch a'Chuillin a mile into large Loch Luichart and out to join the Meig in another mile or so. The fact that Falls of Conon are just at the mouth of Loch Luichart seems to give force to this contention. It is all rather confusing—especially as the river that flows in at the *west* end of the small Loch a'Chuillin is called the Bran, and its valley, all the way to Achnasheen (which one would expect to be on the Sheen) is called Strathbran. Be all that as it may, however, Strathconon, for three-quarters of its length, is the valley of the Meig, with Lochs Meig and Beannacharain therein. Lower Strathconon is wide and green and Lowland-seeming, and is described under the Strath-peffer and Fodderty and the Conon Bridge articles; the long and main Strathconon is purely Highland, but by such standards quite populous in its central reach.

Travellers from the south normally reach this area when they turn sharply northwards, on the A.832, at Marybank, 5 miles on from Muir of Ord, and descend to cross the Conon by the long Moy Bridge. Contin village lies athwart this road 2 miles further—although it is not actually on the Conon but on the Black Water, the quite large but short river which flows out of Loch Garve 4 miles on. The village is not large, but contains, as well as the parish church, a school, hall, post-office, hotel, guest-houses and a quite large modern forestry housing scheme. In the centre, at the road-junction for Strathpeffer, is a tall, cylindrical, battlemented war-memorial monument. The church lies a little way to the west, down at the riverside under a wooded knoll and reached via an old two-arched bridge with cutwaters. It is a very interesting place. The present church, of 1796, is plain, with a large bell in the belfry, plain within also but bright and pleasing, with a very small gallery. There is a tablet erected by the Edinburgh Walter Scott Club in 1912, in memory of William Laidlaw, Scott's land-steward and friend at Abbotsford, who later came up here to factor the Seaforth estates, composer of several songs. He died here. His writing-table is in the vestibule. There is a list of parish ministers since 1614, as at nearby Urray. The original church is first mentioned in 1227, but being dedicated to the Celtic St. Maolrubha (of Loch Maree) had probably a much earlier origin. The older building was the scene of a dastardly incident of clan warfare in 1480, when a raiding party of Mac-Donalds of the Isles burned the old men, women and children who had taken refuge therein. An aumbry of this old building was discovered in the north wall during alterations in 1908, and near by a recess for the recumbent effigy of one Maclay or Maclea Mor, a character who used the crannog in Loch Achilty not far away as his refuge and headquarters. In the graveyard are many ancient stones, including a 15th century wheel-cross, and another of the same period depicting a tree with roots at the base and a cross above, with sword. Many others are difficult to decipher and would repay closer exam-ination. There is a pre-Reformation stone font and what is probably a holy-water stoup lying near.

Above the village to the east is Coul House, now a large hotel, formerly the seat of an important Mackenzie estate, the family of which obtained a baronetcy in 1673. The present building dates from 1821, with later work. The burial-enclosure of the family lies in woodland nearer the village, beside an early burial-chamber.

Half a mile northwards, the main road crosses the Black Water by a fine three-arch bridge, and here is Torrachilty Forestry Centre, with walks and car-park. There is also a large sand-and-gravel works near by, at Achilty, The Black Water is a rushing river, coming down through something of a wooded pass. A dead-end side-road strikes off here, to the west, leading to the Falls of Conon and foot of Loch Luichart. A mile along, in a field at the right-hand side of the road, is a henge monument, now a double circle of grassgrown banks without standing-stones not very impressive. Loch Achilty is just beyond, a mile-long oval sheet of water pleasantly set amongst birchwoods under steep and lowish hills, with the aforementioned crannog, or artificial island, close to the northern shore. The attractive road continues on through Torrachilty Forest another 4 miles, amongst now close-shouldering and steepening rocky hills, passing the Luichart Power Station and a private road and bridge leading to Little Scatwell (normally reached from the other and southern road up Strathconon). This is just above the joining of the Conon and Meig Rivers. Here are the Falls, a series of cascades, and beyond is the large hydro-electricity dam, where the ugly pylons proliferate. The side-road ends at the foot of the 7-mile long Loch Luichart— although the main A.832 joins the loch again 5 miles beyond Garve. Luichart was the first loch in the Highlands to generate electricity.

It is necessary therefore to retrace steps to near Contin, where is Craigdarron Lodge, in woodland, now a hotel. The main road climbs up the Black Water pass, and over a mile up is the car-park for the beauty-spot of Falls of Rogie. It *is* beautiful, too—but unfortunately is distinctly spoiled by the large quarrying operations. There is a footpath and a swinging footbridge across the gorge near the viewpoint. The river itself is most impressive.

Over a mile on, through woodland, the road reaches and follows the south shore of Loch Garve, larger than Achilty but likewise picturesquely wood-girt, belying its name which means rough. On through Strath Garve another mile still, and Garve village is reached. Here there are two large hotels and other accommodation, a post-office, shop and caravan-site, with some modern housing. There is no other village for a very long way. Strathgarve itself, which is the valley of the Black Water, bends away northwards here, to curve round the western shoulder of mighty Ben Wyvis, the A.835 following it on the way to Ullapool, 32 miles away. Up here 6 miles is Inchbae Lodge, a former shooting-lodge now a 13-bedroom hotel in the deep wooded valley. The A.832, however, carries on due westwards from Garve, 15 miles to Achnasheen, where it forks, south for Kyle of Lochalsh, north for Gairloch. It borders Loch Luichart for a little, then Lochs a'Chuilinn and Achanalt, then enters the bleak upland vale of Strathbran. At Achanalt is a little Established church, a branch from Contin. This is the great watershed of North Scotland, with vast deer-forests of Kinlochluichart, Lochrosque and others stretching far and wide, and the Fannich Mountains lonely, roadless, to the north.

To journey to Strathconon, otherwise than on foot, just to the south as it is, it is necessary to go right back beyond Contin, to Moy Bridge and Marybank, where the narrow side-road turns off westwards. It goes for a long way before coming to a dead end at Scardroy Lodge, 21 miles. But still the River Meig probes on beyond, another 10 miles perhaps, up Glen Evaig, to its rise under shapely Moruisg, almost in sight of the western sea. Some 2 miles west of Marybank (described under Urray) the road reaches the foot of Loch Achonachie, where is the large Torrachilty dam and power-station, a very impressive establishment, with a fish-pass which is a favourite with visitors. This is the principal of seven power-stations on the River Conon, and the Group Control Centre. Here was the dam which overflowed in 1967, and fulfilled the Brahan Seer's prophesy. Loch Achonachie is 2 miles long and fairly narrow. Beyond it is the Scatwell area, where there is a little school and a post-office but no village. The large sporting estate here was formerly a Mackenzie seat, home of one of the many Mackenzie baronetcy families, bestowed in 1703. The present mansion is not old, long and low, of two storeys, in trim gardens, with good, wide fields in the vicinity.

Over a mile further is the foot of Loch Meig, also 2 miles long and again very narrow, just a flooded valley, wooded on the north side only. The road crosses the River Meig another mile beyond the loch-head, to the north side, at Bridgend, and the valley between here and Milltown becomes quite populous, something of a community, with a small church, a hotel, a post-office and a number of houses and farms. Strathconon was all populous once, full of Mackenzies, but the lands were largely lost, forfeited after the Jacobite troubles, and later cleared, in the usual grim fashion, by the new owners, to make room for sheep. It is 6 miles more beyond Milltown, the Strathconon centre, to Loch Beannacharain and now the signs of human habitation grow few and far between, wooded Glen Meanich coming in on the right. Beannacharain, like Lochs Meig and Achonachie, is a couple of miles long, and narrow, with a waterfall at its head. Here is Scardroy Lodge, and the end of the road. The great hills soar all around now, the massive six-summit ridge of Sgurr a Choire Ghlais (3552 feet) dominant to the south, with half a dozen lofty little lochs in between.

Contin parish, which goes on yet for many empty miles, is a great place for lochs—for there are about fifty of them, all told, a fisherman's paradise. Included in these is Loch Kinellan, where there is another crannog built of oaken logs, where the Mackenzies once had a small stronghold. Near here, at Blair na Ceann, the Field of the Heads, was the scene of a bloody battle between Mackenzies and MacDonalds in the late 15th century—one of the many, it may be said.

Cromarty. Considering that it for long gave its name to an entire county, and then to a joint county with Ross, Cromarty is a notably remote and quiet-seeming little town, with a rather out-of-this-world atmosphere. Although this is now being considerably modified by the rather hectic activities of the North Sea oil exploiters a mile across the mouth of the Cromarty Firth, with other industrial development in sight and hearing, but as yet these are all taking place beyond the barrier of salt water—though it may be only a question of time until Cromarty itself becomes affected. The town, of course, is placed at the very north-eastern tip of the 20-mile-long Black Isle peninsula, and almost as detached from the rest of Scotland as if it had been on an island indeed. Even Rosemarkie, the nearest little town, is almost 9 miles away, with no villages between.

Cromarty's slightly decayed air may be changing, but it is to be hoped that it will remain the very attractive and characterful place it has always been. It is a little burgh of now only some 600 souls. But it was much larger once, both in population and in area—for the sea has been gaining on it, and much that was once Cromarty is now beneath salt-water. The "Kirk Stanes", below the Fishertown, indicates where a church and graveyard once stood. It was quite a major seaport once—as is not to be wondered at, at the very entrance to one of the finest and largest natural harbours in Europe, the *Portus Salutis* of Sir Thomas Urquhart, and the *Sykkersand* of the Vikings—important enough to be one of the sixteen ports in the land which required a Customs clearance certificate. It was the base of a large fishing-fleet too, with its ancillary trades of fish-curing, rope-works and boat-yards. All this has gone, as has the brewery, the cloth-factory and the two fairs. Even in 1851 the population was 2215. The place was a royal burgh, but was reduced from this high status in 1672 to a mere burgh of barony, though elevated again to a parliamentary burgh in 1833. So the slightly decayed air is natural enough. Cromarty, of course was, in early days, on the main road to the North of Scotland, with a vital ferry here across the Firth. But with all this declension, it has not lost its attractiveness, and it has its stirrings once more, peculiarly enough, particularly as a craft-centre. And it has been declared a conservation area.

Cromarty is also the name of the civil parish, of some 7000 acres, stretching down the centre of the peninsula to just above Rosemarkie, and 5 miles west to Jemimaville, on the north.

The town clusters around its curving-piered harbour, the Fishertown, and the narrow Church Street, which contains the parish church and the town-house, all below the wooded bank of an earlier raised beach which 18th century Cromarty House shares with the roofless Gaelic church in its graveyard. There is a notable wealth of old houses, many very picturesque, and quite a few still awaiting the restorer. The parish, or East, church should be the centre of it all, for it is a historic place—and listed by the Church of Scotland as such—of rather unusual design and with character, but it is kept locked, and its ancient graveyard is badly neglected. It is an early post-Reformation T-shaped building, with much interesting interior woodwork and furnishings, box-pews and its three galleries supported on timber pillars. There are a great many old stones in the kirkyard, and a roofless burial-enclosure.

Just to the north is the whitewashed and thatched Hugh Miller's cottage, now National Trust property and a magnet for visitors. Here the great geologist, writer and reformer was born, in 1802, and here he saw the ghost of one of his forebears, the buccaneer John Fiddes, who had built the cottage. The initials J.F. and J.G., with the date 1711, appear over the kitchen mantel. All is now attractively laid out as a small museum, with a notable collection of fossils and geological samples; also correspondence sent to Miller from all over the world. His bedroom still retains some of his own things, and Bibles. A 40-foot high monument in his memory, with a life-size statue on top stands behind the town, built in 1859, three years after his tragic death. The Cromarty district is unusually interesting geologically, and was fortunate indeed to have had Hugh Miller to explore, chronicle and expound it—although his achievements ranged far beyond geology.

Next to Hugh Miller's cottage is the 18th century town-house, Tolbooth and Sheriff court-house, an attractive whitewashed building with a clock-tower and ogee-roofed cupola. In this is a bell dated 1571. The building is awaiting restoration. In front stands the mercat-cross, a tall shaft on a three-step plinth, retaining its cross finial (which is seldom the case) with the dates 1578 and 1770 thereon. Near by is the Hugh Miller Institute, with public library and reading-room, and the Victoria Jubilee fountain in front. There is a small Episcopal church close by.

Good 18th century houses are thick on the ground. Amongst the shops are those specialising in crafts, pottery, stone-cutting and so on. The Fishertown lies to the east of all this, a picturesque huddle of largely whitewashed and brightly painted cottages, set down at odd angles, and now much frequented by artists and craftsmen. It has been described as a gem of Scottish vernacular architecture.

At the south end of the Fishertown the road proceeds towards the South Sutor of Cromarty, about 2 miles. Where it leaves the little town is a group of old houses of much interest, after passing the position of the former brewery. These were part of the earlier Cromarty House complex. That now known as the Gardener's House, in the garden of the present Colonel Ross's modern house, is the oldest building now remaining in Cromarty, and a very fine example of authentic domestic 17th century architecture on more than the town-house scale; a small mansion indeed, on a variation of the L-plan with a small extra wing projecting to the east in which is the moulded doorway. The building, with its steep roofs, crow-stepped gables, coped chimneys, the drip-stone over a tower window, and other typical features, is evidently of the mid-17th century, but the present laird says that there is still older work included. The basement is not vaulted, however. The house is used in connection with the large gardens, but is not in very good condition. It greatly deserves restoration. There is a tradition that it was the old Vicarage in pre-Reformation times, but it has a totally secular and lairdly aspect. The other old buildings across the road are also interesting and pleasing, likewise connected with the estate.

The road begins to climb thereafter, southwards, and passes on the ascent the extraordinary feature of a lengthy tunnel opening off to the right and leading to the rear quarters of Cromarty House, a major construction. The accepted reason for this is that it was built as a servants' entrance to the mansion, to save its lofty owners having to set eyes on such lowly folk, though there is another suggestion that it was not unconnected with smuggling activities. Cromarty House erected by the Rosses to succeed the earlier castle of the Urquhart lairds, is a very fine 18th century mansion with some notable interior decoration, and a 16th century fireplace from the castle. It has passed from the Ross family. One of its lairds was George Ross, a great benefactor and improver of the town, in the late 18th century. He it was who founded the brewery, "to discourage the natives from the pernicious and injurious habit of dram-drinking". He also set up the ropeworks. Across the road from the tunnel entrance is the little graveyard of St. Regulus, amongst yew trees. Here are many old stones, including one showing a sword and dated 1600, presumably an Urquhart. Also an underground vault, with heraldry, the burial-place of the Ross family. There is no sign now of the chapel of St. Regulus, one of at least four which used to grace the parish in pre-Reformation days. Just outwith the graveyard is one flat stone commemorating one Sandy Wood, who died in 1690, and expressed the desire to be buried *outside* the wall, so that he might have a start on others inside, in order to put his case before the Almighty first, at Navity. St. Regulus's Well is below the knoll, where the former castle's ravine opens out.

The road climbs on to the Mains of Cromarty farm, where it makes a sharp bend to the east, and, passing the former army hutments for the coastal defence batteries which guarded the mouth of the Cromarty Firth naval anchorage, mounts steeply to the lofty viewpoint on the South Sutor, where there is a look-out station for the Coastguard, and the derelict gun-positions. The views from here are magnificent, with seven counties visible. Below are the natural arches and stacks of the Sutors, with the cliff-girt headlands of Blue Head and Red Nose, below the adjoining Gallows Hill, place of baronial execution. At least the victims had an excellent view. It is said that there was a priory of the Red Friars hereabouts, with a St. Mary's Well. Probably it was a hostelry for travellers, combined with a beacon or lighthouse for sea-farers. It was founded in 1271.

Back in the town, north of the Fishertown, is the school, with an ice-house for fish preservation below. Also the main coastguard-station and the lighthouse—this at the site where witches used to be burned. The harbour is not now large, really only a ferry terminal for Dunskaith across the firth, the fishing-fleet having gone. Regattas are still held here annually, for yachtsmen. The large harbour, which used to rival Inverness for foreign trade, is now beneath the sea. The extensive, red-stone ropery premises are now being demolished.

The western part of the burgh is less interesting, of later date, where is the modern housing. Here is the West Established church, formerly the Free church. Outside is a granite memorial to the Rev. Alexander Stewart, an eminent divine who was parish minister and who led in the move over to the Free establishment, in 1843. Up on the hill above is the gaunt shell of the roofless Gaelic church, built in 1783 to cater for the Gaelic-speaking workers who came in to man the industries introduced by George Ross. It is surrounded by a still-used graveyard, with the Hugh Miller monument. The lane past this, down to Church Street, is called The Paye, allegedly derived from the French *le pays*, meaning the road to the country.

Before leaving the burgh something must be said about its most eccentric laird, the famous Cavalier Sir Thomas Urquhart, 17th century translator of *Rabelais*, and inventor of a universal language, who boasted that he could trace his distinguished ancestry right back to Adam. In the Bruce's reign, William de Urquhart was made Sheriff of Cromarty and it became hereditary in the family. Bruce himself was here in 1309 and 1323. Wallace is said to have won a small victory on the hill behind the town. Certainly James the Fourth was often here, on his way to and from St. Duthac's shrine at Tain.

The parish of Cromarty is quite large but notably lacking in population. The coastline south of the Sutor is cliff-bound and inaccessible save by footpaths. Over a mile down is the detached rock called MacFarquhar's Bed, and the Markus Cave, MacFarquhar being a notorious smuggler who used the cave for his imports. Other caves hereabouts are the Drooping, Doocot and Caird's. Further along the coast still is the large farm of Navity, with an interesting story. Here was St. Bennet's monastery and the site of St. Bennet's Well, one of the wishing-wells so popular in the Black Isle, where gifts were offered in the shape of cloths hung on a thorn-tree near by, which still exists. The name Navity comes from the Gaelic *neamhaididh*, meaning heavenly, and refers to the ancient local tradition that the dead will assemble here on the Day of Judgment, before ascension or otherwise. It was here that Sandy Wood was anxious to reach before others! The pleasant large farmhouse on its shelf has magnificent prospects.

A mile further still, southwards, is the attractive glen and still-used salmon-fishery of Eathie, made famous geologically by Hugh Miller. It is a spectacular wooded ravine, with three waterfalls. Miller describes it as "a deeply secluded dell of exquisite though savage beauty". It was allegedly a great haunt of the fairies.

On the high central ridge is mainly moorland, much less planted with trees than is further south-west. At 580 feet is the Grey Cairn, a burial-mound, and there are the remains of enclosures for hut-circles scattered in the area. On the north side of the peninsula, the

B.9163 hugs the shore for almost 6 miles, with fine views northwards but little in the way of features of interest. There is a well at the roadside half a mile west of the town, which has been renewed to commemorate the coronation of George the Fifth, in 1911. Nearly 3 miles along is Shore Mill, with its old mill-wheel still in position. It is now an Admiralty coastguard station, and there is a caravan- and camping-site. Jemimaville village is 2 miles further, but is described under its parish, Resolis.

Dingwall. The royal burgh, and county town of Ross, is an important place, and has been since before recorded time, lying as it does in a highly strategic position at the head of the Cromarty Firth where the Conon River enters the estuary and the hills come close to salt water. So it must be passed through on the way north or south, to or from Sutherland and Caithness. And nowadays, with all the industrial development in the Invergordon–Nigg area just to the north, it has to be passed through still more. In fact, this traffic problem is the principal impression carried away by the casual visitor, unfortunately—like so many another of Scotland's ancient towns, set almost inevitably on river-crossings or at the head of lochs or firths. Which is a great pity, destroying atmosphere, deafening with noise, polluting with fumes. Bypasses may be expensive, but they are vital if the character and entities of our ancient communities are to be preserved.

Dingwall is not a beautiful place, though its surroundings are attractive. But it has much character. Nor, despite its present and past importance, is it very large, having a population of only 4000. Its name is a corruption of Thing Vollr, Scandinavian for meeting-place of parliament. Oddly enough this Viking appellation has stuck, though the original Gaelic name was Inverpeffery. A Papal bull of 1256 refers to it as Inverferan. It seems to have been colonised by the Viking invaders in the 11th century, but they must have been ejected fairly soon, despite the name, for William the Lion built a royal castle here, to keep them away, towards the end of the 12th century. Alexander the Second, his successor, created Dingwall a royal burgh in 1226. This castle in due course became the principal seat of the Celtic Earls of Ross, descendants of the Hereditary Abbots of Applecross, who in turn descended from King Niall of the Nine Hostages, from Ireland—the same line that produced Crinan, husband of Bethoc, whose son was King Duncan the First, and all his line of Celtic kings. The first Earl was Farquhar Mactaggart, or Son of the Priest (Abbot) who came to the support of Alexander the Second. There were five of these Celtic earls, till 1372, when the line failed in an heiress, and much fighting over the earldom developed—in which Dingwall had its part. The chiefship of the Clan Ross passed to the Balnagown line (see Kilmuir Easter and Kildary) but Dingwall remained the county town.

The burgh consists basically of one very long High Street, running east and west with another major street striking off northwards, and

306

carrying the A.9 with it. There are many smaller side-streets, of course. Oddly enough there is absolutely no indication or atmosphere of the sea here, at first sight. Yet Dingwall was quite an important port for a while, and the burgh's arms are a star-fish, with additions. Salt-water in fact is not far away—but not evident unless looked for. The port is now completely gone, despite much money being spent on it in 1733 and again in 1817, when even Thomas Telford took a hand, and a canal was cut, 2000 yards long, through the encroaching mud-flats; and two new wharves were built. The canal is still there, after a fashion, and the wharves too, their bollards standing out forlornly—this at the end of Ferry Road, due east of the town. Traces of the derelict harbour can still be seen. A little bridge crosses the canal-mouth to a small sandy spit. This Conon mouth area was once notable for pearl-fishing. On the way down this Ferry Road, is passed a caravan-park, then the Sheriff Court-house of 1845, a castellated pile oddly ambitious for its site. Then the Ross Memorial Hospital of 1873, and the Queen's Own Highlanders Depot—formerly the Seaforths. At the parting of Ferry Road from the A.9 entrance to the town, is the railway-station, and in its forecourt is the unusual war-memorial of the 4th Battalion, Seaforth Highlanders, of the First World War, a tall and rough timbered cross, brought here in 1924 from France and re-erected, rather effective. Also there is a stone commemorating Sergeant John Meikle, a railway employee, erected by his comrades of the battalion, killed in 1918, unusual likewise.

From here the High Street bends round to the west and quickly narrows. At this east end rises the large and handsome Free church, with clock-steeple, built in 1869, with an elaborate memorial outside, with portrait medallion, to Dr. John Kennedy D.D. Near by is Park House, a somewhat decayed 18th century house with gablets, now partly used as offices. Opposite is the modern county council development department offices, a busy place these days, with so much development being made not far to the north. Here also is the Northern Area headquarters of the Hydro Board, a large hotel and the post-office premises.

Castle Street strikes off northwards, and, as the name suggests, here is the site of the original castle of Dingwall. It seems a markedly flat and indefensible position for a royal and earl's stronghold, but it must be remembered that this was formerly marshland, and the castle would be surrounded by water. Not much remains to be seen, save some fragments of masonry in the garden of the more modern mansion on the site, two-storeyed and crenellated, plus a late doocot. MacBeth was born in Dingwall, presumably in this castle. On the way to the castle is passed, as well as a branch of the Established church, the Episcopal church of St. James, of 1872, smallish with stained-glass in all windows and somewhat dark; also the Catholic church of St. Lawrence. Moreover, further along, the office of the Rosshire Journal newspaper is housed in what was formerly another church—a highly ecclesiastical thoroughfare.

Along the High Street with its shops, banks and hotels, is the rather notable Old Tolbooth tower of the town house, massive and ancient in its lower storeys, still retaining the iron yetts or grilles of its windows, though now provided incongruously with a classical balustrade as parapet. It is said to date from 1703, but there seems to be much older work here. At the top of the building is a wooden clock-tower, and at the foot stands the old Mercat Cross, an octagonal shaft with decorative finial, much worn, on a plinth.

The High Street is not now notable architecturally, but a few attractive features remain of the days when there were many little wynds, closes and entries, leading into back-courts, some of them picturesque. Further westwards is a Georgian house, standing back a little, converted into British Legion offices. And further still the large and very modern county buildings, with clock, and the police headquarters for Ross and Sutherland, opened by Princess Alexandra in 1972—but scarcely prepossessing nevertheless.

The major thoroughfare called Tulloch Street branches off to the north midway along the High Street, carrying the A.9 and most of the traffic—a noisy junction nowadays. Down Tulloch Street are more shops, offices and the public library; and some way along on the left, beside a car-park, is the parish church—for Dingwall is also a civil parish, not very large. The church is a rather dull, square edifice of 1801, quite large, with a steeple and hipped roof. At the entry to its kirkyard stands a Pictish stone, somewhat broken on one side and badly weatherworn, but the symbols of crescent and V-rod on one side, and double-disc and Z-rod on the other, may be discerned. There are many old flat stones in the graveyard, one, at the north-east corner of the church with a hollowed-out basin-like depression in the centre, which may possibly have been used as a baptismal stone—although sometimes these hollowed stones were used for grinding corn and known as knocking-stones. Here are the burial-enclosures of the Mackenzies of Fairburn and Strathconon, succeeded by the Murchisons of Tarradale, including the famous Sir Roderick, the geologist. There are some small remains of an earlier church to the north, said to have been set on fire by a citizen shooting pigeons on its thatched roof. The church is dedicated to St. Clement. Outside, in the car-park, is a monument to Sir George Mackenzie, first Earl of Cromartie, the obelisk dating from 1714 but replaced by a slightly smaller version in 1916, when it developed a list to one side. Perhaps this was a significant development, for the mound on which it was erected is said to have a quite different history. This was the burial-place of another Mackenzie, Sir Roderick, Tutor of Kintail, grandfather of the Earl. One story says that the soil for this mound was brought in creels by women from all over Ross, as a mark of esteem; another that it was put there on the Tutor's own dying orders, to bury him deep, so that the threat of another woman, a dairy-maid he had presumably wronged, to defile his grave, might not be carried out. One can choose one's version.

Near by are the auction-marts—for Dingwall is an important cattle-sale centre, and always was. It used to have many notable fairs, drawing attendance from all the Northern Highlands, some of them having rather unusual names, such as Janet's Market, Colin's, Fell Maree, Martha's and Peffer.

Tulloch Street, now really the A.9, crosses the Peffery and there-after it is mainly residential suburbs. But here are the large modern premises of Dingwall Academy, with other developments in process, including a swimming-pool. The housing rises in terraces where the A.9 curves away eastwards to follow the Cromarty Firth shore, and a lesser road parallels it half a mile inland and 300 feet higher, presum-ably the original road, for Foulis Castle and Ardullie Lodge, Munro seats, are reached therefrom. Above the modern housing develop-ments at this north end of Dingwall, stands Tulloch Castle, in its estate, now used for scholastic purposes, the policies being gradually built up. The castle is large, and a mixture of dates and styles, developing from a simple square keep of the early 16th century which has been somewhat altered, with 17th century and later additions to north and east. The keep is sturdy, with thick walls, and a crenel-lated parapet, now unfortunately spoiled by the heightening of a circular caphouse for the stair-head, unsuitable and unsightly. Also its roof is now flat, replacing a former gabled garret-storey within the parapet-walk. Some of the windows are small and original, others enlarged. There are wide splayed gunloops, some built up, and a curious shot-hole penetrating a chamfered-off angle at base-ment level. The interior has been much modernized to connect with later extensions, but the basement vaults remain, as does the great fireplace of the Hall above. There are some fine decorative plaster ceilings and some early panelling. Tulloch was a barony of a Bain family for many generations until 1760, when it passed to the David-sons, a branch of the Clan Chattan, whose seat it remained until comparatively recent times. One of the later Davidson lairds was known as The Stag. He had five wives who bore him eighteen legitimate children, but he is alleged to have had at least thirty others. Nevertheless Queen Victoria thought highly of him—an interesting commentary on alleged Victorian primness. Oddly, too, the Brahan Seer predicted that "a Laird of Tulloch should kill four of his wives in succession, but the fifth should kill him". Actually Duncan the Stag died of pneumonia after the famous Wet Review at Edinburgh, but his fifth wife did survive him. There is rather a fine stableyard here.

On the corresponding hillside at the other flank of Dingwall, to the south, is the abruptly rising and prominent Mitchell Hill, on the summit of which is the town's more modern cemetery, an unusual site and not very convenient for funerals, with its steep winding access road. It has some similarity to Tomnahurich at Inverness. Rising from it is the prominent landmark for miles around, the lofty battle-mented tower erected in 1907 as a memorial for General Sir Hector A. MacDonald, who came from the Millbuie area near by, entering the army as a private and ending up a most distinguished major-general. The tower is rather like the Wallace Monument at Stirling, though on a smaller scale, and is guarded by six old cannon. The views from up here are fine.

Dingwall has produced other famous sons. Sir Thomas Simpson, of the Hudson's Bay Company, who was one of the discoverers of the North-West Passage and had Simpson Strait named after him, was the son of a schoolmaster here. And some of Gladstone's forebears were natives.

The town is well provided with hotels, guest-houses and tourist accommodation, and has many sporting and recreational facilities. It is a good shopping and services centre, and is the administrative headquarters for a vast area, Ross being the third largest county in Scotland, with even Stornoway in Lewis involved.

Edderton. Edderton is a medium-sized civil parish on the south shore of the Dornoch Firth immediately west of Tain, containing the village of that name to the east, and the historic district of Fearn to the west—the original Fearn, source of some confusion with Fearn parish on the other side of Tain. There is no other village than Edderton, and the population of the parish has never been large. The well-known distillery of Balblair is located here, and there is a scattered community at Ardmore, out towards the Point of that name.

Edderton village lies at the side of the A.9 almost 5 miles from Tain, on the shore of Cambuscurrie Bay, with the wide tidal Edderton Sands at the head. It is not large, but pleasant, with parish church, post-office, shop and, oddly enough, a caravan-sales centre. The present parish church is handsome, dating from 1842, and seeming large for the community. It stands in the village itself, without kirkyard—for this is not the original, which is still in existence almost a mile to the east. A slightly unusual situation developed here. At the Disruption, the protestors—who presumably were in the majority—managed to take over the old parish church, and it was the continuing Established congregation which had to build the new kirk, the reverse of the normal arrangement. The original church is now no longer used by either side, though the kirkyard is still the parish burial-ground, with a modern extension. It stands, beside the highway, on the Edderton Burn a mile west of the parish boundary, and is a fairly typical long, low edifice, alleged to date from 1743 but obviously of older origin. It has an open and now empty belfry, and there is a moulded stone doorway, possibly of the 16th or early 17th century, in the roofless extension to the east. The building is now shut up. In the graveyard are many interesting stones, including a fine Pictish cross-slab in red sandstone, with a wheel-cross in relief on one side, and a horseman on the other, with another cross. There is a stone commemorating an Episcopalean rector named Ross, dated 1679, near the gate, and a memorial to Master Hector Fraser and wife, with heraldry, dated 1716, inset in

Kilravock Castle, seat of the Rose family since the 13th century

Meikle Kildrummie, Nairn, an early 18th century laird's house, pleasingly restored

Cromarty: The Gardener's House, so-called. Typical small mid-17th century mansion, with older nucleus

Dingwall: High Street, with the Old Tolbooth. The royal burgh's Mercat Cross can just be distinguished standing between the pillar-box and the telephone kiosk

the church walling. There is said to be a much older gravestone, possibly 13th or 14th century, with cross and sword, a so-called Crusader stone, but many of the oldest graves are now hidden under grass and moss, as so often happens, and this could not be traced.

At the village, a mile on, a side-road strikes northwards into the peninsula of Ardmore, passing the former Edderton Station. Before this is reached, in a field to the left, stands another Pictish stone, of an earlier or Class One type, a tall unhewn monolith displaying the double-disc and Z-rod with fish, incised, known as the Clach Beorach. This word can mean pointed or sharp, heifer or colt, or again dog-fish—so the choice is open! Near the station is the large and old-established Balblair Distillery, making malt whisky, its premises open to public inspection. Near by is Ardmore Lodge Hotel. There was a harbour at Ardmore which used to import coal and lime and export local produce. The one-time Castle of Edderton probably was near, built by William the Lion to command the ferry here—for the firth is only half a mile wide at Ardmore. It is mentioned in the Scotichronicon.

Inland from Edderton village, another side-road, 4 miles long, lifts through the foothills to join the main A.836 Alness–Struie road at 690 feet. Up this half a mile is the local school. It is an attractive road, with pines and heather and whins, with a bridge over a picturesque burn, but few houses. A hut-circle lies to the west 2 miles up, the mass of Struie Hill (1218 feet) rising behind. Nearer the foot of Struie Hill, a mile along the A.9 past the crofting area of Ardvannie, a lesser road forks off on the left, to the farm of Rheguile, and here a farm-track leads southwards through moorland to the former ha'-house of Meikle Daan, passing on the left a group of burial-cairns, not very obvious. Meikle Daan is interesting. It is no longer lived in, but used as a farm-store. It is a long, now two-storeyed building, although the roof may have been lowered, harled and with an unusual slight projection at the north-west angle, to house a garde-robe. The doorway and two of the windows have chamfered jambs, and over the door is a lintel with the initials A.M. and M.F. and the date 1680. A fireplace lintel from this house was removed to Balnagown Castle. It was a barony of the Munro family cadets of Foulis, later passing to the Rosses. In the house is a very interesting rough stone, loose, with most unusual incisions, three of them of approximate horse-shoe shape with curious additions, all different; no suggestion can be offered as to its significance. The house, although fairly humble in size and aspect, was the seat of the barony of Westray.

Beyond the thrusting, forested shoulder of Struie Hill, 4 miles on from Edderton village, is the broch of Dun Alascaig, hidden on a bank amongst scrub woodland. There was a chain of these Pictish duns along this coastline. Just beyond this, the East Fearn Burn comes down in a steep wooded defile and valley. And a mile on, the West Fearn Burn does likewise, near Fearn Lodge. This Fearn area, beside being picturesque, is interesting in that it was here that the original Abbey of Fearn was established, allegedly by Farquar, Earl of Ross in 1230, though apparently he was only Romanising an already established Celtic monastery; for a Pictish stone from Tarbat churchyard records, in unusual lettering, the Celtic abbot Reodaide, mentioned in the Annals of Ulster in 763, and entitled Ab Fearna. There was a Fern Monastery in Ireland then, and the abbey established here was known as Nova Ferna—a highly interesting case of a Celtic abbey being translated to the Romish polity, and of the transference of names, first from Ireland to Scotland, and then from here to the present parish of Fearn at the other side of Tain, when the abbey was removed there in 1338, allegedly because it was too vulnerable to raiding Highlanders here. Just where was the site of the original abbey is not clear. There is a waterfall about 2 miles up the West Fearn. This Fearn area, which was heavily forested with oaks, cut down for charcoal-burning was where General Strachan's troops mustered and hid prior to his defeat of Montrose at Carbisdale in 1650.

The A.836 road, climbing inland over the hills from Alness, comes down to rejoin the A.9 here, having cut off a major corner, and the views over the Dornoch Firth to Sutherland are amongst the finest on the east coast of Scotland, seen from the view-point, provided by the Automobile Association about 2 miles up. Half-way up to this is a fine single-arch bridge high over the East Fearn Burn. On this A.836 highway over the wide, high, lonely moors, but still in the parish of Edderton, 5 miles southwards is Aultnamain Inn, "in the middle of nowhere", a place of isolation indeed. Near by is a large peat-cutting and processing development. The boundary with Kilmuir-Easter parish is just beyond.

An eye-catching feature of the parish, and Fearn area, obvious from the A.9, A.836 and also the railway, is the large lagoon, half a mile long, formed in a bay of the Firth by the artificial railway-embankment enclosing it, a rather attractive water much frequented by swans and other wildfowl.

Evanton, Kiltearn and Foulis. Evanton, named after one Evan Fraser of Balconie, is a village, founded in 1810, 6 miles north of Dingwall, on the A.9, and now growing rapidly, placed as it is on the edge of the great industrial developments of the Alness–Invergordon–Nigg area. Kiltearn is the large civil parish it stands in, with an area of 30,000 acres, stretching far into the empty hills to the west, and reaching the summit ridge of mighty Ben Wyvis. And Foulis is the castle, former railway-station and district, to the southeast, seat of the chiefs of Clan Munro.

Evanton village is built a mile back from the Cromarty Firth, flanking the A.9 where it has to cross two rivers which enter the firth within half a mile of each other, the Skiath on the south, and the Glass or Allt Grannda to the north. It has a fairly strung-out and not very impressive aspect, with much new housing expansion taking place, especially on the higher ground to the west, and industrial development to the east and nearer the firth. There is little to comment upon in the village itself, with its shops and businesses. The present Established church stands at the roadside towards the north end, unexceptional, and near by, beside the Allt Grannda bridge, an old mill and caravan-park. On the higher area to the west is a former United Secession church of some character, unfortunately now in decay. Also the Diamond Jubilee Hall, near the Free church. There is a very modern school on the Foulis road, and a detached and growing housing development at Culcairn to the north, connected with the Alness expansion. The former airfield area, on the low ground to the east, is now being developed as an industrial estate, with timber-yard, wool warehouse and other commercial establishments, all rather oddly contrasting with the farm which is still functioning amongst it, and the squash-club sited here. Between the rivers, on this low ground, was the site of Balconie House, now demolished. It was originally quite an important castle of the Earls of Ross, but little of that stage survived even before the demolitions. Hugh Miller relates the story of how the Lady of Balconie, in the 17th century, took her maid up to the Black Rock gorge on the Allt Grannda near by, with tragic results, a tale too long to recount here. An oil-rig construction-yard is scheduled for this area of Balconie Point.

The Black Rock of Novar is a highly dramatic feature, lying to the north-west of the village, in Glen Glass, where the river, which has come out of Loch Glass, has carved for itself a deep and fearsome ravine in the soft rock, about 2 miles long and tortuous, in places well over 100 feet deep and sometimes as narrow as 17 feet across, so narrow indeed that it is impossible to see the foot from the top. Its foot is reached by a track from the mill area. Above, it is not to be observed from the side-road which leads westwards up into the hills, to Loch Glass, 6 miles. The river, called the Glass for most of its course and the Allt Grannda, or Ugly Burn, in its lower reaches— for reasons unknown—forms the boundary between Kiltearn and Alness parishes for most of its way, but it is convenient to describe this area under Kiltearn. Two miles up is the small Mackenzie estate of Assynt, a name usually connected with the North-West, its mansion a fairly late cream-washed building in the castellated style, in woodlands. Higher are the modern buildings of the Water Board's filter-station. The little school here is closed down. Glen Glass is rather lovely, wooded and probing into shapely brown heather hills. There are a number of hill-farms. The public road stops short of the loch, at a lodge, with a private road continuing up the west shore. The loch is 5 miles long and less than a mile across, half in each parish, with the great empty hills around. Wyvis Lodge lies at the top end—and Ben Wyvis (3433 feet) is fairly readily climbed from near here. There was formerly an island, possibly a crannog, at the south end, where the Munroes of Foulis are said to have had a refuge.

The parish church for all this area is—or was, for it is now aban-

doned—inconveniently situated down on the shore, where the
southern river, the Skiath or Sgitheach, enters the firth. It is reached
by a side-road a mile long, striking off the A.9 beside the large farm
of Drummond just south of Evanton. Down here is the former
manse, now with the old church bell hanging outside. The roofless
church dates from 1791, though with a pre-Reformation nucleus,
and is still surrounded by the parish graveyard, ancient and modern.
Here is the burial-enclosure of the chiefly Munroes of Foulis, from
1588 to the present day. We are told that from 1126 to 1547 they
were interred at the Chanonry of Ross, in Fortrose. There are
many old flat stones, largely of Munroes, also a memorial to the
Reverend Thomas Hogg, a noted divine of the 17th century, who
was ejected and imprisoned for his Covenanting principles, "a
noted keeper of conventicles", yet who died a royal chaplain in
1692.

The Skiath river is followed up into its own hills, south of Glen
Glass, by another side-road, this valley being called Swordale. This
is a pleasant, open, populated and farmed vale, shorter than Glass
at least as far as the road goes, although the Skiath itself is much
longer, reaching far up into the hills north of Strathpeffer, where it
rises on the south flanks of Wyvis. Swordale House, where the road
ends, is an attractive whitewashed, three-storeyed house of the 18th
century, with attached farmery. The school here is closed, like that
of Glass. There are fine views from the high open valley, over the
Cromarty Firth.

Some 2 miles down the "back-road" from Evanton towards
Dingwall, is Foulis Castle, still the seat of the chiefs of Munro. It is a
very unusual mansion, no longer a castle in the true sense, having
been rebuilt in the Dutch style by the 7th Baronet, to replace the
older castle accidentally burned down in 1750. It consists of an
E-shaped, three-storeyed building within a courtyard, with a tall
octagonal tower projecting from the main block, in which is the main
door, at first floor level. It is scarcely beautiful, being rather gaunt,
but has its own attractiveness. As indicated, the Munroes have been
here for a long time, the first of Foulis dying in 1126. They were
followers of the old Earls of Ross, and were a warlike and powerful
clan, fighting at Bannockburn, Halidon Hill, Harlaw, Pinkie,
Fontenoy and Falkirk, amongst other battles. In 1632 they were
reported to have 1000 men under arms. One charter of the 14th
century refers to Robert Munro of the Tower of Strath Skiath and
Easter Foulis, presumably the predecessor of the present house. The
family gained a baronetcy in 1634, though this has passed to another
branch, and the present Captain Patrick Munro, is the 33rd chief.
They have always been great soldiers, and Robert, the 18th Laird,
called the Black Baron, was actually a colonel of two Dutch regiments
under Gustavus Adolphus, one Horse and one Foot. At that time
there were no fewer than twenty-seven field officers and thirty cap-
tains of the name of Munro in Gustavus's army. The clan was always
strongly Protestant, from the Reformation onwards, and followed

the Hanoverian interest in the Jacobite troubles, the 6th Baronet falling at the Battle of Falkirk in 1746. President James Munroe (the name is not normally spelt with an "e") of the United States, was a descendant of this family.

Ardullie Lodge, a dower-house of Foulis, is situated nearer the coast, over a mile to the south, and just above the A.9, from which it can be glimpsed. It is a quite delightful pink-washed, L-shaped, late 17th century house, typical, with steep roofs, crowstepped gables, dormer windows and good internal panelling. It occupies a terraced site amongst old trees, above the firth-shore. Not far to the north, at Foulis Point, right on the shore, is a large 17th century warehouse-type building, relic of the days when another kind of commerce was practised on the Cromarty Firth.

On the estate of Mountgerald near by, is a group of cup-marked stones. Inland, on the high ground of this end of the parish, the large planted forest of Clach Liath covers much of the hillsides.

Fearn, Balintore and Cadboll. Fearn is the central parish of the Tarbat–Nigg peninsula, of some 7700 acres with a sizeable village and the site of a former abbey; Balintore is a fishing-village, also quite large, at its southern tip; and Cadboll is an ancient barony, castle and estate, with the hamlet of Hilton of Cadboll merging with Balintore. The area is notably flat—even Hill of Fearn is only 50 feet above the sea—and almost treeless, but with its own rural attractiveness. The quite large Loch Eye, almost 2 miles long, lies half in this parish. The soil is a fertile rich loam, and highly farmed.

Fearn village, more properly Hill of Fearn, stands in a fairly central position 3 miles inland from the coast and 5 miles south-east of Tain. It is a pleasant place of cottages and gardens grouped round a green, on which stands the war-memorial. There is a school, shop, services and a small hotel. One of the whitewashed cottages is marked as the birthplace of Peter Fraser, Prime Minister of New Zealand from 1940 to 1949, born here in 1884. To the south-east half a mile is the parish church and the remains of the former Premonstratensian abbey, which gained a certain prominence in the 16th century as being the nominal seat of its 15th Abbot, Patrick Hamilton, the protomartyr of the Scottish Reformation, who was burned at St. Andrews in 1528, for heresy. Actually he was only 19 when given the abbacy, and 25 when he died, and he probably never even visited Fearn—this being quite a common story in those degenerate days. His death, like his life, was probably more concerned with politics than religion. The abbey, dedicated to St. Augustine, oddly enough was first founded at Edderton, about 10 miles to the north-west, in 1221, by Farquhar MacTaggart, Earl of Ross, and moved here allegedly as safer from the depredations of wild Highlandmen, in 1338. The chapel of the abbey is now the parish church, and little else survives. The church is not particularly handsome externally, having been much mutilated from its early appearance both by the efforts of the Reformers and as the result of an accident in 1742 when, during service, the stone-vaulted roof of the nave fell in, killing forty-four people. It was rebuilt in 1772. But despite all this, the interior is impressive, the walls a yellowish stone, with pointed lancet windows, plus a modern timber ceiling. It is now merely oblong on plan, the transepts having been cut off, and remaining in part outside as ruined burial-enclosures. At the east end there is trefoiled sedilia, and holy-water stoup and piscina behind the organ. Some notable memorials to members of the Ross family enhance the east end, in stone and marble heraldry, one to the 13th Chief, who died in 1711, the last of the main line to own Balnagown, who seems to have got into debt partly through his fondness for repairing Ross-shire churches. Flanking this genuine chief are two "usurping" lairds, General Charles Ross and Admiral Sir John Lockhart-Ross, the former a brother of Lord Ross of Hawkhead, in Renfrewshire, who bought his way into the Balnagown property. The General was a notable character however, Provost of Tain in 1715 while at the same time colonel of dragoons—an unusual combination. The Admiral was a nephew, and really not a Ross at all, however gallant. It is all a confused and difficult story. Outside the church are the ruined aisles, one, St. Michael's, containing the fine recumbent effigy, under an arch, of the Abbot Finlay McFead (1442–85), in clerical garb with a crozier above, the other having the mutilated effigy, with shield, of the founding Earl Farquhar.

Half a mile north-east of the abbey, on the B.9165 to Portmaho-mack, stands the Free church of the parish, in an isolated position, typically stern, with a large bell in an open belfry. This is some 2 miles west of the coast, where is the main population of the parish, in the strung-out community of Balintore, Hilton of Cadboll and Shandwick. Balintore is quite large, with a good harbour. Salmon-fishing on a commercial scale continues here, and very successfully, no fewer than 15,000 fish being netted in the last season, by two stations. The little port used to export grain and potatoes, and import coal. There are two small hotels, a caravan-park, and the small modern mission church connected with Nigg parish, Shand-wick being in that parish. The community is growing under the impact of Nigg development. Hilton of Cadboll stretches to the north. Here is the Seaboard Memorial Hall, a modern Free Presbyterian church, a Free church meeting-house, and a fisheries station of fair size. Also the bowling-green and children's play-ground. Most of the houses are of the traditional cottage type. There is a modern and quite large school on the higher ground behind. The site of a former pre-Reformation chapel dedicated to the Virgin Mary lies on a shelf of a grassy bank to the north. From here was taken to the Museum of Antiquities, Edinburgh, via the British Museum, London, in 1921, the renowned Cadboll Stone, a magnificent Pictish cross-slab, depicting mounted chieftains hunting deer with hounds, and even a lady riding side-saddle; also crescent and V-rod, double-disc and Z-rod and Mirror and comb symbols, all amidst the most elaborate Celtic decoration. Anything more apt for giving the lie to the old tale that the Picts were some sort of woad-painted savages would be hard to imagine. At the so-called Ghosts' Hillock here, when digging the foundations for modern housing, were uncovered many human bones of what was probably a Bronze Age burial-place. It is strange that the area had long been a place for local awe, with people who had to pass there dropping a pebble into a hollow, to ward off evil spirits.

Cadboll Castle lies within the steading of the large farm of that name another mile to the north, reachable only by farm-roads. Though ruinous, it has certain unique features surviving. It is a strongly built L-planned structure, with a circular tower and a roofless angle-turret. The original windows are tiny, mere cruciform slits, for defence, even at first-floor level, and there are no windows or apertures at all in the vaulted basement. The first floor, so ill-lit, is also vaulted, which is very unusual, and here was the doorway reached by a removable timber stair and protected by a draw-bar with slot. None of the three chambers here had a fireplace. The upper storeys, where must have been the living and sleeping quarters, are now inaccessible. There are shot-holes and a splayed gunloop. It looks as though there has been a very early type castle here, pre-sumably a semi-ecclesiastical building, much added to and altered in the late 16th or early 17th century. There is an interesting legend about the castle to the effect that no one ever died in it—the last owner had to be carried out in order to expire. A good L-shaped three-storeyed house of the late 17th or early 18th century adjoins to the east. The lands of Cadboll belonged to the Abbey of Fearn, and, as so often happened, managed to "stick to the hands" of the last Abbot, who presented them to his "nephew". Abbot Donald Denoon was quite a notorious character, allegedly a Campbell from Dunoon in Argyll, who had to flee that country, but made his mark in Easter Ross. There are still Denoon families in the area. A daughter of the 8th Ross of Balnagown married John Denoon of Cadboll in the mid-16th century, probably the "nephew". But shortly after the 9th Chief was accused of "cassin down the fortalice and barrailed Tower of Cadboll" and was shut up in Tantallon Castle for his misdeeds—presumably Denoon's brother-in-law. The property later passed to the descendants of the Macleods of Assynt, and the Macleods of Cadboll were quite prominent in their own right, especially in the development of Invergordon. The first Provost thereof was a Macleod of Cadboll.

At the other side of the parish, north-east of Hill of Fearn, lies the farming hamlet of Rhynie, grouped round the quite good Georgian mansion, now the farmhouse, with its fine walled-garden adjoining. A mile to the north is the site of the former castle of Lochslin, or Lochlin, now only a heap of stones on a low ridge. This castle retained its many features up to a comparatively recent date, and in a gazetteer of 1884 is described as 60 feet high and a conspicuous object on the landscape. It is sometimes stated that the famous Sir George Mackenzie, King's Advocate at the end of the 17th century, was born here. The farm of Lochslin is at the east end of Loch Eye. This large loch, 2 miles long and almost a mile wide, is separated from salt water at Inver Bay by only a mile's distance. At one time there were many small lochs in this parish, this is the only one left undrained. Loch Eye is scheduled to become part of a nature reserve, with the coastal expanse of Morrich More, to the north.

Fortrose and Rosemarkie. Fortrose and Rosemarkie—the two names are nearly always used together—small twin towns less than a mile apart on either side of the extraordinary Chanonry Point in the Black Isle, yet each distinct entities, together make up, since 1592, the Royal Burgh of Fortrose. Yet Rosemarkie is much the older, and was originally a burgh on its own. Rosemarkie is also the name of the civil parish, of some 7000 acres, including both.

The story of these two little towns—which between them muster only some 1000 of population could fill a book by itself, and an interesting one. To take the problem of the names first. This emphasis on the word Rose hereabouts is misleading. It has nothing to do with flowers, however salubrious the climate, but is the same word as Ross, the name of the county. The Gaelic *ros* means a promontory, and the very notable feature of the mile-and-a-half-long narrow and low-lying sandy headland of Chanonry Ness and Point, produced the name for the entire great county—the third largest in Scotland—the earldom and the bishopric. The original local names were *Rosmarcanaidh*, the Horse Burn at the Point, and *Fo-tir-ros*, the place beneath the Point. The latter became Fortrose—nothing to do with a fort, or a rose—and was so called at the time of the royal burgh charter. Another complication is the name Chanonry. This of course is the term for a cathedral precinct, or canonry, and seems largely to have displaced the name of Fortrose for a period, when the episcopal see here was at the height of its power, with its proliferating manses of the cathedral clergy. The name has stuck to the peninsula rather than the town, strangely enough. This is an interesting feature in itself, reaching out towards the rather similar Ardersier promontory on the south side of the Moray Firth, on which is sited Fort George citadel. Their tips are in fact less than a mile apart. There are legends, inevitably about these two, which all but turn the Inverness and Beauly Firths into a vast inland loch. Oddly enough, the famous south-country wizard, Michael Scott, comes into this. It is alleged that Michael, for some reason unspecified, called up the Faery host to build a cathedral at Elgin and the Chanonry Kirk at Fortrose—which the little folk did in a single night, unfortunately however making a slight mistake, easily done in the darkness, of erecting the building designed for Elgin at Fortrose, and vice versa. Concerned at the error, Michael suggested that they were such fine buildings that it would be a pity to pull them down again, but that if the little people would build a mound right across the Moray Firth, they could transfer the two erections bodily to their proper sites. This was accepted the next night, but towards

dawn when the great causeway was almost complete a night-travel-
ling Highlander bid the busy workers God-speed—and this promptly
caused all work to be abandoned, and so saved Inverness port's
navigational access. There are variations on this theme. But it is
surprising how the Fife Michael Scott's fame should have become
incorporated in the Gaelic folklore of the North, also that anti-God
forces should have been credited with the erection of these two
cathedrals.

Be all this as it may, the early Columban missionary to the Picts,
St. Moluag, established a cell at Rosemarkie in the mid-6th century,
and about 716 St. Curitan, also called St. Boniface, set up a monastery on the site. In 1124, David the First established the Bishopric
of Ross on this foundation, but chose Fortross as the site rather than
the existing church, which stood on the site of the present parish
church of Rosemarkie. And so the two developed separately, though
so close together.

Today, Fortrose is a very attractive little town, but by no means a
sleepy hollow; indeed it is a popular holiday centre, and deservedly,
and the "capital" of the Black Isle. It clusters, inevitably, around the
ruins of the formerly great cathedral, but actually not much of this
remains, in its pleasant lawn-girt precinct, for that scourge of
ecclesiastical buildings, Oliver Cromwell, demolished most of it to
use the masonry for his great citadel at Inverness. He took most of the
bells too, though seems to have left one, dated 1460, which still rings
at curfew. Another was washed overboard on the stormy voyage
across the Firth, and was later dredged up, and hangs in the kirk at
Avoch. Only the south aisle and the chapter-house and sacristy
now remain, in a rich reddish stone, all now in the care of the Department of the Environment, after being excavated and tidied in
1870. The former dates from the late 14th century, with a much
later little bell-tower and steeple. In the main it was built by the
then Euphemia, Countess of Ross, in her own right, whose recumbent effigy still remains. There is excellent groined vaulting above,
and an aumbry and piscina, with a fine font. Herein is also the
burial-place of the Mackenzies of Coul, and sundry of the later
Seaforth family, from Brahan. The doorway in the south wall is
still provided with two deep drawbar sockets, the upper one still
retaining its long timber bar. The chapter-house is a two-storeyed
gabled building standing a little apart, to the east, with its ground
floor a crypt, with ribbed vaulting and an aumbry. There is a small
mural stairway at the west end. Interesting are the large number of
initials carved on the soft sandstone of the interior, some of them
quite finely done, the work of relays of political prisoners in the 17th
century and later, most of them seemingly Mackenzies, when this was
used as a gaol. The upper storey was used as the Town House for a
time. The entry to the cathedral grounds is by a modern war-memorial gateway.

Surrounding this lovely green square are numerous old houses in
gardens, many of them incorporating parts of the clergy manses, of

which there were over a score. The Bishop's Palace has completely gone, but the Dean's House is represented by an attractive, long, two-storeyed and whitewashed building to the south, with a central pend. Parts of those of the Chancellor, Treasurer, Precentor and others are incorporated elsewhere. At the north end of the square is the present Town House, a Georgian building. In the gable of a cottage near by is built in a panel with the initials C.B.S.

The High Street runs north-east and south-west just to the north of the cathedral square, fairly narrow, with shops, hotels, banks and so on. The Established church is at the extreme north-east end, quite large, having a steeple, and much dark woodwork within, with an end gallery. Opposite are the King George V playing-fields. In mid-town a side-road strikes off northwards, to climb over the Black Isle central ridge, by Killen to Culbokie, and the start of this is a street wherein is sited the Town Hall, a former church, containing a collection of Seaforth family portraits from Brahan Castle, and a print of the original Kenneth, the founder of the name of Mackenzie, rescuer of King Alexander; the quite small Free church, of comparatively modern construction, and the masonic lodge behind. In Church Street too, is the modern fire-station.

Further along the High Street, standing on the pavement near the corner of Academy Street, is the shaft of the old Mercat Cross, a simple, octagonal column, its finial missing. The Academy stands down the street of its name, now mainly large modern premises but with the date 1791 on the older part, a quite renowned school, as is fitting for a town which was a seat of learning in divinity, law and medicine, when this was the ecclesiastical capital of one of the most important bishoprics in Scotland. Before reaching the Academy, two churches are to be noted. The Catholic one is not readily discovered, being down an alleyway at the side of a tall, whitewashed 18th century house of some character, with a weatherworn panel. The church tucked in here, is tiny, dedicated to Saints Peter and Boniface—which is apt, for when Curitan or Boniface set up his establishment here, he dedicated it to Peter; indeed the seal of Fortrose depicts these two saints standing side by side. The Episcopal church of St. Andrew is more kenspeckle, further down the street, in a garden, quite large with some good stained-glass, restored and beautified by Canon Spenser Ross (1843-1929). Below this church a winding hill leads down to the harbour, not very large but attractive, the base of the Chanonry Sailing Club. The former harbour-house is now a pleasing private dwelling and antique shop.

On the north side of the town, on the slope which the side-road climbs towards Killen, are three features, amongst the spreading modern housing. Two are ancient wells, in the quite steep bank, the Doupat (a corruption of St. Duthac's) and St. Boniface's. The third is the burial-ground, quite attractive amongst trees, above the town.

The Chanonry Ness and Point area is interesting in itself, as well as an unusual geographical feature. A road, over a mile long, runs down its centre, with the 18-hole golf course flanking it. Towards the town end, a cluster of houses centre around Ness House, a large whitewashed building which was formerly the Black Isle Poorhouse and is now converted into private flats. A little further east, 200 yards north of the road, is a broken pillar, probably part of a mercat-type cross, where allegedly the last witch-burning in Scotland took place—though this has been claimed for elsewhere. Still nearer the Point is a house which was formerly a fishing-station, with its semi-underground ice-house, very large, still close by. Salmon-fishing was important here. At the Point itself is the light-house, still in use, and a jetty, where formerly a ferry plied across to Fort George. The views here are far-flung and very fine. Near by is a memorial cairn, with a plaque in bronze cast by the boys of the Academy in 1969, to commemorate the famous Coinneach Odhar, the Brahan Seer, said to be burned to death in a tar-barrel here, on the orders of the Countess of Seaforth, prophesying the doom of the chiefly Mackenzies. There is considerable doubt about the date of this event—if little about the unhappy fate of the Seaforths—for while it is usually declared that he died at the end of the 17th century, he seems in fact likely to have suffered a century earlier, at the Reformation period, for there was an order sent north from Edin-burgh, in 1577, commanding the magistrates to seize and try him as a leader in the wicked arts of magic. Be that as it may, the boys of Fortrose did a good job—possibly partly to redeem their forerunners of 1638, when, we read, a party of them rushed into church at sermon-time, the Bishop of Ross himself preaching, collected all the prayer-books and took them down to the Ness and burned them (this at the height of the Covenant–Episcopacy troubles). The Bishop seems to have been much upset, for ". . . he was not long-sum but schort at sermon, and thairefter haistellie got to horss and spak with the bischop of Moray, syne spak with the Marques of Huntlie, and privately disgyssit rodde south . . . and durst not for fier of his lyf returne to Scotland again". So much for the schoolboys of Fortrose.

Rosemarkie, so close to Fortrose, is very different. For one thing, it crouches under high and impressive sand and sandstone cliffs, on a raised beach above the Firth, at a sandy shore, and in conse-quence is much more restricted as to space. Just behind lifts the mound known as Court-hill, now built with houses. The little town, no more than a village really, is compact, with an atmosphere of age. The narrow High Street is not long, and is dominated by the parish church, on the south side, in its old graveyard. This is the oldest ecclesiastical site in Ross, where first St. Moluag and then St. Boniface set up their cells. The present church was built in 1821, large, with a tall square battlemented clock-tower, bright and pleas-ant internally, with a U-shaped gallery and a high pulpit with carved pine backing and sounding-board. There are numerous relics pre-served here, including a pewter communion-cup and patten of 1640, two handsome silver cups presented by the Countess of Seaforth in 1686 (now in safe-keeping elsewhere) a mort-bell dated 1727, a sermon hour-glass, communion tokens and a pewter baptismal bowl dated 1742. Also, in the vestry, the old black mort-cloth. Outside, near the door, is a fine Pictish cross-slab, 8½ feet high, showing on one side a small cross and elaborate decoration, and on the other two crescent and V-rod symbols and a double-disc and Z-rod. This could date from Boniface's time, 8th century. The church is built over a vault discovered in 1735, in which were several old stone coffins, one thought possibly to be that of the saint himself. More certainly the famous Sir Andrew Moray was buried here, in 1338, Regent for Bruce's young son, David the Second. There are many old stones in the kirkyard, including a Leslie burial-place, and one dated 1766 erected by Provost Alexander Houston in memory of his family "and of himself".

Near by there is the large Marine Hotel, with over fifty bedrooms, seeming huge for such a small place, and the small Plough Inn, dated 1691. Near the latter, at the north end of the town, and right underneath the high cliff where the jackdaws and rock-pigeons nest, is a pleasant old-world corner of cottages and trees. This is where the main A.832 turns sharply north by west to climb up through a twisting leafy glen, with branches off, down which the Rosemarkie Burn cascades. This is known locally as the Fairy Glen, and is remarkable for its deep chasms, called the Dens, and soaring pinnacles of boulder clay and sandstone, one group known as the Kaes' Craig, all made renowned by Hugh Miller, of Cromarty, in his geological books. There is a major waterfall here also, about a mile up, below the road-end to Eathie.

No road follows the coastline north-east of Rosemarkie, on account of the unbroken wall of cliffs stretching for about 8 miles, all the way to the South Sutor of Cromarty, these cliffs penetrated by numerous caves, some having yielded prehistoric remains. The side-road to Eathie and Navity parallels the shore-line, about a mile inland and some 600–700 feet higher, serving only a few farms, but a highly scenic road with splendid views southwards across the Moray Firth, and some old Scots pines on the sloping moorland. Another mile further on, the A.832 bends north-eastwards also, to follow the same line, but at a slightly lower level now. There is much planted forest, of the great central Millbuie plantations, flanking both these parallel roads, but few other features—save for the tall T.V. mast and other futuristic devices of the B.B.C. Transmitting and G.P.O. Radio Stations at Craighead on the highest portion of the lesser road. Eathie has its interests 5 miles along this road, but is more suitably dealt with under Cromarty, although in Rosemarkie parish—which is a very oddly boot-shaped one.

Where the A.832 makes its abrupt turn to the north-east, to Cromarty, almost 2 miles above Rosemarkie, the B.9160 carries straight on over the Black Isle ridge, to Resolis and Balblair, at the Raddery area. Here there is a sort of high but open hanging valley, with scattered farms, an old lairdship, with Raddery House, partly 18th century, now a home for backward boys. All this top end of the parish around the 500–600 foot contour, is covered in the vast extent of the Millbuie Forest.

Rosemarkie used to be a noted centre of the salmon-netting industry, with ice-houses for the preservation of the fish, and the farmservants complaining of getting too much salmon in their diet.

Invergordon and Rosskeen. The name of Invergordon is surprisingly well-known, considering the place's size, position and history. Vast numbers of people who have never been near it must know of it, and this over a fairly long period—even though it only received its present name in the early 18th century. For, although it became a burgh in 1864, it developed into a famous naval base only in the First World War, thanks to the magnificent deep-water anchorage provided by the Cromarty Firth, and now, of course, although the Navy has largely gone, for the same reason it is blossoming anew as the site of large industrialisation, with its great aluminium smelter and all the oil-rig development consequent on the discovery of North Sea oil. Nevertheless, it is not so very large a place, even by North of Scotland standards. Its population is growing, but not so greatly, owing to the planning policy of siting the housing for all the incoming people, not at Invergordon itself so much as at Alness, 3 miles to the west. In 1841 the population was 1000; in 1914, 1050; in 1964, 1685; in 1969, 2074. Today it may be 3000. Not very large for so kenspeckle a place.

It lies at a point, mid-way up the Cromarty Firth, where the firth narrows drastically, yet the deep water comes very close to the shore. It is claimed, indeed, that this is the finest deepwater anchorage in Europe. Now that lengthy jetties thrust out, the largest ships can tie up here, very close in, and when the Navy no longer required these facilities, the British Aluminium Company saw its opportunity, for its bulk ore-carriers, and took it, investing £37 million is a huge smelter complex, with more to follow, and offering some 600 jobs. Now the oil consortiums and the engineering firms are moving into the Cromarty Firth also, and the area is becoming a very atypical part of the North, with necessarily large numbers of outsiders coming to man the new projects. But Invergordon has been absorbing newcomers for a long time, and will no doubt manage to retain something of its former sturdy character. A new Cromarty Firth Port Authority is to be set up, to regulate all this expansion.

It was never really typical of the Highland area or Easter Ross, of course. Until the 18th century it was known as An Rudha, The Point, when Sir William Gordon purchased the estate of Inverbreakie Castle here, and things began to change. He was a Member of Parliament and a man of drive and vision. He laid out the plans for his town, to be called after himself in 18th century paternalistic fashion. His son, Sir John, also a politician, indeed Secretary of State for Scotland, carried on the good work, and was the real builder of the town. Later it passed to the Macleods of Cadboll, and it was under their auspices that the harbour was built in 1828, this being extended in 1857 at then great cost, as a flourishing port grew up, exporting timber, farming products, ropes and whisky—for this has long been a great distilling area. Inverbreakie, or Invergordon Castle was destroyed by fire in 1801, but a large Tudor-style mansion was erected on the site in 1873. This in turn was demolished in 1928, and now what is called the House of Rosskeen reigns in its stead. But all around rise the great industrial establishments, the fuel-tanks, workshops, factories and warehouses—and of course the vast smelter complex, dominating all, on its 400-acre site to the north-east of the town.

Invergordon consists mainly of a long and broad High Street, extending for almost a mile, cutting off the base of the Point headland, with most of the earlier development seaward, and the later landward, across the railway line which runs through the burgh, the station, towards the west end, still in use. The High Street is much less cluttered than many, and is enhanced with planted trees. It is a good shopping-centre, with offices, banks, hotels and so on. A drinking-fountain at the west end commemorates the visit of King Edward the Seventh in 1902. St. Joseph's Catholic church, small and modern, stands near the station entrance. The Town Hall dates from 1870 and is in the Italian style, its pediment displaying a sculpture of Neptune. There is not much of architectural distinction here, but this is scarcely to be looked for. The Established church, however is rather fine, a tall Gothic building of 1885, with high steeple and clock, standing to the north of the town, over the railway. Beyond it is the very modern and large Invergordon Academy, in its playing-fields. Unfortunately the serried ranks of great brick-sleeved naval fuel-tanks are an eyesore hereabouts, but some at least are being demolished. The golf course, of 9 holes, lies in an attractive position, with fine views, to the west, with many old trees. There are facilities for tennis, bowling, football, rugby and cricket—as well of course, as angling, both sea and river. There is a boating-club, and the firth makes an ideal yachting water.

The old harbour of Invergordon is now mainly devoted to pleasure boating, with a boatyard near by. But the long jetties which thrust out into the firth are seldom without large ships tied thereto, their great bulk tending to dominate the water-front. The extraordinary access-jetty and conveyor-system for the B.A.C. plant catches all eyes here, with its gleaming overhead corridor conveying the alumina ore from ship to smelter completely automatically on an endless-chain system. 3500 tons of steel went into the building of the £1,200,000 Deep Water Berth, which extends 3400 feet out into the firth, a notable engineering feat by the Edmund Nuttall firm. Despite all this modernity, however, there are still a number of attractive old cottages in this harbour area.

A rather fine war-memorial stands at the road-junction at the east end of the town. A little further on is the little corrugated-iron Episcopal church of St. Ninian. Beyond this are the large modern premises of the Invergordon Distillery, with extensive warehouses, quite a recent development, making grain whisky for blending. There is also the Ben Wyvis Distillery, providing Highland malt whisky. Further still, now on the outskirts, is the quite large County Hospital. An esplanade runs along the sea-front at this end, and here is the swimming-pool.

The smelter complex lies inland here, behind modern housing, not beautiful but a stirring sight nevertheless in this green and fair countryside. This is the Inverbreakie site, where the Gordons first settled. There are four parallel main cellroom buildings in the central block, with six tall chimneys, a casting shop, maintenance buildings, process stores and cell-repair shops. Also carbon plant, gas-storage, alumina silos and so on. The processes use an enormous amount of electricity, supplied by the grid, as much as the entire city of Dundee for instance. The output of aluminium is around 100,000 tons per annum, sheet, bars, sections and foil. Near by is a large factory for the treating and preparation of oil pipes.

Strung out along the coast still further east is the former village of Saltburn with many cottages and quite pleasing in appearance. The Rosskeen parish boundary with Kilmuir Easter is here, that parish, with Barbaraville described separately.

Most of Rosskeen parish has been described under Alness and Ardross. But the area immediately to the west of Invergordon contains the actual location of that name, as distinct from its very large parish area of 34,000 acres. Just over a mile along the A.9 westwards, beyond the golf course, a side-road strikes off, away from the shore and under a railway-bridge, and just beyond is the former parish church of Rosskeen in its old graveyard. This has been a very large and ambitious if somewhat ugly building, of 1832, beside the remains of an earlier church. It was seated for 1600, but now its box-pews are the haunt of pigeons, for it is abandoned and in very delapidated condition. There are many plaques to the Macleods of Cadboll, superiors here up to 1945. The first Provost of the burgh was one of them. The kirkyard is interesting however. Part of the earlier church is now a burial-enclosure, with moulded doorway and Latin inscription, dated 1675, with its fine, small three-light windows. There is a separate red-stone mausoleum for the Munro family of Newmore and Culrain, rather fine, erected in 1664 and restored 1908. Still another enclosure, for the Mackenzies of Kincraig, has also a 17th century moulded doorway with inscription. There are many old tombstones, mainly moss-grown—as well as modern ones, for the cemetery is still in use, with a large extension. Outside the main gate is a louping-on stone, for horse-mounting. Half a mile west of the church, close to the main road, is a small single standing-stone, known as the Thief's Stone, in a field of Rosskeen farm. It has the representation of a pair of tongs carved on it, presumably Pictish.

Behind this main-road area and the golf course, but more readily reached from the road going north through the town, past a large

housing scheme, is the estate of House of Rosskeen, with its comparatively modern mansion in fine policies. The farm lies almost a mile
to the west. At the entry to the grounds, in a small flower-garden, is
a memorial to the Polish forces billeted here during the last war,
with a later renewal to commemorate the millennium of Christianity
in Poland 966–1966, dedicated by the Bishop of Aberdeen. Still
further back from the coast at a cross-roads on the B.817 a mile north
of the abandoned parish church, is the Free church of Rosskeen,
large and gaunt, with a tall steeple, quite a landmark in its rural
isolation, rather dull inside with a U-shaped gallery. And a mile to
the east of this, towards Tain, is Kincraig House, the former Mackenzie mansion, large, whitewashed and distinctly Victorian Scottish
Baronial. At the next crossroads, where there is the large farm of
Tomich with associated cottages, a side-road strikes northwards to
the school and large quarry-workings of Rhicullen, near the Kilmuir
Easter border.

Some account of Invergordon should not end without reference to
its Highland Gathering, held each August, and considered to be one
of the premier meetings of its kind in the professional games circuit,
always attracting large crowds, with competitors coming from far
and near. The pipe-band contest and march-past is probably the
high-spot.

Kessock, Charlestown and Kilmuir-Wester. This part of
the large Knockbain civil parish constitutes the extreme south-
eastern corner of the Black Isle peninsula, and is most conveniently
described separately from the northern part of that parish, centring
on Munlochy. Kessock is well known as the northern terminal of
the regular ferry from Inverness, and is usually called North Kessock
to distinguish it from the Inverness terminal, but of course attaching
the name to the southern side is a modern misnomer, and Kessock
is in fact a district of the Black Isle as well as the terminal village,
with a Glack of Kessock, or little pass, and a Forest of Kessock.
Charlestown is another village near by to the west, also on the coast
—but this has grown of recent years to such an extent that it now
almost merges with Kessock, and is indeed the larger entity. Kilmuir
is likewise on the coast but very different, a former parish, with an
isolated, small, old-world village, quite difficult to reach, beyond
Craigton Point to the north-east.

Kessock—the name derives from St. Kessog, a Celtic missionary—
is not very large, but growing, since it is so convenient for Inverness
folk, across half a mile of narrows, where the Moray and Beauly
Firths join. And it will grow much more, for a bridge is to be built,
which will make this area little more than suburban to the Highland
capital. Meantime there is an excellent half-hourly ferry-service, and
many commuters use it daily. The pier was built at the personal
expense of Sir William Fettes (1750–1836), an Edinburgh man,
founder of the famous Fettes College there, who owned the estate of
Easter Kessock. Near the pier and terminal is a large modern

Community Hall, on the sea-front. A licensed hotel is close by, and several guest-houses, a post-office, shops and a long quite pleasant village stretching along the shore eastwards, with fine prospects scenically. The church is rather odd, part of the Knockbain parish entity, which was contrived in 1756 out of the pre-Reformation parishes of Kilmuir-Wester and Suddie, the main place of worship being near Munlochy. This Kessock church occupies the upper flat of an ordinary old village house on the street, and is now used for evening services and Sunday-school. The ordinary school for Kessock is inconveniently placed for present-day requirements, being sited more than a mile inland, up a winding side-road on the way to Kilmuir, amongst green foothills on the edge of Kessock Forest, pleasant scenically.

Charlestown has been a fishing-village, and some of the typical old low-browed cottages, gable-end to the street, still survive amongst the burgeoning modern housing and villas, all quite attractive. The nearby property of Bellfield, or Wester Kessock, had Mackenzie lairds—like so much else hereabouts—and presumably the name of Charles commemorates one of these. Half a mile beyond Charlestown is the parish boundary with Killearnan, and along here is the Black Isle Boating Centre and restaurant—but this is described under Killearnan.

The road to Kilmuir—properly Kilmuir-Wester to distinguish it from Kilmuir-Easter parish in the Delny area of Ross (though Kilmuir-to-the-South would be more apt)—is a long and winding one, taking between 4 and 5 miles to reach the village which is only 1½ miles as the crow flies from Kessock, rising and falling 300 feet in the process, round the back of Ord Hill and threading Kessock Forest. Half-way there, in a hanging valley less than half a mile from the sea but 400 feet above it, is little Loch Lundie, with a prehistoric earthwork or fort on the wooded hilltop above. Further east along this same ridge is another early enclosure, with hut-circles, also covered in woodland. There is a story that the farmer of nearby Taindore (Tigh an Druidh—the house of the Druids or sorcerers) removed the Basin-stone from the eastmost circle, presumably a font-stone, to his farm, but had to return it because of the bellowing of his cows and barking of dogs.

The road winds downhill, and reaches the ruined former parish church of Kilmuir, in its still-used graveyard beside a farm, on an interesting terrace site high above the sea. The church, as the name suggests, dedicated to the Virgin Mary, has long been abandoned, but it retains at its eastern end the burial vault of the Grahams of Drynie, with the gable still showing a three-light lancet-type window. There are some interesting memorials in the Graham vault, one an early heraldic stone, and another pathetically commemorating "Georges Alexandre Graham de Drynie, Comte de Ross en Ecosse . . ." born in Paris 1840 and died the next year. We read in the second Statistical Account that the Grahams of Drynie lived in France. Yet they seem to have brought this mite home to the Black

Isle for burial. There are many old flat stones in the kirkyard, amongst more modern ones.

No track continues north-eastwards along the cliffs and shoreline, but the road swings sharply southwards, and descends in half a mile to the coast-side small village, now rather decayed but very picturesque, the cottages in their gardens crouching under the high hanging woods, distinctly West Highland in atmosphere. The road ends here. On wooded Ord Hill which reaches 633 feet above, to the south-west, is a vitrified fort.

Back up past the Lundie valley, the road sends off a fork to the right, which in time brings one to Mains of Drynie, where there is a quite imposing large farmhouse, Georgian with pavilion extensions, the former Graham home. Behind, to the north, is the long hog's-back ridge of Drumderfit Hill, this one unwooded, dotted with cairns, and with the site of a former dun, or Pictish castle. Drumderfit could mean the Ridge of Tears, and there are claims that here was fought the renowned battle between followers of the Lord of the Isles and Inverness citizens, in approximately 1400, which the latter won by the expedient of making a strategic retreat and leaving behind a great quantity of liquor—which the temporary victors duly quaffed, became incapable and were comfortably demolished by the returning Invernessians, led by their provost. There may be some confusion here, for there is another battle-site very close, to the south-west, marked on the Ordnance map on the *west* side of the road to Munlochy, on much lower ground. This presumably is the site known as Blair-na-Coi, *cumha* meaning lamentation, which battle, again with the MacDonalds, is said to have taken place in 1340. It seems unlikely that there were two such battlefields so close together, and tradition may be erring a little. On the other hand, this entire period was one of anarchy in Scotland, with a succession of weak kings after Bruce, and the Lords of the Isles seeking to dominate all Highland Scotland.

A mile to the west, as the crow flies, but off the larger B.9161 road to Munlochy, in an isolated position, stands the quite large Free church of the area, at Allanglachwood, red stone with a spire, pleasantly set at the edge of forest in a quiet valley. Artafallie post-office and store further south serves a very scattered community.

Kildary and Logie-Easter. Logie-Easter is one of those quite large civil parishes—in this case of 10,000 acres—which seem to have little real identity, as such, with no village of the name. Logie-Easter might be anywhere—for Logie is one of the commonest place-names in Scotland, *logaidh* meaning merely a hollow. This parish lies on the east side of the Balnagown River from Kilmuir-Easter, in entirely rural country—which, however, is now under threat of development from the burgeoning oil industry—and immediately south of Tain parish, at the neck of the Nigg–Fearn peninsula. The fairly modern community of Kildary is its only village, if so it can be called—though some of the Kildary area is over in

Kilmuir-Easter. The attractive old Ross estates of Shandwick and Calrossie are in this parish, to the east, and the great woodlands of Scotsburn on the high ground to the north.

There is, oddly enough, a plethora of churches, mostly abandoned. The present parish church stands on a bank, at a bend in the A.9 highway, a mile north of Kildary, where a side-road strikes coastwards. It is a quite pleasant, low-set building in pink stone, not old, with a belfry—and was, no doubt, formerly a Free church. Across the road is the war-memorial. Its predecessor is now abandoned, though the graveyard surrounding it is still in use, and stands about a quarter of a mile due north, on another side-road—in sight, in fact. This is a rather ugly edifice of the early 19th century, its windows now boarded up. The only item of interest evident is the former clock, on a sham belfry, the figures for the hours of which are actually engraved on the red stone dial, although the hands have gone. There are no particularly interesting or ancient stones in the kirkyard. The really ancient parish church lay a considerable distance away, almost 2 miles to the west, in a secluded dell or hollow (possibly the Logie of the name) on the north bank of the Balnagown River, reached now only by a farm-track, in the Marybank area, with a walk down through fields required. Here, amongst the cattle pastures, are two gables of a T-shaped building, with thick walling, corbels for the support of an upper floor still projecting, seemingly of the 17th century, though with possibly earlier work also. The reed-grown graveyard is enclosed by an unusual wide embankment of boulders and turf, rather than a normal wall, and may have been something of a defence against the river's spates. There are a number of old flat tombstones buried under grass and moss, none with dates decipherable. The countryside here is picturesque, markedly rough, with woodland and heather and some pasture, for so comparatively low-lying an area. Marybank farm here has now a modern ranch-type house. But Marybank Lodge, a quarter-mile to the east, is a most pleasing pink-washed late 17th century small laird's house, with crowstepped gables, steep roofs, a gablet and other typical features, allegedly on the site of a pre-Reformation religious establishment—hence the name. Another quarter-mile south-east of Marybank, off another side-road, is still one more ruined church, this time lost amongst the heather and rioting broom-bushes, and very hard to find. It is completely featureless, though quite substantial, with fairly thick walling, apparently of no great age, and giving the impression of a Free church of some sort. One last church, Free indeed, and built of corrugated-iron, stands further down this same road, opposite a little used entrance to the Balnagown Castle estate. The reason for all this proliferation of places of worship in a notably under-populated district, is not obvious. Across the road from this is a large sand-and-gravel works, and beyond it is a small loch, near Logie Hill.

Kildary—pronounced with the accent on the first syllable—is a modern housing scheme on a small scale, rather than a village, with a post-office—also, oddly, a large used-car saleroom—and lies on the main A.9 at the foot of this side-road, and not far from the main entrance to Balnagown. The river here is the parish boundary.

Back at the existing parish church, a mile east, a drive heads south-eastwards into the fine wooded policies of Shandwick House, an ancient Ross lairdship, still in the hands of descendants of the old lairds. It is from the Shandwick line that the present 35th chief of Clan Ross descends. The dignified stone mansion, on a pleasant site with fine vistas, dates only from 1936. It contains interesting items, including family portraits. The older mansion stands some distance to the north, of the 18th and 19th centuries, but with an older nucleus, what may be a shot-hole opening in the semi-circular stair-tower at the rear. It is now no longer occupied.

A quite large and modern school stands on the A.9 about a mile north-east of the church, in open country and very flat, the height above sea-level—or Nigg Bay level—being only 40 feet. Another 2 miles on is Calrossie, the other former Ross property, from 1709, near the closed Fearn Station—an area which has been mentioned in connection with industrial or housing development. The present mansion is not exceptional in any way, but the woodlands are very attractive, beeches predominating in the policies, mixed birch and pines growing out of heather, outside.

To the north and west of this parish is the Lamington and Scots-burn area, on quite suddenly much higher ground, the Scotsburn ridge reaching 826 feet, and most of it heavily forested. There are cairns here. The quite sudden and, as it were, hidden Glen of Scotsburn to the north being rather an interesting formation, guarded at its south-west end by the fine and unfinished Pictish fort of Cnoc an Duin, and with the remote St. George's Well—an odd dedication for Scotland—at its north-east end. The Lamington crofting area, just to the south, is one more on which the developers have cast their eyes. With the parish running down to Nigg Bay, it may well be that, in time to come, Logie-Easter will be notable for more than churches.

Killearnan, Kilcoy and Tore. Killearnan is an irregularly shaped parish of the Black Isle, 8000 acres in extent, lying at the south-west extremity of that great peninsula. Its coast runs along the north side of the Beauly Firth for 6 miles, and it reaches up to the Millbuie central ridge, around the 500-foot contour, at its north-ernmost point. Kilcoy is a central district, with a 17th century castle and a hamlet, also a scattered planted forest of the name. And Tore is the only village, although there is another hamlet at Milton, near the parish church. The large estate of Redcastle covers much of the area on the south.

The church is the parish centre only very nominally, for it is situated highly inconveniently for most of the not very large popula-tion—though convenient enough for the one-time laird of Redcastle. It stands on the coast, near the south-west end of the parish, in an isolated position half a mile from the Milton and more than 3 miles from the village of Tore. The red-stone building in its tree-girt kirkyard has a pleasing situation scenically, and is a long, plain, cruciform building, dating from 1450, renewed in 1800 and restored again in 1891. There is an early arched doorway built-up in the south front, with a very weather-worn memorial to the right. Also an empty panel-space on the north transept outer wall. But the main feature of interest is inside, where, at the west end, is preserved a highly unusual recumbent effigy, only about 3½ feet long, and half the size of most, possibly representing a child. The present writer has never seen the like elsewhere. The bell dates from 1676. In the kirkyard are a great many old flat stones so grass-grown as to be barely discernible. The Mackenzie of Kilcoy burial-place is here. The manse near by is large and whitewashed.

Milton hamlet lies to the east, also on the coast, with the little school between. It is a picturesque small place, evidently dependent on the large Redcastle estate which adjoins, old-fashioned, with the shore-road making an abrupt bend through it, where there is an 18th century coachhouse range for the castle. Redcastle, once called Edradour, represents a strange contradiction. For this is a fine and prosperous estate, in good order, belonging to Lord Burton. Yet its large and historic castle is tumbling in ruin and utter neglect. This is the more unfortunate in that the building is particularly interesting. Included in the 16th and 17th century work is the nucleus of the very early castle of Edradour, for which claims have been made that it was the oldest inhabited house in Scotland. This is no longer so, if it ever was—for nothing here seems to date from so early as 1179, when William the Lion's brother, David Earl of Huntingdon, built the first Edradour. The castle, approximately L-shaped, is built to correspond with the contours of the site on the lip of a ravine. The oldest parts are the lower vaulted basements to west and south, with exceedingly thick walling. Above is mainly 16th century work, the gables being surmounted by angle-turrets on elaborate corbelling, well supplied with shot-holes. The 17th century extensions are to the north, with a round and a square tower projecting, and dated 1641, with Mackenzie initials. Collapsing masonry makes a sad picture, but much could yet be saved. Edradour was in Bisset hands by 1230, the local family on whose foundations the Frasers rose to power in the North. The Douglases gained possession for a while, and this property fell to a brother of the famous 8th Earl—whom James the Second stabbed to death at Stirling—and who was created Earl of Ormond and Lord Edradour. On the Douglas fall, all this Black Isle area was annexed to the Crown. It was gained by the Mackenzies, so powerful hereabouts, in 1570, and held till 1790. So much of the present building is Mackenzie work. Presumably they changed the name to Redcastle—and the stone is certainly red enough. It passed to the Baillies of Dochfour, of whom comes Lord Burton. Perhaps traces of the old curse linger here. The story is that, in the 18th century, the estates of Redcastle and Kilcoy were suffering much from a cattle plague, and the lairds agreed with a local sorcerer to cure it—at the price of a human sacrifice. A friendless vagrant was captured, and disembowelled alive before the wizard— but cursing the lairds, to the effect that the day would never come when the family of Redcastle would be without a female idiot and that of Kilcoy without a fool. Redcastle was occupied by troops during the Second World War, when no doubt its fall began.

The narrow but scenic coast-road fringes this estate eastwards for a long way, and in 4 miles crosses into Knockbain parish near Charlestown and North Kessock. This road has markedly few houses, but at Coulmore 5 miles along, where there is a small estate, is the interesting modern development of the Black Isle Boating Centre with its Anchor-and-Chain Restaurant, a very attractive establish- ment, with jetty, sports centre, small swimming-pool, and minor yacht-chandlery shop. There is a caravan-park near by. The pros- pects here are very fair.

This is at the eastmost extremity of the oddly shaped parish. More central, and a mile inland from the Milton, is Newton, at a crossroads on the A.832, and here is the large Free church, rather gaunt, with belfry, and the parish war-memorial opposite. There is a farm called Chapelton near by, so presumably there was once a much earlier church hereabouts. Half a mile northwards is a hamlet, at the former Kilcoy Station, with a hall. Also Kilcoy Mill. The castle of Kilcoy stands to the west half a mile—in a much happier state than Redcastle, despite the curse. For though it was empty and somewhat decayed a few years ago, it is now restored, occupied and in excellent order, a very handsome example of early 17th century fortalice, quite large, built on the Z-plan. Circular towers project at the north-west and south-east angles of the main block, the latter corbelled out to the square to form a gabled watch-chamber. Angle- and stair-turrets further enhance the aspect, and notable are tne two very fine decorative dormer windows. There are many gun- loops and shot-holes, also richly carved gargoyle spouts. A feature of the interior is the Hall fireplace, dated 1679 and carved heraldic- ally for Mackenzie, with the addition of mermaids playing harps and a greyhound and hare. Kilcoy was built in 1618 by Alexander Mackenzie, fourth son of the 11th chief of Kintail, the family later gaining a baronetcy, now extinct.

Half a mile above the castle are three of the many chambered cairns of this area, which was obviously heavily populated in pre- historic times. In one was found, in 1908, a Bronze Age burial with urn. Another mile north-westwards, at the farm of Carnurnan, in its garden, is another good cairn of three concentric rings of stones, showing seven, thirty-one and twelve uprights. The name is said to be a corruption of St. Iturnan or Irenan, allegedly a nephew of St. Columba—from whom presumably the parish takes its name. He is said to have been murdered here—though of course the cairn is greatly earlier. The views from this ridge are magnificent.

East of the Kilcoy area, along the B.9162 from Conon Bridge, lies the crofting district of Muckernish. And at this road's junction with the main A.832 Black Isle highway, is the village of Tore. It is quite small, with an inn and a school, and, down the road towards Kessock, southwards, a modern cemetery designed to serve a number of rural areas. There is another chambered cairn a mile to the east of Tore. The country hereabouts is very pleasant, with wide prospects, much forestry and natural woodland, and always the firth and mountain backgrounds.

Kilmuir-Easter, Barbaraville and Balnagown. Kilmuir-Easter is a medium-sized civil parish of some 10,000 acres, shaped like a long triangle, with its base on the Cromarty Firth just east of Invergordon and its tip high in the hills of Strathrory. Its largest community is now Barbaraville, on the coast, but older than that is the attractive village of Milton, really Milntown of Tarbat, to the east. The Delny area lies inland from Barbaraville. Balnagown Castle, formerly the seat of the chiefs of Clan Ross, stands at the eastern border, and Tarbat House, once seat of the Mackenzies of Cromartie, near Milton. These two great properties once dominated the district—but those days are past. The Strathrory area to the north-west is all but empty hill and moorland.

The parish church, with the school beside it, stands in an isolated position just back from the shore midway between Barbaraville and Milton, on the A.9. The church, on a mound in its old graveyard, in open, treeless country, is plain, save for an extraordinary circular 17th century tower at a burial-vault at the east end, with corbelled belfry having a stone conical roof and tiny dormer windows, somewhat similar to that at Kirkhill in Inverness-shire. There is an eagle's head crest, the legend "G.M.R. beigit 1616"; and on the other side worn heraldry and the initials M.D. It is an unusual and attractive feature, linked with the family of Munro. The base of the tower may be considerably older. The remainder of the church dates from 1798. There is said to be a mort-bell dated 1696, but the church is kept locked and this was not verified. There are many 18th century tombstones here. A modern cemetery adjoins. The church used to be dedicated to the Virgin—hence the name of Kilmuir, Mhuire meaning Mary.

Milton village lies a mile to the north-east, fortunately bypassed by the A.9, and is a tranquil and sequestered old-world place amongst trees. It is quite small now, although growing again, with some modern housing, but it was much larger once, for here were held four annual cattle markets. It presumably was a burgh of barony for Tarbat House, for its mercat cross still stands in the middle of its small green, with octagonal shaft and ball finial, inscribed "Cromartie 1799". Amongst the pleasing scatter of cottages is the old mill, mentioned as early as the 14th century, still with its wheel though no longer working as such. Also an old drovers' inn, abandoned but rather fine, which surely ought to be restored, in this day of burgeoning development in this area. The small present inn is

333

near by. There is a tiny church, just a converted cottage, of 1862, at the back of the old inn, still used once a month. It is all very picturesque.

The entrance to Tarbat House policies is close by, the former seat of the Mackenzies of Cromartie—indeed whence they derived their first peerage title of Viscount of Tarbat, of 1685. The holder of this was the well-known Sir George, later first Earl of Cromartie. His grandfather, equally famous, was the Tutor of Kintail, Sir Rory Mackenzie of Tarbat, of whom its was said that " . . . there are two things worse than the Tutor of Kintail—frost in Spring and mist in the dog-days". Tarbat House, large and massive, an Adam-style house of 1787, is now standing shut up and empty, though there are said to be plans for its rehabilitation. There are modern houses in the fine wooded policies. An earlier castle of the Mackenzies stood on the site.

At the other side of the parish church, a mile westwards along the A.9 is Barbaraville. Old gazetteers refer to this as Bartaraville, but the reasons for this odd name escape the writer. It dates from 1825 and is quite a lengthy village stretched along the highway just a little back from the coast, with it most attractive part shorewards, small lanes with many cottages, old and new. There is a post-office but no church. To the east is the very modern Jackdaw Hotel, built in 1970 in box-type architecture, but quite large, with twenty bedrooms and a restaurant. A mile further west, and near the Ross-keen parish boundary, is the former little port and fishing station of Portlich, near Balintraid. This harbour was constructed by Thomas Telford in 1817, but is now abandoned. It used to export grain and timber and import coal. There is a rather attractive row of cottages here still, beside the former warehouse; but the main part of the small community of Balintraid lies inland a little, half a mile to the west.

From Barbaraville a side-road goes inland from the A.9 to link with the B.817 at Delny, less than a mile. It passes the former railway-station and present level-crossing of that name, and here is a large warehouse development for an American company, for oil-rig equipment. A little further is a fairly large Free church of 1875, in so-called French Gothic, at a crossroads. And nearby Delny House, a far-from-beautiful "castellated" mansion of 1893, successor of a former seat of the Earls of Ross. East of Delny 2 miles is the Kildary area, which is somewhat extended, the more populous part of it in Logie-Easter parish, and dealt with thereunder—though Kildary House and former railway-station are in this parish. The Balnagown River, which is the boundary, is here crossed by the main road and by a lofty railway viaduct.

Balnagown Castle lies this side of the river, in a large estate. It is a famous name, for the Rosses of Balnagown were the chiefs of that clan—even though the castle, in 1711, passed to another family of Ross who were unconnected with the Highland clan. The building has fallen on sad days however, and was for a considerable period little used. Now it has been taken over by developers, allegedly for an Arabian oil magnate—and in the process what was left of its original character largely lost. It was never really a fine example of our castellated heritage—and is less so now, with stucco finish in sham, parti-coloured stone treatment, and drastic alteration within and without. Most of the building dated from the 18th and 19th centuries anyway, although there is a 15th century nucleus, now mainly represented by the thick-walled vaulted basements. The western front, with its crowstepped gables and slender stair-towers is probably the best feature remaining, but probably the less said about the architecture of this renowned house, the better. Whether certain internal features, such as the Wallace Chair and the fireplace lintel from Meikle Daan, dated 1680, have survived, remains to be seen when present alterations are finished. An ancient picture of Balna-gown shows a fairly simple and authentic L-shaped structure with a stair-turret in the re-entrant angle. The castle's history has been exciting, for the Rosses were a lively lot, though not necessarily good neighbours. The first of Balnagown was Hugh, half-brother of the last Earl of Ross, in 1372. Alexander, 8th laird, in particular worried the Privy Council in that he kept the countryside in terror, and, more important, prevented sundry important Crown tenants from paying their rents because they were so "herreit and wrakkit" by Ross of Balnagown—this in 1569. By 1632 the Rosses could field 1000 armed men. On the death of the 18th chief, in 1711, without direct heir, the estates were acquired by descendants of the de Roos Norman family, called Ross, from Renfrewshire, and their descend-ants long retained possession.

The Balnagown River is an attractive one, and is crossed in the policies by a hump-backed but graceful single arch known as the King James Bridge, probably of the 18th century. Further up, the river bends away westwards and in its upper reaches is known as the Strathrory River. The road up follows the eastern bank, in Logie-Easter parish, and is dealt with thereunder. Strathrory itself is a high open valley of no great length, crossed in its upper stretch by the A.836 Struie Hill highway, but otherwise practically empty. Here is a double-arch bridge in bare heathery country. The strath contains the half-mile-long narrow Loch Sheilan. Kinrive Hill (1063 feet) guards its mouth, to the south, and on the long ridge of this are many burial-cairns, as mentioned under Alness and Ardross.

Muir of Ord. Muir of Ord today is the lengthy and not very picturesque village, or extensive community, flanking the main A.9 highway for over a mile, 2 miles north of Beauly, and just over the Ross boundary therefrom, a place busy with traffic and some in-dustry. It centres round an important road-junction, where the A.832 to Garve, Achnasheen and the North-West Highland sea-board branches off in that direction, and its south-eastern continua-tion heads into the Black Isle, for Fortrose and Cromarty. Besides these, lesser roads leave the A.9 in other directions, to serve the crofting areas surrounding. The place is a vital communications hub therefore, and, occupying an extensive area of flat and lowish-lying ground—the moor implicit in the name—has attracted commercial exploitation, not all of it beautiful. Yet it lies in the midst of an attractive countryside, and makes a good centre for exploring a wide and scenic territory. It was long important as the scene of seven great annual fairs or cattle markets—for this was a drove-road junction also. Here, later, was built up the large Duncan Logan contracting and civil engineering complex, which unfortunately suffered a collapse. On its far-flung site has now grown up an industrial estate, run by the Highlands and Islands Development Board. At Muir of Ord is the Information Office of the East Ross and Black Isle Tourist Organisation.

The centre of the village clusters round the multiple cross-roads, with the railway-station near by. Here are the shops and offices, two churches, Established called Urray West, and Free—not the parish church, which is at Urray and dealt with separately, since that parish is very large—the school, hall and so on. Much modern housing lies to the north-west, along the road to Ord itself, which is something of a separate entity, not a village, centred round the large Ord Distillery, dating from 1838, where another side-road strikes off for the valley of the Orrin. Ord House is here, a tall, harled and whitewashed mansion of 1830, incorporating an older nucleus, displaying a fairly modern panel dated 1637. It is now a hotel, with a pond in front, but was the seat of a quite important branch of the great clan of Mackenzie, so strong in this area.

The A.9 runs dead straight, south over the moor for 2 miles, from the village centre, parallel with the railway. To the west of both, less than half a mile along, is the gorse-grown mound which is the site of the Castle-hill. Presumably this was an early Mackenzie stronghold. Not far along, on the east side of the road, is the very modern old folks' home known as Urray House. Then extends the industrial estate area on the east, and the 18-hole golf course on the west. Slightly over a mile southwards, the B.9169 branches off north-eastwards into the Black Isle, and along this half a mile, a farm-road leads to the interesting feature of Kilchrist, or *Cille Chriosd*, once the parish church of a pre-Reformation parish, later incorporated in Urray. The church, restored as a mausoleum of the Ord Mackenzies, is still there, in the midst of an old graveyard— which is still in use. The building is now distinctly neglected, but contains, as well as many graveslabs and memorials, a piscina and an aumbry. The doorway retains its deep draw-bar socket. In the kirkyard are numerous old flat and moss-covered stones which might well repay uncovering. This church was the scene of a savage interlude in clan warfare when, in 1603, the entire congregation of Mackenzies was locked in during service by a force of Glengarry MacDonells, and burned to death, while a piper paraded round the building, playing to drown the screams of the unfortunates inside. The air he played became the family-tune of the chiefs of Glengarry, and is indeed called "Kilchrist"—one of the less picturesque aspects of our Highland heritage.

Half a mile south of this B.9169 road-end is the Inverness-shire county boundary, and just before it is reached, two standing-stones rise on either side of the A.9, close to Wyndhill caravan-site. Local tradition ascribes these to one more incident in clan warfare, but they are, of course, of far earlier origin, typical prehistoric monoliths. The Brahan Seer prophesied over one that "the raven will drink its fill of Mackenzie blood for three days". This seems to be one of his less probable prognostications—if it was made *after* the 1603 massacre. But fair if he died in 1577. However, he did also declare here, that "soldiers will come from the Muir of Ord on a chariot without horse or bridle". The railway, close by, has fulfilled that.

Due north of Muir of Ord village, the A.9, proceeding towards Conon Bridge, passes Chapelton, where a modern house has been contrived out of a former Episcopal chapel, with its metal cross still surmounting. A little further, on the right, in trees, is the later Episcopal church, now abandoned in disuse. Highfield Cottage, a pleasant low-set white house stands on the edge of the former large estate of the Highfield mansion, now gone. A standing-stone is marked here on the Ordnance map, but could not be discovered by the present writer, amongst rioting vegetation. The area to the east, on the moors of Tarradale and Conon, is rich in chambered cairns and other signs of ancient habitation.

Tarradale district itself lies east by south 2 miles, level farmlands on the shore of the Beauly Firth. Here is Tarradale House, a red-stone mansion with an 18th century nucleus, now a field-centre for Aberdeen University. Here was born, in 1792, Sir Roderick Murchison, the celebrated geologist. Near by, at Mains of Tarradale farm, is an interesting steading, also of the 18th century, featuring an octagonal doocot with an ogee-roof above its arched entrance.

The area to the south-west of Muir of Ord is very different from the rest, being a picturesque woodland and crofting country of scattered small farms dotted far and wide amongst the braes, with fine views eastwards over the Beauly Firth and Black Isle. This is the Corry of Ardnagrask, Aultvaich and Rheindown Wood area.

Munlochy and Knockbain. Munlochy is the name of a sizeable village, and also of a very scenic and interesting bay, really a sea-loch, almost 3 miles long and half a mile wide, towards the south-east corner of the Black Isle, 3 miles north of Kessock. Knockbain is the parish in which Munlochy is situated—Kessock also, but the southern part of the large parish is dealt with separately under Kessock, Charlestown and Kilmuir. The parish, extending to 12,600 acres, was formed in 1756 out of the pre-Reformation parishes of Suddie and Kilmuir-Wester. There is no village of Knockbain, only a crofting area.

Munlochy Bay, much of which dries out at low tide, opens quite dramatically between two lofty headlands, the Sutors of Cromarty

337

in miniature, each about 400 feet high. On the north one was sited the once-important Castle of Ormond—but this is dealt with under Avoch, in which parish it lies. The southern cape is called Craigie-howe, famous for its wild goats, and has a prehistoric fortified enclosure on its crest, with hut-circles; also a cave, the alleged haunt of the gigantic Fionns under Fionn MacCoul. Drumderfit, the secondary hog's-back of hill to the west, is the Ridge of Tears, site of a Pictish dun and sundry cairns, and reputedly the scene of a great battle—also dealt with under Kessock. A family called Logan tenanted the farm of the name for centuries. The bay is a noted wintering place for graylag geese and other wildfowl, and there is a heronry here. It is also renowned for its fishing.

Munlochy village is nicely situated at its head, a pleasant place, climbing a hill on the B.9161 road near its junction with the main A.832 Black Isle highway. The parish church stands, not really in the village, at the foot of the hill to the south, a quite large building with belfry but without a graveyard, enlarged in 1816. The village boasts a residential hotel, guest-houses, a bank, a school and shops, with considerable modern housing. Undoubtedly the building of the projected bridge between Inverness and Kessock will cause Munlochy to grow further.

Half a mile west of the village, at the roadside on the A.832, is the interesting feature known as the Cloutie Well. This is a natural spring, much revered for its various qualities. To it revert hopeful folk on the first Sunday in May, to make a wish and to hang an offering of clothing or cloth on the fence near by. The amount of material hanging here is quite astonishing, and bears testimony to the fact that superstition is by no means dead in 20th century Scotland. It was St. Boniface's Well originally. There is another somewhat similar well about 2 miles to the east, in Avoch parish.

Two miles north of Munlochy, on a climbing side-road which crosses the peninsula, is Knockbain itself, now only a community of scattered small farms, with a recently defunct school and a post-office. There is much forestry hereabouts. A mile to the south, on a branch road to the west, on the farm of Muirton, is a good chambered cairn above a burn, with a tight group of nine large standing-stones in the centre. There are lovely prospects from here, southwards. Sometimes this cairn is described as of Balnague, which house is perhaps nearer. Still on this higher ground, around the 300-foot contour, 2 miles to the east, is another chambered cairn, in a field at Belmaduthie, with seven large inner stones and eight lesser outer ones. Belmaduthie used to have its mansion, a seat of the Kilcoy Mackenzies, with a baronetcy, but this has been demolished.

This was the Suddie parish, and Suddie old kirk lies about a mile to the south-east, near the large farm of Easter Suddie. Only a gable of the former church remains, with an obliterated heraldic panel therein, and a nameless mausoleum, locked, with crowsteps and sham gunloops, presumably for Mackenzie of Suddie. The kirkyard has many tumbled 18th century table-stones, and there is also a burial-enclosure of the Mathesons of Bennetsfield, descended from the old chiefs of Matheson, or MacMath. There is nothing of particular interest at Easter Suddie; but Wester Suddie, only half a mile away but reached only by a lengthy roundabout route, is now called Rosskill, for some reason, and has a tall old mansion of the mid-18th century, rather attractive. This was the home of the Mackenzies of Suddie, one of whom, General John Randall Mackenzie, was the Hero of Talavera, in the Peninsular War, with a monument to him in St. Paul's, London.

At the other side of Munlochy, on lower ground to the south-west 2 miles, is the large agricultural estate of Allangrange, once another Mackenzie lairdship, and quite renowned. The old house is still owned by the Fraser-Mackenzie family, but no longer occupied by them. It is a tall gabled whitewashed place with coped chimneys, and a forestair up to the main door at first-floor level, with a panel above dated 1760. There are still good features within. Near by is a ruined private chapel and burial-ground, enclosed by a wall, all now much overgrown, with many Mackenzie graves, including that of James Fowler Mackenzie, 24th chief of the clan, who died in 1907. The chapel is alleged to have links with the Knights Templar. The mansion of the estate is now a little way to the east, at Allanbank, where its laird has established a large cold-storage plant, which has recently expanded to Conon Bridge.

A mile to the south-west, in an isolated position, is the Episcopal church of St. John, of 1816, at Arpafeelie, now looking a little neglected, with one sad tombstone to a young man of 19, of the Allanbank family, drowned whilst fishing. The name Arpafeelie is an odd one, possibly derived from *ard na fhaolinn*, the height of the seagull. Curiously enough there is also an Artafallie, a scattered community about 2 miles to the south-east, which it is suggested means the high place of the sods, *ard tir faillidh*. Neither sounds very likely. In woodland near by are enclosures of early settlement.

Nigg and Rarichie. After centuries of rural peace, the oddly named Nigg—the word is probably a corruption of *An Uig*, The Bay —has of a sudden come into prominence, and had its character drastically changed. This is now the centre of the large and dramatic oil-rig building developments, and other on-shore services connected with North Sea oil, thanks to its sheltered but vital position just within the magnificent deep-water anchorage of the Cromarty Firth, on the north side. It may seem rather absurd to associate the term deep-water with Nigg Bay, which dries out to vast sand and mud flats at low tide; nevertheless, Dunskaith Ness, at the south-western tip of the Nigg peninsula, has deep water right to the shore— indeed a large ocean-going liner is now semi-permanently moored at the jetty there, to provide accommodation for workers, of which the area is in short supply. Only a few yards out from the beach, the water is 10 fathoms deep, a highly unusual circumstance. So the rig-builders have seen their opportunity, like the British Aluminium

Company at Invergordon across the Bay, and all the district suffers major change. Now there are plans to reclaim part of the Bay for development—and also to form a nature reserve and wildfowl refuge in other parts, however mutually antagonistic these may seem.

Nigg is a civil parish of antiquity, of about 9000 acres, forming the southern end of the large Nigg–Fearn–Tarbat peninsula of Easter Ross. It is largely treeless, and dominated on one side by the wide flats of the Bay, and on the other by the long whale-back ridge of Hill of Nigg, rising to 666 feet, with the prominent cliffs of the North Sutor of Cromarty forming its southern bastion. There is no real village in the parish, but there is a fair, if scattered, population on the low ground at the western side, comprising the Kirkton of Nigg hamlet, the farming community of Pitcalnie mid-way up the parish, and the disused airfield and farms of Rarichie to the north. The strung-out hamlet of Nigg Station lies to the west, over the parish boundary into Logie-Easter, but calls for no special description. The eastern flank of the parish, by contrast, is a continuous barrier of lofty cliffs, stretching for over 5 miles, unapproached by any road.

The parish church, which has a stirring history, stands not far above the Bay towards the south-west corner of the parish, in its ancient graveyard, on the edge of a ravine, amongst trees. It is basically a pre-Reformation structure, typically long and low, and very picturesque, rebuilt in 1626 and altered somewhat in 1725 and 1786, but retaining its antique appearance. Its Dutch bell dates from 1624, in a belfry with stone balls on top. Internally it seems small but lengthy, with a central pulpit and now no loft or gallery. Perhaps its most famous feature is the fine Pictish stone which stands outside, under a canopy at the east gable, a cast of which is in the Museum of Antiquities, Edinburgh. This is carved in elaborate high relief, depicting on one side a very decorative cross and bordering, and on the other, more weatherworn unfortunately, a man with cymbals, a doglike animal, a harp, and other symbols—a notable relic. In the graveyard are many very interesting gravestones. One is actually the work of Hugh Miller, the great geologist, who was a mason by training, a table-stone. There are a number of memorials to the old family of Gair of Nigg, one dated 1659, within an enclosure. Highly interesting is the so-called Cholera Stone, a small, round flat and plain stone, somewhat isolated from the rest and in line with the second window west of the church-door. This represents one of those extraordinary stories, in which an elder of this congregation, as late as 1832, in time of plague, claimed to have seen the said plague, in the form of a small cloud which, with remarkable bravery he captured, of all things in a linen bag. It was buried here, under this stone—and, all believed, the pestilence with it. The elder's name was Jasper Vass. Similar exploits are told of other places. In this church, in the troubled 17th century, an Episcopal incumbent stoutly assured his parishioners that, if they resisted the Presbyterians they "would be immortalised so that nothing could hurt them, even the slash of a broadsword, nay a cannon-ball would but play baff with you!" We are not informed whether this gallant prophecy was fulfilled. The manse near by is old and pleasing in appearance. There is a small school here also.

Southwards of the Kirkton a mile is Pitcalzean House, formerly the home of Eric Linklater, the author. And another mile in the same direction is the great development area, engulfing the former fishing hamlet of Balnapaling; also, unfortunately the site of Dunskaith Castle, founded by William the Lion in his fight against Danish invaders, in 1179. American ones, in 1973, are another story. There was not much left of the castle, admittedly. In its place rise the enormous sheds, yards, workshops and cranes of Highland Fabricators Ltd, a Brown & Root–Wimpey establishment, and the Wimpey Welding Training School, all busy as a disturbed ant-hill. Right at the point of Dunskaith Ness is the former small hotel, for the ferry to Cromarty just across the narrows, now blossoming mightily for the workers, with the great liner aforementioned towering near by, renamed the "Highland Queen". The huge car-park for these two features is eloquent. Dunskaith House, and the former golf course, have also been swallowed up. A steep road, not marked on the maps, now climbs dramatically up the great lump of the North Sutor ahead, from sea-level to 450 feet in half a mile, for the contractors' purposes. The Hill of Nigg was once known as the Bishop's Forest, and was a hunting-ground for the See of Ross. It covers one-third of the entire peninsula. Not to be suspected from below are two half-mile-long lochs cradled up on the hill-top.

Back at Nigg kirkton, northwards half a mile is Pitcalnie hamlet, formerly a Ross lairdship—indeed it was the Rosses of Pitcalnie who held the chiefship of the clan until the present 29th (or 35th, by another accounting) chief, David, of the Shandwick line. A former church here, with belfry tower, is now a hall. Nigg Manse is also here, and the post-office. A little further northwards is the mansion of Bayfield House, massive late Georgian and scheduled for development. It is alleged to be haunted. Still further along this same road, which threads the so-called Strath of Pitcalnie (it is no strath, but merely low ground at the foot of the Hill of Nigg) the Chapelhill church of the Rarichie area stands in an isolated position, a large and gaunt Italianate structure, now linked with the parish church. There was much trouble in this parish during the Disruption and other periods of religious controversy, resulting in the usual plethora of churches. Pitcalnie school is at the road-junction not far away.

This junction sends one fork westwards to the small hamlet of Ankerville, once the seat of a branch of the Rosses, descended from Invercharron. This area is also scheduled for development. The right or eastwards fork leads into the Rarichie, or Rarichies, area, which extends for almost 3 miles from the farm of Wester Rarichie to the disused airfield near Fearn, at Loan of Rarichie. This fertile agricultural district was once very famous in the great Ross clan, for Hugh of Rarichies was the first of the name, third son of the fourth Earl of Ross, brother of the fifth and last, who was cheated of his birthright, the earldom, and became first of Balnagown, and first chief of the clan, as distinct from the ancient Celtic earldom. There is now no village or hamlet of the name, but the disused airfield is an obvious target for development, and signs of that are evident. There were two renowned wells here, one called Sul na Ba, the Cow's Eye, with healing properties; the other John the Baptist's Well, near the church at Chapelhill. Above Easter Rarichie farm on a spur of the Hill of Nigg, is the site of a Pictish fort.

Two miles from the school and junction, the road sends off a branch eastwards to Shandwick Bay—not to be confused with the Shandwick in Logie-Easter parish 5 miles to the west. The road curves round the narrow northern end of Hill of Nigg, and reaches the coast in less than a mile. Towards the end of this, above the slope to the shore, in a field on the left, is the Shandwick Stone, a fine Pictish cross-slab 8 feet high, badly weatherworn at one side, but displaying at the other a cross, with two animals, serpents and circles of decoration. The farm near by is called Old Shandwick, and presumably was the original place of the name, the first Ross of Shandwick being a grandson of the aforementioned Hugh of Rarichies near by, *circa* 1486. The name, of course, merely means a sandy bay. There is a hamlet of Shandwick here, but it merges with the larger village of Balintore, in Fearn parish, and is better described thereunder.

The cliffs to the south of this are inaccessible, save to the determined walker and by boat. Sundry watercourses from the lochs on Hill of Nigg plunge over them in sheer cascades. The King's Cave occurs about half-way along, allegedly referring to a Danish king shipwrecked here, whom fancy has linked with the Shandwick Stone. The high-set farm of Castlecraig roosts near the south end.

The south-west boundary of Nigg parish follows the line of The Pot, a burn which meanders through the shallow but extensive Sands of Nigg, in Nigg Bay, for well over 3 miles, vessels of fairly shallow draught formerly using this channel. These sands are rich in shell-fish, flounders and sand-eels. Whether these will survive the advent of industry remains to be seen. The proposed reclamation here will almost halve the mouth of the Bay, and pollution seems to be inevitable. The new Cromarty Firth Port Authority is going to be kept busy.

Portmahomack, Inver, Tarbat and Geanies. Portmahomack is the quite large and attractive village in the civil parish of Tarbat, at the northern tip of the Nigg–Fearn–Tarbat peninsula, east of Tain. *Tairbeart*, of course, means an isthmus, and there are many places so named in the Highlands—indeed one not far away in this county, Tarbat House, in Kilmuir-Easter parish, though just why this should have been so called is hard to perceive. Inver is a former fishing-village at the mouth of the little estuary which drains the Morrich More 3 miles west of Portmahomack, and Geanies is an old barony, estate and district at the extreme south of the parish. The

Fortrose Cathedral. The 14th century South Aisle, with later bell-tower

Invergordon: smelting plant of the British Aluminium Company's great modern development

Kinkell Castle, Conon Bridge, handsomely restored from ruin to be a home again

Munlochy Bay, in the Black Isle

area of all is about 7700 acres, and it has 14 miles of coastline, culminating at the prominent Tarbat Ness, with its lighthouse, the most
northerly point of Ross.

Portmahomack, which is a corruption of Port na Colmac, the
harbour of St. Colmac, is pleasantly situated half-way out the
Tarbat peninsula on the west side, on a small sandy bay looking
across the Dornoch Firth to the mountains of Sutherland, a
deservedly favourite place with holidaymakers. The hamlet of
Balnabruach is a continuation, southwards. Portmahomack has
quite a good harbour at its northern end, improved by Thomas
Telford, with a pier 420 feet long. Twenty-five fishing-boats
operated from here in 1880, and that was a great reduction on
previous days. There are two fine old buildings at the pier-head,
former warehouses from the days when this was a busy little port.
One is of the 17th century, with crowstepped gables, moulded
windows and buttresses, the other more plain. There is a Coastguard
Rescue Station behind the Harbour House. Near by is an old ice-
house for the cold storage of fish, semi-subterranean. A Victorian
cast-iron drinking-fountain stands rather incongruously in the
vicinity, dated 1887. There are two small hotels, one in process of
enlargement. And behind the early 19th century Castle Hotel, on
the quite steeply rising bank which hems in the village on the east, is
the site of St. Colmac's chapel. Only a small scrap of masonry
remains. A little further to the south is St. Colmac's Well, with
stone canopy, now in a badly neglected state. This ought to be
maintained as a show-piece. Near here is the Carnegie Library
building, whereon is a plaque commemorating the heroic rescue by
Portmahomack fishermen, in 1910, of survivors of the wrecked S.S.
Sterlina. Opposite is the presently used parish church of Tarbat, a
smallish, low-set building, fairly modern and no doubt more conveniently placed for the village than the true parish church—but
infinitely less attractive. The typically large and gaunt Free church
stands at the southern end of Portmahomack proper, where the
little dead-end road curves off to serve Balnabruach, with a caravan-
park near by.

Balnabruach, which means the village on the bank, is merely an
extension of former fishermen's cottages along the bay southwards,
rather pleasant. There was once another ancient chapel here, some
50 yards inland, but nothing remains. Opposite the Free church, a
side-road climbs eastwards a little way, to Tarbat old parish church,
on its knoll and surrounded by its ancient kirkyard. The church
itself is now shut up, which is a great pity for it is an interesting and
characterful structure with a long history. But at least it is kept
freshly whitewashed, and the graveyard is still in use and good order.
The church stands on the site of a 7th century chapel, and beneath
it is said to be a 30-foot-long vault, traditionally built by St. Columba
himself—although almost certainly this should be St. Colmac again.
The pre-Reformation church was rebuilt in 1628 and again in 1756.
It has a most unusual large, square and domed belfry, built of ashlar,

apparently of the 17th century. The bell was brought here from Fearn Abbey in 1591. One of former wings or transepts is now a tool-shed for the gravedigger, and within are some mural monuments of character. One shows the Leslie arms, dated 1623; another commemorates James Cuthbert, Provost of Inverness, also 1623; and one displays Mackenzie heraldry, dated 1642. The entire kirkyard is interesting, and herein were found ten fragments of Pictish cross-slabs. How many actual slabs the fragments represent is not certain. They are now in the Museum of Antiquities, Edinburgh. One is particularly notable, about $1\frac{1}{2}$ feet high, with typical spiral decoration, but highly unusual in that it is also covered with an inscription in Hiberno-Saxon capitals, reading thus: IN NOMINE IHESU CHRISTI CRUX CHRISTI IN COMMEMORATIONE REOTETII REQUIESCIT. This is believed to refer to a very early Celtic abbot named Reodaide or Rethaide, mentioned in the Annals of Ulster, in the year 763 and entitled Ab Fearna. There was a Celtic monastery of Fern in Ireland, and the Abbey of Fearn in the next parish to Tarbat was called Nova Ferna. This is said to have been founded by the first Earl of Ross, but it seems likely that it was merely a Romish establishment imposed on a previous Celtic abbey—an interesting sidelight on ancient history. Another of the fragments depicted dogs or hounds within a finely decorative border. The Dingwall Tomb is a later item of interest here; also the burial enclosure of the Macleods of Geanies and Cadboll, descendants of Assynt. There are many other interesting memorials. Near by to the north, on this same bank, at the "suburb" of Gaza, oddly named, is the school. A local minister once referred to his parishioners as "men of Gaza", namely Philistines, for their non-attendance at kirk. The golf course lies just behind this school.

Further along the same road, north-eastwards, is the large farm of Bindal, formerly Bindhill, with Bindal Muir flanking the cliff-bound coast. On these cliffs, south of the farm almost a mile but easily seen from the road, rises the interesting Ballone Castle, allegedly a former seat of the Earls of Ross, but since they faded out in the 14th century, and nothing here is apparently older than the 16th, it seems likely that it was their successors, the Rosses of Balnagown who built this stronghold. At any rate, it is a fine place, though much shattered, and its main features still survive, a Z-planned fortalice with stair- and angle-turrets, perched on the cliff-edge, and notably well provided with shot-holes and gunloops. Notably well-finished too, with fluted and carved window-surrounds, elaborate corbelling and other special features. The Hall on the first floor is a fine apartment, and there was more domestic and sleeping accommodation than normal. Although it would be a major task to restore, this castle should be saved. It was later occupied by the Mackenzies of Cromartie. There is a grave-slab on the shore below, commemorating victims of a shipwreck in 1682. Because it could not be ascertained what the religion of these unfortunates might be, no local minister would agree to bury them in consecrated ground, so they were interred here—a commentary on the bigotry of that grim period in our religious history.

Beyond Bindal this road probes up the long narrow peninsula, with the sea on either side, to Wilkhaven, where there is a farm and cottages, and a road down a steep hill to a little harbour on the east side, with lobster-pots, a pleasant secluded spot. Further still is Tarbat Ness lighthouse, said to be one of the most elegant in Scotland, as well as allegedly the second-tallest in Britain. It was erected in 1830 at a cost of £9361, on a 50-foot knoll, its light being visible for 18 nautical miles and marking the entry to the Dornoch Firth. There is a group of three burial-cairns a mile to the west. There are many caves in the cliffs hereabouts, some with strange stories attached to them.

Not far south of Ballone Castle, but reached from a different side-road which strikes off eastwards just before the parish church, is the former fishing-village of Rockfield, tucked in under the cliffs of a rocky shore, with jetty and slipway and a straggle of cottages, very picturesque. There are proposals to develop this as a holiday-centre. At one time it supported eighteen fishing-boats. Rockfield, or Little Tarrel Castle, however, lies more than a mile to the south and is reached only by the estate-road into the Rockfield lands. The present mansion of the name lies not far from the B.9165 road, but it is necessary to go on for another half-mile to find Little Tarrel, which stands in the steading of a later farmhouse some way back from the coast. It is a small L-planned fortalice, apparently of the early 17th century, possibly containing older work, very plain but substantial, with crowstepped gables and coped chimneys. There are now only two storeys beneath the wallhead, but the presence of a splayed gun-loop high up under the eaves on the north indicates that the roof has been lowered. Indeed the place has been much altered, and was for long used as a farm-workers' tenement. The turnpike stair is gone, and replaced by an outside forestair. Nevertheless, some features remain, and the castle could be saved and made attractive. The arched doorway is in the re-entrant angle, and is guarded by a shot-hole, while another wide gunloop is let into the west gable. There are two vaulted chambers on the ground floor, and a vaulted passage; and the kitchen has a large arched fireplace, now blocked up, and stone water-basin and aumbry. This castle has been called Tarul and Tarradel, as well as Little Tarrel and Rockfield, which much confuses the tracing of its history and owners—and there is a Meikle Tarrel farm a mile to the south. Nevertheless it is described in the early 19th century as one of the two chief mansions of Tain parish—not Tarbat. In view of all this, much research would be required to trace its lairds. It is interesting however, that the Clan Ross list the surname of Tarrell as one of their septs, so at one time it was probably a Ross house.

South of this area, 3½ miles from Portmahomack, is the large Geanies estate, near the parish boundary. There is the site of a castle here also, but is now gone. The mansion stands above the coast, a mile and more back from the road, on comparatively high ground for this low-lying district, amongst trees which are also not very prevalent. It is a charming house, dating from 1680 and later periods, long, centrally tall and whitewashed, with crowstepped gabled wings. There is a square doocot to the west of possibly earlier date, and an octagonal summerhouse above the shore, dated 1760 and said to have been built as a sort of lighthouse also. There was once a chapel at Geanies, or rather, at Cadbollmount near by, dedicated to St. Mary, not now discernible. Here too is a tumulus, a grassy mound 95 feet in diameter and 20 feet high. A family of Murrays have been at Geanies since the 18th century, before which there was a series of Macleod lairds, of the same line as Cadboll nearby. Prior to that the estate was in Sinclair hands—who presumably gained it at the Reformation, it having been part of the abbey lands of Fearn. Kenneth Murray of Geanies (1826–76) was a noted agricultural reformer and improver, extending the arable area of his property from 2016 to 4000 acres. There was much agricultural improvement in this peninsula area in the early 19th century, East Lothian methods and personnel being imported. Geanies post-office is a single small cottage alone at the roadside.

At the directly opposite corner of this long and narrow parish, facing north over the Dornoch Firth, is the Arboll area. This consists now of a few farms, but was once a quite important barony, with the one-time castle of the Corbet family, now only a site. Corbet is an unusual name for these northerly parts, but it is worth noting that Corbett too is an acknowledged sept of Clan Ross. The Rosses of Pitcalnie seem to have obtained the lands, and may have been descendants of the Corbets. There was also a chapel dedicated to John the Baptist, near Newton, a mile west of Wester Arboll. Its grassgrown foundations lie on a bank above the road, at a slight bend and hill. The Gallows Hill of Arboll, near the Mains thereof, is quite prominent, although reaching only 113 feet.

North of the former crofting area of Lower Arboll is the joint village of Inver and Skinnertown, on the shore. Actually, the Tarbat–Tain parish boundary runs through the midst, but it is convenient to deal with this under Tarbat. Inver village, reached by its own dead-end side-road from the main Tain–Portmahomack road, is isolated and quite attractive, strung along the sandy shore, with magnificent prospects northwards to the Sutherland mountains. The houses are all low cottage-type dwellings, in parallel lanes, as this was a former fishing-village. There is a small inn, a post-office, with the school standing by itself away to the west. Holiday accommodation is now the main activity. One of the cottages in the "main street" has on its walling a memorial to the one-time owner's dog. It is impossible to say just where Inver proper ends and Skinnertown begins—probably at the parish boundary. Inver Bay, to the west, is really the estuary of a burn which drains the marshland of the great Morrich More peninsula, nearer Tain, a level and featureless area which is however the seat of controversy over projected gunnery ranges.

Resolis, Jemimaville and Balblair. This oddly named large rural parish of the Black Isle is pronounced with the accent on the second syllable, the name allegedly being from *ruigh soluis*, the slope of light—possibly from a beacon for seafarers. It lies on the north side of the peninsula, towards the east end, marching with Cromarty, and covers 12,000 acres, being a fairly regular rectangular shape. Jemimaville is an equally oddly named village, with its own story, at the very east of the parish. And Balblair is another village, or scattered community, on the low jutting tract of land westwards across Udale Bay of the Cromarty Firth. Included in the parish also is the extensive crofting district of Cullicudden, a third unusual name, flanking the shore. This Cullicudden was a parish of its own once, but was united with Kirkmichael—that is, the Balblair area—in 1688. The united parish continued to be called Kirkmichael for a considerable time thereafter. There is no actual village of Resolis, and there seems no good reason why the parish should have been so renamed, save that the new church, of 1830, was built near Resolis Mains, in a fairly central position.

This church stands back from the main B.9163 road, about 2 miles west of Balblair, plain and harled, with high narrow windows to the south, very uninspiring within, with much dark wood, a high pulpit and sounding board and U-shaped gallery. There is no kirkyard here—but ample cemetery accommodation elsewhere. About half a mile to the south of the church, on a side-road, is the Resolis War Memorial Hall, built in 1959, large, with a playing-field. And further east a short distance, is the school, with a little community around it, near the rear of the Newhall House policies.

Newhall is the largest estate of the parish, well-wooded, a former Gordon lairdship which passed to the Mackenzies, the Shaw-Mackenzies, and is now the home of Major Shaw of Tordarroch, chief of the name and of Clan Ay. It is a large Georgian mansion of character. There were still Gordons here in 1786, but by 1836 the Mackenzies were in possession. The Gordons have left their name at least at the farm of Gordon's Mills, just across the B.9163 from the Newhall grounds and near the shore of Udale Bay. Here one of the lairds installed a snuff-factory which however was not a success. It became a woollen-mill. The Gordons also discovered lead ore in the St. Martins area, but it does not seem to have been worked.

Only a few hundred yards north of Gordon's Mills is the ruined church and still-used graveyard of St. Michael, or Kirkmichael, quite pleasingly sited above the shore. The central portion of the ancient building has been roofed over as a burial-enclosure for the Munroes of Ardoch, or Poyntzfield. Scraps of ruin lie to east and west, and in one has been a recess for a recumbent effigy. Set in the masonry is a stone commemorating the Gordons of Ardoch as well as those of Newhall. At the east gable are two-light, narrow, pointed windows. Here too is the burial-place of the Shaw-Mackenzies. Another enclosure relates to the Dunbar family, with heraldry, dated 1680. There are many old flat stones in the now neglected ancient part of

347

the graveyard, notable being those referring to the Holms of Ferry-ton, covering centuries.

Balblair lies on rising ground about half a mile northwards, at a road-junction. Here is a hamlet with a licensed hotel, post-office and some modern housing. Still further north some way, on the low ground of the shore, is Inverbreakie, with its still-functioning ferry across to Invergordon, only a mile away across the Firth narrows. The village at the point here is small, with a decayed air, a former fishing-community, with an ice-house still at the rear. The contrast with rampant industry across the water is very noticeable.

Further east on the B.9163, on the road to Cromarty and at the parish boundary, is the quite sizeable village of Jemimaville. This place obtained its name from the wealthy Dutch wife of the Munro laird of Ardoch, Jemima Poyntz. The bridegroom seems to have been so pleased with his acquisition, in the mid-18th century, that he renamed his estate Poyntzfield, and the village Jemimaville. Oddly enough, the village post-office is that of Poyntzfield, not Jemima-ville, for reasons unspecified. The place consists of a long row of cottages stretching along one side of the road only. It is a long way to the church. Below is the wildfowl-haunted Udale Bay. The old estate of Udale, whose drive opens southwards from the village, is now a farm. Udale Bay, where there are great zostera-beds, is, along with part of Nigg Bay across the Firth, scheduled to become a nature reserve.

Poyntzfield House stands on high ground about a mile to the south-west, in a wooded estate, an interesting and unusual mansion, rebuilt in 1757 and 1775, by the Dutch-conscious laird—which may account for the strange architecture. It is a great mixture of styles, forming three sides of a square, with a regular and reasonable Georgian front of three storeys, but an odd little central tympanum. At the back, amongst a clutter of lean-to additions, rises a tall harled tower, culminating in an octagonal outlook-chamber, with ogee-roofed cupola. This is known as Jemima's Tower. The house is said to be haunted, with doors which open and shut and on which knockings are heard.

About a mile and a half westwards, reached from the B.9160 to Fortrose, is the smaller estate of Braelangwell, with another Georgian mansion, having a farmery with old stableyard buildings. It was formerly a property of the Davidsons of Tulloch, a branch of the Clan Chattan federation. There used to be a distillery in the grounds, but this has gone.

From Braelangwell, over a mile across the valley called the Den, on a side-road and not very far from the War Memorial Hall, the hamlet of Newmills straggles beside a small mill, rather attractive. And near by, to the west, in an isolated position, is the quite large Free church and manse. The Bog of Cullicudden adjoins to the west, and the Cullicudden area flanks the B.9163 straight road for a couple of miles. Local tradition says that a bloody battle was fought here, but does not specify when. The name is said to mean the creek of the cuddies, meaning here small fish. But the old-time parish was probably originally called St. Martins. Its ruined church and graveyard of Kirk Martin lies down at the shore, below some small farms. Fragments of the red-stone masonry remain, with the date 1609 above a moulded doorway, plus three empty panel-spaces. Also a small window. There are many ancient flat stones, largely moss-grown, including at least one inscribed with a calvary cross. There is a tomb with apparently Gordon heraldry, dated 1658. There were Gordons at St. Martins, as at Newhall. The name comes from St. Martin of Tours, to whom the church was dedicated. The property still called St. Martin's, now a large farm, lies a mile or so to the south, on the other side of the main road, facing south over a pleasant shallow valley of the Resolis Burn, with the foundations of an earlier chapel near by. The burn used to form a small loch at Kinbeachie, where there was the site of a castle, now gone, a property of the Urquhart family. Behind it, on the rising ground towards the central Millbuie forested ridge, is the farming area called The Braes. On the farm of Easter Brae is a long cairn of some dimensions, with whins growing on it. And in the woodland of Millbuie Forest, above Easter Culbo, is a group of six more cairns, with three others, including a long and a chambered cairn, to the west.

Cullicudden has a post-office and school on the main B.9163 road. And down on the cliff above the steep shore, towards the western end of the parish, is the fortalice of Castlecraig, a quite spectacular building, ruined and one wing fallen, but still retaining its main keep to parapet and roof level, even the roofing. It is perched in a highly inaccessible position, and it is strange to consider that this was a palace of the Bishops of Ross—a much embattled palace, for reasons no doubt good. The keep seems to be all that is left of a courtyard-type castle, and consists of a 50-foot-high oblong tower, with a corbelled parapet and walk crowning the west wall only—though there may have been a similar feature to the east, now fallen away. But the lateral walls clearly had no parapet. There are no windows in the west walling. The ground level is guarded by gunloops, and there are shot-holes elsewhere. All the main floors are vaulted, including the top—which accounts for the roof remaining, and small vaulted chambers were contrived in the thickness of the east walling on each floor, beside the warm kitchen flue. This basement kitchen vault had a wide fireplace, with an external water-basin and duct for introducing rain-water. The castle is said to have been erected by the Urquharts, hereditary Sheriffs of Cromarty. When the bishops gained it is not clear, but they were still there long after the Reformation, in 1638. Perhaps it was simply because of the difficulty of ejecting them from their so strong palace.

Strathpeffer and Fodderty. Strathpeffer is a well-known name, famed for long as a spa and holiday resort—it has been called the Harrogate of the North—and rather surprisingly small though attractive, when visited, with a population of only 1100 and not even the status of a burgh. Actually, Harrogate and Strathpeffer have only their waters in common. Nevertheless, Strathpeffer is a characterful and pleasant place, hidden in its hollow of the hills. Fodderty is the large civil parish in which it is situated, extending to 65,000 acres, lying west of Dingwall and reaching far into the mountains to the north-west, taking in the summit ridge of mighty Ben Wyvis. The parish includes also the village of Maryburgh, but this is dealt with under Conon Bridge, of which it is now almost a part.

Strathpeffer is hardly a descriptive name, for the spa could hardly be said to lie in a strath, or wide valley. The small river flowing eastwards here is called the Peffery, and the Kirkton of Fodderty lies midway along its quite pretty valley; but Strathpeffer itself sits in a hollow or amphitheatre amongst green wooded hills to the west, with houses and hotels climbing on every hand. Indeed hills, or hilly streets and terraces, with hotels, are the predominating feature of the place—although this is no criticism, for the effect is pleasing and the surrounding vistas fine. Although it was the mineral springs which first brought visitors here, it is now renowned as a holiday resort in its own right. Catering for visitors is almost the sole activity—but tastefully. There is nothing tripperish about Strathpeffer, it will be noted!

It was in 1819 that Dr. Thomas Morrison, of Elsick and Disblair in Aberdeenshire, publicised the curative properties of the mineral springs here, declaring them to be particularly beneficial for digestive and kidney disorders. A Pump Room was set up. What is more, an Institution for Poor Spa-Drinkers was also established—something not always thought of. It was announced that the waters contained more sulphuretted hydrogen than any other in Britain, with about 30 grains of sulphur to the gallon. However, Dr. Morrison was not really the first to discern all this, for in the late 16th century the famous Brahan Seer—Brahan Castle is near by—prophesied thus of the spring: "Uninviting and disagreeable as it is now, with its thick-crusted surface and unpleasant smell, the day will come when it shall be under lock and key, and crowds of pleasure- and health-seekers shall be seen thronging its portals in their eagerness to get a draught of its waters." Or words to that effect. The Pump Room is still there, with the Spa Pavilion—although catering more generally today than for health-seekers only, with dancing and entertainments in the Pavilion.

The village lies—or rather climbs—around the A.834 Dingwall to Contin road, and the shops and offices tend to flank this, at a part known as The Square, although there is scarcely a square or even a main street. The very large Ben Wyvis and Highland Hotels, each with over 100 bedrooms, rather dominate; but there are numerous other and smaller hotels and guest-houses. There is a Tourist Information Centre. Cricket, bowling and other leisure pursuits are catered for, with angling of course a speciality in the neighbourhood, with a vast choice of rivers and lochs—even on the Golf Course Loch, where there is an excellent and highly scenic 18-hole course just to the north, at Ulladale.

Since nearly all here is built on terraces of the braesides, no consistent scheme of description is possible. The large Established church stands on the A.834 hill to the south-west, not old, with no graveyard—for this was not the site of the original parish church. Near by is St. Anne's Episcopal, quite large also, with an arcaded aisle and much stained-glass. The Free church stands high on the other side of the village, to the east. There is a small Hector Mackenzie Memorial Hospital, of 1890, also on this side.

To the east also, within the grounds of Castle Leod estate, is an interesting feature known as the Eagle Stone. This is a good Pictish symbol-stone of the early or Class One type, showing an eagle and the horse-shoe symbol. It is about 3 feet high, chipped at the top, and stands on a small knoll beside trees, reached from a lane near Eaglestone House. The Brahan Seer prophesied about this too, saying that one day ships would tie their cables to it—which seems highly unlikely. But in fact the stone has been removed from elsewhere, so perhaps this makes a difference. There is a local tradition that this marks a battle between the Munroes and the Mackenzies (the Munro crest being an eagle), but though there may well have been a battle near by, for these were innumerable, this stone was engraved long before Mackenzies or Munroes were thought of.

Castle Leod near by to the north-east is a notable and handsome fortified house of the beginning of the 17th century, mellow red-stone set on a terrace amongst noble trees and parkland, the seat of the Earl of Cromartie. It looks rather more ancient than it is, built at two close periods, 1600 and 1616, by the famous Tutor of Kintail, Sir Roderick Mackenzie of Tarbat, first as an L-shaped fortalice with more typical 16th century parapet and open rounds; then 16 years later filling in the re-entrant angle of the L with a gabled block having conical-roofed angle-turrets and dormer windows. It all rises from a basement plinth, and is guarded by splayed gunloops and circular shot-holes. The entrance is surmounted by a large, elaborately decorative panel, with Mackenzie heraldry. The ground floor is vaulted and the Hall on the first floor is a fine apartment. There is excellent panelling. The castle is more roomy than is usual, owing to the 1616 extension. The grandson of the aforementioned Tutor—himself uncle and guardian of the young first Lord Mackenzie of Kintail, ancestor of the Earls of Seaforth, at Brahan—was the notable Sir George Mackenzie, created Viscount Tarbat and first Earl of Cromartie in 1703, the present Earl being a descendant.

Behind Castle Leod on the rapidly rising ground known as the Bottacks is the scattered little crofting community of Achterneed, once also a railway-station hamlet, with level-crossing. The railway-line to Achnasheen and Kyle of Lochalsh still passes here, though under threat. To the west, the line goes through a long cutting, and almost 2 miles along this is the feature known as the Raven Rock, a bold crag overhanging the railway. There is a legend that here the ravens used to assemble for an annual gathering, when strange music was heard. A certain man who by chance stumbled on this unusual assembly managed to capture the king raven and released the talking bird only when given the secret of the music which charmed him—allegedly the origin of the famous mouth-music of the Highlands. To the east of Achterneed stretches the rather un-usual Heights area, a series of former crofting townships on a sort of extended shelf above the valley—Heights of Inchvannie, of Kep-poch, of Fodderty, of Brae and of Dochcarty. Behind these on still higher moorland are many relics of antiquity in the shape of cairns and hut-circles. At the large farm of Brae, well to the east, are the scanty remains of a one-time small fortalice called Dochmaluag Tower.

The parish of Fodderty was formed out of three early pre-Reformation parishes, Fodderty itself, Kinnettas and Tollie. Kin-nettas is now represented only by the small slantwise graveyard on the hillside at the north side of Strathpeffer, just behind the gardens of some houses. There are some old table-stones, but no signs of the former church remain. Tollie lay to the south-east, of which more anon. Fodderty itself has no real village, and its church has been converted into a private house calling itself Kilvanny Manor, with two large monoliths of a former stone-circle beside it. But near by, across the road, the old graveyard is still the parish's burial-ground and cemetery, with the former old manse behind. The cemetery is entered through rather fine wrought-iron war-memorial gates, with two bronze targes. The site of the original church is in the midst, on a knoll now covered with graves. There are many old stones here, as well as modern memorials. The former manse, now called Fodderty Lodge, is a most attractive house, whitewashed, with steep roofs and crowstepped gables and dormers. The legend "The Manse of Fotterty 1730" is inscribed over the door, and the date repeated on a fireplace lintel. An old mill, still with its wheel, is not far away; also Fodderty school, likewise whitewashed. In the vicinity is Keppoch House, a partly Georgian mansion, pink-washed and very pleasant, on a terrace facing south.

This prospect southwards is bounded by the lofty and abrupt ridge usually called Knock Farrel, but in fact Druimm a Chait, the Ridge of the Cat. Knock Farrel is a Pictish vitrified fort crowning this ridge, measuring 420 by 120 feet, and one of the finest in the land. There are many legends associated with this site, which is supposed to have been a stronghold of the Fionn warriors. The two standing-stones down at the former parish church below are claimed to have been hurled there by the hero Fionn MacCoul himself in a trial of strength. There is a well dedicated to John the Baptist at the foot of the hill, near Fodderty Lodge, allegedly of healing quality. The views from the ridge are splendid.

At the other, southern, side of Druimm a Chait, where the descent is much more gentle, is the extensive crofting township of Gower, above Loch Ussie, now usually called Knock Farrel also, with a post-office, a very out-of-the-way community. The road which circles the loch to the north is also scattered with houses, one of which is now a tapestry-weaving workshop, with a very modern sculpture by Gerald Ogilvie-Laing of Kinkell Castle outside. Loch Ussie is quite large, nearly a mile across, with wooded islets, set in a sort of lofty basin about 400 feet above the level of the Conon valley to the south. It has its own legends, for it was into this that the Brahan Seer threw his famous magic stone when being chased and captured by the servants of the Countess of Seaforth, his enemy and chief's wife. As he did so he predicted that the Seaforths would one day produce a child with four thumbs and six toes, who would in due course recover the stone from inside a pike in the loch, and would thus inherit its magic powers. This matter appears to be still in abeyance. Meanwhile the loch itself is considered to have magic properties, and wishes are made over its still waters. The far sides are heavily clothed with woodlands of the great Brahan estate.

To south and east of Loch Ussie is the former Tollie parish, though the name is now used only in connection with the farms of Woodside, Keithtown and Glaick of Tollie. Somewhere in this area, rather than on the steep slopes of Knock Farrel itself, took place in 1429 one of the most savage battles in clan history, between the Mackenzies and the MacDonalds of the Isles. The son of the 6th Mackenzie chief was married to a daughter of the Lord of the Isles, but she was not beautiful and blind in one eye, so he sent her home to the isles, on a one-eyed horse, led by a one-eyed groom and accompanied by a one-eyed dog. The resultant fury sent 2000 MacDonalds marching on Clan Kenneth lands. The Mackenzies however managed to defeat the invaders, with great slaughter on both sides. A few years later there was another battle, actually on Druimm a Chait this time, between the Mackenzies and the Munroes. A well at the foot of the hill was found to contain nineteen Munro heads thereafter, so presumably the Mackenzies won this one also.

The Tollie farms lie on the east flank of the high circle of rising ground which encloses Loch Ussie. To the south, stretching down to the banks of the River Conon, is Brahan estate. This, of course, is the famous former seat of the chiefs of Mackenzie, first Lords of Kintail then Earls of Seaforth, whose admittedly tragic and long-drawn fall coincided so well with the dire prophecies of the martyred Coinneach Odhar, the Seer, who lived beside the loch. The stories about his death, like those referring to his prophecies, have tended to proliferate, one theory being that he was burned for "heresy" just after the Reformation at the end of the 16th century; another that it was because of the spite of a Countess of Seaforth a century later. But the earldom of Seaforth was not created until 1623. At any rate, he predicted, amongst other things, the downfall of the chiefly house in no uncertain terms—and most of them have been faithfully ful- filled. They are all taken quite seriously locally, still, Brahan Castle itself, as predicted, is now completely gone, like the Earls of Seaforth, and the estate has passed into Matheson hands—although by inheritance, not sale. The former stables have been converted into a delightful house by the present laird. Some of the old stone heraldry from the castle is preserved, together with a cup-marked stone. There are many treasures within, including a fine Bronze Age torque, one of many ploughed up in 1857. The Seaforth portraits have, in the main, been housed in the Town Hall at Fortrose. The terraced and walled gardens sink towards the river, amidst fine parkland. The demolished castle dated from 1621, plus 18th century work. At the west end of the policies, where drive meets road, is a monument on a seven-stepped plinth, commemorating Frances, daughter of the last Earl of Seaforth, who was involved in a fatal pony-trap accident, likewise predicted. There is a stone-circle in the woodland above the road here, beneath the crags of Brahan. The site of the former church and burial-ground of Tollie parish is said to have been on an island in the river Conon, below.

Round at the west side of this lofty land-mass which culminates in Knock Farrel is the hamlet of Jamestown, now a sort of detached suburb of Strathpeffer, having grown out of a crofting community. There is a former Free church here, now roofless, which has been converted into a rather lovely garden and summer-house, very unusual. Jamestown looks southwards over the Conon valley, just a mile east of Contin, and the Fodderty parish boundary passes through it.

All described hitherto has been the southern end of this large parish. To the north stretches the greater part of its area, empty moor, hill and mountain, reaching for many miles up into the deer-forests of Garbat and Inchbae, and including the mighty mass of Ben Wyvis (3433 feet) the most prominent mountain in Easter Ross, an isolated range rather than an individual hill. It has seven principal summits. It is claimed that rail passengers from Inverness to Wick have Wyvis in view for half a day. Although looking lumpish from some angles, it has fine and wild corries and cliffs to the east, and when snow-capped can look extremely impressive. It can be climbed without too much difficulty from the east, from the Loch Glass road, by Evanton, or from the west, from the A.835 Ullapool road, in the Garbat vicinity. Naturally the views from the top are amongst the most extensive in Scotland.

Tain. The royal burgh of Tain is like the other Ross royal burgh and capital, Dingwall, in that it has really two names. Tain is of Scandinavian origin, either from *thing*, a place of assembly, or from *teinn*, meaning osier. But the older Gaelic name was Baile Dhubh-aich, St. Duthac's town—and it is strange that it is the former which has stuck, for the Gaelic influence, of course, persisted, and Tain is permeated with the memories of St. Duthac, even the burgh seal showing his representation. Be that as it may, this is a most pleasant and interesting little town, sited on the Dornoch Firth at the extreme north of Ross, full of character, important centre for a large area and having a stirring history. If Dingwall is the capital of Ross county, Tain is the Ross family capital—indeed every second person you meet here appears to be called Ross. It is not very large, with a population of under 2000. It is also a large civil parish of 21,000 acres, and includes the village of Inver 5 miles to the east—though for present purposes Inver is more conveniently described under Portmahomack and Tarbat which it borders.

Tain is ancient and dignified, and looks it—which is not always the case. It has little to contend with in rivalry, for although Dornoch, capital of Sutherland is only 5 miles away, that is as the crow flies, across the Firth, it is reached only after a 32-mile journey. And southwards, the nearest town is Invergordon 12 miles away. But though the Highlands come close, here is no feeling of isolation or of some sort of frontier town, but an air of settled peace and security. The advent of North Sea oil, with all its onshore ramifications, it is to be hoped, will not spoil Tain.

The town is fairly compact, on a slope which sinks to the east, with two principal streets running north and south roughly parallel and side-streets off, with most of the later development on the higher ground to the west, and the oldest parts on the low ground to the east. But the place is enhanced by trees and gardens, and there are sudden fine vistas. It is said to have been created a royal burgh in either 1057 or 1066, by Malcolm Canmore, but, though its charter is known to have been confirmed by James the Second in 1457, the first extant charter is that of James the Sixth, of 1587. Tain was renowned in pre-Reformation days as the birthplace of one of the last of the great Celtic saints, Duthac, styled Chief Confessor of Ireland and Scotland, who was born about the year 1000 and died in Armagh, Ireland in 1065, his body being brought back to Tain in 1253. Some would have it that he was a much earlier saint, but this is contra-indicated.

The small and early chapel of St. Duthac which stands on a mound in the low ground beyond the railway, to the east of the town, surrounded by the modern cemetery, is said to have been built on the site of his birthplace, and probably dates from the period when his remains were brought back. It is of rude and simple architecture, with ivy-covered gables and massive walls, but apart from two lancet windows no other features remain. This was a renowned "girth" or sanctuary for offenders, also the repository of the famous sacred shirt of the saint, which was alleged to have protective qualities and as such was worn by the Earls of Ross, in battle. When Hugh, 4th Earl was killed wearing it at Halidon Hill in 1333, its reputation presumably took a knock, nevertheless, it was held in such awe that the victorious Edward Baliol and his English friends removed it from the body and sent it back to Tain.

The later St. Duthac's collegiate church, now known as the Memorial Church and no longer used for worship, stands amongst trees about quarter of a mile to the west, within the town, on a shelf of the slope, a fine building in so-called Decorative Gothic, founded by the aforementioned Earl's brother in 1371, and was after the Reformation used as the parish church until 1815 when it was thought to be too small, and the present large church was built higher in the town. It is now, after a period of neglect, used as a show-place and memorial. When a freebooter named MacNeil of Creich burned the original chapel, in 1427, in an effort to capture the Laird of Freswick who had taken sanctuary therein, the relics it held were transferred to this collegiate church, then some 60 years old. This was not the only occasion when the sanctuary rights were violated, at Tain, for in 1306 Bruce's Queen Elizabeth de Burgh, on her flight to Orkney at the depth of her husband's fortunes, took refuge here with her daughter and Nigel Bruce, and were shamefully taken out by the then Earl of Ross and handed over to the English, a betrayal Scotland has never forgotten. The odour of sanctity was transferred, with the relics, to the collegiate church, and it in turn became a place of pilgrimage from all over Scotland. It was to St. Duthac's, in Tain, that James the Fourth made annual pilgrimages for twenty years. This perhaps was not entirely a matter of piety, for he used to much enjoy his journeys to and fro, with hunting, feasting and song—and found it an excellent way to keep in touch with his northern subjects, something no monarch had bothered to do hitherto. Moreover he installed his favourite and difficult mistress, Flaming Janet Kennedy in Darnaway Castle, in Moray, and was able to use her premises there as a convenient half-way house when he felt he had to get away from his unloved wife, Margaret Tudor, Henry the Eighth's sister. He was actually here a month before his death at Flodden in 1513. The building, restored in 1877, is fine within, with splendid east and west windows, each of five compartments and tracery above, and good stained-glass—the latter depicting, amongst other historic scenes, the Scottish parliament of 1560 which adopted the Reformed Confession of Faith, with John Knox and other notables—including the Provost of Tain who was also Commendator-Abbot of Fearn—taking part. There are trefoiled sedilia, a priestly effigy and a fine oaken pulpit presented by the Regent Moray, Mary Queen of Scots' famous half-brother. Also many interesting memorials and slabs. The graveyard outside contains many old stones also.

Close by, in Castle Street, there is an interesting local museum, a labour of love on the part of some citizens, now under the auspices of the Ross and Cromarty Heritage Society. Here is collected a great variety of items, relics, manuscripts, photographs, etc., of local and indeed national interest. At the door is a recently discovered large Pictish stone, from Ardjachie farm 2 miles to the north-west, with many cupmarks and an unusual wheel-like symbol incised. Amongst other interesting items are two mort-bells, a fire-ball and a town-cryer's bell; the huge key of the Tolbooth, and the manacles therefrom; coins of Gustavus Adolphus (1620) found at Ardross, probably left there by soldiers in the Montrose troubles; a notable Stone Age axe-head found at Millcraig, but originating at the famous Langdale

Pikes "manufactory"; an ancient banner of the Earldom of Ross, and other Ross relics left by the late Chief, including the jewel of a Nova Scotia baronetcy of the Rosses, of 1668; and many more. This is an excellent venture, which was started as an exhibition for the visit of the Queen-Mother in 1966, and has become permanent.

The High Street is near by, and here rises the very impressive and unusual Tolbooth building—unusual in that it is so complete and well-preserved, for it is in fact typical of many built during the late 16th and 17th centuries, entirely Scottish in character despite frequent comments that it is of continental design. It takes the form of a tall, square castellated keep or tower, with parapet and walk, plus a clock therein and angle-turrets at the corner, clustered round a conical steeple, all built in good ashlar. Here is the original curfew bell, Dutch, of 1616. Just when the building was erected is not clear, but oddly enough, the General Assembly of 1706 ordered a collection to be made for the repairing of the Tolbooth of Tain. The more modern Town House is attached, in the rather overdone Scottish Baronial style of 1849, replacing one burned in 1833. At the base of the Tolbooth tower is the Mercat Cross, restored in 1895. Also the Seaforth Highlanders' war-memorial plaque.

There are now no other major buildings in the High Street, but just to the south of the Town House is the attractive Rose Garden, opened by the Queen Mother at the 9th Centenary celebrations in 1966; also the Albert Memorial-like monument to Provost K. Murray of Geanies, of 1879. In the parallel Queen Street, to the west, stands the Town Hall, a large yellow-stone edifice in oddly mixed architectural style, allegedly "French Renaissance", with hipped-roofed central block and sham-battlemented wings, dating from 1875, with lawn in front—more attractive than the description makes it sound. Further to the north in Queen Street is the present large and handsome parish church, of 1815, with more battlemented towers, seated for 1200, with a U-shaped gallery and lofty pulpit, with organ behind. There is some good stained-glass here also, including a memorial window to Sir John Fraser, Principal of Edinburgh University 1944–7, famous surgeon and native of Tain. The much smaller Free Presbyterian church, very plain, is near by, with opposite it, at a corner of the street, a small plot of ground whereon are collected sundry stone relics, including an old font and a former pediment with Munro heraldry.

The old Royal Academy of Tain building stands in Academy Street, the northern extension of High Street. This well-known school was constituted by royal charter in 1809, and this building erected in 1812; but it is now the office headquarters of Highland Fabricators Ltd, the oil-rig manufacturers at Nigg, while the Academy itself has moved to large modern and factory-like premises on the high ground to the west of the town. Here also is the fire-station, and there is much modern housing to south and east. The older residential area was to the north-west, but here too are modern developments, one group of council-houses pleasingly set back behind trees, with gardens in front. Hereabouts is the small Episcopal church of St. Andrew, rather dark internally with some quite good stained-glass.

The area to the east, down the quite steep hill below the High Street, is attractive, with leafy lanes, old garden-walls and an air of the old world. Nevertheless, down here is the railway-station, still functioning, the children's boating-pond and playground, and the Alexandra Suspension Bridge, with access to the 18-hole golf course, near St. Duthac's chapel. Tain is well supplied with amenities and attractions for visitors, with bowling and tennis and other sports, and the school swimming-pool open to visitors during the summer season. There are many hotels, guest-houses and a caravan-park. Visitors are also welcome at the Highland cheese-making establishment at Blarliath. Further visitor-directed development is proposed for the neighbourhood, for the oil-boom is bringing many people here.

Before leaving the burgh of Tain it is worth recollecting that it was here that the great Montrose was brought, ignominiously bound on a broken-down nag after his final betrayal and defeat at Carbisdale, to be confronted and harangued by the Covenanting ministers under General David Leslie, and then sent on the long painful journey to his death at Edinburgh, in 1650.

Tain parish is large, but not very populous. Three very extensive tracts are taken up with the forests of Morangie and Tarlogie, to the west and north, and the great salt-marsh and sand-waste expanse of the Morrich More, to the east. The latter is a wide peninsula stretching for 5 miles, to Inver Bay, flat and empty, with the disused airfield of Fendom to its south, a place of winds and wildfowl and waders over which much controversy rages as to whether or not it is to be a bombing range or a nature reserve—or both! Seaward of this, a couple of miles out in the Dornoch Firth, are the notorious Gizzen Briggs, shallows and sand-bars which have been the end of many a ship, and about which many tales have arisen. The name is Norse and means the leaky bridge—and the word gizzen is still used in dialect to refer to leaky through drought or shrinking. South of the Morrich More lies Loch Eye, half of it in Tain parish, a 2-mile long sheet of water, without any especial features but rather pleasant to come across in the surrounding flat country. This is to be a nature reserve, it is hoped with Morrich More as appendage.

To the north of Tain, over a mile along the A.9 is the well-known Glen Morangie Distillery, of 1843, the home of "Highland Queen" whisky, nicely set at the shore, with a pond and a burn. Morangie Forest actually lies much further to the west, amongst the foothills of Strathrory, covering a vast area. There are fine forest-walks here. Further to the north of Morangie is the Tarlogie district, with Tarlogie Wood linking with Morangie Forest, and very large. Here is a Forestry Commission hamlet, pleasingly placed amongst the old woodlands of the former Tarlogie House, once the seat of one Peter Mackenzie, styled Count of Serra Largo (1856–1931). Seaward a

The Falls of Rogie, near Contin, Easter Ross

Tain: the Old Tolbooth
with Mercat Cross below

Portmahomack: the harbour,
the Dornoch Firth and hills of
Sutherland in the background

mile, on the coast and beside the A.9, is the farm of Ardjachie, where was found the Pictish stone now on display at Tain museum. There is a low headland of Ardjachie Point here—but it is quite dwarfed by the extraordinary and lengthy sand-spit peninsula half a mile to the west, called merely the Ferry Point, which juts a mile and a half into the firth to within three-quarters of a mile of the Sutherland shore, where formerly the important Meikle Ferry was run. This is now disused, and the pier and ferry buildings are used as a mussel-fishing and bottling establishment. It is a gallant enterprise in a remote situation, almost as though on an island—yet Tain is only 3 miles from the road-end. The mussel-beds around here are extensive, the Dornoch Firth always being renowned for this; indeed the bay on the east side of the peninsula is called Tarlogie Scalps, meaning mussel-beds. There is a semi-subterranean ice-house out at the Point, for the storage of fish. Also a caravan-park at both the tip and root of the peninsula. The Tain parish boundary with Edderton is about a mile on.

To the south-west of Tain there are few features of especial interest. Aldie House and Mill stand back from the A.9 about a mile south, in the crofting area of Hilton. Aldie was a Ross lairdship from 1628 to 1756, before which it had been Munro land. Latterly the owners were called Mackenzie-Ross. The Aldie Water here is rather remarkable in changing its name, after it flows out of Glen Aldie, to the River Tain—which it is called for only 3 miles, to the firth. South of Glen Aldie is the feature known as The King's Causeway, now a side-road but once only a moorland track, which James the Fourth used to walk barefoot as he approached the celebrated Tain sanctuary—though some claim that it was his son, James the Fifth.

Urquhart and Logie-Wester, Culbokie and Ferintosh. Urquhart is a comparatively common place-name in Northern Scotland—even as far south as Dunfermline in Fife. The name, which used to be spelled Urchard—though there are other forms like Urchany, Urchy and Orchy—derives probably from *airchardain,* or wood-side, or alternatively from *urchair,* violent, meaning a rapid torrent. So it is not to be wondered at that it is common. Logie is even more so, merely meaning a hollow. However, it is possible that this Urquhart takes its name from the family of that name, who in turn called themselves after the more famous Urquhart on Loch Ness-side, for a branch of the family became hereditary Sheriffs of Cromarty, and owned much of this area once. Be that as it may, the large conjoint parish of the name extending to 15,000 acres, was formed out of the early parishes of Urquhart and Logie-Wester as early as 1490, and covers the northern portion of the "root" of the Black Isle peninsula, north and east of Muir of Ord. It actually includes the districts of Conon Bridge and Kinkell, but for convenience, these extreme western portions are dealt with separately. Ferintosh is a familiar name but a doubtful entity. It was a particularly famous barony, with remarkable privileges, sufficiently so to be in-

cluded, oddly enough, in the county of Nairn, for the convenience of
its Forbes Urquhart and Cawdor lairds. But there is only a vague
area known as Ferintosh today, more of a memory than anything
else. There is a village at Culbokie, towards the north-east end of the
parish, and hamlets at Alcaig and Duncanston. The parish is almost
9 miles long by an average of 3 miles wide.

Urquhart itself is situated midway along the Cromarty Firth
shore, and consists of a farm and the old ruined church, with graveyard, and little more. The church remains are very ivy-grown, so
that features are difficult to discern but they are quite substantial
and do not appear to be very ancient, almost certainly post-
Reformation. There is still an open belfry containing its bell. The
kirkyard, still in use, has many early flat stones, one dated 1608, and
some with sculpturing which might repay investigation. There
are some interesting later monuments, one with heraldry dated
1741 relating to the Rev. Alexander Falconer and wife; another
of the early 18th century showing three very chubby angels, two
depicting resurrections and one of death gruesomely spearing the
deceased.

The present parish church lies nearer Alcaig, half a mile to the
west, dating from 1795, a wide, plain building at the roadside, without kirkyard, seated for over 1000, with dark woodwork and a small
gallery. There is the unusual feature, for a Scots parish church, of a
small side chapel at the west end, quite separate. The large manse
is near by, of 1777.

Alcaig hamlet lies between the B.9163 road and the shore, half a
mile to the north, a slightly decayed-seeming place, with a post-
office and sawmill. It used to have a pier, for trading sloops, and a
ferry across to Dingwall—which is only a mile away across the
Conon estuary of the Cromarty Firth.

On the higher ground half a mile south-east of Alcaig, in the
Ryehill area, is the quite famous Free church of Ferintosh, also large
and quite ambitious architecturally, harled, with a very unusual
belfry-tower with large bell. Here officiated Dr. John MacDonald
"the Apostle of the North". This, the local school, and the forested
area on the Millbuie ridge 2 miles to the south-east known as New-
land of Ferintosh, are the only remaining links with the ancient
name. Ferintosh was originally a barony of no less than 4725 acres,
first of the Urquharts, then of the Forbes of Culloden family, which,
as a reward for anti-Jacobite services rendered by Lord President
Duncan Forbes and his father, to the government, and the damage
done to their property, particularly their distilleries, by the said
Jacobites, was given the unique and useful privilege of being allowed
to distil spirits exempt from all excise duty. As a result, Ferintosh
blossomed like the May—hence the large churches! This joy lasted
from 1690 to 1786—when the privilege was unsportingly rescinded,
and the then laird compensated with £20,000. Ferintosh was thus
considered so important as to remain included in far-off Nairnshire,
where is Culloden, until 1889. There are no distilleries now. In the

whinny braes above the Free church is a large chambered cairn, with a number of upright stones and one enormous recumbent.

The parish is threaded laterally by two main roads, B.9163 near the shore, and B.9169 on the higher ground, just over a mile apart. At a side-road junction on the latter, is the Ferintosh school, with a public hall, and over a mile along, to the east, is the hamlet of Duncanston, really only a scattered community with a post-office. To the east of this another half-mile, back from the roadside to the north, is the scanty remains of a henge, the name given to prehistoric monuments consisting of a circular ditch and external embankment, with entry causeways, often, but not always, with standing-stones forming an inner circle. This one is 100 feet in diameter, with three grass-grown circles still evident but no standing-stones. It is in a bad condition, cattle-trodden. There are not many of these to be found in Scotland.

Culbokie village still further east a mile, at the roadside of B.9169, with school, licensed hotel, guest-houses and post-office, is quite pleasant, and expanding with modern housing. Behind, in part of the planted Findon Forest, is Culbokie Loch, half a mile long but narrow. Nearer the village, is the dun of Glascairn, also in woodland. These duns were a much later development than the henges, being Pictish fortified dwellings, usually circular, the brochs being a development therefrom, dating from the turn of the Christian era. There are a great many of these all over the country, usually, as here, sited in a mound or other strong position. There is another a mile to the north, at Milton, also amongst trees now. These had triple rings of defence, with an inner wall 8 feet thick, enclosing an area 55 feet across. The name Culbokie means the nook of the goblin or bogeyman, and no doubt refers to the ancient presences indicated by these dwellings of the past.

The area eastwards and southwards, to the Resolis boundary, is called Findon, Braefindon and Findon Forest. The Findon Burn plunges into a chasm, also allegedly an abode of fairies, with a 20-foot cascade, called *Bhean Sith*, which in fact means fairy—and sounds exactly like banshee! The Findon estate was long a possession of the Mackenzie of Scatwell baronets.

This large parish, generally, consists of fairly good farmland on the lower ground, a dull and featureless shoreline and the heavily wooded high central Millbuie ridge, ranging from sea-level to 800 feet.

Urray, Marybank and Glen Orrin. Urray is an enormous civil parish flanking the Inverness-shire boundary, covering 74,000 acres and stretching from the Beauly Firth shore at Tarradale up the Orrin valley for about 25 miles, to the Wester Ross watershed at Loch Monar. The names of Orrin and Urray may be connected. Muir of Ord is in this parish, but it and its vicinity are dealt with separately. Marybank is a small cross-roads village on the A.832, well-known to travellers to the North-West by Garve and Achnasheen, situated where that road takes an abrupt right-angled bend to slope down and cross the River Conon at Moy Bridge.

There is no village of Urray. The parish church is situated in an isolated position 2½ miles east of Marybank and a similar distance north-west of Muir of Ord, at the roadside, in a not-old graveyard. This was not the original church, which lay nearer the river to the north. The building dates from 1780, with a domed belfry, fairly plain outside and in, but bright, with a small end-gallery. In the vestibule is the old bell, dating from about 1590–1610, made by Edinburgh hammermen and inscribed "Sound well and do well. Urray." There is a list of parish ministers here from Reformation times. Also a fine collection of pewter, all inscribed "Parish of Urray 1810", seven chalices and four pattens. The graveyard, still in use, is pleasant amongst trees, but has no particularly interesting memorials. The parishes of Urray and Kilchrist were united about 1600—the latter being dealt with under Muir of Ord.

Old Urray, the former manse, lies to the north a short distance, with an old stableyard. Still further north, near the Orrin's bank, is the ruined early church, in its ancient kirkyard, just east of the bridge. Only a fragment of the building remains amongst old trees. There are many flat stones here, mainly seemingly of Mackenzies, but most moss-grown. An alleged fragment of an ancient grave slab "with ornamental Gothic cross" could not be traced. The Orrin bridge is here, with a sand-and-gravel works near by. Over the bridge, on the slightly higher ground to the north, near the large house of Arcan Mains, is the remains of a stone-circle, many of the stones moved, in trees across the field. The Arcan area is quite extensive, covering much of the low ground between the rivers Orrin and Conon, which join just east of this, opposite Brahan Castle estate on the north side.

Marybank—not to be confused with Maryburgh 5 miles to the north-east at Conon Bridge—lies at the end of a long straight stretch of the A.832, really an estate village for the large property of Fairburn lying to the south in the mouth of Glen Orrin. Here is a school, hall, post-office, shop and cottages, with associated farms. There is a little Established church where evening services are held, a former chapel-of-ease from Urray.

The Fairburn property rather dominates this part of the parish, richly wooded and occupying the quite hilly land at the entrance to Glen Orrin. There is a large Scottish Baronial mansion of the Stirling family, in red stone. But to the east of this, over a mile, on the summit of the intermediate ridge, is Fairburn Tower, an interesting fortalice of the late 16th and early 17th centuries, ruinous but complete to the wallhead with its main features surviving. It is very tall and slender, five storeys in the main block and six in the wing, which is a stair-tower added in the 17th century. There are circular angle turrets at two of the gables, and a number of gunloops and shot-holes. The original entrance was at first-floor level, reached by a removable timber stair, its doorway strengthened by a draw-bar and slot, with a straight, narrow mural stair down to the vaulted basement, to which there was no other access. There are wall-chambers here also. The later tower carried the stair right to the top storey, where it ended in a gabled watch-chamber. This little chamber has an interesting story. For amongst the famous Brahan Seer's prophecies was that this proud Mackenzie stronghold would one day sink so low that a cow would calve in its loftiest chamber. This was before the stair-tower was built. Sure enough, last century a cow did manage to find its way up the long winding turnpike stair, when the castle had become ruinous, and having got into the watch-chamber could not turn round and get out. It had its calf up there—and a special train was run from Inverness for sightseers to view the event.

The Orrin is a wild and rushing river, much liable to spates. Its lower valley is very picturesque and wooded, but wild also. Most of the long glen is roadless, save for estate tracks, but there is an attractive back-road from the Ord Distillery vicinity at Muir of Ord, which in 3 miles reaches Aultgowrie hamlet, passing the high old bridge over the incoming Allt Goibhre (Gowrie), a major tributary with its own glen, to the south. There is much planted forestry here, Urray Forest. Beyond another bridge, over the Orrin itself, this road climbs up the hill northwards to Marybank, passing near Fairburn Tower. But private roads go up both sides of the Orrin, through the woodland. The Falls of Orrin are half a mile up, not very high but quite impressive in a series of cascades and deep linns and pots, the current strong. In another 2 miles the woodlands cease, and the estate road runs up through empty hills to the loch formed by damming up the river a further 3 miles up. This extends for some five roadless miles, with the Corriehallie deer-forest on one side and the Cabaan Forest on the other. Still the river goes on many miles more through the mountains, probing towards the far watershed area around Loch Monar, with the giant peaks of Sgurr na Choire Ghlais (3554 feet) and its associated summits between this glen and Strathfarrar to the south. Only the very determined walker can penetrate here.

Back at Marybank, where the A.832 bends away northwards, a lesser road continues on westwards along the south bank of the River Conon. Nearly 2 miles along is Muirton Mains, an old Fairburn farm, attractive with a range of good steading buildings beside a pond. The road proceeds on to Loch Achonachie, which is a widening of the Conon, and here is the Torr Achilty Power Station and dam. In 1967 this dam overflowed, and the flood wreaked havoc along the valley as far down as Conon Bridge, drowning hundreds of sheep and cattle and damaging buildings. The Brahan Seer had prophesied this too, saying that a loch above Beauly would one day burst its banks and destroy in its rise a village and its vicinity.

Thereafter this road continues up Strathconon, there eventually to end—but this is getting far from Urray, and moreover moves over into Contin parish, and better dealt with thereunder.

APPENDIX

Places of special interest, some open to the public, others where access or view is usually possible or can be arranged.

(* Indicates property in the care of the Department of the Environment: † indicates property of the National Trust for Scotland.)

BANFFSHIRE

Aberlour: Episcopal Orphanage Church
Banff:
  Castle
  Duff House
  Mercat Cross
  Old Houses restored
Cullen:
  Cullen House
  Auld Kirk
Deskford: *Sacrament House, Old Church
Dufftown:
  Mortlach old church
  *Balvenie Castle
  Glenfiddich and Balvenie Distilleries
Fordyce:
  Old Church
  Castle
Keith:
  Auld Brig
  Milton Castle and Linn
Letterfourie: Craigmin Bridge
Macduff: Fish-market
Pennan:
  Cullykhan site
  Hell's Lum and Devil's Kitchen Rocks
Portknockie: Bow Fiddle Rock
Portsoy:
  Boyne Castle
  Marble Workshop
Sandend: Findlater Castle
Tomintoul: Kirkmichael Kirk and Stone

INVERNESS-SHIRE

Abriachan: Druim Croft Museum
Aviemore: Centre

Beauly: *Priory and Pictish Stone
Boat of Garten:
  Kincardine old church
  Osprey Sanctuary
  Strathspey Railway (local venture)
Carrbridge: Landmark Visitor Centre
Culloden:
  †Battlefield Information Centre and Museum
  *Clava Stones
Dores: Clan MacBain Memorial Park
Drumnadrochit:
  *Corrimony Chambered Cairn
  Falls of Divach
  *Urquhart Castle
Dulnain Bridge: Muckrach Castle
Eskadale: R.C. Church—Sobieski Stuart graves
Fort George: Fort and Regimental Museum
Foyers:
  Falls of Foyers
  Forestry Centre, Walks and Wildlife Exhibition, Farigaig
Glenmore:
  Cairngorm Ski-road and Lift
  Forest Park
  Outdoor Training Centre
  Reindeer Herd
Inverness:
  †Abertarff House
  *Boar Stone
  Cromwell's Clock Tower
  Dunbar's Hospital
  Earl of Mar's Effigy, Friar's Burial-ground
  Museum
  St. Andrew's Cathedral
  Tomnahurich Cemetery
  Town House and Clach-na-Cudain Stone
Kincraig:
  Glen Feshie Forest Walks
  Highland Wildlife Park, Dunachton
  Insh Old Church
  Lagganlia Outdoor Centre
Kingussie:
  Am Fasgadh Highland Museum
  Ruthven Barracks
Kirkhill:
  Mausoleum
  Reelig Glen and Forest Walk
Nethy Bridge:
  Castle Roy
  Old Church

Newtonmore: Macpherson Clan Museum
Petty: Castle Stewart
Rothiemurchus:
  Loch-an-Eilean and Castle
  Old kirk and Shaw tomb
  National Nature Reserve, Trails and Forest Walks
Strathnairn: Gask Ring-cairn

MORAY

Advie: Tormore Distillery
Bellie: Old R.C. Church, Enzie
Birnie:
  Mannochmore Distillery
  Old Church
Brodie:
  Castle
  Rodney Pictish Stone
Burghead:
  Museum
  *Pictish Well
  Moray Sea School
Covesea:
  Caves
  Lighthouse
Duffus:
  *Castle
  *Peter's Kirk
Edinkillie:
  Daltulich Bridge
  Randolph's Leap
Elgin:
  Bishop's Palace
  *Cathedral
  Greyfriars Convent
  Museum
  Old Houses restored
Forres:
  Museum
  Sueno's Stone
Gordonstoun:
  Michael Kirk
  School
Grantown-on-Spey:
  Castle Grant
  Inverallan Kirkyard and Pictish Stone
  Lochindorb Castle
Kinloss: Abbey

Knockando: Woollen Mill, Nether Tomdow
Lhanbride: Coxton Tower

NAIRNSHIRE

Ardclach:
  *Bell-tower
  Dulsie Bridge
Auldearn:
  †Boath Doocot
  Old Church
Cawdor:
  Barevan Old Church
  Cawdor Castle and Church
Croy: Kilravock Castle
Nairn:
  Kebbuck Stone
  Pottery
  Rait Castle

ROSS, EASTER

Alness:
  Community Leisure Complex
  Dalmore Distillery
Ardgay:
  Carbisdale Castle (S.Y.H.A.)
  Croick Church
Contin:
  Falls of Rogie
  Old church
Cromarty:
  Eathie Burn valley
  †Hugh Miller's Cottage
  Old Church
Dingwall:
  Pictish Stone, kirkyard
  Tolbooth Tower
Edderton:
  Balblair Distillery
  Clach Beorach (Pictish)
  Old church, with Pictish stone
Evanton: Black Rock Gorge
Fearn:
  Abbey
  Shandwick Pictish Stone
Fortrose:
  *Cathedral
  Chanonry Lighthouse
  Town Hall Picture Gallery

Invergordon:
   B.A.C. Smelter
   Invergordon Distillery
Muir of Ord: Kilchrist Mausoleum
Nigg: Old Church and Nigg Stone
Rosemarkie:
   Fairy Glen
   Old Church and Pictish Stone
Strathpeffer:
   Eagle Stone
   Pump Room
Tain:
   Morangie Forest Walk
   Museum
   St. Duthac's Church and Chapel
   Tolbooth
Tarbat:
   Ballone Castle
   Old Church
   Tarbat Ness Lighthouse
Urray:
   Fairburn Tower
   Torachilty Dam Salmon Lift

SHORT BIBLIOGRAPHY

A Guide to Prehistoric Scotland, Richard Feachem (Batsford).
The Ancient Stones of Scotland, W. Douglas Simpson (Hale).
The Story of Scotland in Stone, Ian C. Hannah (Oliver & Boyd).
The Stones of Scotland, G. Scott Moncrieff (Batsford).
The Picts, Isobel Henderson (Thames & Hudson).
Early Christian and Pictish Monuments of Scotland (H.M.S.O.).
The History of Celtic Place-names of Scotland, W. J. Watson (Blackwood).
Place Names of Scotland, James B. Johnston (S.R.P.).
The Historic Architecture of Scotland, J. G. Dunbar (Blackwood).
The Fortified House in Scotland, Vol. 5, Nigel Tranter (Chambers).
Scottish Castles, W. Douglas Simpson (H.M.S.O.).
The Highland Clans, Sir Iain Moncrieffe (Barrie & Rockcliff).
The Great Clan Ross, John R. Ross (J. Delyell).
The New Statistical Account of Scotland (Blackwood).
Memoirs of a Highland Lady, Elizabeth Grant (Murray).
The Cairngorms on Foot and Ski, V. A. Firsoff (Hale).
Beyond the Great Glen, F. R. Corson (Oliver & Boyd).
The Scottish Mountaineering Clubs Guides: The Central Highlands, The Cairngorms & The Northern Highlands (S.M.C.).
The Unknown Highlands, Ross Finlay (G. T. Foulis).
North-East Lowlands of Scotland, J. R. Allan (Hale).
Romantic Strathspey, J. A. Rennie (Hale).
History of Aberdeen and Banff, W. Watt (Blackwood).
History of Moray and Nairn, C. Rampini (Blackwood).
History of the Province of Moray, Lachlan Shaw (Hamilton Adams).
History of Nairnshire, George Bain (Nairn Telegraph).
History of the County of Inverness, J. C. Lees (Blackwood).
History of the Province of Ross, Robert Bain (Peffereside Press).
The Findhorn, T. Henderson (Grant & Murray).
Urquhart and Glen Moriston, W. Mackay (Inverness).
Annals of Forres, R. Douglas (Elgin Courant).
Elgin, Past and Present, H. B. Mackintosh (Yeadon).
Old Inverness (Inverness Courier).

INDEX

Main localities are indicated in capitals and bold figures

INDEX

Delnies, Carse of, 258, 259, 277
Delny, 333, 334
Denoon, Abbot Donald, 317
Denoon family, 317
Department of the Environment, 36,
    59, 89, 119, 123, 200, 206, 216,
    319
DESKFORD, 3, 4, 35, 36, 52
Deskford, Lords, 28, 36
Deskie Burn, 13
Deveron, River, 1, 3, 5, 8, 9, 14 et seq.,
    31, 32, 42, 47, 53, 68
DHRUIM or DRUIMM, 135, 136, 178
Diebidale, 292
DINGWALL, 279, 281, 282, 284, 306 et
    seq., 354, 355
Dipple, 249, 250
Distilleries, 1, 6, 7, 8, 11, 12, 13, 22, 25,
    26, 29, 36, 38, 41, 45, 51, 52, 54,
    57, 58, 59, 66, 71, 72, 102, 184, 188,
    194, 195, 198, 199, 201, 203, 221,
    223, 228, 246, 287, 292, 325, 358,
    360
Divach Lodge, Falls, 121
Divie, River, 210, 212, 213
DOCHFOUR, 92, 93
DOCHGARROCH, 81, 92, 93
Dochmaluag Tower, 352
Doe, River, 118
Don, River, 3
Dorback Burn or River, 159, 210, 212,
    213, 236
DORES, parish, Strath, 105 et seq., 167,
    173
Dornoch Firth, 279, 283, 310, 312, 343,
    345, 358, 359
Douglas family, 16, 20, 59, 191, 295, 331
Doune, Hill of, 54
Doune of Relugas, 214
Doune of Rothiemurchus, 171, 172
Doupat Well, 320
Downan, 11, 13
Drachlaw, 48
DRAINIE, 188, 208, 229, 231, 239, 240,
    241
Drake's Nurseries, 143
Druidtemple, 167
Druie, River, 112, 169, 170
Druim Museum, 81
Druim a Chat, 352, 353
DRUMASHIE, 105, 106, 107
Drumbuie, 121
Drumchardine, 149
Drumderfit Hill, 328, 338
Drumguish, 141, 142, 148
Drumin Castle, 11, 12, 13, 72
Drumintoul, 169
Drummossie Moor, 98, 166
DRUMMUIR district, Castle, 24, 25
DRUMNADROCHIT, 119, 120, 121
DRUMOCHTER, 76, 102, 103, 104, 141
Drumullie, 91, 94

Drybridge, 65, 66
Drynachan, 269
Drynie, 327, 328
Duff family, 8, 19 et seq., 25, 28, 35,
    38, 46, 56, 58, 59, 60, 62, 68, 69,
    128, 133, 207, 218, 242, 247, 249,
    250, 254, 255
Duff House, 8, 9, 18, 19, 20, 35
DUFFTOWN, 37, 38, 57, 59
Dufftown-Glenlivet Distillery, 1, 58
DUFFUS, 23, 188, 190, 199, 201, 205 et
    seq., 229, 230, 237, 245
Duffus, King, 226
Duffus, Lords, 206, 219
Dullan Burn, 37, 58, 59
DULNAIN BRIDGE, 96, 108, 109
Dulnain, River, 83, 93, 94, 96, 108
DULSIE, Bridge, district, 191, 259, 260,
    262
Dun Alascaig, 311
Dunachton, 143, 144
Dunain Hill, 92
Dunbar family, 43, 56, 91, 128, 196,
    204, 207, 210, 214, 219, 220, 238,
    242, 244, 245, 249, 260, 263, 264,
    275, 276, 347
Duncan the First, 125, 166, 217, 226
Duncan, John, 256
Duncanston, 360, 361
Dun Dearduil, 77, 177
Dundee, Viscount, 147, 179
Dundreggan Lodge, 117
Dundurcas, 21, 24, 247
Dunfermline Abbey, 35, 253
Dunfermline House, Kingston, 256
Dun Fionn, 139
DUNLICHITY, 104, 105, 107, 181, 182
Dunlugas, 9, 16, 28, 42, 43
Dunmaglass, 176, 181, 183
DUNPHAIL, district, Castle, 212, 213
Dun Richnan, 107
Dunscriben, 121
Dunskaith Castle, Ness, 304, 339, 341
Durn, Burn, Hill of, 3, 40, 64
Durward family, 119
DUTHIL, 93, 96, 140, 168, 260
DYKE, 191, 208 et seq., 229

Eagle Stone, 351
Easter Clunes, 139
Eathie, 305, 322
EDDERTON, 310, 311, 315
Eden, Bishop, 132
EDINGIGHT, 5, 45, 47
EDINKILLIE, 212 et seq., 262
EDINVILLIE, 5 et seq.
Edradour, 331
Edward the First, 119, 206, 215, 219,
    236, 247, 250, 258
Edward the Seventh, 19, 59, 324
Eidart, River, 75, 142
Eight Men of Glenmoriston, 118

376